Action, Gesture and Symbol

The Emergence of Language

Action, Gesture and Symbol

The Emergence of Language

Edited by
ANDREW LOCK
University of Lancaster,
Lancaster, England

Foreword by Jerome Bruner

1978

ACADEMIC PRESS
London · New York · San Francisco
A Subsidiary of Harcourt Brace Jovanovich, Publishers

ACADEMIC PRESS INC., LONDON, LTD.
24—28 Oval Road
London NW1

United States Edition published by
ACADEMIC PRESS INC.
111 Fifth Avenue
New York, New York 10003

Library of Congress Catalog Card Number: 78-52094
ISBN: 0-12-454050-3

Printed in Great Britain by
The Lavenham Press Ltd., Lavenham, Suffolk

Contributors

SUSAN R. BRAUNWALD, *2416 Nottingham Avenue, Los Angeles, California 90027, U.S.A.*

ANNE LINDSAY CARTER, *P.O. Box 5073, Berkeley, California 94705, U.S.A.*

ROGER A. CLARK, *Department of Psychology, Hull University, Hull HU6 7RX, England*

DEREK EDWARDS, *Department of Social Sciences, University of Loughborough, Loughborough LE11 3TU, Leicestershire, England*

HEIDI FELDMAN, *3424 6th Avenue, San Diego, California 92103, U.S.A.*

LINDA FERRIER, *77 Main Street, Jaffrey, New Hampshire 03452, U.S.A.*

LILA GLEITMAN, *University of Pennsylvania, Graduate School of Education, Philadelphia, Pennsylvania 19104, U.S.A.*

SUSAN GOLDIN-MEADOW, *Department of Education, University of Chicago, 5835 Kimbark Avenue, Chicago, Illinois 60637, U.S.A.*

HILARY GRAY, *Derbyshire County Council, Educational Psychology Service, 16 St. Mary's Gate, Derby, England*

PATRICIA MARKS GREENFIELD, *Department of Psychology, University of California, Los Angeles, California 90024, U.S.A.*

PENELOPE HUBLEY, *Department of Psychology, University of Edinburgh, Edinburgh EH8 9TA, Scotland*

DAVID INGRAM, *Department of Linguistics, University of British Columbia, Vancouver V6T 1W5, Canada*

KEITH LAIDLER, *Survival Anglia Ltd., Brook House, Park Lane, London W1Y 4DX, England*

ANDREW LOCK, *Department of Psychology, Lancaster University, Lancaster LA1 4YF, England*

JOHN NEWSON, *Department of Psychology, Nottingham University, Nottingham NG7 2RD, England*

ALICIA NOKONY, *Department of Linguistics, University of British Columbia, Vancouver V6T 1W5, Canada*

FRANS X. PLOOIJ, *Department of Developmental Psychology, University of Nijmegen, Nijmegen, The Netherlands*

M. P. M. RICHARDS, *Medical Psychology Unit, Old Cavendish Building, Free School Lane, Cambridge CB2 3RF, England*

M. M. SHIELDS, *University of London Institute of Education, Department of Child Development and Educational Psychology, 24 and 27 Woburn Square, London WC1, England*

JOHN SHOTTER, *Department of Psychology, Nottingham University, Nottingham NG7 2RD, England*

COLWYN TREVARTHEN, *Department of Psychology, University of Edinburgh, Edinburgh EH8 9TA, Scotland*

CATHY URWIN, *Department of Psychology, University of Warwick, Coventry, England*

Foreword

Though this book contains a rich variety of papers, it maintains an extraordinary clarity of focus. For the authors are all concerned (indeed sometimes preoccupied) with a single great theme—the manner in which the acquisition or the origin of language relates to the uses of language in social interaction and in coping with the world of objects and events and abstractions in which social interaction occurs. What is remarkable about the community of interest is that the papers were prepared in virtual independence of each other, and while the editor doubtless chose the contributors with this general theme in mind, it is still striking how much the papers converge.

They converge on what I take to be the major thrust in developmental linguistics of the past decade. Ten years ago, interest in the study both of language acquisition and its evolution in the animal kingdom centered on syntax—the rules through which strings of constituents in an utterance achieved well-formedness as sentences. The study of syntax emerged, of course, from the interest aroused by the brilliant and pioneering insights of Chomsky's generative transformational grammar. But while syntax and the rules for well-formed sentences are still crucial to an understanding of what language is, there is more to *using* language than knowing its grammar. *Using* language, moreover, cannot be dismissed as the "mere" performance of an underlying grammatical competence. There are rules that govern appropriateness of utterance, felicity, and contextual plausibility. There are problems in testing the extent to which presuppositions are shared with respect to both meaning and speech convention.

In a word, language proper is an instrument for fulfilling various communicative functions. And communicative functions themselves exist as constituents in still broader patterns of social interaction. As always, understanding of a given process depends upon viewing it from top down (what function a particular grammatical form serves in the larger communicative context) and from the bottom up (how does a system of such components make *any* function realizable).

So, in the chapters that follow one finds not only discussions of syntax, but also of the pragmatics of speech, how language interacts with context to achieve its meanings. And one finds research on the nature of speech acts—how we indicate conventionally our communicative intent and how our addressees signal their uptake of our conventional maneuvers. The result is a much richer account not only of the nature and growth of meaning but also of the relation between form and function in language, the diverse linguistic procedures by which linguistic functions can be realized.

If one were to take this volume as a "1978 specimen" from which to generalize about intellectual history in the last quarter of the twentieth century, there are some interesting points to be made. The first is that the new approach to language has sparked a revolt against traditional "cause-effect" psychology and raised deep questions about the adequacy of positivist theories. A central element in the revolt is the contrast between "caused" and "intended" behaviour, a matter that concerns several authors. Perhaps as a result of this revolt, it would be fair to say that psychology and philosophy are closer together in outlook (if not in method) than they have been in half a century. Perhaps it was the line of reasoning that stemmed from the later Wittgenstein and comes in a second generation from Austin, Searle, Strawson, and Grice that has made the liaison possible. A third trend is also discernible: the bridging of gaps that before were not so much empty as they were filled with corrosive dogmatism. The gaps between prelinguistic communication and language proper as the child develops, the gap between gesture and word, between holophrases and sentences, between chimps signing and man talking, between sign languages and spoken ones, between the structure of action and the structure of language. I think that the renewal of interest in language as an interactive, communicative system has made these "gaps" less like battlegrounds where one fights and dies for the uniqueness of man and more like unknown seas to be mapped.

There is a special privilege in writing a foreword: you get the first opportunity to read without having to do any of the work of book making. It is full of riches, this book, riches of many kinds. It is also a harbinger of much good research still to come.

Wolfson College,   JEROME BRUNER
Oxford.
June 1978

Preface

How do children learn to talk? Few questions can have been asked as often as this one, or have been provided with so many possible answers, and yet remained essentially unanswered. Because of its apparently unique features the language system has always resisted a developmental analysis. In recent times the recognition of this uniqueness has led to a view of language development as an unfolding of some innate capacity, thus solving many problems by rendering them irrelevant. Whether that is a satisfactory view or an empirically verifiable one is becoming more and more doubtful. This collection of papers adds more fuel to this fire. The major question around which this book has been built is this: is there a continuity between the preverbal and the verbal levels of communication; is the latter predicated on the former? In a recent paper Schaffer (1977) has noted that "however persuasive the similarity (between these two levels), one should bear in mind that it provides an argument based on analogy—no more. Developmental continuity therefore remains an assumption. . . . Any attempt to 'explain' the onset of language in terms of its developmental precursors is thus still fraught with difficulties." This problem of continuity is the central focus of this current volume.

As editor I must emphasize that the shape into which the contributions concerning this problem have been organized—as outlined in the introduction—represents a personal view. There are many more stories and threads running through this collection than the one I present: thus I can put forward one line of argument knowing that should it be found lacking, each contributor brings so much insight to his or her topic that my fate is independent of theirs. To have worked and corresponded with such impressive talents has been a most rewarding pleasure and honour. I have learned so much from each manuscript that during the preparation stages I regained a child's anticipatory excitement in waiting for the day's post: to each contributor—my sincere thanks.

I am glad to have this opportunity to acknowledge the help I have had from many people during the preparation of this book. I am very grateful to

Professor Philip Levy for his encouragement and for extending to me the assistance, facilities and resources of the Department of Psychology at Lancaster University. Two people have helped me greatly in the preparation of the manuscript and I am most grateful to them: Sandra Wall provided a great deal of assistance with the bibliography; Sue Foster took on the task of constructing an index single handed. Thanks also go to Josephine Woods for many of the illustrations and figures. Last, but by no means least, the typing and secretarial help, most of which was provided by Linda Teale, Mary Howard, Frances Sharples and Deborah Reynolds: their efforts have been indispensible.

Lancaster   ANDREW LOCK
June 1978

Contents

Section 4: Communicative Actions and the Establishment of Gestures

Section 5: From Gesture to Symbol

Section 6: Symbols and Society

Acknowledgements

The editor and the publisher wish to thank the following for their kind permission to reproduce material quoted from other volumes:

W. W. Norton and Co., Inc., for quotations from *The Origins of Intelligence in Children* (© 1951) and *Play, Dreams and Imitation in Childhood* (© 1962) by Jean Piaget; Cambridge University Press, for material from *Speech Acts: An Essay in the Philosophy of Language* (© 1969) by John Searle; New Science Publications for a quotation from *Conversations with a two-month old, New Scientist 62 (896)* (© 1974) by C. Trevarthen; John Wiley and Sons, Inc., for a quotation from *The Social Context of Language* (© 1978), edited by I. Markova; Faber and Faber Ltd for a quotation from *Persons in Relation* (© 1961) by John Macmurray; Penguin Books Ltd, for a quotation from *Cognitive Sociology* (© 1973) by Aaron Cicourel; Mouton Publishers, for a quotation from *Semiotica 3* (© 1972), by Aaron Cicourel and Robert Boese; W. H. Freeman and Co., for a quotation from *Cognition and Reality* by Ulric Neisser (© 1976); Harcourt Brace Jovanovich, Inc., for a quotation from *Language and Mind* by Noam Chomsky (© 1968); University Tutorial Press, for a quotation from *A Manual of Psychology* by George Stout; the British Psychological Society for a quotation in a paper in the *Bulletin of the British Psychology Society 28* by John Newson (© 1975); Almqvist and Wiksell International for a quotation from a paper in the *Scandinavian Journal of Psychology*, 10 by J. Smedslund (© 1969); John Hopkins University Press for a quotation from a Chapter in *Giambattista Vico: an International Symposium* (Eds. G. Tagliacozzo and H. V. White) by Sir Isiah Berlin (© 1969); and quotations from *Mind: an Essay on Human Feeling, Vol. 1* by Susanne Langer (© 1967).

Section 1

Editorial Introduction

1

The Emergence of Language

ANDREW LOCK

University of Lancaster, England

ON BEING PICKED UP*

A relatively short time ago man stood apart from the rest of the animal world by virtue of the pillars of culture and language. But in recent years these cornerstones of our conceived humanity have been greatly eroded. The attack on the uniqueness of our cultures has arisen from recent Japanese research on the transmission of patterns of life in the Japanese macaque monkey (Kawai, 1963, 1965; Kawamura, 1963). There they have observed behaviour which shows a distinct likeness to a cultural tradition. They have seen the development of "cleanliness"—the primate society having adopted what was originally the discovery of one individual. That individual discovered that eating clean food was better than eating it covered in sand. And cleanliness is next to Godliness.

Almost simultaneously an American chimpanzee learnt a language. Maybe not very well, but well enough (Gardner and Gardner, 1969). The interest which this finding has generated stems partly from its effect on the old adage concerning how many monkeys, with how many typewriters and so much time, would be needed to produce a Shakespearian play. Their chances may be only one in 10 million, but, with a little help from their friends, they have taken that chance.

*Revised version of a paper presented at the Association for the Study of Animal Behaviour Symposium "Mother-child interaction in man and the higher animals": London, December 1975. For further details, see Lock (in press).

In both cases questions concerning the evolutionary implications of these findings have arisen. Are we witnessing the beginnings of the evolution of language and culture, beginnings similar to those of our own? Are we seeing these processes beginning for the *second* time? The importance of these questions is often dismissed by pointing at the one great difference between the evolution of our languages (and culture), and its acquisition by chimpanzees: the difference that prompts the question, "Who were the friends who gave language to us?" Ignoring such supernatural speculations, I wish to propose instead that we have not *given* language to a chimpanzee, but have rather provided one with conditions which have enabled her to discover language for herself. Further, I am implying that this is the case with our own infants: that they discover language through the conditions provided by their interactions in the social world. Many writers treat "language" and "grammar", "learning", "acquisition", "discovery" and "invention" as virtually synonymous. For example, Chomsky (1968, p. 75) summarizes a line of argument thus: "In short, the language is 'reinvented' each time it is learned, and the empirical problem to be faced by the theory of learning is how this invention of grammar can take place." I will retain this ambiguity at present, and summarize my argument here with a slogan: *children discover language through a process of guided reinvention.*

My line of thought is as follows: the major problem for any theory dealing with the possible evolution, or development, of language is that of reference. There are very few traces of this ability in the affective communicative systems of either primates (Goodall, 1968; Itani, 1963; Marler, 1969; Reynolds, 1968) or human infants. The ontogenetic gulf between communicating with emotional expressions and communicating with propositional ones thus seems vast: but I wish to argue that this vastness is illusory. It is the Russian psychologist L. S. Vygotsky who provides the ideas that change the scale of our perceptions. He puts forward a "general genetic law of cultural development" as follows: "any function in the child's cultural development appears on the stage twice, on two planes, first on the social plane and then on the psychological, first among people as an intermental category and then within the child as an intramental category." (1966, p. 44)

If he is correct, it follows that symbolic systems have their first expression in the social transactions that go on between us, and in the case of infants, these are initially emotively-based. The implication of this now takes the argument in the reverse direction: if we have evolved from similar stock to our primate initiates, these transactions used to be solely emotional. Thus in some way, language of a referential nature must be implicit in earlier affective, non-referential communicative actions. A theory of either the evolution or development of language would then be aimed at elucidating how what is implicit in prelinguistic communication is given an explicit form (cf. Popper's account (1972) of the development of world 3 and objective knowledge). In the Chomskyean paradigm, the child's problem is "to determine which of the [humanly] possible languages is that of the community in which he is placed" (1965). Here instead, his problem is cast as having to use the language of his community to give an explicit form to the "language" implicit in his own transactions with that community. By using examples of three infant's early dealings with the world I will outline how three of our own contemporaries accomplished this task.

None of us are born with the ability to raise our arms to assist another in lifting us up: an activity that infants are often partners to. Thus in early occurrences of this activity the child's arms only get raised by the physical consequences of the mother pushing her hands under his armpits: he himself shows no active adjustment to her behaviour. But fairly quickly the child becomes familiar with being picked up, and he begins to recognize his mother's actions towards him. This is evidenced by the fact that he now shows anticipation of her reactions: he raises his arms himself, and does not rely passively on her efforts.

At first he responds to the physical stimulation of his mother's hands: as she touches him he adjusts his position, and she very easily slides her hands under his arms. As he grows, he anticipates sooner and sooner in the interaction until his mother only has to stand in front of him for him to raise his arms. At this point in his development a new element creeps into the situation. Because he is able to anticipate his mother's actions so far in advance, he can make a "wrong guess" at what she is going to do: and making a "wrong guess" has a very important consequence. As an example, consider Paul at 9 months and 6 days of age:

Paul is in his baby-walker. His mother comes into the room holding a pair of scissors and stands "absent mindedly" in front of him. She looks at Paul and he raises his arms.
Mother: O.K., just a minute.
She puts the scissors down and comes back to him. Paul has not been watching her, but is scooting across the room. She stops in front of him, and before she starts to bend down and move her arms out toward him, he raises his arms.

This incident was recorded on videotape, and was played back to the mother afterwards. She confirmed that when she came into the room she had no intention of interacting with Paul: she was wondering what she had done with a piece of material. It was only because Paul "signalled" to her that they subsequently became involved together. Thus Paul by his behaviour can create an intention for his mother where previously she had none. But while he has stumbled upon this ability, he cannot use it with any deliberateness. He has created an intention for his mother, communicating something to her, quite fortuitously. In Vygotsky's terms his ability exists at the intermental level, and not at the intramental one. Yet similarly, there are few of his innate, as opposed to acquired, abilities that can be executed with any deliberateness at this time. His bladder, his crying and his laughing are still patterned largely by the spontaneous rhythms of a primates nervous system. (This is an obvious oversimplification: see, for example, Emde and Harrison; 1971.)

But around the time that he shows such sophisticated behaviour as this, the patterning and employment of most of these early actions begins to change. In the case of arm-raising it is initially possible to describe these changes in terms of anticipation again. Thus far the child has shown anticipation within the act of being picked up: his mother must be "physically in the process of doing" for him to raise his arms. But being picked up occurs in the wider context of everyday life. Infants are picked up to be fed, washed, bathed and comforted; and the preparations for these activities occupy a large part of his day. Food is prepared and cooked, tins are opened; baths are drawn: all these activities culminate in being-picked-up. The child now begins to move his arms in anticipation of these: not in response to his mother's actions, but to the sights, smells and sounds of these events. For example, Mary aged 10 months and 15 days:

> Mary is on the kitchen floor while mother is preparing her dinner. Every time mother walks past her or turns towards her Mary raises her arms. Eventually she is picked up and put in her chair ready for feeding.

The final development of this communicative "gesture" can be seen in the next example. Here arm-raising is used by Paul, not in anticipation of being picked up, but in the pursuit of that goal—he makes a request:

> Paul; age 10 (6): Paul crawls to his mother and scratches her leg while she is ironing.
> Mother: What do you want?
> Paul raises his arms.
> Mother: No, I can't pick you up now.

Not only does he make a request of his mother, he leaves her in little doubt as to what that request is. This specificity in the meaning conveyed by arm-raising is important. For example:

> Mary; age 10 (16): Mary crawls after her mother as she leaves the room. She manages to jam her fingers in the door as it closes. She screams. Mother comes back, immediately Mary sees her she lifts her arms.

It may be argued that the action of lifting the arms is irrelevant on this occasion: a crying child would be lifted anyway. But cries on their own are notoriously inefficient:

Paul; age 6 (19): Paul is sat alone in the middle of the living-room. He starts to cry. Mother comes into the room.
Mother: Oh, now what's up, hey? Oh dear, Oh dear, what's the matter? She picks him up.
Mother: Are you thirsty, is that what it is? Do you want a drink? She goes and picks up his bottle and offers it to him. He refuses it and continues crying.
Mother: Hungry? Are you? Do you want something to eat? No? Sleepy then, do you want to go to sleep?
She puts him in his pram but he continues to cry. She picks him up again and walks about comforting him. She stops at the window. Paul apparently looks out but continues crying. Mother tries to attract his attention, and then to direct it.
Mother: Look, there's a pussycat, can you see him? Do you know what pussycats say? Do you? They say "miaow" don't they, yes, of course they do. Paul stops crying during this speech.
Mother: There, that's better, down you go then. She places him back on the floor.

Crying on its own leaves too much of the message "unsaid", too much to be supposed by the hearer. Apparently in response to this problem the developing infant begins to modify his crying, complementing it with other, more specific, communicative actions, each with its separate developmental history. A dramatic example of this is:

Paul; age 14 (23): Mother enters the room holding a cup of tea. Paul turns from his play in her direction and obviously sees the cup of tea.
He cries vestigially and so attracts mother's attention; immediately he points toward her and smacks his lips concurrently.
Mother: No, you can't have this one, it's Andy's.

Here crying functions both to attract attention and convey the message of the child's wanting something. Pointing directs that attracted attention and informs the mother what that something is. For this child, the roots of the pointing gesture can be traced back to earlier direct attempts to pick objects up. Lip-smacking has resulted from a stylization of actually eating or drinking, and its use here leaves the mother in little doubt as to why the child wants the cup.

Similarly, when the crying child runs to his mother with outstretched arms, he conveys a specific message to her through the combination of these different actions: *and to do this is to have mastered one of the fundamental skills of language.* Sentences convey specific messages through the combination of different actions. If we look at the developmental history of the child's ability to combine gestures we find three phases. One in which the ability to use single gestures is developed; a second in which single gestures occur in sequences—the child cries . . . and then points or raises his arms, say; and finally a period in which two or more gestures occur together—the child cries and points "at the same time". A similar sequence is found in language development: the so-called holophrastic period of one-word-at-a-time; the occurrence of two words in a sequence; and that of true multi-word utterances. This is another hint that the two processes—of language and gesture—are very similar. And they are alike in further ways. As noted earlier, the great chasm to be bridged in both speculations on the evolution of language and those on its development is that between affective and referential communication. Here it should be noted that in these gestural combinations the child displays an ability which is transitional between the two. Crying is no longer solely affective: it now both attracts the mother's attention and conveys information. Similarly, pointing directs that attention, and also "refers" to an object. Functionally there is little difference between the child crying and pointing at an object—gestural use, and later saying the name of that object with a whining intonation while pointing at it—language use. What difference there is would seem to be enshrined in the concept of symbolism. Yet the removal of lip-smacking from its original sphere of application to this one of interpersonal communication "smacks" of symbolism itself.

I would suggest that at this stage in his development the child has *mastered* the fundamentals of language: but I would not wish to go as far as saying he now *possesses* language. Whilst he can communicate his intentions in an unambiguous and structured manner, the messages he conveys are not objective in nature, nor are they propositional, and neither are they capable of being judged true or false. Language is still only implicit in his activities, and will remain so until he becomes able to name objects.

This latter ability *seems* to have a totally separate history to the communicative ones I have been discussing thus far. And for 2 or 3 months after they appear in his repertoire, words stay separate from, and are not used in, the communicative pursuit of the child's intentions. During this period they seem to be used only "for the fun of it", in social games with the mother:

> Mary; age 11 (28): Mary is sat on the floor with her mother, who is sat facing her.
> Mother: (holding duck out to Mary) What does the duck say? What does he say?
> Mary: (reaching towards duck) Argh
> Mother: Yes, I know you want it. What does he say?
> Mary: Woraghagh
> Mother: He doesn't, he says "quack quack quack quack".
> Mary: Gh, gh
> Mother: Yes he does. And who's this? (holding out Teddy)
> Mary: Aah
> Mother: And that's aah is it, that's aah Teddy.
> Mary: Aah

It is only after words have been practised in this context for a few months that they are found being used communicatively—and for this purpose they are used in conjunction with the older gestural ability:

> Peter; age 14 (4): Mother is playing with Peter, getting him to fill a box with all his toys. He gathers every object in reach and puts them in the box. He turns to me (I am about four feet away), looks at the toy dog at my feet, waves his arm (a gesture peculiar to Peter, used communicatively to make demands; cf. Lock, 1976) and says "darg". I throw it across to him.

Perhaps, though, this apparent developmental separateness of gesture and word, communicative function and referential function, is illusory. Certainly the child's ability to respond with different noises to differing objects arises from roots other than those underlying his gestural attainments. But how does he make the transition from this primitive level of perceptual discrimination and associative responding to that of actually naming objects, to the level of reference? This transition surely depends on factors involved in his earlier communicative use of gestures and actions. As already noted, pointing, lip-smacking and arm-raising show the rudiments of both reference and symbolism well in advance of the appearance of a linguistic system. When sound and object are associated, these rudiments are capitalized upon, and referential language emerges (cf. Bruner, 1975; Edwards, 1975; Lyons, 1973).

Further, in this period of the emergence of spoken words, the language and gestural systems interact to such an extent that any separateness they may have is immediately lost. Edwards (1975) notes that in the naming of objects, the importance of "reference" is obvious. But, he points out,

> object-naming also has a social relational and cognitive structure which underlie the nature of reference itself. Object-naming typically occurs in the context of what Brown (1956) called "the original word game", in which child and caretaker (usually mother) supply each other with names for pointed-at objects and pictures, or point out things named by the other. Typically the "game" is linguistically mediated by much more than mere object-names; it is full of questions and answers, locative and deictic expressions like "What's that?", "there it is", "that's a kangaroo", "it's a box", "it's over there", and so on. Moreover these expressions are integrated into a context of sequenced looks and gestures which are crucial to their function in the total communication setting . . .
> The game has two complementary versions. In object-naming the child supplies a name for a located object. In pointing at named objects he indicates their location. (Edwards, 1975, pp. 3-7)

Reference, gesture and communication are all obviously intertwined. Finally, certain two-word utterances can be traced back directly to gestural origins. It would be a bit simplistic to say that gestures are translated into words, that words begin to replace gestures in the child's communicative system: but it would not be too simplistic. Consider the utterance "mommy up" reported by Greenfield and Smith (1976) being used by an 18-month-old child. Here "mommy" does not refer to mother, but seems to have developed from the total stylization of crying into a repeated nasal phrase. It retains the same function as crying, that of attracting attention and making a demand. "Up" specifies the child's intention, and thus functions to the same end as arm-raising did earlier. The two-word utterance "mommy up" has thus both the same form and use as the two-gesture communicative act of crying and arm-raising, and developmentally the two abilities appear very closely related.

Through looking at the emergence of language in this way the evolutionary perspective is opened up. Gestures arise in the interactions between people, in the communicative acts they share. At the height of their development these gestures show all the rudiments of language and at least in some cases, patterned speech results from the internalization of the structure of these shared acts—as, in similar vein, Piaget argues that thought arises from the internalization of action. Likewise, meanings initially exist between the interactants—Vygotsky's "intermental level"—and only later with the development of symbols are they internalized and simultaneously given explicit form—Vygotsky's "intramental level". George Mead (1934) maintains similarly that meaning is objectively present in any social conduct between individuals, and that "language simply lifts out of the social process a situation which is logically or implicitly there already" (1934, p. 79). Implicitly there, *both functionally and structurally*, in the interactions between chimp and chimp, chimp and man, or man and child: and given explicit form, first through the gesture and then through the symbol.

Gestures and words may thus be thought of as tools which enable an individual to accomplish the task of making explicit meanings. It is a task that chimpanzees have just started upon, but one which is always set before our own infants. But these tools are not given by us to either chimp or child: rather, we provide the social context in which they fashion them for themselves. From here it is only a short distance to saying that in our own evolutionary past we created the social context in which we, as a species, could fashion these tools for ourselves. Thus, being picked up is a part of every primate's childhood: but being a being being picked up is an integral part of picking up language.

Everyone comes to a book with their own preconceptions, and uses them to construe what they read. That problem is compounded in an edited volume, for it is the editor's own preconceptions which have guided the choice and scope of the contents. The above was prepared as a paper for conference presentation at the time when this book was just getting off the ground. I have included it in this prefatory context to allow the reader some insight into the biases around which this collection has been organized.

ACTIONS, GESTURES AND SYMBOLS

One of the major problems confronting the study of language "acquisition" is that of the relation between the individual and what he acquires: between the subjective, intersubjective and objective worlds. And this is not a problem unique to language acquisition, but one pervasive throughout the social sciences. We can see the issues clearly expressed in the writings of the anthropologist Clifford Geertz. Geertz (1966) views culture not as complexes of concrete behaviour patterns, but as "sets of control mechanisms, plans, recipes, rules, instructions—what computer engineers call 'programs'—for the governing of behaviour". His "control mechanism" view of culture starts with the assumption that human thought is both social and public: not "happenings in the head", but having as its natural environment the market, town square, etc. It is a traffic of significant symbols, which may be anything used to impose meaning upon experience. These symbols are generally given data, being in the community when a man is born, and left relatively unchanged when he dies. They are used, mostly spontaneously, to put a construction upon events, to orient a man to "the ongoing course of experienced things".

This is a sensible view which would gain much support today: yet the conceptual problems are obvious. In some senses, thinking does go on in the head: however I wish to conceive my thought processes, I have ultimately to accept them as cerebral, and hence as my individual property. Again, viewing symbols, the counters in the thought-game, as given data with an objective existence open to scientific scrutiny, is a ploy which is difficult to support beyond the heuristic level. Many linguists who perforce must treat language in this way would have no qualms in accepting that symbols are an essentially social phenomenon, and in doing so lay themselves open to charges of double-think. It is only when we come face-to-face with these problems that we notice the contradictions inherent in our commonsense views. Generally we get by through adopting a rather naïve view of "meaning" and thus sweeping most of our problems under the carpet. We cannot ignore these problems, though, when it comes to the question of language development.

It is these issues which are taken up in the second section. Richards approaches the relation between the biological and social worlds and highlights some of the problems inherent in our current conceptual handling of the issues involved. Newson then takes up the same themes, but from a slightly different tack. He argues that for the purposes of understanding *human* development the problems encountered are so great as to negate the traditional objective scientific paradigms. Thus, instead of being external observers of the processes under study "we must shift perspective so as to look at the process of communication from the point of view of a *participant observer*". The effects of making such a shift will become apparent in the chapters of later sections which discuss more detailed aspects of communicative development in very much this spirit. Shotter goes on to develop the themes of both Richard's and Newson's chapters into a very full account of how one might sensibly investigate communicative development. Drawing on a wide variety of sources he marshalls philosophical, sociological and psychological writings to outline the essential features of an hermenuetic developmental psychology. These three chapters, in recognizing the awful trichotomy between the subjective, intersubjective and objective modes, provide an essential perspective on the rest of the book, and their influence will be apparent throughout. As an example of the ways in which this approach may be put into practice, these opening chapters are followed by Urwin's discussion of the development of the communicative abilities of two blind infants.

The remaining sections of the book are very much organized along the lines of the argument outlined above in discussing the arm-raising gesture. That is, that many of the infant's early actions are effective in the world only through the monitoring and completion of them by another. As a result of this those actions come to be used by the infant in the knowledge that they are effective through the efforts of that other person: thus actions become transformed via interaction into gestures. Finally, the employment of these gestures leads the child to the possession of sufficient social knowledge and communicative expertise as to provide a basis for the symbolization and conceptual articulation of his experience—language proper. Thus language is seen as very much predicated on gesture: reliant as much on social knowledge as on sensori-motor knowledge of the physical world (cf. for example Brown, 1973; Piaget and Inhelder, 1969; Sinclair, 1971).

An intimate relation between gesture and word in the development of language has occasionally been postulated by psychologists (for example Latif, 1935; McCarthy, 1954), but historically it has not gained much favour. However, in the case of the evolution of language, gestural origin theories are currently in vogue (see Hewes, 1973). Interest in these theories has increased due to spectacular successes in teaching sign languages to infra-hominid apes. Bar the siamang and gibbon, the great apes have all shown some "linguistic" capacity. The work by the Gardners, Premack and Rumbaugh with chimpanzees needs little comment. Recently, similar headway has been reported by Patterson of Stanford University with a gorilla. Now, as Laidler points out in Section 3, there is reason to believe that the orang-utan possesses similar capabilities. Laidler's study is unique in persevering with teaching a vocal form of language. His results suggest that greater progress could be made with the more compatible gestural mode. But important as these advances are, it is necessary to note they only demonstrate that the great apes have the capacity to operate at the symbolic level, and that this potentiality can be actualized with the conspiracy of a suitable medium and cultural environment. They do not directly shed light on the possible origins of language in the evolutionary sense: only by analogy and the use of imagination do they point to certain conclusions.

On this question one needs evidence that apes possess a prelinguistic or proto-symbolic gestural system which they employ in their natural lives, and even then there are many pitfalls in extrapolating to events in the prehistoric past. Rambaugh and Savage, of the Yerkes Primate Laboratory, Georgia, have recently reported (1977) a natural sign-language employed by pigmy chimpanzees living under zoo conditions. As yet the extent of this system is unknown, but Rambaugh has already suggested that the progression of evolutionary advancement is from touch alone, to touch plus gesture, to gesture alone: a sequence similar to that in human development, i.e. a progressive development from direct social action to true communication (cf. Klopfer, 1976). Immediately such systems are found in non-humans, all the old problems of objectivity and the like return to the scene. After all, animals are only animals and fit for Occam's Razor because they cannot talk.

Griffin (1976) has recently reopened the question of animal awareness, and suggests that the time is ripe for a cognitive ethology to emerge. Plooij's paper in Section 3 is in this vein. He points to the existence of a natural gesture language in wild chimpanzees, and illustrates its probable ontogenetic history. He does so by making use of the approach of developmental psycholinguists. By taking this line he emphasizes the great similarity between the developmental sequences of both chimps and humans, *up to the point* at which the human progresses to true propositional language. Many contributors to this volume point to the close ontogenetic relationship between gesture and symbol (word) use in human development. Elsewhere I have written at length about the transition to propositional forms (Lock, in press). Speculations about language evolution will always be speculations, but if we dig out Haeckel's much-battered adage that "ontogeny recapitulates phylogeny" our speculations are afforded a great deal of attraction.

Space precludes an exhaustive exposition on these lines, but a brief outline is useful. Romanes (1888, 1897), Darwin's pupil and inheritor of his manuscripts, has advanced a logical model of language evolution and development, seeing them as coterminous processes. In his view, the intentional use of gesture for the purpose of communication is "the protoplasm of the sign-making faculty", containing "the germ of predication" (1897). Gesture use thus implies the proposition, or put the other way round, propositions are implicit in gestures. (See here also

Vygotsky's distinction between inter- and intramental levels noted above.) Popper (1972) conceives both evolution and development as problem-solving situations. Following him, we may view language emergence as a problem-solving situation: how to make explicit what is implicit in earlier abilities; how to objectify and conceptualize the components of abilities. Solving these problems results in the emergence of the symbolic world.

Thus in the framework here, the *evolution* of language can be seen as the solution of these problems by the *invention* (the means by which implicit properties are given explicit form) of the conceptual mode. In terms of development we must take stock of the fact that there are numerous different conceptual systems in use in human cultures (but all these world views are implicit in our social interactions—or *must be* if this line of thought is correct). Consequently, the *development* of language needs to be qualified as the *guided reinvention* of a specific conceptual system, predicated on an earlier prelinguistic communicative ability (for a fuller discussion of this, again see Lock, in press).

The processes of guidance become operative at birth, with human parents immediately placing and interpreting—and thus giving meaning to—their infants actions within a cultural context (see Macfarlane, 1977). Crying, for example, does not appear to have a universal meaning, but takes a different value in some cultures (Konner, 1972) and will doubtless vary in meaning at the microcultural level of individual parent-child dyads (Richards, 1974). It is in this context that the specific developments discussed by Clark, Gray and Trevarthen and Hubley in Section 4 must be placed. It would seem reasonable to assume, however, that while the specific actions under discussion are likely to vary throughout populations, the processes thus elucidated will be of general application. These three chapters are of interest not only in providing a clear picture of the overall progress of the infant to the stage of gestural communication, but also in the substantial agreements and disagreements between them. Some of the points are raised in triplicate, but because of the importance of the topics, and the fact that the chapters were produced independently, I have not edited these out. It is quite clear by the end of this section that around the age of 9 months the infant's social transactions have elevated him to a level at which he is equipped to become a very competent communicator—without being able to say a word.

In Section 5, Ingram outlines the other side of the coin, how the infant's knowledge of the physical world relates to the development of language. Nokony reports a detailed study of one child's transition from prelinguistic to linguistic communication explicitly adopting the Piagetian framework. For a review of the relation between Piagetian theory and the social perspective implicit here the reader is referred to Newson and Newson (1976). Similarly, Carter traces in great detail the passage of one child from being able to direct another's attention gesturally to performing the same function with words. All these writers lend weight to the view that language develops through a continuous process. This does not mean that there are no qualitative differences between, say, crying when hungry and later saying "I am hungry". While the poles of the continuum may show vast differences, developmentally they are linked through a series of small non-qualitative changes. Ginsberg (1976) reviewing the evolution of communicative patterns, concludes that "though many fairly complex situations can be comprehended and communicated by the signing chimp, he is still different in kind as well as in degree from any human potential for language". From this current perspective Ginsberg's view requires qualification, qualitative differences being seen as consequences of quantitative ones, and what qualitative differences there are—for example, the propositional ability—representing the explicit formulations of abilities implicit in phylogenetically and ontogenetically earlier systems.

This problem of differences is a knotty one, and the remaining two chapters in Section 5 bear on it. Firstly, there is the problem of specific linguistic knowledge raised by the Chomskyean approach to language. This paradigm has explicitly raised language to an unique status:

> Anyone concerned with the study of human nature and human capacities must somehow come to grips with the fact that all normal humans acquire language, whereas acquisition of even its barest rudiments is quite beyond the capacities of an otherwise intelligent ape. . . . It is widely thought that the extensive modern studies of animal communication challenge this classical view; and it is almost universally taken for granted that there exists a problem of explaining the "evolution" of language from systems of animal communication. However, a careful look at recent studies of animal communication seems to me to provide little support for these assumptions. Rather, these studies bring out even more clearly the extent to which human language appears to be a unique phenomenon, without significant analogue in the animal world. If this is so, it is quite senseless to raise the problem of explaining the evolution of human language from more primitive systems of communication that appear at lower levels of intellectual capacity. (Chomsky, 1968, p. 59)

A little further on, discussing specific views put forward by Popper (1972), he makes his position quite clear with respect to evolutionary theories:

> There is no reason to suppose that the "gaps" are bridgeable. There is no more of a basis for assuming an evolutionary development of "higher" from "lower" stages, in this case, than there is for assuming an evolutionary development from breathing to walking; the stages have no significant analogy, it appears, and seem to involve entirely different processes and principles. (1968, p. 60)

It is not surprising, then, that the operations underlying linguistic abilities should come to be postulated as specific to the language system. Because of a shift from syntactic grammars in the study of child language many writers have moved away from the view of specific linguistic universals (for example Bruner, 1975; Luria, 1975; MacNamara, 1972; Neisser, 1976; Piaget and Inhelder, 1969; Sinclair, 1971). Greenfield's contribution to this section, along with the evolutionary perspective put forward here, continues this shift, arguing for amodal principles of structural organization. Clearly it is necessary to devote more time in future to the relations between perception, action—physical and social (i.e. gesture)—and language.

In his recent book Neisser (1976) has begun to explore these lines, and in doing so also raises the question of the relevance of gesture to language development. At one point he raises a problem for gestural (i.e. visual) communication versus auditory forms. Words, being sounds, are easily dissociated from the perceptual cycle attuned to the speaker and "appropriated" by that concerned with the referent: "a name is a property of a thing which must be uttered by a person: its charm and its power lie precisely in the confluence of these two perceptual cycles. Words specify their referents as well as the articulatory gestures of the speaker" (Neisser, 1976, p. 165). In the case of visual gestures, the situation is more confused:

> A visual signal, such as a gesture in sign language, might not have this advantage. The child would be naturally inclined to treat it just as something his mother was doing, rather than as somehow connected with the signified object. Of course it is possible for people (or chimpanzees) to learn various kinds of sign-language, but they must be *taught*. The contingencies must be deliberately arranged, at least at first . . . I do not think language would have emerged spontaneously among organisms that could not hear. (Neisser, 1976, p. 166)

This is a very cogent and well-reasoned view, but one, along with many other currently reasonable expectations, that is contradicted by findings reported by Feldman, Goldin-Meadow and Gleitman in Section 5. To find a symbolic communicative system being generated *de novo*, and in a sufficient number of cases to assume that we are not dealing with an aberrant prodigy, will be astounding to many. And to find that this system exhibits grammatical form opens our eyes even wider. This chapter raises so many issues as to make it impossible to list them all here. Further, with the information so new in our consciousness we need time to let it sink in to be able to give it a full and rational appraisal. But having said this, I intend to consider briefly the possible significance of this report with respect to the ontogenetic and phylogenetic issues of concern here.

Cicourel, in conjunction with Boese (Cicourel, 1973; Cicourel and Boese, 1972a,b), has made a distinction between native sign-languages—those acquired and used spontaneously by deaf children—and second-language signers. "The use of a native sign-language is viewed as qualitatively different from the use of oral language in the 'same' ethnographic contexts" (Cicourel and Boese, 1972b, p. 225). Basically, they argue that different grammatical normative systems are involved in each case (for details, see Cicourel, 1973; and Cicourel and Boese, 1972a,b). It is useful to give some of Cicourel's views in detail, as they convey the points that I would want to make.

> The generative nature of sign-language usage for the deaf and the use of non-oral features of communication among hearing persons are not viewed as being tied to a syntactic rule production system, but as having features that mark sign language as a qualitatively distinctive system for the deaf, and as a residual system for the hearing that either adds supplementary information to oral speech or can transcend such speech and serve as an independent channel of communication (Cicourel and Boese, 1972b). I am assuming that the hearing child learns a rather primitive signal system consisting of gestures, quasi-manual signs and vocal cues. As his speech production grows more sophisticated, the use of the signal system becomes residual and subject to minimal control. If speech is not encouraged or is blocked, the manual sign system would emerge as the basic form of communication. I am asserting that the generative semantic principles underlying both hearing and deaf systems of communication are the same. (Cicourel, 1973, pp. 94-95)

> If sign language can be a systematic way of communicating with primates, then native signs unconnected to oral language structure might afford more success. If primates can use signs tied to spontaneous human use of signs, then we might be able to establish some kind of communicative continuity between man and animals of lower complexity that does not presume that oral language is somehow more "natural" or the only conception of "language" available for communication across species. (Cicourel and Boese, 1972b, p. 231)

I believe the evidence presented here tips the scales greatly in favour of this sort of view. Chimpanzees in their natural environment employ a "natural gesture language": the prelinguistic human infant similarly becomes able to communicate gesturally. Further, the developmental processes in both cases appear to have a great deal of complementarity: direct actions being initially fortuitously communicative, and eventually becoming truly so through the meaning they are afforded in their interactive setting. Language would appear to emerge out of gesture through a creative process, doing so with or without the presence of a model, thus legitimately allowing us to cope with both developmental and evolutionary perspectives within the same theoretical paradigm emphasizing the process of invention. As Macmurray has pointed out (1961, p. 60),

> Long before the child learns to speak he is able to communicate, meaningfully and intentionally, with his mother. In learning language, he is acquiring a more effective and more elaborate means of doing something which he already can do in a crude and more primitive fashion. If this were not so, not merely the child's acquiring of speech, but the very existence of language would be an inexplicable mystery.

Two prime factors seem to allow humans to exhibit their facility in language "learning". Firstly the time factor—the historical age of language —has been sufficient to allow the species to genetically adapt itself—or develop its preadaptation—to an environment which it has itself created. It would be foolish for us to expect an infra-hominid to be able, at present, to progress as far and as quickly as we have, given that the apparently inherent potentiality of the human for language is so great as to find expression even under the most adverse of circumstances. Secondly, conversely, or even necessarily, the social environment into which he is born is one which seems tailored to allow the full expression and development of that potential: adults modify their behaviour towards young children in many ways to provide what Edwards (Chapter 16, this volume) terms "implicit language tuition".

The chapters in the final section (Section 6) address themselves to specifically language-related aspects of this interlocking system. That language development can be profitably viewed via the concepts of adaptation and guided reinvention can be clearly seen here. Broadly the child may be viewed as an inventor of hypotheses about possible meanings on the bases of his social experience. His subsequent actions from these foundations elicit guidance or feedback which effects their refinement towards a culturally acceptable set. That guidance or feedback is most likely to be provided in a form which is relevant—or adapted—to his current level of development towards that end. Edwards, Braunwald and Ferrier each deal with facets of the early stages of language development in this light. Shields finishes the book by considering the abilities of older and linguistically more sophisticated children, and in doing so places the work reported here in the larger context of developmental psychology as a whole.

Section 2

Theoretical Perspectives
and a Case Study

2

The Biological and the Social*

M. P. M. RICHARDS

University of Cambridge, England

Social psychology, as an academic training and research activity, has developed as a self-contained and inward-looking discipline which has not only become separated from the phenomena it sets out to analyse but is also sterile as a source of human understanding. It has adopted the ethos and methodology of mainstream psychology and applied them to a restricted series of topics and problems—predominantly those constructed by the manipulation of small groups of people ("subjects") in artificial laboratory situations. Such theory as has been produced can always suggest new experiments which provide new permutations and embroidery on the old themes so the social psychologists can always be seen to be busy. But busy at what?

The field became inward-looking and esoteric because the language of its discussions was not comprehensible to the main body of experimental psychologists and because little that went on seemed to have any bearing on the outside world. This latter point is not simply one of relevance,[†] but is even more seriously related to the generality of the findings. All too often, what seemed to be a common feature of behaviour in laboratory situations has been found not to hold in the real world. So, for example, the ease with which "attitudes" may be manipulated in a laboratory small group seems to have few parallels in everyday life.

·*Reprinted by permission of Penguin Books Ltd. from *Reconstructing Social Psychology* (N. Armistead, Ed.), pp. 233-239 (Penguin Education, 1974). © Nigel Armistead and contributors, 1974.

†Recent attempts to demonstrate the relevance of this kind of social psychology by applying it to everyday situations have only served to underline its triviality (see, for example, Swingle, 1973) and show that it is perhaps a very pompous way of stating the obvious.

It is not too difficult to see why social psychology should have developed in this way. Its practitioners have always had the lowest status within psychology and they were left with the problems that were regarded as peripheral by the higher-status psychologists. These latter people, while concentrating on the topics most amenable to the methodology of classical physics and chemistry, were happy enough to see social psychology exist, for they could hardly deny the existence of a social world, but they always looked down on it as the "soft" end of the subject. In a situation like this it was predictable that the social psychologists should try to gain status by aping the experimentalists—by trying to out-psychologize their more secure colleagues. So the methodology became everything and produced a subject that was all form with no function or, to adopt an analogy from psycholinguistics, it is all performance with no competence. Elaborate experimental designs and sophisticated statistics were used in studies of phenomena that might have no importance—or even reality. (In passing, we may note how often in psychology departments the social psychologists are in charge of statistics teaching.)

In recent years this picture has begun to change. Being the most vulnerable, social psychology was the first discipline to crumble in the face of attacks on mindless empiricism. At the same time interest in the problems of social life has been growing and not unnaturally people have been asking what academic psychology has to offer. So social psychology is being reconstructed. It is my aim in this chapter to argue that if these attempts at rebuilding are to be successful, they must take account of both the social *and* the biological nature of man. To do this I will use a discussion of early development and socialization as illustration.

Social scientists have had a longstanding prejudice against biological views of man which has been fed and justified by numerous misleading doctrines about human nature that have arisen from the theories of the biologists. The identification and analysis of these has become a major theme in the history of science (e.g. Young, 1973) and I have only space to mention a few of the more obvious.

The false translation of theories about evolution into social Darwinism was but one phase in a long tradition which has used organismic analogies for society. In this particular version, the notion of natural selection was used to justify and make seem inevitable, social divisions within society and the exploitation of man by man. Here, as so often seems to be the case, the biological analogy was not used to explore or analyse the structure of society or the processes acting within it but simply as a justification of a *status quo*. This same process may be found in the attempts to see cultural and social differences between individuals or groups of people as an inevitable product of biological differences, a tradition that runs from nineteenth-century anthropology through to the current debate about the heritability of I.Q. (Richards *et al.*, 1972). Here, as well as a misunderstanding about the social nature of social action, there is a misconception about the role of genetic differences in the development of individual characteristics. Those that have argued in this way have not understood that epigenetic processes specify means and not ends, and that therefore genes do not *determine* anything.

Another widespread biologism is obvious in "explanations" of human action that involve postulating a series of innate drives or instincts. Theories of this kind gloss over all problems about the meaning of behaviour (q.v. Becker, 1972) which they see as being immanent in particular configurations of muscle movements. So behaviour is not distinguished from action and such accounts are unable to cope with fundamental questions about intention, the self or self consciousness.*

A final vice that should be mentioned is the use, or rather overuse, of accounts of animal behaviour in discussions of our own species. If these arguments are not based on both a full biological understanding and an appreciation of the social world constructed by man, they will always tend to reduce man to a complex animal-machine. They will underplay the species-specificity of our own behaviour and so ignore the human attributes of language, self-reflection and social communication (Bernal and Richards, 1973).

In a justified attempt to save their concerns from a reduction to biologisms of these and other varieties, many social scientists have moved in the other direction and have constructed entirely social theories of social action and it is this tendency I hope to counteract. Any complete account of man must be able to come to terms with both his social and his biological natures.

A human infant is born with a predisposition to become both adult (Trevarthen, 1972) and social (Berger and Luckman, 1967). Given both the biological structure of the infant and the social world in which he lives and which is necessary for his survival, a social adult will be formed during development. If the biological structure of the infant did not play an essential role in this process, any living organism should serve. But, of course, we find that attempts to rear even our closest biological relatives, the great apes, as

---

*There have been some recent signs that this question is being reopened by some ethologists. Vernon Reynolds (1976) has recently published a text book of human ethology which is based on Weber's distinction between behaviour (Verhalten) and action (Handeln). However, such a view is still rare and usually all analysis is based on the observation and measurement of behaviour, even when working with our own species. Hinde and Stevenson Hinde (1976), for example, have recently re-asserted a purely behaviouristic approach to the study of social relationships on the grounds that concepts like intersubjectivity are correlated with "behavioural meshing" and because they believe that behaviouristic methodology is all that is available. They do, however, concede that behaviourism is insufficient to "solve every question that will come up".

children fail to produce people. Similarly, deprived of human companions, a human infant will not become a person. In order to understand socialization, the process whereby an infant born into a society becomes a full adult member, we must analyse the contribution of biological structure to the process. What is it about an infant that allows him to become a person?

One of the first things to notice about a human infant is his inability to survive on his own and so his absolute dependence on other members of his society which will last for several years (Bruner, 1972). During this time, even his most basic biological needs (for food, for warmth) can only be satisfied by the active intervention of others. So the essence of socialization becomes communication, for it is only in so far as other adults perceive and understand an infant's needs that these can be met (Macmurray, 1961, especially Chapter 2). From birth onwards, adults are involved in a process of interpreting an infant's behaviour. It is through these interpretations, the actions of adults towards him, that an infant is able to perceive the consequences of his activities, and this allows him to develop an intentional structure for his own activities. Through this process, his behaviour becomes intentional action. This is a line of theoretical speculation which is grounded in the philosophical work of G. H. Mead (Mead, 1934; Strauss, 1956; Miller, 1973). Until recently, this work has largely been ignored by developmental and social psychologists and much more detailed theoretical analysis and empirical research is required before we can get beyond the most general statements. But its great advantage and potentiality lies in the fact that it opens the way to a truly human view of social development which may be married with an adequate theory of developmental biology.

However, there are some areas where our knowledge of development is already sufficient for us to see some of the details of the processes by which the social and the biological interact with one another.

The infant's biological structure provides a selectivity in the perceptual processes so that attention is focused on features that form part of adult communication modes and therefore allow the formation of agreed channels for communication between adult and infant. (This is described in much greater detail elsewhere (Richards, 1974).) From an early age one can observe rudimentary dialogue between infant and adult in which there seems to be agreement about how communication is to be effected even if the nature of what has to be communicated is little more than a mutual acknowledgement that there is another person there. Infants selectively attend to faces. This seems so natural to us adults that we seldom pause to consider either the complexity of organization that makes this possible or the enormous importance of this biological preadaptation for socialization and the richness of the face as a source of information about a person's state. Another example of this kind of preadaptation is the infant's preference for speech-like sounds. This provides a structure in (and of) the world for the infant; he does not have to begin from scratch trying to classify all sounds as if they all might have biological and social importance for him. Through this adaptation he is led towards relevant sounds and so into an agreed channel of communication which will culminate in the acquisition of language and his entry into his linguistic community.

To establish communication one needs not only agreed channels or modes but there also must be rules about the temporal use of the channels. Recent observational studies of infants have shown that their behaviour is structured in time and that they are very sensitive to the timing of the alternations and reciprocations of their social partners in communication episodes. Within the first few weeks of life, they come to expect that responses will arrive at particular points in sequences and, if they do not, the sequence may well be cut short. Abilities of this kind are, of course, essential before speech may be developed as a mode of communication, and yet again the indications are that they are made possible by the existence of a human biological structure.

The fundamental role of these biological preadaptations to social life can easily be appreciated if you perform a thought experiment on yourself. First fix in your mind a picture of an infant—say a 9-month-old. Picture his social actions, his powers of communication and understanding, his abilities to make his intentions known to other people. Then consider how these might have developed taking a traditional view of the infant as a creature which is essentially a *tabula rasa*, with a few reflexes and the rest of his behaviour a series of random movements. Add to this the postulates of any stimulus-response learning ("behaviour") theory. Then explain how the infant grows up into the 9-month-old you pictured at the beginning . . . Of course, it won't work. Even if one assumes an enormously structured environment, a glorified conditioning laboratory constructed with the sole purpose of ensuring the learning of a vast array of specific attributes, it still does not seem possible. But even that is ruled out. Observation of the environments of infants provides no evidence that parents systematically respond to their children in the ways that are required by learning theory. No; clearly the infant must play a major role in structuring and organizing his own environment and learning particular things about it and he is endowed with a biological nature that makes this possible.

However, this biological endowment does not determine outcomes—it provides means and not ends. Human development would not be possible without a social world. This is something that is missed by theorists who argue that the infant is a social being and that his behaviour patterns such as crying and smiling constitute social behaviour. Implicit in this view is the idea that the behaviour pattern determines its own social meaning (as it is seen as the determinant of the adult's response to the infant). In contrast to this, I would argue that the infant's behaviour pattern is of biological origin but it is made social by its recognition and interpretation by adults. (This theme is elaborated by Shotter in Chapter 4.) Its meaning is negotiated by those who interact with the infant.

This difference is much more than a quibble, because if one believes that a behaviour pattern arrives with a ready-made meaning, there is no room left for the development of autonomy and self reflection by the infant. Furthermore, the infant's signals (his crying, smiling, and so on) would become a kind of biological imperative and any adult who failed to respond to them would have to be regarded as biologically as well as socially deficient. Of course, these infant signals are not randomly associated with his internal states and conditions. Nobody seems to regard smiling as a signal of discomfort nor is crying seen as a sign of contentment. But in responding to the infant's signals an adult must interpret them, decide what they mean and what, if anything, is to be done about them. As cross-cultural studies have demonstrated, these interpretations vary across society and embody each culture's belief system.

In this discussion I have deliberately concentrated on some of the features of the earliest stages in the process of socialization because it is here that the role of biological structure is perhaps clearest. But all the later stages rest on these beginnings. Often this is forgotten and accounts of socialization emphasize later childhood and the role of school and other institutions. If these alone are considered it is easy to provide a superficially complete account without mentioning biological structure. However, this only touches the surface of the matter because, though a child may change while a member of a school, the total of such changes do not together make up the whole of socialization. These one-sided accounts take as unproblematic the formation of a person and merely consider the rather superficial processes that result from participation in particular social institutions. The central issue in the problem of socialization is the formation of a person.

In this brief chapter I have only had space to sketch out a few points of an extremely complex area but I hope I have established two things: first, that theories in social psychology must take account of man's biological structure. Without this they are incomplete or, worse still, they will tend to drift off, unanchored, in an endless sea of social definitions. And I have tried to show that biological considerations need not lead to reductionism or to any denial of the social nature of social life.

Given the fragmentation of our academic life, in both research and teaching, into the various disciplines, it is extremely difficult to find positions from which to bring together those things that are traditionally kept in isolation. Here, I think, social psychology is ideally placed and in its reconstruction the way is open to build a viewpoint that will cut across traditional tendencies and provide a holistic vision of man.

POSTSCRIPT

When the editor invited me to contribute to this book, I felt that an account of the theoretical work that I was doing with Denise Riley on the social and biological in development would fit in with the overall plan and the editor readily agreed. However, we were too optimistic. As we got deeper into the work we began to realize the extent and complexity of the task we had undertaken and found that, as the deadline for our chapter approached, we were far from reaching a point where we could make any statement that was worth publication. So instead, we decided to follow another course. This is reprinting an earlier statement of mine from Nigel Armistead's *Reconstructing Social Psychology* together with a postscript which would serve to indicate its weaknesses and provide a few pointers in the directions where we feel that resolution of some of the problems may lie. However, we should emphasize that no-one has yet produced an adequate theoretical statement of the way in which one might handle the relationship between the biological and social worlds in developmental theory, so that anything that is said at the present time must be regarded as very preliminary and tentative.

The chapter reprinted above outlines the traditional interactionist approach to developmental problems. Roughly, this involves a division of the factors concerned in development into two categories, the biological and social (nature and nurture, genes and environment, innate and learnt), and opposing these and stating that they are linked by a process of *interaction*. (This should not be confused with the use of the same term to describe a social relationship as in the interaction of mother and child.) For a number of reasons we find this an unsatisfactory approach and suggest that its continued acceptance is a major obstacle to theoretical progress in this area.

There are many variants of interactionism but all of them seem to share the following difficulties:

(a) The nature of the interactive process is almost always left vague and unspecified. Indeed, many writers simply gloss this problem by saying that "complex interactions are involved" but no more. It is not clear, for example, whether interaction should be conceptualized as the putting together of separate elements like the pieces of a jigsaw puzzle or whether it is a process of blending or mixture. (Here the level of analysis is likely to be crucial.) If we are to derive any theoretical strength from the concept of interaction we must be able to conceptualize the process *in detail*.

(b) Often the elements that are said to be involved in interactive process are of such diverse conceptual kinds that they could never meet. For example, interactions between the genes and environment are frequently discussed as if there were some material processes by which the genes and social conditions in the family, for example, could act upon one another. Obviously, one could describe a complex chain of processes which would provide a link between the two but this seems rather different from what is implied by interaction. For interaction to have any conceptual utility it seems reasonable to demand an isomorphism between the interacting elements. The use of various statistical techniques containing interaction terms often helps to conceal this problem. Such mathematical descriptions of interactions have no constraints of isomorphism—one can add any kind of variable—so may be very misleading theoretically.

(c) The implicit (or explicit) assumption of most interactionist formulations is that there are biological given, or starting, points which are acted on by social and psychological conditions. This implies that each has a degree of autonomy which would then appear to rule out the possibility of interaction.

Formulations of this kind do not give an equal status to the two terms of the interaction equation. Biology is seen as being prior both in space and time. This is clear from the wide use of phrases like the "biological foundations of behaviour" or the common view that development and socialization consists of a movement from the biological towards the social. This is paralleled by philogenetic view of an evolution from animals to socialized humans which in many discussions of human action reduces history to the consideration of hunting and gathering societies or, even, non-human primates. This view of the priority of biology is reflected in our language too as biology is seen to be, literally, closer to the bone. Where the priority is linked to determinism the confusions become compounded as in the recurring debate about the significance and meaning of racial differences in I.Q.

More could be said of the conceptual problems of interactionism but perhaps these brief notes are enough to indicate the extent of the problems. Interactionism is a plausible strategy, especially when contrasted with extreme environmentalist or hereditarian formulations, but it is far too loose and muddled to provide anything approaching an adequate conceptual framework for understanding developmental processes.

In beginning to build more adequate theoretical models there are a number of features of developmental processes that we need to consider:

(a) Biology does not have any conceptual priority over social processes. It may appear to because the early stages of development are often described in physiological or anatomical terms (foetuses and newborns) while older children and adults are usually seen in psychological and social terms—at least by developmental psychologists. We perhaps need to re-examine the conventional starting points for developmental description and see that conception, for instance, can be a misleading beginning. In the social world the moment of conception is unnoticed and in terms of human action is not a starting point of any significance. To use it in psychological accounts may simply lead back to a position where individual development appears to emerge from the world of biology.

If the newborn is described as a biological being, this again sets up a framework into which development becomes a movement from the biological to the social. Part of the difficulty here lies with the loose and varying usage of terms like social behaviour. If social behaviour is taken to be behaviour that is characteristic of interchanges between adults or verbal children—as it is, in effect, in many theories—an infant will be seen as something other than a member of a social world and development and, especially, socialization becomes the movement to that world. But if we are less adultocentric in our definitions the problem can be avoided.

(b) Central to many of the confusions that have been mentioned is the notion that there is an autonomous world of biology. But at whatever level one chooses, careful examination reveals that there is no autonomy of this kind. The newborn, for instance, is just as much a product of historical processes as evolutionary ones and his own development as a foetus will have been influenced by the social world in which he lives. We know little of the details of the processes involved but even for the most obvious of "biological" criteria like birthweight and the probability of neonatal survival there are marked correlations with such social factors as the social class of his parents or whether or not they are married.

Evolutionary arguments are often misleading in that they ignore our history and our social life. Attachment processes between mother and child, for instance, have been discussed in terms of a selective advantage in avoiding predation. Leaving aside the point that it is reasonable to suppose that many, many generations have passed since animal predation was a significant factor in infant mortality, arguments of this kind miss the fundamental point that in social species selection is mediated by social arrangements and organization. These have changed rapidly and frequently throughout the evolution of our species making hypotheses about selection hard to sustain or refute but the least we can say is that it is unlikely that selection pressures have operated uniformly throughout human history in the same ways as can be observed today in non-human primate societies.

(c) Interaction implied a rather random and chance meeting of elements. However, randomness is in no way characteristic of development—indeed quite the reverse. Many developmental processes show a high degree of predictability and resistance to change in varying environments. This is an area in which a good deal of theoretical work has been done by biologists, notably C. M. Waddington (1975) but it is only just beginning to have any influence on developmental psychology. However, the kind of epigenetic models that Waddington has proposed appear to avoid many of the problems of interactionism and are one of the most promising lines of theoretical development. But in using models of this kind it is very important that the levels of analysis that are being employed are specified. It is all too easy to combine non-isomorphic elements in conceptual schemes without providing the "transfer function" that are necessary to link psychological and physiological processes or either of these to social analysis. Perhaps, as Waddington has hinted, three-dimensional models will be required for adequate representation of these relationships.

As I warned at the beginning, these brief remarks are intended as tentative and preliminary notes. A great deal of work remains before we can reach satisfactory theoretical formulations. However, the first step in that process is the recognition of the weaknesses of current theories. I have sketched some of these at a very general level. One way of pushing this process much further is to apply a critical conceptual analysis to a specific development problem. The area of the development of communication and language would seem a very suitable place to start.

3
Dialogue and Development

JOHN NEWSON

University of Nottingham, England

The purpose of this chapter is to outline a theoretical approach which puts communication at the centre of the stage in relation to the development of a human infant. The term "communication" is not here being used as a synonym for language, but is intended to refer to a more general human facility upon which language itself seems to be founded. Thus this paper is concerned with the origins of our ability to empathize, to imitate and to share emotions with our fellow men, as well as with our ability to learn to speak any particular language. By talking about "communication", then, I wish to make reference to our power to create shared understandings with other people via interactions which make use of mime and gesture as well as the overt display of emotions and feelings. Thus I shall take it as self-evident that in face-to-face communication we engage in reciprocally prompted actions which include non-vocal as well as vocal signals; while within the vocal mode itself, words are by no means the sole vehicle for our communication.

This approach is certainly not intended to deny the importance of language as a hugely powerful tool of communication so far as human co-operation and culture are concerned; but it does imply that it may be impossible to understand the evolution of formal verbal or written language systems, either in the personal history of the individual or in the evolutionary history of mankind, without recognizing that shared understandings between people pre-date the emergence of language systems. As a developmental psychologist, however, I intend to restrict the discussion which follows to the growth of communicative competence at the individual level, by attempting to describe how shared understandings begin to emerge during the first year of a child's life.

When we consider the question of communication between adults, we can usually take it for granted that they already share all sorts of mutual categories of thought and feeling. Between an adult and an infant, however, we have to try and comprehend the way in which a code of communication may be evolved *de novo*, as it were; and this poses a different problem from that in which one is merely concerned with the specification of some mechanism for translating from one established code into another. To understand how the infant's ability to communicate is first established, where none was before, is not easy. Problems arise at the conceptual level, perhaps because our conventional scientific language of description and explanation is shot through with all sorts of deterministic, mechanistic and behaviouristic assumptions. To illustrate this point, I will first try to tackle the issue of communication using a form of descriptive language which deliberately adopts the perspective of a neutral or non-participant observer, my aim being to push explanation within such an expository framework to its natural limit. Subsequently, however, a rather different account will be offered; and this strategy may enable the reader to judge for himself the relative merits of these two approaches. It may also help to explain why we ourselves have been driven to adopt the second one.

AN OBJECTIVE APPROACH

During the past decade, there has been a great resurgence of interest in psychological studies of human infants; and within this movement, many researchers have been drawn towards the particular study of the complex and sophisticated social activity which all normal babies so obviously manifest when in the presence of their everyday caretakers. For the student whose knowledge of babies is drawn from psychological textbooks, and not from real life, the most striking effect of exposure to ordinary mothers and their infants is the revelation that, by the age of 10 or 11 months, normal babies are highly competent in the art of communication. By this age it is obvious that they deliberately make known their desires and dissatisfactions, join in games, share jokes, imitate all sorts of obviously meaningful actions and gestures, and can even tease their mothers. Furthermore, it is quite clear that they accomplish all this without the help of formal language and without even a passive understanding of words as such. Like researchers in many other centres, we ourselves have been concerned to develop ways of giving an accurate description of how preverbal infants typically develop such complicated social skills in interaction with their mothers. In the Child Development Research Unit at Nottingham, we now have on file a substantial number of video-recordings illustrating mother-baby interaction in free-play settings obtained from regular weekly recording sessions with infants between 4 and 11 months of age. It is on the basis of a careful study of these and other similar records that the following propositions are offered as guidelines for further discussion.

1. It seems to be a necessary condition for the evolution of communication that the two individuals involved are capable of performing discrete and distinguishable actions which can serve the function of signals. Each of the two individuals must have a repertoire of "displays" or potential signals, together with some independent capacity to exercise selective control over the performance of such actions.

2. Equally important, however, is the notion that each individual must be sensitive to the occurrence of similar "displays" when these are offered by the other individual. Furthermore, both partners must apparently be impelled regularly to relinquish their own activity in order to be able to attend effectively to the activity of the other.

3. For communication to develop, it seems to be necessary for the discrete "signals" of the two interacting organisms to be repeatedly interwoven in familiar alternating sequences. This process, in time, gives rise to a recurrence of patterned sequences to which both partners are sensitive and to which both partners contribute.

The whole process may be summarized by saying that adults and infants actually engage in "conversation-like" exchanges. These typically take the form of well-worn rituals of interaction to which the baby clearly makes a real and positive contribution. Even young infants play a highly active role in constructing dialogues of reciprocating activity, and apparently have little difficulty in sustaining that role even though responses are demanded at a rate which frequently exceeds 30 gestures per minute, or one every other second.

In a previous paper (Newson, 1974) I have stressed the debt which developmental psychology owes to Colwyn Trevarthen for highlighting the fact that human babies characteristically exhibit a variety of intrinsic activity patterns which serve as a basis for communication competence. Even at birth, it is possible to detect gesture-like actions which are complex co-ordinations of arm and hand movements, head and eye orientations, mouthings and vocalizations. This activity of the infant is not formless but highly integrated. It is patterned as a function of time, and displays a specific rhythm so that each separate action builds up to a clear climax followed by a subsequent decline. Typically, babies evince such patterned activity when faced with "objects" which are themselves responsive in like fashion: exhibiting, that is, patterns of sound and movement with that particular climactic periodicity which is characteristic of the behaviour of most mammals.

In early infancy these temporally organized patterns may be obscured unless we search carefully for them. They tend to be interrupted by unco-ordinated "jerky" limb movements, and are suppressed or masked by frequent discomfort reactions. Young babies also tire easily. Under optimal conditions of wakefulness and physical support, however, it is possible to demonstrate and record quite perfect gesture-like actions, remarkably similar in form and speed to those habitually used in gestural communication by adults. In practice these gesture-like actions are executed with such rapidity that it seems to be necessary to make use of slowed-down video or film recordings to study them and demonstrate their occurrence with certainty. Trevarthen's evidence is, however, very compelling and suggests that babies are capable of emitting discrete "pre-formed" actions which simulate adult communication gestures. Given that conversation-like gestures can occur in babies, it is obvious that we should ask what factors prompt and sustain them; and to begin with it seems clear that their time of occurrence is not at all random, but timed to accommodate to the reciprocal gestures offered by some person with whom a baby may be confronted. Typically, the infant and his regular adult caretaker come to operate according to an alternating or turn-taking sequence, in which each partner first acts and then attends to the activity of the other (Schaffer, 1974). There is controversy about whether this alternation of activity indicates some intrinsic predisposition for turn-taking in the baby, or is an artefact of a controlling influence exerted by the more sophisticated adult partner. Much neonatal-type activity follows a burst-pause cycle; if the adult merely filled in the infant's own pauses with his own bursts of activity, and inhibited his own gestures when the infant began to be active again, a semblance of deliberate alternation would obviously result.

There is, however, more to this. When an infant is faced with an "object" which is responsive to his own activity, it is clear that he may easily become locked into a sustained sequence of actions; his movements give rise to effects which attract his visual or auditory attention, eliciting an 'orienting response': and as a result of this his previous movements are inhibited. Then, as his attention **begins** to falter, he starts to indulge once more in an active phase of bodily movement which again produces change, and this is likely to attract his attention once more. An easy way to demonstrate the persistent engagement which can take place between an infant and an "environment-ally responsive" object is to link the infant's limb with some device which responds variably at a suitable time delay. When, for example, a string attached to the child's wrist is linked to a mobile placed clearly within his view, thus causing it to be disturbed whenever he waves his arms, it may be observed that even a very young baby seems to be constrained to "work" at operating the device, and his attentive involvement with it will characteristically be sustained over a long period of time (Papousek, 1967; Kalnins and Bruner, 1973).

The precise feedback characteristics which facilitate such "self-rewarding" activity are still but little understood; but they obviously include an optimal time delay between action and consequent reaction, and a variable, but not entirely unpredictable, outcome in the form of some consequent effect to which the infant does in fact attend. This optimal time delay may be related to the natural rate of signal exchange already referred to.

A mobile is, however, only sensitive to the infant's actions to a very limited degree, in this case being merely responsive to gross arm movements above a certain minimum amplitude. As an "environmentally responsive feedback system"; a human caretaker is a lot more sophisticated than a mobile and a piece of string. In particular he or she can, and does, "monitor" other aspects of the activity of the infant and hence is able to respond sensitively to all sorts of things the infant may do in addition to waving his arms. Such a caretaker will be guided by the nature and form of the infant's attention-paying gestures, including associated changes of facial expression, direction and intensity of gaze, etc. It should therefore not surprise us if the joint activity of adult and infant does soon begin to resemble a dialogue in which the partners take turns to act and to attend towards one another, thus producing a very adequate simulation of mature human discourse.

AN INTERSUBJECTIVE APPROACH

Let us now pause to take stock of the kind of account we have been attempting to give. So long as we restrict ourselves to the language of detached observation, we can only say that the infant makes "gesture-like" signals, or that conversation is being "simulated". We cannot assert that the infant himself—or for that matter the adult—attaches *meaning* to his actions, and it is for this precise reason that we have been driven to describe the infant's actions as "displays". By such usage, attention is directed towards the outward form of certain actions which are classed as signals, perhaps because of the consistent effect they can be observed to have on other members of the same species (Smith, 1965). Such a description cannot, however, offer an explanation for the evolution of those shared understandings which constitute the *meaningful content* of whatever is being communicated. To give an account of the ontogenesis of communication in this deeper sense, it is obviously necessary to grapple with the more difficult conceptual problem of how signals first acquire their "significance" within the mental experience of the infant. It should by now be clear, however, that no such account can be given while we restrict ourselves to a form of language which is only suitable for the description of what is outwardly observable. The language of the detached "scientific" observer quite simply contains no terminology for describing the reality of intersubjectively shared experience. In other words, the language which physical scientists so successfully use to describe relationships or interactions between material objects—with which we have no power to communicate directly—must be different from the form of language needed to describe how socially shared understandings can arise between people. A change is required both in the form of language and in the style of exposition, before we can expect further insight. At this point in the argument, therefore, we need a change in standpoint: we must shift perspective, as it were, so as to look at the process of communication from the point of view of a *participant* observer (Newson and Newson, 1975).

Once we are permitted to project ourselves into the role of someone who is trying to communicate with the infant, it becomes clear that such a person is bound to respond selectively to precisely those actions, on the part of the baby, to which one would normally respond *given the assumption that the baby is like any other communicating person*. In other words, the caretaker, being already well practised in the art of communication, will not respond indiscriminately to all aspects of the infant's activity. Instead he or she will selectively attend to those actions to which one would habitually attach significance as gestures which are normally meaningful in ordinary human discourse. Changes in the infant's facial expression will, for example, be attended to closely, because these will be automatically interpreted as changes of state which the infant is assumed to be experiencing. If he begins to look "pained" it will be assumed that he is suffering distress. Similarly with a young baby, one responds in different ways to unco-ordinated jerky movements of one limb and to directed hand-swipes apparently aimed with some degree of intention towards objects in the external world.

The response mechanism of another person is, however, so delicately tuned that it can respond *in anticipation* to what might be called actions-in-the-making. Thus, for example, when a mother sees the beginnings of a turned-down mouth in the facial expression of her child, she may immediately act to distract him *before* his lower lip begins to tremble, and thus may succeed in diverting him before his discomfort irrevocably engages his attention. In this instance the action is deliberately prevented from running its "normal" course. It is in fact a taken-for-granted aspect of normal mothering that distress in an infant may be cut short by using such distraction strategies. Somewhat less obviously, perhaps, actions which the mother values may skilfully be drawn out of the infant. Thus, by judicious anticipation allied with angling for the baby's attention at the right moment, full-blown smiles may be got from a baby by building upon the first incipient smiling gestures which the mother thinks she is able to detect. What eventually leads her to distinguish between a mere grimace and a true social smile is probably that the latter can be reliably elicited in a ritual consisting of nodding and smiling at the infant. In this case it is the context and timing of the baby's gesture, in relation to the mother's attempt to bring it out during the course of a social exchange, which is critical in determining whether a smile is considered "social". It follows that the meaning of a smile, as a social gesture, is inseparably bound up with the infant's ability to use it in a socially appropriate manner, i.e. at precisely the right moment within a dialogue of social interaction.

What is being argued here is that, whenever he is in the presence of another human being, the actions of a baby are not just being automatically reflected back to him in terms of their physical consequences. Instead they are being processed through a subjective filter of human interpretation, according to which some, *but only some*, of his actions are judged to have coherence and relevance in human terms—either as movements born of intentions, or as communications (or potential communications) addressed to another socially aware individual: subjectively filtered and then reflected back. It is thus only because mothers impute meaning to "behaviours" elicited from infants that these eventually do come to constitute meaningful actions so far as the child himself is concerned. Actions achieve this status to the extent that they are capable of being used as communication gestures which he knows how to produce, on cue, in the context of a social exchange between himself and someone else. In a real sense, therefore, gestures only acquire their significance in so far as they can be utilized as currency within social dialogues.

The desire to establish a degree of shared understanding with her baby is normally a powerful motive for the mother. She treats him from birth as a person who can be credited with feelings, desires, intentions, etc., and looks for confirmation that he will relate to her in a person-like way. His social smiles in response to her approaches provide important confirmation of humanness, and the fact that he can produce conversation-like vocalizations when she talks to him provides similar reassurance. By 3 months, many mothers also enjoy playing socially stimulating games with their babies; for instance games of anticipation like "threatening head", in which a warning signal is followed by a mock attack on his person with explosive lip noises and physical contact between the mother's mouth and the baby's face or body—a ritual in which mild alarm repeatedly ends in excited giggles. It is not only in games, however, that the dialogue form predominates. Thus in the serious matter of spoonfeeding, the child will soon know how to play his part in the ritual, accepting or rejecting each proffered spoonful by anticipatory mouth opening or by turning away. In a similar way the baby will now actively assist in the process of cup-drinking, by such actions as clinging to the cup and pulling it towards his mouth, showing impatience for more, pausing and looking up between swallowing bouts, and so on.

In all these activities, the co-ordinated looking activities which the infant performs with his eyes are obviously of fundamental importance in maintaining and establishing rapport with any caretaker. In the situation of direct face-to-face interaction, the infant will be visually attracted to scrutinize his caretaker's face when she is talking to him: it has, after all, the fascinating qualities of being a moving, self-deforming and noise-producing "object" which is also precisely and delicately responsive to his own actions and changes of mood. As we have already noted, however, the infant may be almost equally preoccupied in paying visual attention to an inanimate mobile, especially if it is one over which he himself can exert some form of control. He may be similarly drawn to devote his full attention to the puppet-like actions of a single hand scrabbling about in front of him; and if this is made to approach and touch him in a game-like interaction ritual, a hand in play may hold him spellbound. The interesting thing about this is that at 3 months of age there is little evidence to suggest that the infant understands the relationship between the dancing hand and the person who is controlling it. For theorists of cognitive development, like Piaget, the emergence within the infant of a clear distinction between "person objects" and "thing objects" marks a momentous watershed in mental development; and while it is by no means clear what prompts this "Copernican revolution" in human mental organization, the whole course of subsequent mental development is thought to be altered as a consequence.

From the caretaker standpoint, it is clear that mothers regard their infants' attention-paying gestures as immensely important within the dialogue of reciprocal actions which develops. The infant's tendency to pay them visual regard matters to them particularly, and direct eye-to-eye contact is seen as an especially rewarding and significant interpersonal event.

When between 5 and 6 months their babies begin to sit without support, and hence become rather fully involved in exploring and exploiting all sorts of inanimate objects, handling them themselves with full visual concentration, mothers often seem to suffer a period of relative deprivation as their babies' new-found interests now apparently exclude them. One may even observe mothers bending right down to seek eye-to-eye contact with their infants at this stage. Two important communication-maintaining strategies now emerge, however. One is the use by mothers of some reliable vocal gesture to call the baby's visual attention back towards themselves— the recurrent use of the name of the child is one example of this, although it is not always particularly successful. As an alternative, therefore, some mothers seem to develop an idiosyncratic and specialized auditory signal like tongue-clicking or even blowing noisily on the child's face to make him look up and meet their eyes.

The second common communication-maintaining strategy is to provide the baby with a simultaneous vocal-intonational commentary, which serves to highlight interesting moments relating to what the infant may be simultaneously experiencing *vis-à-vis* the object he is involved with. Here, once again, it is important to appreciate that the mother has the power to *anticipate* effects which her baby may inadvertently be about to produce, not just to react to things *after* they have happened. This means that she is able to offer him a dramatic intonational "marker" at the precise moment when the effect will be registering on the child himself. Certainly it is highly characteristic of this stage of development that mothers do repeatedly offer the baby vocal markers which highlight the occurrence of specific events so as to enhance their salience for him. Frequently also, maternal vocal signals are used as "pacers" to sensitize the child to the time-course of significant dynamic processes which he has inadvertently set in train. An example would be a mother's intonational commentary accompanying the occurrence of an interesting rotary movement set off by the child (for instance, when he begins to touch and explore a roundabout toy). Once again, however, it is in the mother's power to anticipate the likely outcome of the occurrence, before it is actually begun, which permits her intervention to be made with such delicate and precise timing that it coincides maximally with the child's visual attention-paying to the event in question.

The intuitive use of intonational marking and pacing signals by a baby's habitual caretaker provides him with a valuable running commentary on his own actions, even though this commentary cannot yet be effective by virtue of its verbal/semantic content, since the infant can be induced to experience shared states of feeling when a mother's voice-tone is associated with actions he is simultaneously performing. It seems likely, for instance, that in the course of repeated encounters an intonational commentary can begin to impart to the infant's actions a sense of coherence and goal-directedness which they would not otherwise have. Suppose, for example, that a baby is fumbling towards extracting a small object from within some kind of container. His mother's commentary—change of pace, tone of voice, dramatic interjections, etc.—will reflect the relative effort of his initial approach, will serve to sustain him to go on striving when success is judged by her to be imminent, and will express the drama of tension-release at the moment that a meaningful result is finally accomplished. In this way the tone of the maternal voice will convey to him both the need for continued activity and the sense of climax when his efforts are about to pay off. Certainly babies of a few months are highly sensitive to the tensions of audience expectation when they are battling with cognitive problems in the presence of an interested group of onlookers. When one is demonstrating the abilities of babies to students, one is highly conscious of audience-participation effects, of the kind which caused van Osten's horse, Clever Hans, to continue tapping its hoof until it had counted out the correct number of raps to complete the sum which its audience could see on the blackboard. In a broad sense, therefore, it seems that the roots of cognition and of social empathy may be a good deal closer than has hitherto been recognized. After all, many mothers deliberately teach their infants the meaning of "dirty" by registering dramatic disgust whenever the child starts to put some unclean object into his mouth; and if an unexpected happening occurs, they likewise reinforce the baby's sense of surprise, dismay, etc. by the whole quality of their own contagious emotional reaction, particularly through the tonal quality of their spontaneous vocal response.

The fact that marking and pacing signals, when offered in the auditory mode, do not distract the child from giving his full visual attention to whatever events he is himself controlling, implies a powerful and economic use of two independent channels of communication. One feels driven to speculate, therefore, about the peculiar disadvantages which must be suffered by the deaf child at this particular stage of development, because although it is possible to use marking and pacing signals which may be seen rather than heard, their use could be predicted to have a highly distracting effect upon the infant's visual attention-paying strategies, when used simultaneously.

Eventually, of course, even the child with intact hearing must learn to withdraw his visual attention from his own object-oriented activity in order to receive gestural—as opposed to auditory—confirmation about the reactions of his onlooking caretaker; and this clearly demands the operation of a memory-holding function within visual attention-giving, such that the activity may be interrupted while the infant makes a visual check-back from object to person, and be smoothly resumed again in the light of encouragement received or delight shared. In short, the infant must learn to make what we call a "referential glance" towards the caretaking person, thus providing a potent and deliberate act of communication about the effect of his actions on things. One important reason for the emergence of the referential glance could be that a child's play with objects often produces unexpected or mildly frightening outcomes. For instance, something may fall over and make an unexpected noise, or the child may accidentally bang an object into his own face. It may therefore be that reference-back-to-the-caretaker, for reassurance in states of alarm, represents an entrenched and primitive communication strategy which the child simply learns to carry forward from earlier days and put to new use. Perhaps, too, mothers deliberately tend to recruit their children's visual attention, particularly in "emergencies", by using urgent auditory warning signals which the child will be rather unlikely to ignore. This sort of speculative discussion, however, is mainly useful in drawing attention to the general principle that it may be a mistake to look for the precursor of any particular communication gesture, without referring to what has happened previously in the communication interchanges of the two interacting partners. Thus in the development of communication competence the *historical dimension*, in terms of idiosyncratic strategies previously developed by a particular mother-infant pair, is likely to be of fundamental importance in understanding how new strategies develop.

None the less, the ability to refer from thing to person, and back to thing again, must be seen as a significant accomplishment in the communication history of any child. It clearly has a lot to do with the infant's developing ability to distinguish operationally between persons and objects, and probably with his capacity to operate in the light of the even more fundamental distinction between self and other.

Obviously much more could be said about the diverse strategies used by ordinary mothers to establish and sustain communication with their babies. Susan Pawlby, for instance, has devoted a whole project to documenting the development of imitative routines between mothers and babies in order to show how such gestures are routinely used to communicate to the baby similarities between his own actions and those performed by others (Pawlby, 1977). Another study by Hilary Gray has concentrated on the way giving and taking gestures develop within a communicative context. It is not possible to elaborate on all these issues in a single short paper.

To sum up: the dialogue between a human infant and his regular caretaker represents a "cultural construction" of the utmost importance to the infant's whole future mental development. In attempting to describe the complexities of interaction during the first year of life, the very notion of dialogue is inescapable, and can most fruitfully be conceptualized as an alternating sequence of communication gestures. These are initially held together by a determination, on the part of the adult partner, to construe each and every act which is made by the infant as a meaningful signal in the light of the given situational context and of the immediately preceding signals which have been directed towards the baby. In many instances the relevant actions contributed by the baby himself will be indications that he has attended to the communication gestures offered to him or they will be spontaneous acts directed by the infant towards interesting objects or events which have monopolized his attention almost by chance. The caretaker, however, needs to operate within the format of an assumed ongoing dialogue, because as a communicating being this is the only way that it is possible to begin to make sense either of the baby's actions, or of her own in relationship to him.

Furthermore we, as observers, must use an effort of imagination so as to share with the baby's caretaker the general feeling of what it is to engage in an ongoing dialogue with him: otherwise we will not be in a position to describe the evolution of those shared understandings which subsequently begin to develop through this intricate process of interpersonal involvement and negotiation. From the baby's point of view it is only by being continually involved, as a participant actor, within an almost infinite number of such sequences that he is finally brought into the community of language. In short, it is only because he is treated as a communicator that he learns the essential human art of communication.

4

The Cultural Context of Communication Studies: Theoretical and Methodological Issues

JOHN SHOTTER

University of Nottingham, England

If we cannot give good reasons for our actions when called upon to do so by other members of the society in which we are also a member, then we risk more than just embarrassment at appearing somewhat stupid, we run the risk of losing our status as autonomous individuals. For, human societies being what they are, if we cannot justify our actions to others, then they may find them illegitimate, irrelevant, or unintelligible even, and thus rule them "out of court"; and it is then quite legitimate for them to expect us to act as they desire rather than we ourselves would prefer.

Thus to qualify as an autonomous person, not reliant like a child upon others to complete and give meaning to one's acts, having them decree the nature of one's actions, one must be able at some point in one's acting to stop and to deliberate, and, as a result, make clear to oneself (and/or to others) one's reasons for so acting. That is, one must be able to make clear in terms intelligible to other members of one's society the rational connections between what one is doing, its antecedents, and to what one hopes it might lead (and perhaps even the grounds for so hoping). So, psychologically then, if one is interested in the problem of how infants grow up to be "one of us" but also, none the less, themselves, with their own unique position in society at large, then a most interesting topic of study is the process within which the growth of deliberate action occurs; or, as one might call it, the *progressive rationalization of action*, or of experience.

It is proposed here that the developmental process in question is embedded in the communications which take place between the infant and those others in his society who are already (relatively) autonomous individuals. And the thesis that I want to defend here is one drawn, primarily, from Vygotsky (1962, Chapter 6): simply, that the activity which issues from one spontaneously, in the course of acting as one's circumstances require, may be transformed into deliberate action if one can learn from others some *reasons* for it; that is, broadly, if one can learn from them, by the way in which they "reply" to what one does, to what in the social world one's actions may lead, so that later, one may act *in the knowledge of* the social consequences of one's action.

It is worth adding here that such a process is, most interestingly, one in which the progressive rationalization of action may still take place at a practical level, while at a theoretical level, the participants involved in the process remain fundamentally vague as to the "proper" characterization of crucial features of their own nature—vague as to, for instance, the nature of human agency and how it is that people can act as they do, or vague as to the "proper" descriptions, interpretations, or explanations of particular actions. And this is a point which could be of great importance to those of us who as psychologists are professionally concerned with the rationalization of human action: it means that we may be able to live with theoretical vagueness and still be effective at a practical level. In fact, the assumption that certain central categories of the social world—agency, intention, etc.—are intrinsically vague will be elevated in what follows into one of their major theoretical features—for if people ever are to be thought of as being themselves responsible for doing things such as realizing intentions, transforming themselves, or simply making one thing rather than another happen, then it is necessary to assume that social reality is intrinsically vague, *not-yet-fully-determined*: only if it is, is it possible for man himself to be able to determine it one way or another by his actions.

APPROACHES TO THE STUDY OF HUMAN BEHAVIOUR

The Concern with Social Practices:
Man as an Agent in a Social World

In recent years, microanalytic studies of all forms of social interaction have burgeoned (more under the aegis of sociology than psychology; see Cicourel, 1973; Goffman, 1971), and with their burgeoning, implicitly rather than explicitly, a new way of doing psychology is beginning to develop. But now, rather than theory preceding practice as with the initial attempt to institutionalize psychological inquiry (see Koch, 1959, p. 783), practice is preceding theory. And this, as we shall see, is just how it should be if institutions appropriate to the conditions in which they must operate are to be established: they should merely institute what seem to be the effective aspects of the practices people are already performing in the circumstances spontaneously; it is a matter of the reflexive rationalization of the activities concerned.

The concerns of the new psychology are already reflected in the words above: action rather than thought has come to occupy the centre of the academic stage. Rather than an interest in attempting to discover, like Hull (1943) say, just a small number of very general principles by which to explain all "behaviour"—be it that of man, monkey, rat or amoeba—interest has now focused upon man's social practices, upon his ways of doing things, his "methodologies" (Garfinkel, 1967), his ways of making sense to others (Winch, 1958). So now, instead of constructing "theoretical models" that might parallel in their performances, men's forms of life, and arranging experimental situations in which men do just what is expected of them to confirm such models, attention is now turning to the study of what men actually do do in their attempt to construct and sustain a social world (Berger and Luckman, 1967), and conduct their everyday lives within it (Douglas, 1971; Schutz and Luckman, 1974). And of course, the behaviour of those conducting such investigations and attempting to construct accounts of what people do is not exempted from such studies (see, for instance, Cicourel's (1973) account of the ways linguists use speech and talk to construct a grammar that will describe the structure of a language); in other words, the new psychology promises to be *reflexive* (see Mead, 1934, p. 134, and Cicourel, 1973) in the sense of understanding itself and others in the same terms.

Now in the microanalytic study of mother-infant interaction we are concerned with the study (in fine detail) of the social practices in which people construct a way of (or a methodology for) making sense to and of one another. But our investigation of such social practices is itself a social practice, with the same concern. This fact leads to a strange but happy circumstance, for discussion of the general nature of such social practices (i.e. of ways of making sense) is at the same time necessarily a discussion for us of our methodology (i.e. our way of making sense of, and to, them). Thus in our studies, what is sauce for the goose is also sauce for the gander; whatever methods we may propose that mothers and children use in their attempts to make sense to one another, and develop their capabilities in their exchanges with one another, are also methods that we may use in our attempts to make sense of them. Thus the discussions that follow are at once both discussions of method and of theory, for in very general terms our task is to discover methods for understanding the methods that people use for, among other things, understanding one another. Or to put the matter somewhat less cryptically, our task is to find a way to develop the initially vague and inarticulate understanding of social practices we all, as participants in such practices, must have, into a precise, articulate and useful account. And in this we are concerned, not with the *origins* of our knowledge (of social practices) but merely with its *growth*; a point Popper (1963, 1972) emphasizes in his account of the growth of scientific knowledge. How it is that we can act as we do, we do not yet know, nor for the process of development that I want to discuss here does it matter that we do not know; all that matters is how we may develop the ability *ourselves* to "direct" our own processes, whatever they may be, whatever their origins.

Social practices, methodologies, "ways" of acting, strategies, etc. become, then, the subject matter of our new psychology; and, instead of as natural scientists studying the natural world, we study our subject matter as social scientists, from a standpoint in and as a feature of our *social world*.

Now the "social world" differs markedly from the natural world (of atoms and molecules, billiard-balls (?) and planets) in terms of which we have tried to explain human conduct in the past. As is quite clear, collections of atoms and molecules do not, we assume (although theorizing in physics has become exceptionally free in recent years), regulate their interactions with one another in terms of the meanings they assign to each other's behaviour; while equally clearly, people do so act. It is in their account of meaning that recent writers upon the nature of the social world (Wittgenstein, 1953; Winch, 1958; Mead, 1934; Schutz, 1967; Garfinkel, 1967; etc.) depart so much from the natural scientific view: they take "meaning" to be a human activity, a practical activity; it is something that people *do*. They do not take meanings as things which, as the products of processes, could exist independently and in isolation from the processes in which they are produced; as a human activity, "meaning" is best thought of as a verb, not a noun.

Theorists of the "social world" are thus saying two important things: one is that people must be treated as *agents*; that is, no matter what metaphysical notions one may believe about universal determinism, etc. people can—without quite knowing how it is that they can do it—cause at least some of their own motions. And the other thing is that one cannot find the sense in a person's action just by looking at the logical structure of the movements in which it consists; one must study how these movements are put to use in a social context. Thus what one must do if one is to become a member of a society is, among other things, to "learn how to mean" (Halliday, 1975, in which an account not in disagreement with the one presented here is developed).

Now learning to mean, to make-sense-to-others, is not just a matter of learning how to make certain well-defined patterns of responses—that is, learning something objective—it is a matter of learning how to adapt and modify one's actions in the face of continually changing external circumstances while maintaining their relation to some internally held principle, standard, or goal shared by those with whom one lives—that is, one must learn a *practical skill*. And in fact one must learn many different practical skills if one is to relate one's behaviour intelligibly to the behaviour of others in one's social life (whether those others happen to be present at the time or not); one must learn, for instance, how to take one's turn, to agree, to request, to name, to describe, to command, to promise, to negotiate, to love, to hate, to rationalize, to theorize, to carry out in fact a whole host of different practical accomplishments in ways which are both appropriate to one's own circumstances, *and* which make sense to those others. This is what it is to be a social agent. And the whole point about the nature of such activities is that they are only differentiated from one another in terms of the different "ways" of meaning something to others, the social practices, the use of language, involved in conducting them; the knowledge embodied in such practices need not first exist as ideas-in-people's-heads before being put into practice. Practice may precede, and exist, quite independently of theory. Thus when Winch (1958, p. 15) says that "our idea of reality is given for us in the language that we use. [And] it may be worth reminding ourselves of the truism that when we are in fact speaking of what we mean by the expression 'the world' . . .", he is saying something quite problematic, for quite what that *idea* of reality is, still remains to be explicitly formulated. And that is the task of the activity known by such philosophers as Winch as "conceptual analysis". But as for the child, for him to acquire the concepts embodied in our everyday "ways" of acting meaningfully, he does not have to acquire any *ideas* about the reality in which he lives, any cognitive structures or such like, he simply has to learn appropriate practical skills—at least, in the first instance: the advantage sooner or later of having some ideas is discussed in the next section.

The Self and Social Institutions

By constructing the appropriate laboratory (i.e. social) settings, it has been shown that one may elicit all kinds of characteristically human actions from infants at a very early age (Fantz, 1961; Bower, 1966, 1974)—a point to which we shall return when we discuss the role of mothers as the motivators of their infants' activity. But nothing in the results of such experiments would seem to indicate that the infant *himself* had detected and identified, or in other words "monitored" (Harré and Secord, 1972) his own differential responding in the same way as those experimenting upon him; still less would they indicate that he himself had "directed" it, and that he knew what his own activity "meant" for how he might go on to "deal with" the situation (in contrast to merely responding to it).

If one is going to be a person, an autonomous individual, acting in the knowledge of who and what one is, and what one is trying to do in relation to all the others with whom one is sharing one's life, then something more than merely behaving in ways that others can recognize is involved—one must be able to recognise what one is doing, oneself.

In other words, genuine human action is essentially "reflexive" in a way that other organic activity is not. If one is to act *with understanding*, then one must be able to act back, suggests Mead (1934), to influence oneself in the same way as one influences others. Human action is necessarily referred, not to an organism, but to a *self*, a peculiar bifurcated thing that is both agent *and* patient in action, and subject *and* object in thought. And the development of the self is of course, as Mead points out, of quite a different kind to the development of the physiological organism proper.

Now while the child as an organism may seem to be provided innately with the capacities to act in many different ways, "where" might the source of knowledge be located about the different particular uses to which these, otherwise rather indeterminate capacities may be put? The way in which a new member of a social world finds the structure of it already "pre-established" in its institutions, seems to me to be rather well put by Berger and Luckman (1971, pp. 77-78) when they say, following Schutz:

An institutional world . . . is experienced as an objective reality. It has a history that antedates the individual's birth and is not accessible to his biographical recollection. It was there before he was born, and it will be there after his death. This history itself, as the tradition of the existing institutions, has the character of objectivity. The individual's biography is apprehended as an episode located within the objective history of the society. The institutions, as historical and objective facticities, confront the individual as undeniable facts. The institutions are there, whether he likes it or not. He cannot wish them away. . . . Since institutions exist as external reality, the individual cannot understand them by introspection. He must "go out" and learn about them, just as he must to learn about nature. This remains true even though the human world, as a humanly produced reality, is potentially understandable in a way not possible in the case of the natural world.

In other words, the knowledge which the child must acquire if he is to learn how to put his innate capacities to use, intelligibly and responsibly, to do the "done things" in his society, is "out there", in his society, encoded not as ideas in people's heads but, as was said before, in the practical activities of everyday life.

And this is a most important point: the classical image of man that we seem to have inherited from the Greeks, is of man as a thinking subject, set over against the world as an object. In our new approach, man is primarily a doer, immersed in the world as an agent who has the power to act on the world and to change it to accord more with his own needs and interests (Shotter, 1975). Reflective thought becomes a secondary activity, occurring if at all only when man is withdrawn from practical activities; and his thinking then may or may not serve to inform his subsequent doings. Thus, in the view I am taking, practice precedes theory of it.

Ryle (1949, p. 31) also takes a similar view. In discussing the relation between theory and practice, he maintains:

> Efficient practice precedes the theory of it; methodologies presuppose the application of the methods, of the critical investigation of which they are the products. It was because Aristotle found himself and others reasoning now intelligently and now stupidly, and it was because Izaak Walton found himself and others angling sometimes effectively and sometimes ineffectively that both were able to give to their pupils the maxims and prescriptions of their art.

If we are to establish institutions which are appropriate to the circumstances in which they must operate, then efficient practice must precede the theory of them.

We are now in a position to discuss the advantage in having, so to speak, some idea of what it is one is doing: in fact there is considerable point to the attempt to formulate, once practices prove effective, the theory of them. Ryle's comments suggest two reasons: (1) accounts, if their application is understood, may serve to indicate intelligent rather than stupid, effective rather than ineffective action, and thus serve to institute standards of correct and incorrect conduct; and (2) they may also be used as aids in the instruction of others into the practice. But there is another, even more important reason: (3) by using one's theoretical accounts to formulate a plan, one may extend one's practices, deliberately, into areas other than those in which they were initially developed. And this is most important. For if men are ever to be self-determining, and act as they require rather than as their circumstances require, they must develop the ability to *deliberate* before they act; that is, they must develop the ability to decide courses of action in theory before executing their choice in action (Winch, 1958; Macmurray, 1957; Taylor, 1966)—learning how to "direct" one's own thought appropriately, in order to "do theorising", being itself, of course, a practical accomplishment (Blum, 1974).

The advantage of having some "idea", then, of what it is that one is trying to do in one's action, is that one can be more than just a passably competent member of one's society, one may project oneself into the future and attempt to bring into existence new situations, ones which may never have as yet existed, but which none the less would be ones intelligible and relevant to other members of one's society. Thought of a certain organized kind must of necessity accompany action if one is to act as oneself desires, rather than as one must, in "reply" to one's circumstances. And it is the production of the ability to so organize one's thought in relation to one's action that was referred to above as "the progressive rationalization of action or experience".

The Hermeneutical* Approach

Now is an appropriate point at which to discuss an approach to the study of communication of a kind altogether different from that hitherto used by professional psychologists in their studies of behaviour. It is an approach which will at first, perhaps, seem strange—unintelligible even—to the majority of us, trained as we all have been, in that approach to the study of behaviour which allows the use only of objective methods. For, rather than the testing of theories by experimentation, it abandons the search for that kind of knowledge—objective knowledge—altogether. Instead, its central activity is that of seeking, in the course of something like "dialogues" with them, interpretations of the meaning of people's actions—thus to discover from whence their actions issued, and towards what they may be directed. In short, it is just the kind of science needed to find the *reasons* for people's actions. It is called by some (Taylor, 1971; Habermas, 1972; Giddens, 1976; Gauld and Shotter, 1977) an *hermeneutical* approach, for its task is not unlike that which originated in the seventeenth century with the problem of interpreting the meaning of biblical texts (Palmer, 1969), i.e. the task of transforming a superficial, global, and perhaps misunderstood grasp of what a text is about, into an accurate, well-articulated account of its actual

---

*Hermeneutics: "The Greek word *Hermeios* referred to the priest at the Delphic oracle. This word and the more common verb *hermenuein* and noun *hermeneia* point back to the wing-footed messenger-god Hermes from whose name the words are apparently derived (or vice versa?) Significantly, Hermes is associated with the function of transmuting what is beyond human understanding into a form that human intelligence can grasp. The various forms of the word suggest the process of bringing a thing or situation from unintelligibility to understanding. The Greeks credited Hermes with the discovery of language and writing—the tools which human understanding employs to grasp meaning and to convey it to others" (Palmer, 1969, p. 13).

meaning (perhaps even going so far as to seek its meaning not at the time of its production, but its meaning for us today!). The search for "objective knowledge" is irrelevant to such an endeavour; understandings from within a frame of reference, a tradition, or a culture are what are required—hence the relevance of this approach to the title of this paper.

As a science of interpretation, then, the hermeneutical approach does not attempt to predict, control, or to otherwise explain the causes of people's behaviour, as one does—by using the special standpoint of the disinterested, external observer, and by referring to theories about the underlying nature of what one is observing—in the attempt to gain an intellectual grasp of natural phenomena. Instead, it takes it as given that we all have as human beings a certain special "insider's" view of human behaviour, and concerns itself with the task of transforming the vague and perhaps mistaken understandings of *human phenomena* we already possess from that insider's point of view into more precise and effective ones. It thus makes a number of major distinctions ignored by those taking a behaviourist approach to the study of such human phenomena.

First: it distinguishes between those entities (usually, other people) which can be understood directly by communicating with them, and those which cannot, and which can only be studied indirectly by reference to a theory. In studying the latter one must proceed as if they were logically structured in one way or another, and then continually check to see whether one's logical expectations are confirmed or not. Whereas, in communication one's investigations are not guided by a theoretical structure, but by the implications of the "replies" received from one's investigations of an entity so far; we find that "it" can play just as much a part in structuring the exchange as ourselves, and in so doing, reveal itself to us. For instance, suppose one day a man seizes a piece of material and is about to attempt to mould it to his purposes, when it seems to wriggle in his hands. Given the sense of responsibility that people can have for at least some of their actions, we may presume that in this instance, the man senses that he was not responsible in any direct manner for the motions of the matter he experienced. Hence, he immediately drops it. His whole attitude to it changes. Initially, he had committed himself to treating it as inanimate matter, moulding it to one's purposes being one of the things one can do with such matter; but then he discovers, empirically, as a result of his own direct contact with it that it is not. While such a "reply" closes off one general mode of conduct to him, it leaves open, say, whether he then deals with the material as if it were organic, or personal, or one of a number of more differentiated categories of things within these broad categories. And the point here is this: in finding that he cannot now treat the material as inanimate, he does not need to formulate *a theory* of what might now be the nature of the material to be able to go on dealing with it; his idea as to its actual nature may remain utterly vague. All he must do is to switch his mode of conduct from one form of practical activity to another, his investigations being guided (because he does not yet know in any detail the nature of what he is dealing with) only vaguely by the differentiated notions (of inanimate, organic, or personal) mentioned above. Thus to come to an understanding of things in communication, it is possible to begin with only a vague commitment to a particular mode of conduct, and to move in the course of the exchange to a more precisely differentiated one. However, the opposite of vagueness is the order of the day in understanding things from the outside, via theories: only if one begins with a well-defined logical structure, is it possible at all to be certain about the relation between one's predictions and one's observations.

It is worth adding here a comment about the nature of *commitments* in human relationships: if, for instance, we meet a stranger, even a slight smile (to what things do we "give" slight smiles on encountering them?) is sufficient for us to indicate to him that we have acknowledged his humanness, *and this commits us to going on with him as a human being.* We cannot, at least not without breaking that commitment, change to treating him as an animal, or as an inanimate thing. But our commitment here is unsystematic, indeterminate, and knowing that we are dealing with a human being, still leaves it open to us as to how to go on to make more sense of him; or to him. Rather than face ourselves with such a task unnecessarily, we are thus careful to whom we "give" such smiles.

The next important distinction made by those taking an hermeneutical approach but ignored by behaviourists is this: as mentioned before, there is a sense of knowing something from the "inside" which is quite different from that knowledge we may have of things from the outside. Hence there is a sense in which it is possible to understand human phenomena (because we are "inside" the processes of their production) in a way not possible with natural happenings. Berlin (1969, 1976) attributes the discovery of this form of knowledge to Vico; he says (Berlin, 1969, p. 375):

> To apply the old medieval maxim that one can only fully understand what one has made to such provinces as mathematics, mythology, symbolism, language, is evidence enough of philosophical insight, a revolutionary step on which the cultural anthropology and the philosophical implications of the new linguistic theories of our time have cast a new and extraordinary light. But Vico did more than this. He uncovered a sense of knowing which is basic to all humane studies: the sense in which I know what it is to be poor, to fight for a cause, to belong to a nation, to join or abandon a church or a party, to feel nostalgia, terror, the omnipresence of a god, to understand a gesture, a work of art, a joke, a man's character, that one is transformed or lying to oneself.

This kind of knowledge, the knowledge of actors involved in human affairs as opposed to those who merely observe them, is, Berlin argues, knowledge of quite a unique kind, irreducible to any other. Possessing it, as Gauld and Shotter (1977) point out, we can "understand", for instance, that people who have intentions will do what they believe will be most likely to fulfil them, for we know "from the inside" that this is a part of what it is to have an intention. And there is no other way of knowing what is involved in having an intention; certainly it is not possible in any simple sense to observe people consulting their beliefs. So here again, as above, we meet the divorce between explaining a particular event by relating its occurence to a general law or principle, and understanding it, not by subsuming it under a generalization at all, but as arising from one particular intention rather than another. It is understood when we know what in particular the person was trying to do, and what in particular were his beliefs in trying to do it.

Implicit in the above is the distinction between natural and human processes that behaviourists also ignore to their cost. It is a distinction, for instance, de Saussure (1960) makes when he distinguishes between *language* and *speech*. "Language, once its boundaries have been marked off within the speech data," he says (1960, p. 15), "can be classified among human phenomena, whereas speech cannot." Speaking is a many-sided natural *process*, a wilful act on the part of the individual, requiring many different disciplines (physics, physiology, psychology) in its study; language, on the other hand, is a human *product*, and, as a man-made entity may be treated as a unified whole—hence the possibility of linguistics as an (almost) autonomous discipline. If Vico is right, and we can only understand that which we ourselves make, then language, law, etc. and indeed all social institutions, are understandable in a way quite impossible with natural processes (which we have not, of course, created). And this was de Saussure's point: by assigning to linguistics just the task of analysing language but not speech, linguistics has been able to make great progress while psychology, failing to distinguish human from natural phenomena, has languished.

The hermeneutical approach is concerned, then, not with explaining natural phenomena but with interpreting human ones; with the task not of prediction and control, but of helping men to increase their own self-awareness: to understand, for instance, that to treat many forces of society as natural processes is to radically misinterpret them, and that interpretations may be possible in which our part in them is made more clear to us. In psychology, however, we are not at all clear into which category our phenomena fall. But this is not because we are muddled (which we are) and in any case do not bother with the distinction, but because, as we shall see, the distinction is in a most interesting and important way, an intrinsically vague one; and it is a fundamental and continuous task in any culture to devise ways of maintaining a boundary between ourselves and Nature. Indeed, elsewhere (Douglas, 1966; Shotter, 1975) is described some of the social, cultural, and political consequences of drawing this essentially uncertain distinction with arbitrary precision. We may see the nature of our uncertainty simply by considering the nature of the standard questions we often set ourselves in psychology: "Why do we act as we do?" "What is it that enables/makes/causes/etc. us to do what we do?" As stated the questions are ambiguous in that we might be asking:

(1) "What *in us* enables us to do it?" or
(2) "What enables us *ourselves* to do it?"

(1) is of course the classical form of the question and requires as an answer a description of some "mechanism" within us. Whereas (2) requires a description of some process of social exchange productive of increased self-directed, self-regulated, or self-determined activity; an account of something that goes on *between* people rather than *within* them. In (1) and (2) then, one has two quite clearly different foci of interest, with two quite different aims, needing in their pursuit, two quite different frameworks of thought. It should be noted too that in (1) and (2) two quite different images of man are involved: while in (1) man is treated as a special collection of causal mechanisms, in (2), he is treated as a peculiar bifurcated thing, manifesting partly natural processes or natural powers (Harré, 1970) outside of his personal agency to control, and partly human processes or personal powers which are within his own self-control—and with the possibility of the former being transformed into the latter (Shotter, 1973). It is thus perfectly legitimate when confronting such bipartite beings as these to ask, "What is it that will enable such beings to act as they *themselves* rather than their circumstances require?" in a way not possible when addressing merely causal mechanisms.

If man does have the peculiar bifurcated nature suggested above, then it will not be possible to use any one single approach in attempting to understand/explain the reasons/causes of his activity. At different points in what follows, *theories* of man's essential nature will, on the one hand, be offered (in the attempt, for instance, to account for the fact that he is a being capable of being motivated by others, as well as himself), while on the other, the importance of *interpretations* (especially the interpretations mothers place upon their infant's activities in the course of their exchanges with them) will be explored also. But it should not be thought that these two approaches are simply alternatives, able to exist independently of one another. The hermeneutical approach is irreducibly basic (Gauld and Shotter, 1977), for a theory is a human phenomenon, a man-made entity, and as such the terms in which it is couched present a task for hermeneutical analysis; they cannot be given an interpretation free from frames of reference, traditions, or cultures. To explain, say, developmental processes we must already "know" what it is to concern ourselves with developmental phenomena from a position within, presumably, a tradition concerned with their study; there is no pre-suppositionless knowledge to be had.

The Beginning and the End of Developmental Studies

I want to propose that our aim in studies of mother-infant interaction be described as an attempt to account for the social practices by which human abilities (including our knowledge of them) are transformed from more primitive into more developed forms. But what should be the starting point for such studies? In accord with his concern only with the growth of knowledge not its origins, Popper (1972)—along with all those concerned with the study of everyday social practices—has argued for *common sense* with all its vagueness and error as the starting point for all scientific investigations; for its inadequacies may be eradicated in the course of its growth.

Is such a methodological maxim any help to us here in studying the development of young infants? Surely before infants acquire any human knowledge, they must first be accounted merely as organisms and investigated as such? In that case, is not a starting point in common sense useless to us? Must we not begin from some theory of organismic functioning? Well: perhaps not. For "what we are attempting is a descriptive analysis", said Stout (1938, pp. 407-408), who considered in his "genetic" approach to psychology many of the issues we are considering now:

> of the process through which knowledge of the material [and the social] world in all the essential aspects of its being passes from more primitive to more developed stages. What we are emphatically *not* attempting is to show how such knowledge is or might be generated from a prior experience in which it is not present. . . . The psychologist need not and ought not to start from metaphysical assumptions in his descriptive analysis, descriptive analysis itself leads up in the long run to metaphysical problems. . . . But they are not properly psychological.

Thus we must begin by taking the common sense view that mothers take of their infants at birth, that they begin life as in some sense *persons*—albeit, as very primitive ones. For if we do not, and we take him to be an organism, then we face, as Stout pointed out, not simply the task of describing how his knowledge grows from primitive origins, but how something essentially organic is transformed at some point into something essentially personal. So, rather than concocting metaphysical assumptions about the special organic nature of the human child at birth, to be true to our starting point in common sense, we must assume that babies are born as persons—or at least, as Macmurray (1961, p. 50) puts it, they live "a common life as one term in a personal relation".

But if we begin by assuming infants to be already competent to participate in social exchanges, what is it for them to become more competent than they already are? What is it for any of us to become more competent than we already are? The point is entirely general, and raises the question of our aims in developmental research. For what is it in general that we may hope to do as a result of our investigations, more than we can already do? To an extent an answer to these questions has already been sketched in previous sections: men may develop intellectually by becoming more and more able themselves to determine the form of their own activity, rather than having to rely upon their circumstances (including other people) to elicit it from them. Men develop from beings able only at first to essay short sequences of action with vague and elementary meanings, into beings able to essay longer and longer sequences of activity, involving more and more people, with greater and greater precision of meaning. This seems to be the true mark of human intellectual achievement: to be able to maintain one's commitment to the realization of an intention involving a long sequence of activity in which each and every act in the realization of the intention can be seen as meaningfully related to each and every other act—a sequence in which, as we shall see, acts are related to one another act by an hierarchical structure of implications (Smedslund, 1969). And men may gain the ability to do this, as was suggested earlier, by constructing explicit accounts of already established practices (not necessarily written accounts), and use them in constructing plans of action. This I take to be the whole point of developmental research: to extend our ability to decide for ourselves how we will act by making clear to ourselves the nature of the different goals available to us, so that we may choose from among them what to do next.

ASPECTS OF MOTHER-INFANT COMMUNICATION

Life as one Term in a Personal Relation

Now while mothers may treat their babies in a personal manner from birth (Macfarlane, 1974), it is not an assumption that has as yet found much favour among scientists studying child development. Many have assumed that the child *is* at first "asocial" (Schaffer, 1971, p. 13), "animal matter" (Richards, 1974, p. 51), developing as an aspect of "embryogenesis" (Piaget and Inhelder, 1969, p. vii) only later into a person. Trevarthen (1974, 1975) is one of the few to insist that infants must be treated both practically and theoretically as persons right from the start. And a part of what it is for the infant to be in a personal relationship right from the start, is for his mother to treat his activity, not in organic terms as merely reaction to a stimulus, but in personal terms. That is, regarding the form of his activity as personal, she does two things: on the one hand, she acts to elicit from him certain forms of no doubt innately organized activity, but activity which makes sense to her and which, without her intelligent adjustment of the eliciting circumstances would undoubtedly remain unexpressed (see example from Newson and Newson (1975) described below). In other words, she acts to *motivate* certain types of activity in her child—Schutz (1953) would say, she provides a *because-motive*; he acts because of what she does. On the other hand, having motivated some characteristically human activity, she now acts to interpret it as having a *meaning*: "Oh, look," she says, after having got her infant to look at her by cooing and smiling at her, having placed her face in his line of regard, "he's looking at me". So she replies to his (?) look with a "Hello, hello you cheeky thing". The point here being that whatever she does to motivate her baby's activity, when he responds she still interprets it as something which he himself does, not merely as something which she has succeeded in eliciting from him; it is thus treated as activity worthy of being an expression in a dialogue, an expression requiring a meaningful reply. She thus supplies him with what Schutz (1953) would call an *in-order-to-motive* as well; for in this situation he can learn what he can bring about by his actions.

The process above, because it entails the mother acting contingently upon what the child does, may seem to some to be like the reinforcement learning, *á la* Skinner. Nothing could be further from it: it is the way in which the mother replies in terms of her *interpretation* that is crucial. Only by replying in socially proper terms to his responses is he presented with an opportunity to learn the proper social use to which his activity may be put. If, for instance, every time he made a pointing-like movement he was given a reward, a sweet, say, or anything, other than his mother attending to the object he was looking at (or in some contexts giving him it), then one may indeed increase the frequency of his pointing-like movements. But the infant could never possibly learn that such movements were something that could be used, not for getting sweet rewards, but for the social purpose of directing someone else's attention.

As another example of the way in which the intelligent adjustment of the adult to the child's own activity may function to elicit complex human action from him, that he might not otherwise express, Newson and Newson (1975, p. 442) have described well the task of getting a supine 4-week old infant to follow a dangling ring with his eyes:

In this superficially simple task, the test demonstrator will carefully attend, not just to the general state of arousal of the infant, but to his precise focus and line of regard. Having "hooked" the attention of the infant upon the ring, one then begins gingerly to move it across his field of vision in such a way that the infant's eyes continue to hold the object with successive fixations until eventually the head follows the eyes in that co-ordinated overall movement pattern which denotes successful tracking. If the test object is moved too suddenly, or is left static too long, the visual attention of the infant will flag and the attempt will have to begin all over again from scratch. In this instance, what is in fact happening is a highly skilled monitoring by the adult and a consequent adjustment of the dangling object, moment by moment, depending on the feedback which is being obtained from the spontaneous actions of the infant.

And, as they go on to say, "the resulting action sequence of the infant is therefore a combination of his own activity and an intelligent manipulation of that activity by the much more sophisticated adult partner". It is in the sense, then, that the child can be a competent participant in such interactive exchanges as these, in a way that, presumably, other organisms could not, that he may properly be counted as one term in a genuine personal relationship.

Thus it would seem, even when the infant's initial activities may seem so unlike those of an adult, we can still begin our studies from the common sense assumption that, *within the context of a personal relation*, there are similarities to be found from birth. Thus as a methodological point, we should seek in early exchanges, and not be surprised to find, precursors to all adult forms of social exchange (Bruner, 1976).

Human Nature, Intrinsic Motivation, and Implication

Beginning our studies as suggested above—by treating the infant as a competent participant in early social exchanges—leaves open the question of the infant's specific nature at birth. But this is a question we want to avoid facing if we can, for it is a question about the nature of *origins* rather than processes of growth. And we can avoid it if we assume that at birth the child has no *definite* form to his nature at all, that it really is vague and indeterminate—but not indeterminable. And the most obvious fact about the human infant at birth is his helplessness, he seems to have no specific, "ready-made" answers to any of the stimuli that impinge upon him. "There must, however," says Macmurray (1961, p. 48):

be a positive side to this. The baby must be fitted by nature at birth to the conditions into which he is born; for otherwise he could not survive. He is, in fact, "adapted", to speak paradoxically, to being unadapted, "adapted" to a complete dependence upon an adult human being.

And in some way, mother and child develop together in such a way that, within the institution they construct between them, the child develops as a person. That is, he develops his *persona*, his knowledge of his *self*, his knowledge of who and what he is and what he can do in relation to all those with whom he shares his life. Now it is not that lacking such knowledge he would be totally unable to react to the actions of other people, but without such knowledge of himself, and of his social position, to inform and structure his actions in those situations he shares with others, he would be unable to join in their attempts to realize communal projects, to bring new conditions for human existence into being. But what is there in the nature of human beings such that they undertake the task of bringing about such a development in themselves, what motivates them to it? Surely the child could just remain dependent on others, couldn't he?

As White (1959) remarks, theories of motivation have an unhappy history in psychology. While "drives" may be postulated to account for what an organism might do at any given moment—if enough different drives are postulated *ad hoc*, that is—there is no "drive" which can be postulated for what seems to structure an organism's behaviour over some long period of time. In other words, the concept of drive takes no account of growth and development. "We need," says White (1959, p. 297),

> a different kind of motivational idea to account fully for the fact that man and the higher mammals develop a competence in dealing with the environment which they certainly do not have at birth and certainly do not arrive at simply through maturation.

And the new motivational idea White proposed is that men and the higher mammals should be thought of as being innately capable of developing *competence*; "competence" here being taken to mean, in a broad biological sense, an organism's fitness to interact effectively with its environment. In organisms capable of learning only very little, this capacity may be considered to be an innate attribute; such organisms come into being already adapted to their circumstances. But in mammals and especially in men, as White points out, fitness to interact with the environment on one's own is only slowly attained through prolonged feats of learning. And it is in view of the directedness, and the persistence, of the behaviour that leads to these feats of learning, that White considers it necessary to treat men and mammals as motivated to develop competence. But we have here a form of motivation to be conceptualized in quite a different way to the sources of free energy thought of as the drives or instincts needed merely to activate short-term behaviour.

Let us attempt to elucidate such a concept of motivation: in the most general sense, a motive is that which tends to move anything. Thus in mechanisms, the wind is the motive force that drives the sailing boat, exploding hydrocarbons the motive force driving the motor car engine that powers the car, etc. (while it is the helmsman or the driver who *directs* the course of such things). The motive of an action in this sense is the free physical energy available to "drive" it, and without which movement would be impossible. Or, putting the matter in even more general terms: in a world of matter in motion, it is the energy available to produce changes in motion. Thus, given the mechanistic framework of thought classically adopted by psychology, the "drive" model of motivation is the one only to be expected. However, the organic world is more than a world of matter in motion; it is a world of forms in transformation, being born, growing, dying. It is *rhythm* rather than simply uniform motion that characterizes such a world. And as Susan Langer (1967, p. 324) describes it:

> The essence of rhythm is the alternation of tension building up to a crisis, and ebbing away in a graduated course of relaxation whereby a new build up of tension is prepared and driven to the next crisis, which necessitates the next cadence. If the series of actions thus engendered consists of alternating contraries, such as rise and fall, push and pull suction and expulsion, and each element in spending itself prepares and initiates its own converse, the resulting rhythm is a dialectic.
>
> Dialectical rhythms, like rhythms *per se*, are not limited to the actions of vital systems . . ., but they play such a major role in vital functions that their importance in the activity and even the physical existence of organisms makes them an essential mark of the living form in nature . . . the parabolic curve which expresses the typical act form emerges again and again, at each level of integration, in the physiological rhythms of every organism; and this form, with its main phases of inception, acceleration, consummation and cadential finish, is what makes the rhythmic pattern, and is accordingly the basis not only of the distinguishable unit acts in a continuous activity, but also of their self-concatenation, and consequent self perpetuation of the continuum.

Rather than simply matter in uniform motion, Langer suggests, the organic world contains agencies executing rhythmic acts. Taking this form of "motion" as basic gives rise as one might expect to a rather different concept of motivation. Instead of "drives" motivating movements, in the organic world *acts motivate other acts*.

It may at first seem unusual to say this, for usually we say that all acts arise from a situation, an organism is motivated by its circumstances. But what a situation is for an organism is determined by its acts-in-progress (Dewey, 1896; Mead, 1934). And, says Langer (1967, p. 283):

> The only way an external influence can produce an act is to alter the organic situation that induces acts; and to do this it must strike into a matrix of ongoing

activity, in which it is immediately lost, replaced by a change of phase in the activity. The new phase induces new distinguishable acts. This indirect causation of acts via the prevailing dynamic situation is "motivation". It may arise from intraorganic sources, too, which is to say from autogenous acts that radically alter the general activity, inducing a new phase (i.e., a new situation); in that case, overt acts of the organism may be motivated by entirely covert events.

Thus, only if one holds in the back of one's mind the idea that all motions are essentially mechanical ones, does one find it necessary to postulate a special external "motive force" to account for changes in activity. Just as uniform motion is given in the physical world, we may take rhythmic activity as given in the organic world; and thus motivation—the capacity of an overarching act to motivate within itself subordinate acts—becomes an intrinsic part of that world. Then our task becomes that of accounting, not for organic activity *per se*, but for, of all the possible acts that might be executed, the ones that are actually executed.

As Langer points out, White in his discussion of *competence motivation* draws back from this extreme position of *intrinsic motivation*—"We could go further", says White (1959, p. 318), "and say that each item of behaviour has its intrinsic motive—but this makes the concept of motivation redundant." He clearly rejects such a move, and wants to place alongside say, hunger, thirst, etc., *effectance*, the motivational aspect of competence. So that for him, while some actions may be motivated by hunger, those directed towards competence may be motivated by "effectance". We shall not follow White's lead here, for it leads, mistakenly I feel, to a search for the extrinsic causes of people's action. Instead we shall pursue the view already stated, which may be summed up by saying: an act may be motivated by the superordinate act of which it is a subordinate part. For example, one's act of reading this chapter is motivated by one's act of studying mother-infant interaction which is . . . ultimately . . . motivated by one's act of living.

Chein (1972), like Langer, suggests that acts are motivated by the acts to which they are subordinate; or, to put it another way, they are motivated by the acts within which they are included. The recent analyses of act-structures in cognitive psychology (Miller *et al.*, 1960) and linguistics (Chomsky, 1965, etc.), depicting hierarchically arranged systems of elements in tree-diagrams, describes their structure well. But as mentioned earlier, the analyses distort the true state of affairs if they depict the act-process as consisting of one act followed by another act followed by . . . another act, and so on, as if the first act was the cause of the second, etc. (see Dewey, 1896, for a critique of such a view). As Smedslund (1969) points out, mental (act) processes are logically related to one another *by implication* not causation: an act is known for the kind of act that it is in terms of the future acts that it implies. Or, to put the matter in Smedslund's own words (1969, p. 8):

Having a belief or wish in itself *implies, contradicts,* or *changes the likelihood of* many other beliefs and wishes. Believing that something is a stone implies a belief that it will sink if thrown into the water, and wanting to have one's cake contradicts (conflicts with) wanting to eat it. . . . A crucial difference between a cause-effect relationship (A causes B) and an implication (A implies B) is that the former involves logically independent phenomena, which must be shown empirically to succeed each other, whereas the latter involves logically dependent phenomena. Physical phenomena may be linked by a theory from which it follows that A leads to B. On the other hand, a mental phenomena A in itself implies B, without any theory.

Intrinsically motivated acts are necessarily intrinsically related, logically, rather than extrinsically related—a characteristic reflected in the fact that linguistic categories, as Chomsky (1965, p. 55) insists, are structure-dependent; they are known for what they are only in terms of their relations to one another.

Now the force of the discussion above for our studies in mother-infant interaction is this: if actions are to be known for what they are *in terms of their implications*, then we should expect to see mothers (without any theory) interpreting their children's acts for their implications. Also, of course, we may see them check, if they so desire, the validity of their interpretations by testing them for their further implications—e.g. "my baby's reaching for that object implies he wants it, thus if I hand it to him (given that I know he can grasp things) he should grasp it, thus I'll hand it to him, and . . . he does grasp it"; her insider's knowledge of grasping being a help here.

The situation for the interactants in social processes is, then, one where their acts are motivated by being included within the rhythmic structure of more overarching, ongoing acts. Being thus situated, acts have a meaning; they "point to" or imply other acts, necessarily, without a theory, as a logical part of what it is to be an act. Thus it may seem, even in quite unreflective exchanges, as if the interactants are continually making "inferences" about one another, although strictly, they are not (see William James, 1890, II, pp. 111-113, criticism of "unconscious inference"). They are merely acting within a shared field of implications. A person's acts imply, contradict, or change the likelihood of the other person's possible replies to it, intrinsically, as a necessary part of what it is for social exchanges to occur at all. And this, clearly, is what Mead (1934, p. 77) means when he says, "the mechanism of meaning is present in the social act before the emergence of consciousness or awareness of meaning occurs. The act or adjustive response of (a) second organism gives to the gesture of (a) first organism the meaning it has"—the adjustive response of the second organism is "implicated", as he says earlier (p. 76), in the act of the first.

Mead's analysis of meaning repays careful study, though there is not space to conduct such a study here. Briefly, he suggests that meaning emerges in the way in which the adjustive response of one organism "completes" or "fulfils" an act begun by another; the way in which what follows from one organism's activity is developed by another organism in *its* activity. Meaning is not, for Mead, a psychical addition to a given act, nor is it an "idea" as traditionally conceived; an act is known for the kind of act that it is in terms of the future acts it implies—for instance, the way the clucks of the hen (to use Mead's example) are completed by the flight of the chick to the hen, gives, he would say, the meaning of "danger" to the hen's clucks; although, clearly, the chick has no awareness that this is the nature of their meaning, for it shows no signs at all of having deliberated upon its response in theory before executing it in practice. So, although it is clear that, given an organism's particular activity, only certain kinds of particular further activity may be developed from it, neither organism need be aware of the *nature* of the development being executed. Only if possible developments are to be considered in theory before being executed in practice, to repeat an earlier point, is an awareness of meaning necessary. We may expect to find, then, that people merely acting in accord with pre-established social practices, with "ways-of-going-on" which have already been decided, act without an awareness of the meaning of their acts, although their acts (as with the hen and chick) may be "seen" by others to have a meaning. Thus we may find mothers responding (adjustively) to their children's acts quite unreflectively, in unproblematical, "taken-for-granted" ways (Berger and Luckman, 1967; Schutz, 1967) which reflect the goals and techniques of the social tradition of which they are a part. And while we, as investigators of a mother's exchanges with her child, may "see" an intention in the character of her (adjustive) responses to her child, she may be aware of no such intention, she may merely declare herself to be doing what seems only "natural", the "taken-for-granted", matter of fact "way" of going on. The source of her intention must be sought, not in her emotional states or intrinsic nature, but in the history of the development of the social practices of which she is an exponent (Shotter, 1975; Taylor, 1971). We must understand the ideological context within which mother-child interaction takes place (Busfield, 1974); the ideas, beliefs, and values in terms of which such interaction is conducted.

Now while it is the task of mothers to *live* with their babies, it is our task to study them; we are not participants in the same process as that in which they are engaged, even though at times we ourselves may need to enter into exchanges with them. Thus to view ourselves as participant observers is quite incorrect. Our task is to carry out critical investigations of these everyday, taken-for-granted practices in an attempt to produce rational methodologies; to produce, if not mechanically precise specifications, at least maxims and prescriptions for efficient practice. But if, to recall some earlier remarks, we are to establish such rational methodologies, to institute such practices in a way appropriate to the circumstances in which they must operate, we cannot afford to ignore the actual intentions in the mother's practices. For it is only in terms of such intentions that their meanings may be assessed—for example, in an attempt to realize an intention, a mother may execute a succession of acts, judging all activity in the sequence, except the last act, as a failure of one kind or another. But to elucidate the actual intentions sustaining the mother's social practices, we must, besides carrying out other studies of an historical and cultural kind, involve ourselves in exchanges with her. We shall turn in the last section of this essay to the task involved in negotiating such accounts with those we study. Next, we shall turn to a discussion of early social practices in the light of all the comments above.

Early Social Practices

The baby lives, we have assumed, "as one term in a personal relationship". If this is so, then we must look from the very start for evidence of a personal relation, even if at first it is evidence only of the fact that babies present themselves as appropriate recipients of personal ministrations. Recently, some of that evidence has been forthcoming. Macfarlane (1974) discusses the way mothers greet their babies immediately after delivery. "One can observe," he says, "how the mother verbalises her inspection of her child . . . imitates the child and puts her own interpretation on the child's behaviour." Whether he intends them or not, from the moment of birth the child does things capable of bearing personal attributions. And, as Macfarlane remarks, mothers are good observers of these sorts of activities in their infants (even though they may misdescribe their own abilities when drawn into a discussion of them by investigators!) He notes, for instance, that many mothers remark upon their child's ability to visually follow the motions of their faces (while saying at other times that of course babies so young could not see). Or, that the 1-month-old's ability to appreciate a three-dimensional object is noticed by the mother as the baby "reaching out" with his lips when a bottle is brought up to them. Mothers, whether they would admit it in rational discussion with psychologists or not, clearly treat their young babies in a personal manner from the moment of birth—they do not, like animal trainers, act for the first 6 months of their life as if they must condition them, and only later turn to treating them in a personal manner.

Wolff (1969) has studied the natural history of crying in very early infancy and has shown that, within broad categories, mothers interpret different types of cry in different ways. Although, as he points out, the mother's personal style (and hence her past experience) is far more important than the form of crying in itself in determining how she will care for her crying baby. Her interpretation of what the crying means is based just as much upon the events (the exchanges between them) in the preceding three hours as the actual pattern of the cry. In other words, as we may expect to find time and time again at this stage, the meaning a mother develops from or assigns to a child's action (or utterances) is highly context-dependent: an act's meaning depends upon the past history of its development.

Now the essence of human social action is not islands of sharing in a sea of otherwise separate individual activities, it is manifested in the long, interlaced sequences of exchange in which both parties remain engaged with one another throughout. Very early on such "interactional synchrony" (Condon and Sander, 1974) has been observed to occur in neonates simply exposed to speech. The fact seems to be that, not only do people move their whole bodies in an hierarchically organized, rhythmic fashion in self-synchrony with their own rhythms, their listeners also move in interactional synchrony with them. This hierarchical, rhythmic organization of action is to be expected if human acts really do have the dialectical form described by Langer (1967), whom we quoted earlier. What is perhaps surprising at first, but perhaps should not be so when we pause to consider the way in which of necessity organisms exist in a state of dynamic exchange with their circumstances, is that the rhythms of one person may entrain those of another. This interactional synchrony certainly begins as early as the first few hours after birth, and may, Condon and Sander suggest, exist even earlier. Thus, as Condon (1974, p. 627) points out, the neonate

> participates developmentally (through complex, sociobiological entrainment processes) in literally millions of repetitions of linguistic forms long before he will use them in speaking and communicating. By the time he begins to speak he may have already laid down within himself the form and structure of the language system of the culture.

But not only speech rhythms, the rhythms associated with other forms of action too must surely, under circumstances remaining to be investigated, be capable of affecting the child.

If long, interlaced sequences of exchange are to be established as activities people can themselves *do* rather than simply have happen to them, then people have to learn how to "turn-take", i.e. how, on the one hand, to submit onself to the influence of another, and, on the other, how to initiate appropriate action oneself. Involved is what one might call an "ontological skill"; the ability to change one's own mode of being oneself, in this case, from being a patient to being an agent. Newson and Pawlby (1972) have studied the development of these "turn-taking" games. Often, mothers seem to seize upon opportunities offered by their infants to establish a back-and-forth sequence of acts. For example, they describe the exchange between Tilly (at 28 weeks) and her mother as below:

> (Following an exchange involving some play with a rattle)
> Tilly makes a vocalization (like a cough)
> Mother repeats vocalization
> Tilly repeats it
> Mother repeats it
> Tilly puts rattle to mouth
> Mother: "Are you going to eat that one?"

Inserted into the episode with the rattle, then, is this short back-and-forth exchange in which Tilly took her turn and did, clearly, what her mother expected (required) her to do. Tilly manifests here, then, in some small degree, that she can be an agent in her own right, that she can *herself* do something appropriate to the social situation that she is in, that she can make herself what can be interpreted as a sensible response. Here she repeats the vocalization only once, and then her attention shifts elsewhere (and the mother follows, giving again a routine interpretation to what she does). Perhaps later she will be able to sustain the intention involved over indefinitely many exchanges—then we shall find the mother elaborating the game, as in the imaginary example below:

> Baby: Ugh!
> Mother: Ugh!
> Baby: Ugh!
> Mother: Ugh!
> Baby: Ugh!
> Mother: Ugh! Ugh!
> Baby: Ugh! Ugh!
> Mother: Ugh! Ugh! Ugh!
> Baby throws food on the floor.

Schaffer (1974) who has also studied turn-taking emphasizes, like Condon and Sander, the natural periodicity of the infant's activity. He notes that babies emit bursts of vocalizations, and it is left to the mother to fill in the pauses. Thus the establishment (the institution) of turn-taking is not so much a matter of the mother *imposing* such a structure upon the baby's activity as of finding it within it. She must let herself be paced by the infant's behaviour. But more than this: as Kaye and Brazelton (1971) remark in their study of the exchanges that go on between mother and child in the child's pauses in sucking, the *timing* or *phasing* of what the mother does is important. If what she does—say, jiggling or stroking her child—comes too soon after the beginning of a pause, it will (contrary to the mother's intention) retard rather than speed up the next burst of sucks. As we mentioned earlier, when discussing Langer's account of acts, what a situation is for an organism is determined by the nature of its acts-in-progress, and presumably the *phase* they have reached. Attempting to "trigger" the baby's activity during the relaxation phase of an act rather than just as tension begins to build up again, seems to delay the completion of the relaxation phase rather than initiating immediately a new build-up of tension. Thus here again, the dialectical, push-pull structure of acts is an important consideration: mothers, it seems, appreciate at least to some degree how to motivate an act by intervening at the appropriate phase in their babies' ongoing activity, catching them in the outgoing or incoming phase, as they see fit.

Trevarthen (1974, 1975) is another worker who has emphasized the fact that the foundation for interpersonal communication is "there" at birth, terming it "innate intersubjectivity". In particular he has studied the distinctively different modes of responding infants manifest in the presence of people; 2-month-old infants seem not only to perform a rudimentary form of speaking by moving their lips and mouths (what Trevarthen calls "prespeech"), they also make many hand and arm movements that are developmentally related to the gestures of adults involved in animated conversations. Again, as with other workers, Trevarthen emphasizes that in the exchanges in which these movements occur, it is the mother that continually imitates the baby—the baby coming only later (6 months) to imitate the mother, and then only with difficulty and special instruction.

All the examples mentioned above illustrate, I feel, what it is for the very young infant to be treated as one term in a personal relationship right from birth. But more is involved than just the way in which the infant is treated; he must also "reply" to his treatment appropriately. We may feel, understanding interactional synchrony as we do and the need to insert our interventions into the ongoing stream of the infant's activity at the right phase, that we could interact now with nonhuman organisms to bring them up in a human fashion. But as we shall see, how the human infant answers in his own right in his exchanges with his mother is also important, for there seems to be another factor of importance in the developmental process: *the mother's concern with her child's development of a self.* In their exchanges with their children, mothers seem to test the character of their child's responses to them to see if the child has any knowledge of the social significance of what he is doing, whether "he" is doing it deliberately, whether "he" knows the nature of what he is doing, and why. It would be the failure of nonhuman animals to develop self-consciousness, quite apart from the discouraging bodily form, which would disturb human mothers' attempts to bring them up.

In an incident Shotter and Gregory (1976) describe, a mother is attempting to show her young child (Samantha, aged 11 months) how to place shaped pieces on a form-board. Having just physically helped her little girl to place one of the pieces, Samantha's mother says "Oh, clever girl". But Samantha had not paused in her activity and signalled by eye contact and smiling that she knew she had done something socially significant, she just went straight away on to manipulating something else. So her mother leant forward, caught her eye, and repeated her "marker": "AREN'T YOU CLEVER?" Samantha then stopped and smiled.

Mothers are not just satisfied with their children doing the tasks that they require of them. They must give, also, indications in their actions that they did what they did as a result of trying to do it, that "they" knew what was required of them, that their actions were based in some knowledge of the socially defined requirements of the situation. Thus children must come to show in their actions, not just awareness of their physical circumstances, but *self*-awareness: an awareness of the nature of their relations to others. People are not like other organisms, dealing directly with nature, they must deal with nature from known "positions" within a culture, in terms of a knowledge of the part their action may play in relation to other people's actions in maintaining or progressing the culture. Such a quality of their consciousness cannot, of course, be directly observed. In terms only of observational criteria, people do not differ from organisms in the structure of their activity. But indirectly, people demonstrate their self-knowledge by the way in which they respond to the consequences of their own actions. It is in terms of what it implies for future action that the knowledge informing people's actions is revealed; often, for instance, in the way they "mark" their own acts as socially significant ones, or, perhaps, the surprise they manifest when the result is not as they had expected. Thus here, mothers do not just attempt to get their children to complete socially acceptable actions, they "analyse" the concepts that they are developing just as concepts should be analysed: by testing them for their implications—"If he knows that what he's just done is significant then he should expect and accept acknowledgment from me . . . I will give it . . . he does accept it . . . thus he does know"; again using her insider's knowledge.

In acting like this the mother may be said to be acting as a "double-agent" (Newson and Shotter, 1974): she acts both on her own behalf and also on her infant's behalf in what goes on.

At first, an infant clearly has little power to satisfy his own needs. But to the extent that a mother can interpret her infant's behaviour as having an intention to it (no matter how vague and indefinite it may be on his part), she can help him to complete or fulfil it, and in the process "negotiate" a satisfaction of his needs with him. The child's action is thus made to eventuate in a consequence that is at least intelligible to her; and she does it by rendering herself available to him as an "instrument" or "mechanism" acting to produce a result which she feels may be one "intended" in his activity—whether it is the actual, precise intention in his activity, no-one can say, least of all the child, for his activity is so diffuse and uninformed that any intention there may be in it at all must be presumed to be, at this stage, really indeterminate.

As a result of her help, as a result of the way in which a mother completes the realization of what might possibly be her child's intention, his actions may become incorporated into the circle of reciprocal exchange between them both. Thus he learns to act, both in expressing himself and in manipulating the things about him, in such a way that *at least it makes sense to her*—the child himself not understanding till later the nature of what it is that he is actually doing, it being enough at first that he understands how to do it. And thus the process continues, with the child being "helped" by his mother in this way to *retrospectively evaluate* his states of feeling and the consequences of his actions. Now it is not so much in this process that he experiences new states of feeling or performs new patterns of action that have never occurred to him before, that would otherwise be biologically unavailable to him, but that he learns meanings or *socially significant uses* for feelings that he may have or movements that he might make any time. He comes to learn the way other people fulfil the meaning in his movements, so that later he may fulfil their meaning himself—as Mead (1934, p. 46) puts it: "the . . . gesture becomes a significant symbol . . . when it has the same effect on the individual making it that it has upon the individual to whom it is addressed . . . and thus involves a reference to the self of the individual making it". In acquiring knowledge of how to order his activities in relation to others, the child himself learns how to act; he learns, gradually, how not to rely upon others to complete and give meaning to his behaviour, but to relate what he does and what he feels to his own knowledge of his own momentary "position" in his culture; he relates his own activity to his own self.

Institutions and Projects

In urging that the basic forms and functions of human action and expression are differentiated *in play*, Bruner and Sherwood (1975) are surely correct. In the course of playing games, mothers establish specific forms of exchange with their children; sometimes person-to-person exchanges, other times person-to-object exchanges. They establish between them, I would like to say, an "institution" in Merleau-Ponty's (1970, p. 40) sense of the term given below:

Thus what we understand by the concept *institution* are those events in experience which endow it with durable dimensions, in relation to which a whole series of other experiences will acquire meaning, will form an intelligible series or a history—or again those events which sediment in me a meaning, not just as survivals or residues, but as the invitation to a sequel, the necessity of a future.

For, as we remarked earlier, of necessity, each human act unfolds or develops within an implicational field of possible subsequent acts. And what I would like to argue in a moment is that, rather than any very precise innate foundations for the structure of human exchanges, there are precise foundations to be discovered in the *institutions* we establish between ourselves and others; institutions which implicate us in one another's activity in such a way that, what we have done together in the past, *commits* us to going on in a certain way in the future (Winch, 1958, p. 50). But of course, the members of an institution need not necessarily have been its originators; they may be second, third, fourth, etc. generation members, having "inherited" the institution from their forebears. And this is a most important point, for although there may be an intentional structure to institutional activities, practitioners of institutional forms need have no awareness at all of the reason for its structure—for them, it is just "the-way-things-are-done". The reasons for the institution having one form rather than another are buried in its *history*.

I make these preliminary comments about institutional acts here—acts with an "invitation to a sequel"—in relation to the child's task of making a transition from the playing of games to the execution of *projects*. For I take it that, although human development may be distinctive by the degree to which it occurs in the course of play, the true mark of human achievement is this: that one becomes able to commit onself to the realization of an intention involving a long period of sustained activity, in which each and every act is related to each and every other act in the activity by an hierarchical structure of implications. In other words, more than playing one's role competently in games, people can execute a sequence of actions, all perhaps quite different from one another, but nonetheless all connected to one another in a unity of action and experience by a thread of meaning, by a system of implications. Thus we may agree with Chein (1972, p. 289) when he says that,

> The essential psychological human quality is . . . one of commitment to a developing and continuing set of unending, interacting, interdependent, and mutually modifying long-range enterprises.

Except that we would want to add that it is, of course, man himself who develops his own enterprises; he is not a victim of enterprises which develop in and of themselves. And, of course, men may commit themselves to projects, the realization of intentions, *the precise character of which they cannot imagine (or describe) until they have given them a satisfactory realisation*—for instance, as a painter, or the writer of a book must essay forth, and, in a back-and-forth dialectic, modify his productions until they possess a satisfactory form. It is the ability to direct oneself through the course of projects to do with bringing new, socially intelligible situations into existence, being truly creative, that may be taken to be the true mark of humanness. In the rest of this section, I want to discuss how the child may become not only a socially responsible agent, able to at least some degree to realize intentions in the world, but an *autonomous* agent also; able when acting all alone to be creative and to fulfil for himself the meanings in his own actions; rather than being reliant upon others to complete their meaning. But first I would like to make some brief comments about innateness, case-grammatical categories, and agency; social institutions may be just as influential in shaping our linguistic categories as innate factors. Fillmore (1968, p. 24) defines the following "cases" thus:

> *Agentive*, the case of the typically animate perceived instigator of the action identified by the verb.
> *Instrumental*, the case of the inanimate force or object causally involved in the action or state identified by the verb.
> *Dative*, the case of the animate being affected by the state or action identified by the verb.

And so on, for a number of other cases, remarking that "additional cases will surely be needed" (p. 25). About such cases Fillmore (1968, p. 24) says,

> [They] comprise a set of universal, presumably innate, concepts which identify certain types of judgments human beings are capable of making about the events that are going on around them, judgments about such matters as who did it, who it happened to, and what got changed.

One is irresistibly reminded here of Aristotle's notion of "the four causes".

Now whereas Fillmore, like Chomsky, feels that language has its own innate roots, so to speak, modern psycholinguists are looking for evidence of case-grammatical categories in the prelinguistic social exchanges of mothers with their infants (Bruner, 1976). But even this latter endeavour may not be as methodologically straightforward as it might at first sight appear, for, in a very important sense, the roles and relations may be in the eyes of the psycholinguistic beholders. Their cultural tradition must influence the different types of roles they can discriminate. For instance, consider our notion of agency: for us agents instigate action and operate on things, making what they will, happen. But, says Carpenter (1966, p. 206):

> Eskimos have no real equivalents to our words "create" or "make", which presuppose imposition of the self on matter. The closest Eskimo terms mean "to

work on", which also involves an act of will but one which is restrained. The carver (for instance) never attempts to force the ivory into uncharacteristic forms, but responds to the material as it tries to be itself, and thus the carving is continually modified as the ivory has its say.

This is the Eskimo attitude not only to ivory, but towards all things, especially people: parent toward child, husband toward wife.

Whereas we think of our actions as having to do with gaining possession and control of things, doing with them as we like whatever their nature, Eskimos think of their actions as working *to reveal what is already there*—just the concept of agency we need, but find so difficult to grasp, to understand the actions of mothers who "reveal what is already there" in their babies.

I take the force of the above comments to be as follows: while it may be quite true that the "grammar" of our language is inherent in certain aspects of our social practices, we may only be able to "see" them there because we are *already* practitioners of those self-same practices. In another culture, quite incommensurate with our own, the categories inherent in their practices may only become clear if, in some way, we can reconstruct a "view" of their whole "form of life" within which such categories play their part. So while we may study the growth of Fillmore's *Agentive* case, we can only elucidate what its character is *for us*, in our community, at this particular moment in history—which, if developmental research were to be generally influential, may be very different in a few years time. Thus again, this leads to the view that, rather than seeking *in the child* the innate foundations for the structure of social exchanges—syntactic categories (Chomsky) or semantic categories (Fillmore)—the foundations for our forms of social life must be sought *in the history of the institutions between us*.

To return now to the development of autonomy, the ability to execute projects on one's own: Hess and Shipman (1965a, b), drawing upon Basil Bernstein's (1971, 1972) distinction between elaborated and restricted codes, have studied the consequences of the different instructional strategies used by mothers of different social classes with their children. They characterize their main finding as a relative lack of cognitive meaning in the working-class mothers and children: that is, one of the features of the behaviour of the working-class mothers and children is, they say, a tendency to act without taking sufficient time for reflection and planning. Rather than deliberating, they act impulsively in the sense that a particular act seems unrelated to the act that preceded it or to its consequences. In this sense it lacks meaning; it is not sufficiently related to the context in which it occurs, to the motivations of the participants, or to the goals of the task. For example, in a shared task, a mother may silently watch her child make an error then punish him, rather than anticipating his error and warning him, telling him to look ahead and avoid the mistake. In summarizing their findings, they say (Hess and Shipman, 1965a, p. 885):

> [The working-class] environment produces a child who relates to authority rather than rationale; who, although often compliant, is not reflective in his behaviour; and for whom the consequences of an act are largely considered in terms of immediate punishment or reward, rather than future effects and long-range goals.

And they go on to suggest that enrichment programmes must overcome a "deprivation of meaning". What is needed, they say (Hess and Shipman, 1965b), is not more varied stimulation, but "experiences which give stimuli a pattern of sequential meaning", which "show children how ideas and events are related to one another".

But, one may add here, in learning language, in learning how to mean, one is not learning to grasp a general *idea* of language which, once grasped, may be put to use to inform any utterance, for any use, at any time. One is learning simply to participate in a great rag-bag of different linguistic institutions. And what particular linguistic practices one learns depends upon one's particular, everyday life linguistic exchanges: one may learn to joke and commiserate, for instance, but fail to learn to describe or to command others—at least, in some contexts. "Showing" the child how ideas and events are related to one another would not seem to be enough; the child will not learn how to do it himself as a practical skill. If one is going to learn theorizing, for instance, as a practical skill, especially theorizing about the nature of one's own social life in order to deliberate upon, and to plan one's future courses of action, one must engage oneself in exchanges with those in whom this is already an everyday life activity. Being instructed in the theory of a practice is of little use if one is not being also instructed at the same time in the practice itself. Thus it is that children may fail to learn things if they miss the opportunity to engage actively in certain kinds of social exchange.

But what is it that conditions the style of the instructional exchanges in which one is involved in one's early life? Tulkin and Kagan (1972) in investigating whether the social class differences in childhood discussed by Hess and Shipman were also the case in infancy, found that they were, and suggested that one important source of such differences was the mothers' concept of their infants. They suggest that working-class mothers tend not to believe that their children cannot express "adult-like" emotions or to communicate with other people. Some felt that it was only important for a mother to speak to her infant after the infant began to speak. Furthermore, working-class mothers seemed to feel that they could not have much influence on the development of their children, they saw themselves as somewhat powerless and helpless in this respect. "Thus", say Tulkin and

Kagan, "a mother's attitudes are not independent of social and economic conditions." They are participants in social institutions which have a long history, and they act in a way that seems to them the only "natural" way to act, as their continued membership in their institution requires them to do. And as "carriers" of the institutional practices they have "inherited", in their exchanges with their children they pass on their ways of going on.

While much study is now being conducted in psychology in relation to the game-playing analogy—with its references to rules, roles and relations—little work has been conducted on the ability to execute *projects*. Yet it is the person's ability to essay his actions into the future, his ability to act in relation to an end which does not yet exist, on his own, that is the mark of autonomous action. It is the process in which people's individual personalities develop that needs to be studied as well as their membership of a culture, their ability to pursue projects as well as play games, their autonomy as well as their interdependency.

Conflict and. Negotiation

If a child is to become an individual personality, a person among many like himself but not indistinguishable from them, then he must not only grasp "the-way-things-are-generally-thought-to-be" in his community (at that moment in history), but also "the-way-things-seem-to-him". The child may learn "methodologies" (Garfinkel, 1967), ways of seeing, ways of feeling, thinking, acquiring knowledge and communication, all kinds of social practices inherent in the conduct of everyday, communal life. But he must also learn how to express *his* own particular version of the communal world, as experienced from the momentary position he and no-one else occupies in it.

There is an intrinsic conflict, then, between an individual's interpretation of the world and the communal world of which he is only a part. And we might expect that, in mother-infant relationships, before the child has acquired much knowledge of the way things are thought to be in his community, there will be a degree of conflict in the relationship requiring resolution.

We suggested earlier that the interpretations mothers put upon their child's activities was important in determining the meanings the child learnt for his actions. But now we must suggest that the process cannot be just a simple "one-pass" affair; it must be a matter quite often of an initially wrong or inadequate interpretation being modified in the light of subsequent "investigations", until a result acceptable to both parties is achieved. In other words, there is a social practice of *negotiating* interpretations involved. But here we must be careful about the sense in which we take the word "negotiate". As Taylor (1971, p. 23), from whom much of the emphasis upon social practices here is taken, remarks,

> Our notion of negotiation is bound up . . . with the distinct identity and autonomy of the parties, with the willed nature of their relations; it is a very contractural notion. But other societies have no such conception.

In fact, it would seem, ways of negotiation must themselves be something put under investigation in the developing child. As Taylor points out, our ways of negotiating are not necessarily the only ways that there are: the traditional Japanese village, as he describes it, for instance, puts a high premium on unanimous decision; such a consensus would be considered shattered if two clearly articulated parties were to separate out, and one win out in opposition to the other. And besides these different practices, in our own society, ways of negotiating settlements are different in relation to different kinds of conflict. Thus to be an effective personality, the child must learn the proper practices of negotiation with others (as indeed must mothers with their babies), i.e. the rules of all the games in micro-social power politics.

And the point here about negotiation is quite general: the meaning of an action (or utterance) is not just a matter of the intention it expresses, but also of how it is taken. The character of people's activities is something to be negotiated amongst those (here, mother, child *and* those who study them) who are concerned with the meanings being communicated and the commitments being undertaken. It is this more than anything else which will distinguish the nature of the investigations we propose from those that have gone before in psychology: there will be no one, single, true account of the situations being studied, only an account true for certain "practical intents and purposes" *in a community*. The same activity may be seen as having any one of a number of different interpretations according to the overarching projects or intentions it can be seen as tending to realize. So, not only will we mislead ourselves, methodologically, if we set out to characterize mother-infant exchanges in purely formal terms, we shall also mislead ourselves theoretically if we think that we can obtain the one true account of what is happening. We must remember that subjective accounts (if forthcoming) of "the-way-things-seem-to-each-of-us" are different from the objective accounts of "the-way-things-are-thought-to-be" in the community. While it is the mother's task to negotiate her child's development with him as best she can, in terms of how "things-seem-to-her", it is the scientist's task, not to render her actual experience explicit, but to give an account of how "things-are-thought-to-be" for the proper development of a child in our community. The scientist's aim is thus quite different from the mother's. Nevertheless, this does not mean that he need not negotiate his account with those he is studying, for his aim is an account that *all* can see as applicable, especially those whose practices he is meant to be producing the theory of.

SUMMARY AND CONCLUSIONS

In this essay I have concentrated upon the human actions involved in social practices, the actions involved in doing things in ways which make sense to other people. But more than this: for our concern has been with the way in which social practices may grow and be developed in the course of exchanges between people. Thus, in general terms at least, our concern has been with the methodologies, both our own as psychologists and other people's, involved in directing the course of human development. Like Popper, we may avoid discussing the *origins* of human nature, if we concentrate our attention upon what human nature now is and apply ourselves to the problem of its further growth. And this does seem to be a feasible project, for unlike all other animals, man seems to have no species-specific nature, thus no *Umwelt*, and in being capable of bringing new conditions for his own existence into being, is capable of changing his own nature.

To account for the fact that man does seem to develop himself we must postulate that he is *intrinsically motivated* to do it. But it is not just a matter of man increasing his competence, his well-fittedness to his environment, for often, rather than developing his competence, man changes his environment. Thus to find a guide, a direction to the future for his action from the past, man must consider the *meaning* of his actions, what it is that his past actions "point to", so that he can go on in a way sensibly connected to what he has already done in an attempt to complete his projects. Thus placed, within a field of meaning, men may direct the course of their own lives, subject to few specific biological directives. While non-directive, though, the biological matrix of which they are a part and in which they have their being, seems to give man's motions in the world a specific, *rhythmic* character. Their actions show a temporal development, such that each action unfolds from a determined past towards an as yet undetermined future, in a back and forth, in and out, dialectical movement. It is the work of Condon and Sander (1974), more than anything else in recent years, that provides perhaps, the key to many mysteries in understanding the character of human interaction. For behavioural synchrony, taken together with its hierarchical structuring and the concept of intrinsic motivation may help to explain many puzzling phenomena to do with the way that people find themselves, necessarily, committed to act in certain ways, given what they have already done so far in a situation. It is the temporal development of life processes we understand the least at the moment, in its progress from less to more realized states.

Situating himself in one field of meaning rather than another, man may construct for himself one direction into the future rather than another, and in living it, make himself into one kind of being rather than another. But the way in which man projects himself depends upon his interpretations. However, while they are matters of human skill and ingenuity, they are not matters for the individual alone. The centrality of interpretation in any science of man (Taylor, 1971) makes any such science unbelievably complex; and turns us away from considering processes just *within* individuals to those *between* them as well. It is this complexity that simplistic, reductionist, mechanistic approaches to cognitive psychology have tried to ignore. But such a psychology, as Allport (1975) and Neisser (1976) recently (among many others) have pointed out, has still failed to establish any secure facts or foundations. And what Neisser (1976, p. 92) has to say about our ability to attend seems to be true about our abilities in general:

> [They are] not limited by any fixed mechanisms at all, and therefore *no* specific hypothesis about such mechanisms can be correct. Instead, performance depends upon the skill of the observer [or person]. Practiced subjects can do what seems impossible to the novice as well as to the theorist.

And earlier (p. 91) he suggests that, "the fact that people do not notice something is no evidence that they could not have noticed it if they had tried."

These comments of Neisser return us to our initial concern with the nature of human agency, intentionality, skills, beliefs, motives, etc. and the centrality of an hermeneutical approach (Gauld and Shotter, 1977); for these are all processes which *we* are partly "in" and partly "out" of. Although all presumably natural in their origins, we seem able to appropriate them to our own social world, knowing them only in terms of their appropriations, hence in terms of our interpretations—there is no escape from the "hermeneutical circle", although it may be much enlarged (Taylor, 1971).

The hermeneutical approach is concerned with the analysis and description of those phenomena that we are "in"; that we can understand "from the inside". As for those things "outside" us, all we can legitimately do, it seems, is to ask what follows logically from conceiving their reality to be structured in certain ways, and then proceeding as if it were so structured— detecting and correcting errors in our formulations as we proceed (Popper, 1963); absolute truth being theoretically unattainable.

But even the phenomena that we are "in" are vague and open to our interpretations. Only negotiation can settle such matters for practical intents and purposes, so that communal life may continue, until the next conflict between interpretations requires resolution. And the task of the scientist in all of this? Rather than merely accumulating knowledge in the attempt to construct the one true view of how it all is for all time, our science must be seen mainly as a way of extending the kind of contact we have with the world in our ordinary, everyday common sense. The social scientist's role becomes, not that of replacing everyday common sense with an absolute truth, but of analysing, refining, and enlarging upon it, so that we know more clearly not only what we *are* doing, but also more clearly what we *might* do instead (Shotter, in press).

5

The Development of Communication Between Blind Infants and their Parents

CATHY URWIN

University of Warwick, England

INTRODUCTION

Reactions against the psycholinguistic approach to language acquisition have called for redefinitions of the "task" for the child (Nelson, 1973) and the appropriate subject matter for developmental inquiry. Seeing language acquisition in relation to other aspects of the child's functioning has directed attention towards developments which precede and make possible its first emergence. At the same time, notions of "social development" in infancy have broadened. The significance of many of the "Attachment" systems has been re-interpreted to emphasize the opportunities for communicative exchange which they provide (Bruner, 1969; Jaffé *et al.*, 1973). Studies of parent-child interaction now aim to encompass the origins of agency, intentionality and meaning through which the child becomes an active participant in the social world, beginning to interact on the basis of rules and acquiring language as used in his own environment (Bruner and Sherwood, 1975; Richards, 1974; Newson and Newson, 1976; Shotter, 1974). The opening of preverbal communication as a research area has thus allowed a meeting of interests between those concerned with early social relations and socialization on the one hand, and early language development on the other.

For blind infants and their parents there are severe constraints on establishing social relations. Language is particularly important as a system of communication, but its development is often problematic in the early stages. This chapter will explore how two blind infants began to speak. It attempts to describe the development of social relations in communicative terms and to place parent-child interaction and the emergence of language within the life-worlds of the families concerned.

BLINDNESS IN INFANCY: THE EMERGENCE OF LANGUAGE

In the infancy period, many of the constraints which lack of vision poses for development are particularly evident. Clinical literature highlights the blind infant as extremely vulnerable to deviant development and stresses the importance of establishing active exploration (Fraiberg, 1971; Wills, 1970). But while the blind baby must rely on sound to gain information as to the existence and location of objects beyond the range of touch, the development of co-ordinated reaching on sound cue alone is a more complex operation conceptually than visually guided reaching; in both blind and sighted infants, reaching for objects on sound cue alone does not emerge before 8-9 months (Bower, 1974; Fraiberg, 1968). For blind infants delays in mobility are typical, further restricting their access to the environment. The opportunities for extending the blind infants' experience provided by the parents become particularly important. But their baby's blindness has severe implications for their developing relationship with him. While the parents cope with the shock, grief and fears for the future consequent on the diagnosis, the baby does not return their gaze, must be coaxed to smile, and in many ways lacks means for initiating contact with them. Under these conditions the emergence of language is particularly important, "providing the parents with a form of longed for contact which they have missed" (Burlingham, 1961). And for the blind child, the development of language increases his opportunities for interacting with others and facilitates his understanding of the environment. But for many blind children with no additional neurological damage, their speech is initially delayed and restricted to their own body movement or familiar routines. The propensity to imitate is particularly marked, and extreme cases of echolalia are not uncommon (Wood, 1970). Some blind children play with the sounds of words at the expense of using them to communicate, and often the blind child's early language consists entirely of ready-made phrases which he may use inappropriately (Urwin, 1976). While sighted children vary in the kinds of words which dominate their early vocabularies (Nelson, 1973), most blind children are comparatively late in acquiring nominals, and use them reluctantly in communication (Burlingham, 1961; Wood, 1970; Wills, personal communication). It is extremely rare to find the blind toddler delighting in "naming for naming's sake". If development is proceeding well in other areas, language acquisition may progress rapidly to incorporate talk about objects and events: "and it is amongst their achievements that by the time they reach nursery school age they may even out-do the seeing in this respect" (Burlingham, 1961). However, there is an apparently universal delay in the blind child's using the I-You pronoun distinction appropriately (Adelson and Fraiberg, 1973).

Many of these language difficulties are most marked in the early stages (Urwin, 1976). This implies that essential conditions for the emergence of linguistic communication as a generative system may not have been fulfilled. Constraints on the development of active exploration may result in delays in cognitive functioning responsible for some of the language problems. But cognitive development alone does not explain language development. The implications of the babies' blindness for the development of social interaction in the preverbal period may also be related to his difficulties in acquiring language.

THE DEVELOPMENT OF SOCIAL RELATIONS
IN COMMUNICATIVE TERMS

In formulating an account of preverbal communication as it relates to the emergence of language, crucial questions concern how one conceptualizes the "meaning" of the child's first words, and the processes involved in the child's use of symbols which bear an arbitrary relation to reality. While this arbitrariness makes possible further developments in creative language, the use of words in communication depends on reciprocal recognition. Speaker and hearer must comprehend the significance of the symbol and the communicative import carried in the way it is used, both from their own position and that of the other at the same time (Habermas, 1970). To understand the "structure of intersubjectivity" presupposed by all successful communication (Ryan, 1974), we must turn our attention towards the evolution of negotiating processes and shared experiences which precede the emergence of speech.

Despite the many and varied approaches in preverbal communication, we may now acknowledge that adults and infants can communicate from birth onwards, "even if the nature of what is communicated is nothing more than a mutual acknowledgement that there is another person there" (Richards, 1974). Early established mechanisms for regulating social contact, mutual attention and reciprocal exchange may be taken to represent some of the earliest means available to adult and infant for achieving mutual recognition. Developmental questions concern how the parameters of communicative exchange evolve.

Whatever the age of the infant, communicative exchange has particular characteristics and a potential "completeness" by virtue of the parent's adjusting her own communicative repertoire to the infant's developmental level. As many authors point out (Bruner, 1975; Newson and Shotter, 1974; Snow, 1975), interpreting the baby's action "as if they were 'intentional'" seems to be a prevalent component in the adults attempts to sustain the interaction with a very young baby. But in making decisions about how and when to interact with the baby, the parent selectively "interprets" his actions as significant, through her own system of meanings (Richards, 1974), and increasingly according to her own understanding of the child and what has already been established between them. During the infancy period, broad dimensions of developmental change in the baby create openings for new forms of interchange to emerge. At the same time, while social interaction may promote developmental change in other spheres, many of the baby's developing interests may compete with his involvement with the parents. But crucial changes concern the processes through which interactions are initiated and sustained by the child acting as "communicant" rather than by the mother acting as "communicant interpretor" (Sugarman-Bell, 1978), across an extending range of situations. This implies a realization of his own agency in relation to that of the other, and developments in his ability to relate to her perspective. Exploring reversibility in operatory procedures and differentiation of roles within increasingly complex forms of reciprocal exchange may show how these developing processes are realized in interaction. Developments in representative functioning provide conditions through which, "the infant changes so that he begins to need language to extend other communicative means already available to him" (Sinclair, 1971). General cognitive changes may underlie the emergence of symbolic functioning; but it is manifested in particular forms which are themselves significant by virtue of the interaction through which they have evolved.

This approach would predict that the history of social interaction between a particular child and his immediate family may bias him towards acquiring certain specific forms‍ rather than others in the early stages. The interpersonal nexus underlies the "meanings" expressed in the child's early words, and provides the basis of mutual agreement as to the communicative effects of interaction later exploited in word usage. It also follows that changes in the child's relations with others may create "needs" (Merleau-Ponty, 1964) for particular words as much as the cognitive changes which are more generally emphasized. Although only concerned here with the "one-word stage", this perspective views language acquisition as an aspect of socialization itself. It is now recognized that "helpful" adjustments in adults' speech to young children result from their attempts to promote "conversation" (Lieven, 1976; Snow, 1976); the notion of the "context" in which the child is acquiring language has broadened to include the shared assumptions upon which parent-child talk is based (Ferrier, 1975; Lieven, 1975; Ryan, 1974). While the child learns to make himself understood, what he says must be relevant to those around him. He is acquiring language which serves to maintain social reality through the roles and social relations which realize and perpetuate it.

THE IMPLICATIONS FOR BLIND INFANTS AND THEIR PARENTS

From the earliest available means for establishing social contact and reciprocal exchange (Stern, 1974; Brazelton et al., 1974) to regulating mutual attention to objects and events across a wider spatial field (Schaffer et al., 1975) the visual channel plays a dominant role in early communication. Almost all the topics covered in this book, from offering a baby a rattle (Gray, Chapter 8) to the emergence of gestures (Clark, Chapter 10) imply its importance. The baby's lack of vision may impose considerable constraints on establishing reciprocal exchange between them, requiring considerable adjustments from his parents. At the same time, the adults will largely rely on vision. Many cues telling them of the significance of an event will not be available to the baby, and different aspects of the same event may be significant to him. While looking towards the mother is one of the most irresistible means of initiating interaction which the sighted infant has available to him (Dunn, unpublished data), the blind infant's access to other people's activities and opportunities for learning through imitation and observation are severely restricted. For sighted infants, the broad dimensions of developmental change create their own momentum as the baby's emerging interests in objects and developing mobility imply changes in the parent's participation (Blount, 1971; Escalona, 1971; Trevarthen, 1974). For the blind infant, the later emergence of co-ordinated reaching and self-initiated search, and the typical delays in mobility may bias social interaction further. And while the blind child's relation to society will always be problematic, many of the parents' assumptions about their child's development and their own role in it are severely threatened, questioned, or called into play.

TWO LONGITUDINAL STUDIES

The accounts which follow explore these factors, presenting some of the findings from intensive longitudinal studies. Steven and Jerry were visited at home at fortnightly intervals. This presentation concentrates on developments between 7 to 20 months, covering a large part of the preverbal period and the "one-word" stage of language usage. Each session involved informal interview, audio- and written observational recordings; videotapes were made each month of the children in interaction with one or other of their parents. Methodological details are not given here, but observations taken from the video-recordings and observation measures are used illustratively. Accounts are presented in case history form, guided by the theoretical considerations previously outlined.

STEVEN and JERRY and THEIR FAMILIES

Both children are registered as blind, are first born children, and are normal in all other respects.*

STEVEN has a little sight in one eye. Since the defect is obvious, diagnosis was made shortly after birth. No adequate tests of the visual functioning of young babies are available, and it is not yet clear how efficient Steven's is. It appeared to improve considerably after the first 6 months, and by 8 months one could capture his gaze for brief periods. From the first months Steven was given toys to hold and by 5½ to 6 months could reach for them if held close in front of his "good eye". This, of course, sets Steven apart from the majority of blind children. But his mobility was delayed, forward progression not beginning until 14 months (Fig. 1). In this and other areas, Steven shares the developmental problems of many blind children.

Steven's parents live in a small market town. They are both school teachers. Both parents were initially very upset by the baby's blindness, and withdrew from their own family and friends somewhat. Steven's father has found it hard to come to terms with the diagnosis. His mother has expressed her feelings very much less. She soon became fully occupied with looking after a very difficult baby, who cried excessively for the first 8 months. Steven's mother plays the major role in managing the home and taking care

---

*Roughly 2,000 children in England and Wales are registered as blind, the classifying definition being "requiring education through means not involving the use of sight". The majority of these children will have some vision, and an increasing proportion have additional handicaps.

of the child; but both parents believed that one of the most important things about family life was "doing things together". They recognized Steven as a handicapped child, and felt there were particular things which they could do themselves to promote his development.

JERRY is totally blind and has well formed eyes. Diagnosis was made at 3½ months. Jerry's parents live in London. Jerry's mother worked for a short time before meeting up with his father, who has a skilled trade. Both parents

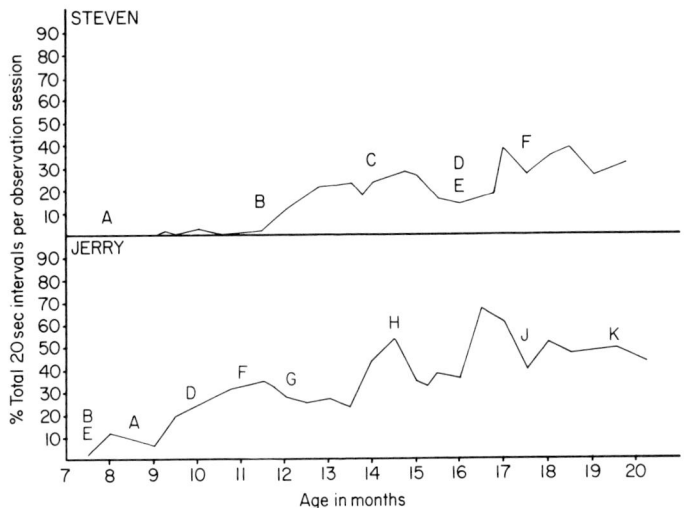

Fig. 1. Self-initiated gross changes in body position and mobility during observation periods.
A, Sitting without support. B, Rolling. C, Forward progression prone. D, Pulls self to stand.
E, Takes steps with support. F, "Walks" supported by furniture. G, Walks without support.
H, Walks freely across room, climbs on and off furniture. J, Occasionally walks from one room to the other. K, Walking freely from room to room.

could not believe that "nothing could be done" for Jerry, and felt that no-one understood. Both parents came from large families and most of the relatives live nearby. Patterns of visiting were such that the maternal grandmother, often accompanied by other daughters, would drop by virtually every day when Jerry was young. While this gave Jerry's mother some support, throughout the study period she has been through periods of relatively severe depression. But Jerry's blindness was only one of the contributory factors. The father was out of work several times and they were often short of money. The mother hated being so confined to the house, and the marriage went through periods of considerable strain. Nevertheless, the importance of Jerry's relationship with his father should become clear in later accounts.

Co-ordinated reaching for sound making objects was established by 9½ months, and active search to retrieve lost objects began towards the end of the eleventh month. These developments occur within the typical age range (Fraiberg, 1968). With respect to mobility, however, Jerry did not show the typical delays. He was standing by the end of the first year, and although initially inclined to topple over, was taking steps across the room by 15 months (Fig. 1).

In the first months of the study, Jerry's mother did not think there was anything "special" she should do to help Jerry's development. She thought the most difficult thing would be helping him not "mind" that he could not see. They thought they might have to teach him to walk, but the main thing was to "treat him like a normal child" which meant "not letting him get too dependent on you", and encouraging him to look after himself.

The two children thus differ in crucially important respects. Steven has a little vision, there are marked differences in developmental rate with respect to object skills and mobility, and the families' day to day lives are very different. Their comments suggest different assumptions about the development of children and the role of parents.

Both mothers felt that the children were initially slow in speaking and commented on how little they seemed to understand. By 20 months each child had acquired a relatively large vocabulary and had just begun to produce two-word combinations. Steven had amassed a large repertoire of "names" of objects. Jerry had acquired a large number of names of friends and relations and social-ritual phrases. To a greater or lesser extent, their early word usage reflects the implications of limited or lacking vision. The final section of the chapter summarizes developments in word usage through the one-word stage for each child.

The sections which follow summarize developments in social interchange between each child and his parents. Accounts are presented under headings which typify "communicative events" (Hymes, 1974) of different sorts.

"Social Play" is loosely defined as heightened mutual exchange for its own sake, excluding situations in which objects are incorporated. "Joint Action Involving Objects" discusses task situations of varying degrees of complexity or play activities in which both the parent and child act on the objects in question. Situations in which the parent relates to or participates in the "Child's Own Object Projects" and ongoing explorations of objects, and when communication takes place about objects and events in the "More Distal Environment", outside the immediate sphere of action of them both, are also discussed.

In each of these spheres particular difficulties may be anticipated because of the babies' blindness. While discussing the kinds of adjustments made by the parents, the accounts attempt to illustrate the age-specificity of communicative exchange, to highlight continuities, and to describe factors pertaining to its evolution.

The first section describes characteristics of the development of social play between each child and his family, through the whole study period, then presents examples from both children from 7 to 12 months. Over this age period, many of the features of the development of social interchange were common for both children. Thereafter, the two children's development diverged, and the accounts are presented separately for each child:

STEVEN

Further Developments in Social Play for Steven describe developments from 13 to 20 months. However, their interaction was rapidly dominated by various forms of *Joint Action Involving Objects*. These developments are discussed in the two sections which follow, covering the 7-12-month and 13-20-month periods.

JERRY

In Jerry's case, little of his interaction with his parents involved the incorporation of objects or things. Developments in *Joint Action Involving Objects* are discussed in one section. However, as described in *Further Developments in Social Play* for Jerry, many forms of social play persisted to evolve throughout the study.

SOME CHARACTERISTICS OF SOCIAL PLAY

While the phenomenon of "social play" is difficult to define, it is easier to talk of its characteristics, which of course are shared by many modes of communication, including language itself.

Steven and Jerry's parents use of touching and speaking raises many questions about the integration and potential substitutability of communicative channels. Varying temporal sequencing, rhythmicality, tempo and mood, techniques for promoting smiling were, of course, particularly important. But both mothers would make extensive use of changing gradations in the baby's facial expressions and body movement, speaking in "reply" to the child's actions, or to "match" their nuances. The parent's techniques undoubtedly exploited age-related perceptual sensitivities and specific response tendencies in the infants. But it was characteristic of both mothers that, once they discovered particular devices which "worked" they would use them again and again. Many forms of play became routinized, persisting to evolve throughout the study.

By 7 months there were striking similarities in each mother's repertoire of routines. Both used phased touching routines to alert the babies' attention; they would trace their fingers around the babies' mouths, blow on their faces, and encourage them to explore their own body parts. Both mothers would mock-imitate the babies' fusses, coughs, splutters and sneezes to "dramatize" the babies' actions. And as consonantal sounds began to appear, they elaborated ritualized imitative frames for "Dadda" "Babba", glottal noises and greeting sounds. Both parents made use of songs and well known nursery games. And while Steven played "Patacake", Jerry played "Clap hands till Daddy comes home". But particular interchange frames were idiosyncratic to each child and his parents.

Steven

Steven's limited vision offered extra opportunities within many of the forms of play introduced above. In addition his mother elaborated devices explicitly designed to enhance visual attention. For example, she would wiggle her fingers, prompting him to catch them, and would whisper in his ears to get him to turn to look at her. Of the many routines in their repertoire, "Arr" deserves specific mention. In the first 6 months the mother used this affective vocalization to coax the baby out of distress and encourage his attentiveness. By 11 months, long bursts of "Arr-Arr" were sustained by the baby. "Arr" was later exploited by the child to gain attention, appearing in a variety of contexts by 20 months.

Jerry

Modes of play initially similar for the two children took on a different form to encompass Jerry's rapid development in mobility. At the same time, many additional forms of body play involved his parents using speech to encourage the child to co-ordinate his actions with theirs, and their responding to his body movements as communicatively significant.

Sequences built around "Hello—Bye-bye", for example, first emerged as the baby made more efforts to roll over into a crawl position. Loosely speaking, the mother's "Bye-bye" accompanied motor efforts resulting in his moving away from her; "Hello" accompanied his turning back towards her, putting her face close to the child's and later turning him upside down and back again. "Lay there!" involved the mother pulling the child back towards her to tease him as he rolled away.

There were differences in Jerry's parents' repertoires. Jerry's mother made extensive use of rhythmic touching and stroking. As to his father, "He plays rough with him and Jerry comes back for more." Initially, perhaps, it was not appropriate for her to play in this way. "He plays *those* games with his Dad." Jerry's father combined extreme sensitivity and warmth with provoking the child to the limits. He used play exchanges to maximize conditions in which the child could dictate "the next step", and also to assert his own authority. As Jerry got older, his mother teased him more, and took over some of the father's modes of play. But some of the routines remained the prerogative of Jerry and his Dad, and these will be referred to later.

The Evolution of Well Established Routines

As the children got older, some of the early established routines declined, and new forms emerged. But for both children, particular routines persisted to become generative, the exchange frames carrying with them the conditions of their evolution. Functioning to sustain heightened social contact, predictable procedures maximized opportunities for building expectancies and anticipation. This allowed and required the parent to exploit new variations. Since many routines involved touching, speaking and physical contact, an element of one could be substituted for another. The babies' developments in other spheres opened new contexts for the routines to be exploited, at the same time acknowledging the child's new range of interests with particular pertinence. But within the familiar interchange frames themselves, as the babies showed increasing anticipation and control, the parents began to push them towards making their intentions explicit. The children came to play an increasingly dominant role, and by the second year, were exploiting variations themselves across a widening range of situations. They lifted elements of well established routines out of context, to control interaction, and to accompany their own solitary activities. Eventually they appear transformed in the earliest examples of the children's "pretend play".

Steven and Jerry: 7-12 Months

Examples taken from Steven at the beginning of this period serve to suggest how the babies' attention and responsiveness could be captured through subtle phasing and timing of the adult's actions.

    (1) STEVEN at 0;7(3) (i.e. seven months and three days)
        Steven, on his mother's lap, coughs, "Oh, what a bad cough you've got!"

S. smiles and looks up. She mock imitates his cough, which sustains his smiling. He vocalizes. "Yes they do!" He vocalizes. "They have awfully bad coughs." S. vocalizes. "Yes!" He breaks the exchange by looking down.

By 8 months the babies anticipation and active control are more evident, and sequences are sustained longer.

(2) STEVEN at 0;8(13)
During feeding, the baby coughs. The mother mock imitates. The baby smiles, looks towards her, and jerks his body. "Who's got a bad cough?" The baby vocalizes. "*Who's* got a bad cough?" The baby vocalizes and she wipes his face. Shortly afterwards he coughs again. She imitates; S. imitates the mock cough. "Oh dear." S. coughs again. "Is it choking you?" He looks towards her, coughing. "Did it choke you?" He smiles, and coughs again. "Oh dear dear." S. vocalizes, smiling. "Have some more."

For Jerry, many routines are well established by this age. These find new openings with developments in mobility, and new routines emerge.

(3) JERRY at 0;8(9)
Jerry is across the room on the floor. His mother has been calling "He's coming to getya." "Where is he?" J. swings into a crawl position. "Where is he?" J. begins moving his legs. "Go and get him." J. vocalizes. "Arr, go." J. vocalizes. "Ta-ah." J. squeaks and part rolls. "Bye bye." J. vocalizes, raises his head and shifts his feet. "Bye bye. Bye." J. vocalizes. "Going to the market?" J. vocalizes. "Yeah? Going to the market? Jerry?" He lies still, and his mother goes in and attempts to get him to lift his head up.

By 9 months Jerry will stand unsupported for a few moments. "Ready steady go!" begins as his mother uses "go" to catch him as he topples. Using this action procedure, an old established routine, "He's coming to getya" finds a new expression, with the new action accompaniments.

(4) JERRY at 0;9(4)
The mother stands J. up again, and lets him go. He stands steadily. "There's a doggie come"—"And he's coming to get you!" and she catches him as he falls forward.

By the end of the first year both babies take more active control over well established procedures. The parents introduce new constraints as they take advantage of what the baby "knows already", so that the exchange will remain interesting to them both. They begin to assert the differentiation of roles between them, extending the babies' discoveries of the effects of their actions in relation to theirs.

(5) STEVEN at 0;11(13)
The child on her lap, the mother introduces the clapping routine. Appealing to his "knowing all about it", she introduces new variations, varies her role to

emphasize the child's, and simultaneously requires him to recognize hers. "Are you going to clap my hands for me?" She puts her hands up in front of him. "Clap my hands." S. takes hold of her hands, and she claps, one two, three, one, two, three. She speeds up her clapping. S. takes control, smiling, and speeds up her claps. "There!" S. lets go, and claps his own hands on the outside of hers, pushing them together. He manipulates her fingers. She pinches his nose, "Boo! Cut his nose" and repeats it, "Boo!" S. pulls his mother's hands apart; she resists. S. laughs. His mother laughs, and claps. The child reaches for her hands, and pushes them together, lets go, and flaps them. The mother claps. S. lets go and swings his hands hard at the mother's. She leads him into "Patacake".

Sitting astride his father's leg, from the simple repetitive sequence based on synchronized action, Jerry can now restart the routine; to some extent he can respond to his father's varying the pace as he teases him to promote responses from the child which would confirm his active participation.

(6) JERRY at 0;11(16)
Jerry's father has been giving him rides, holding the climax through "Ready, Steady, Go!" The father calls a halt, removing his hands. "And no more. No more. No more. ALL STOP." J.'s head is down. He clenches his fist. Teasing him, his father jerks his leg three times and pauses. J. bounces three times and pauses. J. then bounces four times and pauses. His father does the same. His father jerks his foot to make a noise three times, and pauses. J. smacks his legs three times, and lifts his hand out. His father takes it, and J. begins bouncing and vocalizing: his father co-operates in restarting the procedure.

Thus, by the end of the first year, within well established routines, each child was able to reinitiate and in some measure control the actions of the parent when in close physical contact. Up to this point, developments could be described in similar terms for each child. Hereafter, the two accounts diverge.

STEVEN

Further Developments in Social Play: 13-20 Months

In the following months, Steven would initiate many of the routines himself. He would vocalize "Arr" in reaching for his mother's leg, call with "Cuckoo!" and deliberately force out coughs to gain attention. Clapping hands, and playing "Brr brr" with his lips, appeared in his own play and new routines emerged as his mobility improved. In many respects the first half of the second year was a period of "showing off". But in general, the extent to which Steven and his mother engaged in these forms of play declined; their interactive repertoire, was rapidly dominated by object-centred activities. But the early established routines did not entirely disappear. Always there to fall back on in times of distress, songs such as "Ole MacDonald" provided frames for encouraging his "joining in" to produce the appropriate noises. Body play, centred on fingers, toes and body parts, gave way to naming games. And many attempts to create fun about objects or to attract the child's attention involved incorporating the object into well established social routines. For Jerry, the story is different, as will become clear in later sections.

Joint Action Involving Objects

Steven's mother believed that playing with toys could provide important conditions for enriching the child's experience and understanding. Throughout the study period providing the child with toys to play with was a major means of keeping him entertained, and various forms of joint action involving objects was a dominant theme in their interactive repertoire (suggested in Fig. 2).

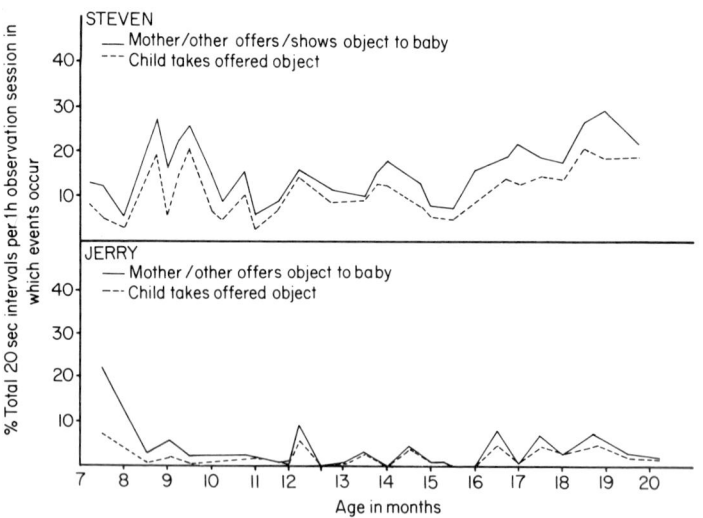

Fig. 2. Exchange of objects during observation sessions.

From early attempts to encourage the child to reach for objects, to the later elaboration of more complex forms of co-operative activity, the mother would tailor her selection of tasks and presentation of objects to maximize his involvement of the moment and promote his efforts. By gradually changing the form of her own participation and definition of appropriate procedures, she attempted to take him towards her own model of how the activity should be performed.

Throughout the investigation, Steven's mother capitalized on being able to capture the child's visual attention. Nevertheless she is operating under considerable constraints; and for the child there are delays in the development of reversibility in action procedures involving objects, and persistent problems to his appreciating the locus of the other's attention.

7-12 Months

By 7 months Steven was already reaching for objects, but this depended on his mother's presenting them close enough to his "good" eye. At the same time she used her voice extensively to alert his interest, work up excitement and promote his efforts. As he began to smile when objects were presented (towards the end of the eighth month) and later to vocalize, she would imitate his noises and comment in response. Eventually she took the child's smiles to indicate recognition. She now began to use the "names" of toys to comment on his involvements; forms such as "There! That's your fish!" replaced "Isn't that a nice thing?" as she referred to what she took to be particular favourites.

Over this period, as the baby's reaching skills became relatively firmly consolidated and his efforts persistent, his mother introduced new variations into the object exchange. She would offer him another object while he was already holding one, coaxing him to hold two at once (8 months onwards). She would attempt to encourage him to bang two together, to bang one object on another, to bang his xylophone with a hammer (11 months), and to pull the cord of his musical toy (12 months).

At the same time the presence of objects might serve as an "excuse" for exploiting interpersonal relations, to which potential instrumental functions are subserved. For example, she began to tease the baby, by deliberately presenting objects out of reach, laughing with him (9½ months onwards); to put objects in unexpected places, on his head and under his jumper (10 months onwards); and to give his toys characters and make the animals make noises.

Over this time, *the child's own object projects* (Fig. 3) would keep him occupied for longer periods, and his mother would "leave him to it". She

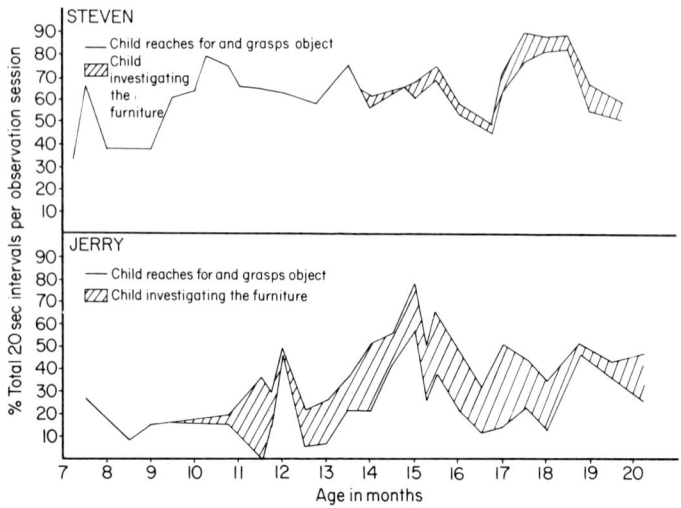

Fig. 3. Children holding objects or investigating the furniture during observation sessions.

would seldom interrupt his sustained investigations but would comment when his attention lapsed, during bursts of exuberant activity, when he smiled and vocalized at an object or if he looked towards her, as he began to do occasionally by the end of the first year.

In spite of the advantages given by Steven's limited vision, his field of exploration was severely restricted. In the *more distal environment* his attention was sometimes caught by bright objects. Picking up these cues, his mother would bring them close. But when he became fascinated by coffee cups, he was regularly warned away with "Hot!" Further afield, the lights would draw and sustain his attention. As to sounds, he would pause for prolonged periods to listen to the clock ticking, its chiming, and to the cars outside. Detecting changes in the child's attention, she would talk of these things. "They're the clocks. Hush. Listen. Tick-tock, tick-tock, tick-tock." "Is that a car outside? Is it? Is it Daddy's car?" While the mother could respond to these cues, the baby could not exploit the system deliberately to direct the mother's attention. Neither could he follow the direction of her gaze or her pointing.* Although Steven's tenacity with toys was evident, the decision to provide them rested largely with the mother. Occasionally he fussed as he dropped an object, which his mother would return. But the child

---

*Steven's mother sometimes tried hard to get the child to follow her pointing towards objects at places further afield. Even by 20 months, Steven would remain staring at her extended finger.

never exploited fussing as a demand for a particular thing, and by the end of the first year, no clearly unambiguous communicative means equivalent to request gestures emerged. Neither did he offer objects towards the mother as characteristic of sighted infants initiatives by this age (cf. Bates *et al.*, 1975).

13-20 Months

By 13 months Steven would search for particular favourite toys as his mother prompted him with the "name" of the thing. By 14 months he produced what his mother considered his first attempt at a "proper word". Staring hard at his "gonk" (a floppy soft toy with big ears), he imitated her. From this time onwards she created situations to see what he could recognize. She made books with pictures of familiar objects, encouraging him to search for the things she named. She used the "gonk" to draw attention to body parts (e.g. "Where's his eyes? "Find gonk's nose", and so on), and ultimately used such situations to teach him to say the appropriate words.

But over the same time period significant changes in other forms of joint action involving objects also occurred, and Steven became mobile. While this widened his arena for exploration, his mother would use objects to promote his efforts, calling to him across the room. She began to build towers with his coloured beakers for him to come to knock over (14 months onwards). As he began to show signs of trying to fit the pieces together she attempted to coax him to put one on top of the other. She built on the child's interest in exploring containers and their contents, bringing with it more complex task situations. Initially she would introduce the proceedings with "Let's do . . . shall we?" when referring to her own actions, and would dramatize their effects with exclamations, completing them with "There!" She would encourage him to copy her, "Steven do it", giving the child the object, pointing to the place where it should go, and they would "push" together. Rapidly introducing another object, sequences became relatively regularized as the child came to anticipate the procedure. While "Another one?" or "More" was sufficient to cue the child, gradually she raised her criterion. Using more imperatives and directives, she demanded that the child do more by himself, as his understanding of the relations became more evident. By 20 months, the child would turn to take objects from her and put them in their places.

But these changes must be seen in relation to preceding developments in reversible exchange. Around the beginning of the second year, Steven's mother began to coax the baby to give up the objects he was holding. Initially this produced nothing but distress. But by 14 months he would allow her to take things from him. Shortly afterwards he would put objects into her open hand and the first signs of his offering objects emerged. Ritualized exchange sequences, the child initiating and controlling the routine (Bruner, 1974) appeared occasionally, peaking in the sixteenth month, with accompanying "Da-da" and later "Thank you" as the child handed the object over. But the ritual was rapidly subsumed under the child's exploiting the mother as agent within the more complex action projects. He would hand her a ball to put in the toy, for example, or a book to initiate looking at picture books together.

Studies of sighted children have implied that the flowering of reaching gestures, communication through pointing and the beginnings of "showing" around the end of the first year represent parallel developments (Bates *et al.*, 1975) indicating changes in the child's ability to co-ordinate his interactions with people and his actions towards objects (Sugarman-Bell, 1975). No signs of Steven's pointing towards distal objects appeared. But between 19 and 20 months he began to occasionally exploit a reaching gesture to demand his "drink" and his "book" when he could see them. This gesture to demand a particular thing, though late in emerging, and restricted to specific usages, sets him apart from totally blind children.

The Beginnings of Representative Play

Within well-structured situations, because the operations were difficult for Steven, his mother had to make the procedure explicit and sustain her guidance, clearly defining what actions were appropriate and how they should be performed. However, she continued to "create fun" in object play situations. His toys now had familiar characters, his animals made noises, and the cars went "Brm brm". Often she would incorporate objects into a previously well established play routine. She might vary the "finger game" described earlier:

> (7) Steven's mother raises the lid of the post box, wiggles her finger through it. "Hello!" The child laughs.

To sustain the child's attention in playing with nesting beakers and boxes she would, for example, slip objects into inappropriate places, dropping his cow in, sticking the wooden man from the car on top of the tower of beakers, and hiding it inside them.

Over the same time period, Steven begins to exploit similar principles of substitutability, incorporating familiar procedures into novel contexts, in his own reconstructions suggesting the beginnings of "pretend play":

> (8) Age 1;4(2)
> Steven plays "Patacake" with the washing tongs.

(9) Age 1;5(11)

   Steven says "Arr" to Teddy.

(10) Age 1;6(15)

   Steven says "Hello" to Teddy and "gonk".

(11) Age 1;7(1)

   While the child is beginning to combine objects, build towers, put things inside each other, he also begins to "flaunt" the rules. Smiling he puts the ball from the hammer toy where the pegmen should go.

(12) Age 1;7(14)

   Steven raises the lid of the pegbox to his "good eye", peers through it, and says "Arr!"

(13) Age 1;8(1)

   Steven says "Hello" to "gonk" and gives him a book to read.

JERRY

Joint Action Involving Objects: 7-20 Months

At the beginning of the study Jerry had few toys and his mother felt he was not much interested in them. She herself spent little time in encouraging his interest in toys, though she left them with him in his cot. But before the child was mobile and prior to the emergence of active search, she would encourage him to play with his toy squeaky cat when he was fretful or bored. Once reaching to sounds was established, like Steven's mother, she would tease him, but as much to promote his body movement and mobility as well-executed reaching. As the baby began to search for objects when he dropped them, and spent more time in active exploration, his mother left him to his own devices, pleased that he could keep himself occupied while she got on with the housework. Figures 2 and 3 show the marked contrast between the two parents and children in this respect.

   Although Jerry acquired more toys as he got older, little of their interaction involved both mother and child acting jointly on particular things. An important exception occurred between 12 and 17 months with the evolution of "Gis it me", their own version of "give and take" or, more properly, "drop and retrieve". This had been preceded by forms of teasing in which the mother would tickle the child with his squeaking toy or a bottle, coaxing him to give it up. Prior to the emergence of the routine, Jerry had begun to deliberately experiment with dropping and retrieving objects in his own play. During its peak period, successive turns were under the baby's control, as he would deliberately drop an object for the mother to retrieve and return with a climax of excited tickling. However, initiating the routine in the first place depended on the mother's decision. And although the baby took control once under way, he would not reverse the procedure by offering or returning the object to her.

By 17 months, the child became more resistant to giving up objects, and new interests to some extent competed with his involvement with the parents. Combinatorial activities were emerging in his object play, and from 18 months onwards his own explorations showed clear hallmarks of representative functioning.

Having to get on with her own work, the mother's definitions of what toys were for certainly contributed to the relatively limited extent to which she participated in the *Child's Own Object Projects*. At the same time no initiative came from the child inviting her participation. While there were no equivalents to pointing to things, reaching in demand, or looking up towards her during his play, like many mothers of blind children she found investigatory strategies such as biting, prolonged chewing, and repetitive flapping of things against his face effectively excluded her.

As to establishing mutual attention to *Objects and Events in the More Distal Environment*, the parents would sometimes detect the child's listening to the cars and people outside. But in general this depended on their attention already being involved, when someone's arrival was expected, or when they were producing the sounds themselves. Thus, for the major part of the study period, Jerry's explorations of objects and the furniture proceeded largely independently of interchange with his parents. But by 20 months there were indications that Jerry was beginning to incorporate objects into these exchanges. He would now give up objects on request; an occasional instance occurred when he attempted to offer with "Ta" in accompaniment. But one of the most successful innovations was the arrival of a trolley and bricks. He and his father would push it about, checking the bricks in, carrying on long vocal exchanges, "Mote Mote, beep beep, brmm brmm" around it. Jerry would use these phrases to accompany his own play with the trolley when by himself. As such it stands as the closest example of "pretend play" involving objects which I have been able to identify.

Further Developments in Social Play: 13-20 Months

While Jerry's parents found it irrelevant, unnecessary or difficult to encourage his interest in toys, many of the early established play routines involving vocal interchange and body play persisted.

Developments in Vocal Interchange

In Steven's case, the relative extensiveness of mutual imitation between parent and child declined towards the end of the first year, rising again with the advent of standard words from 14 to 15 months onwards. For Jerry and his parents, ritualized forms of vocal interchange set apart from ongoing action remained a dominant feature of their interactive repertoire. A large part of the mother's speech to the child involved prompts and acknowledgements within such frames as "Where's Dadda? Where's the Babba?" and later "Golly golly golly" and "Logger logger ligger lugger". Other routines, based on varying intonation patterns, such as rising and falling contrasts, were incorporated as the mother capitalized on Jerry's vocal differentiation. If he was distressed she would "carry on a conversation like" from the adjoining room. By the beginning of the second year, such "dialogues" might last up to 15 minutes at a time. Although the child's willingness to imitate fluctuated, eventually this provided a vehicle for encouraging him to repeat standard words and ritual phrases.

Further Developments in Body Play Routines

By the beginning of the second year, Jerry came to exploit the rhythm of and to dominate play sequences when in close physical contact with the parent. This now invited new forms of teasing from the parents.

(14) Age 1;0(20)
Jerry has "Lay there!" off pat. Rolling over to one side, his mother pulls him back, "Lay there!" J. repeats the movements again and again. His mother won't let him get away with it, pressing him down so that he struggles, "Lay there! Lay there! Lay there!"

New constraints now require the child to make his demands more explicit. In the following example, Jerry's father acknowledges the child's intentions, encourages his persistence, prolongs the dialogue, and then thwarts his expectations, thereby asserting his own authority.

(15) Age 1;0(20)
Jerry now uses prolonged demand-vocalizations to request more play. Standing holding his father's knees, he whines, "Do you want to come up?" J. whines. "Do you want to come up more?" J. whines again. The father continues in this vein, and then apparently gives way to the child's frustration. "Alright then. Just once more yeah?" J. whines quietly, and his father puts his hands round his waist. "Ready?" as if to lift him. Then he drops his hands, sitting back. "No, I've changed me mind. I've decided not to." J. protests vigorously, then shows distress, and laughing the father picks him up.

With the upright posture and the beginnings of independent walking, nursery games incorporating rhythmic body movement replaced the early "baby games". By 13 months Jerry would stamp in time to "Lydee dydee diddel dee dy", his mother holding his hands. The routine well consolidated, she would push the child to perform the actions independent of physical support.

(16) Age 1;2(1)
> "Jerry boy do it on his own" and laughing she sends him away from her, and begins singing again. He can sustain a few steps, but then lunges forward to reach for the mother again.

By 17 months Jerry would stamp in time from across the room, varying the beat and control the pace of his mother's chanting. He would drop on his bottom to "Bump on his bum" or the "Down" of Ring-a-Roses. He had come to exploit signs of excitement which previously his mother's initiative had been tailored to promote. He would flap his arms and bounce to build the crescendo of vocalization and tickling. He took action patterns from regularized play exchanges which he had come to control, exploiting them in altered form in new interactive situations. In the following example, Jerry reproduced movements originally part of "Lay there!" to sustain the interaction.

(17) Age 1;5(0)
> Jerry's mother has been holding his fingers so that he can "jump" to "Ready, Steady, Go!"
> "Ay up!" and she stands him on his feet. J. leaps forward, curls up in a ball on the floor and waits for his mother. She laughs, takes hold of him, and turns him over. "Gotya!" J. pauses, then turns on one side. "Again?" she turns him upside down. "Gotcha!" and lets go. J. rolls on to his side again. She turns him upside down. "Gotcha!" J. rolls on to his side again. The mother turns him upside down. "Gotcha!" She turns him all the way round, and puts him down. "Gotcha! And J. rolls over the other way.

The altered movement pattern stands to represent the past history of interaction, from which it derives its meaning. But it is still dependent on the immediate interaction context. Inherently ambiguous in themselves, Jerry's attempts to exploit pre-established interaction routines were even more so because he could not first be sure of his mother's attention.

(18) Age 1;5(12)
> J. has been clapping while his mother has been giving him chocolate. Having been given some more, he continues to clap. But the mother's attention has been caught by something outside the window. With rhythmic movements, J. thrusts himself forward again, several times. He pauses. His mother is looking out of the window. He swings himself round in a circle and pauses, his

mother still looking out of the window. J. stands still for several minutes, then bursts out in frustrated crying. The mother gives him more chocolate, but he continues to fuss.

By 18 months, Jerry begins to use "words" to make requests for particular routines: "Up Down, Daddy" as he stands at his father's feet. And in play with his mother "Clap hands" and "Lay there" now serve as unambiguous invitations to specific forms of social play independent of physical contact.

While his mother's play with him has become more vigorous, routines particularly important to Jerry and his father were also emerging. For simplicity's sake, three of these may be called "Are you sure?", "Don't you do that" and "Come and fight him". "Don't you do that" and "Come and fight him" involved mock threats as the father encouraged him to fight back. "Are you sure?" first encouraged the child's attempts to stand; later the father would deliberately put him in precarious positions.

By 19 months, Jerry's father would stand Jerry on the table with "Jerry, are you sure?" Jerry would answer "Surr, Dadda" and leap off to be caught by his father.

By 20 months, where the parents have previously built up the child's anticipation, approaching him from across the floor with "I'm coming . . . I'm coming!", in action Jerry will now take the dominant role.

(19) Age 1;8(6)
> Jerry gets up from the floor, some way from the father. "He's coming", the father says, "He's coming", as Jerry speeds up. "Oh he's got him! Oh he's caught his Daddy!" as Jerry does so.

Jerry now has words for "Ready" "Steady" and "Go". In play with his father, his use of words extends his opportunities for controlling the pace of the routine and building the climax.

(20) Age 1;8(6)
> Jerry is standing by his father. "Are you ready?" his father drops his hands with a thump. Jerry takes over: he pauses before building up the anticipation. Then produces "Steady . . ." Again, Jerry pauses and with a climatic "Go!" leaps at his father.

Though tied to the immediate context, Jerry's use of words expresses a reversibility of perspectives dependent on the past history of interaction through which the "meaning" of the words has been derived.

While no examples of symbolic transformations could be found for Jerry, through dialogue he reconstructs past social encounters, expressing a differentiation between self and other.

(21) Age 1;6(2)
> While his mother has left the room, J. reconstructs with variations past

episodes of play with his mother and father, occurring in the previous hour. He uses a low voice for his mother and a "gruff" voice for his father.

Jerry: "Don't you do that."
"Mother's voice":   "Don't you dare!"
Jerry: "*Don't* you do that."
"Mother's voice":   "Don't you dare!"
And with the father—
"Father's voice":   "Are you sure?"
Jerry: "I sure!"
"Father's voice":   "Are you sure?"
Jerry: "I sure."
"Father's voice":   "Are you sure? Jerry? Are you sure?"
Jerry: "I sure! I sure, Dadda!"

and bursts of hysterical laughter.

CHARACTERISTICS OF EACH CHILD'S EARLY LANGUAGE USAGE

Steven

In the final months of the study, Steven rapidly acquired a whole range of new words. The majority of these were nominals. Prior to this time Steven found new uses for early acquired forms as rapid developments opened new situations. When inappropriate in adult terms, his mother corrected him. The bases for generalization might be perceptual, according to actions he performed himself, and actions inherent in the objects themselves. "Brrm" came to include many moving things, and his actions on them. First appearing at 16 months, he used "Hot" at every available opportunity as he caught sight of coffee cups. He eventually included the iron (17 months 4 days) and the refrigerator (17 months 11 days). He also exploited his own idiosyncratic forms which his mother said meant "anything nice to look at" to draw her attention to the thing in question; she would comment accordingly. It was to such a use that Steven put the majority of words available to him. As he caught sight of particular toys or objects he would excitedly repeat its "name" again and again. The rapid accrual of nominal forms paralleled changes in combinatorial activities with objects, more sophisticated forms of representative play in which the child exploited the relations between objects and their properties, and used animated toys to reconstruct, with variations, past interactional experiences.

In many respects, the broad outlines of Steven's developmental progression shares features characteristic of many sighted children, and this vocabulary bias suggests a language learning strategy which K. Nelson (1973) has characterized as "referential". The rapid accrual of nominals is uncharacteristic of the majority of totally blind children. Clearly, Steven's limited vision has been very important to establishing communication about objects. But throughout, constraints emerge with respect to the particular "words" he acquires, how he uses them, and the point at which new developments emerge.

Steven vocalized prolifically; his speech when it emerged was poorly articulated and very repetitive. He exploited ritualized greeting sounds and calling devices, and later "Hello" to a marked degree, repeating them again and again until his mother answered.

The build-up of the child's vocabulary reflects his limited vision to a greater extent than at first appears. This restricted his access to many of the objects and events in his surroundings, and at the same time to the conditions which might elicit productions of the appropriate "words". While he had a large repertoire of ritualized noises, many of the nominals referred to things with particularly salient sounds. From the clocks to the cars and the rain, Steven would produce the words as the clock struck, as cars passed by and as he heard the rain outside. Though he had a few words for the furniture, the majority referred to his toys and to the pictures in his books. There were particular difficulties in his co-ordinating interaction with people with actions on objects. He did not begin to offer or present objects to his mother until comparatively late. There were similar delays in his appealing to his mother as a source of agency outside himself to gain help in object oriented activities. Normally we infer such developments through the child's gestures such as pointing, reaching and other actions towards others as he attempts to gain or direct her attention, demand particular things, or help with projects of his own. Steven came to exploit looking, vocalizing and smiling at objects to draw his mother to comment in acknowledgement. But this could not function outside his limited visual range. Restrictions or delays in the child's acting to draw the adult to help in manipulation of objects is reflected in the restricted range of interpretations which can be given to the child's use of words. For sighted children, using words to demand particular things appears to be one of the earliest communicative functions to be established (e.g. Bates et al., 1975; Dore, 1975; Carter, 1974). For Steven, no use of words to make requests could be discerned (by either the mother or myself) until the emergence, at 18 months, of the "demand" gesture which he used restrictively for his "drink" and his "book", saying the words at the same time. This depended on his being able to see the object in question: by 20 months he was not yet initiating references to non-present events or objects himself.

It is tempting to conclude that the lack of communicative functions manifested in joint action has restricted the availability of "functions" which the child can exploit in his early language usage. This, of course, is to assume that the two forms of communication can be equated. Such a conclusion ignores the totality of development change in which its emergence takes place, the impact of the child's emerging language on communicative exchange itself, and that the power of language usage lies in its making possible an integration of communicative functions transcending many levels of abstraction.

In the following example, Steven can now accomplish with language what he could not accomplish with the limited gestural means available to him:

> (22) Age 1;7(15)
>
> S. is now conducting the familiar "post box" operation himself. By now, once under way, the mother sits back, as S. plainly "knows all about" what is to be done. He turns to her for each peg in turn, saying "Thank you" or "more' as he takes them. He produces one of his first two-word combinations, "More men, more men" to comment on recurrence as he puts them in the box and takes the lid off. He decides the enterprise is over, and attempts to replace the lid. It is heavy. He cannot quite manage it. He pummels, pushes, slides it, but the mother does not interrupt. He stops, peers hard at the lid, and tries it again. He stops, and looking hard at the box with the lid half on, says "Thank you. Thank you." His mother interprets this as a request for help. "Do you want me to help you? Alright then", and she replaces the lid for the child.

Jerry

Jerry's early speech was highly imitative. He acquired ready-made phrases rapidly and easily. By 20 months his productive vocabulary consisted primarily of names of familiar people, words for his own body movement, songs and ritualized forms associated with particularly well established routines. By this time Jerry had acquired a few nominals and rarely used them. Although one might hear him say "door" or "telly" as he contacted the objects in his own ramblings and exploration of the furniture, he never volunteered these words in interaction. Neither, of course, did he use words to "ask" for objects, or to refer to them when not in contact with them. This was in spite of the fact that Jerry's own play with objects was now clearly representational.

The lack of words to refer explicitly to objects confused the parents. But in fact they rarely used the names of objects or toys in referring to them until he was 18 months old. By this time he was speaking, so they began to teach him to imitate the names of things. Taking his involvement with toys more seriously, they would now use appropriate names to draw his attention to particular favourites.

The high reliance on imitation, the predominance of ritual phrases, and restricted use of nominals are characteristics common to many blind children. However, for a blind child of his age, Jerry's early speech was prolific, relatively articulate, and displayed a generativity of function and structure which suggests that many developmental problems had been circumvented.

Much of Jerry's early speech was biased towards sustaining interaction through basic rules of dialogue maintenance. He would use "Hello . . . Bye bye" to open and close encounters, and vary intonation patterns to regulate and express a variety of communicative effects (cf. Sacks *et al.*, 1974). Imitation served as a mode of communication in its own right (cf. McTear, 1976). Jerry would dictate the mother's response, exploiting the alternative forms available, running through the names of familiar friends and relations himself. At the same time he would call "Mum" and "Dad" in distress, to gain attention, use the words in greeting, and could also identify familiar people with their names.

While this framework for communicating through vocal exchange was established in the preverbal period, the body action games had contributed to the build-up of a vocabulary of words and phrases centred around his own body movement. But developments within the exchange frames themselves allowed him to use such forms as "Clap hands", "Up-down" and "Lay there" to initiate and control interaction. With "Don't you do that!" he would "reverse the roles" to protest at the rough actions of his father.

As in Steven's case, the earliest acquired forms extended in range of usages, to new contexts of interaction and as accompaniments to his own play. By the final months of the study period, Jerry was occasionally incorporating words and phrases initially based in play routines into object oriented activities.

One of Jerry's earliest acquired forms, "Surr", derived from "Are you sure?", shows the most extensive range of usage. At 17 months while Jerry was in his cot, one might hear "oo sure? oo sure?", and rush in to find him on the edge of his cot. In interaction, Jerry would use "Sure? I sure! Sure!!!" to call attention, to appeal for more, or to shout defiance. By the final months:

(23) Age 1;7(20)
    J. is testing the security of a box on the arm of a chair, to see whether it will topple. "Surr?" he pushes gently, and removes hands. "Surr?" and he tests it again.

But Jerry's language is undeniably restricted in what he was able to talk about and the extent to which it was meaningful to those outside his familiar interaction environment. The history of interaction through which the child has begun to speak has precluded the emergence of language explicitly referring to objects and physical events. This may change since object centred activities are now emerging. Dialogue itself may consolidate his understanding of events to which his access is restricted, allowing them to become mutually accessible.

> (24) Age 1;8(6)
>> Through "dialogue" about a familiar event, J. and his mother elaborate the theme of "non-existence" or "completion". Finishing his feed:
>> Mother: "It's all gone. Sorry. You can't have no more. No more eggs. Sorry."
>> Jerry: "No?"
>> Mother: "No."
>> Jerry: "Inart?"
>> Mother: "No."
>> Child: "No."
>> Mother: "No." (laughing)
>> Child: "No."
>> Mother: "No. All gone."
>> Child: "All gone."

SUMMARY AND CONCLUDING DISCUSSION

> The vernacular of everyday life is primarily a language of named things and events . . . referring to the relevance system prevailing in the linguistic ingroup which found the named thing significant enough to provide a separate term for it. (Schutz, 1967, pp. 13-14)

This chapter has explored the evolving communicational nexus through which each child began to use particular arbitrary symbols in communication. Prior to the emergence of speech, both babies' blindness posed constraints on establishing communication about objects and events located outside their own immediate sphere of action. This was reflected in each child's early word usage.

For both children there were delays or difficulties in their incorporating objects into their interactions with adults and establishing reversible exchange involving action on objects. Forms of "showing" did not emerge spontaneously in either case. Steven began to reverse actions of "giving" and "taking" after specific training from the mother. Jerry was just beginning to do so by the end of the study as more extended opportunities for interaction about objects, supported by dialogue, emphasized their mutual accessibility and the role of the other.

Here we have seen the implications of the absence of such forms of initiative from the child on the parent's participation in interaction. It is one manifestation of the difficulties posed by the babies' lack of vision for establishing communicative exchange about objects. The kinds of constraints operating between these children and their parents are likely to underlie many of the early language difficulties found for other blind children. Other complications reflect the implications of lack of vision less directly. Excessive imitation, for example, often results from the parents and child relying on this to maintain contact between them. In more extreme cases, little social interchange may develop.

Relative to the general population of blind children, both Jerry and Steven's early language is developing extremely well. I have attempted to highlight processes of mutual discovery through which the children came to exploit speech to communicate. In establishing interchange with their babies, the parents capitalized on potential substitutability of communicative channels, without which language as a semiotic system could not develop to stand apart from ongoing events. Within the interchange frames themselves they related to find and extend what was already established between them. As the babies showed increasingly evident control, the parents exploited alternatives and encouraged their children to take more active roles. Examples have shown the children capitalizing on the communicative significance of their own actions, beginning to reverse operatory procedures over an extending range of conditions, freeing communicative acts from their contexts of origin, and showing increasing sophistication in their ability to exploit their own agency in relation to that of others according to "rules" elaborated between them. But throughout the process is dialectical. While the parent must adjust her mode of participation to developmental change in the baby, the child takes over and transforms procedures first consolidated in social interaction to extend them to a wider range of situations. This is particularly evident during the early part of the one-word stage. Examples have suggested how the past history of social exchange is reflected in the child's exploiting the boundary between the "real" and the "unreal", the "appropriate" and the "inappropriate" in his early pretend play. By 20 months each child is reconstructing the distinction between "self" and "others" and is using words in an arbitrary sense, while beginning to participate in "conversation". Dialogue principles underlie communicative exchange throughout the preverbal period. With the evolution of representative functioning, they now serve to support the children's realizing in language mutual understandings consolidated in social interaction, extending their uses to new situations and forming new combinations.

The history of social interaction creates the "meanings" expressed in each child's early words. At the same time they are learning particular forms as they relate to speech as it is used in their own environments. Throughout, the parents have made different decisions about how and when to interact with their babies, resulting in different biases in the relative dominance of the kinds of communicative events outlined, and the ways in which they used speech themselves in these situations. This reflects the different living conditions of the parents and the meaning systems through which the child's actions are interpreted as significant. Differences in the history of social interaction through which each child began to speak resulted in their acquiring different particular words and their using them in different ways. *Steven* has amassed a vocabulary for talking about objects and their properties, and is generating combinations making connections between them, elaborated by his mother in dialogue. *Jerry* has words to sustain his relations to significant people, and his early language is closely tied to familiar routines. Mastering basic conversational rules for "taking turns" extremely early, Jerry has language to initiate interaction, to maintain phatic exchange, to call for more of the game, to protest, to make threats and to tease. In learning particular arbitrary symbols to refer to "named things and events" the child acquires language relevant to the life-world in which he is growing up. This must also apply to the uses he finds for speaking itself.

Section 3

The Evolutionary Background

6

Some Basic Traits of Language in Wild Chimpanzees?

FRANS X. PLOOIJ

University of Nijmegen, The Netherlands

INTRODUCTION

In this chapter some observations on the behaviour of free-ranging chimpanzees leading their natural community life are presented. These observations stem from a study of the development of communication of the.chimpanzees living in the Gombe Stream National Park, Tanzania, East Africa. They are intended to add fuel to the debates concerning chimpanzee language (e.g. Fouts, 1973; Gardner and Gardner, 1969; Premack, 1971; Rumbaugh *et al.*, 1973): whether any forerunner of this remarkable ability is manifested under natural conditions; and concerning the position of gestures in both the evolution (e.g. Hewes, 1973) and development of language (various authors, this volume).

The first assumption that must be made is that whatever aspects of language chimpanzees may possess, these must be inherent in certain parts of their social practices. To uncover these aspects may be a very difficult task indeed. For as Shotter notes (this volume), we may only be able to see those aspects when we are ourselves practitioners of the selfsame social practices. As will become clear later, gestures lie at the forefront of this discussion. But *a priori* it is very difficult to surmise what these gestures might look like. Shotter)this volume) rightly points to that fact that an act is known for the kind of act it is in terms of the future acts it implies. Consequently "no-gesture-at-all" may be a very important part of the communicative process. It may imply that a chimpanzee mother is not prepared to allow her infant to suckle, that an infant has to solve its own problem, that a male is about to attack, and so on. In the case of "non-behaviour" it is all the more clear that one has to be familiar with the implied future acts in order to perceive it as significant. On the other hand, if it is possible to study profitably the pre-verbal development of communication in humans, as Bates *et al.* (1975), Bruner (1976), Dore (1975a) and various authors in this volume have done, it should prove possible to study the non-verbal development of communication in chimpanzees as well, and to do so from a similar perspective.

The present chapter adopts this line and suggests that chimpanzee infants initially go through a sequence of communicative development similar to that of human babies: that is, from being perceived by their mothers to be com-municating—communicating unintentionally—to later being able to put their earlier perceived actions to the end of deliberate and intentional communication. There is thus to be found a perlocutionary as well as an illocutionary phase in the non-verbal development of imperative and declarative performatives. Further, examples from adult chimpanzee behaviour illustrate that the use of gestures in totally different contexts as well as combinations of gestures also occur.

DEFINITIONS

Throughout this chapter some philosophical and linguistic technical terms are used. I find it useful to define them here. As it took me, as a non-linguist, some time to understand them, there may be other readers who find them-selves in the same position.

The following definitions are from Bates *et al.* (1975):

perlocution = a signal issued by one person which must have some effect, intentional or unintentional, on another (receiving) person;

illocution = intentional use of a conventional signal to carry out some socially recognized function (e.g. indicating the presence of objects or events, commanding);

imperative = using signals as a means of controlling the receiver's behaviour;

declarative = the use of an object as a means of obtaining another's attention. (Note that Austin's (1962) definition differs from the one given here.)

In the ethological literature the following terms were introduced by Smith (1965, 1969):

display = acts in the behavioural repertoire of an animal that have become specialized in the course of evolution to convey information. These acts include postures, movements, vocalizations and other sounds, the release of volatile chemicals and so on;

message = the information available to an individual as a result of having received only a display;

meaning = the information available to an individual as a result of having received a display together with other, contextual sources of information.

These terms from two different disciplines are not as far apart as they may seem at first sight: only after a baby has gained knowledge of the links between his own message and those contextual sources of information which his mother selects, through her reactions to his acts, in other words, only after a baby has started to understand the meaning which his own acts have to his mother does illocution by the baby become possible. This is what I mean by the phrase "message and meaning overlap" further on in this chapter.

CHIMPANZEE BABIES versus HUMAN BABIES

First I shall present some facts about chimpanzee babies. The chimpanzee baby is a "naked ape". All his time is spent on his mother's body: he is, though, very poor at clinging and has to be supported most of the time or even carried while the mother is moving about. He sleeps most of the time and wakes up every one to one-and-a-half hours. When awake, the infant engages in "mountaineering", "rooting" and "whimpering". Prechtl's descriptions (1953, 1964) of "mountaineering" (in German, *"Kletterbewe-gungen"*) and "rooting" in the human newborn fit the behaviour of the infant chimpanzee extremely well. Through "mountaineering" he moves upwards over his mother's body, and through "rooting" he gets a nipple in his mouth: but in no sense could he be thought of as going in this manner "straight for the nipple".

Often the end result of whimpering is that his mother pushes him closer to her body and simultaneously upwards. However, as with the human infant, there is no evidence that the infant is aware *a priori* of the signal value of his whimpers. It is useful here to make a distinction between message and meaning as Smith (1965, 1969) has done. On the one hand the infant performs behaviours that carry messages about his state. On the other hand his behaviours may serve as signals with a certain meaning for the mother. Message and meaning do not necessarily overlap.

The latter is also true for the human baby. In his development it appears that more and more overlap occurs between message and meaning. The human infant's behaviour acquires value from the actions it engenders in the mother, and concurrent with the development of these values intentional communication appears to arise. Related to this is the transfer of the initiation of dyadic exchanges from mother to child. The child begins to use actions which initially occurred at his mother's "prompting" to request those "prompting" actions. For example, Clark (this volume) notes how the infant develops the ability to take an object by reaching out for one when it is offered. *When* he is offered an object is initially dependent upon his mother's whims. Later, however, he uses the action of reaching out to prompt his mother to give him something. In both examples, the child develops the ability to make requests: an ability which may well be a prerequisite to the later linguistic expression of requests. The obvious question at this point is whether wild chimpanzees exhibit similar developments.

DEVELOPMENTAL SEQUENCES IN THE CHIMPANZEE

The data demanded by this question is currently somewhat thin on the ground, but we may tentatively formulate an answer to it. There appears a definite sequence in the early development of chimpanzee mother-baby interaction that slowly progresses, in linguistic terms, from perlocutionary to illocutionary communication: from the infant unintentionally eliciting actions from his mother to his doing so deliberately. One example is "whimpering". Through the social effect of "whimpering" the infant gains an awareness of its signal value, and will thus progress to whimpering *in order to* engender his mother's interaction. However, the sequence may best be illustrated in the development of "play-tickling", which occurs as follows. From the age of about 6 weeks, the infant chimpanzee begins to bite simply everything that comes close to or touches his face, perioral stimulation being especially effective. Social as well as physical objects are bitten without any discrimination, with the objects that are most frequently close at hand, or rather close at face, being most frequently bitten. Obviously, parts of his own body such as the hands and feet come first, parts of the mother's body come second, and so on. This biting serves to trigger a specific interaction between mother and infant. Before the age of 6 weeks the mother directs only maintenance activities—grooming, for example—towards her baby. But soon after the onset of biting she begins to show special attention and starts poking and tickling her infant *as a reaction to his bites*.

At the age of 7 to 8 weeks grasping was first observed accompanying biting, being initially very clumsy with an enormous lateral deviation as shown in Fig. 1.

In the case of human infants Bruner (1973) and Trevarthen *et al.* (1975) would argue that a goal is prefigured in this motoric form. And in fact very soon a goal appears to become evident: the infant reaches after his mother's hand once it has retreated from him. Normally this results in her tickling him

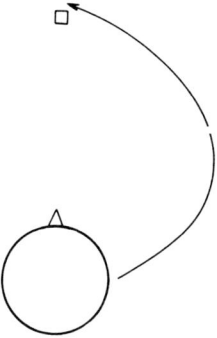

Fig. 1. First *observed* grasping accompanying biting.

again. What the status of this reaching is *vis-à-vis* making a request is difficult to ascertain. However, around the age of 3 months biting becomes restricted to social objects, that is to parts of the mother's body. This restriction in the objects to which the action is aimed is similar to the development of crying Piaget describes in the case of his son and daughter (Piaget, 1952, p. 60, Obs. 27) and suggests that the infant chimpanzee is beginning to use acquired knowledge in guiding his activity (for a more detailed account of the above, see Plooij, in press).

However, this is not the end of this developmental sequence. It continues, and results in the infant not only being able to *maintain* the interaction, but in his being able to *initiate* it. He becomes able to initiate "play-tickling" sessions with his mother by using behaviours whose values have been established in earlier sessions. He develops this ability as follows. When the mother is tickling her infant, he will "defend" himself: if the mother tickles his belly, for instance, he will arch his back and pull up his legs so as to repel the stimulation with hands and feet. If she tickles his neck-pocket, he will bend away while bringing his hands backwards over his shoulders towards her hands or head, trying to push them away. This produces a characteristic posture. Around the age of 11 months, infant chimpanzees start to initiate play sessions by directing this posture towards their mothers or other individuals, as can be seen in Fig. 2. Other postures, developed in a similar way, may be used as well.

Thus we see the infant chimpanzee using a signal as a means of controlling his mother's behaviour. That signal has developed from earlier behaviour

Fig. 2. Female-infant chimpanzee (in front) tries to initiate a play session by directing this posture "Hands around head" (= HOH) towards another individual.

employed in interactions with his mother, and in a similar vein to the functions outlined for human infants by Lock and Clark (this volume). That development is well described in Vygotskian terms: through social interaction the infant chimpanzee's action has progressed from the intermental level to the intramental one. According to Bates *et al.* (1975) this current use of the action would be in accord with most definitions of an imperative, and the border between perlocution and illocution thus seems to have been crossed.

Comparable developmental sequences are shown by the infant chimpanzee in other contexts. One such context is that of grooming. When grooming her infant, a chimpanzee mother frequently puts him in the characteristic posture shown in Fig. 3. In order to groom his side and armpits, she takes his arm and pulls it upwards. By the age of 6½ months the infant may be observed adopting this posture unaided while his mother grooms him. This is a prelude to what is to follow. At the age of 11 months an infant was observed who came up to his mother, sat down in front of her and adopted this posture, more or less as shown in Fig. 4. Almost predictably, his mother groomed him! Other writers in this volume (Lock, Edwards) note the development by human infants of an arm-raising gesture which at first appears in the infant's repertoire as a passive response to being picked up and later becomes an active request to be picked up.

At this stage one cannot help but become suspicious that processes exist common to the development of communicative behaviours in both man and chimpanzee. These suspicions are strengthened when considering yet another gestural example that suggests the use of an imperative. This gesture may be described literally as "lies down on back": an individual lies down on his back while keeping his head lifted and extending his hand and arm towards another individual whom he is also looking at. The meaning of this gesture becomes clear if one knows how very young infants interact with older infants. In the first half year of life chimpanzees hardly interact with anyone but their mother. When they finally start making excursions away from their mothers and towards other individuals, interactions can only be sustained if that other adopts a very passive role: as soon as a "stranger" takes hold of the infant's arm (in order to pull it close and cuddle it, for instance), the infant withholds and retreats. Apparently, the infant does not like being restrained in these situations. The only thing the older individual can do to maintain such an interaction is to lean backwards and allow the infant to walk over him and lie on top of him. It is in this context that the older individual leans backwards and extends his arm. This gesture, "lies down on back", is usually given at a distance of a few metres—the reason for this probably being that the younger infant would retreat towards its mother were the older individual to approach him. This gesture was observed being used by chimpanzees as young as 12½ months towards younger infants. It seems

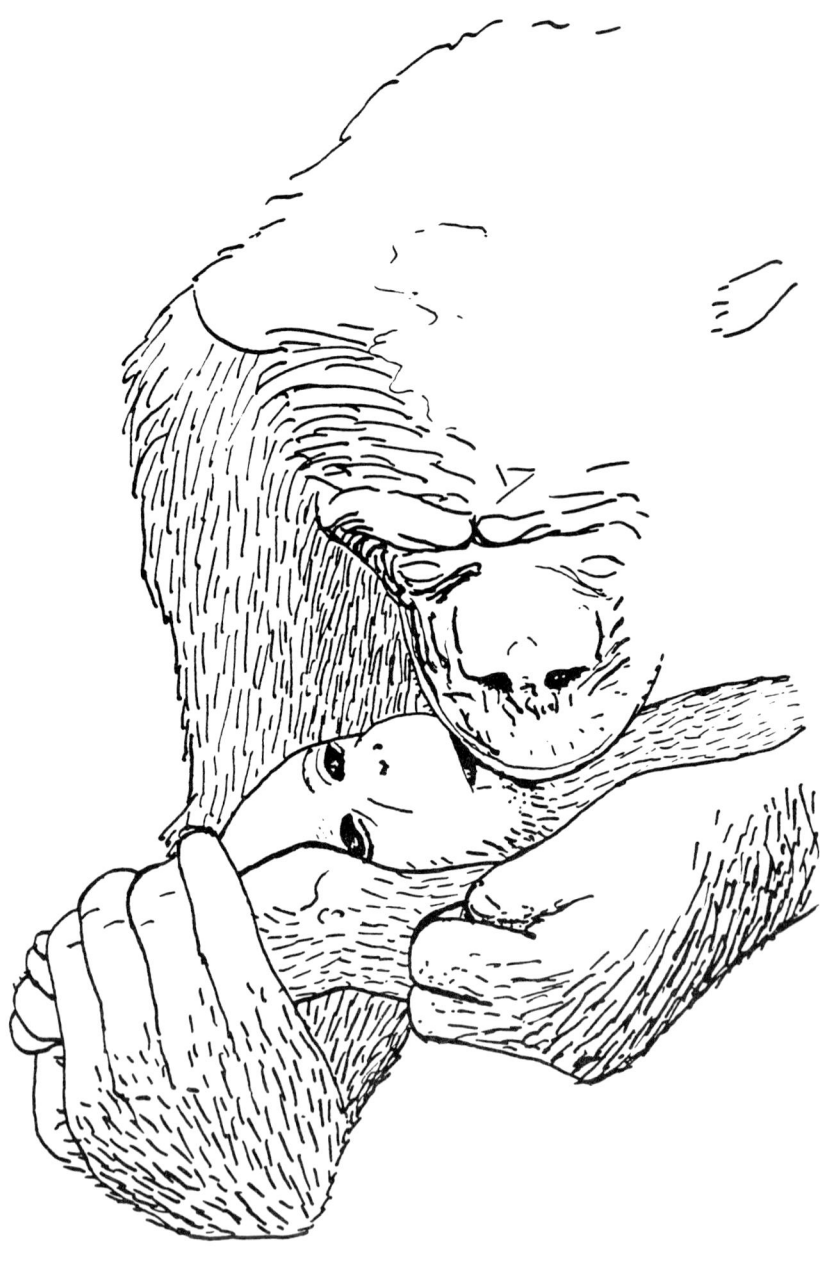

Fig. 3. Mother chimpanzee "puts arm high" (=DAO) of her baby with her right hand and grooms his right armpit with her left hand.

Fig. 4. "Arm-high" (=AOH) gesture.

unlikely that this gesture represents an innate signal which is released by an infant as a stimulus object since it is so context specific. More probably it arises through a process of "social negotiation", the older infant finding almost by trial and error the means of initiating a successful interaction. Whether the younger infant reacts to the meaning of the gesture, or merely takes advantage of the opportunity thereby afforded for interaction is, of course, another question.

Comprehension of the Agentive Role

Yet another question that may be posed at this time is whether the infant has any comprehension of the agentive role played by another. The attracting and directing of the mother's attention plays an important role in the communicative development of the human infant (Bruner, 1976; Edwards, this volume; Schaffer, 1975). Bates *et al.* (1975) have argued that one cannot infer that a child understands the role of an adult as agent unless he "looks up into the mother's face" at times when he wants something of her. Does an infant chimpanzee do this, however?

Again, the answer is yes: and in fact, the strategy develops even earlier than the other examples given so far. Its occurrence is very well illustrated in the developmental sequence which culminates in "begging". If the young infant wants, say, the mother's food, he simply takes it. To begin with, the mother allows this. Soon, however, she will passively prevent the infant from taking the food by not letting go of it, or by withdrawing her hand from his advances. In such cases the infant keeps trying to obtain the food directly, without ever looking up into the mother's face. A change in this behaviour was first observed by the age of 9 months when the infant starts "begging": he will touch the mother's hand or mouth and look intermittently at her face (eyes) and hand (or mouth). Thus the infant no longer attempts to directly attain his goal, but uses his behaviour communicatively and indirectly for that purpose—a development occurring, again, in human infants. We have no pictorial record of this "begging" by infants, but an idea of what it is like may be gained from Fig. 5 which shows begging in adult chimpanzees.

Thus with the onset of begging between the age of 9 and 12½ months, followed by the use of the other three gestures initiating tickling, grooming and approach, it may be assumed that the chimpanzee infant understands the role of his mother (and others) as an agent; that he starts using imperatives; and in crossing the border between perlocution and illocution that he possesses a true communicative ability—in Smith's terms (1965, 1969) message and meaning now overlap.

Fig. 5. "Begging" in adult chimpanzees. From left to right: Hugo, Figan and Mike. Mike is begging from Hugo.

Proto-declaratives

According to Bates *et al.* (1975) one may define a proto-declarative as "the use of an object as the means to obtaining another's attention". Two candidates for this function appear in the case of chimpanzees: "leaf-grooming" and "running away with an object". In the case of leafgrooming an individual will suddenly, as if out of the blue, take a leaf and begin grooming it intensively. In the majority of cases this results in another individual coming over to him or her and observing closely what is going on. Nothing special was ever observed to be on the leaves groomed in this way: it seems more likely that what is special is nothing intrinsically to do with the leaf itself, but more to do with the role leafgrooming plays in social inter-action. The leafgrooming individual obtains the attention of others, which is often a prelude to an interaction of some sort—grooming or rough-and-tumble play, for instance. The earliest age at which leafgrooming was observed was 17 months. Carter (this volume) notes a similar use of objects by human infants in her description of what she terms an "attention-to-object" schema. The difference with the human infant is that it appears that an attempt is being made to direct attention to the object itself. However, Clark and Gray (this volume) both note the early introduction of objects into the interchange between human mothers and infants. Newson (1972) points out that before the infant arrives at a communicative use of objects in the manner described by Carter (this volume) there is a period in which objects are implicated into "the games infants play" with apparently the sole purpose of attracting attention. This *mélange* of development brings us back to Shotter's point (this volume) that the significance of an act can only be uncovered in terms of the future acts it implies. Chimpanzee cultures are not nearly as object oriented as human ones, and they thus have little "incentive" to go beyond the social aspects of attracting attention.

The second candidate here, "running away with an object", is self-explanatory. An individual takes an object (any object, the most ridiculous little twig will do) and starts running away from another individual *while looking back* at him or her. This other may then rise and run after the first individual, and generally interactions similar to those engendered by leafgrooming follow. The earliest age at which "running away with an object" was observed was 14½ months. One sequence was observed where an individual aged 21 months firstly ran away with an object and then, failing to gain the attention of the other, he began leafgrooming. This gained the attention of the other. The active individual then ran away with another object, and the other followed, with rough-and-tumble play ensuing.

USE OF GESTURES IN OTHER CONTEXTS

The following examples show how gestures such as those just described may be used later in life in totally different contexts. The first example concerns the arm-raising gesture which is normally used to ask another individual for grooming.

> Goliath, an old male, and Flint, an adolescent male, have been engaged in rough-and-tumble play for a long time. At one point Flint screams repeatedly: Goliath has become too rough. Quickly, Flint runs away, and Goliath immediately runs after him, as he had done several times before as part of the rough-and-tumble play. Now, however, Flint screams even louder and runs faster. Goliath immediately sits and makes the "arm-raised" gesture while looking towards Flint. Flint stops at some distance and stands there, looking at Goliath. He approaches Goliath, and when he has nearly reached him the latter runs away from Flint with the "relaxed open mouth" face showing. Flint runs after him and the rough-and-tumble play starts all over again.

No grooming takes place here whatsoever, and this is surely a significant fact. In raising his arms Goliath was not asking to be groomed but was using this gesture to indicate that he was not intending to hurt or chase Flint in any way. The use of arm-raising here beyond its original context would merely be grist to the mill were the actor human and the perspective a pragmatic one (cf. Bates, 1976a; Braunwald, this volume).

The second example concerns the gesture "lies down on back". Usually this gesture is used by infants towards younger infants. In adult life it takes a different form and is referred to as "beckoning": the original "lies down on back" gesture is ritualized (as are many human gestures, for example, pointing; cf. Carter, this volume; Werner and Kaplan, 1964), in the sense that a beckoning individual only leans slightly backwards instead of lying down. (The term "ritualize" as used here is different from the one used in the ethological literature.) This beckoning is used in many contexts, the following being but one example. When an adult male of the Gombe population under consideration demands a sexually receptive female to come close in order to be mated he is not very demonstrative: except for the fact that his hair goes up and he shows an erection, he does little beyond shaking a branch or small bush while sitting. A receptive female may then approach him until she is a few metres away. She then turns her hindquarters towards him while crouching down and looking back at him. The male may then beckon and she may locomote backwards in his direction, with copulation resulting from it. This behaviour is shown in Fig. 6.

Fig. 6. "Beckoning" (=BEC) by the male (on the right). The crouching female is already approaching.

COMBINATIONS

One of the characteristic features of human languages, both verbal and signed, is that of the combination of meaningful units into larger wholes—words are combined into sentences. In language development words are first used singly by the infant and only later do they gradually begin to be used in combination. Deaf children acquiring communicative skills of equal complexity progress through the same stages—apparently both with and without an environmental "input" (Schlesinger and Meadow, 1972; Goldin-Meadow *et al.*, this volume). Lock (this volume, and in press) notes a similar sequence for the child's prelinguistic gestures: once meaning and message coincide, gestures are employed singly, but later they are used in combination. The exact relationship between these gestural developments and the later emergence of syntax is presently a matter for speculation, but the mere possibility of such a relationship is exciting in itself. Given this possibility, and the fact that the combination of different communicative actions, either in sequence or simultaneously, in order to convey a specific message to another individual is one of the fundamental skills of language, then the question as to whether wild chimpanzees show similar abilities in their communicative system becomes of interest.

In the case of humans there are two important interpersonal functions, those of attracting another's attention and of directing that attention, which are fundamental for successful communication. Often the two functions are served by separate true communicative actions: an infant cries (thus attracting another's attention) and then points (thus directing it). The following example of adult chimpanzee behaviour concerns a request for grooming being made in a different fashion to that earlier described.

> Two individuals are sitting together and have been engaged in self-grooming for some time. Presently one of them turns her back towards the other, *scratches at a certain spot and makes a tonal grunt*. At first the other continues his/her self-grooming. The first individual keeps her hand on the same spot, her back still turned towards the other, and waits. Finally the other starts grooming her where she has indicated. She then takes her hand away.

Presumably the tonal grunt serves to attract the other's attention almost immediately—and the hand to direct it. Note also how the context in which the actions are performed add to their effectiveness.

However, humans need not perform two true communicative actions to convey a message successfully: if our attention is caught by something we need only say "Look" to another. The word attracts and in combination with our stance directs the other's attention quite efficiently. It is not always necessary to say "Look" and point, for example. Searching for examples of pointing in chimpanzees is not very fruitful. According to Menzel (1973), "one good reason that chimpanzees very seldom point manually is that they do not have to": being quadrupedal their whole body is "pointing". Thus we are more likely to find examples such as the following, as opposed to occasions in which a true communicative action is used to direct another's attention.

> A mother and adolescent daughter walk side by side through open undergrowth, a few metres apart, looking upwards searching for a tree with ripe fruit. The daughter emits a tonal grunt while looking upward. The mother looks at the daughter: simultaneously both dash off, climb via different routes up into the tree canopy, and reach the same spot where there is ample food.

While this observation may not show directly a true combination of gestures it does give evidence of the basic ability which underlies the efficient use of gestures for the two functions under consideration: that attention can be attracted *and then redirected*.

Two further examples may be given which show equivalent behaviours in different contexts; firstly:

> The Flo family has been resting for some time. Flo, who is either mother or grandmother to all of them, rises and walks two metres in their direction while looking at them. Then she makes a tonal grunt, turns around and leaves the spot. The others follow her.

Secondly:

> A mother who (i) lowers her bottom, (ii) looks back at her infant, (iii) reaches back towards him/her and (iv) makes a tonal grunt. The infant approaches her and climbs on her back.

A further insight into the sophisticated nature of chimpanzee "interpersonal" communication is provided in the following example.

> A mother walks away from her infant after a period of rest. Her infant does not follow her as he should. The mother stops and looks fixedly at the ground, making tonal grunts. Initially her son only looks in her direction but soon he approaches her, as if to take a closer look. Just as he reaches his mother she walks away rapidly, and he follows her. An immediate inspection of the spot where she was looking revealed that there was nothing there!

Shields' (this volume) discusses the topic of "the child as psychologist": maybe a similar approach to chimpanzees is warranted. Such a paper could well begin with an observation by van Lawick-Goodall (1971, pp. 96, 97) of two individuals in the same group:

> One day, sometime after the group had been fed, the youngster Figan spotted a banana that had been overlooked but Goliath (a high-ranking male) was resting

directly underneath it. After no more than a quick glance from the fruit to Goliath, Figan moved away and sat on the other side of the tent so that he could no longer see the fruit. Fifteen minutes later, when Goliath got up and left, Figan without a moment's hesitation went over and collected the banana. Quite obviously he had sized up the whole situation: if he had climbed for the fruit earlier, Goliath almost certainly would have snatched it away. If he had remained close to the banana, he would probably have looked at it from time to time. Chimps are very quick to notice and interpret the eye movements of their fellows, and Goliath would possibly, therefore, have seen the fruit himself. And so Figan had not only refrained from instantly gratifying his desire but had also gone away so that he could not "give the game away" by looking at the banana.

While this suggestion is put forward in a slightly frivolous manner it is not nearly as foolish as it might first sound. The apparent social knowledge and expectancies a chimpanzee has of his companions would appear to be on a par with those attributed by Shields' to young children.

CONCLUSION

Wild chimpanzee babies go through a similar developmental sequence as human babies do in the first year of life, albeit in a different form. By the end of the first year both show the use of performatives.

Furthermore, adult chimpanzees show the ability to combine gestures and to use one gesture in totally different contexts. This indicates the ability to understand and to produce *new* meanings and this suggests openness, which is one of the most characteristic design features of human language.

DISCUSSION

"From a comparative zoological point of view, the great apes are, in their behaviour, strikingly related to man, and very different from the monkeys" (Kortlandt, 1960). This chapter shows that this is evident in, among other things, a similar, formal course of some aspects of non-verbal, behavioural development over the first two years of the life of free-living chimpanzees in the Gombe Stream National Park. This together with the admittedly meagre evidence that these same free-living chimpanzees show some basic traits of language causes me to doubt statements that wild chimpanzees, as opposed to chimpanzees in captivity do not posses the ability "to communicate the unseen things in their minds" or, in other words, the ability to "create the very essence of genuine language, including conceptualization and symbolization, in a non-verbal way" (Kortlandt, 1965, p. 332).

I agree with Kortlandt's (1973, p. 14) conclusion that "the manipulatory potential of the wild chimpanzee hand is far from fully exploited in its expressive behavior", but he himself pointed out that "the same function can be achieved in various ways" (Kortlandt, 1965, p. 324). I hope to have shown that the free-living chimpanzees do have "a lot to say to each other" in terms of looks and glances, gestures and postures, touching, grooming, *and* soft vocalizations (grunts). Anyway, why would the capacity as shown for instance by Washoe, Moja and Pili (Gardner and Gardner, in press) have evolved if it served no function for the feral ancestors of laboratory chimpanzees? (Menzel, 1973)

Although we are far from decoding this gesture language completely, hopefully I have shown how to proceed in order to crack this code. If the discrepancy between the capacity shown by Washoe, Moja and Pili (Gardner and Gardner, in press), for example, and the communication system of wild chimpanzees is not to be found in the chimpanzees themselves, where does it come from? It is much more likely that a discrepancy is to be found in the methodologies used by the different field-workers and in the way different scientific disciplines look upon language and communication.

First let us examine methodologies. Kortlandt (1962) was observing from a hide. Consequently, he was far from being a practitioner of the social practices in which aspects of chimpanzee "language" show up (see Shotter, this volume). Contrastingly, I followed the chimpanzees on foot wherever they went, and did this regularly for 20 months (see Plooij, in press). I witnessed so many instances of social practices together with the contexts in which these were embedded that I started to know the future acts which a certain behaviour (or non-behaviour) implied. This directed my attention to aspects of the chimpanzees' behaviour which I did not notice before. This is in accord with Schneirla's (1972) opinion that a field-worker is not merely a "watcher" but always a "perceiver". The best argument in favour of this methodology, however, is offered by the chimpanzees themselves: when adolescent males start to leave their mother at about the age of 7 years, they do so to join other (adult) males of their own community. However, they do not participate in all the interactions that are going on between the males. It is very common to see a group of adult males sitting together and all grooming while an adolescent male is lying at a distance of some five to ten metres and *observing* the adult males. What is more, I observed one adolescent male who followed an adult male wherever that male went and it was as if the adolescent male could not take his eyes off his "favourite". He observed every little move the adult male made. *And* he imitated that male.

Once I observed the adolescent male come back after his favourite, together with a whole group of adult males, had "displayed" in the crown of a tree (vigorous leaping and jumping from branch to branch), jumped down to the ground and slapstamped down-slope. He repeated the whole sequence three times before running after the males again! It is very likely that the adolescent males learn the rules and the social practices of the adult males during the time that they follow the males in general and one "favourite" in particular. It will take at least one year before an adolescent joins in all the social practices of the adult males. If an adolescent chimpanzee needs over a year, it is not surprising that human observers need at least as much to "grasp" certain social practices.

The second reason for the apparent discrepancy between wild and captive chimpanzees may be found in the way different scientific disciplines look upon language and communication. Primate field-workers use the social-releaser approach, whether explicitly or implicitly. This approach leads to the view that communication involves the simple elicitation of responses from the recipient of a signal (Hinde, 1974, p. 87). However, there is more to communication than social-releasers alone and other aspects of communication processes must be studied (Hinde, 1974, p. 85).

In linguistics and related disciplines, on the other hand, workers focused mainly on the internal logic of the structure of our natural languages. Consequently, no biologically pertinent bases for comparisons between primates were present (Bastian, 1965).

Recently the concept of "speech-act" was developed inside psycho-linguistics, which drastically changed the ideas about the role played by preverbal communication in language development (see Bruner, 1975; Dore, 1975b). In my study of the development of early non-verbal communication in wild chimpanzees I grew more and more aware of the fact that the social-releaser approach was too limited to be of much use. First Catherine Snow (1977) and later Andrew Lock (this volume) introduced me to the studies of preverbal communication which led to the production of this chapter. This may serve as an example how

> knowledge of human behaviour can sometimes give us increased understanding of that of animals. Students of animal behaviour are so aware of the horrors of anthropomorphism that they sometimes shy away from the most interesting aspects of their subject matter: the over-simple view they get could be corrected by a little disciplined indulgence. (Hinde, 1974, p. 6)

That my indulgence *was* disciplined may be witnessed by the fact that I only gained the knowledge of human behaviour after the field period was finished.

"But is it language?" ask the Gardners (in press). As Seuren (1976) has pointed out, "This can be no more than a matter of interpretation . . .

human language is characterized by a highly specific and quite complex set of restriction . . . these linguistic restrictions reflect a species-bound, innate set of strategies and expectations with respect to language, which forms part of the cognitive equipment of every newborn human being" (my italics). He speculates that "in part, they [these restrictions] are a consequence of the structure of underlying thought processes on the one hand, and of physical and physiological properties of vocal production and auditory perception on the other".

I would like to discuss the latter two points further. As for the physical and physiological properties of vocal production, babbling in particular deserves attention. I observed no babbling at all in the wild chimpanzee babies (data forthcoming in dissertation). This contrasts with remarks made by Hayes (1952) about the chimpanzee Viki. It brings back to us an old and important question: why do humans *speak* and why do chimpanzees only make use of soft grunts, looks and gestures. Kortlandt (1965) reformulated the problem of the humanization of the hominids in terms of the appropriateness of the mechanism insuring survival in a given type of habitat. He suggested a vast field of non-speculative scientific research. For instance, one could investigate "whether the young of nidicolous, den-dwelling mammals do or do not vocalize more than the young of related nidifugous and/or lair dwelling species in similar habitats". However, "there are several reasons for doubting that language was launched directly in the audible channel, and for seeking protolinguistic beginnings in the *visible* rather than the audible portion of a putative hominid repertoire" (Shafton, 1976, p. 102). My findings are in accord with this remark.

As for the underlying thought processes, Seuren (1976) suggests that "man's language faculty . . . is the result of certain more general principles of cognitive functionality". One of the general principles that characterize human language is the ability for digital communication (Bateson, 1972, p. 342). Watzlawick (1967, p. 104) pointed out that "rituals may be the intermediary process between analogic and digital communication, simulating the message material but in a repetitive and stylized manner that hangs between analogue and symbol". Now I consider the gestures described in this chapter as rituals developed over the many, regularly recurring, social practices between mother and baby. Therefore, chimpanzee infants are on the verge of digital communication. The question of whether the adult chimpanzees do or do not use digital communication seems worth pursuing. My study focused on chimpanzee babies and infants and my observations of adult chimpanzees were not as intense as they could have been.

According to Shafton (1976, p. 98), "the target of emerging hominid language must consist of culturally acquired, voluntarily emitted (audible oral) signals, with culture-specific, holophrastic social meanings." Apart from being visual, the Gombe chimpanzee signals do fit this definition! Some evidence for them being culture-specific comes from observations by McGrew (personal communication) of a chimpanzee population approximately 100 miles south of the Gombe Stream National Park (at Kasoge point, one of the Japanese chimpanzee-observation sites). The form of their "arm high" gesture differs from the one used by the Gombe chimps, in that two chimpanzees both put their arms high and hold each others' hands. However, the meaning of the signal is the same.

How do these data fit the widely held hypothesis that an arid habitat and armed co-operative hunting were the crucial selective pressures in the evolution of a so-called "environmental language"? Shafton (1976, p. 90) supports an alternative theory that "language in the first instance was a set of acquired social rituals, with the function of sustaining the fundamentally stable, nonviolent mode of hominid social life". He argues that *sociogenic changes* may have played a major role in the evolution of language rather than heavy ecological pressure. This accords with my earlier suggestion (Plooij, in press) that the typical ape mother-infant play which seems to be absent in most monkeys, is related to the group-structure or social environment.

ACKNOWLEDGEMENTS

The data on which this paper is based were collected in the Gombe National Park, Tanzania, at the Gombe Stream Research Centre, whose existence is due to the permission and co-operation of the Tanzanian Government and its officers in Dar es Salaam and Kigoma.

This research would have been impossible without the initial encouragement of Dr H. Albrecht. Dr H. C. J. Oomen, lector in Animal Ecology, University of Nijmegen, and Professor Dr G. P. Baerends, Professor of Zoology, University of Groningen, have given me invaluable help and support throughout the project. I am grateful to Dr Jane van Lawick-Goodall for allowing me in the Gombe Stream Research Centre to carry out my project. I am indebted to Dr A. Kortlandt and Professor R. A. Hinde for their constructive discussions and to Mrs H. H. C. van de Rijt-Plooij and Miss R. Dumont for their help in analysing the original records. Finally, I am grateful to Mr F. Mooren for doing the line-drawings.

This research was financially supported by the Netherlands Foundation for the Advancement of Tropical Research (grant No. W 84 - 66), and the Dr J. L. Dobberke Stichting voor vergelijkende Psychologie.

7

Language in the Orang-utan

KEITH LAIDLER

Survival Anglia Ltd., London, England

INTRODUCTION

Linguistically speaking, apes, and especially the chimpanzee, have come a long way in a short time. Not 15 years ago their progress towards language was at best, abysmal, with the Hayes' chimpanzee Viki mastering only three sounds (apart from natural chimp noises) in six years. Then in rapid succession, Premack showed what appeared to be linguistic skills in his chimpanzee, Sarah, the ape successfully mastering (amongst others) proper nouns, verbs, adjectives, prepositions, particles and conjunctions; Gardner and Gardner demonstrated the efficacy of A.S.L. as an effective medium of communicatory exchange between man and chimpanzee (Gardner and Gardner, 1969, 1971), with aspects of sign language uptake bearing resemblances to infant human verbal language acquisition (Brown, 1970). And Lana, again a chimp, began to "talk" to a computer in Duane Rumbaugh's laboratory (Rumbaugh, 1973, 1974). Whatever the finer points of the argument, these animals seem to be revealing a hitherto undreamt of potential for communication, orders of magnitude greater than that so far analysed as "usual" for primate species below man.

Marler (1965) has stated that a repertoire of approximately 10-15 basic signals occur within the infra-human primates, much the same as in other vertebrate groups, e.g. Prairie dog (10 sounds), chaffinch (15 sounds). Smith (1969) has found that of the displays used in social communication in infra-human vertebrates, all can be subsumed into 12 major message sets. Each set is said to be crucial to the survival of the species, and ambiguities between sets are therefore maladaptive. If Smith's hypothesis is accepted, then at 10-15 signals in primates below man, no other signal-type can be allowed to evolve. The chimpanzees Lana, Sarah and Washoe have clearly transcended such evolutionary limitations.

It is of interest to note that all the above work has been carried out on non-vocal methods of communicatory exchange. This has been done, it seems, to circumvent the limitations which chimpanzees apparently possess in producing voluntary, vocal responses. The work of Hayes and Hayes (1951, 1970), in attempting to teach an infant chimpanzee to talk, has held much sway in this regard. Speech training of their subject Viki began at 5 months. Progress was extremely slow, and it was a further 5 months before Viki achieved what seemed for her an extremely difficult feat, the production of a harsh staccato grunt each time food was offered. Following this, a so-called shaping method was instituted, Viki's mouth being manipulated during vocalization and only successively closer approxima-tions to the model required by her parents were allowed. From this came the word "mamma". At 3 years of age, (i.e. 30 months after speech training began), Viki could produce "papa" and "cup". She subsequently learnt "up" and at the end of the experiment, aged 6, had these four "words" plus a clicking of the mouth and a "tsk" sound in her "vocabulary". To judge from cine recordings, the sounds were not well-formed, and in at least two of them Viki had to place her hand across her mouth to prevent the escape of air. This would seem to indicate an inability to close off the nasal chamber by raising the velum.

Such disappointing results led to the popular belief that apes are incapable of vocal language. This assumption seemed the more probable owing to an extensive collection of data, all of which apparently indicated anthropoid incapacity in this regard.

Neurobasis of Language

Evidence from brain lesions (see Geschwind, 1970 for refs) and from electrical stimulation of the brain (Robinson, 1967; Brickner, 1967) all point to much the same conclusion: that in all but the living Hominidae the loci for vocalizations are to be found in the limbic system of the C.N.S. the same area wherein are found the loci for emotional states. Such a system speaks for the mediation of the diverse types of vocalization with the various emotional states of the animal. There is no evidence that neocortical areas participate in the production or origin of such sounds in the infra-human primate.

By contrast, the neocortex appears to be in almost sole charge of vocalization in man, except for emotional ejaculations which originate, as in other primates, from the limbic system. Man's neocortex is larger than any other primate, and further, this advantage is accompanied by an absolute increase in the number of cortical cells (twice as many as in the Great Apes). The highest increase in both area and neurone counts in the neocortex are in the frontal and temporal lobes, and the inferior parietal regions; these latter two are known to be implicated in language production.

Man's brain also shows unique asymmetry, at least among the mammals. Not only is the asymmetry functional, language and handedness being the usual province of the "dominant" left side, it is also anatomical; as both Geschwind (1970), and Wada and Rasmussen (1960) have shown, the area behind the primary auditory cortex in the upper surface of the temporal lobe is approximately one third larger on the left than right side. The same is apparently true for human neonates (Wada, 1960).

Geschwind (1970) has put forward evidence which to some degree correlates language function with neural topography in Wernicke's and Broca's areas. The same author has also argued that language is based on the angular gyrus of the brain and, more pertinent to this chapter, that a fore-runner of this region exists in the macaque.

Anatomical Correlates of Vocalization

Although the Pongidae and man show gross morphological similarities in the anatomy of the vocal tract, there are several respects in which species differ one from the other.

The chimpanzee possesses double vocal cords (which are homologous with the true and false cords) and can produce double-toned sounds, though only where there is a high build up of air pressure as is seen in emotional states. Vocalization in inspiration (possible but painful in man) is easily voiced in the chimpanzee due to its well-developed aryepiglottic folds (Lenneberg, 1967).

The laryngeal morphology of the Orang-utan is marked by quite heavy calcification of the cartilagenous structures (Nemai and Kelleman, 1929) more so than is found in either *Pan* or *Homo*. The aretynoid cartilages are relatively small. Laryngeal musculature is weak and undeveloped, and the vocal folds, while lined with muscle fibres, show a dissimilar orientation when compared to man. Nemai and Kelleman opine that, because of such calcification and under-developed musculature, the Orang-utan's larynx would be incapable of producing delicately modulated or controlled sounds.

DuBrul (1958) has mentioned three main characteristics of man's speech apparatus not seen in any living primate: the bending of the vocal tract so as to produce three chambers, the descent of the larynx allowing the full resonating potential of the larynx to be utilized (see, however, Stark and Schneider, 1960), and the capacity for voluntary movement of the distal part of the soft palate, the velum. In addition, Lenneberg has remarked upon the streamlining of the hominid vocal tract: the shape of the cavities and fixed resonating chambers are so designed, there is but a single set of functional vocal chords, and they are set across the stream of air so that, when adducted, they produce sound on expiration only.

The buccal cavity and lips of both apes and man also differ. The dental arcade is parabolic in man, whereas it forms a ∩-shape structure in the Pongidae. Lenneberg (1967) claims that this structure is essential for the spirant sounds such as f, v, s, sh and th. The tongue of man is well-represented in the cortical motor areas, reflecting its importance in speech articulation. Histological difficulties preclude a comparison of functional anatomy, but, as Lenneberg has noted (Lenneberg, 1967), its attachment and suspension seems to be different in man as opposed to the Pongidae.

The facial muscles are more distinct among the Hominoidea than among any of the monkeys, with the greatest degree of differentiation being seen in man. The area showing the highest degree of differentiation is the perioral region, the greatest complexity being found in the muscles in the corner of the mouth (the modiolus). Lightholler (1929) has stated that the musculature of man most strongly resembles that of the chimp and gorilla, although both Huber (1931) and Duckworth (1910) have indicated areas where man's facial musculature is either more differentiated or more prominent.

Clearly, above all other primates, man seems uniquely possessed of the anatomical endowments for the production of the complex range of sounds present in speech. Whether such perfect preadaptation automatically precludes other species of primate (or infra-primate mammals) from the learning of simpler "working-languages" remains, in most cases, to be heuristically tested.

Pongid Vocal Competence Reassessed

In one respect, the assumption of vocal language non-competence in the Pongidae has greatly aided research on the language capacity of these creatures in the form of investigations into the variety of symbolic communicatory modes referred to above. However, such neglect of vocal language potential may be an important oversight. Two bodies of fact counsel caution on the topic of ape vocal language:

1. *Overgeneralization.* Viki's vocal performance was not designed to increase confidence in chimpanzee vocal capacity. However, it has been almost universally taken as evidence of *Pongid* non-competence. This is a very different matter. The chimpanzee might conceivably be congeneric

with the gorilla, as has been argued by some authorities, but *Pan* is most certainly not *Pongo*. The large evolutionary distance separating the chimpanzee and the Orang-utan is such that a generalization on this capacity is clearly unwarranted. Indeed, we already have evidence to this effect.

A paper by Furness (1916) on the vocal language potential of the Orang-utan is sometimes cited during discussion of this subject, but rarely amplified. This worker apparently achieved as many trained sounds (papa, cup, th) in 11 months with his unnamed Orang-utan subject as did Viki during 6 years of experimentation. The subject could apparently produce sounds only by physical occlusion of the nose using its finger (compare Viki). Unfortunately, the animal died of unspecified causes 4 to 5 months after learning its first word.

2. *Improvements in Speech Therapy Techniques.* Even if the above over-generalization were accepted, advances in speech therapy for the establishment of speech in humans would still suggest methods by which Anthropoid vocal language performance might be improved. The training procedures of Hayes and Hayes, and of Furness are by no means the apex of language tuition techniques. A much greater degree of success has been achieved recently using methods based on operant conditioning theory. These methods have been used to treat a wide range of severely disturbed children ranging from schizophrenic (Isaacs *et al.*, 1960) to autistic children (Hewett, 1965). With language training it has been found that imitation is probably the best means of achieving language-type responses, and of co-ordinating these with the total behaviour of the child. One very efficacious method for developing this function is to train the child to imitate complex motor movements first, then to imitate sounds, mouth positions, words, phrases and sentences, in that order (Hewett, 1965; Risley, 1966; Bricker and Bricker, 1966; Baer *et al.*, 1967; Guess *et al.*, 1968).

METHODOLOGY

Language Tuition for an Orang-utan

General Considerations

The work of Hewett (1965) was chosen as being the most applicable to the task of producing appropriate vocal responses in the Orang-utan. The research was well planned, successful, and, more importantly, it was carried out on an autistic child, in a setting which would allow replication with materials and resources within the compass of the present study. It was my impression that, superficially at least, the infant Orang-utan of the study resembled in many respects an autistic human child, primarily in its self-directed, rather than other-directed actions.

Experts at Newcastle speech therapy clinic endorsed this general assessment (M. Edwards personal communication). Most interestingly, work cited at these meetings showed that a "shaping method" within the reinforcement theory paradigm (similar to the Hayes' regimen with Viki) produced in human subjects "only a very restricted vocabulary" (Lovaas, 1966) whereas the new methods were much more successful.

From the outset, it was decided that a functional approach to vocal communication would result in the most efficient use of time and energy. Thus:

(a) Correct articulation and pronunciation of English words were not sought; the subject was required to produce only a distinct, well-formed and consistent sound. It seemed redundant during the early stages of tuition to teach, for example, both "ff" and "dd" sounds, and then to combine them to give an approximation of the English word "food", when "ff" in the relatively uncomplicated *umwelt* of an infant would serve equally well as an unambiguous designator of the object-class food.

(b) The sounds taught were arbitrary, and based on their ease of articulation and tuition. This produced a bias towards unvoiced sounds.

(c) The sound produced was to be utilized to designate a specific referent or class of referents.

(d) Sound-object matching was arbitrary, but wherever possible attempted to follow the first phoneme of its English equivalent (e.g. "kuh" for "cup", "fuh" for "food").

Experimental Situation

The talking booth was modified from Hewett (1965). As a two-roomed booth was impractical for the Orang-utan subject (violent screaming attended any enforced contact-breaking as would have occurred in a two-compartment booth) the Orang "talking box" was constructed as a small room (1·8 × 1·2 × 1.2 m) built of natural wood. The teacher, sitting cross-legged, instructed the infant, who sat facing the teacher, on his lap (Fig. 1). Being the sole object in an otherwise dull, homogeneous environment, the teacher became at once the centre of interest, greatly facilitating tuition. In addition, restriction of the infant's movements, mouth manipulation, and time-out procedures were all enhanced by the constraining dimensions of the booth.

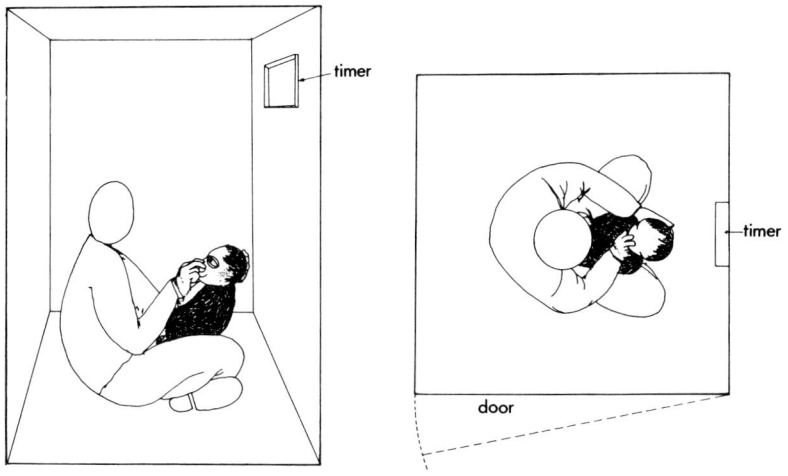

Fig. 1. Training booth situation.

Plan of Study

This took the form of seven stages. In stage 1, which proved unsuccessful, voluntary unformed vocalizations were looked for, using a method similar to Hayes (1951). When such vocalizations proved impossible to elicit, stage 2, an attempt to elicit mouth (buccal) breathing, ensued, with the infant's nose closed by the teacher. This was successful, and the infant began, in addition, to produce an approximation to the "kuh" sound. This sound was rewarded. Stage 3 was a simple physical imitation of the movement "hand on head". Stage 4 the combination of physical imitation "finger over nose", with buccal breathing and "kuh" vocalization (i.e. a combination of stages 2 and 3, with nasal occlusion performed by the infant himself). Stages 5, 6 and 7 were essentially the training of three different mouth positions which, when accompanied by buccal breathing gave the three sounds "puh", "fuh" and "thuh" respectively. Although at the beginning of each stage much aiding and prompting was necessary for successful completion of the action required, by the end of each stage, the infant was able to perform the movement and vocalization without help. In addition, buccal breathing became possible without nasal occlusion for each stage, resulting in the infant producing the four sounds trained using only the usual "speech" movements of lips, tongue, etc.

Table I
Times to mastery of each stage

Phase	Title	Initiation	Mastery
1	Shaping	3 January	Aborted 7 April
2	Buccal breathing	18 January	10 June
3	Physical imitation	28 March	17 June
4	Physical imitation plus "kuh"	5 June	7 July
5	"Puh" vocalization	7 July	30 July
6	"Fuh" vocalization	13 August	21 August
7	"Thuh" vocalization	30 September	2 October

RESULTS

Learning Competency

Figure 2 tabulates graphically the total training time (omitting stage 1) for each stage. Because each stage is concerned with the achievement of a particular ability, it is difficult to compare stages. However, it is possible to assess stages 2 to 4 as showing increasing difficulty for the infant. Stage 2 requires the single action of opening the mouth and (latterly) "kuh"

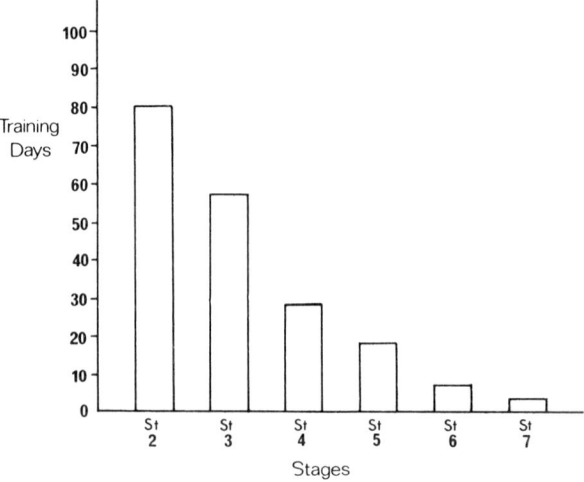

Fig. 2. Total training times for consecutive stages.

vocalization. Stage 3 demands imitatory movements requiring a greater degree of physical dexterity. Stage 4 requires all the attributes of the preceding two periods. The remaining stages may be rated as offering at least as complex a challenge to the infant as stage 4. Hence a comparison of the times of achievement of the different stages is of interest.

A rapid and consistent decrease is at once noticeable in chronologically later stages, indicative of increasing ease of mastery as each succeeding stage is attained.

Usage

Usage can be most usefully analysed by dividing sound emissions into (i) appropriate and (ii) novel emissions.

Appropriate Emissions

An emission was termed appropriate if it occurred during an event for which the teacher had trained the infant. As an ongoing part of the experiment, each time the infant mastered a new sound, it was transferred to a definite object- or activity-class. The infant was then required to match vocalization with the appropriate object/activity. As the sounds were learned in series and not in parallel, it was necessary that one word should initially "stand for" all desired objects and activities and that limitations on the number of referents subsumed under this original "magic word" should occur as more sounds were learned. The sounds, and their presumed meanings at various stages are shown in Table II.

At each point in time situations were engineered that required the production of a specific sound (e.g. feeding periods (eventually) required a "puh" to be lifted up and carried to the feeding place; a "fuh" for solid food; and a "kuh" when milk was offered). Appropriate and inappropriate responses were noted and are shown in Fig. 3. An inappropriate response of 30% (i.e. 70% appropriate response) was taken as the limit of competency.

As is evident from Fig. 3, inappropriate emissions were held below the 30% level on 47 of the 56 training days covered by the graph (taken from the beginning of "puh" tuition, 7 July) a percentage of 83·8. Likewise is 88·7% (47 of 53 training days) for "puh", 91·9% for "fuh" (30 of 33) and 61·5% for the thuh-sound (10 of 14 training days).

Several peaks of inappropriate response remain above the 30% level. Those occurring at the initiation of training any new sound are ignored for the purpose of this analysis as indicative only of non-competency in the

Table II
Presumed meaning of sounds at various stages

Date	Sound	Meaning
Up to 7 July	Kuh	All desired objects/activities
7 July to	Kuh	All desired objects activities without cagoul
13 August	Puh	All desired objects/activities when cagoul worn
15 August	Kuh	Contact-comfort; all desired objects/activities
to		without cagoul
22 August	Puh	Contact-comfort
	Fuh	All desired objects/activities when cagoul worn
22 August	Kuh	All desired objects/activities without cagoul
to	Puh	Contact-comfort
30 September	Fuh	All desired objects/activities when cagoul worn
30 September	Kuh	Milk and other beverages in mug
to	Puh	Contact-comfort
2 October	Fuh	All pan and solid food
	Thuh	All food and milk, when cagoul worn
2 October	Kuh	Milk and other beverages in mug
to	Puh	Contact-comfort
15 October	Fuh	All pan and solid food
	Thuh	Brushing continuation

sound, and of the novelty of the situation. Remaining points above the 30% level are:

   (i) six peaks in "kuh" training (peaks A, B, C, D, E and F);

  (ii) two peaks in puh-sound tuition (G and H);

 (iii) two peaks in "fuh" tuition (I and J);

 (iv) one peak in "thuh" training (K).

In addition the minor peaks (a - e) seen during "puh" training, although below the 30% level, are thought to be significant owing to the usual zero rating of this sound.

The six major and five minor peaks of inappropriate response show a marked temporal correspondence. It was hypothesized that certain events occurred during training which produced serious upsets in appropriate emission. After careful checking of the diary records, no consistent traumatic or anomalous events outside the training situation were found to correspond with peaking. During the training procedure changes in feed, or meal times were not deemed causative agents. Two events did, however, provide a good fit with the peaking data, acting either alone or in concert.

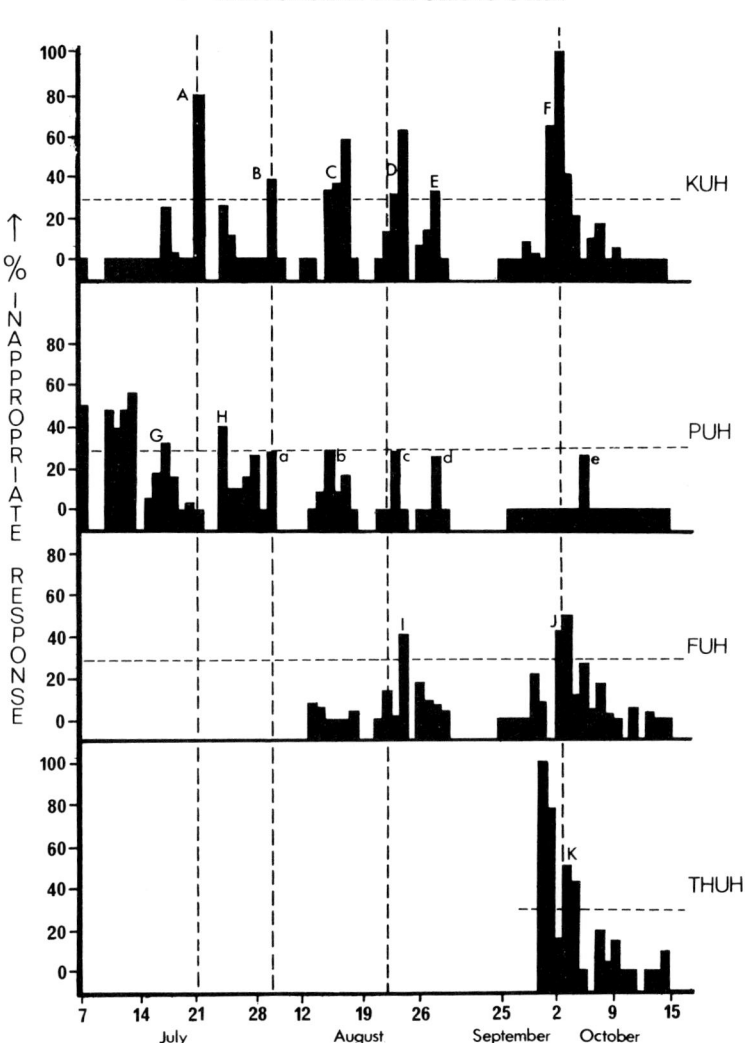

Fig. 3. Appropriate and inappropriate use of sounds during the training period.

(a) *Unaided production of a new sound.* When the dates of unaided production of the sounds "puh" (two given as the sound required relearning —see p. 153), "fuh" and "thuh" are marked, four of the six peaks of the "kuh" graph fall either on (A, B and F) or within one day (D) of their occurrence. Similarly, "fuh" mastery falls within one day of an increase to 28% inappropriate response in "puh" emission (minor peak c) highly suggestive of a causal link. Mastery of "thuh" production also demonstrates a major "fuh" peak (J) and a minor peak of "puh" (e). Thus, five of the eleven major, and two of the five minor peaks are accounted for by the mastery of a new sound. In addition, just as a new sound produces repercussions on the previously established vocabulary", the ability to produce the new sound voluntarily also seems to affect its own production immediately thereafter. Thus, major peaks H, I and K occur within one training day of mastery of the respective sounds, as does the minor peak (a) when relearning the "puh" sound.

(b) *Transfer of a sound to a narrower referent.* Table II details the redefinition of sounds already learned from the simpler sound-for-everything to a situation where reward was made contingent upon the production of a specific sound for a more narrowly defined referent. The four dates corresponding to this training demand are: 15 August ("puh" for contact comfort, partly transferred as "kuh" also serves); 22 August ("puh" for contact comfort); 30 September ("fuh" for solid food, "kuh" for milk); and 2 October ("thuh" for brushing continuation). These dates marry well with peak inappropriate dates. Thus, 15 August with major peak C and minor peak a; 22 August with major peak D, minor peak e; 30 September with major peak F and 2 October with major peaks J and K.

The two remaining major peaks (G and E) and the singleton minor peak (d) are somewhat conjectural. At no time during the date in question or the previous three days was any great emphasis placed upon the sounds which formed the bulk of the inappropriate response. Indeed, on occasion, more weighting was given to the sound against which errors were made.

Errors. The type of error-word given in each peak also shows a pattern indicated in Fig. 4. Only sounds previously learned by the infant figure as errors in the graph, i.e. there is no attempt to systematically produce the emotional "inborn" cries of which the infant was capable.

When only two sounds are known to the infant, the error sound is obvious. However, when the third sound ("fuh") is available, there is then a choice of errors ("kuh" or "fuh", "puh" or "kuh", and "puh"·or "fuh"). Considering the "kuh" trials, it can be seen that following the monopolistic position of "puh" during the early stages, the fuh-sound immediately achieves primacy during peak D (i.e. immediately following "fuh"-mastery) and attains a complete monopoly at peak E. However, upon achieving voluntary "thuh"-production, "fuh" errors fall to the equally low level of the puh-sound (2·55% of the total error on peak F) and "thuh" errors supercede.

Similarly, with "puh", the first error peak following "fuh" mastery shows a 50-50 split between "kuh" and "fuh", after which "fuh" takes over.

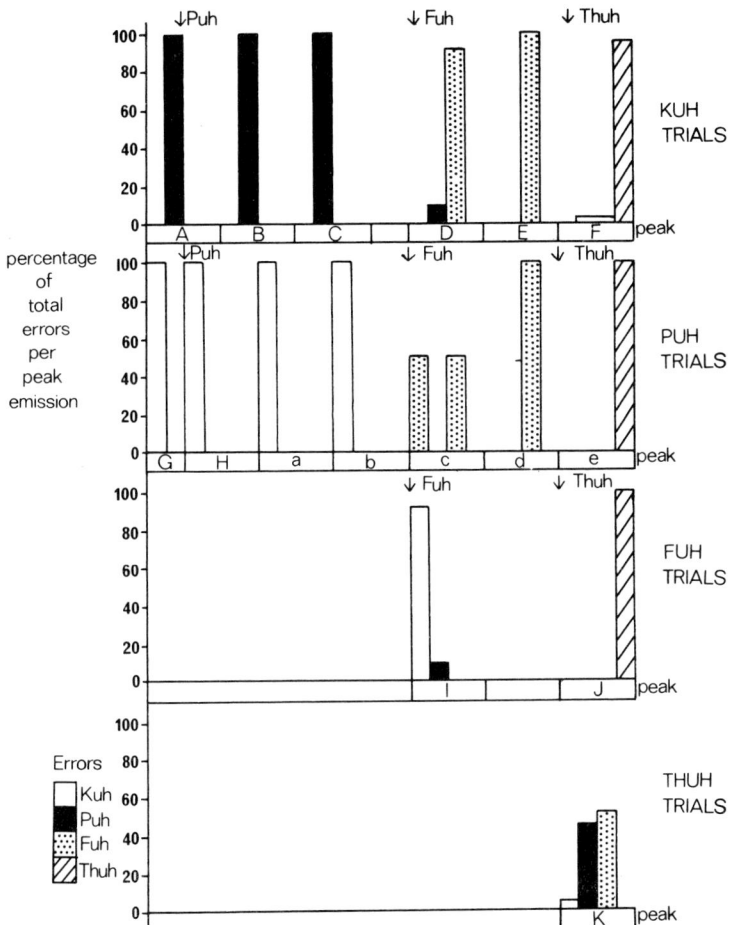

Fig. 4. Distribution of inappropriate use of sounds during the training period.

Following "thuh"-learning, "thuh" replaces "fuh" as the source of error. The same is true for "fuh" trials after "thuh" is mastered; errors on "fuh" trials (previously "puh" and "kuh") are usurped, and "thuh" errors predominate at the 100% level. Thuh-sounds cannot be compared on these grounds as no newer sound was taught.

Novel Usage

Novel emissions are defined as those uttered outside the teacher-engineered situations and normal training demands. Emissions so defined are in excess of 171 sounds for the period 28 June (when novel usage began) to 15 October (experiment's termination). The emissions may be divided into three categories.

Category 1. Phenomenological Requests: Sounds produced when a non-training object in a novel situation was denied the infant, *without* the teacher or second person being involved in the exchange, e.g. looking towards a door he had tried (and failed) to open and voicing two "puh" and one "fuh" apparently in an attempt to open it.

Category 2. Spontaneous Emissions: Sounds voiced by the infant for no apparent reason, e.g. whilst sitting quietly or climbing around the cage.

Category 3. Novel Requests: Sounds produced as in Category 1 but *with* involvement of the teacher or second person, e.g. voicing a "kuh" when a piece of paper he had been chewing was removed by the teacher.

Emissions. Cumulative totals for all categories of novel emissions reveal phenomenological requests to be uttered a far greater number of times (78) than novel emissions (46) with spontaneous sounds (56) occupying a middle position.

Emissions per day. The total time that novel emissions took place can be divided into four periods, each corresponding to the learning of a new sound. These periods are not equal in length, but by dividing the number of emissions by the number of days in that period, the number of emissions per day can be calculated, and the figure for each period is then directly comparable.

When this is done (Fig. 5) average emissions per day are seen to fall steadily with each successive period in all but one category, novel requests. Emissions in this latter case were produced at a relatively high level during period 4, in sharp contrast to the zero rating of period 3. This result affects *total* average emissions per day, resulting in the increase seen in period 4. More definite is the finding that a greater number of novel emissions took place during periods 1 and 2 as opposed to periods 3 and 4. This is true for all categories. When the periods are summed in this fashion (Fig. 6) the discrepancy becomes even more obvious. On no occasion do periods 3 and 4 comprise more than 25% of the total emissions of any one category (novel emissions) and in the case of spontaneous emissions, vocalization occurred solely in the first two periods.

Occasions. Emissions per day and number of emissions are not necessarily the best measures for all aspects of novel vocalization. Simple numerical superiority conveys something of the infant's use of his sounds, but the number of occasions on which vocalizations were made adds another facet. An example may make this clearer, contrasting number of emissions with number of occasions.

6 July: 5 "kuh", each time I stop brushing (5 emissions, 1 occasion).

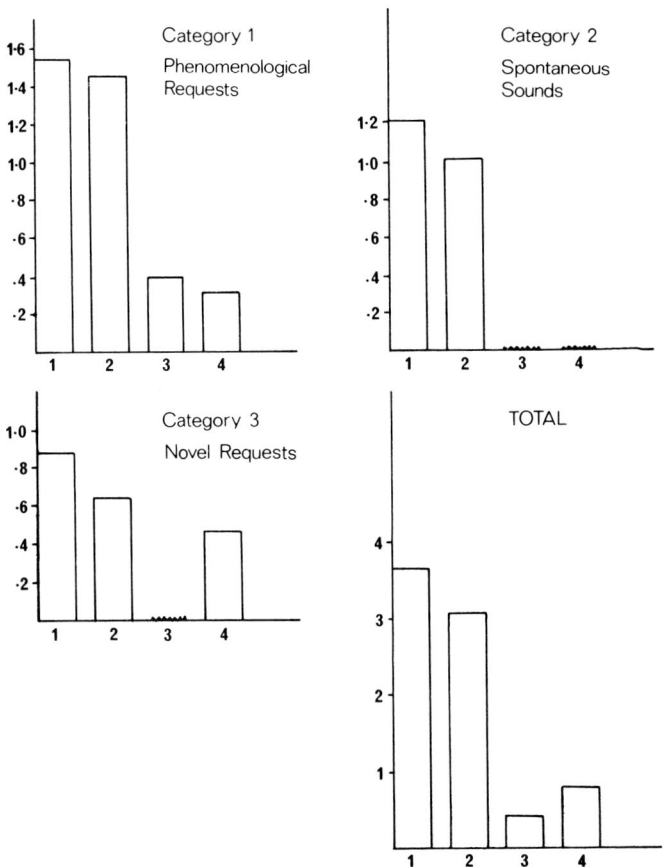

Fig. 5. Cumulative emissions/day for periods 1, 2, 3, 4.

7 July: 1 "kuh" while standing watching people; 1 "kuh" after biting wall; 1 "kuh" during ring and string experiment (3 emissions, 3 occasions). Thus, the number of separate occasions when the infant produces a sound is considered more important in this regard than the actual number of sounds produced.

When analysis is conducted in this fashion, the disparity between the three categories decreases, and their relative positions change, with spontaneous vocalizations numbering 19, and phenomenological and novel requests occurring 15 and 18 times respectively.

When the number of occasions per day during each period are computed (as was done with emissions, p. 146) several points emerge (Fig. 7). It is clear

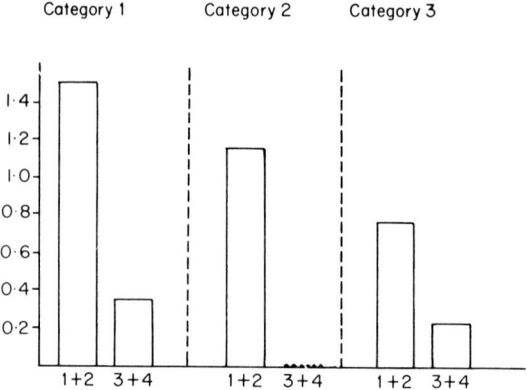

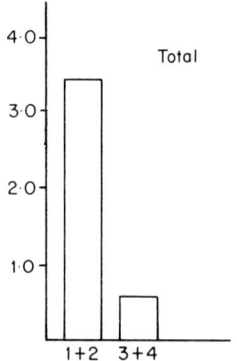

Fig. 6. Cumulative emissions/day for periods 1 + 2 and 3 + 4.

that, as with emissions, certain periods are characterized by far greater numbers of novel emission than are others. The pattern of the total occasions histogram is similar to that of the total emissions, but there appears to be a reversal of relative positions with regard to periods 1 and 2. This pattern corresponds with no single category of emission occasion.

On comparing average occasions for each category during the same period, a marked correspondence between periods 1, 2, 3 and 4 is seen for the phenomenological and novel request categories. The figures for each period are 0·37, 0·27, 0·1 and 0·2 for category 1 (phenomenological requests) and 0·37, 0·21, 0 and 0·23 for novel requests. No such similarity exists for category 2 except perhaps in period 1 (0·33 as opposed to 0·37 for categories 1 and 3).

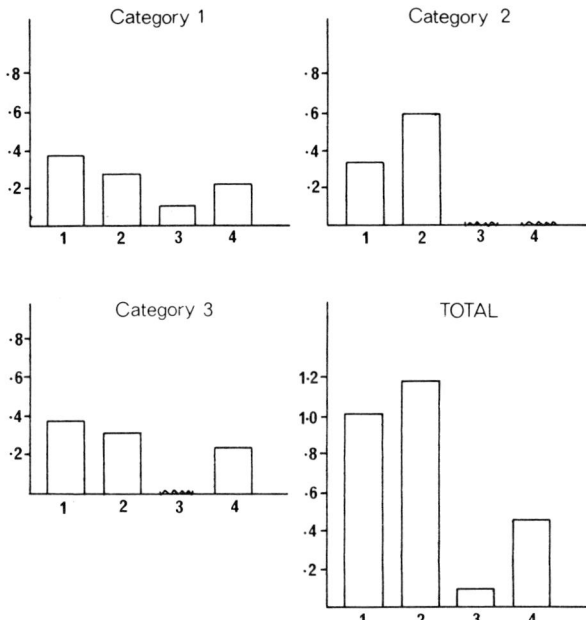

Fig. 7. Cumulative occasions/day for periods 1, 2, 3 and 4.

As with emissions, there is a much larger proportion of occasions when emissions took place during the first two periods of each category. The average for each two-period grouping is shown in Fig. 8. The discrepancy between periods 1 and 2 and 3 and 4 is not so great as in emissions, the latter varying between 0 and 35% of total occasions in any category, and *in total* 21·5%.

DISCUSSION

Learning

Cody's learning of the different training stages at a faster rate with each increasing stage (Fig. 2) is very reminiscent of Learning Set (Harlow, 1949), i.e. as training proceeds the infant learns to learn what is required of him. This hypothesis is strengthened when comparison is made of the phases

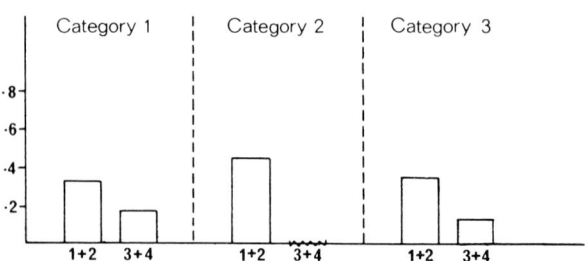

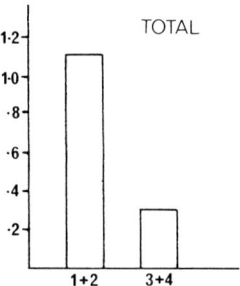

Fig. 8. Cumulative occasions/day for periods 1 + 2 and 3 + 4.

within various stages; here each phase is of shorter duration than the correspondingly earlier phase. This finding also suggests that had further work been possible with the subject the sound-gains may have been commensurately greater for any given time period.

Usage

The data show that the infant produced a sound corresponding to that "indicating" the object/activity he required at greater than a 70% level (more often 80%) throughout the period following initial tuition and training in the sound. It is important to realize that these vocalizations were *not* produced in a standardized training environment (i.e. not in the talking box), once mastery had been achieved. Once tuition was complete, the infant was required to produce his sounds in a variety of situations, and he achieved this at a greater than 70% competency level (except where otherwise indicated, and for the reasons stated). In all, Cody requested food, milk and contact-comfort with the appropriate sound in no less than 14 different rooms in 7 locations: Flamingo Park Zoo (3 rooms); Thames TV London (2 rooms); Granada TV Manchester (2 rooms); Weardale (2 rooms); Northern TV Leeds (2 rooms); Pullman Train (1 room); Sunderland (2 rooms).

Neither was the infant person-bound; appropriate sounds were elicited by at least three different keepers while the teacher was out of sight but within auditory range, and by the teacher's wife, mother and sister in the teacher's absence. Neither was object-limitation seen, in that the subject would produce the fuh-sound equally well for fruit (usually apple or pear), for vegetables, biscuits, meat and toffee; "kuh" for milk or other liquid in a variety of cups (more than three), or for his bottle (maxi or mini) and "puh" for contact-comfort to three keepers and the teacher's mother. It seems, therefore, that the infant possessed a class-concept (Rosenstein, 1961) with regard to the three sounds taught. "Thuh" was not tested for a sufficiently long period to allow such a conclusion.

This ability was not apparently shared by Viki, who was extremely stimulus and situation bound (Lenneberg, 1967). Hayes (1970) also makes telling comments on Viki's capacity. "At the age of 30 months [she] . . . used only 3 words and these not always appropriately. In fact, some days she either refused or was unable to say anything."

By virtue of the chosen experimental set-up, Rumbaugh's subject, Lana (Rumbaugh, 1974) is likewise stimulus and situation bound, as is Sarah (Premack, 1969). It is the Gardner's chimpanzee, Washoe, with whom Cody is most similar in this respect. Washoe is reported (Gardner and Gardner, 1969) as producing her signs spontaneously, signing with a variety of persons (and when alone) and possessing the ability to generalize from specific object-sign combination taught to the object-class from which the teaching object had been taken.

For himself, Cody very rarely used his sounds to request some object presently out of sight, nor did he use one sound so as to put himself in a position to emit a second sound. This is considered due, in part, to the immaturity of the subject who was 15 months at termination of the experiment. Exceptions to this state were few, but did, nevertheless, occur, the protocol given below falling within the last week of the experiment, and suggestive of a developmental, rather than an absolute limitation on ability. Thus, on 15 October the infant twice refused the last of his pan-food, voicing "kuh" each time. When placed on the floor, he immediately made his way to where the milk bottle was located. Later, after termination of the experiment, but before Cody had been left to return to a more natural state with a second infant Orang, the infant came across to the teacher when he offered pan-food, voicing two "puhs". The teacher replied "No, fuh" on two separate occasions (the correct sound for pan-food) but the infant replied each time with a "puh", attempting at the same time to climb up the teacher. When allowed to do so, and settled on the teacher's right hip, he turned and, without being prompted, uttered a good fuh-sound with his eyes directed towards the food.

Comparison with "Language" Acquisition in Primates

When rate of sound acquisition is considered, it is found that Cody mastered sounds at a much faster rate than Viki, the infant chimpanzee for whom we have most data on sound acquisition. Her first sound was learned at 10 months (5 months after initiation of training) in approximately the time taken to teach Cody his first sound (Hayes, 1970). However, the second sound did not appear until 14½ months of age (Cody—12 months), the third sound being achieved at 23 months (Cody—12 months 3 weeks). Cody's rate of acquisition is far more comparable with Furness' Orang-utan subject, who took 11 months to learn four sounds. Such a result may reflect a difference in the relative efficacy of the training methods administered to the subjects, or a natural propensity in the Orang-utan for voluntary vocal production. I am inclined to favour the former hypothesis for several reasons.

Phylogenetically the chimpanzee is closer to man than is the Orang-utan (Young, 1971), and might therefore be thought to possess more points of similarity than does its Asian cousin. This in itself is not, of course, a strong argument. Wolves, for example, because of their similarity in hunting technique, are far closer to man in many aspects of social behaviour than are the Lorisidae, although these latter are phylogenetically much closer. However, the chimpanzee is a social creature (Goodall, 1963, 1965), much more so than the Orang-utan (Harrison, 1961; Mackinnon, 1971; Davenport, 1967), and it is thought likely that a much greater selection pressure towards communicatory competence would be seen in *Pan* than in *Pongo*. (This may indeed be the case, but the work of Gardner and Gardner (1971) and Fouts (1973) has shown that such communicatory skill may well have been channelled into gestural rather than vocal communication.) However, both chimpanzee larynx and facial musculature are more like those of man than are the Orang-utan's, and the buccal manipulations of human language might be supposed easier for the chimpanzee than for its Asian relative (see Introduction). In addition, Kortlandt (1965) has drawn attention to the early babbling of the chimpanzee infant (confirmed by Hayes, 1951), and speculates that it disappears early after its appearance because of the selective disadvantage of such self-advertisement to predators. No such babbling was heard in the Orang-utan subject here discussed. Further, Viki-type instruction, when used on human subjects, is equally inefficient (Lovaas, 1966). The evidence reviewed above does seem, therefore, to support the argument that the chimpanzee may produce as good a vocal showing as the Orang-utan if similar operant techniques are utilized.

As a general rule, the acquisition of sounds in this Orang-utan subject seems to follow the pattern: a time of passivity or non-co-operation; unsureness and partial co-operation in the production of a sound; success at sound production; unsureness as to the correct context for sound production; and success at sound production in the appropriate context. Once achieved, the sounds were emitted (with the exception of periodically "confused periods"— see below) at an acceptable level of correctness until termination of the experiment.

An exception to this pattern was the puh-sound, where, upon mastery, "kuh" was lost; when "kuh" was retrained, "puh" was lost completely and immediately, and had to be partially retrained. It is considered that the most plausible explanation for this anomalous behaviour is that the acquisition of the second sound occasioned the first challenge to the infant's omnipotent "magic spell"—"kuh". Until this time "kuh" had been, as it were, the giver-of-all-good-things. Whatever object or activity the infant required would be supplied on production of this sound, and the infant had become accustomed to this happy state of affairs. The second sound is thought to have initiated a conflict within the subject—"kuh" was no longer the giver-of-all-things and, because of the preponderance of "puh":"kuh" trials at the time of "puh" acquisition, "kuh" was dropped in favour of "puh" as Cody's "Panacea". Training was then initiated to reinstate "kuh", whereupon "puh" dropped out and had to be retrained. In short, it required a period of several days to inculcate in the infant the realization that *both* "kuh" and "puh" were required *on specific occasions*. Subsequently, following mastery of a third sound, Cody was not unversed in the ways of redefinition of sounds for a more specific referent, and the addition of further sounds did not cause total loss of any sound for periods greater than one session. During this latter period, however, the "magic word" phenomenon (using the most recently learned sound) was still evident. It would be of great interest to know if such conflict occurs among human infants, either during the period before the acquisition of approximations to adult words (Halliday, 1973), or at the so-called "holophrastic stage". The same query may be advanced with regard to the conclusions of the following two paragraphs.

The finding that, when one sound was newly learned it took over from the preceding sounds (albeit briefly) as a "magic word" was depicted graphically in Fig. 4. It appears that the learning of a new sound produces, initially its use as a "magic" sound, and, concurrently or very soon thereafter, a reappraisal of all sounds known to the infant, until a new *status quo* is achieved.

Redefinition of sounds already learned to a more specific referent, as occurred on 15 and 22 August, 30 September and 2 October can also be seen as an event likely to require reappraisal of such sounds as are presently possessed. It is just this event that seems to contribute to, or be solely responsible for, peaking of inappropriate response on the four dates mentioned (see Fig. 3) and for confusion in sound-class matching.

When Cody's linguistic development is compared with that of a normal human infant of the same age, a great fall-off in the former's abilities is seen. Halliday (1973), researching language acquisition prior to the mastery of approximations to words in adult usage found that he could divide all such utterances into the categories: Instrumental, Regulatory, Interactional, Personal, Heuristic and Imaginative. Of these, the first four appeared during 9½-10 months of age, and all six of them from this age to 15 months.

Cody, by comparison, seems to have possessed primarily the Instrumental mode, i.e. "give me" (with the sound signifying which object/activity was desired). A speculative regulatory (command) role might possibly be given to the infant's use of the "thuh" sound ("do brushing again") but it is thought more likely that the sound was used simply as a fourth command ("more brush"). Interactional emissions *were* heard, but only rarely. To quote from Diary 13 (October, infant's age 15 months) verbatim:

> Cody bites me hard—I slap, then turn my back on him. He says "thuh", runs round to face me, climbs on my knee and, looking straight up at me (at my face) says "thuh" as if this would appease me and assuage my anger.

During the whole experimental period no sound was heard produced in a personal, heuristic or imaginative context. It seems, therefore, that Cody's "linguistic ability" during the duration of training consisted of two, perhaps three, of the four functions seen in a human child of approximately the same age. It is notable that of the functions observed, only one (Instrumental emissions) had been trained, the other(s) being the infant's own creation. This is not to say that the subject possessed language, which even accepting the loosest functional definition would require the capacity to recognize and use new words, to understand and generate sentences, and by means of language to learn more about language. However, it is unlikely that Halliday's subject, Michael, or Lock's "children" would also fulfil such criteria at a similar age. From this viewpoint, Cody's achievements become far more similar to the human condition. And while such comparability is unlikely to persist, it is also extremely improbable that Cody had yet reached his limiting point as far as language development was concerned.

Glottogenesis

The evolution of language is a long-standing problem, the main points of which have been lucidly reviewed by Hewes (1973). Of all twelve major theories, he chose a gestural origin for language, basing his conclusions, in part, on the findings of Gardner and Gardner (1971) and Premack. Lock (this volume) also seems to incline to this view, combining gesture with vocal signals. The human child does appear to be placing an essentially emotional sound (crying) under voluntary control when he cries and raises his hand to be picked up. The Orang-utan of this study also resorted to this ploy, hand raising while crying appearing at the age of 4 months, and for the same reason. Later, the puh-sound plus arm-raising was used to "ask for" contact-comfort.

The human infant may voluntarily use a sound to communicate to another its needs, but what of those creatures wherein language is thought to have arisen, Dart's "Southern Apes", the australopithecines? Were these hominids, whose brain size approximated that of the present-day Great Apes, able to equal the capacities of Lock's children (this volume)? The nub of the problem seems to be the question "at what level of neuronal complexity can a primate begin to use voluntary vocalizations to signify to another an object or an action?" No matter how skilled in gestures, voluntary vocalization is the *sine qua non* of man's primary communication system, i.e. vocal language. The work described in this chapter would seem to show that, given a neural matrix of equal complexity to the Orang-utan infant (and sufficient training), it is possible for the association of specific sound to specific object to be formed. This may be regarded as a form of proto-naming. It is unlikely that such an ability (given the necessary environmental and selective pressures) would have been beyond the australopithecines, whose brain volume was comparable to that of an adult Orang-utan.

It is, perhaps, an opportune time to say a few words in favour of a multi-theoretical approach to language evolution. Why any one theory must account *in toto* for glottogenesis seems obscure. It appears far more likely that various skills and abilities acted in concert to initiate the communication system which led ultimately to the vocal system we know today as language. To divorce vocal language from gesture in this context seems both artificial and unnecessary; there is a place for each. In the behaviour of Lock's subjects, with their intergradation of gesture, emotional and referential sounds, we may see a pale shadow of the processes which shaped the initial stages of glottogenesis. These abilities seem, moreover, to be within the bounds of the Orang-utan so that, given "some millions of years under suitable environmental conditions" (Hewes, 1973), vocal, as well as gestural competence could have developed, in parallel, within such proto-hominid species as eventually led to *Homo sapiens*.

Section 4

Communicative Actions and the Establishment of Gestures

8
Learning to Take an Object from the Mother

HILARY GRAY

Educational Psychology Service, Derby, England

The baby's learning to take an object from his mother can be viewed from two perspectives: firstly as the mastery of one of the earliest skilled movements that changes his environment, and secondly as the beginning of communication between mother and child about that environment. Since the public world of objects is also the mother's environment, these two perspectives on the developmental process may not be entirely separate.

Consider the referential function of communication to which the child is moving. Following Austin (1962) and Strawson (1950, 1964), there have been several attempts to analyse the logical structure of referring speech acts. At its simplest, such an act is directed to another person either explicitly in words, or by establishing eye contact, or just because the speaker can reasonably expect that his voice will be heard, and the act directs the other's attention to an object. The referring act may also be performed gesturally by pointing. For a successful communication in this case, the referrer's attention to the object is demonstrated by the manual gesture, and either before or while pointing he will also gain the attention of his communication partner to himself, so that the gesture is seen. Each person's attention is therefore given both to the other and to the object of reference. While recognizing that the complete structure of a referring communication is far more complex (Strawson, 1950) it is useful to look at the child developing this minimal skill of integrating attention to an object and attention to a person, and I shall repeatedly refer to these as the two "behavioural requirements" of reference.

Because he can integrate visual and manual behaviour, the normal person can perform both simultaneously in the pointing gesture. When "eye pointing" is used by physically handicapped children, the two behaviours must be performed sequentially. But when this happens, it is assumed that there is also simultaneous integration of looking at communication partner and looking at object of reference, in that the child presumably remembers the communication partner while looking at the object, and vice versa. I hope to suggest how this ability to integrate attention to object and attention to person may develop, firstly by looking at four relevant theories, then by quoting sequences of mother-infant interaction about an object.

THEORY

I. Vygotsky's theory of how the infant comes to be able to perform a referring gesture has been seminal in recent discussions of the development of communication.

> In the beginning the pointing gesture is merely an unsuccessful grasping movement aimed at an object and signifying forthcoming action. The child tries to grasp too distant an object but its hand reaching for the object remains hanging in the air and the fingers make grasping movements. . . . This situation is the point of departure for the entire subsequent development. Here for the first time arises the pointing gesture in itself. Here is only the child's movement objectively pointing at the object and nothing else.

> When the mother comes to the aid of the child and comprehends his movement as a pointing gesture the situation essentially changes. The pointing gesture becomes a gesture for others. The child's unsuccessful grasping movement gives rise to a reaction not from the object but from another person. The original meaning to this unsuccessful grasping movement is thus imparted by others. And only afterwards, on the basis of the fact that the child associates the unsuccessful grasping movement with the entire objective situation, does the child himself begin to treat this movement as a pointing gesture.

> We might formulate the general genetic law of cultural development as follows: *any function in the child's cultural development appears on the stage twice, on two planes, first on the social plane and then on the psychological*, first among people as an *intermental category* and then within the child as an *intramental category*. (Vygotsky, 1970, pp. 43, 44)

Vygotsky gives neither age nor developmental status of the child when the change from intermental to intramental functioning occurs. However, he seems to be saying that the child learns the motor skill without reference to a person, and because the mother assists when the skill is inadequate, the child associates his inadequate act with the "entire objective situation" of the mother and unreachable objects. Referring is therefore effected at the intermental stage only because the mother sees the child attempting but failing to reach, and treats his behaviour "as if" it were a referential gesture. Thinking in terms of the two behavioural requirements of reference, the child's attention is given to the object; the second requirement is fulfilled and the two requirements integrated only because the mother sees and interprets the child's behaviour. Furthermore, the eventual development of the child's ability to intentionally direct another person's attention to an object (the intramental stage) causally depends on the earlier stage, the child by association, presumably according to laws of classical conditioning, learning that when his mother is watching him it is worth making such movements.

Other writers have discussed in this volume and elsewhere (Clark, this volume; Lock, this volume; Newson, 1974; Shotter, 1974) the importance of the mother treating the child's behaviour "as if" it were an intentional communication. The work of Bower, on the other hand, suggests an alternative mechanism to that proposed by Vygotsky for the development of the pointing gesture. Trevarthen's descriptions of neonatal behaviour show how radical is the development of the ability to integrate, as in pointing, the two behavioural requirements of reference, and Bruner offers a theory of the mother's part in the development of the motor skills themselves. Vygotsky, on the other hand, seems to suggest that the ability to reach develops first. He refers to such motor skills as "lower mental functions" and, for the sake of argument, I shall read him as implying that only when the ability to reach is fairly well developed are failed reaches treated "as if" they were gestures. Thus, although I shall not question his two-stage theory, it may be possible to characterize the *intermental* phase of referential communication in more detail than he did. The theories of Bower, Trevarthen and Bruner are considered in order to explore this possibility.

II. Bower's work suggests that there is more to the story than Vygotsky tells. Firstly, he shows (Bower, 1972) that at a few days of age, infant's motor behaviour is, very roughly, appropriate to the distance of the object they are looking at. Why, then, should an infant try to grasp too distant an object, the hand reaching for the object remain hanging in the air and the fingers make grasping movements? Is this observation of Vygotsky's correct? Bower (1973) suggests that such "failed reaches" for more distant objects may be different from reaches for nearby objects in respect of (1) pattern of hand movement, (2) associated emotional behaviour of the child and (3) his social context. He quotes informal observations of 5-month-olds seeing an interesting distant object, but the shape of the hand reaching for the object being more like pointing than like grasping and the child making "pleading" sounds. Other work by Bower (Bower and Paterson, 1972; Bower and Wishart, 1972) shows that infants of this age have the neurological means to remember an object when it has disappeared from view, and it would therefore be reasonable to suggest that they could be aware of a person even though they were not looking at the person but visually attending an object.

Bower (1973) suggests formal investigation of whether such arm movements towards objects out of reach occur only when the child is in the presence of a person, to establish whether they are "indicator gestures intended to affect the behaviour of nearby adults". This infers that such experiments would establish that 5-month-olds make referential communications.

Whatever the results of such experiments, there is here a significant contrast with Vygotsky's view. The latter holds that the child needs the experience of the mother responding helpfully and that referring behaviour occurs because the child has learned to associate his mother with the experience of wanting and failing, then receiving. The extreme statement of Bower's case would seem to imply that the infant is in some unlearned way aware of the presence of the adult, and that, presumably because of neurological programming, this awareness results in gesture-like hand movements, and in vocalizations that sound like the emotion of wanting. The two behavioural requirements of reference are thus performed by the infant, who needs only the *presence* of another person. Although I am perhaps exaggerating Bower's position, this reading seems not an unreasonable statement of his case, in that he nowhere suggests investigation of the role of the adult.

Whatever the outcome of testing, Vygotsky's and Bower's theories are useful, then, in contrasting the traditional associationist and maturational approaches to the nature and development of communication. Like many polar opposites, however, they share at least one feature. Vygotsky fails to suggest that the adult may be involved in the development of the motor behaviour which she, in turn, responds to so that it constitutes an intermental gesture, and Bower fails to acknowledge that the child, being able to fulfil and integrate the two behavioural requirements of reference, to take account of the presence of an adult while attending to and reaching towards an object, may have a developmental history that similarly actively involves the adult.

Lock (this volume), for instance, cites observations which suggest that an account, showing a developmental sequence of different structures of communicating interaction, can be given for the arm-raising (asking to be picked up) gesture. I am suggesting, *contra* Bower, that it is not simply a matter of the child being aware of the adult, and, *contra* Vygotsky, that it is not simply a matter of the mother seeing the child's behaviour towards the object. Rather, the intermental phase of referential communication can be characterized so as to show how the action of the mother and the action of the child, *vis-à-vis* each other and an object of reference, each change, and change in relationship to each other, as the child develops. Where does this developmental story begin?

III. Trevarthen (1974) has described the movements of infants when socially stimulated compared with those when he is looking at an interestingly moving object of graspable size. These movements are most clearly observable at age 2 months but occur neonatally. Facial expressions, hand movements, and the integration of mouth movements with breathing show both similarities and differences in the two modes. Socially stimulated (by his mother) the baby smiles, his hand moves horizontally, in a lateral plane from side to side, as though he were waving, and mouth movements occur with exhalation of breath, as in speech. Richards (1971), referring to his joint work with Trevarthen, has described how the baby's social behaviour is sequentially inter-phased with that of his mother, depending on her sensitive response to his behaviour in order to move on to another phase in the inter-action sequence.

Optically stimulated by an object, on the other hand, the infant shows different facial expression and hand movements, which Trevarthen calls "prereaching". The face looks attentive, the mouth taking on an "A" shape that gives, at least to observers, the impression of concentration. Hand and arm movements are different from waving and in temporal terms highly determinate. The hand moves vertically, opens at the apex of the movement, then descends, closing in a pincer grasp at the base of the movement. These movements occur in discrete stages, at roughly three stages per second, the same as motor reaction time, and it takes about two seconds for a complete swipe. Legs also join with eyes, hand and mouth in these movements. Thus, the infant responds as one integrated system: synergistically. Legs and arms, eyes and mouth, all focus on a spatial position about three inches in front of the baby's upper chest and in the body midline. When objects are presented in this position, which for convenience I shall call the "hot-spot", the prereaching activities described above are clearest and most frequent.

Trevarthen regards it as important that in temporal respects prereaching has similarities to, as well as differences from, prespeech. In particular, from a few hours after birth, as in the adult, eye movements, at ten per second, are completely compensated by head movements, which occur at roughly the reaction time. Together with the spatial and temporal similarities between infant and adult social and reaching behaviour described above, Trevarthen claims to describe a shared spatio-temporal system, the importance of this being, in his view, that it enables the mother to read her infant's behaviour from a very early age indeed.

Trevarthen's highlighting of the synergistic quality of the activity of very young infants, with its correlate of clearly observable differences between behaviour in the social and object modes, excluding as it does simultaneous integration by the infant of attention to object and attention to person, has most significance for this chapter, and in two respects. Firstly it suggests the earliest form of intermental referential communication. The mother observes and interprets the baby's behaviour. Whether or not the parameters of neonatal and adult behaviour are identical at the neurological level, the meaning of the baby's behaviour is clear to the mother because he can respond only in one mode at a time, and because he responds to the context which she shares, in fact which she *is*, in the social mode, and almost certainly *provides* in the object mode. Thinking of the two requirements of reference, the baby only shows (by his hand movements, facial expression and mouth movements) his interest in or boredom about the object: direction of attention to the mother does not occur in the object mode. This requirement, and the integration of both requirements, is performed by her because she provides objects of interest and watches his movements and expressions.

Secondly, Trevarthen's work focuses three changes from this early stage to the intramental phase of referring. (1) The baby somehow learns to integrate attention to object and attention to person so that he can refer another person to an object. When eventually he can point to an object and look to his mother, behaviour is no longer synergistic, but one body part (hand and arm) is enough to make the gesture, while another, the eyes, performs the task of directing the latter to a person. (2) The context dependance of infant communication, well recognized in the literature, is clear. Eventually, in making referring speech acts (though never in gestures) communication will be about objects and events not present to the communication partners, and the success of the referring speech act will depend on the partners sharing a set of semantic and syntactic rules. (3) Finally, the developmental process involves also the integration of emotional behaviour with object directed behaviour. Bower's observations recognize this, and classically, in both psychoanalytic and learning theory, early communication has been thought of as the adult's response to the child's emotion. Vygotsky's description of intermental communication, by contrast, does not include the child crying on failing to reach the object, and, in Trevarthen's account, emotion (in this case pleasure) occurs only in social mode. For him there is no wanting of *objects*, only the continuum from interest to boredom. Perhaps emotionality is one clue to characterizing the development of intermental communication about objects from the very early stage described by Trevarthen. Newson and Newson (1976) write of the enormous pleasure experienced by the *mother* in the baby's emerging ability, which they date at about 6 months, to switch his attention between herself and their mutual environment, the world of objects. This "makes her feel that communication between herself and her infant is at last a real possibility." This hints that there are problems for the mother in helping her baby through the intermental phase of referential communication. We shall now ask how she is involved in the development of the ability to reach for an object, one of the two requirements of referential communication.

IV. Bruner has extrapolated from his problem-solving theory of skill learning, a set of hypotheses regarding the mother's part in the development of those motor actions which she will treat as referring gestures. His view of skill development is consistent with Trevarthen's descriptive work in so far as he regards the components of skilled behaviour (direction of hand to object, shape of hand, etc.) to be within the child's repertoire before he has had the opportunity to practice those components and thus to benefit from feedback (Bruner and Koslowski, 1972). Such practice has a function, however, namely the "modularizing" of components, that is, regularizing the time required for performance, so that there is better concurrent and sequential "orchestration" of components, and thus attention is eventually freed from the particular task for further task analysis. Because of this task analysis, one well practised strategy, is, at its own point of maximum efficiency, replaced by a new one that may ultimately be more efficient.

Bruner (1974) sees four roles for a helper in this process. Because the unskilled operator has to choose from a set of component actions which are not yet "orchestrated", the mother may reduce that choice by either (1) imposing a strategy or (2) performing some of the components herself (scaffolding the task). Bruner regards such help as having a long-term effect on a child's development, because it maintains in him the expectation that he will be effective in his interactions with his environment. The mother further helps by (3) maintaining freedom from distraction for a highly distractible learner and (4), since the substitution of new, more efficient, strategies occurs only under conditions free from emotional stress, the mother maintains these during play.

Already some similarities and differences between this assistance with skill development by the mother and her part in intermental communication can be identified. One difference is in respect of emotionality, a basic factor in communication but, according to Bruner, a hazard in skill development. Some similarities are the scaffolding of the motor task which, as Shotter has pointed out, has the same form as Vygotsky's "intermental" communication, and the context dependence of both early communications and early help with skills. In both cases the mother only knows what her baby is trying to do because she perceives the whole context of his behaviour.

Bruner (1974) cites the "mastery play" of infants during the second half of the first year of life to exemplify the mother's four roles. Mastery play is "playful means-ends matching, such that to any object is applied all activities in the child's repertoire and vice versa".

Consider, however, the mother's task in helping the even younger infant, who, during the first half-year of life, is still learning those actions, including reaching, which he will himself playfully permutate, and to which she will respond "as if" they were gestures. I would maintain that the greater distractability and greater helplessness of the younger infant together imply a more difficult and more involved role for her. For she cannot, by merely looking at his behaviour, understand his intentions and scaffold his actions or maintain freedom from distraction or emotional stress. Rather, she is involved in the creation of an intention, in that, in his helplessness, she provides the material for action and presents it in an interesting manner. Thus she is present—a potential distraction—and she is interested in his behaviour—a potential source of emotionality.

Shotter (1974; this volume) following Spitz (1965) has discussed this period of development as one of "psychological symbiosis" between the mother and her child: the mother *qua* mother, and her child if he is to develop, have certain needs which they satisfy for each other. The following quotations of interactions between two mothers and their infants are presented to suggest how it may be possible to characterize in more detail one part of that symbiosis—intermental referential communication—bearing in mind the following questions. Can an account be given of the mother's part in the young baby's learning to perform the motor acts which, in turn, she will treat "as if" they were gestures? In particular, how does she scaffold the child's actions when she not only completes but also creates his intentions, and how can she carry out these tasks if her presence is actually detrimental to her goal and without totally disrupting the task by introducing an emotional element? Can a developmental account be given of changing forms of inter-action with respect to objects, beginning with the mother watching and responding to the "synergistic" baby, up to her response to the baby who can himself integrate the object and social behavioural requirements of reference? If such an account can be given, does it confirm either a maturational or an associationist view of the development of communication?

OBSERVATIONS OF GIVING AND TAKING

The following descriptions are taken from video-recordings, the illustrations being direct copies from video frames, indicating the changes in the mothers' and babies' behaviour to which I wish to draw attention. A brief account of

how these were made will facilitate understanding of the descriptions themselves, and also of their theoretical significance. Ruth and Kathryn were the
first of several babies who came for study twice a month, beginning when
they were 2 months old, until they were 5 months old. At the latter time all
the babies could reach for an object reasonably proficiently. For pre-test
purposes, the babies were first video-recorded alone, facing a rattle—fixed
on a bracket—five inches from the baby's chest. This enclosed a small
speaker wired to a tape recorder so that the rattle could be made to sound.
Subsequently, the mothers were asked to "play with the baby and while you
are playing, give her the rattle a couple of times". For this "social session" a
quite normal rattle was available, and the pre-test rattle referred to above
was moved away, high on the wall above the infant and on the side opposite
the mother. I mention this "pre-test rattle" only because it played an
interesting part in one of Ruth's sessions with her mother (see below).

Under these conditions mother-baby pairs developed stable, individually
different forms of giving and taking the rattle, which, when viewed in terms
of Bruner's theory, were predictive of the infants' rates of learning to reach
for objects, and which also reflect the different ways in which the mothers
solved the problem of integrating communication with their babies with the
babies' attention to objects.

Kathryn: 3 Months Old

At 3 months, Kathryn's mother first played socially with the baby, tickling
her, talking to her, responding to her vocalizations and changes of facial
expression, until the baby had reached a state of vigorous motor activity,
happy smiling to the mother and long intonated vocalizations. I shall subsequently refer to such play as "dyadic interaction". It is closely related to
Trevarthen's "prespeech". At this point the mother introduced the rattle,
markedly reducing her own vocalizations, including her responses to the
baby's own behaviour. Such responses as did occur were always short,
excited, whispered comments on the baby's activity in respect of the rattle,
rather than the longer, fully intonated utterances she used earlier.

If she failed to attract the baby's attention to the rattle, if Kathryn moved
her hands towards the rattle but then fixated her hands, or if she took the
rattle then held it without further attention to it, the mother would put the
rattle aside and return to dyadic interaction with the baby. Periods between
the mother offering the rattle and either the baby taking it or the mother
laying it aside and resuming dyadic interaction are referred to as Giving and
Taking episodes. Here is the fourth such episode during the first recording

session when Kathryn was 3 months old. It was the first time during any of these recordings that Kathryn gave the impression of taking the rattle herself.

During dyadic interaction, Kathryn, all limbs active, looks away from her mother, who then takes the rattle and sounds it just to the left of the hot-spot (see p. 163 for definition). Kathryn immediately fixates the rattle and her hands, fisted, stop moving (Fig. 1).

The mother immediately moves the rattle to the hot-spot, re-orienting it so that the handle is offered to the baby. The baby's hands, both fisted, move towards the hot-spot (Fig. 2). At the midline, the hands are still while the right hand opens. Mother excitedly whispers, "Oo, what is it?"

The right finger tips touch the rattle handle and loosely close, missing the stem. Mother manoeuvres the rattle into the loosely closed fist (Fig. 3).

The hand grasping the rattle moves down to the baby's side and the baby visually follows it (Fig. 4). The mother comments in her normal voice, "You've got it now, haven't you?"

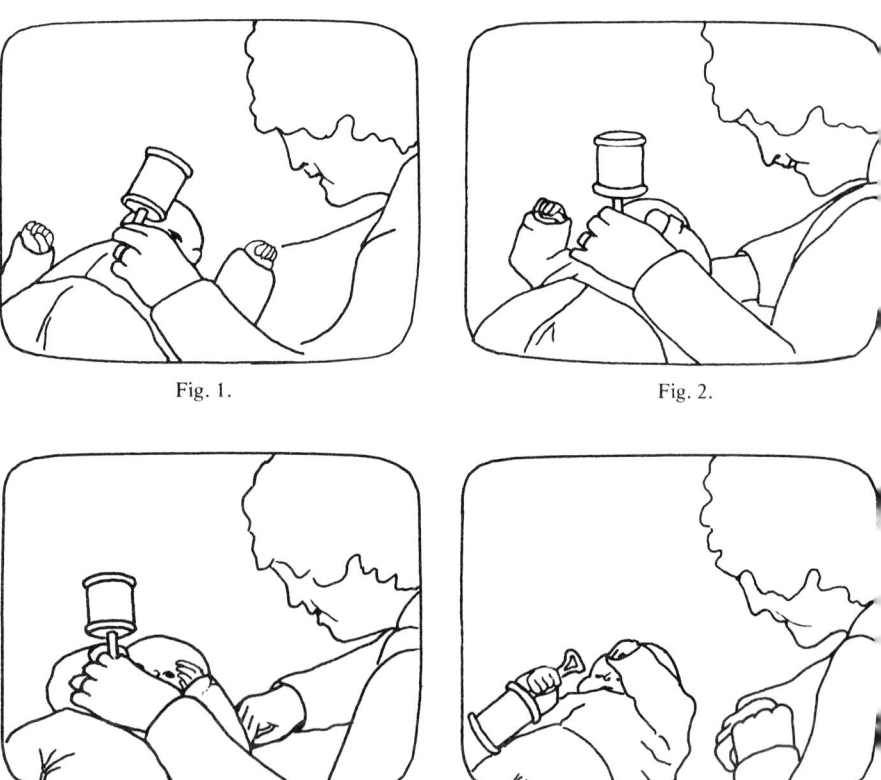

Fig. 1.   Fig. 2.

Fig. 3.   Fig. 4.

Kathryn and her mother's behaviour during the second session at 3 months, a few days later, was very similar.

The pattern shown in clumsy form above was subsequently refined and by 5 months occurred as an exceedingly smooth interchange. It constituted this pair's stable form of giving and taking and its characteristics can be viewed in the light of Bruner's theory. The almost total distinction between dyadic interaction and activity with the rattle means that the mother effectively combines, by sequencing them, arousal of the baby with freedom from the distraction that her own presence could cause. That the rattle is offered at the hot-spot means that the task of directing her hand to it is made as simple as possible for the child, visuo-motor co-ordination presumably being supplemented by each hand kinaesthetically guiding the other. Finally the mother scaffolds the entire task, completing the reach by manoeuvring the handle into the baby's hand. Bruner writes of children's expectations of success: in this case the mother also learns that her baby can be successful at this task, and her pleasure is apparent.

Ruth: 3 Months Old

In contrast, Ruth was much slower in learning to reach for the rattle. At 3 months, her mother moved the rattle almost constantly around the baby's visual field, continually shaking it. This shaking and moving was visually interesting to Ruth, and she made swiping movements at the rattle during the periods when it was relatively still, that is, when it was being shaken but not simultaneously changing in position. The mother responded to these movements by briefly moving the rattle nearer to the swiping hand, but the task of reaching for the rattle was not otherwise scaffolded for the baby. The rattle was rarely still, never at the hot-spot for very long, and in any case never near enough for the baby to easily reach it.

Furthermore, in that she frequently spoke—inviting the baby to hold the rattle, to talk to it or to herself, commenting on her watching the rattle, or describing it—Ruth's mother maintained far less freedom from distraction during presentation of the rattle. Consequently, unlike Kathryn, Ruth's visual fixation frequently shifted away from the rattle to her mother. Indeed, this mother actively attempted to gain the baby's attention away from the rattle to herself, as in the following sequence.

Mother, whose head can just be seen in the top right hand corner of the photo, moves the rattle round to a position high and slightly to the left of the hot-spot and Ruth visually follows. In Fig. 5, her left hand can just be seen, slightly raised to swipe at the rattle. The mother, all the time shaking the rattle, says "There", then "Can you hold it?" then "Mm? can you?", as Ruth visually follows and swipes with her hands (Fig. 5).

Ruth glances away from the rattle to her mother who bends in her face saying, "Are you going to talk to it then?" (Fig. 6) Mother says, "Are you going to talk to me then" nodding her head and her voice warmer and deeper, suggesting intimacy. During the mother's speech Ruth's eyes switch between the rattle and her mother, who repeats, "Are you?".

Mother moves the rattle over her own shoulder (the rattle stem can just be seen in the mother's hand) (Fig. 7). The rattle is thus hidden from Ruth, who begins to cry. Mother immediately shows the rattle to Ruth again saying, "You don't want to (talk to me); there's your rattle again" (Fig. 8). Ruth sees the rattle and immediately stops crying. Mother says, "There" and returns to moving the rattle interestingly around the baby's visual field.

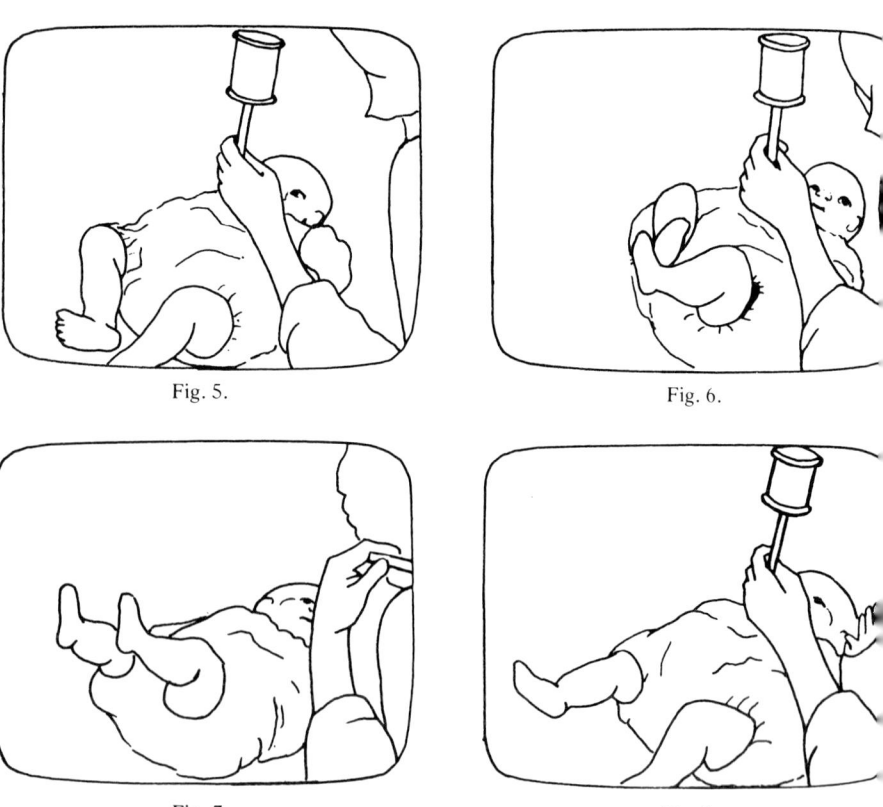

Fig. 5.

Fig. 6.

Fig. 7.

Fig. 8.

The behavioural characteristics of this pair's interaction regarding the rattle that I want to draw attention to are the mother's frequent movement of it, with shaking, around the visual field; the fact that it is rarely at the hot-spot and even when there, is not still; and her frequent speech, inviting and commenting on activity by the baby, and quite realistically *questioning* her ability to hold the rattle—realistically in that it is an ability that Ruth is never given the chance to show. Ruth shows frequent switching of visual attention between her mother and the rattle, and although there is no clear contingency between the mother's speech and the baby looking to her, there is almost certainly a connection. As far as the skill of reaching is concerned, the task is more difficult for Ruth than for Kathryn. When she wants Ruth to hold the rattle, the mother still shakes it, still speaks, and does not use the hot-spot. There is less control over strategies and less freedom from distraction. Similarly, when she wants Ruth to attend to herself, this mother does not, unlike Kathryn's, put the rattle completely out of the baby's visual field.

At all times, Ruth's mother gives the baby choice over whether she will attend to the rattle or to herself. In complement to this, she is highly sensitive to that choice, even when for an inanimate rattle over herself. I shall discuss the form of this sequence again (Ruth at 4 months and Conclusion). Notice, however, how the second time the rattle is shown it is in response to Ruth's own crying. Early in the sequence, Ruth had, by her alert attention to the rattle, let her mother know that watching it satisfied her. Later when she cried her mother treated this as if she was actively rejecting dyadic interaction and "wanted" to see the rattle. The mother is vindicated in this interpretation of Ruth's behaviour when the crying stops. The mother's involvement in the sequence, so that Ruth's behaviour looks like and is treated as a request, is active as well as interpretative: she herself interestingly displays the rattle, tries to initiate dyadic interaction, and, experiencing rejection, re-introduces the rattle.

Ruth: 4 Months Old

When Ruth was 4 months old, she and her mother were also developing their stable pattern of giving and taking, as follows:

> During the pre-test, Ruth on her own had been very happily watching the rattle on the bracket on the wall, smiling and gurgling to it, moving her whole body and limbs.
> Then the pre-test rattle is moved high to Ruth's right (just out of sight at the top left of the drawings) and her mother sits on the other side of her. Ruth immediately

begins to whine, looking first towards her mother, then towards the pre-test rattle, and right hand stretched towards the latter, as in Fig. 9. Mother distracts with a game then she introduces the normal rattle at the left of the baby's midline and shakes it there, saying "Here, have this one" (Fig. 10). The baby immediatedly fixates that rattle, vigorously moving all her limbs. Facial expression and limb movement give an impression of excited interest in the rattle. The mother intersperses her characteristic comments ("That's nice") and invitations ("Can you hold it?") while she displays the rattle by moving and shaking it, and Ruth shows her interest in it.

Then the mother makes a slight but definite movement of the rattle in towards the baby's left hand, and holds the rattle still. The baby stops moving her hand (Fig. 11).

The baby's hand is now open and still and the mother places the rattle stem against her palm. Ruth's hand closes, the mother still supporting the weight of the rattle. The mother says, "That's it, you hold it". Ruth is now having difficulty seeing the rattle. Mother releases the rattle, which, still in the baby's hand, falls under gravity out of Ruth's visual field. Ruth looks first to her mother (Fig. 12).

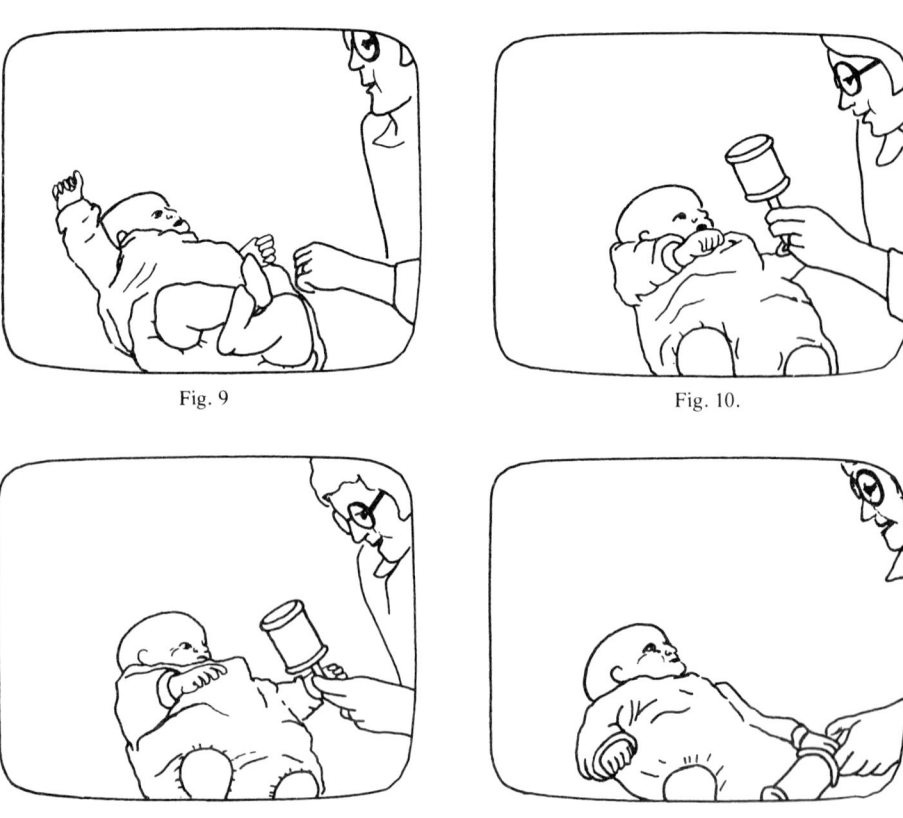

Fig. 9

Fig. 10.

Fig. 11.

Fig. 12.

Then Ruth rolls onto her back and raises her right hand and begins to cry. She turns again to her mother.

Mother smiles, says, "It's all right; you've not lost it", moves the rattle up into Ruth's visual field (Fig. 13). Ruth sees the rattle and her face relaxes in contented interest as her mother says, "Have it again, then".

Fig. 13.

Consider two features of this pair's interaction, firstly the mechanics of getting the rattle from mother to baby. The mother's long display of the rattle by shaking it, to which Ruth responded with excited interest, then her small but definite movement of it towards the child's left hand, to which Ruth responded by stilling her body and apparently giving attention to grasping the rattle, were all repeated in every episode of giving and taking when Ruth was 4 and 5 months old. In fact, in later episodes, the pattern was for her mother to end the period of displaying the rattle with the small but definite movement, but not to put the rattle against the hand. Rather, Ruth would herself respond with an accurate movement of her left hand to the now still rattle, the mother just re-orienting the rattle to accommodate to that hand movement. In terms of skill learning, Ruth, in comparison with Kathryn, was less protected from distraction, and the position of the rattle away from the hot-spot made the task less easy. Probably it was the stilling of the rattle which as much as anything acted as a cue for Ruth to grasp it. It is interesting, however, that in object constancy games at 10 months this mother would similarly give minimal, almost symbolic help when, as she frequently did, Ruth became distressed over the searching task. For instance, when an object was hidden under a cushion, Ruth first looked hard at the cushion, bending her head to look under it, then uttered a demanding cry. Her mother simply patted the cushion and Ruth, her attention having been re-directed, lifted the cushion and retrieved the toy.

The second stable feature of this pair's interaction is that (as at 3 months) the rattle is shown to Ruth in response to her own crying. Furthermore, the form that this takes has developed between the 3- and 4-month recording sessions. At 3 months, Ruth simply cried, eyes screwed up, when her mother attempted to replace her visual entertainment by the rattle with dyadic interaction. At 4 months, her cries are often simultaneously coupled with eye contact with her mother, or with visual fixation of the pre-test rattle, and with arm extension towards the latter. Bower's work (in particular Bower and Paterson, 1972; Bower and Wishart, 1972) suggests that infants of about this age can in some way remember the existence of an object when it is out of sight, and can combine that memory with relevant arm movements. This cognitive memory structure seems to be involved here. In any case, visual fixations and directed arm movements certainly provide the mother with richer grounds for interpreting the baby's unhappiness. However, to understand her baby she must still rely heavily on the physical context (both her own position and that of the pre-test rattle), and on the sequential context. She relies on the latter in two respects. Firstly there are the individual instances of lose sight of rattle—cry towards pre-test rattle and/or mother—see rattle—contentment, but also there was an accumulation of nine such instances over the recording session as a whole. On seven of these occasions, when the pre-test or the ordinary rattle moved out of Ruth's visual field (because I had removed the pre-text rattle, or because the mother tried to initiate dyadic interaction, or because Ruth could not control the orientation of the rattle in her own hand) she cried and only stopped when her mother showed her the rattle; on the other two occasions her mother forestalled the crying by lifting the held rattle back into the child's visual field immediately it had moved out.

As Richards (1974) suggests, the mother uses a complex variety of cues in interpreting her baby's behaviour. The nine instances when Ruth lost sight of the rattle, two of which are described above, presumably accumulated for this mother into a tiny part of that complexity. But the individual sequences of interaction behaviour fall into no tidy pattern. In this respect, there will be a marked contrast with Kathryn at 5 months. On the one hand, Ruth's mother was once successful (mentioned at the beginning of the quotation above) in temporarily distracting Ruth from crying when the pre-test rattle had been moved away from her. On the other, there were two occasions later in the session when Ruth actively rejected such invitations to dyadic play, by crying, looking to her mother or to the pre-test rattle, and sometimes stretching her arm in the direction of the latter. Thus the sequence "lose sight of rattle—cry—see rattle—contentment" was not uniform. Neither did a tidy pattern emerge at the level of Ruth's combining arm movements and visual fixations with crying. Certainly, reminiscent of the Newsons' observations (although a little earlier as regards age), Ruth's visual fixations moved between her mother and the pre-test rattle, but with no clear pattern, and sometimes she just cried "into space". Although the impression that Ruth wanted to see the rattle, and that she was in some way aware of the importance of her mother in attaining that end, could be clearly felt by an observer, there was no neat switching of visual fixation on which such an impression could have been based. Similarly, although there was the moment at which, like an adult making a referential pointing gesture, Ruth cried with her face and eyes turned to her mother on her left, while her right hand was extended to the pre-test rattle on the opposite side, there was no clear pattern in her combinations of arm movements, visual fixations and crying. For the referential communication whereby the mother understood that the baby wanted to see the rattle did not depend on such individual moments. Rather there was for the mother an accumulation of times when she had interpreted the baby's behaviour (crying, attention to the non-social rattle, etc.). Furthermore, as at 3 months, this interpretation itself depended on the mother's own actions (show rattle or initiate dyadic game) and on Ruth's response to those actions. This accumulation of interactions between the pair, with the mother playing an active as well as an interpretative role, occurred fairly complexly within this recording session, but must have occurred much more complexly and with greater effect at home.

Kathryn: 5 Months Old

Finally, compare the above referential communication with that which developed between Kathryn and her mother. The following episode occurred during a recording session when Kathryn was 5 months old. Like their earlier sessions, this one took the overall form of clear alternation between dyadic interaction and play with the rattle.

   The first time during this particular recording session that the rattle exchanged hands was an extremely neat instance of the pair's stable form of giving and taking. That is, the mother showed the rattle well out of the baby's reaching range and Kathryn's hands were immediately raised, open and palms towards each other on either side of the hot-spot. The mother slowly moved the rattle up the midline, its longitudinal axis parallel to the midline. Meanwhile the baby's hands moved towards each other. Probably both partners mutually accommodated in respect of speed, for as the rattle arrived at the hot-spot, the baby's hands closed on the rattle head. There followed a period of "mastery play" with the rattle. Repeatedly, Kathryn moved the rattle to her mouth, then, watching it, extended her arm and shook the rattle. Very occasionally Kathryn looked to her mother; when she did, her mother made a simple non-committal response—"Is that nice?" or the like. There was clear repetition of the hold rattle at mouth—extend arm—shake rattle sequence. Each time the arm was extended further, until in the end the rattle was dropped.

The first time the rattle was dropped the mother handed it back, varying slightly the couple's stable form of giving and taking by presenting the rattle with its longitudinal axis across the midline. Such "elaboration" was seen in other pairs, after a smooth method of passing the rattle had been achieved. I attribute it to the mother avoiding the danger of their interaction becoming mechanical (and inhuman). At the same time, she was, of course, extending her child's abilities. Similar elaboration seemed to be at work in the following episode, which shows an interesting consequence of their stable form of giving and taking on their referential communication.

> The baby drops the rattle to her right, by her waist, so that it is hidden from view by her arm. Her mother clearly thinks this the natural moment to re-initiate dyadic interaction, and begins to speak to and tickle Kathryn.
> But Kathryn turns away from her mother, and she visually searches the area where she seems to know that she must find the rattle (Fig. 14). It is, however, hidden from her by her own arm (and it is just off the figure). Her mother recognizes that she wants the rattle saying, "D'you want it back?"
> Kathryn turns back to her mother. Her hands are raised expectantly (Fig. 15).
> Kathryn orients her hands around the hot-spot and looks to them as her mother says, "Kathryn find it" and moves her own hand across to silently re-position the rattle so that Kathryn will more easily see it (Fig. 16).
> Kathryn turns her head to the right, and reaches towards the right, so that her hand still hides the rattle from view (Fig. 17).
> Then Kathryn immediately turns back to her mother and again orients her hands around the hot-spot (Fig. 18).
> Mother reaches across to re-position the rattle again but Kathryn is again fixating her hands, still clearly oriented around the hot-spot (Fig. 19).

Even when Kathryn eventually sees the rattle, she does not immediately reach for it, as her mother, elaborating their stable pattern of giving and taking, seems determined that she should. Rather, the mother's determination is coupled with a succession of different kinds of sensitive help to Kathryn beginning when she silently moved the rattle so that it could be more easily seen. The help culminated in the mother continuously shaking the rattle until eventually Kathryn had made a strenuous reach which was successful in touching it, then immediately re-orienting the rattle so that the handle could be grasped.

All Kathryn's attempts to see the rattle and to reach for it are interspersed with fixations of her mother, and then fixations of her hands oriented around

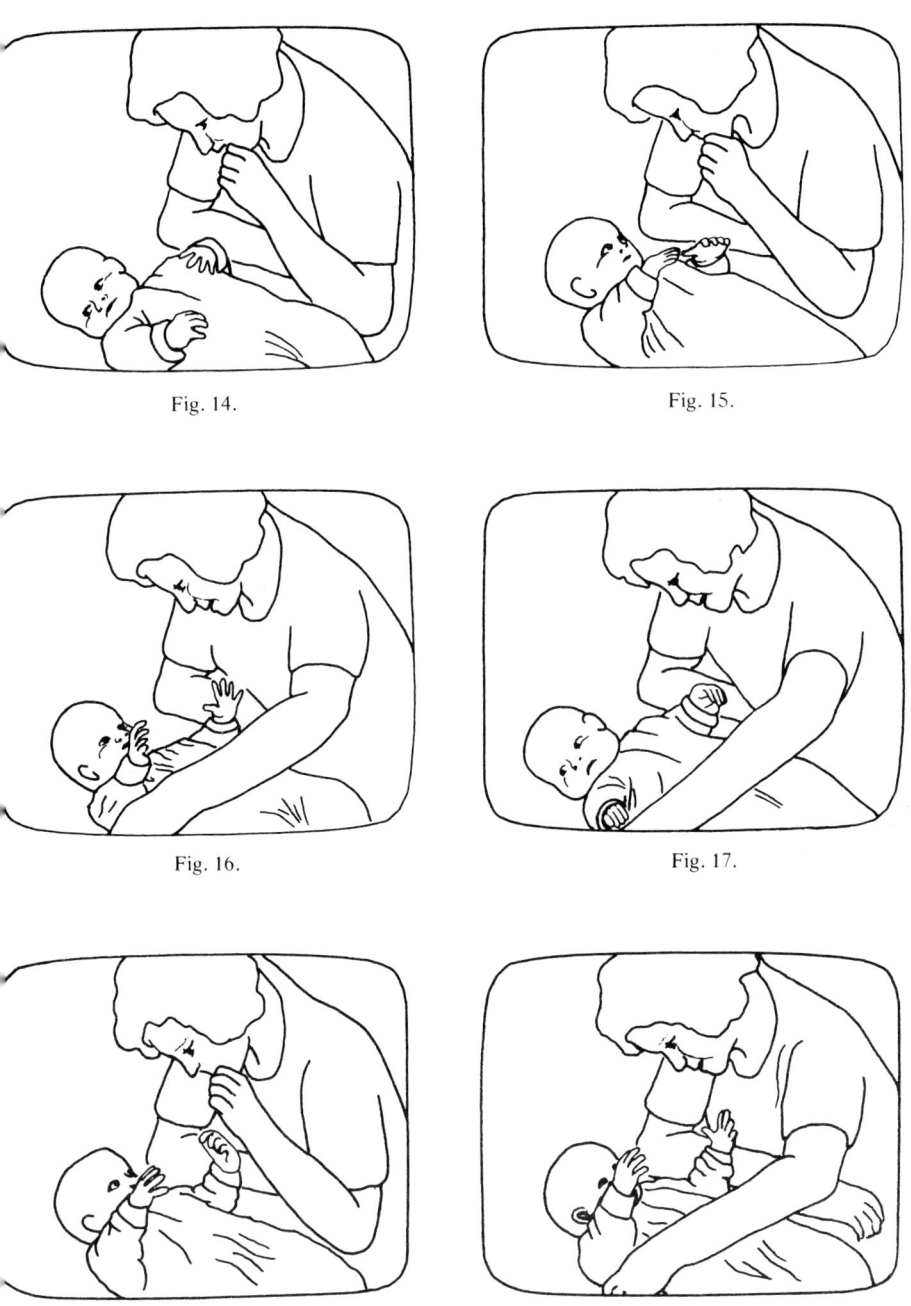

Fig. 14.

Fig. 15.

Fig. 16.

Fig. 17.

Fig. 18.

Fig. 19.

the hot-spot, their usual position in the stable form of giving and taking. Unlike the observation of Ruth at 4 months, there is a sequential pattern to Kathryn's visual fixations and manual behaviour.

Firstly, there were in all six instances of visual fixation of the hands at the hot-spot, and five occurred *after* Kathryn had fixated her mother. It would be tempting to regard such switching between her mother and her hands as Kathryn asking her mother to give her the rattle in the position they had customarily used. But the sequential analysis reveals that things are more complicated. It should be noted that the mother always spoke almost immediately *after* Kathryn has looked at her. That is, Kathryn looked at her mother *spontaneously*, and always when either a search or a reach had failed. The simplest sequential analysis that can be made of all these giving and taking episodes is as six recurrences of: baby tries to see or reach rattle—baby looks at mother—mother speaks but baby is already looking to her hands oriented at hot-spot—mother helps, first by silently moving, later in the episode by shaking, and later still by shaking and holding the rattle up at the right hand side.

My main concern at this point is with the significance of this hand orientation and its visual fixation, which clearly had its origin in the stable form of giving and taking. Again, Bower's work suggests (see pp. 161 and 174) that by 5 months the baby's memory for the rattle can be mature enough to withstand interruption by the mother. But why did the baby, on failure, look spontaneously to her mother, and why did she then look spontaneously back to the position where her mother had always given her the rattle? Are these two micro-sequences really a single action in which Kathryn was deliberately switching visual attention in order to ask her mother to give her the rattle? Was she "eye pointing"? (see p. 160).

Neither the behavioural evidence nor our understanding of communication can allow that conclusion. The behavioural evidence simply shows that, on failure, Kathryn's attention returned to her mother, and that for some reason her seeing her mother re-activated her interest in the rattle, not surprisingly leading her to expect to see it where her mother had usually given it. The other part of the behavioural evidence is the mother's response to the fixation of hands oriented at the hot-spot. Viewing the video-recording gave no impression that this behaviour had any significance for the mother, except to show her that Kathryn did not want dyadic interaction. I have mentioned that elaboration of the stable pattern of giving and taking was a feature common to several pairs, once that stable pattern was smooth, and that this elaboration was probably in part because the mothers, treating their babies as humans, wanted to avoid mechanical giving and taking. By "refusing" to give the rattle in the easy position at the hot-spot, Kathryn's mother avoided mechanical repetition of their give and take.

Furthermore, our understanding of how we communicate can explain this "refusal" more fully. Two features of communication were absent from Kathryn's neatly patterned behaviour. Firstly, the visual switching between mother and oriented hands was not accompanied by crying, so there was no emotional pressure on the mother to make the child's re-gaining the rattle easy. Secondly, the "hands oriented around hot-spot" is not a *publicly* acknowledged sign. In these respects, Kathryn's behaviour contrasts with Ruth's at 4 months, for Ruth cried, and both her crying and her hand extensions towards the pre-test rattle, have publicly acknowledged meaning.

Bower (1973) writes as though behaviour towards an object that occurs discriminately in the presence of persons sufficiently constitutes communication. Kathryn's visual switching and orienting her hands around the hot-spot almost certainly occurred because she was aware of her mother, and probably this behaviour could have been the beginning of a "private language" between the pair. After all, many mothers do respond to particular actions by their children which have meaning for no outsiders, and Lock (quoted in Shotter, 1974) once did this deliberately in interaction with a baby.

In mentioning the possibility of a private language, however, my reference to Wittgenstein is deliberate. According to him, communication is only possible at all because we can understand behaviour according to publicly agreed rules of meaning: the latter essentially human capacity, is a fundamental condition for all communication, including any restricted language games that may happen to occur (Wittgenstein, 1958, § 199).

Kathryn's hands oriented around the hot-spot, coupled with visual switching, depended on the pair's stable form of giving and taking and could have been developed by the mother into a sign that she could recognize as the child asking to be given the rattle. But, in understanding the behaviour of an immature human being, mothers must usually depend on the public agreement to which they themselves are parties. Kathryn's mother's "refusal" to give Kathryn the rattle in the easy position can be seen as yet another way in which she treats her baby as a human being: a potential party to this public agreement.

SUMMARY CONCLUSIONS

I have suggested that mother-baby pairs develop stable, individually different forms of giving and taking objects. Full evidence for stability would depend on comparing the sequential form of Giving and Taking episodes both within and between different occasions at each age level, and in contrasting forms across pairs. These stable forms are refined and elaborated and evidence for these two processes would depend on comparing within and between ages for each pair.

The above selective evidence can only illustrate these points. I want to summarize in terms of the questions posed at the end of my theoretical discussion. Consider first the mother's part in skill learning, her creating and scaffolding of intentions and her own emotionality and potentially distracting presence. Kathryn's mother, who made a clear distinction between dyadic interaction and offering the rattle, preserved freedom from distraction and emotional pressure; she also made the problem as easy as possible for the child, and scaffolded the child's movements in respect of the reaching task which she herself intended the child to perform. She was skilful in creating and scaffolding that intention in Kathryn, and in preserving freedom from distraction; her own pleasure was clear. In contrast, Ruth's mother gave the child greater choice between herself and the rattle, so that there was less freedom from distraction. The rattle was presented in a manner (with much movement) and at a place (at the side) that made it harder to reach. This mother seemed to need to feel confident of the child's interest in the rattle before suddenly making it available for her to take.

Regarding reaching as a motor skill, these individual differences are consistent with Bruner's theory, in that Kathryn learned to reach more quickly than Ruth. These differences in styles of interaction regarding problems with objects were still clear when the babies were 10 months old. Then, if Ruth was perplexed, she behaved in such a way that her mother could treat her behaviour as a demand for help; with similar object constancy problems, Kathryn frequently persevered until she found the solution, but a problem she could not solve alone was abandoned without complaint.

Such individual differences are significant to the problem of referential communication in several respects. Perhaps most importantly, they serve to emphasize that early communication is frequently a very private affair, taking place between the individual person and another, and usually with the same person. That there should be individual differences in such a private mode of exchange is not surprising.

Then, the individually different patterns of communication about objects described above show two stages in the intermental phase of referential communication and its particular problem of integrating attention to person and attention to object. This answers the next question raised at the end of my theoretical section, the possibility of a developmental account of intermental referential communication. First let us characterize the four episodes. At 3 months, Kathryn happily responds to her mother, then the mother introduces the rattle and Kathryn responds to that. While Kathryn is attending to the rattle and reaching towards it, the second requirement of reference is performed only because her mother watches. Consistent with Trevarthen's descriptions, Kathryn's attention is not divided between object and social partner. Ruth happily watches the rattle, objects by totally disintegrating into crying when her mother tries to introduce herself, and again responds contentedly when her mother re-introduces the rattle. Ruth's attention is not simultaneously given to object and mother (she does not, for instance, as at 4 months, move her hand towards the rattle while crying, and her eyes are closed). However, there is more for Ruth's than for Kathryn's mother to "work on" regarding the baby asking for the rattle, both in that its disappearance is actively rejected and its reappearance accepted, and in that the mother can reasonably interpret the whole sequence as suggesting that while crying Ruth was "remembering" the rattle, that the two requirements of successful references were being fulfilled concurrently by the child. But for the mother to be in a position to draw this conclusion, she herself must see the whole sequence, connecting earlier and later contentment and contrasting it with the crying: in fact she takes an active part in it, instigating dyadic interaction, receiving the rejection and then displaying the rattle again. Shotter wrote of the mother and baby completing each other's intentions. Because Ruth seems to reject her mother's intention (dyadic inter-action), her mother has stronger grounds for inferring that Ruth cries with the intention of seeing the rattle, and so she completes that intention for her, reasonably treating the cry "as if" it were a request to see the rattle. Kathryn's mother, on the other hand, has no grounds at 3 months, for inferring that the baby remembers the rattle. In this case the *mother's* intention that Kathryn should take the rattle is completed, but only because of the mother's skill in establishing an intention in the baby.

There are two aspects to the next stage in the development of referential communication. (1) There is some spontaneous switching of attention between the object and the communication partner, and (2) visual attention to object and person is accompanied by other behaviour, vocal and/or motor. The latter is such that it can be interpreted as relevant to the child getting the object—Ruth's crying and raising of her arm towards the pre-test rattle and Kathryn's orienting of her hands around the hot-spot. It is not surprising that Ruth should reach this stage of intermental referential communication first, for she and her mother have long been involved in situations such that Ruth's behaviour looks like and is treated as referential. I have suggested, too, that it is more likely that the mother will treat the baby's behaviour as a sign, if it is such that it can be publicly recognized as having a meaning. Surely the most basic agreement between human beings is about emotions. Ruth's cry therefore influences her mother's behaviour more effectively than does Kathryn's hand orientation.

Such switching of visual attention, accompanied by object-relevant behaviour, still counts as intermental communication in that neither child has learned that she must establish *that* her mother sees her gesturing behaviour: the contrast is with Lock's subject, Paul, who at 10 months first scratched his mother's leg for her attention and only when she looked at him made his arm-raising gesture. Ruth's crying with visual fixation of her mother seems to be rejecting the invitation to dyadic interaction, rather than saying "look at me". Similarly with Kathryn at 5 months: although there is an ordered sequence of searching for the rattle, looking to the mother, then to her hands where she expects to receive the rattle, the visual attention to the mother is probably at best a *response* to her own failure, rather than an active capturing of her mother's own attention.

It seems possible, then, to characterize the intermental stage of referential communication more fully than Vygotsky did, by describing forms of interaction that developmentally increase in complexity and which are nevertheless dependent on the mother's action and on her attending to and interpreting her child's behaviour.

My final question was whether such characterization supports either an associationist or a maturational view of this development. The mother is actively involved in the developmental process, and I would suggest that the effect of this involvement can be seen in the stable individual differences between the babies' referring behaviour, in particular, Ruth's resorting to crying and Kathryn's hand orientation. The passive adult is not, as Bower seemed to suggest, enough. On the other hand, the interaction is cumulative in effect, but whether the process can be regarded as classic "association" is almost certainly purely academic.

It seems likely that referring to objects should be investigated neither as an *a priori* function dependent only on the maturing nervous system, nor one occurring suddenly when the child has just about learned to reach. For each mother, by sensitively teaching her child about objects, by responding to his emotions, as well as in dyadic interaction, treats her own baby as a human being from the beginning.

ACKNOWLEDGEMENT

This research was undertaken at the Child Development Research Unit, University of Nottingham, with a grant from the Medical Research Council.

9
Secondary Intersubjectivity:
Confidence, Confiding and Acts of Meaning in the First Year

COLWYN TREVARTHEN and PENELOPE HUBLEY

University of Edinburgh, England

INTRODUCTION

This paper examines a change in human communication which takes place about 40 weeks after birth, well before speech begins. Detailed film evidence favours the view that developments of brain functions at this time cause the infant to accept persons in a new way. The change is apparently not primarily a reflection of input from the social environment. It is, indeed, an active regulator of all experience, adapted to create a new form of communication that leads not only towards understanding of language but also to developments in the infant's ideas of objects. The infant's new reaction to persons is voluntary, not reflexive. It may be withheld when appropriate stimuli are present, and it tries to gain expression when circumstances are opposed to it.

A 1-year-old infant is extremely alert to stimuli from its own acts, whether arising from the manipulation of objects or from communication with persons. Moreover, mental activities at this age appear to be preadapted to relate these two different forms of experience, and to develop under their joint influence. The behaviour that starts at 9 months is a rudimentary outline of exceedingly complex cognizance-sharing acts of adults that we normally consider to be both consciously intended and bound by rules of cultural origin. For example, it includes prototypes of pointing to an interesting event and addressing a comment on it to another, giving and taking with acknowledgement of the shared intention, and accepting a word as specifying a particular experience.

The mysterious, forward-looking, innate determination of psychic growth is here manifest in a most elaborate form. Indeed, psychological functions that remain central to the highest intellectual and moral achievements of adults in society are expressed in a 1-year-old on the threshold of spoken language. An accurate account of the intelligence of infants at the end of the first year must, therefore, specify elaborate features of their behaviour that are both uniquely human and directly concerned with the un-self-centred sharing of initiative on which human society and its cultural evolution depend. Prelinguistic infants make acts of communication that show well-controlled grammatical forms adapted to speaking and the understanding of speech, but this is only one aspect of these acts. They are also adapted to non-linguistic forms of co-operative behaviour in which images and intentions are oriented to and specified for others by gesture and by the direction, rhythm and mood of purposeful movement.

The most important feature of the new behaviour at 9 months is, then, its systematically combining of interests of the infant in the physical, privately-known reality near him, and his acts of communication addressed to persons. A deliberately sought sharing of experiences about events and things is achieved for the first time. Before this, objects are perceived and used, and persons are communicated with—but these two kinds of intention are expressed separately. Infants under 9 months share themselves with others but not their knowledge or intentions about things.

In other papers, findings have been reported on Primary Intersubjectivity—the earliest form of interaction between the 2- to 3-month-old infant and persons, and its relation in the infant's mental life to interactions with objects (Trevarthen, 1974a, b, 1977a, b, c). Here we shall present observations from a film and TV study with one baby girl, to show developments beyond 6 months. These and comparable findings on other infants will be related to what has been described by others for this period of infancy. The reader should understand that this is a preliminary account. The highly complex process we are concerned with will require more extensive and more exact treatment.

METHODS

We film infants with their mothers in a quiet room equipped with studio lighting, a TV camera and microphone. Black and white 16 mm cine films are made with a telephoto lens from an adjacent darkened room through a window which isolates subjects from the observers. Each infant is supported in a specially designed seat which allows free movement of all limbs while the infant's trunk is firmly supported in a near vertical position. A front view of the infant is combined with a side view of the mother in a large mirror beside the baby. In biographical (i.e. longitudinal) studies, as described in this paper, both mother and infant become highly familiar with the recording room which is comfortably furnished and carpeted for sound recording. The mother is given no instructions apart from a simple request that she play with and talk to her infant.

The largest sample of behaviour is obtained on TV with sound. This record, carrying an electronic digital indication specifying the date and time to 1/100 second, is replayed to obtain a transcript of vocalizations and a running account of the behaviour of both partners. The smaller sample of the behaviour on film is subject to slow motion or frame-by-frame analysis on a specially constructed projection console using a Perceptoscope variable-speed projector with frame counter. Illustrative photographs are obtained by enlargement from the cine film and printed onto direct positive paper. Further details of our method are given in another paper (Trevarthen, 1977a).

The tapes and films of the present study were viewed independently by both authors, and Mrs Hubley was present at all the recording sessions. Doubtful interpretations were subject to repeated examination until we reached agreement.

During her first year Tracey made 32 visits with her mother for video-recording and filming.

The First 6 Months

Tracey, a first infant, was induced with oxytocin at full term on 21 August 1973. Her mother had previous mild hypertension, was conscious during the birth, but afterwards was briefly anaesthetized for removal of the placenta. There were no complications and they were discharged on Tracey's sixth day. The mother, married to a medical statistician, was then 25 years of age and had been studying for two years at teacher training college. Both parents had university qualifications. Tracey's birth was unplanned and caused her mother, who had just qualified as a nursery school teacher, to give up her intention to begin work.

Details of Tracey's behaviour with her mother during her first 6 months are reported in the Appendix. The following is a summary of the main changes in her reactions to objects and to her mother.

At 1 month Tracey made active stereotyped prereaching movements aimed to a coloured ball suspended in front of her. She tracked the ball attentively with her eyes and adjusted the aim of her rudimentary reaching (Trevarthen and Hubley, in preparation). She also responded to her mother's baby talk by fixing her eyes on her mother's face, periodically cooing and making face expressions, including prespeech coupled with gesture-like movements of her hands. Her mother's speech was affectionate and it demonstrated a conceptual personification of Tracey's actions. The interchange was regulated by the reactions of both partners.

In her second and third month Tracey developed normally, showing interest in her surroundings and subtle communicative interactions of primary intersubjectivity (Trevarthen, 1977c). However, while very alert and active she also showed a wariness with people. She frequently avoided her mother, withdrawing her gaze or pulling away from contact. This may have been a consequence of her mother's slight anxiety and lack of confidence during her pregnancy and through the early months after the birth. She said she feared Tracey, who was breast fed, was not getting enough milk. When Tracey was 11 to 15 weeks of age her mother felt too unsettled to attend the recording sessions and asked that we cancel them until she felt better.

In the fourth and fifth month, when her mother was much happier, Tracey was intently interested in objects and she quickly achieved controlled use of her arms and hands to grasp objects. Tracey also played games with her mother's hands and mouth (cf. Fig. 2). Hand and mouth play was picked up and developed by her mother and other partners.

At 21 weeks Tracey played with a familiar puppet which she watched as she made it move by pulling a cord (Fig. 1; cf. Fig. 4). She showed enjoyment at the effect she made, clearly expressing herself to her mother who held the toy. She also picked up objects offered to her, but made no attempt to give them back. Several times she pushed offered objects aside. She frequently held objects to her side, and dropped them (cf. Fig. 6), sometimes turning this into a joke shared with her mother by a look of amusement passed between them. Objects were incorporated in games by the mother who often touched Tracey with them playfully. Communication was most often mediated by way of play of this kind (cf. Fig. 4).

In her first 6 months Tracey not once handed an object to another person deliberately, nor did she do any other act that combined orientation to a person with her own use of an object. In games Tracey shared her enjoyment of the actions given by others to objects, but she did not separately acknowledge persons and she looked at her mother only after withdrawing completely her own interest in an object. Interest in objects and interest in persons seemed to be conflicting. At 5 months Tracey was just beginning to accept a form of game in which an animated object was accepted both as a mediator of what her partner intended and a focus of Tracey's own interest for manipulation, etc. (cf. Fig. 4).

Tracey at 6 Months

We obtained 110 minutes of videotape and 25 minutes of film of Tracey at weeks 25, 26, 27 and 28. Tracey, seated in the infant chair, was either in front of her mother, or at a four foot square table covered with soft felt while her mother sat to one side. A half-circle was cut out of one side of the table to fit Tracey's waist, thus providing a surface for her to play with objects. During these weeks Tracey concentrated intently on the manipulation of objects of various sizes placed near her. As in previous weeks these included her favourite toys brought from home (Fig. 1).

Fig. 1. Tracey's toys. (Tracey used a rabbit instead of the frog shown. All the toys are commercially available.)

When concentrating on objects Tracey was generally unsmiling, her brows relaxed or contracted to give her a puzzled expression, her upper lip slightly protruded and lower jaw relaxed. She also opened her mouth and oriented her lips when grasping or when bringing an object up to her mouth. Two-handed pulling-in of a suspended object to her mouth was less common than at 1 month previously. Tracey preferred to explore the effects of touching and moving objects under close visual attention, repeating regular cycles of the movements of touching, turning, displacing and releasing. When evidently less alert, or when tired, she watched her hands or feet while they moved slightly. This "hand-regard" or "foot-regard" was a separate function from the handling of objects monitored by vision.

With her mother, Tracey behaved as if self-possessed and contented, but, in contrast to her behaviour at 2 to 3 months, she refused direct face-to-face communication with sharing of mood. Often she looked away, avoiding eye contact (see Fig. 6). At the same time the two of them joined repeatedly in the two kinds of highly co-operative game mentioned above. The first of these used Tracey's marked interest in her mother's *person* as a goal for interest and a source of stimulating activity. The second obtained the same result through mediation of an *object* which thus became a toy, or vehicle of play.

Games of the Person (Fig. 2)

These involved a sharing of communicative intent. The mother captured Tracey's attention, not directly by confronting her, looking at her gently and following her smiles and eye-to-eye contact as in primary intersubjective exchanges, but indirectly by exaggeratedly moving her head in-and-out and by making emphatic face or mouth movements and strongly marked sounds of surprise. For example, she held her head back and opened her mouth widely three or four times in succession, making loud sounds of exclamation, or she put her finger in her mouth and pulled it out to make a "pop", or wiggled her nose. Her mother's hands, too, interested Tracey and they were moved in a rhythmically marked way in these interpersonal games. The mother offered an animated echo to Tracey's expression and excitement, simplifying and exaggerating acts that both recognized as forms of communication.

Tracey concentrated on and *imitated*, more or less faithfully, aspects of each kind of her mother's expressive activity. Most often, however, she replied in a reciprocal way with her own acts of animation; raising her eyebrows, smiling, gesturing or posturing and laughing. Usually she looked away for a moment as she did so. The details of these exchanges demonstrate how a partner in a game must adjust her behaviour closely and appropriately to the baby's signs of interest and enjoyment which have a high degree of self-determination. Occasionally, after looking back several times and exciting her mother to more emphatic play, Tracey looked away and stopped smiling. At other times she rejected the initial solicitations and then the mother either waited for Tracey to look at her, or tried to catch her attention with an object and dropped personal play.

At the same time as Tracey imitated face expressions and hand movements, she also frequently reached to touch her mother's mouth or chin. In previous weeks Tracey had become very attentive to her partner's hands as well as to her face. It appeared that some differentiation of perception of the expressive parts of the body led to the formation of the games in which some of the mother's signals were ritualized to obtain a sharing of excitement and pleasure. Tracey's eagerness to reach for close objects combined with her attention to the face led to various hands-to-face games. Tracey was not seen to reach for her mother's eyes as many babies do at this age. She also tended to look solemnly at people with a "searching look" (Kris, cited by Mahler, 1963, p. 313) or to avoid eye contact. Her interest in hands led the mother to hold up an extended index finger for her to grasp and pull at or chew. Movement of the finger or nose or mouth in her grasp could trigger her laughter immediately. Incidentally, this game illustrates how the essence of an infantile "joke" lies in the sharing of pattern and coincidence in intentionality, i.e. the formation of a climax or paradox in mutual intentionality.

Voice games, profiting from Tracey's interest in her own sounds formed an important source for interpersonal play, with the advantage of permitting play with someone not being watched. Usually, however, her sounds and the mother's speech were part of a complex of expression and coupled to head and body movements, gestures and grimaces, all of which reinforced the communication.

Tracey showed normal development of vocalization, making either excited shouts, crying and laughter, or more subtly modulated trains of hooting or cooing which rose and fell in intonation to create "utterances" that were fitted to concurrent gestures and manipulation of objects. The latter kind of declarative vocalization developed, at about 6 months, into rhythmic, syllabic babbling, made while Tracey was more calm, and often accompanied by concentrated play with objects. In our recordings she babbles infrequently, probably because the circumstances of our observation were not suited to private self-entertainment. However, Tracey did vocalize while playing with objects, and her play with the vocalizations that others made while they expressed themselves with visible movements of face and hands, appeared to follow this development.

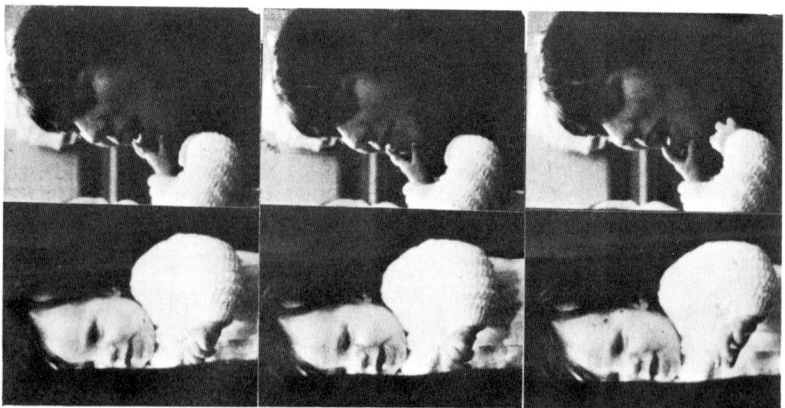

(b)

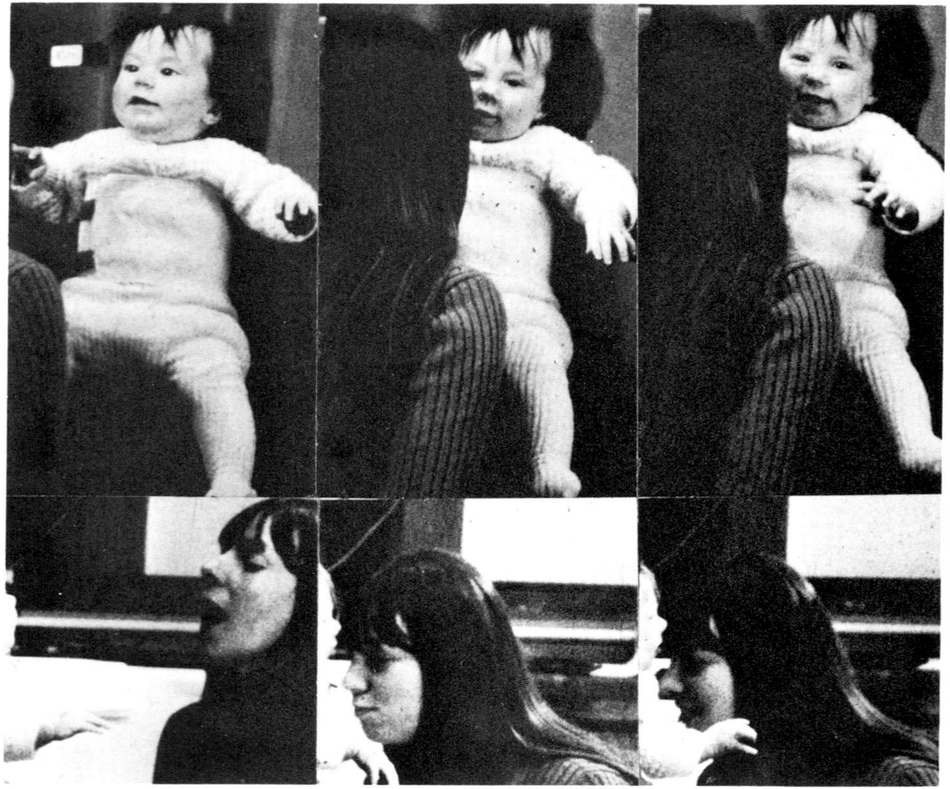

(a)

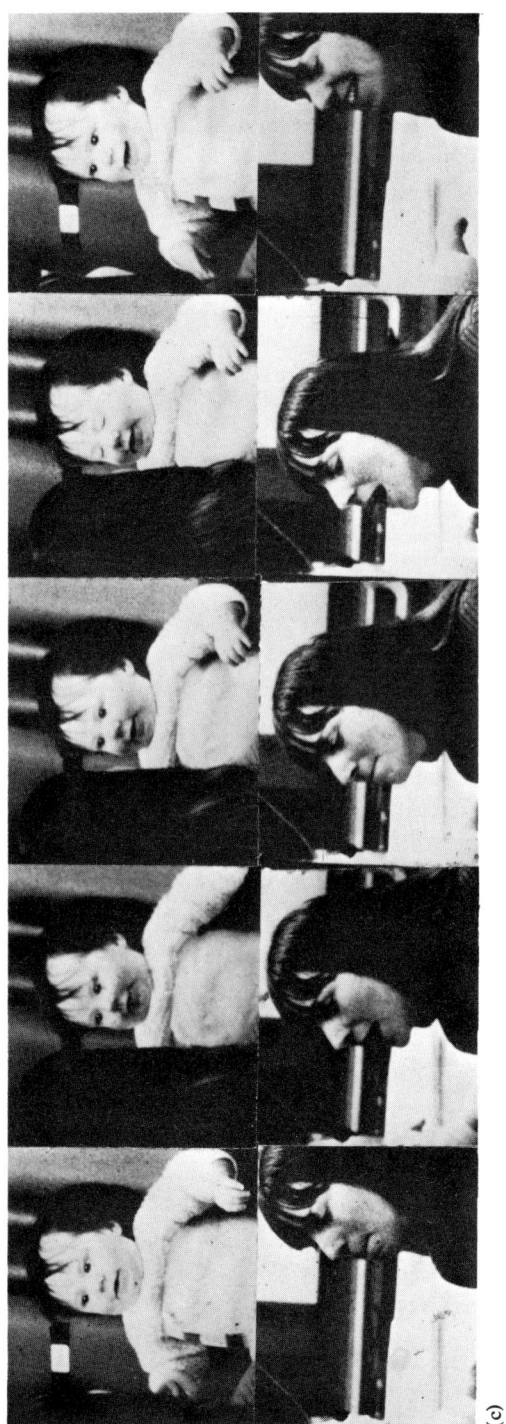

(c)

Fig. 2. Games of the person; 25 weeks.
(a) Tracey touches her mother's moving mouth, looks at it and imitates a protruded jaw.
(b) Mother throws her head back, then rapidly to Tracey's chest, vocalizing. Baby turns away and smiles.
(c) mother repeats plosive sounds, approaching baby's face. Baby replies.

After 16 weeks, when Tracey was making a grunting sound with her efforts at reaching, her mother increasingly used nonsense speech to engage Tracey's interest, and they played games in which the pattern of body movement (e.g. face or hand moved in and out to Tracey's face or stomach) was marked by nonsense sounds and by words sung with exaggerated rhythmic intonation (Fig. 2). The following extracts from the transcript at 25 weeks indicate the variety of her mother's sounds matched to touching of Tracey's body (cf. Sylvester-Bradley and Trevarthen, 1977).

Mother's Acts and Speech: Tracey 25 weeks old

"Ma!" (widens eyes in mock surprise and moves her face towards Tracey)
"Boo!" (leans forward almost touching Tracey's chest with her chin)
"Beri beri, beri. Ba!" (leaning forward, smiling broadly on "Ba")
"Ah—Phht!" ⎱
"Ah—Phoo!" ⎰ (approaches rapidly to touch Tracey's belly)
"Whooo!" ⎰
"Aber, aber, aber, aber." ⎱
"Awer, awer, awer, awer, ptt!" ⎰ (rising pitch, approaching)
"Amer, amer, amer, a mo!" (approaching, head bent low)
"Aah, Tracey!" (taps Tracey and whistles)
"Tch, tch, tch, tch, tch" (looks aside and swings back, sounds in a crescendo)
"Tic, tic, tic, tic, tic" (crescendo, tapping gently along Tracey's neck)

Games with Objects (Fig. 3)

In the month between Tracey's visits at 25 and 28 weeks she joined in games in which objects were animated by her mother (Fig. 3). Their function as foci for Tracey's visual interest was brought under her mother's control, this being subtly adjusted to Tracey's predictions of how the object would displace or make sounds, or how she would touch it. The same formula was observed as with games of the person, the object being endowed with repeated rhythmical cycles of motion, of change in proximity, direction or orientation, and caused to emit patterned successions of rattles, bangs, etc.

For example, the mother held up a toy and instead of handing it to Tracey either moved it in swoops or jumps to Tracey's face or chest and suddenly away, or made it "fly" from side to side above Tracey's head as she turned about to look at it and made gestures to reach for it (Fig. 5). The following vocal accompaniments occurred at 25 weeks:

"Oh! Tickle!" (object suddenly down to Tracey's chest)
"Thup!" (object touched on Tracey's nose)
"Choo!" (catching ball dropped by Tracey)

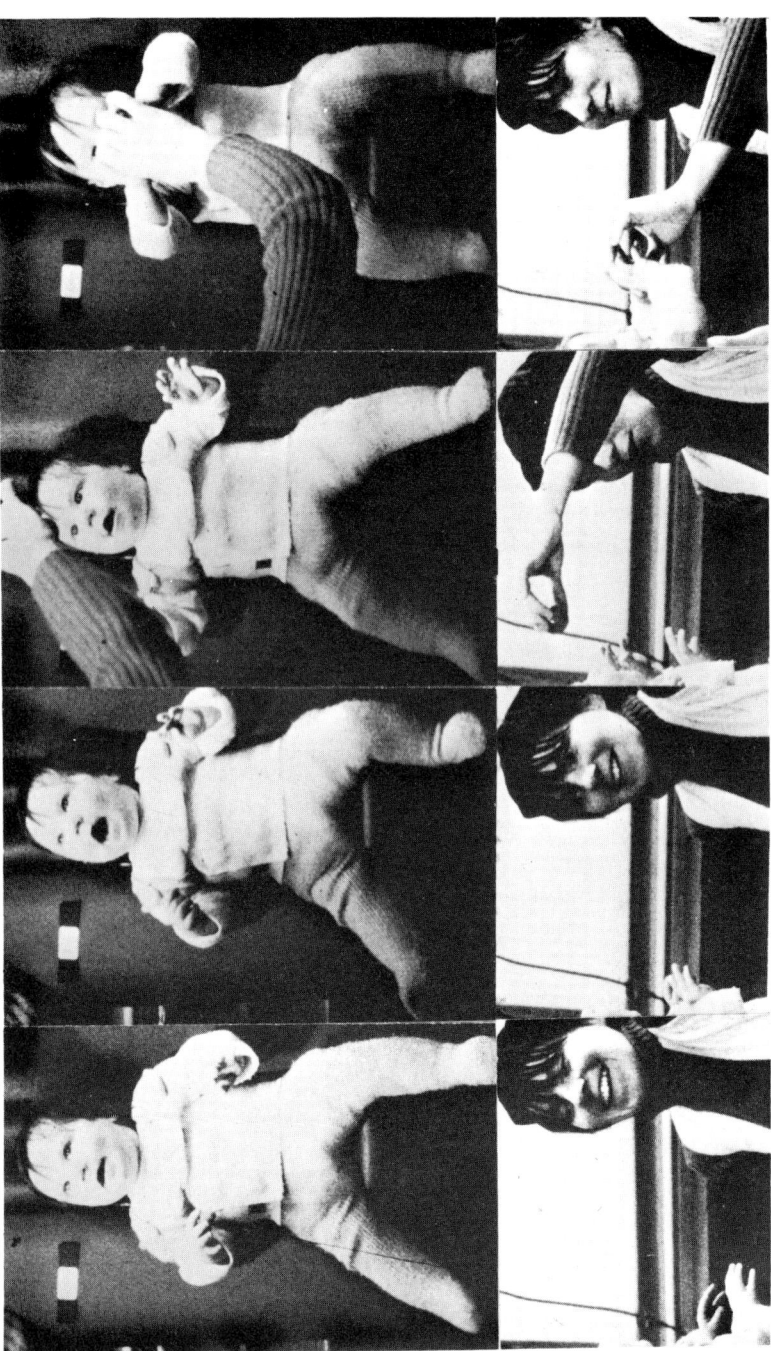

Fig. 3. Object animated by mother; 27 weeks. A wooden ball is carried up in the air then down towards Tracey's reaching hands.

"Up in the sky . . . Da ooh! Tickle!" (ball held and shaken while lifted for Tracey to track, then swooped down)

At 25 weeks Tracey was mostly seriously intent and unamused, but several times she "joined the fun" of play with an object and then smiled, vocalized and finally laughed and moved her body vigorously. Sometimes the "interest" of the game was more concentrated and subtle as the mother made an object produce a series of small movements while Tracey watched intently, unsmiling.

There was a definite gradient of obedience of the mother to Tracey's will. Sometimes the mother merely suspended a thing or placed it on the table passively, for Tracey to manipulate. Then there were excited games with the mother using formulae of progressively organized enjoyment geared to follow the pattern of Tracey's interest. Finally, there were times when they more equally shared intention, Tracey reflecting the action of the mother with changing expression and quite two- to three-syllable babbling sounds, but without smiling or looking at her mother's face. In this sharing kind of play Tracey allowed the mother's inventions to create her experience and did not try to take over herself. This is a foretaste of co-operation to be fully achieved only 4 months later.

All these games were created out of Tracey's interest in the effects of her own and her mother's action on objects. Though motivated by her pleasure in achieving perceptual mastery, they were inside an interpersonal framework. As with games of the person, Tracey co-operated closely with her mother, but she did so without giving more than an occasional glance to her mother's eyes and without looking at her mother's expressions to observe feelings or interest concerning herself. She appeared unable to attend to the other's purpose directly, or else resistant to it.

Both kinds of game appeared to grow out of the touching, sound-making and object-presenting of her mother that we saw when Tracey was 4 or 5 months of age. Even though the mother's adaptations were undoubtedly influenced by knowledge and ideas imported from her cultural experience away from Tracey, the strong regulation of the play by Tracey's acts makes it unlikely that the games were invented by the mother. The games appear to follow development in the object-seeking and person-recognizing functions Tracey has exhibited since her first month, and to depend on the mother being interested and sufficiently aware to adapt to these functions.

What the Mother Says about Tracey

In the sixth and seventh month Tracey was perceived by her mother to be wilful, intensely interested in exploring objects and disinterested in interpersonal communication for its own sake, but able to join happily in games. Detailed evidence about these perceptions came from what the mother said to Tracey while they played together.

She made humorous nonsense sounds, word games sometimes charged with mock anger and surprise as well as fun, and exclamations of delight or laughter. A further striking feature of the mother's language was her use of *questioning*. She repeatedly asked if Tracey did not want to do things, or if she would respond to her. Often she pleaded. She said, "Come on, can I have it back?" after handing Tracey an object. Tracey, in this instance, as in all others at this age, did not give the object back. Her mother took it, or caught it when Tracey dropped it, saying "Thank you". In handing an object to Tracey she said, "Do you want it? Here you are then." The verbal and non-verbal utterances of the mother were distinctly different from her talk to Tracey at 1 or 2 months (see Appendix), reflecting her attempts to respond to Tracey's clear signs of changing interest in and use of surroundings.

Inverting the Game with a Toy (Figs 4 and 5)

At 27, 28 and 32 weeks Tracey's mastery of games with toys shows a complex inversion of roles with her mother. Tracey at this age practised "secondary circular reactions", e.g. shaking and banging objects she was holding. When she shook a cage with a bell in it, her mother, looking at Tracey, synchronized her head with the movement and the sound. This caused Tracey to pause and "think". As soon as she moved again her mother moved her head in synchrony saying, "Bang, bang, bang!" Tracey watched her mother closely and the effect became a game, leading to eager smiling and laughter. Then the mother made Tracey laugh heartily by zooming the toy to Tracey's

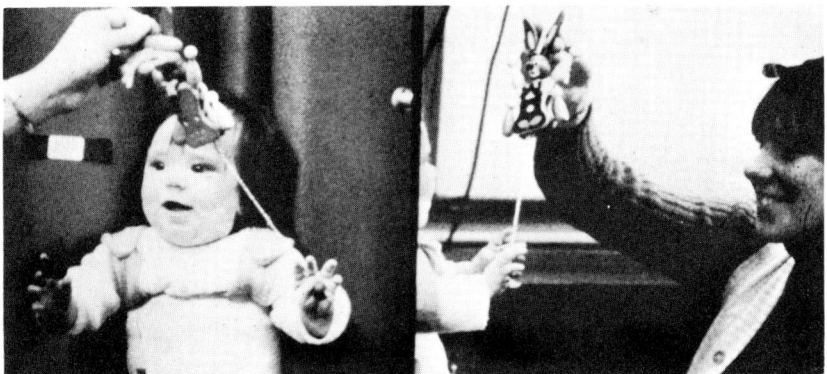

Fig. 4. Object-person games.
(a) Tracey pulls puppet string, watching mother's face and smiling; 27 weeks (Fig. 1B).

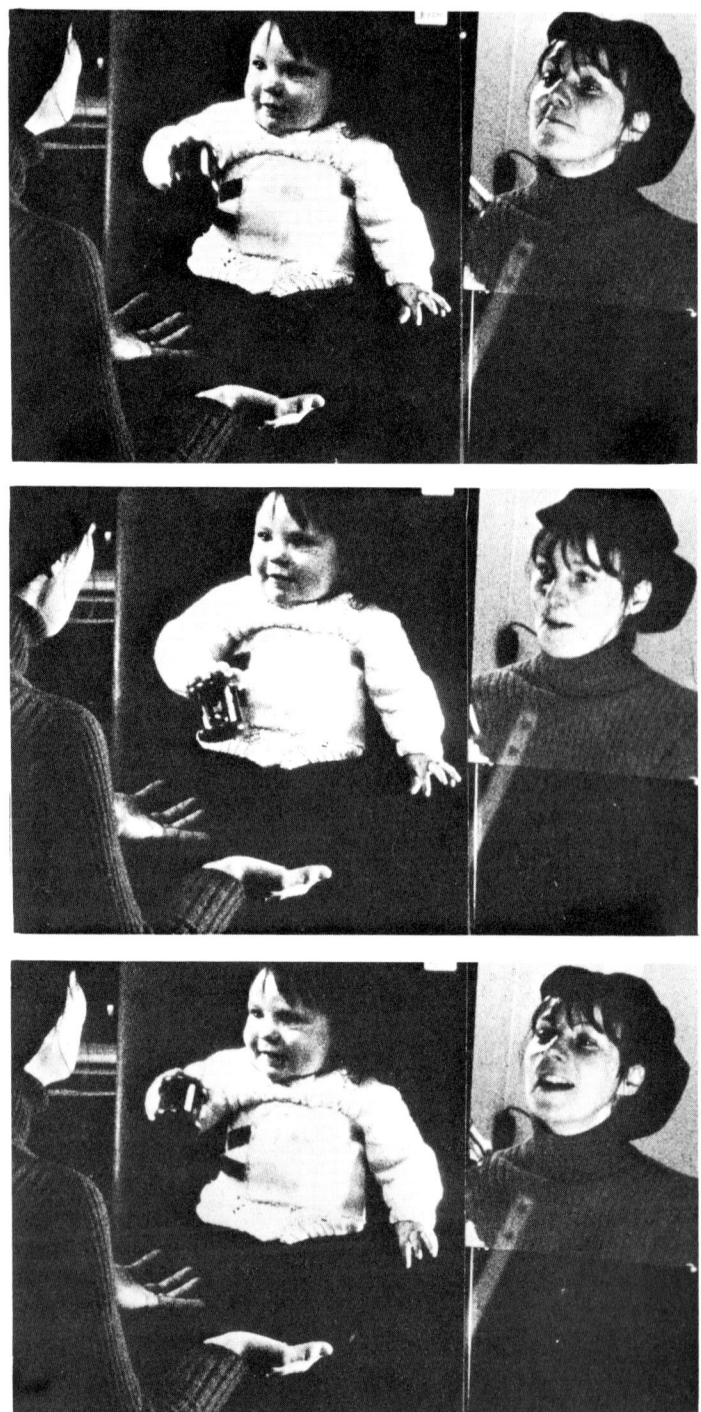

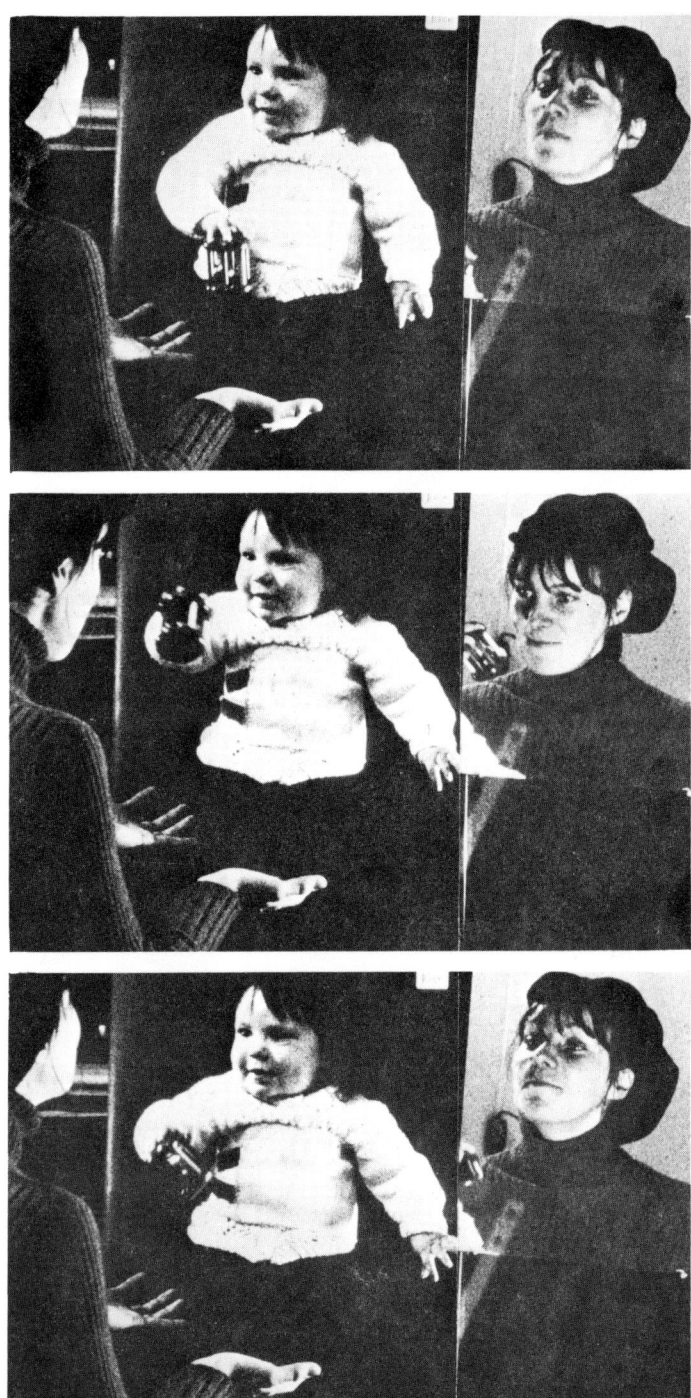

Fig. 4. (b) Tracey shakes rattle (bell in cage) and mother nods in synchrony. Tracey watches mother's face closely, and lags; 32 weeks (Fig. 1A).

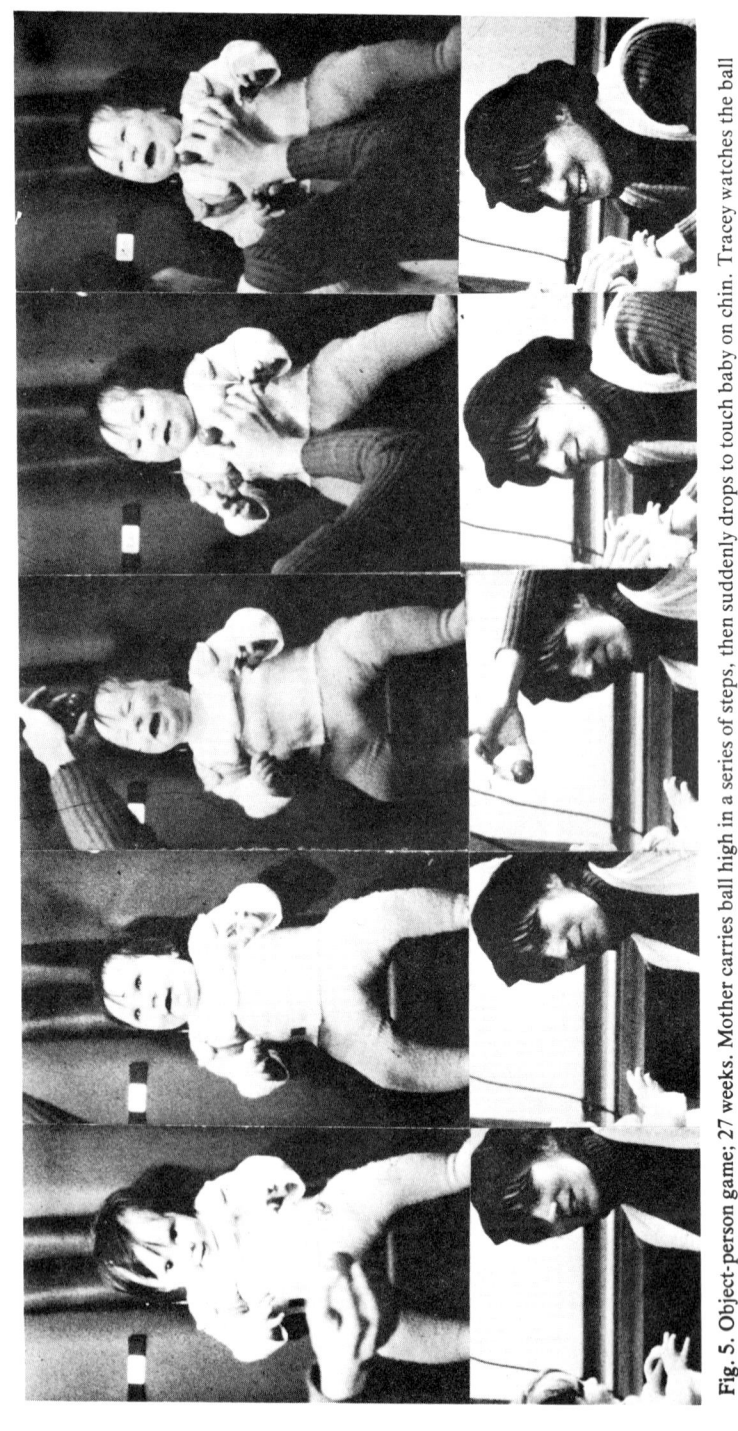

Fig. 5. Object-person game; 27 weeks. Mother carries ball high in a series of steps, then suddenly drops to touch baby on chin. Tracey watches the ball closely, then laughs twice.

stomach repeatedly (Fig. 5). In both games the object was a means for transmitting action interpersonally, but in the first Tracey, evidently cautious because of the novelty or "complexity" of the concept, saw her mother bring a game of the person to match her (Tracey's) object play. The latter was then repeated so that it became a cause or trigger for the shared excitement. In another form of this game the mother shows mock fright at Tracey's banging, which Tracey then repeats. This happens three times and Tracey laughs at her mother's mockery on each occasion.

Obviously such a game brings the mother to the same kind of function as the puppet which, at 5 months, Tracey had learned to activate "remotely" by pulling the string while she watched it (Fig. 4). The significant change is her acceptance of the mother as the puppet and her face as the centre of an effect which Tracey's movements can "cause". Up to this stage Tracey had been unwilling to focus on her mother's face while playing with objects, except in looming games where the face was the "object" Tracey was watching.

At 32 weeks Tracey showed several other signs of willingness to share the fun of her play. She smiled conspiratorially while her mother watched her move an object, and she accepted replacement of objects of play by her mother more readily than before. Her increased friendliness was shown by her delighted participation in the "zooming-object" or "swinging-ball" games animated by her mother, who in turn was very gay and demonstrative. Occasionally Tracey glanced at her mother while enjoying the effects, and this caused her mother to laugh.

Tracey's increased fluency of expression about the task she was doing was also shown in a succession of grimaces and smiles made when she had difficulty dealing with an object. Moreover, both her babbling and her visual control of hand groping after objects were more elaborate than in the previous month. The new expressive behaviours were matched by more complex programmes for praxic behaviour, so the whole of Tracey's intentional mechanism was undergoing important development. She attempted to generalize discoveries between objects, as when she shook a solid wooden block as if to rattle the bell in the cage. Failure to get the effect she expected caused her to give up this action quickly.

In spite of clear developments in control of her actions, and in consciousness of their effects and in spite of the above signals to her mother, Tracey still failed to act reciprocally in giving objects to her mother's open hand. Except for her sharing of mood or humour, she still communicated as if contained within the circle of her own experience and of effects immediately related to her acts. She showed subtle perception of her mother's communication, but this was shown mainly in indirect, or even negative ways, strongly regulated by herself. She was not truly co-operative since she failed to attend directly to the intentions of her mother.

The Development of Sharing of Acts with Objects

At 34 weeks Tracey played with objects at the table, banging them and groping with both hands as she shifted attention fluently between goals. Her mother took the role of observer or assistant, sitting back to pass comment, or dub in suitable voice-effects, like "Bang, bang, bang!" (Fig. 6). Occasionally she brought in a new object or changed the arrangement of things for Tracey. A small brightly painted wooden trolley with four wheels and three round men in holes was offered, and Tracey was shown how it could be pulled along by the string (Fig. 1). Tracey watched but did not imitate. While banging objects together and handling them with two hands, Tracey was beginning to look about, accept her mother's gaze and exchange smiles. This was a prelude to a new level of interpersonal exchange accompanying the handling of objects.

At 36 weeks and at 38 weeks Tracey played with the wooden men while her mother held the trolley. She banged them against the trolley while her mother made matching voice sounds. Tracey grinned then laughed without looking up and her mother laughed. Another prelude to shared action of a more complex kind was seen in an exchange of banging on the table at 38 weeks. Tracey and her mother banged hands on the table in alternation and Tracey, while looking at her mother, grinned at the effect they produced.

Now Tracey was adept at two-handed play and exchanged objects between her hands many times. She often rotated objects in her hand, tending to explore them this way, using distal (wrist and finger) movements, as well as simply transporting or banging them by proximal (arm and shoulder) movements. She also twisted her hands at the wrist in a clear gesture of impatience when frustrated, looking up and vocalizing at the same time. Later she looked up again and wrinkled her nose in "disgust" while shaking her leg in impatience. She looked about the room avoiding a small (½ in.) bead swinging on a thread, which was too small for her to grasp. She took objects offered by hand but held them back and dropped them, failing to return them (Fig. 7). A zooming-object game interested and amused her; then she looked away, self-possessed. She watched demonstrations of how to move the wheels of the trolley, which squeaked, and how to place the men in the holes, but did not imitate.

At 40 weeks Tracey's mother became an acknowledged participant in actions. Tracey repeatedly looked up at her mother's face when receiving an object, pausing as if to acknowledge receipt. She also looked up to her mother at breaks in her play, giving the indication of willingness to share experiences as she had never done before. Tracey pulled the cart in by the string, watching it move remote from her hand. She accepted many changes

Fig. 6. Mother watches while Tracey is engrossed in play. Tracey vocalizes. She does not look at her mother; 34 weeks.

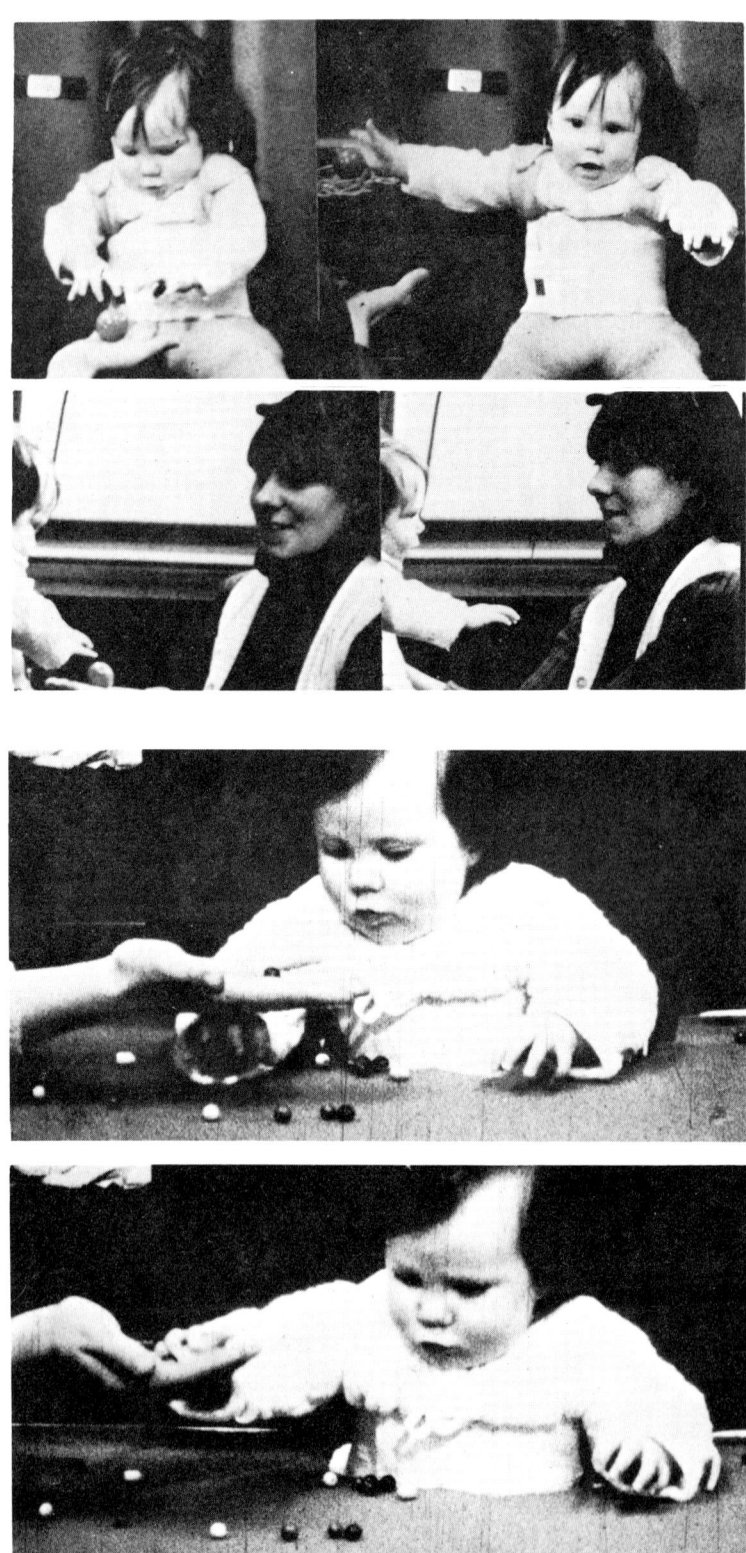

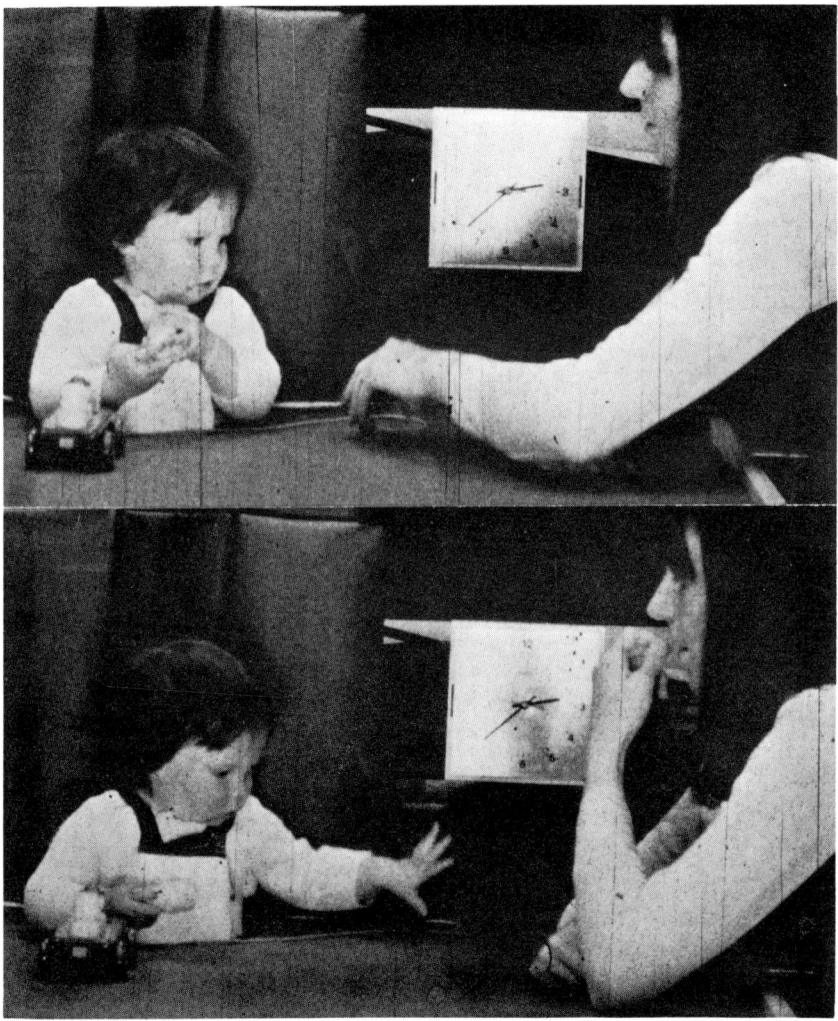

Fig. 7. Refusing and assisting.
Opposite page, top: Tracey takes a ball then holds it back and drops it; 27 weeks.
Opposite page, bottom: Tracey pushes mother's hand away, without a smile; 26 weeks.
Above: Mother pushes bead aside and Tracey imitates to aid with a deliberate sweeping movement; 45 weeks.

among coloured beads by her mother, pausing in her manipulation to look at what was shown to her. She followed when her mother pointed to a bead while speaking, and calmly accepted removal of an object without loss of interest in the shared play. At one point she gently moved her mother's hand aside so she could get to beads beneath it. When her mother showed her how to make the wheels of the inverted trolley turn and squeak, Tracey watched closely and touched the wheels. When her mother eagerly said "Pull it!", Tracey made a move to draw the trolley towards her, but failed because the string was not taut, at the same time, expecting success, she looked up and smiled eagerly at her mother. This was clearly a learned anticipation of the pleasure they usually shared when she did the trick of pulling in the trolley correctly. Throughout this session the mother was showing and giving things to Tracey who was more docile than ever before, and more "interested". In playing with objects they shared the effects almost equally, Tracey looking up at her mother and smiling when an entertaining effect was produced.

At the same age Tracey and her mother played a new game in which the mother was both giving and taking back. Her mother repeatedly offered an object, then quickly drew it back. She watched Tracey who looked up and laughed.

Much of the interplay between Tracey and her mother was carried by vocalization. Tracey hooted with excitement while banging, or grunted with concentration, and then, when trying careful variations in manipulation, made gentler cooing sounds and more articulated babbling. She did this co-operatively in a joint game. Her mother talked in a relaxed way and added sound effects (e.g. "What are you doing? . . . Bang, bang, bang") but she asked what Tracey wanted much less frequently than before, saying instead things like "Take this one" or "There you are" as she showed and gave.

At both 45 and 47 weeks a large transformation in the balance of Tracey's communications with her mother was completed, and the effect on her mother was very great. For the first time Tracey gave a play object happily to her mother when asked to do so (Fig. 8). They played with one of Tracey's toys, a rattle with a clear plastic globe, and a ball inside it (Figs. 1 and 9). The globe could be unscrewed from the handle to take out or put in the ball. When the ball was offered to Tracey she promptly put it in the globe, and when her mother assembled the two parts she eagerly shook it. The mother made the following commentary which lacks questions (except for one rhetorical one), and is full of instructions and declarations:

"Put it in there. Take it out. There it is. Shake, shake, shake!" (Tracey hands the globe to her mother who requests by gesture.) "Put it on there, put it on there. That's it!" (Tracey takes out the object and puts it in again.) "That's it. In again. Out. Mmm! Put it in. No? That's it. Out again. Thank you!" (as Tracey hands it over to her without being asked).

Then tracey's mother rolled a cloth ball to her saying, "Ready, steady, go!" Tracey caught it in two hands and grinned delightedly banging the table with both hands and the ball, and looking up at her mother's face (Fig. 8). As her mother held her hand out palm up to receive the object saying, "Where's the ball?", Tracey hesitated a moment and, distracted by the sound of someone entering the room to her side away from her mother, turned to hold out the ball to the visitor. Her mother continued, "No, here; over this side." Tracey looked at her mother's hand, quickly reached to give her mother the ball, looked to her face and smiled. "Thank you!" said the mother, and Tracey gave a triumphant vocalization and hit the table (Fig. 8).

Later they played a game to demonstrate how Tracey had recently gained the trick of selecting objects named by her mother. A toy duck and fish belonging to Tracey were placed on the table. Tracey's mother said "Where is Duck-Duck?" several times. Tracey looked from object to object, "thinking" but not reaching. Her mother said "Where's Fish-Fish?", then "Where's Duck-Duck?". After behaving in a hesitant, absorbed manner for a moment, Tracey grasped the duck and handed it to her mother (Fig. 8). Tracey often made errors in this game which her mother corrected, but she clearly tried, and sometimes her choice was deliberate and correct. The significant new achievement is her grasp of the principle of the naming game. Her mother reported that in the last couple of weeks Tracey had been co-operating in a number of naming games developed out of familiar acts of giving and taking. For example, she would correctly obey the instruction "Pull the plug" after having a bath. Her mother had quickly learned to cultivate this new interest in words.

Throughout this session the giving-and-taking game was played many times, the mother uttering directions and naming the topics for exchange. They also repeated the truck game, the mother saying "Weee!" as Tracey, smiling eagerly, pulled the string to draw the truck towards her.

Frequently Tracey made vocal commentary in a quiet pause while her mother silently observed her. When her mother pushed the bead on the string of the truck to get it out of her way, Tracey immediately turned to imitate the act co-operatively (i.e. to aid) (Fig. 7). This is in total contrast to the same gesture used 4 months previously to push aside (to refuse) a bead offered by the mother (Fig. 7).

In contrast to her earlier *reactive* regulation of Tracey's behaviour, reflected in a questioning and coaxing manner of speaking, Tracey's mother now regulated in a *directive* manner, issuing instructions and asking rhetorical questions. Tracey, for her part, acted as if she happily accepted the leadership of her mother in a joint definition of experience. We believe the mother's behaviour to be a response to Tracey's acceptance of or seeking for directives.

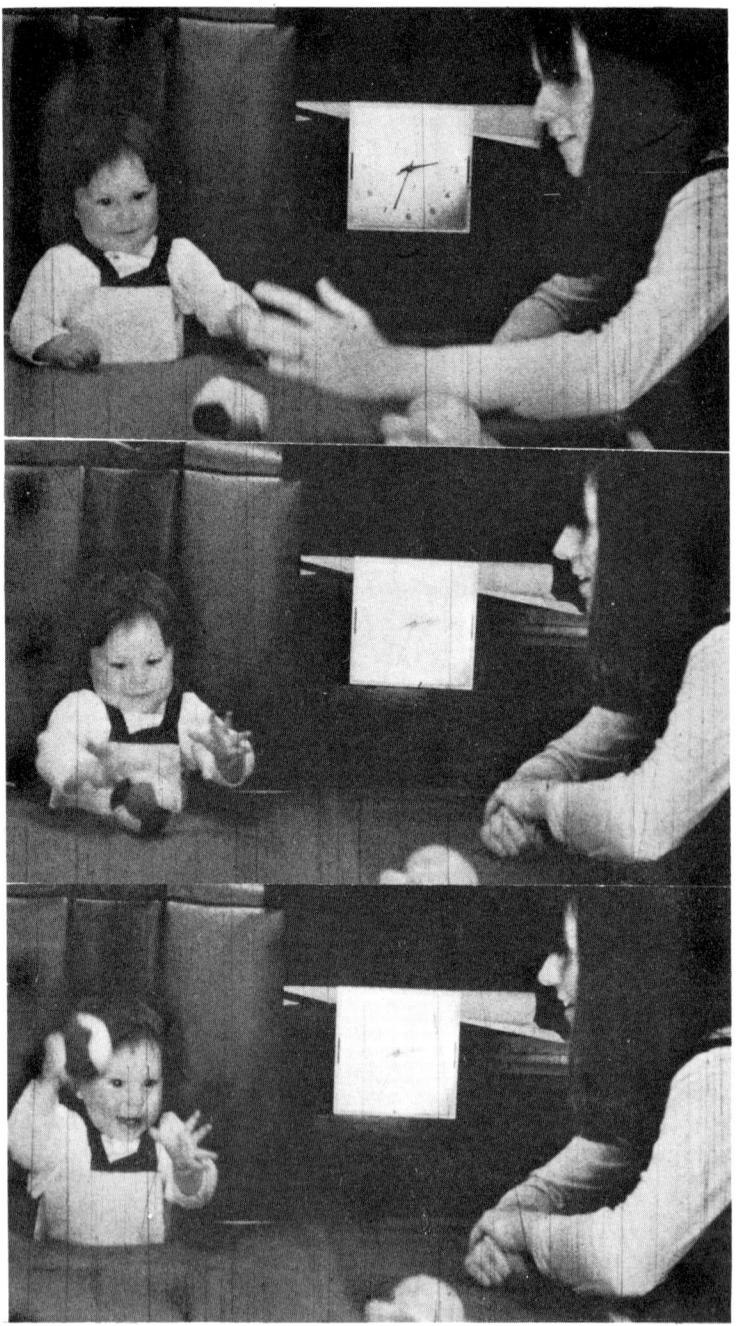

(a)

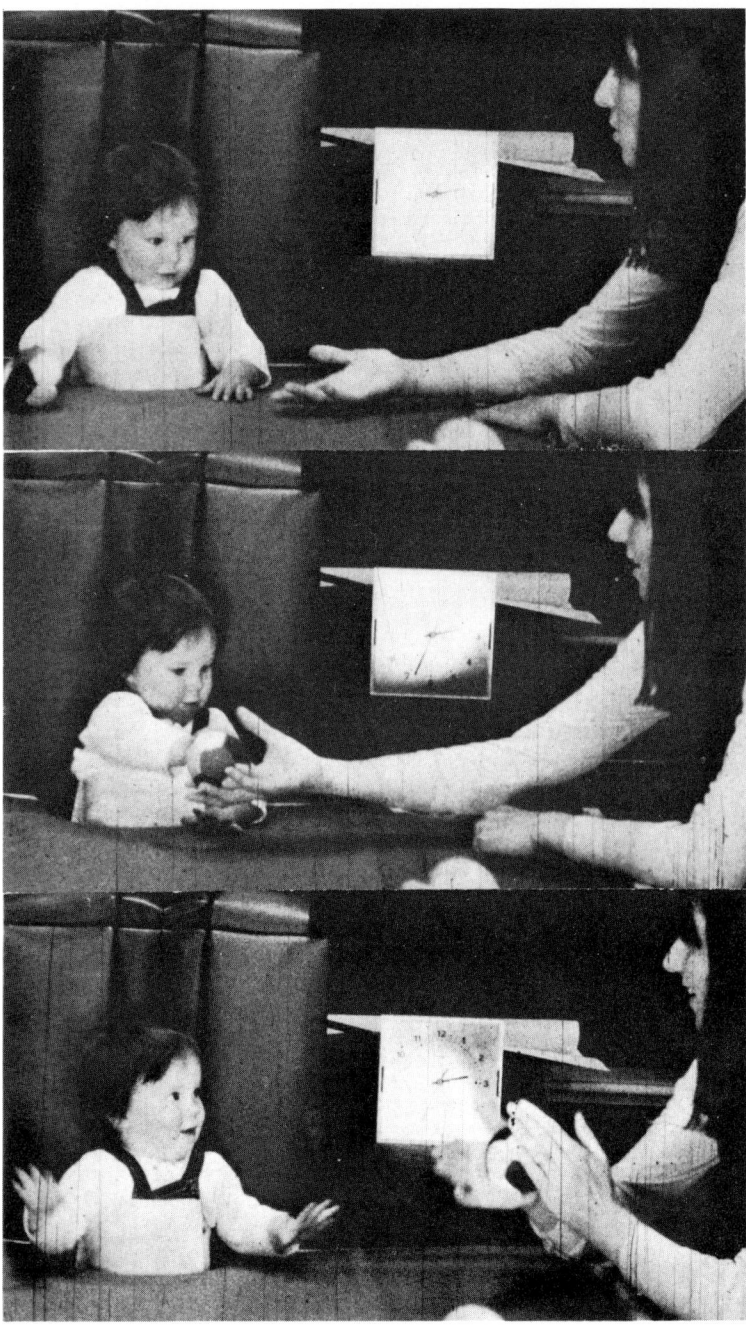

(b)

Fig. 8. Accepting and giving; 45 weeks.
(a) Tracey accepts a ball in a rolling game. Beats the table in triumph.
(b) Tracey places ball in mother's hand when a request is made. Beats the table, smiling at mother.

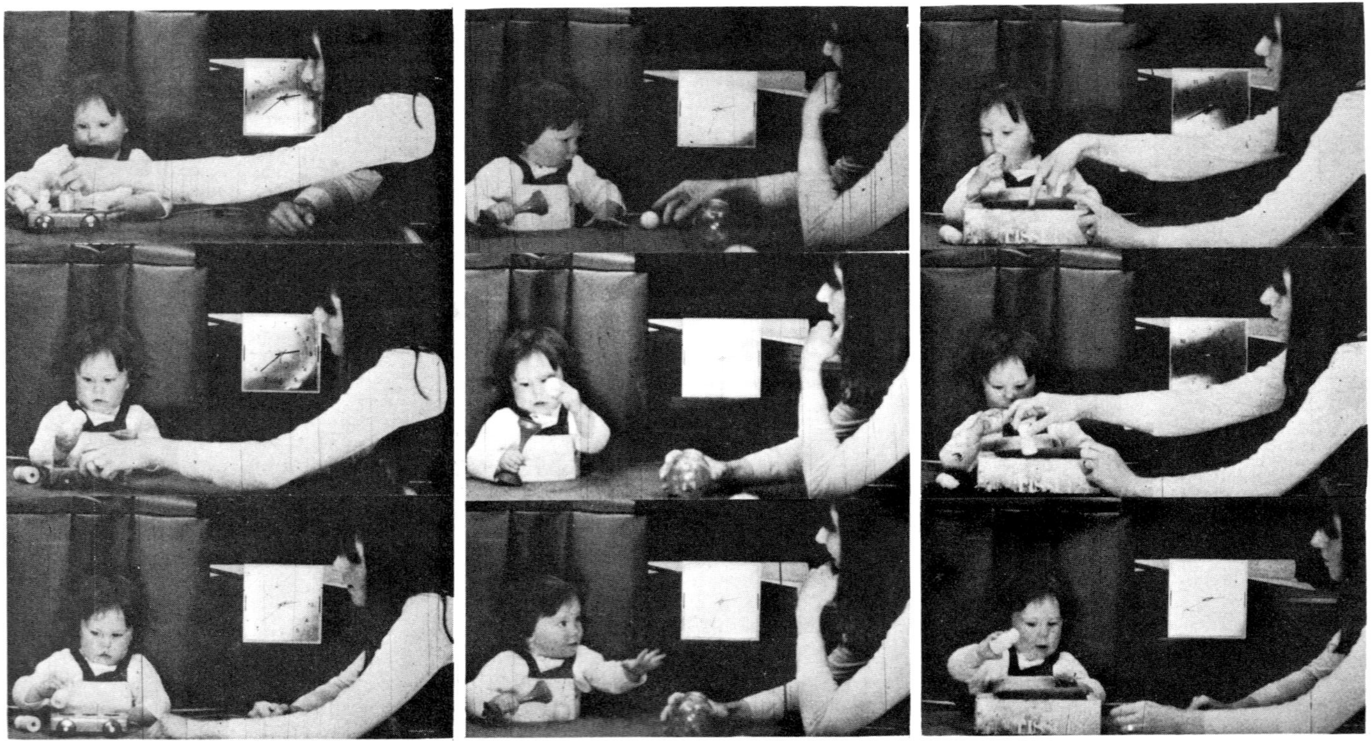

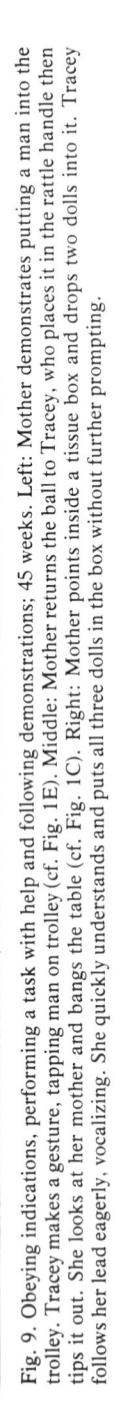

Fig. 9. Obeying indications, performing a task with help and following demonstrations; 45 weeks. Left: Mother demonstrates putting a man into the trolley. Tracey makes a gesture, tapping man on trolley (cf. Fig. 1E). Middle: Mother returns the ball to Tracey, who places it in the rattle handle then tips it out. She looks at her mother and bangs the table (cf. Fig. 1C). Right: Mother points inside a tissue box and drops two dolls into it. Tracey follows her lead eagerly, vocalizing. She quickly understands and puts all three dolls in the box without further prompting.

With this new co-operation came new games: a most interesting example, for its cognitive implications, being the hiding and finding which arose as a variation of putting in and taking out (Fig. 9). The little wooden men were placed in a tissue box. Tracey was led to "find" them by her mother and she showed her grasp of the communication of the game by a look of surprise and vocalizing. This imitated her mother's mock surprise and high pitched "Oh!". They played a long game in which the men were repeatedly hidden, the mother overturning the box with the men inside leaving Tracey to lift it up and "discover" the men. Tracey was a willing participant. The mother vocalized "No" with a shake of her head and downward intonation, or "That's it" with rising voice. It is obvious that Tracey's co-operation and imagination of the mother's role permits her to share in a rich variety of shared climaxes in experience and many modes of action, each marked with a distinctive vocal comment from the mother.

Comparisons with Other Infants

Tracey's development between 6 and 10 months is summarized in Table I.

Closely similar findings have been obtained from biographical films made with one other female baby and two of the first author's own boys. Prior to 9 months, when manipulating objects and babbling, each of the four children was playful in games developed by a familiar partner out of what they were doing. After 9 months they rapidly developed a more observant social behaviour, adjusting their interest in objects to their partners' interests by complex acts including handing of objects to others, and pointing while vocalizing, both these acts being combined with looking at the partner's face and smiling.

The consequence of this new level of awareness of the mother appears to have been that it was the mother who learned a new set of rules.* After 9 months each baby made new steps of behaviour imitated from the mother, became obedient to directives such as pointing and verbal instructions, and learned to respond correctly to a few, often repeated, names of objects or actions. The efficiency of communication and learning was enormously increased, first, by the infant taking on an active role of giver, shower or agent, with voluntary recognition of the mother's interest, and, secondly, by the mother adapting to this.

In the previous 6 months, complex changes took place, some of which,

---

*This account is based on behaviour with the *mother*, but this does not mean that other persons were not treated in similar ways. I have not studied other relationships, except for observations of my own infants with me. (C.T.)

Table I
Tracey and mother

	25 Weeks	45 Weeks
1.	Baby only occasionally initiates face-to-face interaction. Does not interrupt own activity to do so. Smiles and looks at M during person games or games using animated objects at climaxes determined by the motion.	Baby looks and smiles at M often during joint activity with objects, greeting her readily. Will interrupt own activity with objects to do so.
2.	Baby's looking at M's face is unpredictable. It elicits an immediate response of pleasure.	Baby looks at M's face in response to an instruction and to solicit assistance. M often takes these looks of recognition for granted.
3.	Baby shows resistance to M's social attentions by turning away.	Baby does not turn away to refuse attentions from M.
4.	Baby may show extreme interest in objects to the neglect of M. Does not combine attention to objects and M.	Baby can integrate attentions to M and objects in co-operative activity.
5.	Baby's handling and explorations of an object are limited; reaching, grasping, putting to mouth, holding at side, banging and dropping. M must follow B's changing interest in effects produced. May develop games, but there are no equally balanced transactions.	Baby's handling and explorations of objects are more complex, involving sequences like pulling in the truck and then taking out the men. M can develop B's interest into elaborate joint activities where M knows the overall plan and directs B to fit in. B also anticipates the sequence and may direct parts of it.
6.	Baby watches M's activity with an object, especially if activity lies within B's "secondary circular reaction". B does not imitate.	Baby watches M's activity and will use it as a model, especially if encouraged to do so by M. Imitation by B is easily obtained.
7.	Baby takes object offered by M, almost invariably drops it. Does not give an object.	Baby takes an object offered by M, gives it to her when asked, and in a sequence of action when they come to M's turn.
8.	Baby may follow M's pointing to an object in front of B and pick up that object, though not reliably.	Baby easily follows M's pointing to an object and picks it up. B is highly responsive to directive gestures of M.
9.	Mother has to be very soliciting to engage B's interest in a social game.	Baby is far more easily socially engaged, sometimes inviting a sharing of pleasure.
10.	Baby smiles and laughs at games and "jokes", orienting laughter and smiles to M, but needing support of M's involvement in B's actions.	Baby laughs and bangs table triumphantly, in demonstration of pleasure in mastery of a joint occupation with M. B's humour is also more autonomous; smiles when carrying out an act herself.

| 11. | Mother's speaking is turned into "baby-talk" games with body movements and changes of face expression. | Mother's ordinary speaking is more likely to attract B's attention, even when not reinforced by other acts of expression. |
| 12. | Baby does not understand words. | Baby shows she knows the names of some toys. |

from the point of view of a fellow communicator, seem negative or rejecting. Tracey's dropping of received objects at 21 weeks and refusal to give objects until after 40 weeks was, however, not abnormal because the other infants did the same at this age. Tracey's playfulness at 6 months and later development of a rich triadic person-person-object style of play shows she was not more avoidant or withdrawn than the other infants in spite of her mother's slight depression when Tracey was 2 to 4 months of age.

The avoiding shown by all the infants at 4 months, compared to their eager acceptance of eye contact in conversation-like exchanges at 2 months, started just prior to the maturation of arm control and effective prehension of objects. In several cases, the refusal to look directly at a partner was most marked in relation to the mother. This may be partly an artifact of our method of observing in staged encounters, but it certainly is proof that the withdrawal was not due to perception of a "stranger".

By 5 months, objects and events selected by the infant for attention were taken up as mediators or token for interaction of feelings or intentions between infant and mother. For the next 4 months person games and object games excited the infants and provoked signs of pleasure. The infants also clearly enjoyed being in the presence of familiar people and in familiar surroundings, and they fretted when left alone. Being in familiar company encouraged play with voicing, mouthing and handling, all of which were presumably enriched by the development of new capacities for perception of both people and objects. But in all this time the infants often withdrew from intimate face-to-face communication, and they usually did not seek the eyes of people or smile to them while interested in objects. Except for their union in games, objects and people were focused on separately.

If personal confrontations are forced on infants at this age, they resist or withdraw. Withdrawal is not restricted to strangers. At 3 to 6 months the unfriendly behaviour may elicit comment from mothers who say, spontaneously, that they felt "hurt". We have repeatedly recorded a mother to spontaneously grasp her 4- to 5-month-old's head in an attempt to regain eye contact by forceful head turning. This manipulative tactic always failed. The mothers had to accept less direct forms of communication, and then the babies responded well.

With babies in the second and third month, most mothers we have filmed played games that involved touching the infant's body, like pat-a-cake with the hands, bouncing the legs, shaking the cheeks, prodding the nose or stomach. Gradually, it would seem the mother herself is accepted as a game object as she mirrors the infant's acts of expression. After this the play incorporates objects that the infant has accepted as foci for interest. We found that by 6 months these games via objects, or with parts of the mother's body treated as objects, became the infants' preferred form of play. Then, at 9 or 10 months, they started the deliberately co-operative form of interest in objects which transforms play into exchange of acts of meaning.

DISCUSSION

It remains to be seen if the above apparently endogenous changes in inter-subjectivity during the first year are universal in human development. Obviously some forms of cognitive development of the infant are cultivated or facilitated in our society by presenting infants with special toys, like coloured balls, rattles and soft effigies of animals or persons, and infants must be affected by the custom of leaving them on their own in playpens or cots surrounded by toys. Professor Mundy-Castle of the University of Lagos has told us that in West African cultures there is a great emphasis on social interaction with babies, who are handed round and played with verbally by everyone present. There is not much emphasis on object games. Annette Hamilton reports the same for Australian Aborigines (Hamilton, 1970). In spite of such differences in treatment of infants, we believe that certain conclusions drawn from Tracey's development must have wide implications for all humans.

We believe that Tracey's changes were emergent in her mind, and that her mother, though sophisticated by artifacts and ideas from her family, social group and culture, was unconsciously tutored and changed by the changes in Tracey. We conclude that traditional games and toys (like "Pat-a-cake", "Ride-a-cock-horse", rattles, dolls, balls) may best be understood as responses to the infant's innate human talents for play. We would describe the mother's acts we have seen as adaptations to the infant's changing play, and this in turn reflects the infant's changing understanding of her mother as a person. This is not to deny that what a mother does may be essential for the infant to expand his knowledge at an optimal rate. If she acts with spontaneity and freedom in responding, she cannot help creating a series of demonstrations fitted to the infant's cognitive and interactive schemata and stimulating to their growth. Helpful play appears to be her natural response to the infant's communicative personality and it can take many particular forms. Indeed each mother—infant pair we have observed created together a unique repertoire of games. The habits of play evidently became the basis of a unique companionship in each pair.

A nativistic interpretation of infant development fits what has been seen with younger infants. The changes of communication throughout the first year appear to be principally due to differentiation of a highly complex, general intersubjectivity which is manifest very early in rudimentary form (Trevarthen, 1977c). This function identifies persons, regulates motivation and intention toward them, and simultaneously forms rudimentary acts of speech and gesture in patterned combinations and sequences. It also provides internal images of face and hand movements for the identification and imitation of the expressions of others. Acts of adults that signify interest and understanding to other adults are selectively perceived by 2-month-olds, too, and taken as analogous to their own acts of like form. When the mother expresses excitement or pleasure it stimulates a function in the infant that is capable of generating a mirror or complementary act. Proof of these propositions is to be found in the communications of *primary intersubjectivity* that develop into elaborate form in the second and third months after birth (Trevarthen, 1974a,b, 1977a,c).

The elementary dyadic interpersonal function is evidently changed as infants develop effective prehension and an increased facility for observing events and the useful properties of objects (Trevarthen, 1977b). We conceptualize this development to be by differentiation of a fundamentally coherent field of intentionality which is, however, already anatomically partitioned at birth into three modes out of which three kinds of experience and action are generated postnatally. These modes are probably three real systems of the brain that achieve functional differentiation by interaction with each other and with the environment. Forms of action and perceptual processing appropriate for (1) knowing and using objects (praxic mode), for (2) communicating with the human world (communicative mode), and for (3) acting in self-directed or thoughtful manner (reflective mode) appear as distinct rudiments in the newborn. Of these three, the communicative mode appears to undergo greatest elaboration in the first phase of infancy (second and third months). Then it becomes adjusted to developments in the other two modes, especially the praxic. In consequence infants show specific withdrawal from proffered interpersonal contact, and they relegate sharing of experience to more indirect channels. With increased interest in looking at and handling objects comes a playfulness that eventually permits the infantile intentionality to achieve a new level of integration.

Once free interaction between communicative and praxic modes of action is achieved, the infant suddenly shows behaviour that is unique to man in its complexity, and full of potential for the development of knowledge, joint enterprise and language. When a 10-month-old offers an object to the extended palm of another, makes a vocal and gestural utterance in the form of a command or declaration, responds with precise co-operation to a request expressed by facial signs and in gesture and speech, plays a give-and-take game, or obeys learned instructions of speech or gesture to choose objects or perform specific manipulations with them, the expressive manner of what the infant does gives these acts a co-operative form seen in the behaviour of no other species. We believe the same developments will be found in all human societies, but think it likely, too, that cultural differences will take root at this stage of infancy.

Figure 10 is a diagram of the proposed transformations of the intentional mechanism that take place in the first year.

This view of the formation of what we call *secondary intersubjectivity*, linking mother, infant and object on an equal plane of importance, is not compatible either with behaviourist (Watson, 1924) or pragmatic (Mead, 1934) views of the development of human social intelligence, nor does it relate except superficially to the Piagetian theory of cognitive development in the "sensory-motor" period (Piaget, 1970). It requires an innate interpersonal or intersubjective function lacking or unstated in these. The assumption that the young infant is isolated in egocentricity is quite incompatible with our observations.

A significant growth transformation of the infant mind at about 9 months has been detected by all who have made adequate biographic observations. However, different theories lead to widely different interpretations. Excluding extreme learning theories which offer no explanation for such a change, the two principle structuralist (or constructivist) theories for mental development both acknowledge the complexity of the infant's cerebral endowment in principle, but they attribute change in behaviour to progressive attainment of skill; that is, to the integration of practical experiences into representations and concepts. The first theory, that of Piaget, concentrates on cognitive growth—growth of knowledge in the private mind of an actor-perceiver. The other, identified with Mead, emphasizes social and communicative interactions between the infant and the mother of other persons. Society is taken by Mead to be the principal source of rules for knowing people and communicating with them.

A third theory, that of the psychoanalysts, was at the start more concerned with the pathology of adult personality structure. Freud, of course, presented a developmental theory of instinctive motivation, based on his case materials. Psychoanalytic theory is so different from the other approaches to infancy that it must be considered separately.

Piaget (1952, 1962) has captured, with wonderful precision, almost all of

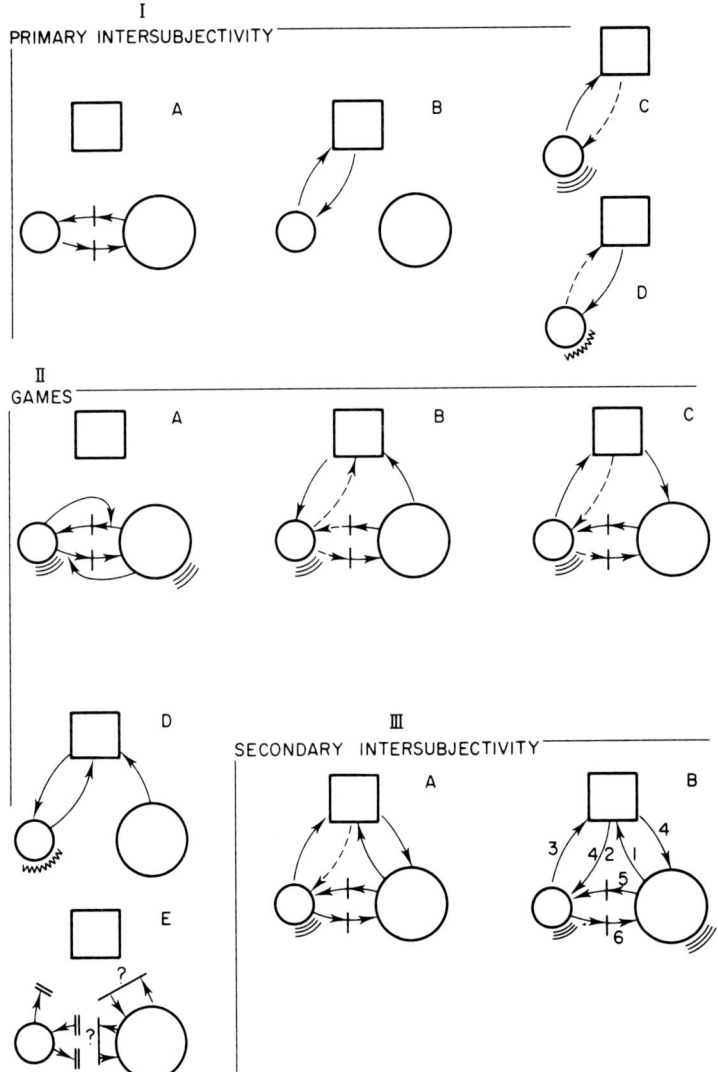

Fig. 10. Functions in the development of secondary intersubjectivity.

(IA) Communicating: baby and mother interact face-to-face; no interest in object. (IB) Acting on an object: baby acts; mother watches. (IC) Piagetian Assimilation: play with "pleasure in mastery". (ID) Piagetian Accommodation: imitation, tracking with "serious intent".

(IIA) Person-Person Game: baby acts on mother's acts to baby. (IIB) Object-Person Game I: mother moves object to amuse baby and watches the baby's face. (IIC) Object-Person Game II: baby moves object and mother tracks it; baby watches mother and is amused. (IID) Baby takes offered object without acknowledgement of mother's intention to give. (IIE) Baby is asked by mother to give and refuses, avoiding mother.

(IIIA) Baby gives object and shows pleasure when it is accepted. (IIIB) Full person-person-object fluency, e.g. mother shows baby how to do a task (1 + 2), baby accepts (3 + 4), then looks at mother and both are pleased (5 + 6).

the events we observe in Tracey's behaviour, except those concerning adjustment of her attentions to her mother. Indeed, Piaget presents himself as a responsive but invisible examiner of the developing imagination and reason of the child. Even when studying imitation and play, he makes his analysis in terms of a "thinking" that allows the infant no special awareness of humans as persons having a unique potentiality for shared awareness and shared intention (Piaget, 1962). The essential process in early infancy is development of imagery for perception of objects. This is built up by amalgamation of cerebral reflexes that guide movements of the eyes, hands and mouth through the senses of sight, hearing, touch and taste. Objects are perceived through effects they produce in sensory-motor reflexes when the infant orients to or manipulates them.

Piaget describes a major transformation in the child's mind at about 9 months. This brings into being "the concept of the object". Before this (Stage III) the infant practices "secondary circular reactions", repeatedly transporting objects held in the hand to cause interesting perceptions of graded novelty. Objects are not yet conceived by the infant as substantive with intrinsic capacity for displacement or persistence in time and have no fixed shape or size. Interest in them ceases when they are covered, and they are not expected to have a given form from one appearance to the next. After about 6 months, the inertial, sound-making, appearance-changing properties of objects transported by the infant cause mental images that are retained to represent objects with constant intrinsic properties. At 9 months (Stage IV) the infant begins to observe the effects of exercising skills of visual exploration (grasping, holding, dropping, hitting, etc.) in sequential combinations. This results in the definition of certain "instruments" that add meaning, for an observer, to the infant's acts (Piaget, 1952, 1970).

The infant, Piaget says, *enjoys* the power of exercising control over the perceptions of objects, so must have a means of evaluating control. By this evaluation, Piaget explains the differences between the "serious intent" (intentional accommodation), by which an infant will explore the experience of an unfamiliar object, and the laughter or smiles that accompany play with a familiar object. The properties of something familiar, being correctly predicted by the infant, offer no further scope for serious investigation (Piaget, 1962).

Piaget, failing to recognize that humans are essentially different from other objects in the infant's world, does not register the fact that infants aim their emotional expressions (of "joy", "serious intent" or "surprise") to persons. Moreover, for him imitation begins very simply as the accommodation of orienting to the displacement of an object, or the mindless re-creation of the sound of a model that itself matches one of the infant's own sounds (e.g. contagious crying). More complex imitations are achieved by associative learning and reinforcement from adults who selectively reward acts of the infant that, by chance, reflect their models. Likewise, the ability of a 10-month-old to give an object on being asked, which Piaget reports, is no different, he believes, from the ability achieved at the same time of placing a ball in a container. Laughter in a game with the mother's face or with an object animated by the mother, is simply due to the infant having a power to predict what will stimulate him after he does something—once again, a private experience of the power of mastery causes joy.

At Stage IV the infant will snatch a cover off a hidden object, and enjoy this instrumental act for its sake. This leads to experimentation with means (intermediate steps) for doing things. This is, Piaget concludes, the first time that the infant can imitate an act seen by movement of a part of his body he cannot see. The achievement is simply due to learning of the mental link between each such act and some other movement which causes a stimulus like the model. Thus, poking out the tongue to imitate is said to involve prior observation of the combination of tongue protrusion with making of certain voice sounds. We now know, however, that silent tongue protrusion (and other "self-invisible" expressions) may be imitated by 1-month-olds (e.g. Maratos, 1973).

Piaget (1932) defines morality as "the logic of action". He suggests that "we can find, no doubt, even before language, all the elements of rationality and morality" but "it is persons external to him who channelize the child's elementary feelings; those feelings do not tend to regulate themselves from within". Moral reciprocity, according to Piaget, is a rational achievement of the child several years of age, when he moves from an egocentric to a socio-centric condition. Kohlberg (1969) likewise considers the infant to be wholly egocentric and lacking in moral sense.

Close followers of Piaget's theory of cognitive development may note significant changes in the mental functions of infants in the last trimester of the first year, but add nothing of significance to his theory of infancy, even when they apply it to development of knowledge of persons or "the self" or to the development of protolinguistic functions (Kagan, 1971; Hunt and Kirk, 1971; Flavell, 1974; Kohlberg, 1969; Bates et al., 1975; Schaffer, 1971; Lewis and Brooks, 1975). As an example of how the cognitive theory is applied, experiments on the attending of infants to events undergoing mechanical or electronic change indicated that babies become more observant and more expressive about what they perceive towards the end of the first year (Zalazzo, 1977). This is considered to be due to development of "thinking". Bates et al. (1975) similarly consider that the ability of a 10-month-old to perform illocutionary acts of communication, intended to make others act as instruments or recipients of information, follows from development of the Stage IV or Stage V object concept.

Bower's studies of cognition in infancy (Bower, 1974) lead him to propose a revision of Piaget's concept of development (Bower, 1977; Bower and Wishart, 1977). Experiments with visual tracking, prediction and reaching of infants less than 6 months old show that some concept of an object, located outside the body, capable of displacement over time and with its own size and form, is present in what Bower calls "abstract" formulation for the whole infant from the start. It is, therefore, not constructed by assembly of sensory-motor reflexes, even though the object perceived does gain in specificity with experience of instances and contexts. This does not seem to totally contradict Piaget's views and it resembles Werner and Kaplan's idea of differentiation (Werner and Kaplan, 1963).

Bower (1977) in reviewing the evidence for an alternative general theory of psychological growth, has suggested how it may explain infants' interest in persons and the development of individual attachments or relationships. He uses evidence from the powers of young infants for imitation and their varied expressions of pleasure with human, non-human, reactive and unreactive stimuli. Nevertheless, Bower's analysis remains rational and impersonal. His infant is developing propositions. When explaining what he means by a more abstract representation, Bower refers to Russell and Whitehead's logical theory of Types and its use by Gregory Bateson (1973) in psychology. He does not distinguish intersubjective functions as requiring a distinct mechanism, except to say that humans are probably born with a need for human company. He observes that "set patterns of interchange" with people are acquired, but generalized detectors for human speech are present from birth. Taking the experimental findings of Lewis and Brooks (1975) on reactions of infants to photographs of people, he concludes that gender identity is acquired by specification within a general recognition of humans that is all that is expressed in early months. Overspecification of the identity of the mother and of the relationship to her is responsible for fear of strangers and separation anxiety.

The formulation of this theory is itself too abstract to help us explain the emergence of secondary intersubjectivity. However, in developing his thesis Bower makes an important point with respect to apparent losses or repetitions of conceptual skill in infancy and childhood. For example, infants change in their ability to predict relations between an object's perceived form and size, and its mass. When reaching and grasping at 18 months, an infant knows an object's mass from its appearance (Mounoud and Bower, 1974). Speaking at 4 years, the same child doesn't know. Such fluctuations in ability mean that incomplete study of a given development, missing early manifestations of a function, may give a false indication that the function in question is built up by the child learning how to combine elements. Repetition of any one ability considered separate from the whole pattern of psychological development is analogous to a cycle of differentiation and reintegration in morphogenesis of one organ in the whole body of an embryo (Weiss, 1939).

A comparable analysis may be applied to epigenesis of the precursors of communication. Halliday (1975) describes "previews" at about 5 months in the attainment of early protolinguistic abilities. We have observed decline in eye contact, smiling, prespeech and gestures, between 3 months (primary intersubjectivity) and 6 months, and then increase of these behaviours at 9 months (secondary intersubjectivity) (Trevarthen, 1977b). At the same time that primary intersubjectivity is declining, the infant loses an inclination to imitate mouth movements and voice sounds (Maratos, 1977). The second form of intersubjectivity is not acquired by assembling reflex reactions to persons and objects. It requires formation of new kinds of function combining preformed intentions to objects and preformed intentions to persons.

In contrast to the Piagetians, those who concentrate on the contribution of the social environment of the infant to development include pediatricians with concern for assessment of the adaptation of infants to their caretakers and the prospects of artificial management of infants in hospitals. Developmental psychologists now seek specifically social explanations for the development of language, and confront such socio-political questions as the genesis of race and social class differences in school performance, or the causes of differences between intellectual developments in different cultures. Infants are increasingly seen to be highly responsive to human contact from birth and their development is now known to be profoundly affected by isolation from the mother or failure to form an emotional attachment to her. A baby is thought to enter quickly into a web or network of social interaction with his or her immediate caretakers, then within the first few years this extends to include their peers and other family members.

All kinds of psychological functions are now seen to develop in dependence on this social context (e.g. Lewis and Freedle, 1973; Schaffer, 1977). It is generally believed that interaction with people permits a baby to learn rules for sharing, teaches them how to use objects and eventually transmits a language code to them. The infant's development is supposed to depend on the mother teaching reciprocation in dialogue, how objects may be used, what effects they may create and how to speak about them. Knowledge of the infant about people as well as about objects is said to be developed by socialization which depends increasingly on transmission of the acquired knowledge, techniques and social conventions of persons close to the infant. The process of acculturation is continued in childhood by formal schooling.

In recent accounts of communication in the first year a special innate ability to sense persons and to communicate is granted to infants (Bell, 1968;

Newson and Newson, 1975). Nevertheless, the acquisition of rules of exchange, in the sense of symbols with shared social significance, is still thought to be due to training or continuous progressive adaptation (Bruner, 1975; Newson and Newson, 1975). The endogenous base for this acquisition is still unknown. Some consider the original response to persons to depend on a refined but automatic sensitivity of the infant to the cadence and contingent responsiveness of stimuli emitted by attentive persons (Condon and Sander, 1974; Watson, 1966, 1977). When confronted with the patterns of actual communication this explanation is seen to be insufficient. The infant has elaborate regulatory power and a capacity to adjust to or imitate the form of communicative expressions of adults (Trevarthen, 1977c).

Ideas about language acquisition were changed by Chomsky's arguments for an innate language acquisition mechanism that could be held responsible for the grammatical form of human language intentions (Chomsky, 1965). Lenneberg's (1967) biological observations on language development were also influential. Subsequent studies of early language (Bloom, 1970; Brown, 1973) and of mothers' speech to infants (Snow, 1972) suggest that the psychological rules of communication necessary for the start of speaking are more concerned with establishing semantics in patterns of joint interest in surroundings. Claims for an innate syntactic function have weakened. The mother, in constant attention to the infant over 1½ years before the baby speaks, has been found to be extremely perceptive of opportunities to give meaning or impute intention to what the infant does in relation to her or the environment. She is thought to codify the infant's adventitious and imitative acts in words and to guide the formation of syntactic structures (Ryan, 1974; Snow, 1976; Newson, 1974; Newson and Newson, 1975; Holzman, 1972; Bruner, 1975; Ninio and Bruner, 1977; Lieven and McShane, 1977). The mother also begins the process of transmitting rules of culture to the infant (Shotter, 1974; Newson and Newson, 1975).

Such an explanation of the development of communication as an acquired social skill linked to experience requires careful assessment in the light of what has been found by accurate descriptions of what infants do. There are extraordinary regularities in development. Changes are initiated, not by the adult rule bearers, but by the infant and child. The changes reported here in the infant's intentions at about 9 or 10 months transform the opportunities for communication and cause the infant to perform deliberate, self-conscious and reciprocal sharing of a focus or topic with another. Apparently the infant offers to others the general structure of language behaviour, and then regulates a developmental timetable for acquisition of its differentiated subverbal rules. Nevertheless, most psychologists prefer to explain the changes as originating from the social environment.

By 2 months the infant takes turns in expression and vocalization, generating rudimentary utterances in a dialogue-like exchange (Stern, 1974; Snow, 1976; Bullowa, 1977). This is regarded by Schaffer (1977) to be a learned ability, but there is only circumstantial and highly selective evidence for this interpretation which begins with a denial of an innate inter-subjectivity. By 9 months the infant is co-operative in distributing attention to objects even following another's gaze or pointing (Scaife and Bruner, 1974; Murphy and Messer, 1977). Although infants make the movement of pointing from 6 weeks (Trevarthen, 1977a,c), deliberate employment of this kind of act in an exchange with the mother does not occur until 9 months. In the intervening period, play involving imitation is thought to be essential to "elaboration of a rule structure in communication" and "development of signalling and sequencing rules" (Bruner, 1975), or kinds of "standard action formats" (Ninio and Bruner, 1977). Early forms of "ostention" (e.g. pointing) in this period are used by the mother in "helping the child to master the concept of a label" (Ninio and Bruner, 1977). But no theory of rule learning can explain how the process begins or why it has a regulated rate of growth. Harré, the author of the "ethogenic" concept of the creation of rules in society, admits that after one has accepted that rules govern human social behaviour "there would still remain the question of the explanation of the universality of certain social types and presentation styles" (Harré, 1974a, p. 182).

At 9 months the child within the already practiced turn-taking format of communication, reciprocates efforts to give communication, e.g. by handing over an object. The child "learns to deal with deixis in an action situation; shifting from the role of recipient to being agent, with the previous agent as recipient" (Bruner, 1975, p. 15). This is an accurate description of the behaviour, but the word "learns" is gratuitous unless the emphasis is carefully maintained, not on the origin of deixis, but on how to "deal with" or control it.

There is, indeed, a seemingly endless list of new achievements at about 9 months, all of which require the baby to identify with and reciprocate attentions of others, or to treat his or her own intentions as objects of interest (symbols?) in a field of communication. How could the following be mastered for the first time at about 9 or 10 months by infants in different societies and different decades unless the common "rule of sharing" were innate and regulated by growth to be active at this age?

Invokes adult help in performing a task with an object (Piaget, 1952; Bates et al., 1975);

lies down on a pillow pretending (for other's benefit?) to go to sleep (Piaget, 1962);

performs "functional" play with toys (e.g. a telephone), using them in "adult determined purposes" (Zalazzo, 1977);

returns affection in the learned form of an embrace or kiss;

waves "bye bye";

plays appropriately with cup, spoon and saucer showing awareness of the function;

obeys simple requests, e.g. "Give me cup";

removes inappropriate clothes, e.g. a bonnet put on indoors;

imitates demonstrated actions on objects including pointing to an object with exclamatory vocalization;

marks paper with a pencil in imitation, paying close attention to marks made (Griffiths, 1954);

plays peek-a-boo, hiding own face for another to watch;

opens and closes a book, looking at mother after each move;

holds a cup to the mother's or doll's mouth;

shows toes when these are named by the mother (Bruner, 1975);

points to indicate objects that are beyond reach or in a picture form and unmanipulable (Bates *et al.*, 1975; Ninio and Bruner, 1977).

Everything in these acts is specified to a referent person or is in a recognized system of meaning.

The development, at the same time as these shared acts, of the ability to understand words and then to name is evidently dependent on the achievement of communicative "reciprocation" about topics. Ninio and Bruner's (1977) study of talk with a picture book is an excellent demonstration of how the infant's knowledge of entities and the development of distinctions between and within them may be facilitated in a game of saying names while intentionally exchanging interest about shared foci.

Nine months is the time of appearance of Halliday's "protolanguage" in which his son, lacking words, could yet vocalize a number of distinct functions in joint action (instrumental "I want"; regulatory "Do as I say"; interactional "Me and you"; personal "Here I come"). All of these depend on interaction of communicative intent to define "acts of meaning", a more general achievement than the understanding and sharing of names for recognized entities (Halliday, 1975). Dore (1975) has also emphasized that well before they speak children can vocalize acts of speaking and quickly adapt prosodic inflections of subtle meaning.

In a detailed study of the development of acts of communication in three female infants in Rome, Bates *et al.* (1975) find evidence that attainment of the ability to perform "illocutionary" acts, acts that have a consciously intended aim to command assistance of another, or to transmit a declaration of experience or intent to another, depends upon attainment of Piaget's Stage V at about 10 months. There seems to be some confusion of chronology, but understanding how to use adults as tools (means controlled with respect to a specified end) is stated to depend on mastery of the object schema, achievement of intentionality and ritualization of acts of orienting or prehension so they become "more appropriate for communicating desire to an adult". Halliday describes the same kinds of behavioural change, without reference to Piaget, as steps in emergence of a language function. In one study "proto-cognition" is primary, the other says "protolanguage" is fundamental.

There is undoubtedly considerable agreement about what infants do in communication during the first year, now that the behaviour is being studied with sufficient attention to its subtle patterns. But none of the published accounts satisfactorily explain the consistent changes.

Given what 2-month-olds can do in mutual awareness with their mothers, it seems simplest to conclude that at 9 months there is attainment of functional control, of intrinsic origin, for the use of innate and practiced communicative abilities so they can be related to physical objects that have been brought inside the field of shared experience and shared knowledge. All of the above examples fit the hypothesis of Fig. 9 that development of the infant mind brings together newly elaborated intentions to things and the giving of messages to people. We see no evidence that this achievement is the result of practice of specific rituals (rules of conduct) learned with a consistent companion. We think the acquisition of specific practices gives necessary definition to a process which is caused by change in the structures of intelligence at a deeper level; one which is basically the same for all infants. If there is insufficient opportunity for the infant to communicate, the developing function might well be weakened or even permanently disfigured. This does not mean it is not inherent and self-regulating in growth.

Further evidence concerning the growth of a fundamental mechanism of infant personality and person-perception by infants comes from observations of the few psychoanalysts who have actually studied infants, principally those of the British Object Relations School. Although analysts tend not to study the world-perceiving cognitive systems of infants adequately, they do sensitively observe personal co-operation or resistance of the infant with the mother. Since Freud made his revolutionary inferences about infant sexuality, psychoanalysis has projected findings from dissection of adult psychodynamics and from observation of regressive changes into preverbal states of the self. Direct observation of infants did not come until after a set of developmental notions had been obtained in this downward or backward way. Meliane Klein was the first to postulate infantile neuroses (Segal, 1967). She observed that after 9 months the baby was capable of remorse for causing pain to a loved one ("depressive position"). This requires that the infant develop a concept of relationship between a distinct self and another (object relation). Interestingly, this is the age at which an infant first shows self-consciousness in a mirror (Amsterdam, 1972).

It is even more recent that a few psychoanalysts, experienced with psychoses of childhood, have explored developments in normal infancy to test basic assumptions of personality development. Spitz (1965) was a pioneer, but he does not have a detailed account of the changes we are concerned with. He attributes the attainment of autonomy (the ability to say "No") to a stage toward the middle of the second year. He underestimates the personal consciousness of the infant and overstresses, as Bowlby (1969) too, has done, the specific instinctual bond to the mother as a caretaker who imitates what the infant does. His classical study of smiling (Spitz and Wolff, 1946) is surpassed by that of Peter Wolff (1963) which brings the true interpersonal communication, through vision, to the fore.

Margaret Mahler (1963) found the mother and infant to form a symbiotic community that achieves a climax of intensity between 6 and 8 months. The mother, fused to the infant's mental organization until "separation-individuation" of the infant's ego, is considered the catalyst of this process in which the infant develops a distinction between his own body, its sensations and functions, and the mother. This is close to the orthodox Freudian position. Mahler attributes changes in the emotional dependence of the child on the mother, and panic when she is felt lost, to the process of separation driven by both sensory-perceptive and motor changes. Locomotion at 9 months, for example, may pull the child too far out of a "security base" and cause panic in the child.

Winnicott (1965), who took a balanced view of all psychological functions in infant personal relations, insists on the need to treat the mother and infant as a unit, with the infant and child moving from absolute dependence through relative dependence to independence, the mother changing in parallel. He claims that if the maternal care is "adequate in important respects", "all stages of emotional growth can be roughly dated". From the "holding phase" of the neonate, in which the mother is in a state of "primary maternal preoccupation", the infant attains a "unit status" as a person "living with" the mother; that is, from being merged with the mother to being relatively separate from her. In the condition of relative dependence the infant can be aware of details of maternal care and relate them to personal impulses. This would appear to acknowledge a rudimentary intersubjectivity. The mother adapts by regulating a "steady presentation of the world to the infant" (as in the games we observed with Tracey). The first sign that the infant knows about dependence is, Winnicott believed, in manifestations of anxiety when the mother is away "beyond the time-span of (the infant's) capacity to believe in her survival". When the infant is 6 months to 2 years old the need for a healthy mother is "fierce and terrible". This is the period of special attachment to the mother or principle companion, when deprivation effects are severe (Spitz, 1965; Bowlby, 1969;

Rutter, 1972). The effect of the new mental mechanisms of the ego "is that the infant can allow for events that are outside his or her control. . . . Then speech becomes understood." In an intermediate stage of healthy development, a most important experience in relation to a potentially satisfying object is refusal of it. Then, as the object changes from being subjectively to objectively perceived, two new things appear, "the individual's use . . . of communication, and the individual's non-communicating self". These would match the communicative mode on the one hand and the praxic and reflective modes on the other.

Winnicott's account of normal development records a change in communication between the infant and mother from "active non-communication" regarding topics of interest during transition (4 to 6 months), to acceptance of reciprocal communication when the infant's separation as an independent experiencer and actor has reached an initial stage of completeness. Apparently this stage is arrived at, at least in our film situation where there can be unhurried enjoyment of each other and toys by mother and infant, when the infant is about 9 months of age. It is, according to Winnicott, a maturational change of the infant, dependent on the quality of the facilitating environment provided by the mother and other family members.

Fairbairn (1949) considered the ego to be governed in its functions not by impulses of pleasure but by relationships to "objects". That is, the fundamental property of the ego is to govern relations (between persons) and there is no need to postulate a separate unorganized "id" as a generator of primitive impulses. Thus Fairbairn arrives at a theory of innate predisposition to relate interpersonally and to social circumstances. Social life for him depended on the mechanisms of relating. Feelings of pleasure-seeking or aggression represent failures of the "object relation", not sources of personal energy. This comes close to Macmurray's theory of the innate "field of the personal" (Macmurray, 1961) and leads on to a view of the infant as inherently sensitive to the opportunities which personal relations offer.

The importance of the analytical perspective for our present purpose is that it emphasizes that the infant's ability to master objects in acts of developing intentionality must be closely tied to growth of independence from interpersonal symbiosis with the mother. Interpersonal communication must develop in some conflict with the emergence of separate, individual acts of conscious intent by the infant for himself. Co-operative use of experience, essential to language, involves joint control of these two modes of action.

CONCLUSION

The behaviour of infants in relation to others shows that they possess a rudimentary but complex understanding of persons, and that they are adapted to co-operate in joint intentions. Out of this person-relating ability, a baby develops a will to share the foci of interest in situations and to define objects of use within acts of meaning.

In the development of fundamental human skills, a regulated pattern of change is clear in the first year of life. A large step towards confidence in "self" and confiding in others is expressed at about 9 months. It is significant that the word *confidence* means both skill in making acts as an independent self, and a sense of being in a trusting relationship to another self.

Developments of personality and of communication in infancy cannot be explained by attending only to the cognitive achievements of the infant as an isolated perceiver and intender. They are probably not dependent on explorations with objects and acquisition of schemata for constant properties of objects.

The discoveries outlined in this paper illuminate a philosophic mystery that often has been made unapproachable by one-sidedness of interest in socially transmitted experience and a catalogue of learned social skills.

As Hamlyn (1974) and Habermas (1970, 1972) have argued, human understanding of people, linguistic or otherwise, requires an ability to stand in relation to a person as a person, and to act with intersubjectivity when relating to rhythms and patterns of experience. Habermas' "dialogue constituent universals" or Vygotsky's "intermental" processes (Vygotsky, 1962), are to be seen as outcomes of infantile knowledge of persons and of how to act with confidence in relation to them. The intrinsic pattern of infant initiatives and responses is as much a creator of the mother's play, baby talk or instruction as any pattern of intention, inherent or acquired, in the mother.

The vocabulary of **language**, games, toys and all other cultural artifacts enrich the possibilities of life of an infant because they meet the infant's habits of intersubjectivity. Changes at certain ages, such as the change at 9 months, cause the rules of interaction to change. People in the social world react by becoming affectionate, co-operative, interested and talkative, adapting to the forms of social action that seem most natural to an infant at each age.

APPENDIX

Details of Tracey's Development in her First 6 Months

In weeks 3 and 4 Tracey was alert for brief periods in a vertical chair and she oriented to and tracked a coloured 3 in. ball suspended 8-12 in. from her face. Co-ordinated *prereaching* movements which she aimed to this object have been analysed in detail to reveal a regular, periodic temporal programming and precise sequencing of movement in limb segments (Trevarthen and Hubley, in preparation).

At 4 weeks a quiet interchange lasting 1½ minutes was filmed while Tracey was lying supine in her mother's lap. She looked up at her mother who, leaning over, watched Tracey's face closely and spoke quietly to her. Tracey fixed her gaze on her mother's face and every few seconds made small gestures with arm and hand with gradually increasing regularity and strength, and smiles and mouth movements of *prespeech*. These communicative acts were waited for and responded to appreciatively by her mother, whose periodic phrases of speaking certainly stimulated Tracey in return. This reciprocal exchange has the typical affectionate intimacy of *primary intersubjectivity* (Trevarthen, 1977a). The "personalization" of Tracey by her mother is shown by the following transcript of her speech:

> Pushing are you? Feet cold are they? Hey? Oooh! (softly) Is that better! Oooh!
> Is that better? Oh yes, indeed yes! Ooooh! Hum? Come on! Poor feet! Oooh! Hum,
> hum? Why did it have to happen? (said when Tracey looks fretful) Are you not
> sitting up right?

In the next few months Tracey showed normal development of interest in objects and communication with persons. However, though she smiled and made gestures and prespeech to her mother and to other persons who spoke gently to her, she was more inclined to look at people in an absorbed, unsmiling way than some babies we have seen at this age and often she withdrew her gaze. This correlates with anxiety and distress of her mother who, at this time stated that she was neither happy nor fully confident of her ability to care for Tracey. At the end of the third month Tracey's mother was worried that she was not feeding Tracey sufficiently, and she woke at night fearing Tracey had died. In spite of these signs of strain in **adapting** to her baby, Tracey's mother provided affectionate care and support.

At 10 weeks our film shows Tracey looking down with an eager playful but unsmiling face avoiding her mother's gaze most of the time they were filmed together. Tracey's mother twice tried to attract Tracey's attention by touching her on the nose, and once Tracey abruptly pulled away. She grasped her mother's extended finger and held it while looking down with a slight smile.

At 16 and 17 weeks Tracey was again preoccupied and wary with people in the lab, though smiling. She looked intently at her mother's mouth and at the mouth of a friendly female partner who spoke gently to her. Tracey's mother held up her watch on her wrist and moved it about for Tracey to "track". This captured Tracey's intense interest but she soon looked away, then made a characteristic friendly glance to her mother's eyes with raising of the eyebrows and a slight smile before looking away again. Once she grinned at her mother with a "resistant" teasing expression then looked down to avoid her mother's gaze. She was strongly attracted to nearly suspended objects making jerky attempts to reach, and aiming her mouth. She oriented her hands visually and made grabs, once successfully hooking her partly opened hand round a hanging ball to pull it to her mouth.

Tracey was probably not greatly distressed or disturbed in development by her mother's mild anxiety, but all who watched her closely felt she may have been affected. We believe she was less fluent in primary intersubjective behaviour at 2 months than she might have been. At 3 months when other infants have shown avoidance of eye-to-eye contact (Sylvester-Bradley and Trevarthen, 1977) Tracey's mother was most anxious. We do not know what was the relationship between the two effects, but it is possible that the mother's confidence, already shaky, fell significantly when Tracey became more self-absorbed, or interested in use of her own body, and looked at her mother less. Tracey's visual attending to objects in the third month and early reaching at 4 months were vigorously healthy.

At 21 weeks, after a vacation of 4 weeks over Christmas and New Year, Tracey joined in a social game in which her mother held her hands up high, moving them about and waggling her fingers while Tracey tracked closely looking from hand to hand, moving her own hands and laughing. The mother accompanied her hand movements with clicking of her tongue and a hissing sound "Pss, psss, psss!" In this game her mother gained communication by adapting to Tracey's visual interest in objects and to her readiness for tracking them with strong head and eye movements, and was also exciting a preference Tracey had shown in watching hands, both her own and other persons. Tracey's behaviour was eager and excitedly happy.

Next Tracey's mother held up for her a puppet motivated by a dangling string with a bead at the end. At home Tracey had quickly learned to grasp and pull the string to make the arms and legs flap up and down. With help from her mother Tracey made the puppet move, watching it intently with open mouth and smile. Now Tracey's extension of the arm to reach was well controlled and she groped accurately adjusting her hands precisely to approach and withdrawal of the suspended ball.

She also picked up an object from her mother's extended palm but plainly refused to return it to the hand when requested to do so. Instead, she held it back to the side to drop it on the floor. This taking and dropping was repeated several times. Most of the time Tracey's attention was firmly on the objects presented, but once she looked at her mother's face and grinned at her instead of returning the object as requested, then absent-mindedly dropped it into the well-positioned waiting hand while looking away to the background. The act of returning the object was not deliberate. Immediately Tracey postured with extended arms and a pursed lip, teasing expression as if aware of resisting her mother's will at the same time as she acquiesced in a grudging apparently uncontrolled way, to the request to give the object. While taking offered objects, she only glanced occasionally at her mother's face and failed to place the object back in the open hand. On several occasions, after dropping the toy, she looked up an grinned to her mother who laughed as soon as Tracey's gaze met her own. There can be no doubt that Tracey's expression of pleasure at the effect she achieved was *shared*. It was deliberately oriented to her mother.

Tracey's mother played a game, poking the object on Tracey's stomach. Later Tracey pushed aside an offered object and then took an object with an introspective, unwilling manner, looking away. A moment later she looked quizzically at her mother, unsmiling, and then suddenly laughed. Her mother was very happy about this and Tracey, in turn, vocalized excitedly, holding her head back and making large gestures. Finally they played a game with an object which the mother animated by waggling it in her hand.

The take-and-drop game was also played with a female stranger who received eager but unsmiling interest from Tracey. When this person offered an object on her open palm and looked at Tracey, Tracey looked away flapping her hand. Then she stared at the object, head down, hands held out to the side moving. For some seconds Tracey gently resisted offers by hand, then she grasped the object when it was dangled from a thread. Later she took the object from the stranger's palm several times, each time dropping it without attempting to respond to the request that it be "given" back. Tracey was less eager to play a game with the stranger than with her mother just before. She did not join in an exchange of pleasure with the stranger as she did with her mother.

10

The Transition from Action to Gesture

ROGER A. CLARK

Hull University, England

This chapter could be thought of as an extension of, and a tribute to, the highly original thought of the pragmatist philosopher George Herbert Mead. At around the turn of the century, when psychology was searching for ways to be respectably scientific, he pointed the way to a conceptual system that could eliminate the bugbears of determinism and mind/matter dualism from a scientific psychology. In other words, he offered a new paradigm in the most global and encompassing sense of Kuhn's (1962) term. It is a matter of history that psychology, as an academic discipline, opted for the Watson solution, which was to continue with the old, inadequate paradigm but include a directive to ignore those aspects of it which were uncomfortable and unscientific seeming. That solution, I believe, accounts for the unsatisfactory nature of much contemporary psychological theorizing and so-called scientific psychological investigation (see Chein, 1972; Koch, 1961). The only method that science has is to attempt to *understand*, and the approach presented here is to be judged by its potential in helping the understanding of the nature of language and of communication.

The first section points to what I believe is the most serious inadequacy of cognitive-type conceptions of language development, and presents a radically different view of the nature of communication. This is followed by a brief description of the method of this particular study and a consideration of the nature of adult giving and taking, since it is by means of focusing on giving and taking that the "paradigm", or conceptual system, will be presented. The second section considers the construction of the communicative structures which organize mother-child interaction in the first months of the child's life. The third section will point to the possibilities of this framework being developed here in the understanding of communication in a broader, evolutionary perspective. This leads on to a description of the first major transition in type of communication in mother-child interaction, the emergence of gesutres, and concomitantly of intentional communication. The final section concerns the next transition, from gesture-mediated communication structures to those mediated by arbitrarily selected noises which is, of course, language proper.

A FRAMEWORK FOR A STUDY OF COMMUNICATION

Sooner or later anyone who is trying to understand communication processes has to ask and to answer one fundamental question about communication: what is it for? The kind of answer given will condition to a great extent the kind of study undertaken. Up until very recently, the answer which informed most psychological study was that communication is for allowing individuals to express themselves. This derives quite naturally from our experience as language-using adults, in that we find we have things to say and sometimes we have difficulty in finding the means to express them. Applying this conception to the development of communication leads to a particular sort of study, in which the child is viewed as a cognitively functioning entity who is trying to deduce from what goes on around him the appropriate means of expressing himself. For example, Brown and Fraser (1964) surmise that the growing child hears a sample of the sentences of a language and "induces" from these an implicit grammar, using the perceived regularities in the sentences. "First language learning so conceived, reminds us of two other operations with language: that of the linguist in the field and that of the adult learning a second language."

Brown and Fraser point out that this is only an analogy, but implicit in its use is the notion of the child approaching language already in possession of some highly sophisticated cognitive equipment, and the attempt to explain the acquisition of language through the child's exercise of these abilities. In contrast, it may seem to some people that these abilities are the very ones that human beings possess as a result of being language users!

The basic elements of this fundamental conception are the child and his environment. The child is a detective attempting to logically derive from his environment the means to express what he has inside himself. Even the addition of a "social" element does not change the basic conception. For example, if one looks at ongoing interaction it is very tempting to analyse situations in terms of what the child was "really" trying to express, the effect his behaviour has on the other person and what this person was trying to express. This, of course, amounts to successively applying the same individualistic model to one participant and then the other.

In real-life situations it is common for an observer to hear the child utter a noise which to him appears unintelligible but which the mother obviously interprets as significant. The observer then has the problem of deciding whether the infant was really saying a word or whether the mother was reading in more than was there. Obviously, the only way to decide this is to see if the noise functions as a word. If the function of communication is to express what is inside, then one will need to know whether the "word" expresses what the child wanted it to express in order to know whether it is really that word. This could prove difficult, to say the least. I feel that this problem is *in principle* insoluble, and furthermore that this undermines the viability of the whole approach. Consequently, this particular attempt to answer the question of the function of communication should be abandoned in favour of an approach which allows a child's earliest utterances to be considered *indeterminate* in intent until made determinate by the interpretations placed upon them by adults (see Ryan, 1974, for a discussion of the role of interpretation in psychological theories of language acquisition).

Mead also objected to this view of the function of communication, which he expressed graphically thus (Strauss, 1964):

> The philologist . . . has often taken the view of the prisoner in a cell. The prisoner knows that others are in a like position and he wants to get in communication with them. So he sets about some method of communication, some arbitrary affair, perhaps, such as tapping on the wall. Now, each of us, on this view, is shut up in his own shell of consciousness and, knowing that there are other people so shut up, develops ways to set up communication with them.

It is apparent that the "prisoners in cells" concept of communication is at the root of most contemporary theories of language development, and that it is an inadequate and misleading notion. By contrast, I start here from the proposition that *communication is that which is involved in the co-ordination of the separate activities of two or more individuals into a single social activity.* In the course of this chapter I hope to be able to show that this apparently innocent statement represents a radical departure from the usual mode of psychological theorizing but a full discussion of these issues is not possible here (see Clark, in preparation). The first practical effect of this view is that it directs attention towards instances where activities are meshed together rather than to those, usually ambiguous, instances where an infant is thought to have "expressed" something.

An important idea incorporated into this framework is the notion that the complication of this basic communicative function in the course of development gives rise to the feeling in an individual that he has something to express and the means to express it. What is meant by "complication" in this context can be conveyed by an analogy. The basic life function of metabolism is effected in many different ways in different life forms. In single-celled organisms it is at its simplest with the ingestion of complex molecules, elimination of waste product, catalysis and the release of energy to the organism. In the case of, say, a cow the process is considerably more complex involving the intricacies of the bovine digestive system, respiratory system and so on. However, the basic metabolic function underlies the process in the higher organism as in the single-celled organism. In precisely the same way, I suggest that the basic function of communication as described above underlies all communication, and human language represents a complication of this function. The development of language can be viewed as a progressive complication of the basic communicative function, and the emergence of certain abilities in conjunction with this. Instead of assuming at the outset that the infant has abilities by the exercise of which he can *fit himself* into social structures, I shall try to explain how the child comes to possess certain abilities as *a result* of being already immersed in such structures. This approach bears a close relation to Mead's (1934) pragmatic analysis of the nature of language and language derived abilities, and is also related to some extent to Vygotsky's (1966) writings.

The Transfer of Objects

It is easy to see co-ordination of activity when the outcome is concrete, so for this reason I have concentrated on the transfer of objects between mother and child as an instance of the application of this framework. Furthermore, this kind of activity seems to occupy a large proportion of the non-essential activity of a mother and her young child. However, in considering this type of activity one must take care *not* to treat it as separate from the rest of the infant's experience simply because it is analytically convenient to take it as a self-contained set of observations. This is because developments in this sphere are important in other aspects of the child's experience and there is no reason to suppose that the child separates it.

The data upon which this discussion is based are naturalistic, longitudinal observations of three mother-child dyads. Videotape equipment was taken into the children's homes and the mothers were asked to do with their children as far as possible what they normally did with them when giving them full attention. The mothers were not told that they themselves were an important part of the observations, so care was needed to ensure that they did not just sit back and let the child "get on with it". We will be concerned with the development of these children up to about 18 months old.

By word of justification, the phrase "the transfer of objects" is used here rather than "giving and taking" because of the imprecision of the latter terms. When we speak of giving and taking something, we impute a fairly sophisticated knowledge of social relations to the actors. We assume they act in relation to a nexus of possibilities which might be described thus: (1) I offer this to him, (2) He requests this from me, (3) He offers this to me, (4) I request this from him. For the adult, "giving" is part of this interrelated knot of social possibilities, that is, if one offers an object it is in the full knowledge of what being offered an object is like. The two situations are instances of the same social act with merely a reversal of roles. This is an important point when it comes to evaluating the child's behaviour. As outlined above, adult giving and taking involves two components: (1) from whom and to whom the object goes (who takes which role), (2) whether the act is initiated by the intending recipient or the intending donor. This structure is set out diagrammatically in Fig. 1. If an adult initiates one of these forms it is in full knowledge of its relation to the other forms whereas it seems quite conceivable that the young child does not relate situations in which he gains an object to those in which he loses one. That is to say, he may well treat them as separate kinds of situation instead of the same situation with a reversal of role. I think that the child cannot be said to be giving and taking (with their adult implications) until he has related these four situations together, so here I use the more neutral term, "transfer of objects".

DIRECTION OF TRANSFER

		FROM A TO B	FROM B TO A
INITIATOR OF EXCHANGE	A	A OFFERS AND B ACCEPTS	A REQUESTS AND B COMPLIES BY GIVING
	B	B REQUESTS AND A COMPLIES BY GIVING	B OFFERS AND A ACCEPTS

Fig. 1. The four possible situations arising in the transfer of an object between adults A and B.

Social/Communicative Structures

It will be convenient here to say something about the notion of a "communicative structure" (which is central to this exposition) since structure is one of those highly useful words with a certain plasticity of meaning. The four quadrants of Fig. 1 could be said to be social/communicative structures at a low level, and the four quadrants together in relation to one another as a single higher order structure. A communicative structure is a negotiated co-ordination of activities which "belongs" to the community whose social activity it helps to regulate. Members of the community can call upon such structures to give order and sense to their interactions. What a scientific psychologist can observe in any real situation is only partially regulated in terms of such structures. This is because part of the interaction is moment to moment, opportunist and unstructured and provides the material for the (unreflective) negotiation of new structures. This is important to realize when dealing with developmental issues. One could draw an analogy between the visual and the social worlds. In order to make continuing sense of the visual world, the organism needs an interrelated set of expectations which allow it to perceive a stable world. Similarly social/communicative structures make possible for the individual a stable social world, in which he can have long and short-term expectations as to the outcomes of his own activity.

ACTION

Much of the interaction seen between mothers and their very young infants (before about 5 months) is difficult to see as communication, but is nevertheless directly important for later communication. These interactions appear to an observer as abortive or very clumsy attempts to achieve what is smoothly and easily achieved at a later date. For example, the mother may be seen to pick up a rattle and try to get her baby to grasp it, while the baby puts his hand in the wrong place, closes his fingers at the wrong time, gets distracted and so on. The ways of transferring the object to the baby vary widely from occasion to occasion because of the general incompetence of the infant and the accommodations the mother is forced to make to his only partially structured activity. However, at a later date "baby have object" is achieved in a highly stereotyped and efficient manner, that is to say there has developed a stable social/communicative structure such that the behaviours of the participants can mesh together smoothly. When the child is born many of his activities are structured, but the contexts in which his activity can be exercised have yet to be determined. For example, Trevarthen (1974a) in his microanalytical studies of infant behaviour has isolated modes of activity which he calls "prereaching":

> Reaching for and manipulating objects seen begins about the end of the fourth month. Before this time there are highly structured movements of "prereaching", as we call it, which show that the infant can intend to reach for an object. But, the performance is inadequate.

Though it is arguable whether these movements show the child to be intending to reach, Trevarthen has described something of great importance. There is no doubt that responsive adults construe these activities as "wanting" the object, as if the child had intentions which it was physically incapable of implementing, and it is this *interpretation* of the child's activity that is of paramount importance. Thus the mother takes it upon herself to fulfil the apparent intentions of her child and many situations arise in which the mother is accommodating the world to the activities of the child. In a sense, then, the mother takes the activity of a baby and places it in a behavioural context such that it becomes comprehensible to herself and to the infant. She will adjust the orientation of the object, its place of contact on the infant's hand and generally use any means at her disposal to arrive at the point where the child has the object in its grasp. In other words, she arranges things such that the child's actions *in fact* become effective in precisely the way that she interpreted them. In this way the child can do things and intend to do them before he is physically capable of success on his own: social activity precedes individual capacity.

A mother, then, will take the grasping and reaching movements of a neonate, movements which are not yet related to the physical world, interpret them as evidence for intelligible intentions from her cultural standpoint and by manipulating the environment *construct* the action that the movements imply. Having performed these actions with mother's assistance the child has been shown a relation between his body and the world. Thus he can now *intend* to do this thing, having done it before, though he may be unable to achieve a successful completion of his intention without assistance. This process, the induction in the child of socially intelligible intentions, can easily be seen as an instance of Vygotsky's (1966) maxim:

> Any function in the childs cultural development appears . . . first among people as an intermental category and then within the child as an intramental category.

Furthermore, this process is such that there is necessarily a certain mutual intelligibility of intentions between mother and child, which is a fundamental prerequisite for their further development of communication.

This view does not accord very well with other views on the development of reaching. For example, Bower (1974) argues that: "the development of reaching can be described as the result of maturational processes with sharpening due to simple learning effects." He notes that very many studies show that neonates reach for objects quite a lot with a rather poor hit rate and then there seems to be a decline in reaching until about 20 weeks, when it again becomes productive and with a vastly improved hit rate, despite the apparent lack of use. However, in his own experiments infants exposed to the experimental situation every day showed no decline so "The decline in reaching that is normally observed must therefore result from lack of use of the behaviour, rather than from inevitable neural growth processes." Thus he seems to argue that the considerable evidence for this decrease in reaching in experimental situations reported by other workers arises because most children are deprived of objects to reach for!

What this type of analysis overlooks is that the experimental situation bears little relation to real life as experienced by the child. Mothers actively assist their infants, whereas the "objectivity" of the experiment denies this possibility. We can reinterpret his results in this way: most objects are out of reach for the young infant, but he is assured of 100% hit rates with objects held by people. Thus we need not be surprised if he seldom reaches outside of the social context, though within that context he is learning much about reaching and manipulating objects. Infants exposed to the peculiar and unhelpful experimental situation every day learn of its possibilities and show no decline simply because they are getting experience that other infants rarely get. It is evident that this is a case of objective experimental methods giving rise to a distorted account of development, because they isolate the child from his social context and assume that aspects of the child's development that in fact have a social history are manifestations of the solitary organism.

In the early phases of communication development, the kind of process described above, i.e. the induction of socially intelligible intentions, gives rise to a structure exemplified by Fig. 2. This is a stable structure of smooth, co-operative activity with considerable anticipation on the part of the child which was previously lacking. We can now talk of a social/communicative structure having been negotiated. Both the child and the mother have expectations in this certain situation which lead to a smooth interaction. This structure corresponds to the adult type situation "A offers and B accepts" in Fig. 1, except that there is no interchangeability of role. It is more limited than the adult structure. The object passes from mother to child with the mother taking the relatively more active role. Whereas in the early stages the mother did most of the work, she now requires more from the child before helping. Typically, she holds an object in front of the child at about eye level and somewhere near the limit of the child's reach. Then she waits for the child to reach out toward it. When the act is well established and providing she has the child's full attention, she will not have to wait long since sometimes the child is reaching even before she has completed the act of bringing the object to eye level and within reach.

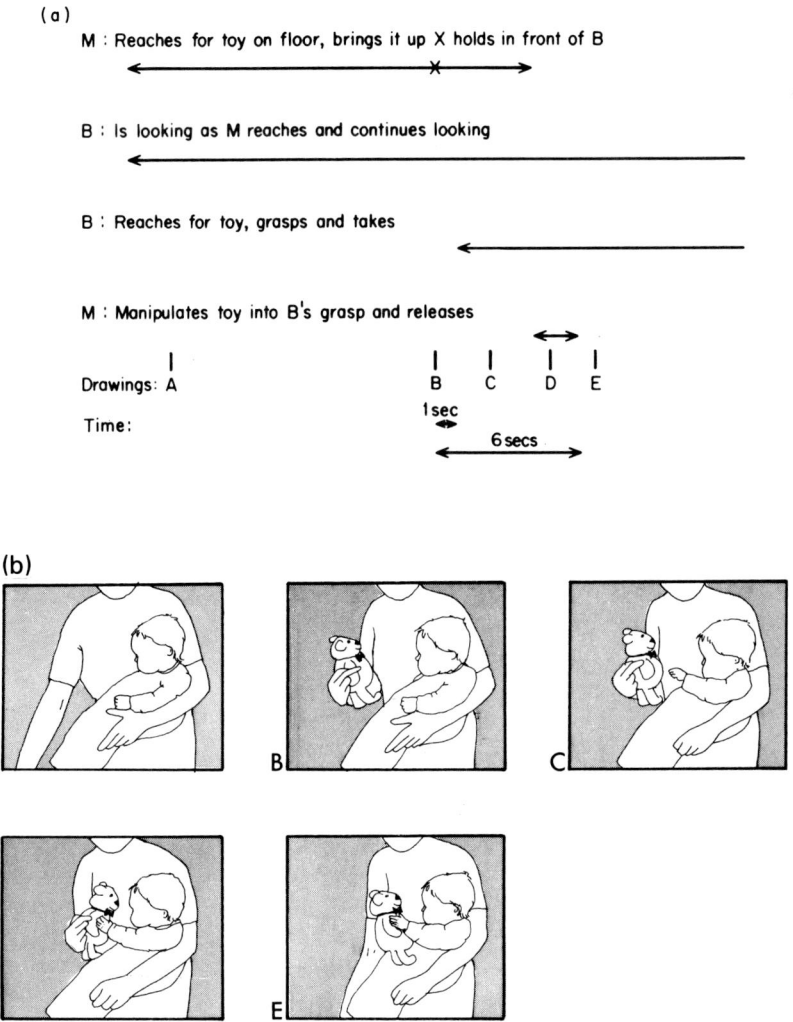

Fig. 2(a), (b). The smooth transfer of an object from mother to infant (age 0;4(11)), with the infant taking the relatively passive role. An actualization of a primitive communication structure. (All drawings by Josephine Wood from videotape stills.)

Transcription

There is a problem, in any observational type of study, of how to write down what is observed in a way that does not pre-judge too many issues. There has been, up to now, a consensus that "units" of behaviour can be isolated and a real-life interaction can plausibly be represented as a succession of such units. Newson (1977) has pointed out the many shortcomings of this method, but the most serious is the least obvious: that this method leads one into thinking of the ongoing *activities* of two organisms as the successive "emitting" of object-like "gestures" which are treated as if they were automatic "responses" to previous "gestures". It is very important *not* to think of the child as learning a "response" to a stimulus provided by the mother, but as coming to organize his activity in a certain way (which he can extend to other contexts) and co-ordinating this activity with the corresponding acts of the mother. It was in order to transcribe sequences in a way amenable to this *active* conception of human behaviour that the method used in the figures here was devised.

In this method, I essentially describe the ongoing activity of the mother on one line and the activity of the child concurrently beneath. Each organized segment of an *individual's* activity can be represented as a line indicating its duration and a few words describing its nature. The relative timing of the individuals' respective acts is accurately represented and it can be seen that each instant in the time scale (i.e. a line drawn vertically) intersects the acts of individuals in different stages of completion so that a still photograph (now converted into drawings) can be precisely located within the scheme. In this way the written description and the drawings complement each other, the diagrammatic scheme providing a context for the drawings and the drawings giving substance to the written descriptions. Separate phases of an individual's organized act can be indicated by a cross where one phase replaces the other. For ease, successive acts of the same individual are described on different lines while maintaining a single time dimension across the diagram. This method is fairly time consuming but has the overwhelming advantage that it can convey a full description without the distortions entailed by other methods.

The Construction of Primitive Communication Structures

The process being described here has its end point represented in the above fashion in Fig. 2. In the early stages of the process the mother makes effective the movements of the infant in the way that she interprets them, but although the object usually does pass eventually to the child, the route is highly variable and there is a series of moment to moment co-ordinations unified only by the mother's intentions. In the fullness of time there evolves from this a stable structure of social activity which is essentially the same in form on different occasions, and of course many different objects are assimilated to the same structure. The mother decides upon the object and holds it before the infant, somewhere around the limit of the child's reach and she maintains this posture until the child reaches for the object. She then adjusts the distance and the orientation of the object so that the child can grasp it. She then releases it.

The details of this evolution are a matter for investigation, but it is certain that it involves *anticipation* of the other's action by the child. In fact, we find that often simply reaching for an object is enough to direct the child's attention to it so that sometimes the child is reaching for it before it is actually offered and there results a beautiful synchrony of activity. Lock (this volume) has also described this increase of anticipation by the child of the end result of a mother's activity with respect to arm-raising to be picked up.

The importance of this communicative structure is that it is a stable element in the interactions the infant is involved in, in a sea of moment to moment reactions of one to the other. It can be described as a social object, that is, an enduring entity in the field of possible interactions. This must be the first major step in the development of communication. There is a change from moment to moment co-ordination of activity, a basic form of communication which suffers from a lack of structure over time, to stable, repeatable segments of social activity.

These structures involve a kind of communication which, for want of a better word, can be called "primitive". Primitive communication structures are characterized by the fact that they do not involve the use of "gestures" by the child. The term "gesture" is used here in a very specific way in the sense of being the means of *intentional* communication. The meaning of the technical term "gesture" will be expanded upon later, but for the moment the above statement can be justified by considering this: having arrived at this stage there would seem to be no reason why the child could not reach toward an object of his own choice in order to have the object fetched *if* he was aware of the communicative significance of his own actions. If he were to do this the child would have determined the object and what was required of the mother and would impress an observer with his communicative abilities. However, at this stage this does not happen except in the very limited circumstances exemplified in Fig. 3. In this instance it is necessary for the object to be close by, since the child pays scant attention to distant non-mobile objects, and it is necessary that the mother is closely monitoring her child's activity because the child *does not persist with the reach if it fails him.* The implication of this is that the child *is not aware* of the communicative significance of his own actions. If he happens to sight some object almost within reach and reaches out to get it, and if the mother happens to be looking and sees that he is interested in it, then she may get it for him. But if she delays, the reach is terminated and not maintained for the mother to see. The reach is not produced for the mother's benefit and the child does not monitor her to see whether she is looking. In Fig. 3 the child's hand goes up and down as the

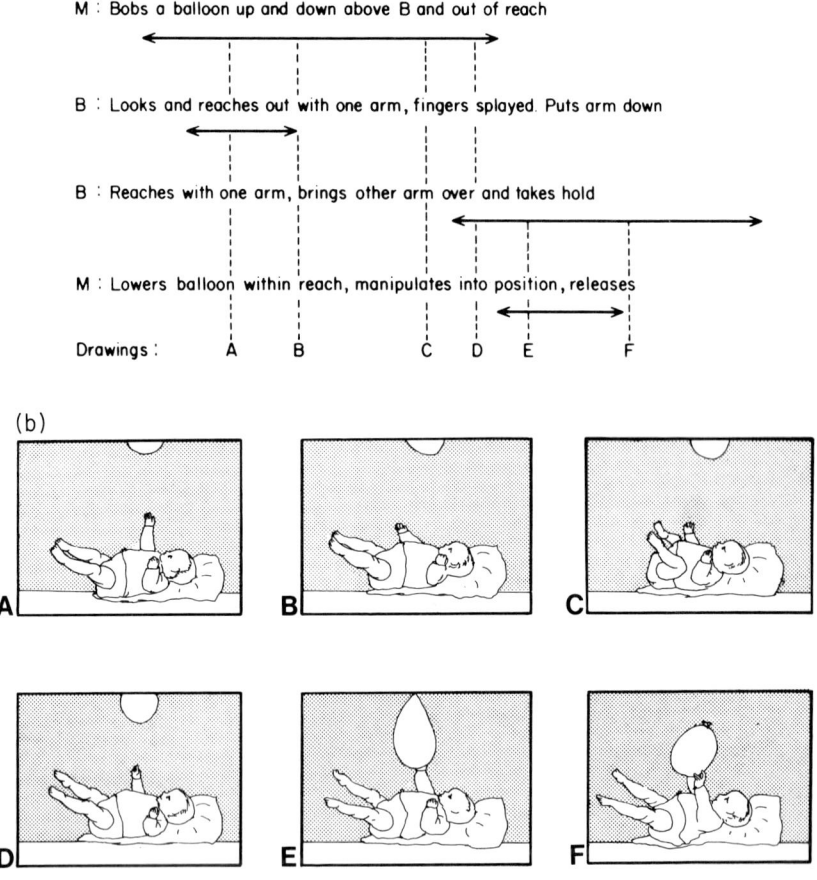

Fig. 3(a), (b). In the primitive stage the infant appears not to persist with an unsuccessful reach. Here Janet (0;6(9)) withdraws her arm on finding the balloon out of reach, and reaches again when it approaches. Although the child may seem to initiate a transfer, at this stage he does *not* reach so that M will see the reach.

balloon approaches and retreats almost as if the two were physically connected. There is a great deal more that needs to be known before this situation can be entirely understood, but for the moment all that needs to be said is that this is tied in with the nature of primitive communication structures. The main feature of primitive communication structures is that, although the reaching of the child *functions* communicatively the child is only concerned with it as part of the action scheme relevant to getting objects. His action is all of a piece and *directed toward the object* rather than to the mother, and he communicates accidentally as a by-product of these attempted actions in the physical world. On the other hand, the mother's action in holding the object up is gestural, since she is doing it in order that the child will see and do something about it. The path from action to gesture is one where the secular or technical functions of the child's behaviour become differentiated from its communicative functions. In this early stage of the development of communication the child does not separate parts of his activity in the same way that an observer can. An observer can see the child's straining toward an object as a discrete element of behaviour, but for the child his whole activity is centred upon getting hold of the object and at this stage he cannot analyse this all of a piece action into components, one of which has an important communicative function. In the next stage the child comes to "analyse" his actions such that the initial reaching part of the whole act becomes an element of intentional communicative activity, i.e. a gesture. I shall return to this later.

From Infant to Mother

I have looked so far at the transfer of an object from the mother to her infant, which is the first element of the "give/take" complex to emerge. The ability to relinquish an object on purpose, and the wish to do so, does not appear until some time later. The child is much more aware of his surroundings by this time, but the establishment of the primitive communication structure involved in the transfer of an object from the child to the mother, with the child in the relatively passive role, seems to follow the same general lines as the above. This is the situation where the infant complies with the mother's request for an object in the infant's grasp. The transcription below indicates one possible way in which this structure could be established:

> Janet (age 0;8(12)) is sitting up on the floor playing with a partly filled, plastic bottle of baby shampoo, which she seems to find very interesting.
> M: "Janet, give that to mummy, darling." Holds her hand, palm upwards, toward the bottle.

J: Looks at M and then at the hand.
M: "Give that to mummy." Moves hand forward to hold the bottle.
J: Is watching the hand as it moves.
M: Pulls gently at the bottle, J having made no attempt to give it to her. "Thank you."
J: Is reluctant to let go and tries to keep hold of the bottle as it is taken. This leaves her arm outstretched as the bottle is pulled from her grasp.

Apparently, in the early stages of setting up this structure in this dyad, the mother, in any one instance, starts by making the "palm-up" conventional gesture. When this is unsuccessful, which of course it must be as the child does not as yet have any means of anticipating the implications of this posture, the mother takes hold of the object. The child still fails to release so she then gently removes the object. In this way, the child can come to anticipate the consequences of the palm-up gesture and place the object therein. This is not necessarily the only path to the final structure, in this case or any other. For example, one often sees the mother's upturned palm waiting to collect accidentally dropped objects. Presumably the child learns to drop things, or propel things, on purpose through having done this accidentally, so cases where the child drops or propels things on purpose and the mother, anticipating this, catches them in her open palm would seem not at all unlikely. This situation would seem well suited to the development of this communication structure, where the mother proffers her upturned palm, and the child places an object in it. The final product, the fully developed primitive communication structure, is exemplified in Fig. 4.

By the observation session following the one from which the above transcription was taken, Janet would reliably place an object in her possession into her mother's upturned palm, though with rather more a throwing away action than a placing, thus showing the complete establishment of this particular primitive communication structure. She would also throw/place objects into other receptacles and do the same at her mother in the absence of a palm-up gesture. What she did *not* do was to hold up the object, wait for her mother to cup her palm and then place the object into it. As in the mother to baby situation, the technical and communicative functions of her actions are not yet differentiated and the child's behaviour is all of a piece and aimed *solely at propelling an object toward a receptacle.*

The Productivity of Primitive Communication Structures

The two quite distinct structures described above are not merely empty rituals but are productive in two senses. In the first place, very many objects can be incorporated into them, so they can be used to give the infant visual

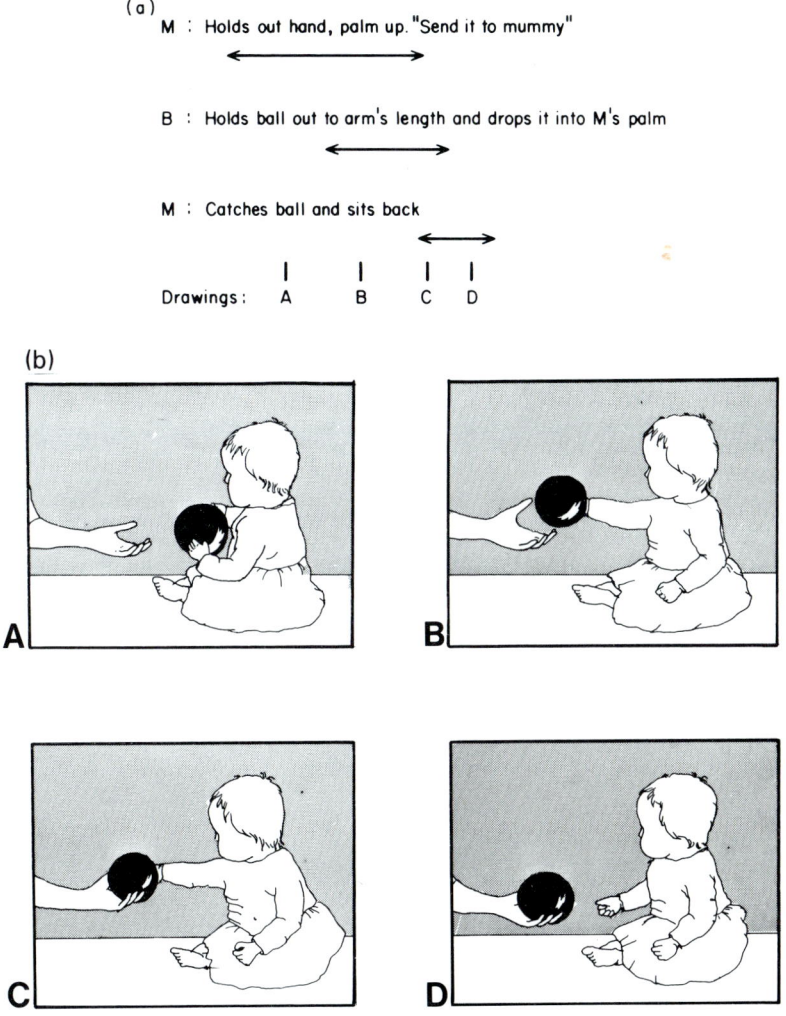

Fig. 4(a), (b). The transfer of an object from the infant to the mother, with the child in the relatively passive role. The child does *not* employ a gesture (0;11(1)).

and tactile experience of a wide range of objects. Secondly, they are extremely useful to the mother as a means for setting up other, more idiosyncratic, structures. A powerful example of this is the way that a mother can, instead of proffering her upturned palm, hold out, say, a box of some sort. She can offer the child in turn objects from a particular set of objects, perhaps a set of coloured bricks, and induce the child to place each in turn into the box. In this way she can use these general purpose transfer structures to educate her child into more complex ways of dealing with the environment. These basic structures act as tools which make it easy for the mother to teach the child the esoteric and very unobvious (to the child) intentions and actions that are appropriate with various toys, such as putting shapes with holes in onto sticks and so on.

Other Structures

Primitive communication structures are by no means confined to situations involving the transfer of objects, but this is one of the most productive situations and one with a lot of potential for future development. Other situations, such as that shown in Fig. 5 may become redundant after the child has physically developed far enough to do these things for himself. In this instance the child is on his back on the floor and the mother takes hold of his hands, pulling gently. She pauses expectantly and the child strenuously pulls himself upward against the hands, using his arms and legs to effect this. The mother then completes the infant's actions and pulls him to a sitting position. Once the child can sit up by himself, he need no longer involve the mother.

GESTURE

Any account of the ontogeny of human communication would, I feel, be greatly strengthened if it could be shown to have a place in the development of communication on an evolutionary scale. To try to relate human communication and animal communication by listing similarities and differences seems no more useful than, say, looking at the similarities and differences of the three-toed sloth and the duck-billed platypus! However, to try instead to place human communication within a general phylogenetic framework would be a step toward understanding its nature. I believe that the theory under discussion here would be very suitable as a first step toward a satisfactory theory of the evolution of language, and although I shall not outline an explicit argument, I think that the following observations of an intriguing congruence in animal behaviours to that of child behaviour would be a good way to introduce this section.

Cullen (1972) has noted that: "If we turn from complicated displays to the simplest signals, we find on the one hand that the signal action may be

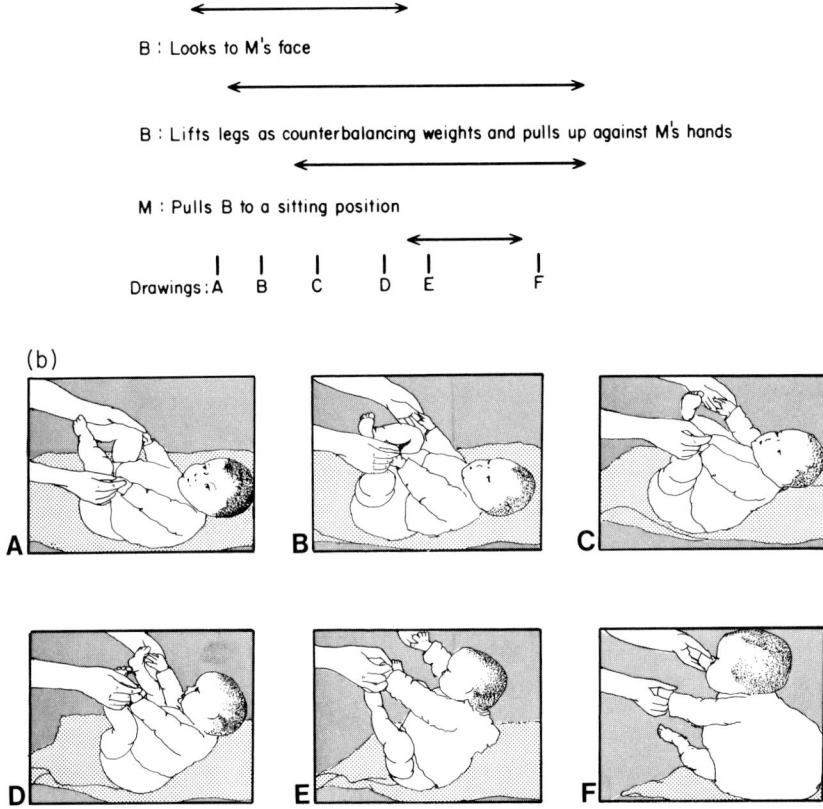

Fig. 5(a), (b). Transient primitive communication structure with the function of putting the infant into a sitting position (0;6(9)).

identical in form with or in fact be, an action with a secular function" and that: "many of the simple displays of birds and fish can be seen as being modified locomotor acts relevant to the situation at the time." Along very similar lines, Ploog and Melnechuk (1969) have observed:

> One way in which signal function, or meaning, changes is through the ritualisation into a communicative act of an originally technical action. Aggressive patterns demonstrate how some signals can be derived from what was originally direct activity. Hamadryas baboons slap the ground and make incomplete dashes at other animals when threatening to attack, and all three baboon species grind their teeth during an intermediate stage of aggressive behaviour. These are formalised signals derived from the activities of actual attacking and biting.

The phylogenetic question that these comments refer to, and the ontogenetic question with which we are concerned are very similar, namely, how is it that individuals can have knowledge in common such that the response is appropriate to the signal? The answers attempted are also very similar, that the more sophisticated forms of communication derive from direct, secular activity. Observation of animals shows stylized patterns of behaviour, or signals, on the part of one individual which reliably imply a particular behaviour by the other. The comments above suggest that this amazing congruence comes about because the "signals" derive from direct behaviour in the world. Thus the form of these "signals" derives from these activities, in that they are ritualized, incomplete acts, and their function (or meaning) is also clearly related to the real acts from which they derive. In lower species it seems plain that the emergence of "signals" from secular activity does not take place within an individual's lifetime, but that the result of the process is somehow "in" the individual at birth. Higher animals might well be equipped to carry through the process in their own lifetime, a point which many dog owners would agree with.

The relevance of this to our current concern is that I suggest this process definitely occurs in the course of the development of human communication. It would be quite reasonable to maintain that this similarity in phylogeny and ontogeny was not merely fortuitous, and that this is a very general process which is fundamental to the very nature of higher forms of communication.

Gesturally Mediated Communication Structures

The primitive communication structures which have been discussed have within them the potential for developing into gestural forms. The child's first gestural usage derives directly from primitive communication structures by changes in the form and function of the child's role within these. It must be emphasized here that the term "gesture" has a very specific meaning in this theoretical framework. In psychological studies the term is often used to refer to any fragment of behaviour in which the investigator might be interested, either in the sense of a physically described movement or of an organized action. The "gesture" in these studies is normally thought of as having some communicative value, and would probably be produced intentionally. However, there is no distinction made between *intentional action* and *intentional communication*. In the specific sense that "gesture" is used here, it is a component of an act of *intentional communication*. It is produced in order that another may act upon it. Here "gesture" is a unit, if you like, of communicative action and refers *only* to contexts of communicative intent. It is most important to bear this restricted usage in mind as it is the crux of the distinction to be made between primitive communication structures and their successors.

I have outlined so far the setting up of two quite distinct communicative structures with different roots but both concerned with the transfer of objects. The first of these is the transfer of the object from mother to child, where the child fits into the mother's suggestion relatively passively. The child's part in this is to reach for and to take the object. It is the initial part of this secular act that becomes stylized and functions as a newly emerged entity, a gesture, in the transformation of the primitive structure into a vastly more sophisticated form of communicative structure. I can do no more than describe the end product of the process here, and leave the process itself as a subject for future research.

In the primitive phase, the reaching of the child is effective through the mother's acting upon her interpretation of its significance, but the child has no cognizance of this essential role that the mother plays and of those aspects of his own behaviour that are instrumental in securing her co-operation. In passing from the primitive phase to the gestural the child becomes *aware* of the communicative aspect of his own behaviour, which has always been there in reality. In other words, whereas before there was co-ordination of activity, i.e. communication, the child was not aware of the relation between his own activity and his mother's monitoring of it. In a far-reaching cognitive restructuring he gains insight into the consequences of his own activity and the "mechanics" of the situation he finds himself in. A gesture, in this case the reach, emerges as a gesture because it is not simply produced in order to get an object, but in order to produce an effect on another in order to get an object. It would be rather as if a Skinnerian rat realized that it had to do things to please the experimenter so that he would give it food. Thus we find that whereas in the primitive phase the child communicates *incidentally*, in the gesturally mediated phase communication is *intentional* and is effected through the newly emergent gesture. Naturally the discovery by the child that activities such as communicating exist is of an importance that cannot be overstressed.

From the point of view of the investigator there is a difficult observational distinction to make. Although there might be no doubt in the lay observer's mind that there has been a change from a situation in which the mother *pretends* that her child is asking for things to a situation where the child *really* does ask her for things, the "scientific" observer sees superficially rather similar behaviours which are supposed to derive from totally different mental organizations. In the second case the behaviour is a gesture but in the first case it is not. One is trying to connect the observer's outside view of a communication structure with his theory of the nature of the child's experience within that structure. I think that one could develop ways of demonstrating that there are real differences while allowing that circumstances might conspire to produce formally identical sequences (though I think this latter to be unlikely with sophisticated enough observations). For example, if one were to interrupt the smooth functioning of the communicative act, one would expect that the child will monitor the mother a great deal and that he will persist with the reach when not immediately successful in terms of procuring the object (given that he is interested enough in having it). This is distinctly different from the situation at the primitive stage as described above and as in Fig. 3. Furthermore, we should find the child sometimes taking a relatively more active part in the transfer in that he determines which object and demands that the mother should play her part in the social act which leads to its possession (Figs 6 and 7).

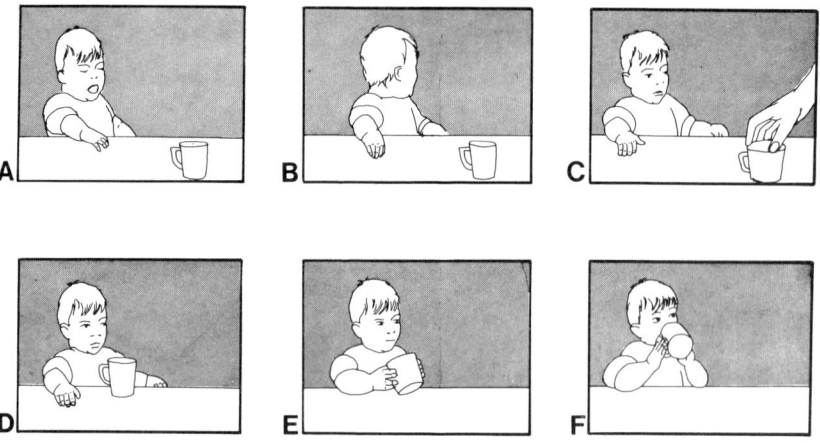

Fig. 6. Transfer from adult to child with the adult in the relatively passive role. The child communicates intentionally through the use of a gesture. From Lock (in press).

Finally, it is worthwhile to point out the relevance of Vygotsky's maxim (see above) to this process, but at a higher level than before. We have, in the primitive phase, communication at the intermental level. It is objectively there, i.e. there is already a co-ordination of the activities of mother and child, but the child is not yet aware of it. In the gestural phase there is communication at the intramental level. The child becomes aware of what is implicit in the social structures in which he is already immersed. Precisely how the change from primitive structures to gestural structures comes about is, of course, a matter for investigation, and is one of the main areas of interest that the present approach focuses interest upon.

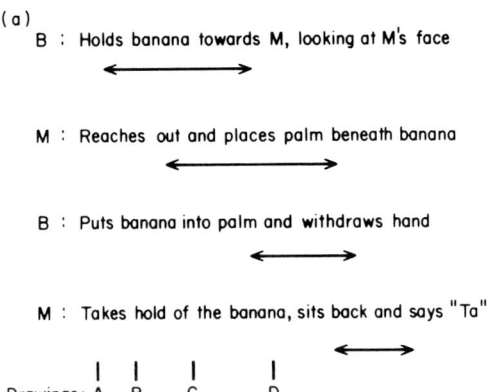

(a)

B : Holds banana towards M, looking at M's face

M : Reaches out and places palm beneath banana

B : Puts banana into palm and withdraws hand

M : Takes hold of the banana, sits back and says "Ta"

Drawings: A   B   C   D

(b)

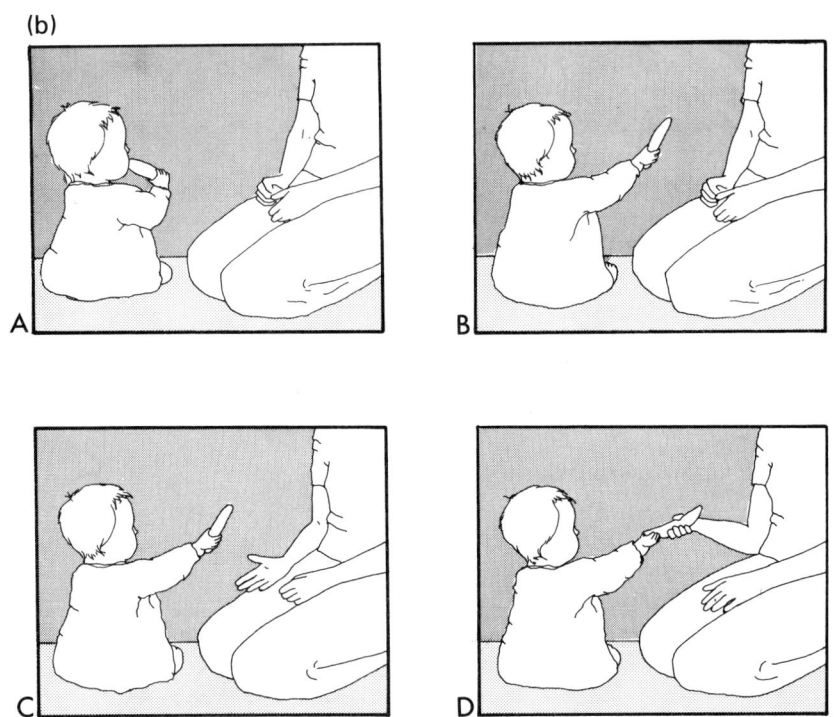

Fig. 7(a), (b). Transfer from child to mother with the mother in the relatively passive role. The actualization of a gestural communication structure (0;11(8)).

In summary then, the gestural form of the transfer of an object from the mother to the child involves the child taking on the more active role. Whereas before he reached for the object proferred by the mother and his act was unitary and directed toward the object alone, now part of this secular action becomes isolated from the rest of the act, stylized, and directed toward the mother so that she will act upon it. The reach-as-part-of-getting-object becomes a reaching *posture* which is *maintained* whereas a reach as an integral phase of a secular act is not maintained when unsuccessful. The establishment of gestures is the first step in the separation of communicating activity from other activity, while maintaining a relation between the two which is essential to *meaning*. A gesture is distilled from a pre-existing social activity involving two organisms behaving in the physical world, and as such it comes into existence already equipped with its "meaning".

The sequence in Fig. 6 was observed by Lock (in press) and is a very clear example of the actualization of the mother (adult) to baby communicative structure entailing the infants use of the reaching gesture and his taking of the relatively more active role in the exchange. The second, and separate, root structure in the transfer of objects, i.e. where the object goes from child to mother, undergoes precisely the same transformation. In this structure, the child holds an object out towards the mother, the mother brings her upturned palm forward and then, in an action entirely separate from the holding out of the object, the child places the object on the palm. The gestural part, the offering, is the stylized posture derived from the placing of an object into the palm as an action equivalent to putting an object into anything. Again, the gestural form, though necessarily bearing a resemblance to the previous form of the social act, reflects an entirely different mental organization on the part of the child. The use of the gesture is exemplified in Fig. 7.

In this way it can be seen that the transfer of objects develops from two entirely separate roots, being the transfer from mother to baby on the one hand, and transfer from baby to mother on the other. These two situations are initially entirely separate in the child's experience, though for an adult they are the same situation with a reversal of role. In the first phase primitive communication structures are erected as often repeated co-ordinations of activity with a well defined role for mother and for infant, with the infant taking a relatively passive part in the proceedings. In the second phase, the communicative potentialities inherent in the primitive form are apprehended by the child such that each primitive structure produces a gestural structure as an outgrowth. At this point there are four structures in which the child can play an appropriate role, which correspond in function to the four aspects of adult giving and taking discussed above (Fig. 1). Two of these involve the child initiating the exchange with a gesture and two of them are of the primitive form (though one suspects that the child's experience of them must have changed with the advent of their gestural forms). It will be noticed that gestures used by the mother and the child are not the same. The gesture appropriate to requesting an object from the other is a reach in the child's case and a palm-up in the mother's. This fact precludes the possibility that the child might acquire his gestures through some form of imitation. It also indicates that the child has not at this stage attained the organization of experience that will relate the structures derived from the two roots together in the adult form i.e. direction of transfer is still important in determining the form of the exchange and there is not yet a perfectly role-reversible "give-take" structure.

DIRECTION OF TRANSFER

		FROM M TO B	FROM B TO M
INITIATOR OF EXCHANGE	M	M OFFERS BY HOLDING OBJECT OUT, AND B TAKES	M REQUESTS WITH PALM-UP GESTURE, B PLACES IN PALM
	B	B "REQUESTS" WITH REACHING GESTURE. M HOLDS OUT AND B TAKES	B OFFERS BY HOLDING OBJECT TOWARD M. M PALM-UPS AND B PLACES OBJECT IN PALM

Fig. 8. The four possible transfer situations at the gestural stage of the infant's development of communication. The baby initiated exchanges involve the use of gestures by the child.

The gestural repertoire of children would seem to vary widely, since within my own small "sample" one child learned to speak rather late but had a compensatory varied gestural repertoire, while another learned to speak early so the development of a gestural repertoire was curtailed. Some observed gestures may be idiosyncratic in form and meaning (though produced by the same process), whereas others, such as those associated with object transfer and the arms-raised gesture to be picked up (see Lock, in press), seem almost universal. What appears to be general in all gestures is the process described above, a biological process that characterizes one stage in the development of communication.

The Importance of Gestures

The account given above is, of course, vastly oversimplified. The complexities of the development of a real child are staggering and the child does not respect the neat compartments that make investigation easier. Every aspect of the child's experience affects every other aspect. As an example of the complexities of real life, and of the potential richness of a study of childrens' gestural usage, I offer the following observations of Cassy aged 11 months. I was lucky enough to observe Cassy use two different gestures to achieve the same end on the same day. In both cases Cassy was being held by me and apparently wanted to go to her mother. In one instance she looked to me while *pointing* at her mother, thus effecting the desired change by communicating to me. In the second case she looked at her mother and *raised her arms* towards her, thus achieving the same end through communicating to her mother. It seems to me that it is unhelpful to talk of rigid stimulus-response chains in considering a child's gestural usage when such instances can be observed.

The importance of gesturally mediated communication structures developmentally (and phylogenetically) is two-fold. Firstly, they establish an important relation in that instead of child-world and mother-world relations existing side by side, so to speak, there is a three term relation, mother-child-world, involving a world in common. Secondly, the step involved in going from primitive to gestural structures, although large, is in some sense natural. A gesture has a *meaning* and a *form* which is directly related to the action-in-the-world from which it derives. I have described how a gesture comes into being at the same time as its meaning. The meaning is not arbitrarily assigned to the "gesture" after its appearance as mind/matter dualists would have us believe, but is an inseparable aspect of the gesture itself. I will stick my neck out here and say that it is not possible to establish a functioning gesture in a child's behaviour except through the process described here, where that gesture is intimately related to an earlier doing-of-things in the world. I also believe that gesturally mediated communication is a necessary intermediate step in establishing communication through arbitrary sounds. It is also the step that relates human communication to animal communication, since there is at present no satisfactory notion of how language could have evolved. The biggest problem in the way of such a theory is the apparent complete discontinuity between the communication of non-human species and language, which is further delineated by the emergent abilities of the language user. If, however, we can take gestural communication as a mode distinct from more primitive forms and from language but *intermediate* to them, then there is the possibility of discerning an evolutionary (and developmental) progression of forms of communication. Up to this point in this exposition, an attempt has been made to distinguish primitive and gestural communication structures and to show how the latter derive from the former. To distinguish gestural and language communication is much easier, but it remains to be shown how language might be derived from gestural communication.

FROM ACTION TO GESTURE TO SYMBOL

What has been attempted so far is to describe the child's part in, and the important features of, primitive communication structures and gestural ones so that sensible questions can be asked about the transition from one to the other. The general framework for the development of communication that has been offered has three phases. Firstly, there is a phase of primitive communication where direct action is developed and co-ordinated with the action of others into stable social/communicative structures. Secondly, there is a phase where communication is, at least in part, mediated through the child's use of gestures. These gestures derive in form from primitive communication structures and the actions employed therein. Their usage, or meaning, also derives from the primitive forms but in using them the child demonstrates that he has learned what it is to *communicate* as a separate activity under his control. The last phase is that of communication structures mediated through arbitrary sounds, which structures derive in some way from the abilities developed in the gestural phase.

In this exposition I have described only clear instances of the kinds of structure with which I am concerned. Since one does not expect that the child will wake up one morning suddenly knowing what a gesture is, there is of course an extensive fuzzy area between the two types where the transition is taking place. Simply describing the extremes fully can be of help in uncovering the processes at work. We have seen so far that to employ gestures the child needs to separate the communicative and technical functions of his actions and to relate them at a higher level. Although the main concern here is with the transition from action to gesture, it seems appropriate to suggest some ways in which gesture could lead on to language and so complete the outline of this framework.

Edwards (1973, 1975) has looked at "social-relational" sources of meaning in the child's first utterances. He has examined in detail the social and cognitive basis of the "original word game", which is recognized as the first manifestation of language abilities. Edwards states:

Typically the "game" is linguistically mediated by more than mere object names; it is full of questions and answers, locative and deictic expressions like "what's that?", "There it is", "That's a kangaroo", "it's a box", "it's over there" and so on. Moreover these expressions are integrated into a context of sequenced looks and gestures which are crucial to their function in the total communication setting. . . . The game has two complementary versions. In object-naming the child supplies a name for a located object. In pointing at named objects he indicates their location.

Here, we shall consider this aspect of the development of communication in terms of social/communicative structures mediated by arbitrary sounds. What we need to know is how such structures are derived, or grow from, gesturally mediated structures. I will suggest here that this involves uniting and organizing two separate aspects of the child's preverbal abilities.

Firstly, there is vocal "imitation". As Newson and Pawlby (1975) have noted, those situations in which the mother makes a sound and the infant makes an attempt at producing the same sound, have a developmental history. This is, of course, a communication situation where the child has to come to know what is expected of him. Mead (1934) has surmised that sounds are eminently suitable for this "imitation" game because they show a similar aspect to producer and hearer, that is, the producer hears his sound in a similar form to the way the hearer perceives it whereas one perceives one's body movements differently to the way an observer sees them. Whatever the logical basis, it is certainly true that mothers and children are capable of entering into a structured social exchange such that the mother produces a sound and the child then produces a facsimile recognized as such by the participants. It is important to realize that this co-ordination of sound productions is not in itself a possible basis for language. As a communication structure it is about on the same level as direct co-ordination of action, except that here we have "sound action". Since sounds do not intrinsically have much effect on the world, this succession of sound forms is not in itself a very useful kind of communication. Of course, when sounds are related to action they become very powerful.

Secondly, I have observed in mother-child interactions an analogous congruence of action. I refer to situations in which the pair are looking at a picture book for example. One can observe the mother point to some part of the picture and the child touch that same part. This structure naturally has a developmental history, but it is sufficient here to say that this structure involves the child using a gesture so that the mother will simply attend to a particular part of the environment and *vice versa*.

It seems natural to suppose that the mother can put the sound imitation and the joint attention structures into juxtaposition such that when she points she can at the same time make the sound that is that object's name. It also seems obvious that the child could play his part in both structures by imitating the sound on the one hand, and pointing to the object on the other, without in any way treating the sound as the name for the object. But again, if this kind of complex structure is set up by the mother *the naming relation is implicit in it.* She becomes confident that the child is aware of the naming relation when the child can *point to the named object*, or can *give the appropriate sound when an object is pointed to.* These are just those aspects of the "original word game" singled out by Edwards. It is not just a question of the child "associating" a sound with a referent, but of the child being involved in a social exchange where he has to provide the sound at a particular point. When the naming relation is firmly established for any word-object conglomerate, then the pointing becomes redundant in some contexts for the word itself implies the activity of pointing. Thus there opens up the possibility of talking about, i.e. verbally pointing to, objects and relations that are not immediately present to the senses.

The arbitrary sound which is now the name for the object (as agreed between the mother and the child) can now be incorporated into other activities than the initial game. Carter (this volume) has described how certain other kinds of word develop in conjunction with gestural forms. For instance, she describes the "object request schema" which is a complex pattern involving the conjunction of certain sounds with what can be seen as one of the gestural communication structures described above. She traces a development and differentiation that produces the words "more" and "mine" and the use of object names to make requests for the object (i.e. incorporating the naming relation into other activities).

Overview

Having considered some ways in which gestural structures might lead on to language mediated structures, the outline of this framework for the development of communication is complete. The course of the development of communication has been represented in this way: (1) action leads to (2) gesture implying action, leading on to (3) arbitrary sounds (implying gestures) implying action. This last relation is in accord with Mead's (and many others') view that the meanings of language, in the last analysis, reside in the actions implied thereby. In this way, language can be seen as a complication of the basic notion of communication; whatever it is that enables the activities of individuals to be co-ordinated with one another.

Section 5

From Gesture to Symbol

11
Sensori-motor Intelligence and Language Development

DAVID INGRAM

University of British Columbia, Canada

INTRODUCTION

In three classic works, Piaget (1952, 1954, 1962) has described six stages of intellectual development during the young child's first two years of life. Together, they comprise what Piaget refers to as the "sensori-motor period". (A brief summary of these appears in Table I; the Appendix contains the major behaviors of the last four stages.) Regarding language, Piaget proposes that development in these stages provides the cognitive precursors to language. Piaget states (Piaget and Inhelder, 1969, p. 85): "articulate language makes its appearance . . . at the end of the sensori-motor period, with what have been called 'one-word utterances'." Active language development is based upon, and occurs after, the sensori-motor period.

At the same time, it is also well known that children's first words typically appear around 10 months to 1 year of age. If sensori-motor development proceeds up to 18 months or 2 years, then clearly a good deal of vocalization and communication is taking place during the sensori-motor period. If so, Piaget's theory implies that the nature of this language is somehow qualitatively different from that which follows it. Indeed, Piaget (1962) has addressed this issue, and has described this transition as one from (personal) "symbol" to (social) "sign". The goal of this chapter is to examine more closely the nature of the language that occurs during the sensori-motor period in terms of whether or not particular linguistic milestones occur with

Table I

A summary of Piaget's six stages of sensori-motor development

Stage 1 (birth to 0;1) *The use of reflexes*: Child shows reflexes that are the foundation of future development, e.g. sucking reflex, vocalization.

Stage 2 (0;1 to 0;4) *Primary circular reactions*: Child develops abilities focused on its own body, such as thumb sucking. Will vocalize when adult does, and will turn head towards sounds it hears.

Stage 3 (0;5 to 0;8) *Secondary circular reactions*: Child's activities on external objects creates reactions which hold its interest. The activities are repeated to make the event occur again, e.g. swinging arms to make a rattle move.

Stage 4 (0;9 to 0;11) *Co-ordination of secondary schemes*: Child uses activities of previous stage as means to achieve ends, e.g. hitting or moving parent's hand to move it away from an object the child desires. Child begins to attempt imitation of novel sounds.

Stage 5 (1;0 to 1;4) *Tertiary circular reactions*: Interest develops in nature of objects. Through exploration with new events and objects, child attempts to determine their novelty. Also, child develops new means to achieve goals, such as using a stick or string to obtain an object. When confronted with a problem, will actively experiment to solve it.

Stage 6 (1;4 to 1;6 or 2;0) *Invention of new means through mental combinations*: Child can solve problems through reflection and anticipation of events. Object permanence is obtained—child is aware of the independent existence of objects. First instances of symbolic play appear, e.g. child will pretend to sleep, eat, etc. In general, child develops a mental representation of reality.

particular sensori-motor stages. In general, it attempts to determine the extent to which sensori-motor stages represent cognitive precursors to language development, and just how closely cognitive and linguistic milestones are related.

SOME BASIC ASSUMPTIONS

To begin, it is necessary to explain in more detail the way in which the relation between language and sensori-motor development will be treated in this study. First of all, this will be an *empirical* approach to the problem. In recent years, there have been several very interesting papers that have speculated on the relation between language and cognition during the first two years of life (e.g. Sinclair, 1971; Lézine, 1973; Bloom, 1973; Edwards, 1973; Morehead and Morehead, 1974; Moerk, 1975). This speculation has varied from predictions on what cognitive developments must occur for language to proceed (e.g. Bloom, 1973) to theoretical discussion and elaboration of what Piaget's theory really predicts about language development (Sinclair, 1971). Here the focus will be on actually observing children's cognitive and linguistic behaviors simultaneously to see what the relation is. Whether or not Piaget's theory is ultimately the correct explanation for cognitive development, his work is highly valuable for the empirical observations it has made on children's development. This chapter will focus on the empirical side of his work and attempt to establish the cognitive behaviors that will occur along with linguistic ones.

Secondly, the approach to sensori-motor stages that will be taken is *general* in nature. In a study of this sort, the decision needs to be made whether to look at particular cognitive developments (e.g. stages of object permanence) or at Piaget's broader notion of sensori-motor stages. Most work done in recent years on sensori-motor development has tended to take the former approach (e.g. Décarie, 1965; Užgiris and Hunt, 1975). This is understandable in light of the fact that Piaget's own discussion of this period tends to break down into separate sections on each behavior (cf. Piaget, 1937, in particular). This chapter, however, will try to correlate linguistic development within the idea of general stages of sensori-motor development. There is a certain risk in taking this approach which needs to be mentioned at the outset. This is the fact that Piaget's notion of general stages is one of the more criticized aspects of his sensori-motor theory (see discussion in Užgiris and Hunt, 1975). One reason for this is that behaviors are occasionally proposed as occurring at the same stage where it is difficult to see any cognitive relation between them. The fact remains, however, that general sensori-motor stages are an important part of Piaget's theory, and Piaget consistently attempts to point out relations across behaviors within individual stages. Since few studies have taken a general approach, it will be necessary in the next section to discuss in some detail how this is done.

A third characteristic of this chapter is that it takes an *observational* approach to sensori-motor development. It is important to point out that this is not done with the idea that an observational approach is inherently better than an experimental one. There have been several studies in recent years which indicate that an experimental method is necessary to understand better Piaget's work (e.g. Bower, 1974; Užgiris, and Hunt, 1975). At the same time, however, it is necessary to keep in mind that the empirical basis of Piaget's theory is the ability to observe and interpret virtually all the child's spontaneous behavior. That is, the stages are not interpretations that result from examining children's behavior under highly controlled circumstances at isolated times, but actually the reverse. All of a child's behavior is subject to interpretation under Piaget's theory. The observational method has two outstanding advantages for the study of the relation between language and cognition. One is the fact that it makes it possible to get an idea of a child's cognitive stage from diary studies that mention cognitive behavior. Secondly, it makes one's determination of a child's sensori-motor stage highly consistent with the way that Piaget actually determined these in his own work. This point is not often appreciated by those who apply the experimental method in this area. As will be shown in the next section, the child's success on a task of a particular stage does not necessarily indicate attainment of that stage.

THE DETERMINATION OF SENSORI-MOTOR STAGES

Despite three long works on the sensori-motor period, Piaget never dealt in great detail with the problem of determining when a child is at a general sensori-motor stage. There are, however, some basic remarks he has made on this issue. One is that behaviors of one stage will first appear in the previous stage.

> It is perfectly normal that these first behavior patterns of the fourth stage are constituted sporadically from the middle of the third stage, except that these episodic productions are only systemized and consolidated one or two months later. In the same way we shall see that the behavior patterns of the fifth stage are foreshadowed from the apex of the fourth and those of the sixth are foreshadowed at the fifth stage. Inversely, it is evident that the behavior patterns belonging to a given stage do not disappear during the following stages but conserve a role whose importance only diminishes very gradually (and relatively). (Piaget, 1952, p. 214)

The last comment concerning the continuation of behaviors into the next stage reflects Piaget's position that these stages are not composed of autonomous behaviors.

> In a general way, the fact should be emphasized that the behavior patterns characteristic of the different stages do not succeed each other in a linear way (those of a given stage disappearing at the time when those of the following one take form) but in the manner of the layers of a pyramid (upright or upside down), the new behavior patterns simply being added to the old ones to complete, correct or combine them. (Piaget, 1952, p. 329)

The determination of a general stage is not established by isolated behaviors but rather by a cluster of behaviors at the same time.

From these remarks, it is clear that the study of a child's general sensori-motor development through stages can only be determined by looking at a wide range of behaviors. A sensori-motor stage is one which begins with increasing use of behaviors that have already occurred sporadically during the previous stage; it reaches a peak when this collection of behaviors dominate the child's activities.

Despite these points, Piaget never presented his data in a way that reflected each of his children's general sensori-motor stages. Since Piaget's books provide numerous observations with ages, however, it is possible to isolate his data and construct a chronological record of the cognitive development of each of his children. This, in fact, was done in Ingram (1975). Table II provides an example of this data, presenting Lucienne's cognitive progress during her thirteenth month.

An examination of the data in Table II reveals examples of both of Piaget's points mentioned above. First of all, behaviors of one stage sporadically appear a month or two before the stage itself, as seen in the stage 6 observation at 1;0(0). Also, the stage itself consists of a variety of behaviors across several skills that dominate the child's spontaneous activity. These behaviors will continue to occur and develop, right on into the next stage. An observational record of this sort makes it possible to see quite clearly the general stages of each of Piaget's children.

THE USE OF LANGUAGE BY PIAGET'S CHILDREN

The determination of general sensori-motor stages in the way just discussed makes it possible to observe simultaneous linguistic developments. Even though Piaget never concentrated on linguistic events, his observations contain sporadic references to the language of his children. The data in Ingram (1975) contain several observations made by Piaget on the language of his children, although most are taken from Jacqueline, the oldest child. An examination of these linguistic examples in relation to each child's general cognitive stage makes it possible to achieve a first approximation of the relation between language and sensori-motor development. I will first discuss each child individually and then make some general observations.

Jacqueline

The observations on Jacqueline in Piaget's published works are nearly three times as frequent as those on the second child Lucienne. A summary of her linguistic development in relation to her sensori-motor stages is contained in Table III.

Table II
Summary of Piaget's observations on Lucienne at 1;0

Age	Observation	Stage
1;0(0)	When accidentally fell back, grabbed pillow and got into sleeping position. Smiled. Later practised and did intentionally, holding hands, instead of a pillow, eyes open, smiling. (1962, obs 65)	6[a]
1;0(3)	Sight of chain sets in motion a search for watch and the action of pulling. (1952, obs 155)	5
1;0(5)	Lucienne hit her head. Piaget imitated, and L. imitated in turn. (1962, obs 49)	4
	Detailed examination of use of supports, showing she will pull support. (1952, obs 150)	5
	Difficulty in use of wooden box as a support. (1952, obs 152)	5
	Fails to use stick as an instrument. (1952, obs 157)	4
	In search for hidden object, looks only in place B, not in A. (1954, obs 54a)	5
1;0(11)	Imitates placing cardboard on head and hitting head with hand. (1962, obs 49)	5[b]
	Solves how to slide a box to herself, through experimentation. (1952, obs 152)	5
	Again succeeds at finding hidden box after visible displacement. (1954, obs 54b)	5
1;0(12)	Piaget hits his head with hand. L. imitates by putting chain on head. (1962, obs 49)	5
1;0(14)	Piaget opens and closes eyes. L. blinks, opening and closing mouth at the same time, then covers eyes with pillow. (1962, obs 29)	4
	L. wants Piaget, who is holding carriage with his hand, to shake it. She looks at his hand, shakes herself, and waves her hand. (1954, obs 166)	3
1;0(16)	When Piaget opens and closes eyes, L. opens and closes mouth, and covers face with pillow. (1962, obs 29)	4
	L. removes first of two cushions to pull second to reach watch. (1952, obs 151)	5
	Piaget hides chain in his hand, then puts his hand under a cover, leaving the watch chain there. When he opens his hand, L. is surprised that the chain is gone. No search for it. Fails all ten attempts. (1954, obs 57)	5

[a]First stage 6 behavior observed.
[b]First instance of stage 5 imitation.

Table III
Linguistic observations on Jacqueline and the sensori-motor stage of their occurrence

Stage	Age	Linguistic observation
3	0;8(2)	Imitated "papa", "baba", which have no meaning for her. (1962, obs 11)
	0;8(3)	Says "aa" as soon as door opens, anticipating entry of someone. (1952, obs 109)
4	0;8(16)	Says "apf" when examining new objects. (1952, obs 136)
	0;10(0)	Blew bubbles of saliva, saying "méhê, méhê". (1962, obs 23)
	0;11(20)	Imitated "papa", which had no meaning for her. (1962, obs 32a)
5	1;1(0)	"Tch tch" for passing train. (1962, obs 101a)
	1;1(4)	"Tch tch" for any vehicle passing outside window, even a man. (1962, obs 101a)
		"Tch tch" for playing peekaboo. (1962, obs 101a)
	1;1(6)	"Tch tch" when hearing noises from the street. (1962, obs 101a)
	1;1(20)	"Birdie", said pretending to hold bird. (1962, obs 101a)
		"Bow wow" for dogs. (1962, obs 101a)
	1;1(29)	"Bow wow" for neighbor's dog. (1962, obs 101a)
	1;2(1)	"Bow-wow" after looking at horse. (1962, obs 101a)
	1;2(3)	"Bow wow" for open tram with visible infant, later for design in rug, later at sight of two horses. (1962, obs 101a)
	1;2(4)	"Daddy" to a man, used several weeks for all men. (1962, obs 101a)
		"Mommy" to a strange woman. (1962, obs 101a)
		"Bow wow" at the sight of hens. (1962, obs 101a)
	1;2(8)	"Bow wow" for dogs, horses, prams, cyclists. (1962, obs 101a)
		"Tch tch" for cars, trains. (1962, obs 101a)
	1;2(12)	"Bow wow" for anything seen from the balcony. (1962, obs 101a)
	1;2(15)	"Bow wow" used for trucks pulled by railroad porter. (1962, obs 101a)
	1;2(25)	"Bim bam" said seeing lamp swaying from ceiling; swayed her own body. (1962, obs 56)
	1;3(7)	"Bow wow" for rug pattern. (1962, obs 101a)
	1;3(11)	Asked for pot and laughed each time it was given to her. (1962, obs 63)
	1;3(15)	Began to actively imitate meaningful sounds that were new to her—imitation takes place through trial and error. (1962, obs 41)
	1;3(18)	"Papeu" for *parti* (gone). (1962, obs 41)

continued

Table III (*continued*)

Stage	Age	Linguistic observation
	1;3(25)	"Bou" for *bouche* (mouth) (later "bousse") "Mou" for *mouche* (fly) "Menou" for *minou* "Sa" for *chat* (cat). (1962, obs 41)
	1;3(29)	"Bagba" for *bague* "Bagam" for *boite* (box) "Caca" for *canard* (duck) "Papin" for *lapin* (rabbit). (1962, obs 41)
	1;4(0)	"Cacain" for *canard* "Bimbam" while pretending to fall. "Aieu" for *oiseau* (bird). (1962, obs 41)
6	1;4(8)	Said "in step" when walking, never had said before; no immediate model. (1962, obs 54)
	1;4(10)	"Nose", pointed to mother's nose, said for first time. (1962, obs 54)
	1;4(14)	"Flop" to a dog she knew; subsequently deferred imitations became more frequent. (1962, obs 54)
	1;5	(No observations given for this month)
	1;6	"Bimbam" used for branches, hanging objects, and even grass. (1962, obs 64b) "Papeu" used to mean "gone away" for people leaving room, vehicles gone away, matches blown out. (1962, obs 101a)
	1;6(8)	"Cane" said upon seeing Piaget's cane. (1954, obs 156) "Papa" when saw Piaget. (1954, obs 156) "Poterre" for *pomme de terre* (potato). (1954, obs 123) "Inine" for *grenouille* (frog) said while looking for a toy one that was missing. (1952, obs 183)
	1;6(9)	"Panene" said when she wanted something to amuse her. (1962, obs 101a)
	1;6(10)	"Fish" for marks on ceiling. (1962, obs 101a) "Frog" while looking at mark on wall. (1962, obs 103)
	1;6(11)	"Papeu" when put tongue in and out. (1962, obs 101a)
	1;6(13)	"Panana" whenever she wants something. (1962, obs 101a)
	1;6(15)	"Mama" said calling mother. (1954, obs 173a)
	1;6(16)	"Ring, ring, where is it?" said during tests searching for hidden object. (1954, obs 58)
	1;6(17)	**First example of linguistic play**—Piaget asks what several animals say, e.g. "How does the cow go?" and J. correctly, e.g. "moo", then Piaget asks how J. goes and she says "mama" and smiles. (1954, obs 173a)
	1;6(28)	"Avon" for *savon* (soap) pretending to wash herself. (1962, obs 64a)
	1;6(30)	"Cry, cry" pretending to cry. (1962, obs 75a)

Stage	Age	Linguistic observation

Representation

	1;7(13)	First reference to past events—in bed by herself, said look, look, "uncle G, aunt A, uncle G", then "nono". Then sat up again and said "look, mummy, daddy, grandma, uncle G, etc." for 10 minutes. (1962, obs 104)
	1;7(14)	When having nap, she went through the list of food she had just had. (1962, obs 104)
		Moved forefinger an inch or so away from thumb and said "little istine" referring to new born cousin. (1962, obs 104)
	1;7(25)	Presses to bear's cheek and bites it, as she does to her mother, and says "oh, oh" for bear (Type 1A play). (1962, obs 75a)
		Picks up blade of grass and puts it in a pail, as she does with grasshoppers a cousin gave her, and says "totelle, totelle, jump, boy" where "totelle" = *sauterelle* (grasshopper), the meaning here is the grasshopper jumps like the boy I saw jumps. (1954, obs 173)
	1;7(27)	Chased after her shadow, saying "Jacqueline"; made shadow of her hand and said "hand"; when Piaget said "where is Jacqueline?" she got off his knee and pointed to her shadow. (1962, obs 132)
	1;8(11)	Sees fog on mountain and says "mist smoke papa", i.e. mist is like papa's smoke from pipe. (1954, obs 158)
	1;8(12)	Same scene as above, says "mist papa". After this, in following days, says "smoke papa" when Piaget smokes. (1954, obs 158)
	1;8(14)	When in bath, pointed to steam and said "mist smoke". (1962, obs 115)
	1;8(15)	Pretended to eat various things, e.g. a piece of paper, and said "very nice". (1962, obs 64a)
	1;8(20)	Pointed to mule, boy, dog, cat, and each time said "gone". (1962, obs 103)
	1;8(30)	Stroked her mother's hair, saying "pussy, pussy". (1962, obs 77)
	1;9(0)	Saw a shell and said "cup" (1962, obs 77)
		Saw a "pussy" in the pattern of a dress, and then said "gone". (1962, obs 103)
		From this day on, said "clouds daddy" or "mist daddy" whenever she saw mist. (1962, obs 115)
	1;9(3)	Took empty box and pushed it to and fro, saying "motycar". (1962, obs 77)
	1;9(10)	Stopped saying "clouds papa". (1954, obs 158)
	1;9(20)	Rubbed floor with a shell, then with cardboard lid, saying "brush Abebert" (like the cleaning lady). (1962, obs 76a)
		Filled hand with shells and said "flowers". (1962, obs 77)

continued

Table III (*continued*)

Stage	Age	Linguistic observation
	1;9(24)	Felt need to introduce people and things to anyone who entered room e.g. "daddy, mommy, nose (of doll), mouth, etc." (1962, obs 105) Would bring doll to parents and say "little man". (1962, obs 105) Would bring object and name it, e.g. "stone". (1962, obs 105) First said "what's that?" to herself, e.g. "what's that? Jacqueline, what's that?" "there"; (knocking down a block). "what's falling? a block"; (touching a necklace) "not cold". (1962, obs 105)
	1;9(28)	When Piaget made a shadow with his hand, J. said "daddy", pointing to the shadow. (1962, obs 132)

There are several important points deserving mention in these data. For one thing, the first words appear during sensori-motor stage 5. Piaget himself was quite explicit on this point: "It was, as a matter of fact, during this fifth stage that J., L. and T. began to make their first clumsy efforts to reproduce the words of adults." (Piaget 1962, p. 53). For Jacqueline, most of stage 5 revealed only the words "tch tch", "bow-wow", "daddy", and "mommy". It was only toward the end of this stage that other words were added. Even then, the pronunciations were quite variable. Stage 6 was marked by a gradual increase in vocabulary and the onset of deferred imitations, i.e. the first uses of words by the child without teaching or an immediately preceding model. Toward the end of the stage, words began to be used in reference to an object not immediately present or visible (cf. 1;6(8)). Also the question "where is it?" occurred (probably as a memorized formula), and the first case of linguistic play took place at 1;6(17) (see Davison, 1974, for an insightful discussion on linguistic play). Several further developments occurred during early representation. The first multi-word utterances appear in examples, and the first references to past events occur. These indicate that Jacqueline is managing to represent the world through language. Another development is the analogies Jacqueline makes at 1;7(28) and 1;8(11) and (12) (cf. Trân Duc Thao, 1973, for an elaborate discussion of the significance of these examples for symbolic development). Lastly, the first "what's that?" question is asked, an important advance in Piaget's view.

The best indication of progress in conceptualization is therefore the appearance of the question "what is it?" which involves both the name of the object and the concept (the class to which it belongs). (Piaget, 1962, p. 223)

Lucienne

The data from Lucienne is far less extensive than that for Jacqueline. Table IV presents the linguistic development of Lucienne as reported by Piaget.

Table IV

Linguistic observations on Lucienne and the sensori-motor stages of their occurrence

Stage	Age	Linguistic observation
4	0;10(16)	Laughs at Piaget's sticking out his tongue; says "bla bla" and puts out her own tongue. (1962, obs 28)
	0;10(6)	Says "tata" when Piaget opens and closes his mouth. (1962, obs 28)
	0;11(5)	"Tata" when Piaget opened and shut his eyes. (1962, obs 29)
5	1;3(2)	Points with finger to objects that are far away so that they are brought to her. (1954, obs 153a)
	1;3(4)	"Ha" to real cat and toy elephant, but not to hen or horse. (1962, obs 101b)
	1;3(9)	Mother asks "where is papa?" and L. points to window where Piaget usually is. (1954, obs 51)
6	1;3(14)	Said "no" not only when refusing something, but also when failed to find something. (1962, obs 101b) "Avoua" for *au revoir* to refer to people leaving, herself going out of a room, touching a door, or getting up from a seat. (1962, obs 101b)
	1;3(19)	"Ha" to horses and toys. (1962, obs 101b)
	1;6(25)	"Hehe" replaced "ha" and refers to all animals except cat and rabbit, and all kinds of people, including her sister. (1962, obs 101b)
Representation	1;11(28)	Recounting of past event. (1962, obs 104)

Similarly to Jacqueline, no language appears before stage 5. Even at stage 5, however, the only word that Piaget mentions is "ha". At the age of 1;3(2), when she is far advanced in most stage 5 behaviors, she is still pointing to obtain objects. It appears that the onset of language for Lucienne is even later than for Jacqueline, and that stage 6 had begun before any kind of rapid linguistic development.

Laurent

Table V presents Laurent's language development up to stage 6. Laurent's development is similar to that of both of the other children. Stage 5 shows the onset of a small number of words, in this case "tata", "mummy", "daddy", and "bow wow". Even in early stage 6, language development is at its very beginning.

SUMMARY

The study of the language used by Piaget's three children indicates why Piaget has claimed that rapid language development takes place after stage 6 of sensori-motor ability. In each of his children, the first words appeared in stage 5, but these consisted of usually less than a dozen for any child. Even well into stage 6, the language consisted primarily of single word utterances. It is be because of these facts that Piaget (1962, p. 221) has claimed:

> Once he is in possession of the semi-signs described in obs. 101 and 102 [stage 6 behaviors; DI], the child will quickly learn to speak, his progress following the lines with which Stern's investigations have made us familiar, word-sentences, sentences of two words, and complete sentences which soon come to be linked one with another.

Based on these observations and the above quote, we can say that Piaget's theory is fairly explicit about the linguistic milestones that occur along with the sensori-motor stages. These are summarized below:

> Stage 5: first words appear, highly variable in usage although context-bound at very onset, not usually more than ten or so in number.
> Stage 6: onset of acquisition of more words, although utterances are still one word at a time.
> Representation: first reference to past events; use of linguistic play; appearance of multi-word utterances; use of "what is it?" questions to ask the names of things.

FURTHER EVIDENCE FROM OTHER DIARY STUDIES

The previous examination of language used by Piaget's own children has provided some predictions on the correlation between linguistic development and the sensori-motor stages. The next question is whether or not other

Table V
Linguistic observations on Laurent and the sensori-motor stages of their occurrence

Stage	Age	Linguistic observation
4	0;9(21)	Said "papa" but it had no meaning for him. (1962, obs 30)
	0;9(30)	While examining toy cat, babbled "papa, baba". (1952, obs 137)
5	1;0(0)	"Tata" said for all successful actions, e.g. getting hold of a toy with a string. (1962, obs 102)
	1;2(22)	"Mummy", exclamation of surprise when saw his mother swing. (1962, obs 102)
	1;2(23)	"Daddy" to Jacqueline who held arms out to him as his father did; to male visitor, and to peasant lighting pipe. (1962, obs 102)
	1;2(24)	"Bow wow" to a dog, as he had during preceding days, also to hen, cow bell, cows, guinea pig, and cat. (1962, obs 102)
	1;3(2)	"Mummy" began to be used for anything he wanted. (1962, obs 102)
	1;3(5)	"Bow wow" for anything moving, from an ant to a tractor in a field. (1962, obs 102)
	1;3(13)	"Moo" for cows, deer head, stag antlers, "pussy" for cat, pigs were either word. (1962, obs 102)
6	1;4(4)	"Mummy" said with pointing when wanting something. (1962, obs 102)
	1;4(10)	"Mummy" when giving mother piece of paper; also when saw mother's clothes in the closet. (1962, obs 102) "Ali" (pillow) as expression of achievement. (1962, obs 102)
	1;4(23)	"Daddy" when saw father shaving; few days when father was swinging him; also when saw father's rucksack. (1962, obs 102)
	1;4(23)	"Nono" said when closing eyes. (1962, obs 102)
	1;4(29)	When friend of Piaget visited, Piaget asked L. "who is it?" and L. said "daddy". (1962, obs 102)
	1;5(19)	"Daddy" for all men 15 to 20 yards away. (1962, obs 102) "No more" meant going away, throwing something on the ground, then something overturned without disappearing. (1962, obs 102)
	1;5(25)	"Daddy" for all men. (1962, obs 102)
	1;5(30)	"Nono" for all sleeping dolls. (1962, obs 102)
	1;6(23)	"Mummy" to father, pointing to light he wanted lighted. (1962, obs 102) "No more" when he wanted something that someone was holding. (1962, obs 102)

children show similar development. To study this issue requires enormous amounts of information on individual children. Not only do longitudinal records need to be acquired, but also active experimentation on both language and cognition. Adequate research of this sort will take a great deal of time and effort, and some researchers are already attempting this task (e.g. Bates *et al.*, in press; Ingram *et al.*, in preparation). There is, however, a preliminary way that findings can be obtained at this time. This is through the examination of published diaries that report on both linguistic and cognitive developments.

At the beginning of this century, when the study of child development was in its origins, several parents decided to keep records of their children's development. These early diaries reported on everything from language to motor development. In fact, one of these, Preyer (1895), remains possibly the most detailed baby diary ever published.

To further examine Piaget's theory, three of these older diaries were selected for close study, i.e. Shinn (1900), Hogan (1898) and Preyer (1895). Data were extracted from these diaries in the following fashion. First, chronological information on both language and cognition was removed and recorded in the same way as the data from Piaget had been as found in Ingram (1975) and exemplified in Table II. Next, the particular stage of sensori-motor development for each cognitive behavior was determined. This was done by using a checklist of common behaviors that occur during the sensori-motor stages. This checklist is provided in the Appendix of this chapter. While the diary parents were not doing the kinds of experiments reported by Piaget, it was still possible in many cases to establish sensori-motor stages. For example, Preyer comments that his son Axel took off and put on a cover of a can 79 times at age 1;1. This is obviously a stage 5 behavior. This procedure provided data for each child that is a broad way was very similar to that for Piaget's children. The results for each child will be discussed individually.

Ruth Shinn

Shinn (1900) studied the speech and cognition of her daughter Ruth up to 1;0. Like Piaget's children, Ruth did not use any words until around stage 5. For example, the following behaviors all occurred before any spontaneous language:

0;7: dropped objects to watch them fall (197);
0;7: used a stick to move distant objects (197);
0;8: pulled tablecloth to bring a paper to her (212);
0;9: carefully examined objects by turning over, putting finger inside (217).

While she showed several stage 5 behaviors in increasing numbers from 0;7 to 0;11, her language consisted of only a handful of words. These were as follows:

0;9:	"Dă!" first word, accompanied by pointing, marked
(end of month)	expression of discovering, admiring (225-226);
	"nă-nă-nă!" refusal and protest;
	"mă-mă-mă!" "a special kind of wanting which slowly gathered itself about the mother in particular" (226);
	"mgm" or "ng-gng" when someone left or disappeared. (226) later became "A-gông" "It meant disappearance, absence, failure, denial, and any object associated with these." (227-228);
0;10:	"kha!" messy fingers;
0;11:	"É!" for *yes* or consent,
	"By!" for *bye bye*.

This language is similar to that of Piaget's children's, except that there are no referential terms in the data from Ruth. She appears to be an expressive child, in the sense of Nelson (1973).

Besides providing evidence for the appearance of a small number of words during stage 5, Shinn's data also add a new aspect for consideration. This concerns the issue of language comprehension. By 0;11, Ruth is in stage 5 of sensori-motor development and has a vocabulary of seven words. At the same time, Shinn makes some very specific observations on her language comprehension. At 0;10, she found that Ruth would respond to the syntactic frames "Point to the . . ." (236) and "Bring the . . . to Aunty". She determined that Ruth understood 84 words, consisting of 51 names of people and things, 28 action words which she obeyed such as "give" and "sit down", and a few others such as "where" and "allgone". Shinn states: "She understood them in simple combinations, too, such as 'Bring mamma Ruth's shoes'" (236). These observations suggest that while productive speech may be quite minimal during stage 5, linguistic comprehension may be more advanced.

Harold Hogan

While Shinn's diary of Ruth covers development up to 1;0, Hogan's diary (1898) of her son Harold mostly deals with the period of 1;2 on. Harold's language at 1;2 consisted of the following eight words which had been acquired since 0;9:

1. "Oh mammam"
2. "hab'em" (this word and next both used for handing over something or wanting something)
3. "Gib'em"
4. "ups-a-dada" (said when lifting something, or jumping up and down)
5. "Wow wow" (word for dogs)
6. "Bow wow"
7. "ba" or "baba" (used to call father)
8. "bye-bye"

According to Piaget's theory, he should be in stage 5 or early stage 6. The following behaviors were all observed during 1;2 and indicate that this is in fact the case (23-30):

puts blocks in basket one by one;
builds with blocks;
got shoes for someone who was dressing;
voluntarily took shoes from sofa to closet where they belonged;
took keys on chain to bed by pushing chain through posts and pulling it to get keys;
shows interest in putting things together and pulling them apart.

His level of development is most clearly seen in the examples of symbolic play that also occurred at 1;2:

pretended to drop things and pull them up, saying "ups-a-dada";
pretends something is in his hand and he gives it to people;
pretends to wash hands.

A particularly interesting example of early representation occurs at the end of the month when Harold wanted his father, who was sleeping, to wake. He ran to his father's bed, saw him sleeping, and paused a few moments quietly, and then said "up, up" several times. When this did not work, he again stood quietly, then went to the closet and got his father's slippers. He held these up, saying "up, up". Here he is solving his problem by mental reflection.

Between 1;2 and 1;4, Harold acquired an additional thirteen words. At 1;5 26 new words appear, and it is clear at this point that he is suddenly entering an active period of vocabulary growth that continues throughout the rest of the diary. If he had been on the verge of stage 6 as indicated, this growth is predictable. At 1;6, the fiftieth word is acquired, and with it appear the first attempts at two-word combinations. At this time, his mother states the following regarding Harold's comprehension: "He seems to understand all that we say to him, but we are careful to use words that we think he will understand." (37) What is specially interesting is her comment on his under-standing at 1;4, when his vocabulary was around 20 words or less. She states that he understood the following commands:

shut the door;
kiss the cheek;
bring mama's shoes;
bring Harold's shoes.

Also she says that he could point to either his or his mother's eyes or nose upon request. While obviously not well documented, this suggests that he is understanding two elements in these commands at a time when his spoken language is quite minimal. These observations are consistent with Shinn's comments on comprehension ability around late stage 5 of sensori-motor development. They are also similar to the result found by Huttenlocher (1974) in a study on the comprehension of children with very little productive language.

Axel Preyer

The diary of Preyer (1895) documents the acquisition of both production and comprehension (of German) as well as detailed observations on cognitive growth. It is much more detailed on language than Piaget and consequently can provide more insight into the linguistic events that occur alongside cognitive ones. Table VI provides a detailed account of Axel's growth on each of these aspects from 1;1 to 1;5.

During this period, Axel is doing a variety of behaviors which suggest stage 5 development. At this time, his language productivity is virtually non-existent, although two recognizable words appear. This is reminiscent of Ruth Shinn who also had very little language during this stage. Shinn states the following about Ruth's communicative system at this time: "For talking to us she used a wonderfully vivid and delicate language of grunts, and cries, and movements" (237). Compare this with the following remark made by Preyer on Axel's speech at 1;5:

> Characteristic for this period is the precision with which the various moods of feeling are expressed, without articulate sounds, by means of the voice, now become very high and strong, in screaming and crowing, then again in wailing, whimpering, weeping, grunting, squealing; so that the mood is recognized by the voice better than ever before, especially desire, grief, joy, hunger, wilfulness, and fear. (131)

Communication at this time is taking place but not through a system of recognizable adult words.

The steady growth of comprehension shows very clearly how this ability is developing. Here Preyer carefully documents Axel's ability to understand words by noting whether or not he points to the object mentioned or obeys the

Table VI
Summary of cognitive and linguistic behaviors of Axel Preyer from 1;1 to 1;5

Age		Behavior
1;1	Cognitive:	stage 5 behaviors occur:
		fear of falling;
		takes off and puts on cover on can 79 times;
		pulls out and pushes in a drawer;
		turns leaves of a book;
		recognizes mother's image in mirror as image.
	Production:	one word, "atta", meaning "going".
	Comprehension:	several words and phrases:
		adult: "where is papa? mama?" correct response, will takes adult to it by hand;
		Adult: "where is papa? mama?" correct response, will lift hand and point;
		"piano" will lead to piano playing;
		"nose" causes him to snort;
		"give" he responds by holding out object in hand to adult (first with just ring and biscuit, now with anything);
		"How tall?" will reach up and show.
1;2	Cognitive:	stage 5 causality:
		when he wanted adult to hit glass with ring, he handed ring to adult, looked at glasses to be struck, and said "hay-uh";
		also hunts for missing scraps of paper.
	Production:	new word "heiss" (hot).
	Comprehension:	has added several new words:
		"give a kiss" makes him near head and pucker;
		understands "where is the . . .?"
		moon eye light
		nose clock
		understands following activities:
		"cough" he coughs
		"blow" he blows
		"kick" stretches out legs
		"give the hand" or "hand" leads to his holding out his hand.
1;3	Cognitive:	further stage 5 behaviors:
		puts ring on head in imitation;
		opens and shuts cupboards;
		pretends to read newspaper (probably a stage 5 imitation);
		turns around to see father whose image is in the mirror.
	Production:	no new words.
	Comprehension:	when told to "bring, fetch, give" will go and obtain object.

Age		Behavior
1;4	Cognition:	first stage 6 behavior;
		when could not reach playthings, child went and got travel bag, got on it, and reached what he needed.
	Production:	no new words.
	Comprehension:	the following 33 words are now consistently understood: "clock, ear, shoe, chair, shoulder, foot, forehead, chin, nose, blow, beard, hair, hat, meat, eye, arm, hand, cheek, head, mouth, table, light, cupboard, flower"; obeys the following: "run, kick, lie down, cough, blow, bring, give, come, kiss".
1;5	Cognition:	pretends to water flowers with an empty watering pot; takes a stick of wood to the stove and puts in with great satisfaction.
	Production:	no new words.
	Comprehension:	can point out the following: "glass, door, sofa, stove, carpet, watering pot". will also follow the following commands: "find, pick up, take, lay down, smell".

particular command. At 1;5, when still only two productive words exist, Axel comprehends about 50 words or expressions. These observations support Piaget's claims and add to them additional facts regarding comprehension. The latter, of course, also forces revisions in his theory that will not be attempted here. For all six of the children discussed so far, stage 5 is marked by the appearance of a small number of words. Also, comprehension develops more rapidly than comprehension at stage 5, with the latter around 50 words at the onset of stage 6.

Jacob

The decision to use diaries such as the last three discussed is based on the assumption that good observations are timeless. This point is exemplified in Ferguson (1976) where some interesting points are made about the acquisition of phonology, in part based on the diary of Lindner (1898). At the same time, however, there is a strong suspicion about older studies, as shown by the brevity of references to them in most current literature. In this case, one could argue that the diaries were made without either audio or video equipment, and that the data may be inaccurate because of this. Also, one could raise questions about attempting to establish cognitive stages on the basis of random observations and a checklist of behavior patterns. The next child, however, is not subject to either of these criticisms.

Menn (1976) is a detailed study of a child named Jacob. Jacob was observed weekly by Menn from the age of 1;0(8) to 1;8(22). During that time she made audio-recordings of his language and occasional video-recordings. Based on these recordings, she provides a detailed and valuable account of the acquisition of his first words. Also, Jacob received standardized Piagetian tasks on his sensori-motor development at five different times, based on the work of Užgiris and Hunt (1975). Table VII provides a summary of his performance on these tasks as well as his language at the time of testing.

At the first test session at 1;1(23), Jacob appears to be at stage 4, in transition to stage 5. At this time he has six primitive "proto-words", a word used by Menn to mean a vocalization used by the child in specific contexts without suggestion of adult usage. This situation suggests that the first words may appear in stage 4. The next two sessions show clearly that Jacob is at stage 5. Since the time difference between the first and second sessions is only 14 days, it is suspicious that Jacob changed stages in such a brief time. It may be that strangeness of the tasks and the testing situation may have resulted in lower performance in the first session. In any case, it is possible that Jacob may have been at stage 5 at the first session so that the suggestion that words may occur in stage 4 needs to be considered cautiously.

In the last two sessions, Jacob shows stage 6 performance. There was such confidence in this point by 1;5(2) that only scale I was attempted. Notice that during this entire period Jacob's language was quite limited. At 1;2(28), when he was showing both stage 5 and 6 results, his spoken vocabulary was only 11 words. This data from Jacob supports the findings established so far by very different methods that stage 5 is the stage for the acquisition of a small number of early words.

A COMPARISON WITH LINGUISTIC STAGES

In Ingram (1974), I reviewed various studies on linguistic milestones in the first two years of life, and proposed three periods of development. These are summarized below:

Period 1   0;10 to 1;5

One word at a time; words are used in a variety of functions, e.g. as wish, request, etc. Small vocabulary.

Period 2   1;6 to 2;0 or later

Table VII
Cognitive and linguistic development of Jacob from 1;1(23) to 1;5(2)
based on Menn (1976)

Age	Scale[a]	Step	Stage	Language development
1;1(23)	I	6	V	"six proto-words—'thank-you' in the giving game, 'Jacob' in playing peekaboo, 'no' and 'don't' while contemplating or engaging in forbidden behavior, 'there' when putting objects down, and 'toast' on one occasion, apparently a request." (238)
	II	4	IV	
	IV	2	IV	
	V	3	IV	
1;2(7)	I	8	V	"added two more (proto-) words, 'down' and 'round', both used to accompany his own actions of knocking down block towers and rotating objects." (240)
	II	7	V	
	IV	4-5	IV-V	
	V	10	V	
1;2(28)	I	10	VI	"acquired three new action-accompanying proto-words [ioio], 'up', and 'top-top', and the label 'doll'. He had also been reported to use 'down' as imperative, comment on action of others, report of object falling, and aged 1;2(24) as a commentary as he peered out of a eight-story window; this one word showed autonomy." (243)
	II	7	V	
	IV	5	V	
	V	10-11	V-VI	
1;3(26)	I	14	VI	"Jacob had added only three words to his active vocabulary . . . 'hello', 'here' as an accompaniment to giving an object, and the predicate 'hot'. But in terms of function, these four weeks had seen a good deal of progress. Jacob had begun to regularly use his action words with rising contour to request action and permission to act, and to ask for confirmation of his predications." (245)
	II	12	VI	
	IV	6-7	VI	
	V	no results		
1;5(2)	I	14	VI	"Eight words, seven of them object names and the one demonstrative 'what's that' had been acquired in the interim; the object names were used only as labels, but the action words continued to be used in a variety of ways." (245)
	only scale given			

[a]The scales are: I, Visual pursuit and permanence of objects; II, Development of means for obtaining desired environmental results; IV, The development of operational causality; V, The construction of object relations in space.

One word at a time at onset; use of single words in semantic roles such as Agent, Object; use of sequences of one-word utterances; rapid growth of vocabulary; (month or two later) vocabulary up to 50 words; onset of multi-word utterances; (several months later) onset of information function; onset of references to absent situations.

Period 3 2;0 onwards

One-word utterances no longer used; onset of ideational and textual functions (cf. Halliday, 1975).

A comparison of these with the present study reveals the following similarities: stage 5 (and possibly stage 4) correlates with Period 1, stage 6 is similar to the early part of Period 2, and representation covers the latter part of Period 2 and Period 3. The discrepancy stopping a one-to-one correspondence is the length of Period 2 which seems to cover both stage 6 and representational development.

There is, however, a way that this discrepancy may be resolved. During the course of this study, an important problem arose regarding the establishment of stage 6 and representational behavior. This is because of that fact that in many ways stage 6 is the most poorly defined stage in Piaget's theory. In Piaget (1954), for example, stage 6 *is* representation, i.e. there is no qualitative difference between them. Since stage 6 is an important transition stage between sensori-motor and representational intelligence, it should be expected to have some unique qualities of its own. In a perusal of all of Piaget's books, only two were found. One of these concerns symbolic play. In stage 6, the onset of symbolic play appears in symbolic schemata, which are symbolic activities focused on the child's body, e.g. pretending to wash one's hands, pretending to sleep, etc. In the representational period, symbolic play extends away from the child and onto a variety of other kinds of play discussed as types I, II, and III in Piaget (1962). The second difference concerns the nature of the first words. During stage 6, these are called verbal schemata; they are highly personal to the child and highly variable in meaning. Later, in representation, they become verbal preconcepts and are used as social signs in communication.

Another problem that arose concerning stage 6 was its length. Reviews of Piaget's theory, including his own, often refer to stage 6 as lasting from around 1;6 to 2;0. This is reasonable given the important role it plays in cognitive growth. The examination of the actual chronological records for the three children, however, showed this stage as lasting only around two months. This is because types I and I symbolic play soon overcome those of symbolic schemata. In general, Piaget's data create an impression of stage 6 as a brief and poorly defined stage of development.

Given these problems, it is clear that stage 6 needs to be re-defined. One fruitful possibility which I would like to suggest here is that stage 6 is essentially

Period 2, one that lasts several months, and that representation begins with Period 3. Symbolic schemata and types I and II of symbolic play are seen as occurring in the same stage, with the former occurring first. This is consistent with other stages of Piaget's theory where new behaviors occurs first focused on the child and later on others, e.g. children first only try to visually pursue objects they drop themselves, and only later those dropped by others, all within the same stage. The question then arises about how stage 6 is seen as distinct from representation. The answer to this may be found in the interesting distinction made by Halliday (1975) between the mathetic function and the information function. The former characterizes his Phase II which is highly similar to Period 2. By the mathetic function, Halliday means that the child in this period from around 1;6 to 2;0 uses language primarily to comment on the world around him, rather than use it to communicate information. This function is a transition one that leads eventually to the information function which is the basis of adult language use. It may be that the mathetic function could be the most effective way yet to capture the nature of language in stage 6 during the important transition to symbolic ability. A re-defined stage 6 along these lines might look something like this:

Stage 6 (re-defined)
   onset of mathetic function;
   onset of symbolic play, including symbolic schemata and linguistic
      play;
   (later)
   references to past events;
   wider range of symbolic play (types I and II);
   appearance of "what is it?" for names of things.
Representation
   appearance of information function;
   use of advanced symbolic play (type III).

Given the lack of detail from Piaget on stage 6, this suggestion is not that incompatible with his more general remarks on this stage.

COGNITIVE PRECURSORS

Before concluding, it is important to comment on what the results of this investigation mean for the notion of cognitive precursors to language. Since the findings indicate that certain linguistic milestones occur along with certain sensori-motor stages, one could conclude that there are specific precursors to language. For example, Bloom (1973) has speculated that object permanence must be achieved before rapid vocabulary growth can take place. Since the seven subjects of this study do not show rapid growth of vocabulary until stage 6, the results seem to support this proposal. It is necessary, however, to be cautious about drawing such conclusions. Given the small number of subjects that are involved, the safest conclusion is that there are certain linguistic and cognitive developments that appear to occur together. The results suggest a trend that is worth further investigation.

Concerning specific precursors, some recent research has provided some interesting results on this issue. Synder (1975), in an important study on this subject, collected data on verbal and non-verbal communication from 15 normal children ranging from 1;1 to 1;6 years; she also gave the subjects the Uzgiris and Hunt scales of sensori-motor development. After statistical analysis, she found that only one skill correlated with language development, that of stage 5 means-ends. This finding is quite reasonable since language can be seen as an instrument to achieve goals, much as physical instruments discussed by Piaget. This finding is also in agreement with the discussion of the language of stage 5 found in Bates *et al.* (1975). Its function is limited to pragmatic usage, however, as the information function will require further advances.

As for object permanence, Corrigan (1976) has found in a study that longitudinally collected language and tested for object permanence in three children from approximately 0;10 to 1;6 that object permanence did not necessarily correlate with language growth. One of her subjects, for example, was using multi-word utterances before object permanence was achieved. The latter situation was also found in Ingram *et al.* (in preparation) with one of four subjects who were observed longitudinally from 0;7 to 1;7. Our subject was using syntax at stage 5. In her case, there was only one striking difference between her and the other three subjects in the area of sensori-motor development, and that was in her imitative ability. The diaries discussed earlier also report advances in imitation around the time of rapid linguistic growth.

Preliminary findings such as these support the need to be cautious in interpreting the results of this study as evidence for specific precursors to language (cf. Bowerman, 1976, who also advises caution in this area). So far, though, it appears that there are certain cognitive and linguistic developments that occur together, and that the ends-means and imitative achievements may be important in the appearance of pragmatic and syntactic forms of language.

APPENDIX

A Checklist of Prominent Behaviors that Appear in Piaget's Sensori-motor Stages 3 to 6

Stage 3: Secondary Circular Reactions

General

1. Reproductive assimilation (circular reactions)
   a. rubbing objects against surfaces
   b. shaking of objects
   c. striking objects with hand
   d. hitting two objects together
   e. putting object in mouth
2. Recognitory assimilation
   a. fear of strangers
   b. recognizes footsteps, opening of door, etc.
   c. recognizes bottle
   d. knows presence of someone when touched

Object Permanence

3. Visual accommodation to rapid movements
   a. search for fallen objects (by self, others)
   b. search for lost trajectory
   c. memory of positions
4. Interrupted prehension
   a. grasps for objects pulled away
5. Deferred circular reactions
6. Reconstruction of whole from visible fraction

Displacement

7. Lack of assignment of trajectory
8. Lack of ability to rotate objects

Causality

9. Causality by imitation
   a. imitation of bye bye to make adult continue

Imitation

10. Systematic imitation of sounds already made by the child

11. Systematic imitation of movements seen by child
    a. clapping hands
    b. opening and closing of hand
    c. wave bye bye

Stage 4: Co-ordination of Secondary Schemata

General

1. Removal of objects that are obstacles
   a. hold hand in way of visible object
   b. hold object in hand
   c. move hand to grasp object
   d. put cover over object to make it invisible
   e. child pushes medicine away
2. Intentional rejection of object
   a. give child one object, then a second
   b. give child two objects, then a third
3. Use of other's hands (etc.) to achieve goal
   a. gives adult box to open, pushes hand of adult
4. Prevision
   a. recognizes someone getting up is leaving
   b. recognizes medicine
5. Exploration of new objects—4 steps:
       visual exploration
       tactile exploration
       movement of object
       secondary circular reactions applied
6. New secondary circular reactions
   a. swinging
   b. letting go (at end of stage)

Object Permanence

7. Search for hidden object
8. Search for hidden object with visible displacements

Displacement

9. Reversible operations
   a. hands object back to adult
10. Study of constant shape
    a. moves objects to and from eyes
    b. moves head side to side
    c. intentional rotation to see reverse side
    d. errors in judgement of distance

11. Relations of depth
    a. looking over or around screens
12. Movements of translation
    a. can follow complex movements of object
    b. side to side anticipation of movement behind child
13. Unawareness of "placed upon"
    a. can't grasp small object placed on another object
    b. can't balance one object on another
    c. can't use supports

Imitation

14. Imitation of non-visible movements already made by the child
    a. opening and closing of mouth
    b. putting out tongue
    c. sucking thumb
    d. opening and closing eyes
15. Imitation of new sounds
16. Imitation (with effort) of new visible models
    a. forefinger against thumb
    b. bending and straightening of finger
    c. marionette movement

Stage 5: Tertiary Circular Reactions

General

1. Tertiary circular reactions
   a. dropping objects to study their trajectory
   b. exploration of new objects (experimentation)
   c. study of sounds of objects
2. Use of instruments
   a. use of supports ("placed upon")
   b. behavior pattern of the string
   c. behavior pattern of the stick
3. Experimentation to solve problems
   a. pulling sticks through bars of playpen
   b. putting chain into container
   c. correctly stacking cups
4. Advanced prehension
   a. object will fall if not handled carefully
   b. hat indicates leaving

Object Permanence

5. Success at visible displacements
6. Failure at invisible displacement

Displacement

7. Relation of contents to container
   a. takes objects out of container
   b. puts objects back into container
   c. dumps out container
8. Object rotation—objects in relation to other objects
   a. stands doll in relation to floor
9. Complex operations
   a. can find new path to object
10. Experimentation with visible displacements
    a. carry object one place to another
    b. drop and re-drop objects
    c. slide objects along a surface
    d. roll ball
11. Position and equilibrium of bodies
    a. stacking of objects
    b. study of vertical position (standing up and knocking down objects)

Causality

12. Objective causality of objects
    a. let object go so that it can slide
    b. expectation of movement of objects
13. Objective causality of people
    a. assumption of expectant attitude
    b. hands object to adult to operate it

Imitation

14. Systematic imitation of new visual models
    a. remove and replace jar lid
    b. hit objects with stick
    c. scribble on paper with pencil
15. Systematic imitation of new auditory models
16. Imitation of new non-visible models
    a. putting hand on head
    b. touching chin
    c. tongue against side of mouth
17. Complex movements
    a. circle around face with forefinger

18. Awareness of mirror reflection
    a. knows adult is behind
19. Facial parts
    a. explores facial parts of others, then of self

Stage 6: Invention of New Means Through Mental Combinations

General

1. Invention of new means to solve problems
    a. use of chair to stop door from moving
2. Evocation of absent objects
    a. looks for object that is misplaced or put away

Object Permanence

3. Success at single invisible displacement

Displacement

4. Representative groups of space
    a. goes around to back of sofa to retrieve ball
    b. detours to reach object
5. Acts of orientation
    a. can point to places of family members who are no longer in sight

Causality

6. Mental reconstruction of causes
    a. sees actions and immediately looks for causes
    b. solves problems where unseen objects block gate, etc.
7. Mental foresight of effects

Imitation

8. Immediate imitation of complex models
    a. cross and uncross arms
    b. imitate facial features of photos
9. Deferred imitation
    a. says words for first time without an immediate model
10. Representational imitation
    a. of objects and situations, to better understand them

Play

11. Pretence centered on child's own activities
    a. washing, eating, sleeping, drinking

Representation

General

1. Recounting of past events
2. Awareness of names
   a. need to know names of all objects
   b. use of "what's that?" question

Object Permanence

3. Success at multiple invisible displacements

Play

4. Projection of symbolic schemata onto new objects (type IA)
   a. make animals cry, eat, etc.
5. Projection of imitative schemas (type IB)
   a. has doll brush floor, read paper, etc.
6. Identification of one object with another (type IIA)
   a. call block a car
7. Games of imitation (type IIB)
   a. child pretends to be someone else
8. Symbolic combinations
   a. Type IIIA simple combinations
      —construction of whole scenes
   b. Type IIIB compensatory combinations
      —re-enacts forbidden acts
   c. Type IIIC liquidating combinations
      —symbolic transposing of unpleasant events
   d. Type IIID anticipatory symbolic combinations
      —accept order, but play out consequences

12

Word and Gesture Usage by an Indian Child

ALICIA NOKONY

University of British Columbia, Canada

INTRODUCTION

Recent studies of child language acquisition which have turned to a Piagetian model in examining the relationship between cognitive and linguistic development have centred largely on the problem of determining meaning in the child's early utterances. There is, however, another aspect of Piaget's theory which is also of considerable interest to child language researchers—his position that language is just one part, although the principal part, of a larger symbolizing capacity and that language acquisition, therefore, is inextricably a part of semiological genesis. Sinclair (1971), Morehead and Morehead (1974) and Ingram (this volume) have focused on the emergence of language as part of the symbolizing function using a Piagetian framework. Other researchers, such as Halliday (1975), Bates (1976b) and Greenfield and Smith (1976), have considered the evolution of symbolic behaviour in the context of the child's social development. It seems that the semiological analysis of early child behaviour and speech, both from the cognitive and the pragmatic points of view, provides a powerful way of accounting for certain aspects of language acquisition. The goal of this chapter is to demonstrate how instances of gestural imitations occurring with the speech of one child can be analysed as proto-words according to Piaget's descriptions of the evolution of the linguistic sign.

Index, Symbol and Linguistic Sign

The ability to symbolize—that is, to substitute some *form* (the *signifier*) for some *content* (the *signified*)—characterizes a significant development at the end of the sensori-motor period (roughly towards the end of the second year of life). The child moves beyond sensori-motor intelligence, which operates through immediately present stimuli, to conceptual representation or thought; he can then work out mental combinations through evoked stimuli and is able to start predicting the future and re-enacting the past. According to Piaget, the symbolizing function is organized in a similar way to other cognitive functions, which means that the ability to symbolize evolves through a process of assimilation and accommodation co-ordinated by the child's activities and developing internal logic. The origins of this function can be observed in the behaviour of sensori-motor children, especially during the last two substages of this period, substages V and VI, the transition period between intelligence based on sensori-motor activities and intelligence which is representational, i.e. sign-based.

Sign is a generic term referring to a unity of some signifier with some signified. In semiological terms, there are different kinds of relationship which may obtain between a signifier and its signified, among which are the *index*, the *symbol* and the *linguistic sign*. The *index* is a relatively "primitive" signifier-signified relationship such that the signifier is a trace of the signified. The neighing of a horse or the imprint of its hoof are indexical signifiers in that they indicate, to someone familiar with animals, the existence (proximal in the first instance, though not necessarily so in the second) of some hoofed animal that neighs. Developmentally, the index makes its appearance in Piaget's sensori-motor substage IV in the form of what Morehead and Morehead (1974) call "shared features"; that is, the child is able to recognize features of an event which are common to his own action schemata. The meaning which he then draws out of the event is that which is attached to the particular schema with which it shares features. The index (or "shared features") operates as a mediator between the outside models and the child's own behaviour. The appearance of this phenomenon is taken to be the first evidence that some relationship exists for the child between a signifier and a signified, although such a relationship is not yet representational and is still attached to the here and now.

The *symbol* is a representational sign in that the signifier re-presents, or is substituted for, the signified and may be used purposefully to communicate the latter. In classical semiological terms, symbol refers to a sign in which the signifier physically or functionally resembles the signified. An example is the scales of justice, a symbol of impartiality, but an utterance such as "There's a . . ." where the imitation of a horse neighing is embedded in the sentence frame is also an instance of a motivated signifier-signified relationship. Here, the signified "horse" is represented by an imitative signifier "neighing". The appearance of *deferred imitation*, marking the beginning of substage VI, is the first evidence that the child is capable of representation. Imitation of an absent model (or signified) implies that the model has been replaced by a *mental image* (the signifier) upon which the imitation is based. The mental image is necessary for any kind of symbolizing, and it is from a phenomenon which first appears in substage V—adultomorphic, or adult-like, behaviours —that stable and specific mental images can start to be inferred.

Whatever shape the child's early signifier-signified relationships assume, they reflect in various ways his distance from the collective sign system which is the adult language. A word of an adult language is called a *linguistic sign*. Like the symbol, the linguistic sign is representational. However, it differs from the symbol in two important ways. Firstly, unlike the symbol the linguistic sign is not based on a necessary resemblance between the signifier and signified; rather, the signifier-signified relationship is unmotivated and arbitrary. There is, for example, no motivation for the connection between the signifier /hors/* and the signified, the mental image of a horse. Secondly, whereas the child's first signs are private and individual, the linguistic sign is collective, or conventional; that is, all speakers of English have agreed more or less that /hors/ designates a four-legged solid-hoofed animal that neighs.

Piaget's work implies that there is a time in development when the child's knowledge of language may be more accurately determined from his imitative and play behaviours. This means that even the adult-sounding words and word combinations which a child uses at this time might be described as motivated because of their identity with the situations in which they were first introduced to the child's symbolic system and in which they are subsequently used.

Symbolic Behaviour and Social Interaction

Although the ability to symbolize may function in the early stages primarily to extend the child's knowledge of the world, it soon becomes the core of his social interactions. Successful symbolic communication is the result of a complex of social and experiential factors among which are: (a) the child's

*In this chapter a mixture of American and I.P.A. symbols have been used: c = tʃ; š = ʃ; o = ɔ and o′ = primary stress, — = difficult to translate. In the morpheme by morpheme translations / / have been inserted around deviant pronunciations and " " around English words used in Dakota sentences.

realization that symbols can be exchanged not merely for expression of needs and desires but for giving and getting information (what Halliday, 1975, has labelled the Informative Function); and (b) the evolution of what is a private and individual system of symbols into the arbitrary, conventional and rule-governed system of linguistic signs which is the adult language.

This chapter deals with phenomena in the developing communicative system of one child, Gabriel, which exemplify the transition from private sensori-motor representations to true linguistic signs. His imitative and play behaviours are characteristic of Piaget's substage VI and a significant portion (over 20%) of his approximately 100 observed morphemes are clearly unconventional—some imitative, some idiosyncratic word-like inventions. The most striking aspect of Gabriel's system, however, is his use of gestural imitations in verbal syntactic frames, as contrasted with other types of gestural behaviour. These phenomena will be examined from the perspective of the evolution of the linguistic sign from its indexical and symbolic precursors and in the context of Gabriel's developing discourse abilities.

Gabriel is acquiring an American Indian language, Dakota-Sioux (Santee dialect), as his first language. Since most other studies in this area have been based on acquisition data from English or related languages, it is intended that this present study will show that tentative conclusions reached in these investigations are supported by cross-linguistic findings.

THE STUDY

Data

The discussion of Gabriel's communicative system is based on analysis of detailed transcriptions taken from 32½ hours of tape-recorded data. Gabriel's corpus size is 7,130 utterances (when gestural and onomatopoeic representations are included). The data are from 16 playsessions, 15 during a three-week period when Gabriel was 2;4(0) to 2;4(22) and one further session 5 months later when he was 2;9(0). These sessions averaged two hours in length and were conducted under similar conditions in the presence of the child's aunt, Wilma, and at least one other peer who interacted with Gabriel using various play materials. The author was present at all tapings and kept a running transcription with contextual notes, as well as playing with and talking to the children. Sometimes older children and one or two other familiar adults were also present. Wilma assisted in transcribing and trans-lating the tapes; each session was transcribed the day it was recorded. Table I

Table I

	Age	MLU	Upper bound	No. of utterances
Session				
1	2;4(0)	1·38	3	409
2	2;4(1)	1·30	4	122
3	2;4(4)	1·24	4	554
4	2;4(5)	1·17	3	510
5	2;4(6)	1·27	3	315
6	2;4(7)	1·48	3	463
7	2;4(8)	1·82	4	736
8	2;4(11)	1·29	3	113
9	2;4(12)	1·32	3	555
10	2;4(13)	1·59	4	686
11	2;4(14)	1·46	3	241
12	2;4(19)	1·50	4	452
13	2;4(20)	1·42	4	535
14	2;4(21)	1·23	3	669
15	2;4(22)	1·18	3	487
16	2;9(0)	1·42	4	283

gives sessional information; mean length of utterance (MLU) is included here for comparative purposes. It must be noted that calculation of MLU is difficult across languages and that standard criteria (Brown, 1973) have been departed from to a certain extent, most particularly in the morpheme status we have assigned to interactional vocalizations and gestural morphemes. Gabriel is the third of five children. During the data collection he was healthy and good-natured and appeared to be developing normally both physically and mentally. A more detailed account of Gabriel's linguistic development can be found in Nokony (1977).

As the low MLU indicates, there are many one-word utterances in the corpus. The multi-morphemic utterances which occur fall into a few basic patterns, the most predominant of which are "ká . . . ", " . . . ye/ya", " . . . eyá", or "ká . . .$\left\{\begin{matrix} \text{ye/ya} \\ \text{eyá} \end{matrix}\right\}$", where the unspecified element(s) can be one of any of Gabriel's other morphemes, including the gestural and onomatopœic symbols. "Ka" in the adult language is a deictic meaning "that farther away", but Gabriel uses it so generally it seems improbable that he has attached a fine semantic distinction to it. "Ye" is the female declarative sentence-ending particle with the rough meaning "it is a fact"; however, Gabriel appears to use this element as a morpheme boundary as well as an utterance boundary and it is likely that it performs a syntactic rather than a semantic function in his system. "Eyá" is very difficult to interpret because of its phonetic similarity to many adult forms. It seems to be confined to those utterances of Gabriel's which refer to actions rather than to objects; Wilma translated it as "it says or goes like that".

The predominance of these patterns gives Gabriel's morpheme combinations a pivot look. Brown (1973) observed that early multi-morphemic utterances are often referential rather than relational and thus appear pivot-like. Bloom (1973) suggested, however, that early syntactic strategies are correlated with how much the child imitates, that referential patterns (function word plus substantive word) are typical of the child who imitates a lot. The fuzziness of what might be Gabriel's function words—"ka", "ye/ya", and "eyá"—lends support to an interpretation made by Dore *et al.* (1976); that is, these forms may be placeholder morphemes, allowing the child to produce longer utterances without having to deal with semantic complexity as well.

Overview of Dakota-Sioux

Dakota-Sioux is a member of the Siouan family of languages (Hokan-Siouan phylum). It is spoken extensively in the mid-western United States and in seven communities in mid-western Canada. The Dakota-Sioux population has been estimated variously to be between 5,000 and 10,000 people, the majority of whom are Sioux speakers. It is still the first language of many children growing up in Sioux communities, although the influence of English is spreading. Only Dakota-Sioux was spoken in Gabriel's home and it was the principal language in Wilma's home where most of the taping sessions took place. Gabriel was exposed to English on television, however, and during play with older neighbourhood children. In the final session there is evidence that he is becoming bilingual.

A few features of the adult language are given here, but readers are directed to Riggs (1893), Boas and Deloria (1941), Buechel (1970) and Carter (1974) for more detailed descriptions of Dakota-Sioux and the closely related Teton dialect.

Dakota-Sioux is an SOV language. There are basically two classes of verb stem—the stative and the active—which may be followed by any of the approximately 30 grammatical clitics indicating number, aspect and mode. There are sex-appropriate variants of some of these clitics, which form the basis for the male and female speech forms. Abbreviations are used in this paper in the translations of those clitics which occur in example utterances. "Ye", the female form of the sentence-ending particle meaning roughly "it is a fact", is represented by "F."; "ha", the female form of the interrogative particle, is represented by "Q."; "kte", the potential marker which basically indicates the future tense, is represented by "Pot."; "šni", the negative particle, is represented by "Neg."; and "ce", a particle which seems to give generic meaning to verbs it is used with, is represented by "G.". The pronouns fall into two main categories—separate or incorporated—the latter breaking into subgroups according to the verb stems with which they are associated. The pronominal elements are italicized in the examples given here, and infixed pronouns have been set apart from the element in which they occur by "+" markers. The third person is unmarked in Dakota-Sioux. Basic syllable structure in Dakota-Sioux is (C)CV. The rules for morpheme combination and stress movement are fairly complex and will not be dealt with here.

The Sioux language has a small set of baby words, some of which Gabriel uses; these are appropriate only if used by a child or in conversation with a child. There are also records of an adult sign language system that was used among the Sioux tribes. The author observed its being used on only one occasion, however, and that was between two elderly men. There is no reason to believe that the gestural symbols used by Gabriel have any connection with this sign system.

The following are typical adult Dakota-Sioux sentences taken from the corpus:

(i) declarative:
Cicí   *ni* + yáxte   kté   ye.   "Monster will bite you."
mons. you   bite   Pot. F.

(ii) declarative-negative:
Wašté   šni   yé.   "It's not good."
good   Neg. F.

(iii) interrogative with question word:
Táku   *detkã*   há?   "What are you drinking?"
what   you-drink   Q.

(iv) interrogative (yes-no):
Cã + *ní* + ze   há?   "Are you angry?"
you-angry   Q.

(v) interrogative (yes-no), negative and complex:
Duksá   o + *yá* + kihí   šni   há?   "Can't you cut it?"
you-cut   you-are able   Neg. Q.

(vi) imperative:
Haáke   õyé   káya.   "Make some clothes."
clothes   some   make

(vii) imperative-negative:
Íyã   ű   šni.   "Don't run."
run   do Neg.

(viii) complex:
Wa + hdé   kãhã   wašté   kte   dé.   "If I go home, this one will be good."
I-go   home if   good   Pot. this

RESULTS

Gestural Imitations as Words in Formation

As we mentioned earlier, Gabriel's use of gestural imitations appears to provide a most interesting demonstration of the transition between sensori-motor intelligence and sign-based intelligence and thus of the connection between language development in particular and the symbolizing function in general. The discussion of these phenomena begins here with the establishment of Gabriel's ability to represent as indicated in behaviours which are characteristic of early substage VI. These first examples are also grouped together because they occur outside of dialogue and, at first glance, may seem unrelated to the formation of linguistic signs. Assuming the correctness of the semiological approach, however, these data and the curious mixture of gestures and adult-sounding words which Gabriel uses in dialogue appear to be precursory to his use of linguistic signs.

The actual imitations will be italicized in the examples.

Evidence for Representation

Although Gabriel has been "located" in the representational substage VI, we can find instances of what would be taken as the first evidence that he has this capacity—adultomorphisms from which we can infer the formation of stable and specific mental images (examples 1, 2 and 3), and deferred imitation, which indicates that signifier and signified can be separated from one another in time and space (example 4).

(1) Session 1   2;4(0)
Gabriel sees a cup, goes over to it, picks it up and drinks from it.

(2) Session 16   2;9(0)
Gabriel picks up a broom and starts sweeping the floor with it.

(3) Session 7   2;4(8)
Gabriel picks up an LP record album, takes it to the stereo and tries to lift the lid which covers the turntable.

(4) Session 1   2;4(0)
(The model for this imitation is the male "fancy-dancing" performed at the summer pow-wow dances which are held across the Prairies. We cite this as an example of deferred imitation, although the possibility exists that Gabriel's first imitation of the model occurred in its immediate context but was not observed.)
Gabriel starts to dance, shifting his weight from one foot to the other for every two beats he is marking out with his arms; arms are held close to his sides,

elbows bent and hands clenched as though holding shakers. To finish the dance, he suddenly throws back his arms and jumps, landing with feet spread, and says /hah/.

Just as imitation occurring removed in time and space from its model is evidence that the model has been replaced by a mental image, immediate and precise imitation of new models (examples 5, 6 and 7) suggests that Gabriel has internalized the model *before* imitating it-rather than *by* imitating it. Examples 5 and 6 are not social, however, in that Gabriel makes no effort to secure the attention of either the model or other potential interlocutors; example 7 is social because he interacts in play with Esther, but there is no dialogue.

(5) Session 13   2;4(20)
Esther (Gabriel's 4-year old cousin) puts a box of crayons under her chin and holds them there by pressing her chin down against her chest. *Gabriel watches her, then picks up his own box of crayons and does the same, still facing her.*

(6) Session 9   2;4(12)
I fan my face with a notebook. Gabriel is close to me watching. *He picks up a tape reel box, turns to face in the same direction as I am facing and starts to fan his own face with the box, looking back at me once or twice.*

(7) Session 13   2;4(20)
Esther burps after eating a doughnut and drinking some juice. *Gabriel makes burping noises while looking at her.* Then they both laugh.

The elements of *double knowledge* of objects (Gabriel treats as a fan in example 6 what he otherwise treats as a box) and of *play* (Gabriel's games with Esther resemble a kind of turn-taking process based on mutual imitation as in example 7) are further evidence that the separation of assimilation and accommodation has taken place, thus allowing the differentiation of signifier from signified necessary for language and representational thought.

Representations in Dialogue

The examples which have been given thus far are functionally distinct from those which follow in that the latter occur in dialogue and are instances of the use of symbols to give information. It must be noted that Gabriel does not yet ask questions; the rising intonation in which certain of his words are uttered indicated that he is seeking verification of these utterances rather than further information. Much of the support for analysing the gestural imitations here as proto-words or proto-linguistic signs comes from their appearance in symbolic exchanges. This status derives from their being part of Gabriel's efforts to re-present his knowledge of the world to others. In these examples, Gabriel displays a knowledge of elementary dialogue rules for turn-taking and question-answering, although a fair amount of modelling on the part of his interlocutors is still required in order to sustain dialogues with him.

Gestural imitations as responses to questions which have elicited imitative behaviour. Examples 8 and 9 have been grouped together because Gabriel's imitative responses here could well be considered appropriate in light of the questions which preceded them, questions which elicited imitative responses. It is possible that Wilma's use of this strategy for building dialogues with Gabriel is an influencing factor in his first dialogue-initiating attempts. But it is also possible that Gabriel responds more readily to this kind of question and spontaneously reports the sounds and actions of people and objects because he is cognitively oriented toward these properties.

(8) Session 4   2;4(5)
   (Wilma and Gabriel are looking at pictures in a mail-order catalogue.)

   W: (pointing to picture of combs)
   Táktuk   hũ + p +   cé   ye   hé?   "What do they do?"
   what   do   plur. G. F.   Q.

   G. *Pretends to comb his hair with his hand from his crown to his forehead.*

   W: Eyá   há?   "Like that?"
   —   Q.

(9) Session 1   2;4(0)
   (Wilma and Gabriel are looking at the mail-order catalogue.)

   W: (pointing to pictures of guitars)
   Íŝ   táku   há?   "What's this?"
   this   what   Q.

   G: Eyá.   "Goes."
   —

   W: Eyá há?   "It goes like that?"
   —   Q.

   G. Eyá.   "Goes."
   —

   W: Tókex   ecṹ + ca   há?   "How is it used?"
      how   do   G.   Q.

   G: *Goes through actions of playing a guitar, holding his hands close to his chest and wiggling his fingers.*

   W: Aké   iyá.   "Do it again."
      again go
   Tókex ecṹ + ca   há?   "How is it used?"
   how   do   G.   Q.

Dé	dową́	kta	yé.	"This will sing."
this	sing	Pot.	F.	
Dową́	kta	yé.		"It will sing."
sing	Pot.	F.		

G: Hą́.   "Yes."
   yes

W: Tókex	ahíya	há?	Décex?	"How does it sing? Like this?"
how	sing	Q.	like-this	

(Wilma points to more guitars.)

G: Eyá.   "Goes."
   —

The element "eyá" has been cautiously translated here as "goes", although it may in fact not have this meaning for Gabriel. Its appearance with many of the gestural imitations which occur in dialogue situations is a curiosity. As was pointed out earlier, it seems to function as an action morpheme. When used with his imitations, it may serve to elevate them to the status of comments on actions.

Gestural imitations in spontaneous speech. Before Gabriel has the adult words for various objects and events, he can symbolize them through gestural and vocal imitations. He has also learned that these symbols can be used in social interactions to convey information to others. While representation ciearly need not be verbal representation, not all children manifest the gestural and verbal combinations which Gabriel uses in dialogue. The fact that he does is particularly revealing of just how words might evolve.

(10) Session 7   2;4(8)
   (Gabriel sees a baby on television clap its hands together.)

   G: Bibí   yá?   "Baby?"
      baby   —

   W: Hą́.   "Yes."
      yes

   G: Ká   bibí   *he claps his hands together* eyá.   "That baby 'claps'."
      that   "baby"   —

   W: Eyá há?   "Goes like that?"
      —   Q.

   G: Hą́.   "Yes."
      yes

   W: Óh.   "Oh."

   G: *Claps his hands together again.*

(11) Session 3   2;4(4)
(Esther is teaching Gabriel how to wave good-bye.)

E: Gabriel.   Gabriel.   Gabriel.   "Gabriel. Gabriel. Gabriel."
[wã́ka]   "Look."
(= wãyáka, "look")
(Esther demonstrates waving action.)
G: "Héy!"   "Hey!"
(Gabriel secures Wilma's attention.)
He waves to her   eyá.   "'Waves.'"
                    —

Ká.   (He points to Esther.)   "That."
that
W: Tókex   hecṹ   há?   "How did she do it?"
    how   do   Q.
Tókex   eyá + ci + ya   há?   "How do they say it?"
how   say   G. —   Q.
G: /babáị/   "Bye-bye."
    "bye-bye"

There is still instability of person forms in Gabriel's system; that is, proper names are not entirely consistent in either phonetic form or reference. Gabriel uses the name "Andrew" for his cousin Esther, perhaps because of the difficulty of pronouncing "Esther". The form /nɛt/, derived from the name of another cousin Annette, is used rather generally when Gabriel is referring to familiar females other than his mother who are from 10 to 30 years old.

(12) Session 7   2;4(8)
(Esther is playing with toys on the floor. She knocks some of them over.)

G. Ká   /páːjáː/.   (He gasps.) Kó.   "That falls-breaks."
    that   (= ixpáye, "to fall")   that
W: Táktuk   hṹ   ha?   "What did she do?"
    what   do   Q.
G: /ắʔú/   /çi̥/   *he falls over on his side on the chesterfield*   eyá.
    "Andrew"   —   —
                                              "Andrew 'falls' goes" (or perhaps
                                              "Andrew causes-to-fall goes.")
W: Eyá   há?   "Like that?"
    —   Q.
G: Hã́.   "Yes."
    yes

(13) Session 16   2;9(0)
(Gabriel watches a man on television make a face, dropping his mouth open and widening his eyes in an exaggerated way.)

G: "Hey!" *He makes the same face* eyá.   "Hey! 'Makes a face'."
/mæ̃/ *he makes face again.*   "Man 'makes face'."
"man"
/nɛ́t)! (He gets Marina's attention.)   "Annette!"
"Annette"
He makes face   eyá.   "'Makes face'."
—
He makes face.   "'Makes face'."
/æ̃ndú/. (He shakes her arm.)   "Andrew!"
"Andrew"
(Esther looks at him.)
Gabriel makes face again eyá. Eyá.   "'Makes face", 'makes
                                                   face'."

These examples demonstrate how Gabriel is able to comment on events he hasn't yet got the words for. His efforts are systematic. He gains the attention of a potential interlocutor and then makes his "statement" using a combination of verbal and gestural elements, usually ending with the form "eyá". It appears that some rule for sentence formation using gestures is operating here, perhaps of the form:

$$\text{Sentence} \longrightarrow \left(\left\{ {\text{"ka"} \atop \text{N}} \right\} \right) \text{Gestural imitation "eyá"}$$

This sentence pattern provides Gabriel with a frame in which he can at some point substitute linguistic signs for the gestural symbols he now uses. Example 11 may in fact indicate this possibility, where Gabriel uses both an imitation of waving "bye-bye" and the word itself in reference to the same event.

The next example, 14, is cognitively more complex than those which have been presented so far. It shows Gabriel's ability to reconstruct a cause he hasn't observed when he is given only the effect. In order to do this he must form a mental image of what might have happened, and then communicate this version to Wilma. Because Gabriel has been witness to the events preceding the effect (another little boy Raymond crying), his misrepresentation of the situation may be deliberately misleading. This would require his reconstruction of what might have happened and then deformation of that mental image in order to reassemble the misleading version.

(14) Session 6   2;4(7)
(Marina, a Dakota woman, has brought her younger brother, Raymond, to Wilma's house, intending to leave him to play. When she gets up to go, however, he starts crying, possibly because he is afraid to stay alone. Marina comes back to him and they leave together.)

W: (to Gabriel)   Táktuk hũ   há?   "What's he doing?"
                  what   do Q.

G: Ábu yá.   "Sleep."
 sleep —

Dé / $\tilde{\text{æ}}$ ndu/ *he pretends to strike someone with his hand* eyá kó.
this "Andrew"   — that
                   "Andrew 'hit' this."

W: Táktuk hũ ha?   "What did she do?"
 what do Q.

G: /έ/ *he performs same hitting action* yáya. "Goes 'hit'."
  —   goes

W: "Oh", eyá há?   "Oh, like that?"
 "oh" — Q.

G: Hã.   "Yes."
 yes

Deferred gestural imitation in dialogue. So far we have presented examples of gestural imitations which have occurred closely after their models or signifieds. In these cases, Gabriel's references are fairly easy to interpret. However, the limitations of the personal symbol, as opposed to the arbitrary and conventional linguistic sign, become apparent when Gabriel attempts to use his private gestural representations to relate an event of the recent past to his mother. Wilma reported this incident after she had taken Gabriel home following the first playsession at her house.

(15) Session 1 2;4(0)

(Gabriel and Esther and I had been playing a turn-taking game of "kiss and wake up".)

When Wilma took Gabriel home, his mother was waiting on the front step. He secured her attention and said /nɛt/, pointing to Wilma's house which is next-door. *Then he reached up and kissed his mother's cheek and said "Eyá",* pointing to Wilma's house again.

Wilma found it necessary to "translate" for Gabriel's mother what her (Wilma's) shared experience with Gabriel had led her to interpret from his gestures and words. In fact, many children who use personal symbols in early speech, either verbal or gestural, are only comprehensible to their caretakers. A corollary to this is that the length of time that personal symbols persist in the speech of a child may be a function of how far his social interactions extend beyond the immediate family.

Onomatopœic Imitations as Words in Formation

Besides the gestural morphemes, Gabriel has invented onomatopœic symbols based on the sounds that certain objects make or sounds which are attached to certain of his routines; for example, one such "word" accompanies his blowing out the match whenever Wilma lights a cigarette.

(16) Session1   2;4(0)
(Wilma has lit a cigarette and leaves the match burning for Gabriel to blow out.)

G: "Hey" ka   /p^{h}ú̥/   yá.   "Hey 'blow' that."
    "hey" that   *blow*   F.

(/p^{h}u̥/ is both the act of blowing and the symbol for it.)

We have previously suggested that linguistic signs eventually replace personal symbols in the child's speech. One of Gabriel's onomatopœic representations, co-existing with first one, and then two, adult word equivalents, perhaps provides an example of how a personal symbol is eventually phased out and a linguistic sign is phased in.

Gabriel uses both an imitation of a horse neighing, phonetically of the shape /ʔʌʔʌm/, and the form /kóka/ or /kúka), derived from the adult Dakota word /šṹká̃), "horse", to refer to his toy horses or to horses he sees in pictures. These two forms are used interchangeably in a number of syntactic frames or as one-word utterances throughout the sessions. In Session 15, however, /ʔʌʔʌm/ appears only briefly, along with /kóka/, just prior to what appears to be the introduction of the adult English word /hɔrs/ into Gabriel's lexicon.

The example is rather lengthy and has therefore been edited in order to present the following two observations: (a) the use of all three forms for the same referent, and (b) the "practising" of the new form /hɔrŝ/ in syntactic environments both of the old forms have been used in.

(17a) Session 15   2;4(22)
(Gabriel picks up one of the small toy horses; its tail is broken off.)

G: "Hey!"   /kóka/   /bóya/.   "Hey! Horse broken."
    "hey"   horse   (= ixpáya, "fall down")

W: "Hey?"   "Hey?"

G: /kóka/   /bóya/.   "Horse broken."
    horse   fall-down

W: /šṹká̃/?   "Horse?"
    horse

G: Há́.   /kóka/   /bóya/.   "Yes, horse broken."
    yes   horse   fall-down

W: /šuká̃/   ixpáye   há?   "Did the horse fall down?"
    horse   fall-down   Q.

G: Há́.   /kóka/   /bóya/.   "Yes, horse broken."
    yes   horse   fall-down

W: Hã̌, šũkã̌ ixpáye yé.   "Yes, the horse fell down."
    yes   horse   fall-down   F.
G: "Héy."   "Hey."
W: "Héy?"   "Hey?"
G: /pápi/.   "Puppy."
    "puppy"
W: /pápi/?   "Puppy?"
G: /2ƛ2ʌm/, /2ƛ2ʌm/, /2ƛ2ʌm/.   "Horse, horse, horse."
    (He picks up another toy horse.)
    "Héy." "Héy" /hórŝ/   iyá.   "Hey. Hey horse goes."
    "hey"   "hey"   "horse"   —

(17b) Session 15   2;4(22)
    (The following utterances of Gabriel's have been removed from the dialogue
    in which they occur but represent spontaneous utterances using the new form
    /horŝ/ in old syntactic frames.)

    G: "Héy"   /hórŝ/   /babáį/.   "Hey horse bye-bye."
       "hey"   "horse"   "bye-bye"

    /hórŝ/   /dʒidʒíŝ/.   "Horse monster."
    "horse"   (=cicí, "monster")

    "Héy"   /hórŝ/.   "Hey horse."
    "hey"   "horse"

    "Héy"   /hórŝ/   iyáya.   "Hey horse goes."
    "hey"   "horse"   goes

    "Héy"   /kórŝ/   /pajá:/.   "Hey horse broken."
    "hey"   (= ká + "horse"?)   (= ixpáye, "fall down")

    "Héy"   pótet   /hórŝ/   iyá.   "Hey two horses go."
    "hey"   two   "horse"   —

The new word /horŝ/ is brought into Gabriel's system through the old
structures in which its predecessors have been used, a strategy which has
been noted of other children (Slobin, 1973). We have suggested earlier that
gestural morphemes may be replaced by linguistic signs in this same way;
here we have an example of what may be this transition from personal symbol
to linguistic sign.

CONCLUDING REMARKS

In this chapter we have been interested in examining the emergence of
linguistic signs or words. The point we have been trying to establish, using

selected evidence from the data of one child acquiring Dakota-Sioux as a first language, is that any symbol, whether verbal or gestural, can potentially evolve into a linguistic sign. A semiological approach seems to account for what might otherwise be dismissed as idiosyncratic phenomena in the developing communicative system of this child. These phenomena, gestural and onomatopœic representations, match the descriptions given by Piaget of transitional behaviours between sensori-motor intelligence and sign-based or representational intelligence; they thus appear to be precursors to linguistic signs. We have tried to show that data from this child provide convincing evidence that there is a connection between the child's early imitative behaviours and his eventual capacity to use linguistic signs as a speaker of an adult language.

ACKNOWLEDGEMENT

The research described in this chapter was supported by Research Grant No. S74-0377 from the Canada Council.

13
From Sensori-motor Vocalizations to Words:
A Case Study of the Evolution of Attention-directing Communication in the Second Year

ANNE LINDSAY CARTER

University of California, Berkeley, U.S.A.

The percentage of human communication that involves pointing out or drawing attention to an immediately perceptible object is undoubtedly extremely high. There is in fact an informal sense in which virtually every communication of any sort involves or implies the expression of reference to something in order to convey one's ideas, feelings or whatever is communicated about it, and very often this indicated "something" is a concrete entity in the immediate environment of both sender and receiver. Among the other types of communication, this observation holds also for linguistic communication, in which the functioning of the referential expressions may even then be characterized as "pointing" (cf. e.g. Searle, 1969). The act of drawing attention to an object within the sender's and receiver's conjoint visual field has in addition to its pervasiveness a plethora of surface forms and underlying uses. Most important for the present study, however, is its early role in the development of language.

In line with widespread current interest in the developmental role of the attention-directing act,* this chapters treats the common, gesture-based,

---

*Recent language development studies exhibiting a pronounced emphasis upon early object indicating behavior are those by Clark, 1973; Greenfield, 1973; Lyons, 1973; Atkinson, 1974; Bates, 1974; Griffiths, 1974; Sugarman, 1974; Bruner, 1976; Collis and Schaffer, 1976; Kaye, 1976; Ninio and Bruner, 1976; and this list is far from exhaustive.

origin of attention guiding prelinguistic vocalizations and their separate evolutions into attention guiding words which were observed for one second-year infant named David. Broadly speaking, the issue underlying both the present and previous analyses of David's communicative development (Carter, 1974, 1975a,b, in press a,b,c) concerns the nature of processes by which the system of intentional human communication comes to be dominated by conventional linguistic structures; the specific goal is to characterize a few of these processes for a single child. On this account, the aim of the present chapter is to systematically document some of David's evolving communicative structures, both gestural and vocal, and where possible to provide evidence of operations whereby each temporary developmental structure was supplanted by its immediate successor in the developmental sequence. Similar to that in the work of Halliday (1973), Dore (1973) and Griffiths (1974), the focus in this chapter will be on cognitive structural change rather than social-interactive learning procedures, although a few comments on sociolinguistic implications in the findings will be provided in the conclusion.

THE STUDY OF DAVID'S PRELINGUISTIC COMMUNICATIVE BEHAVIOR: BASIC FINDINGS

The data of the study of David—a healthy, intelligent, only child of middle-class college-educated parents—were obtained from detailed narrative and code transcriptions of ten videotaped one-hour playsessions (henceforward labeled PS1,2,3 etc.) that covered his second year at fairly regular intervals. The scheduled unstructured sessions occurred in a nursery school playroom and involved the presence of David, his mother and two or three other mother-infant pairs. Videotaping took place in a separate room behind a one-way window, with sound input from a single microphone in the playroom ceiling.

A previous report of this study of David's communicative behavior (Carter, 1974) documented a prelinguistic communication system abstracted from the 12-16 month range, comprising eight distinct classes of communicative behavior. Each class was defined in terms of its unique contextually deter-mined goal, doubly represented in both a class-specific gesture and a class-specific monosyllabic vocalization. During this time, although the gesture was the primary or only indicative member of the dyad, in most (i.e. on the average over 80% of) observed instances of any class the characteristic gesture and vocalization were produced *concurrently* by David, an observation producing the rationale both for their combined treatment as a unitary cognitive act and for attributing the gesture's pragmatic significance to its predictable vocal accompaniment. To indicate that their initial indicativeness was basically gestural, however, the eight classes of gesture-vocalization acts were labeled *communicative sensori-motor schemata*, utilizing the cognitive developmental terminology of Piaget (e.g. 1952).* The originally primitive and mysterious but progressively more indicative and ultimately conventional-looking vocalization or, more accurately, vocalization class of each schema was labeled a *sensori-motor morpheme* because it initially met within the sensori-motor system the three criteria of frequent recurrence, fixed significance (essentially that of the co-occurring gesture) and irreducibility proposed by Bloomfield for the fundamental definition of morpheme.† (For brevity, observed instances of each vocalization class are also usually termed morphemes.) Between 12 and 16 months 91% of David's bids for interaction could be characterized within this dyadic system of prelinguistic schemata.

The eight (simplified) schemata of this system are presented in Table I, showing for example that [m]-initial utterances tended to accompany his reach for an object; [b]-initial utterances, to accompany hand motions indicating the wish for an object's riddance, etc.‡ A detailed analysis of the complete prelinguistic system is provided in Carter (1974). For present purposes, however, exclusive attention will be given to second year developments in the Attention to Object (AO) schema, defined by the goal of directing the receiver's attention to a particular object, and represented by the combination of pointing or showing gestures and [l]- or [d]-initial monosyllables.

Unity in the Attention to Object Schema

At first glance, the categorical unity ascribed to the AO schema may seem unwarranted in comparison with the greater unity of gesture and vocalization

---

*Inter-judge reliability obtained for characterization of schemata in the first four playsessions has been assessed at 93%. This and all related obtained reliability measures for the coding categories of utterance transcription, gesture, gesture-vocalization time relationship, gesture contour, object of regard, receiver, location of sender and gestural object are presented and discussed in Carter (1974).

†When describing the morphological units of adult language the term "morpheme" has numerous technical ramifications. In this study, however, morphemes are intended to be understood for the most part simply as the smallest units of significance within David's not-yet-conventionalized system of communication.

‡A broad phonetic transcription is used here which subsumes minor phonetic differences (such as degree of voicing) that were often impossible to discern on the tapes.

Table I

Simplified description of David's eight communicative schemata in the period 12-16 months (reproduced with permission from *Development of Communication: Social and Pragmatic Factors in Language Acquisition*, by N. Waterson and C. Snow. Copyright © 1978, by John Wiley and Sons Limited)

Schema	Gesture	Sound	Goal	No. instances (PS1 to 4)
1. Request Object (RO)	reach to object	[m]-initial	get receiver's help in obtaining object	342
2. Attention to object (AO)	point, hold out	alveolar ([l] or [d])-initial	draw receiver's attention to object	334
3. Attention to Self (AS)	sound of vocalization	phonetic variants of "David", "Mommy"	draw receiver's attention to self	142
4. Request Transfer (RT)	reach to person	[h]-initial (constricted and minimally aspirated)	obtain object from, or give to, receiver	135
5. Dislike (Disl)	prolonged, falling intonation	nasalized, especially [n]-initial	get receiver's help in changing situation	82
6. Disappear-ance (Disa)	waving hands, slapping	[b]-initial	get receiver's help in removing object	32
7. Rejection (Rej)	negative headshake	[ʔʌʔʌʔ]	same as for Dislike (above)	20
8. Pleasure-Surprise-Recognition (PSR)	(smile)	flowing or breathy [h] sounds especially *oh, ah, hi, ha*	express pleasure	20

Frequencies, representing total (both simultaneous and non-simultaneous) instances of each gesture vocalization pair, were derived from four videotapes of play behavior, recorded at approximately one month intervals. The total length of videotaped data from which these frequencies were obtained came to less than three hours. (The sound track of each of the four tapes was less than the full hour in length.)

classes exhibited in Table I by other schemata. However, certain considerations help somewhat to reduce its apparent heterogeneity. The configurational similarity and proximity of articulation of the two criterial sounds of this class, for example, would undoubtedly make them less discriminable to an infant forming them on a kinesthetic as well as acoustic basis than to the adult hearing them as separate phoneme classes. More specifically, David's [l] and [d] sounds fell into a superordinate production class having a common, alveolar ridge, place of articulation. Extrapolating developmentally backwards from the many later phonetic differentiations observable in Fig. 1 for this schema, it appears possible, assuming the significance of tactile as well as auditory sensation in the infant's earliest perception of his own articulation classes, that a similar differentiation prior to PS1 could have engendered the [l] and [d] sounds out of this broader alveolar category.* †

It should be mentioned that in addition to [l] and [d] sounds, David very occasionally produced [s] and [y] sounds conceivably also belonging to the AO schema, although their relative frequency was so low they seem by comparison barely worth mentioning. Interpretation of the [s]-initial class as a full-fledged AO variant with the same developmental status as the others is rather questionable for a number of reasons: (1) it was represented by only one form, the word "see"; (2) it had no occurrences either before PS5 (approximately 17 months) or in PS6 to 9; (3) there were only four correctly pronounced instances, two in PS5 and two in PS10. Approximately nine other instances involved the substitution of [ʃ] for [s]. Perhaps the two biggest deterrents to including this category—represented by an AO form frequently noted in other infant studies, e.g. by Bullowa (1967), Griffiths (1974), Huttenlocher (1974)—were its conventionality from the outset and greatly delayed appearance, both of which prevented tracing it back to a similar or common origin with David's other, prelinguistic, AO vocalizations. Like (l) and [d], [s] is alveolar. As [y] by contrast has a more displaced (palatal) articulation, the apparent inclusion of [y] sounds in the AO category could counterindicate an origin in an undifferentiated alveolar protoclass. However the very few observed [y]-initial utterances were usually produced in a sequence of [l] sounds, suggesting that the [y] signified no more than a

*Despite their described articulatory similarity, [l]- and [d]- initial utterances were analyzed as members of separate branches even at the outset, because of their clarity and stability, and also a difference in distribution of their co-occurring vowels over the first four playsessions, suggesting that each consonant had already acquired a different most-likely vowel set. With [l] sounds, [a] was by far the most frequent trailing vowel, with the next being [u], whereas with [d] sounds [æ] and [a] had an approximately equal likelihood. It is therefore probable that some shaping of these two consonant sound classes had begun even before PS1, possibly as a result of the tendency exhibited by David's mother toward high frequency AO use of the words "look" and "that". Because of evidence that they were phonetically divergent, incipient meaning differences for these consonant classes, although unobserved, was also a possibility.

†The term alveolar is used to indicate articulation made at or in the general area of the alveolar ridge, and is intended to be sufficiently loose to include sounds which would correspond to well-defined alveolar and dental articulations in the adult language.

(literal) slip of the tongue in an attempt at alveolar production, as illustrated in the PS3 incident in which he produced the Attention to Object sounds [lae. la. ya. la. la. la. la. a.]. In any case, the structural importance of the few tentative [s] and [y] instances to his AO schema development seemed negligible.

With regard to non-uniformity in the AO gestural class, in spite of their obvious differences, both AO gestures involved a basically similar body area and configuration (an upwards or outwards closed-handed reach) and as a result the bare possibility of a similar origin. The general origin of the AO point hypothesized by Werner and Kaplan (1963) is a touching reach. One can see a hint of this touching or contact origin in the extended index finger, and also perhaps in the infant's predictable tendency to use this finger to touch or tap pictures in books. In a similar vein, David's alternate showing gesture—holding an object up or toward the receiver—seemed intuitively to demonstrate subject-object contact as much as anything else, suggesting that its origin too might have been a touching or contacting reach. Therefore, because under these two hypotheses in conjunction both AO gestures would have differentiated out of a common origin, an underlying unity (although speculative rather than, as with the sounds, descriptive) is through them bestowed upon the gestures as well. Of course, although suggestive, such arguments do not prove that the classes were internally coherent. Regardless, however, of whether their developmental, structural or physical similarities were true indicators of underlying relationship, the classes of both gestures and vocalizations demonstrated an unarguable unity in the single most critical respect for this study, i.e. having the contextually ascertainable Attention to Object goal.

Attention to Object Schema Development: General Perspectives and Processes

In this chapter the second year evolution of several conventionalized vocalizations out of David's prelinguistic [l]- and [d]-initial morphemes will be described. In all degrees of formation throughout the year these AO morpheme derivatives were also often accompanied by pointing and showing; however, their phonetic and functional developmental continuity generally permitted inferring the Attention to Object significance at all levels of development even when, for reasons such as otherwise occupied hands or (in later sessions) the use of multiple word referential utterances, gestures were not manifested. At the same time, their divergent directions of development (cf. Fig. 1) gradually extended and stabilized their overt differences,

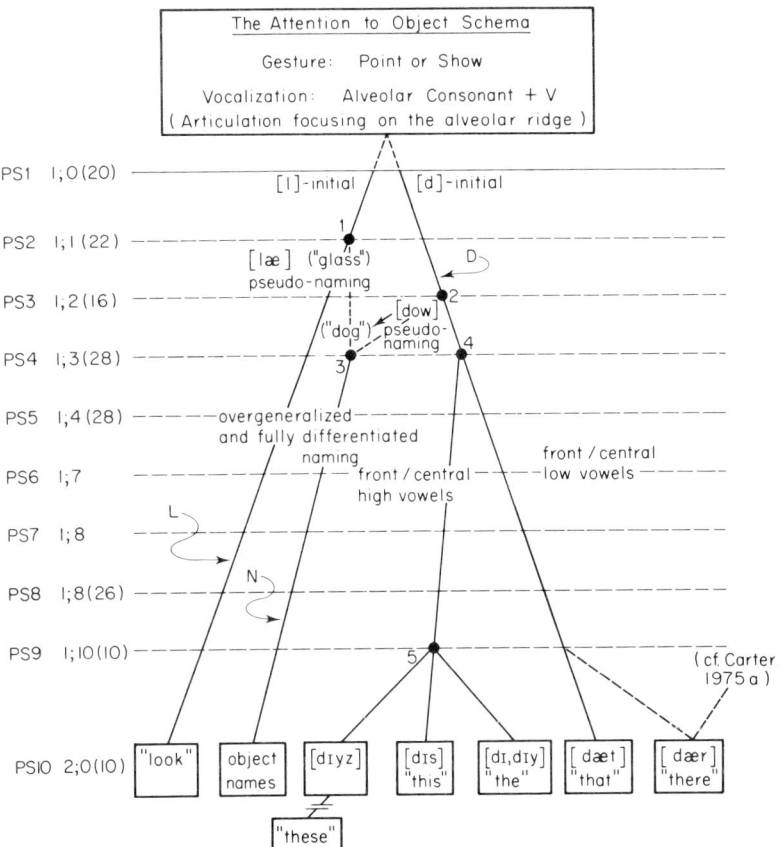

Fig. 1. The differentiating and integrating evolution of Attention to Object schema morphemes into words of the adult language.

The terms "differentiating" and "integrating" are merely descriptive, with "differentiation" indicating a proliferation of variants of an initial class, and "integration" indicating a convergence of two branches of behavior into one product behavior. The criteria of both differentiation and integration are based on form changes, with differentiations defined strictly phonetically, and integration in terms of the establishment of object naming as an autonomous mode of referring.

In each of the differentiations recorded here (Nodes 1,2,4,5), the differentiating node was located in a certain playsession on the basis of the introduction of a close phonetic variant of pre-existing forms, having at the time of the initial appearance the same use as previous forms, yet representing (on the basis of later phonetic developments) the antecedent of a semantically distinct adult word. (The suggested behavioral mechanism underlying this differentiation was the subject's assimilation of a phonetically similar, and use-related, adult form into his pre-existent class.)

With regard to integrating Node 3, because both l and d sounds were observed in pseudo-names, this development seemed initially to be occurring in branches L and D independently. However, what appeared to be the immediately subsequent developments (extended pseudo-naming and semantic overgeneralization) were found to lead step-wise toward the development of true or fully differentiated naming, a behavior which could not be incorporated into branches L or D (consisting of [l]- and [d]-initial utterances exclusively), and which therefore required a separate representation in the diagram. For these reasons, pseudo-naming is treated here as a hypothetical phenomenon which derives from branches L and D, but which has as output a separate branch, N. The basis for locating Node 3 in PS4 is discussed in the text.

increasingly obscuring from superficial observation the fact that they had shared a single pragmatic origin. In terms of the adult language toward which they were progressing, their separate classifications were in fact decidedly contrastive: deictic pronouns and adjectives ("this" and "that"), object names, a verb ("look"), an adverb ("there") and the article "the".

Major outlines of developments underlying the production of these developing forms and their antecedents are given in Fig. 1. Surprisingly, an exhaustive survey of second year utterances associated with pointing or showing revealed that like the original (12 to 16 month) pointing morphemes all *new* AO elements excepting object names and the few tentative [y] instances were also alveolar- (essentially [l]- or [d]-) initial, suggesting that for David: (1) the phonetics of a newly observed or acquired utterance—in particular, its phonetic similarity to pre-established morphemes—was an important (though not the only) determinant of its significance; (2) as suggested by the defining parameters of the prelinguistic classes themselves, the most salient early parameter of morpheme sound structure—and hence his phonetic basis for the recognition of morpheme similarity in adult words—was the initial consonant; and (3) the class of words potentially assimilable from adult modeling as AO sounds in particular was delimited to those beginning with the described alveolars. These observed phonetic constraints (resulting ultimately in exclusively alveolar-initial words), the order of emergence of new morphemes, and numerous heterogeneous but convergent inferences to be presented below provided the basis for postulating the structured development of Fig. 1.

While Table I shows the AO schema's high relative frequency, Fig. 1 reveals its fundamental developmental significance in an unusually large number of branchings, nodes and linguistic products. The most salient of the Fig. 1 processes is the schema *branching*, represented in a single-input, multiple-output node, i.e. Nodes 1,2,4,5. In all cases, including those of the development of pseudo-names (Nodes 1 and 2), a branching node indicates the first appearance of a new AO morpheme which demonstrated three properties: (1) it was, in keeping with the above indicated constraints, a close phonetic variant of an earlier AO morpheme; (2) it exhibited the same AO use as the pre- (and often still-) existing alveolar utterance; and (3) it represented (on the basis of subsequent developments) the phonetic antecedent of a semantically distinct adult word. The introduction into the corpus of a new AO element with these properties was inferred to indicate that an imitative fragment of an attention-directing word had been assimilated into David's own pre-existent alveolar class. In any given instance the assimilatory mechanism could have been either the incorporation of a slightly deviant sound, which would phonetically increment the original morpheme class, or class subdivision into more finely discriminated sounds. For descriptive purposes however, the results of either process will be referred to (and diagrammed) as a differentiation or branching.

Demonstrating its unusual qualitative as well as quantitative complexity, only in the case of the AO schema was a development found which could be characterized as a convergent or *integrating* node. Developmental outlines of other schemata analyzed to date (e.g. Carter, 1975a,b) contain only branchings; however, in addition to (unusually many) branchings, AO development produced evidence at one point that two subschemata had converged into one (in Node 3) to produce the open class of object names. The developmental basis for inferring this particular occurrence, however, was a parametrically distinct process from that underlying the four AO differentiations. Many additional factors must be considered when characterizing this transformation, some of which will be discussed in the subsequent sections.

Attention to Object Schema Development: Outline of Specific Findings

Briefly previewing the specific sequence of AO developments to be examined, the evolution represented in Fig. 1 by branches L, D and N, can be described as follows: With respect to *branches L and D*, development of the [l]- and [d]-initial utterances consisted primarily in gradual phonetic refinement of the earlier primitive forms, together with indicated sub-branchings marking the origins of one or more alveolar-initial words. With respect to the *naming branch* (N), PS1 produced, in addition to [l] and [d] forms, a few apparent AO object names. However, while the [l] and [d] sounds appeared in both increasing numbers and increasingly refined and differentiated forms in PS2 to 4 (roughly 14 to 16 months), object naming suffered a setback in these sessions, if it could in fact be said to have existed in PS1. In its place, however, PS2 to 4 contained some variant [l] and [d] forms that were systematically ambiguous between the sort of AO forms observed earlier and similar sounding ([l]- and [d]-initial) names of objects. Perhaps instantiating the "quasi-reference" phenomenon hypothesized by Lyons (1973) and Atkinson (1974), these few systematically ambiguous utterances, characterized by a name-like appearance but uncertain significance, were labeled *pseudo-names*. Having the force neither of clear AO morphemes nor clear names, and represented in Fig. 1 development therefore as transverse branches linking branches L and D to branch N, this type of ambiguity marked most PS2 to 4 acts that might be considered naming. Beginning in PS4, regular or unambiguous names were dominant though sometimes overgeneralized, a development marked in Fig. 1 by Node 3, having the two converging [l] and [d] pseudo-naming branches as input and naming branch N as output. From PS5 (approximately 17 months) onward David made no observed naming mistakes of the sort that result from semantic over-generalization. At the same time, a steady increase in correctly named objects implied that the gestural aspects of his attention directing com-munication were becoming dispensible. It is probably at least partially due to this increase in true naming acts that, although seen in all playsessions, the accompaniment of pointing and showing gestures diminished in frequency over the year (cf. Fig. 2) thus moving the burden of communication originally carried by the gesture increasingly into the vocal channel.

In order to both convey the texture of these developmental trends and also pinpoint evidence for specific mechanisms of change, in the following sections the three basic AO strands of development are documented in detail with a selection of chronologically ordered events and related discussion. In contrast to the direct longitudinal procedure used in previous reports of David's other schemata, it is presently necessary to treat developments in each branch separately because of the overall developmental complexity of this schema. Accordingly the central body of this chapter is divided into three essentially independent sections. First, in the section immediately following, the development of [l]-initial utterances is traced into the verb "look". This survey is followed in the subsequent section by a description of the evolution of [d]-initial demonstratives, whose development is further subdivided on the basis of trailing vowels into three subclasses producing (1) pseudo-names, (2) "that" and "there", and (3) "this", "these" and "the". In the third and last section, the development of object reference is analyzed as it passes through four main phases, resulting in the use of stable and fully differentiated names. In addition to allowing a closer inspection of the developmental relationships in each branch, breaking up the analysis in this way has the further advantage of demonstrating that the overall trend from gestural to vocal communicativeness in this schema consisted of parallel transforma-tions occurring in all branches simultaneously.

In operational terms then, the criterial behaviors for including any event in the Attention to Object category were: (a) *gestural*: acts of pointing to or holding out for observation an object, and (b) *vocal*: [l]-, [d]-, [s]- or [y]-initial utterances and their derivatives, and object names. As stated and as examples will show, most often the vocalization and gesture co-occurred, meeting the two criteria redundantly. Whenever the gesture was missing, as became increasingly the case in later playsessions, the context was analyzed for Attention to Object significance; up to the last playsession interactional bids were determined exclusively in this way to be AO acts. Excepting instances of one complex and infrequent [d]-initial variant and one highly tentative [y]-initial form to be treated elsewhere, all thus-inferred Attention to Object acts throughout the entire year were included in the data base for the following longitudinal analyses.

[L]-INITIAL UTTERANCES: [lɛ], [læ], [la], [lə], [lʊ], (BRANCH L)

The development of [l]-initial utterances was for the most part straight-forward, producing simply higher order approximations to and more instances of the adult directive "look". The only deviation in this trend was the tendency between PS2 and 4 toward ambiguity with object names. In particular the vowel portion of some [l]-initial AO utterances began to resemble that in the name of a frequently pointed out object having an [l]-initial (or consonant + [l] initial) name, resulting in an apparent imitation of that name. This pseudo-naming phenomenon will be treated separately in the *object names* section. A few instances of this simple but high-frequency AO branch (excluding pseudo-names) are provided in the following subsections with for the most part no comment necessary.*

PS1   1;0(20)

(1)   1/1. David points across the room in a vague direction and says, softly and breathily, [la! la!] (He starts pointing before looking where he is pointing.)

PS2   1;1(22)

(2)   2/1. David turns around to Mother, says [la.], pointing to object outside.

(3)   2/2. One of the other mothers lifts up the flap of her purse on the floor beside her to reach inside. David points at it, says [la] (or [lʊk]).

PS3   1;2(16)

(4)   3/1. David, looking at Mother, bangs his hammer on the table, then turns and holds it out to her, saying [wʊk!]. Mother: "Um-hmm, that's nice. That's a hammer."

The two or three observed [w]-initial AO utterances resulted from the replacement of [l] in "look" or its variants by [w] (due to articulatory

---

*Transcription Representation:
(a) *Phonetics*, in square brackets or, when feasible, by English orthography.
(b) *Intonation:* (1) declarative, by periods (.); (2) rising final, by question marks (?); (3) exclamatory, by exclamation marks (!).
(c) *Stress:* (1) primary, by acute accents(´); (2) Secondary, by grave accents (`).
(d) *Timing:* (1) Pauses, by semi-colons (;); (2) Rapid succession, by the symbol‿.
(e) *Repetitions*, by a number and a multiplication sign in parentheses following the utterance, e.g. (3×).

assimilation to the following vowel). Representing apparently no more than extremely occasional articulatory slips, they are assumed to have held no special significance for the infant.

(5)   3/2. David, holding a book, walks over to another mother, saying [dae. lʊ. bʊk! lʊk! lʊk!]. Woman: "Look?" David then looks up at the ceiling, points and stage-laughs, then says [lʊk. layt. ("light") layt.]. He then looks at the woman, and again stage-laughs. Woman: "Uh-huh."

PS4   (1;3(28)

During the interval PS2 through 4, David manifested a behavior that was inconsistent with previous or subsequent tendencies, in occasionally using the pointing gesture and AO morpheme to request objects (see example below), an act for which in previous and subsequent sessions, the reaching gesture and Request Object (RO) schema morpheme were used almost exclusively. This development may have been either progressive or regressive. He was from one perspective indicating not only *that* he wanted, but with more emphasis and specificity *what* he wanted, in general conformity with a gradual movement from general to particularized reference. On the other hand, the action may have represented a confusion paralleling at the gestural level the vocal ambiguity of the pseudo-name.

(6)   4/1. David looks at the juice table, and then while repeating [la] (9×) points to the table, and then pulls his mother to it by the hand. She gives him a cookie and he quiets.

PS5   1;4(28)

(7)   5/1. David, across the room from his mother, picks up a toy, holds it out toward her, saying [la. lʊ mama.] ("camel", apparently). Mother: "That's a camel? Well not exactly. That's a goat. A goat."

(8)   5/2. David rings a bell he is holding, then holds it up for a nearby peer to see, crying "Look! Look! Look!"

PS6   1;7

(9)   6/1. David climbs up a small tier of steps toward the owl picture on wall, then points to the owl, saying loudly [la! aw!] ("owl!") [aw! aw! aw!] while continuing to regard the owl.

PS7   1;8

Further phonetic refinement in the convergence of AO [l] sounds toward the sound of "look" was seen in the fact that from PS7 onward all vowels in these morphemes approximated the vowel in "look". No more [la]s or [læ]s were to be seen except for one reference to "glass" by a regressive [əlæ] in PS10.

(10)   7/1. David holds up a train, and while regarding it, says "wook. look.; [may] train."

PS8   1;8(26)

(11)   8/1. David sets a drum in his mother's lap. As the drum falls and he rescues it, he says "Luh! Dwum.; Dwum‿Mommy."

PS9   1;10(10)

In PS9 "look" was included in larger utterance units, making gestures unarguably optional.

(12)   9/1. While leaning over to pick up a block, David says "Look at (drowned out by room noise) block."

PS10   2;0(10)

The inclusion of "look" in even more complicated utterances occurred in PS10. In the following example, the greater complexity of the utterance as a whole apparently absorbed some attention or processing "space" that would ordinarily be given to articulation, resulting in a phonetically diminished "look". From the perspective of functional development the explicit attention-directing function of utterances containing "look" was invariant throughout the year. Even though many year-end utterances in which it participated were appropriate in type and form, well organized and fairly complex, the word "look", by now almost always correctly pronounced, would undoubtedly later develop meanings not yet demonstrated in PS10, when it was apparently still an attention guiding directive exclusively.

(13)   10/1. David holds up a long chain of beads which he has just connected, saying, [ʊk hay meyd mɔwɪy; ʊk hay meyd mɔwɪy; ay meyd.] ("Look what I made, Mommy . . .").

[D]-INITIAL UTTERANCES: [dɪy], [dɪ], [dɨ], [də], [dæ], [da], [dɔ], [dow], . . . (BRANCH D)

Many researchers have noted the cross-linguistic pointing or deictic significance of the infant's prelinguistic [d] sounds (cf. Wundt, 1900; Stern, 1930; Lewis, 1936; Leopold, 1939; Werner and Kaplan, 1963), and in my own experience with English-learning infants, pointing gestures have almost invariably been accompanied by [d] sounds. Noting this pervasiveness, Stern in fact even suggested that [d] and [t] formed natural or language-independent demonstratives, owing to their "outwardly-directed" character. Although the same might be said of David's [l] sounds, it is possible that the latter constituted an unusual class of AO markers which initially differentiated out of the original alveolar class for perhaps idiosyncratic reasons, such as exceptionally frequent parental modelings of "look". Comparison of their respective products in Fig. 1 suggests at any rate that his AO [d] class had a more central developmental significance.

It also had a much more complicated developmental history, demonstrating at least three stages of differentiation over the second year. (As indicated previously, the term "differentiation" is used only descriptively, to signify an increase in the variants of a pre-existing class, and hence does not refer to the actual mechanism for their proliferation.) The first differentiating node (in PS3) marked the development of two subclasses: (A) *[d]* + *back vowels* ([dɔ], [dow], etc.), sounds which became pseudo-names of the D branch, and (B) the remaining [d] + V sounds, still simple AO morphemes. In PS4 the latter class was itself composed of two distinct categories: (1) a *[d]* + *low front-to-central vowel* branch ([dæ] → [da]), ultimately producing the words "that" and—with further qualification—"there"; and (2) a *[d]* + *high front-to-central vowel* branch ([dɪy], [dɪ], [dɪ/ə], etc.). In PS10 the latter class contained three variants which, although similar in sound and significance, were nevertheless phonetically distinctive and produced in slightly different ways: (a) [dɪs], becoming "this", (b) [dɪyz], the phonetic antecedent of "these", and (c) [dɪy], the phonetic antecedent of "the". These developments are examined in the following subsections.

A. [D] + Back Vowels ([dɔ], [dow], . . .)

AO [d] + back vowels occurred only in PS3 and 4, in which they were, like pseudo-names of the L branch, ambiguous between AO morphemes and object names. This class will therefore be treated along with the [l]-initial pseudo-names in the object names section.

B. [D] + Low Front-to-Central Vowels ([dæ], [da], . . .)

The products of the low front/central branch were "that" and "there". An observed ambiguity throughout the year between the meanings of identification, location, success, etc. (essentially the meanings of "that" and "there") for any of the precursors of these two words resulted probably from an incomplete differentiation out of the more general AO class. The semantic opaqueness of the [d] + low front/central vowels was especially noticeable before PS7. At that time all instances of the class moved closer to "that" phonetically, in manifesting a final [t], and presumably also semantically, in that their subsequent uses tended toward increasingly acceptable adult uses of "that" (although never fully contrastive with "this"). This situation obtained until PS9 or 10 when the form [dær] (and "there") also showed up.

What sort of meanings might these forms have had prior to PS9 or 10? Although their pragmatic attention-directing function was easy to see, after repeatedly combing the data for cues it is still impossible to specify their semantics. However, it may not have been merely a methodological problem that prevented pinpointing the semantic (as opposed to physically or pragmatically functional) meaning for many of David's early utterances; this difficulty is in fact to be expected, given that, as Piaget (1952) stresses, at first the concrete effect of an infant's action is its most (or only) significant determinant. In the early playsessions David probably had no need to uniquely specify the meanings of forms such as, for example [dɛś wɔn!], whose alternate adult interpretations (e.g. identification for "that's one!" vs. location for "there's one!") would produce the same AO response in his hearers, because of not only the predictably pragmatic nature of sensori-motor intelligence, but also the independent observation that an AO response, i.e. object acknowledgement, usually seemed from contextual analysis to be all that he was seeking from the hearer. Furthermore even as late as PS10, and despite their phonetic and probable semantic development, the pragmatic connection between sound and effect remained for many utterances a more salient and seemingly more important determinant of linguistic categories than the semantic connection between sound and meaning. These observations are supported by the lack of any tendency toward either utterance-initial or utterance-final position of the AO[d] + vowel forms in the following events.

PS1   1;0(20)

(14)   1/1. David, holding a coat he has just obtained, looks smilingly toward one of the other mothers, saying [adá]? and patting the coat (an action suggesting the AO showing act contact origin mentioned previously).

PS2   1;1(22)

(15)   2/1. He looks at the owl poster on the wall and says "[dæ]; owl".

PS3   1;2(16)

(16)   3/1. David picks up a book, and holding it out in front of him, walks to one of the seated mothers, saying "[dæ.] [lɔ:]; book! look! look!"

PS4   1;3(28)

(17)   4/1. David sees a hammer he likes, says [dæt!, dæt!; hæmda].

(18)   4/2. He sees a cookie on the floor, says while bending to pick it up, "[da! da! da! da!] cookie!" and then triumphantly (it seems) holds the cookie up above his head at arm's length for the woman in front of him to see.

(19)   4/3. David sees a peer pointing to (touching) a picture in a book that is resting on a table. David then walks up beside him, tapping with his index finger on the

book, first apparently on the same picture to which the peer was pointing, and then to something else on the same page, saying "look [dæt!]" and then, increasingly loudly, [dæt!; dæt!; dæt!; dæt!; dæt!]. (Note contact origin implications for pointing act.)

PS5   1;4(28)

(20)   5/1. He carries a toy across the room, babbling ([æ (4×) awda; æ æ] (3×)) then says [dæ!] (or [dæt]) (3×), this latter while holding up the toy for the woman in front of him to see, and then, "See [dæ]"?

(21)   5/2. He holds up his cup for a peer to see, saying [dɪydá!].

PS6   1;7

(22)   6/1. Pointing to a picture in a book, David says [da!; lʊ!; læt!].

PS7   1;8

Although several [dæt]s were observed prior to PS7, from PS7 to 9, as previously indicated, *all* observed [d] + low front/central vowel variants ended in the consonant [t], while the included vowels shifted away from [a] and toward a more consistently produced [æ], both seemingly permanent changes marking an important step in the phonetic movement of these morphemes toward "that". Moreover from PS7 until year end and presumably thereafter, every [d] + low front/central vowel form whatsoever exhibited a final consonant, revealing [da], [dæ], etc. to have become fully superceded forms.

(23)   7/1. David is holding a train that he wants fixed in his mother's lap, but his mother is talking to the other mothers. He looks up at her saying "dæt.; fɪk;] mummy?!"

PS8   1;8(26)

No AO [d] + low front-to-central vowel forms were observed in PS8.

PS9   1;10(10)

The participation of "that" variants in larger utterances was noticeable in PS9 and 10. The very different functions of some multi-morphemic utterances containing [dæt], for which a pointing gesture not only did not co-occur but would often in fact have been inappropriate, suggested that the AO significance of this form was becoming subordinate to its use as a neutral object marker, indicating a shifting focus at this time from its effect (pragmatic usage) to its referent object connection (semantic usage; cf. Peirce, 1932; Morris, 1946).

(24)   9/1. David looks at the recording equipment carried by a sound man (recording this session for a television program), then says "What him doing [dǽt]?"

(25)   9/2. David, struggling to wrest a bucket from a peer, yells loudly "Gimme [dæt!; máhə!;] gimme [dæt!]; gimme [dæhæhæhǽ!]" (crying)

The form [dær] was first seen in PS9 in an utterance implying for it a similar significance to [dæt]: (cf. event (24) above).

(26) 9/3. David sees a peer across the room playing with a toy, and says "What Dot doin [dǽr]?" (or [dǽər])

This particular instance of [dær] was originally inferred to have spatial significance, as reported in Carter (1975a). However, because of the subsequently noticed phonetic, rhythmic and structural similarity of its utterance frame with that in event (24) above—in David's protocol, a condition frequently indicating similarity of significance as well—its function can no longer be considered unambiguously locative. With this additional evidence a more probable interpretation is as an AO directive which had acquired locative properties only partially, i.e. to roughly the same extent that [dæt] in event (24) of the same playsession had become a neutral object marker. Therefore, although the evidence is a bit too thin to describe its structural relationship to the AO schema, [dær] is assumed to have derived from the AO schema as well as from the closure-marking category described in Carter (1975a). In support of this position, all other PS9 [dær]s, although manifesting the success or completion and (hint of) locative significance described in Carter (1975a), also demonstrated AO schema sound and meaning influences.

(27) 9/4. David, standing over his wagon, encourages a peer to put a toy in, saying "here", then as the child drops it in, [doy], and afterward [dær].

PS10   2;0(26)

Instances of [dær] or "there" showing up in PS10 indicated as in PS9 both AO and success or completion (and perhaps locative) significance. The two meaning contributions to this developing word, both influences noted also by Griffiths (1974) in another infant's development of the word "there", are represented in Fig. 1 by dashed lines converging toward the PS10 product "there". A few representative instances of "that" and "there" variants are included in the following PS10 events, in which despite any semantic shifts, their Attention to Object use was still visible even without the accompaniment of a gesture.

(28) 10/1. David sees a peer hold a toy up to David's mother. He says "Here.; I have it.; that."

(29) 10/2. David, trying to remove a portion of a toy that does not come off, raises the toy to his mother, saying "[dǽt] off.; take [dǽt] one."

(30) 10/3. David looks at the mothers' reflections in the mirror, then turns to look at them directly, looks again at their images, and again at them directly, saying [dær].

C. [D] + High Front-to-Central Vowels [dɪy], [dɪ], [dɪ], [de], . . .)

The remaining branch of the [d]-initial morphemes began around PS4, in which the first instances of [d] + high front/central vowels were seen in the following events:

PS4   1;3(28)

(31)   4/1. His mother has just picked him up after he had been crying. In her arms, he looks at the juice table, points, and says [ba:bɪý (?) dadɪý; dadɪý; (5×)].

(32)   4/2. Immediately afterward she sets him down and he gets a bell and hands it to her, saying [dɪy.; dɪy.].

PS5   0;4(28)

A use of [dɪy] similar to that in PS4/1 above is documented in the first event from PS5:

(33)   5/1. He looks at the cookies across the room, then reaches to his mother to take her hand and draw her across the room, saying [ow. yadɪý.; dadɪý.].

The second event from PS5 exhibits his first observed instance of [dɪy] in utterance-initial position, demonstrating perhaps a new usage pattern, one that would later allow this sound to develop the significance of the modifiers "this" or "the". The possibility of this developmental trend is further supported by the third event immediately following, in which [dɪy] is produced prior to the name of an object to which it also refers.

(34)   5/2. David holds a cup for a peer to see, saying [dɪy da!].

(35)   5/3. David and mother are looking at a picture book together, with David saying [lala! (2×) Adah!]. His mother then closes the book and drops it into the wagon beside him. He reaches for the book, saying [dɪy.;. bʊ].

PS6 (1;7), PS7 (1;8), PS8(1;8(26))

PS6, 7 and 8 produced no instances of [d] + high front to central vowels. The usual basis for classifying utterances has been their consistency of use and form over several consecutive playsessions. This consistency has also allowed the usual inference that later playsession utterances similar in form and identical in use (or identical in form and similar in use) were developmental products of the earlier well-established forms.

By the same token the lack of [d] + high front/central vowels in these three playsessions weakens the inference that PS9 and 10 instances of this phonetic class were developmental products of earlier instances. However the exhaustiveness of the protocol analysis provides several bases for believing that this hiatus resulted from a sampling limitation problem rather than a real discontinuity: (1) The [d] + high front/central vowel class of AO utterances was in all playsessions the one with the lowest frequency, making it the most vulnerable to elimination from statistical fluctuations occurring in all classes. (2) Based on co-occurring gestures and context, these utterances had the same AO significance in PS9 as in PS4 and 5. Thus, despite a (progressive) incremental phonetic change in PS9 (see below)—one which paralleled phonetic developments in both the [l] and [d] + low front/central vowel branches—the significance of these sounds was invariant in play-sessions before and after the PS6-through-8 gap. (3) No other forms were used for drawing attention to an object in PS6 through 9 except for variants of "look," [dæt], [dær] and object names, demonstrating both the confinement of AO significance to pre-established forms and their refinements and an observable continuity in the other much higher frequency branches. The combination of these three findings implies for the [d] + high front/central branch both developmental continuity and a sequence of phonetic developments closely matching that of the other AO branches. It is assumed therefore that the [dɪs] of PS9 was not an independent emergence, but resulted rather from the continued development of the [d] + high front/central vowel branch throughout the 19-22 month interval in which it was missing from the sample.

PS9   1;10(10)

In PS9 the only [d] + high front/central vowel element was as indicated [dɪs], manifesting in its final consonant a phonetic similarity to "this" (also first seen in PS9), and in its seeming free variation with "this" a functional interchangeability as well. The lack of any other [d] + high front vowel elements suggests that elements phonetically less like "this" had been dropped in this period just prior to the stable acquisition of "this", leaving as the sole residuum of earlier developments this evolving form's phonetically closest subvariant. "This" and [dɪs] were seen in both utterance-initial and utterance-final position just as other [d] + high front/central vowel elements had been previously (cf. PS5). Now, however, because the juxtaposed sound in each utterance was a morpheme that was almost an adult word, the collocation with other morphemes presaged development of underlying linguistic structures having more than one pragmatic function—and there-fore (as with [dæt] in the same playsession) the transformation of [dɪs] (or "this") from AO directive to neutral object marker. At the same time however, each instance of [dɪs] (or "this") was still marked by a primary Attention to Object significance seemingly independent of the morpheme with which it was produced. (Again, as with [dæt], this attention-directing significance was contextually inferable without the aid of gestures.)

(36)   9/1. David grabs a rope that he wants removed from his wagon and shakes it,

saying "rope.; this off.; this off.; this off." Mother: "Want it off now?" David: [ʔeeee]. ("unghhh"). Mother: "Huh?" David, stretching the rope toward her as much as he can: "This.; [wowp]." Mother (not understanding the underlying purpose of this AO act): 'Um-hm."

(37)   9/2. David, mounting the rolling giraffe, sees a toy on the floor, and says, while dismounting, "here.; this.; this.; this.; this."

(38)   9/3. Apparently then seeing another object on the floor that he wishes, he says "Found dıś!"

PS10   2;0(10)

By PS10, although its subvariant [dıs] was still being used as well, a few additional instances of "this" demonstrated that the fully developed sound structure of this mature form was within closer reach even though not yet stable. In most instances of either form, however, both by now exhibiting contextually appropriate usage for the pronoun or adjective modifier "this", the final [s] was clearly pronounced.

(39)   10/1. David, holding something, says to his mother, [1 dıś] "Mommy."

(40)   10/2. Apparently trying to remove a stubborn piece from a wooden puzzle, "[dıś] off.; [dıś] off.; [dıś] off."

(41)   10/3. In connecting a large string of beads, David says when attaching one, [dIś wun!], when connecting the next, [dIś bIy!], then [dǽt bIy], and for the next addition, [dIś bIy]. (There is as yet no observable distinction in use of the variants of "this" and "that", even though these forms have become phonetically distinct and stable.)

Unlike later playsession instances of the [d] + low front/central vowel forms, all of which exhibited a final consonant, the final [s] was clearly missing in a few instances of the PS10 [d] + high front/central vowel forms (e.g. [dıE], [dı], [dıy]). In each such case the morpheme's utterance position, in terms of both word order (preceding a noun) and intonation contour, suggested an imitation of the adult "the". The developmental connection between AO morphemes and these [dıy] sounds was the most difficult to confirm of any second year [d]-initial utterance. However, even the PS10 [dıy]s were always at least associated with AO significance, in being produced immediately prior to the name of an object to which the entire multimorphemic utterance drew attention and to which a pointing gesture would therefore still be applicable (see events below). Further, there was no independent situational or overall behavioral evidence that the significance of these simple [d] + V sounds actually differed from that of his noun-preceding [dıs] having the appearance—if not yet quite the true function—of an adjective modifier (cf. example 10/3). Taking into account the utterance, associated behaviour and situation, the only consistent difference between productions of [dıs] and [dı] (or [dıy]) was that of stress, with [dɪs]—like [dæt]—invariably receiving primary stress, and [dɪ] (or [dɪy]) being unstressed.

The phonetic form [dɪy] had been seen previously in PS4 and 5, when it was an inferred antecedent of [dɪs]. By PS9 and 10 however, the more developed [dɪs] (and "this") had become preferred and stable. If the PS10 [d] + high front/central vowels represented simply a developmental continuation of earlier forms, why then would David have revived this by now regressive form among them to serve a purpose which was already easily accommodated by one of the more advanced forms? Perhaps the utterance frame may provide some cues. For example, a possible partial reason for the PS10 occurrence of [dɪy] (and its [d] + V variants) in place of the more usual noun affiliate [dɪs] was its consistent location between two words in longer utterances, a position making the production of [dɪs] more awkward and effortful. Moreover, longer utterances were found as a rule to result in phonetic reduction of included morphemes, caused perhaps by limitations on memory or processing capacity (cf. event (13)). Constraints on his memory as well as articulation may therefore have contributed to the inevitable influence of adult "the" modeling in accounting for a phonetically reduced [dɪs] in these instances.

As with virtually all of David's developing vocal forms therefore, evidence suggests that as a result of his observation of adult modeling and other factors, the differentiation of a specific sound preceded the development of its differentiated meaning in this case as well, with the immediate phonetic antecedent—and a later variant form—of "the" being no more than a phonetic reduction of "this". However, it must be added that their lack of stress made PS10 [dɪy]s look less like regular AO variants than any other branch D product since David did not ordinarily use unstressed sounds to draw attention. Although because of the previously observed pattern of morpheme derivation, a further advance in AO development is strongly suggested by this new distinction, it at the same time precludes ruling out a separate origin for PS10 [dɪy] utterances even though the latter alternative seems far less likely. At any rate, because, unlike the other [d] variants, it could not actually function as an attention-gaining device, nor therefore as an attention-directing device, it was no longer possible to claim for certain that the utterance [dɪy] had a referential object at all. Because of its uniqueness in this respect this late-appearing class—of whatever origin— provided the strongest evidence among the [d]-initial utterances that a qualitatively different linguistic development was or would soon be taking place, allowing the infant to devote as much attention to the relation between successive utterances (characterizing the "syntactic" level of linguistic description as represented by Morris (1946)) as to that between utterance and either effect or referent. In the case of the AO schema both latter types of relation, representing respectively the pragmatic and semantic levels of signification observed earlier in the year, would by their nature have presupposed the existence of a referent object.

(42)   10/4. David shows a key to his mother; "heré [dɪy] (or "the") key; heŕe [dɪy] key; heŕe [dɪy] key; [moy]."

(43)   10/5. "[dǽr dɪ] (or [de]) television; (2×)" was said while regarding the TV from across the room.

(44)   10/6. After having connected a long string of beads, he sticks the end in the chimney of a small doll house, and holding up the beads, still anchored in the chimney, for his mother to see, says [hae un dɪy hmowk!] ("House and the smoke!")

Finally, [dɪyz], another new variant of [dɪs], was seen, although only once:

(45)   10/7. David says [dow wã̌ dɪyz] ("don't want these" (?)) as he removes one in a series of disks which he is taking from a spindle and throwing aside.

This new variant differed from the previous one in being utterance final, but resembled it in lack of primary stress. (It received secondary stress here.) The single instance of what looked like an imitation of "these" would not justify a claim that it yet represented for David a plural form of [dɪs], even though this significance was suggested by its phonetics, utterance position, and behavioral context. Because it might have referred to the disk he was removing momentarily rather than to the whole series of disks, all that can be confirmed is that [dɪyz] was functionally and phonetically similar to, and a probable antecedent of, the adult "these".

The survey of the second year development of [d]-initial utterances is completed with the emergence of [dæt] ("that"), [dær] ("there"), [dɪs] ("this"), [dɪy] ("the"), and [dɪyz] (for "these"). In it most of these forms continued to be used as AO markers throughout the year, although evidence of an incipient meaning shift was seen in [dær] and [dɪy], while [dæt] and [dɪs] were transforming from pragmatic AO directives to semantic object markers. Concerning the latter, however, a review of events (28), (37), (40), (29), (36), and (41) reveals that even though the antecedents of "that" and "this" could be treated as separate phonetic classes from 16 months, their semantic functions were not observably contrastive even by 24 months. In this case therefore as with many other schema differentiations, two clearly and stably distinct phonetic forms developed prior to any observable distinction between them in use. Because of the contrastive adult usage of "this" and "that", it may be inferred that, like "look" in Branch L, these Branch D AO derivatives were still developing semantically at 2 years.

OBJECT NAMES (BRANCH N)

The only two schemata to produce object names in the first months of David's second year were the Request Object (Carter, 1975b) and presently considered Attention to Object schemata. It will probably be no surprise to find that David's AO schema manifested a relatively large number of both naming instances and different objects named, since this schema represents the usual name-learning communicative vehicle. Typically, for example, a mother points to a horse and says something like, "That's a horsie. Horsie!" soon after which the infant also points to the referent object and emits an imitation of "horsie"; the primary evidence that the name "horsie" or phonetic approximation thereof has been learned usually seems to reside in the infant's spontaneous production of the same AO form in the appropriate linguistic and situational context after some unspecified period of time. Additionally however, the AO schema seems to have been the ontogenic structure that supported David's gradual acquisition of basic object-denoting skills. The following sections outline evidence in his AO schema development for an isolable succession of increments in referential competence leading finally into the level of fully differentiated naming.

PS1   1;0(20)

Not only did the AO schema produce the largest number of object names but over all ten playsessions object naming was its most frequent manifestation. As with most other PS1 phenomena however, little can be concluded about the development of naming in that first playsession, wherein schemata were so vaguely and variously manifested that it was difficult to develop any adequate classification system, or even to be certain that at that level the concept of separate schemata of communication could have validity. Illustrating the problem was the sound [bæ], produced by David when approaching the basin, which presumably meant "bath" or by association "water". However neither possible interpretation was satisfyingly supported by contextual evidence, the caliber of which is illustrated in the following event.

(46)   1/1. While looking at his mother, as he walks away from her, he raises his arm to point vaguely in the direction he is walking, at the same time saying [bæ]. He then turns in the direction he is pointing and walking, again says [bæ!], reaches up to the sink, and while his hand is on the sink, yells [bæ] (approximately 8×) and then babbles rhythmically.

The clearest (and most startling) PS1 naming event took place at the end of this session, in which utterances had consisted entirely of equally or more ambiguous sounds than those in the above example. In this event David not only produced what appeared to be the names of two objects, but produced them in a close juxtaposition which (in seeming to indicate a single communicative intent under their combined production) implied a rudimentary form of conjunction or class inclusion. However if its interpretation is correct, this type of noun collocation was not seen again until after PS7 (1;8).

(47)   1/2. David looks at a poster on the right wall, depicting a reclining leonine animal with a smiling, clown-like face, he says [əlæow] (or [klæow]). Then he leans on his elbows in his mother's lap, and turning to look at the poster on the back wall depicting a comical owl, says "[la] (or [lʊ] or [lʊk]); owl.; owl clown (or [klæ])". His mother is looking at him, but seems not to understand, as she does not respond.

PS2   1;1(22)

There were some apparent naming attempts in PS2 taking the same [bæ] or [ba] form observed in PS1, many of which referred to objects with [b]-initial names and therefore looked like true names. Not all of the thus "named" objects had [b]-initial names however.

(48)   2/1. David picks up a ball, then runs to his mother, saying [baa] in a soft and sustained (soothing) tone, and holding the ball up in front of him. His mother, apparently thinking he wants to give it, tries to take it from him, but he doesn't let go.

(49)   2/2. He walks toward the basin, pointing to and looking at it, while saying [la. ba. ba. ba. ba.].

(50)   2/3. David sees a peer's bottle across the room, points to it and says [ba. ba. ba.ba.].

(51)   2/4. He holds up a block for his mother, saying [blæ]. Mother: "Aren't those nice blocks?" He then holds up a cookie, says [ba. ba. ba. ba.]. Mother: "That's a cracker." He eats it.

It is difficult to select any one explanation of the final AO act in the last event, because there are so many possibilities and nothing in the context that supports the selection of one and exclusion of another. The sustained and inappropriate use of [b] sounds when showing the cookie could be accounted for by phonetic perseveration, tentative overgeneralization, deliberate misnaming, the development of a temporary or experimental AO morpheme and undoubtedly other processes as well. Moreover except for objects having [l]- or [d]-initial names (cf. following discussion), it was almost entirely objects having [b]-initial names that were "named" in PS1 to 3. Hence even those [b]-initial AO utterances that looked like legitimate naming events require explanation, since their frequency suggests that he was drawing attention to objects at least partially on the basis of the sounds of their names. Descriptively speaking, it may be noted that the referential extention of one sound to many objects was a property not only of sensori-motor morphemes in general, but also of pseudo-names (cf. next subsection) and semantically overgeneralized names. The high frequency of what looked like [b] names therefore corresponds to a pattern of broad use for a single sound that applied to practically all utterances during this interval. The question remains unanswered, however, as to why his referring acts should have been phonetically determined in this particular way. Since, unfortunately, evidence of an underlying structural development of which the [b] phenomenon could have been symptomatic is presently lacking, the question must be left without even a tentative answer at this time.

Pseudo-naming

[l]-Initial Utterances: Type a Pseudo-naming

It is advantageous at this point to deviate from the playsession-by-playsession longitudinal format in order to examine in some detail the superficially similar phenomena of *pseudo-naming* seen in PS2 to 4 and *semantic overgeneralization* seen in PS4 and after. Beginning with the pseudo-names of Branch L, as indicated previously the only deviation in the straightforward phonetic movement of AO [l] sounds toward "look" was the tendency between PS2 and 4 for some to be consistently ambiguous between AO morphemes and object names. The possibility that this special ambiguity was developmentally significant is suggested by the combination of four factors in the pattern of development: (1) its appearance only during the interval PS2 to 4; (2) its fairly regular occurrence during this interval; (3) its occurrence during the same interval in the mostly independent Branch D as well; and (4) the significance of PS4, the endpoint of this interval, for the development of naming in the entirely separate, Request Object, schema (cf. Carter, 1975b). The concurrence of related phenomena in other streams of development implies that these morphemes were not just ambiguous, that is, difficult to interpret, but in certain respects homonymous, that is, alternately AO morpheme and object name, or simultaneously both. They might have represented a confusion between the pragmatic and semantic levels of signification, or even a fairly stable interim mode of representation between them. At any rate, they appeared after the full development of the AO [l] sound, but before the observed permanent and systematic use of names (cf. Carter, 1975b); hence in at least a chronological sense they mark a transition between purely pragmatic level of sensori-motor morpheme signification and the essentially semantic level of fully differentiated naming.

As illustration, it may be recalled that even in PS1 (event (47)) one of the possible phonetic representations of (what was taken to be) the name "clown" was something like [læow], a sound which could also be an [l]-initial AO morpheme. The same phenomenon was also observed in the two PS2 events below in which David referred to the same clown-like poster animal as [læo] and his cup of juice as [læ], presumably an imitation of "glass".

(52)   2/5. Leaning on his elbows on a table, he points at the animal poster across the room, saying [læo]. Mother: "Hm?" He turns to look at the owl poster on the back wall, saying "[dæ.]; owl", and is then distracted by a peer.

Because of its leonine aspect, David might at this point have been naming the animal "lion" instead of "clown", although the context provided no evidence one way or the other. However, it doesn't much matter in this analysis which word was the actual target. The more important point is that he was in all probability at least partially intending the sound of *some* name, and not just an [l]-initial AO morpheme, because the [æo] or [æow] diphthong elaboration occurred only when referring to this particular animal. The same argument applies to [læ] in event (53).

(53)   2/6. He stands at the juice table, pointing and reaching for his cup and saying [læ].

On the other hand, although in either of the preceding two events independent phonetic evidence suggests that he was attempting in some sense to name the objects referred to (in that in PS1 and 2 [læ] was used in reference only to his cup; and [læow], only to the clown-lion), interpreting either sound to be a pure AO morpheme would also result in a behaviorally consistent overall picture of the interactions. In PS3 the same [læ] sound occurred, along with a more accurate pronunciation of "glass", in an utterance sequence containing AO morphemes, names and pseudo-names in one seemingly undifferentiated and singly directed burst of energy, hinting at an either confused or deliberate cognitive interconnection between these three utterance types.

(54)   3/1. He produces a gesture intermediate between point and reach toward the cup on the juice table, saying, [la. glæ. la. glæ. glæ. glæ. glæ. glæ. a. da. la. mæ, glæ, læ. lʋ. læ læ] (whimper)

[l]-Initial Utterances: Extended Type a Pseudo-naming

Although evidence for them was weaker, two variant types of pseudo-names were suggested by a few PS3 and 4 incidents. In PS3, although [læ] was used almost exclusively to refer to his cup, David twice used this name-like AO morpheme to refer to cookies as well. Its apparent extention to a different referent object seemed to represent in essence merely the substitution of one sound (of the name "glass") for another (the regular AO morpheme). It would in general be very easy to interpret this utterance type to be an over-generalized name. However, in this study one could never be sure that such utterances were truly representational names—overgeneralized or not—unless they were phonetically unrelated to their gestural morpheme predecessors. True overgeneralization, the type that has recently been most frequently discussed in the literature (cf. Clark, 1973, 1974; Nelson, 1973, 1974; Bowerman, 1976) indicates a categorization problem of an essentially semantic nature. However the apparent or pseudo-overgeneralized naming presently hypothesized would have resulted instead from a signification level confusion, manifested initially merely in the substitution of an object name for the sound of the gestural morpheme, but with no basic change in its general attention-directing significance.

[l]-Initial Utterances: Type b Pseudo-naming

Type a (and extended Type a) pseudo-naming thus involved his treating the sound of a name, e.g. [læ] ("glass") as though it were an AO morpheme, a behavior presumably resulting from phonetic assimilation of the name into the pre-existing AO morpheme class. In the same interval, however, the inverse phenomenon was also seen, in which David treated [la], the most frequent AO morpheme variant, as if it were a name. Specifically (as suggested in the events below), [la] seemed to signify "cookie" (especially in the second event, in which he produced what appeared to be an ostensive definition for this sound). It is possible that [la] had become name-like through phonetic similarity to the semi-naming [læ] in a reverse or feedback process of assimilation. Since evidence of its range of application is lacking, this hypothetical utterance-type will be treated simply as a straight, or Type b, variant of pseudo-naming.

(55) 4/1. David looks at the juice table, saying repeatedly, [la], while first pointing to it, and then grabbing his mother's hand to pull her toward the table. When they arrive at the table, he watches her silently while she is getting him a cookie, and eats quietly after she hands it to him.

(56) 4/2. After having obtained another cookie, also requested by [la], David is eating silently. One of the other mothers, who has been watching him, asks David's mother, "What does [la] mean?" David immediately stops eating the cookie and holds it out for her to see, looks directly at her and says, [la.] (3×).

[d]-Initial Utterances

In the same interval a similar ambiguity was observed between object names and the [d]-initial morphemes of the other major AO branch. In an apparently related (Type a pseudo-naming) trend, the AO sound [dɔ] or [dow] was used, which might have meant "dog" in those instances in which the referent object was a (picture of a) dog, but which could also have served the more general demonstrative purpose of previous [d]-initial utterances. In PS2 to 4 either interpretation seemed equally plausible in instances of actual reference to a dog. Use of these utterances with (pictures of) other referent objects on the other hand might have resulted from either pseudo-naming or the beginnings of semantic overgeneralization. Note in this regard the following two events, each containing a seemingly undifferentiated mixture of AO morphemes ([dæt]), Type a pseudo-names ([dow]), perhaps Type b pseudo-names (name-like uses of [dæ]), and true or perhaps overgeneralized names ([dɔgɪy]), together producing an utterance sequence similar to the [l]-initial sequence observed in event (53). As before, this amorphous juxtaposition of utterance types hints at cognitive overlap in their underlying intentions.

(57)   3/2. David, sitting in his mother's lap, points to four different pictures in a book he is holding, saying for each picture, [dɔ]. For each the mother would say, "That's not a dog there. I think that's a birdie (or boy, etc.)." He points to three more items, turning the pages, and saying for each, [dæt!], then to three more, saying for each, [lʊ!], and then finally to an item for which he produces four [dɔ]s. Mother, agreeing in seeming relief: *"That's a dog."*

(58)   4/3. Looking at a picture book with his mother, David says, [do;gɪy!] ("do-ggie!"). Mother: "Uh-huh." Looking and pointing at another picture, David says, "Oh. [dæ.]", then, "Oh. [dow.]", then, looking elsewhere and pointing, [dɔgɪy!] Mother: "Uh-hm". He turns the page, points to a picture, and says, "Uh.;[da; . . .], is distracted by a peer, and then [. . . gly].

Semantic Overgeneralization

In the previous two events the variety of referent objects for the utterance [dɔ] and its variants hinted also at the beginning of a new type of extended use for the [d] morpheme that was yet further removed from its gestural AO origins, specifically, that manifested in the frequently observed phenomenon of semantic overgeneralization. However, it was not possible to conclude that true but overgeneralized naming (as opposed to extended pseudo-naming) was taking place unless David used a sound that was unlike any of his gestural AO morphemes. In PS5 (1;5) one could see a more definite semantic overgeneralization when David called a number of playgroup children by the name of one of them, which he pronounced [mɪyma].

(59)   5/1. His mother has named all the children in the room for him, one of whom is named M _____. After her name is given to him, he produces the imitation

[mɪyma.] (3×), pointing to the child while saying it. Later as another infant walks by, he calls him also [mɪyma] while pointing to him, and repeats this naming act several times. After a few repetitions, his mother tries to correct him, but he persists in naming [mɪyma] not only the infant his Mother named M_____, but other infants as well.

A playfulness in David's attitude suggested that he was making a joke in this perhaps deliberate over-extension of the peer's name, but it also suggested that he was by this time familiar with the problem of determining the nature and extent of the category to which a given name applied. The wide separation in sound between [mɪyma] and his AO morphemes demonstrates that [mɪyma] was not yet another pseudo-naming example, in contrast to the [dɔ] example in the immediately preceding event, which might have represented any of several developmental categories or a transition stage between them. For another PS5 example of semantic overgeneralization, compare David's use of "camel" in events (7) and (65).

Fully Differentiated Naming

Resuming the playsession-by-playsession examination for the description of regular naming, the ordinary object names produced in PS3 to 10 can be quickly sampled. Throughout the year the only basic changes observed in his AO naming acts were gradual phonetic refinements and a large increase in vocabulary. Although their functioning naturally became more subtle with the advent of multimorphemic utterances, the basic use of names was still clearly, even in PS10 and with or without gestures, to draw the hearer's attention to the referent object. No comments are needed therefore for the one or two events selected to illustrate this category in each remaining playsession.

PS3   1;2(16)

(60)   3/1. Looking out the window and upward, David, says [lʊ.; bʊ!] ("bird" (?)).

(61)   3/2. Picking up a ball, he holds it out to his mother, saying [ba.].

PS4   1;3(28)

(62)   4/1. He points to and looks at the juice, saying [ja!].

(63)   4/2. Having pointed to the juice table, he grabs his mother's hand to take her there, saying [da.; duw.; duw.; duw.; duw.] ("juice").

PS5   1;4(28)

(64)   5/1. He holds up a toy bee in front of one of the other mothers, saying "bee".

(65)   5/2. He holds up a toy horse in front of his mother, saying [la. lʊ mama] ("camel"). Mother: "That's not a camel. That's a horse."

PS6   1;7

(66)   6/1. He points out the owl on the wall to the other children, saying loudly, [la!; aw!].

(67)   6/2. He holds up a block for his mother to see, saying [bak!].

PS7   1;8

(68)   7/1. He looks at the picture of a cat on a book cover, then suddenly looks up at his mother and says "kitty".

(69)   7/2. He sees a peer reaching out to take one of his train cars, then turns to his mother, points to the peer and says in an alarmed tone, [beybɪy!].

PS8   1;8(26)

(70)   8/1. He holds the hammer out toward his mother, saying "Hammer, Mommy."

(71)   8/2. He sees a toy tow truck across the room, walks toward it, talking to his mother behind his back, saying "Tow twuck,; Mommy."

PS9   1;10(10)

(72)   9/1. He stops in front of a camera man, looks up at him, then looks and points at his toy train on the floor, saying "twain", and looks back up.

(73)   9/2. He sees a duck across the room, and says "duck". (This may have been egocentric speech, as it seems to have been uttered too softly to have reached his mother, who is behind him talking to the other mothers.)

PS10   2;0(10)

(74)   10/1. He holds out a ball for his mother to see, in an attempt to distract her from her conversation elsewhere, saying "Ball, Mommy; ball."

CONCLUSION

With the conclusion of the evolutionary development of naming skills, the description of David's AO schema development as a whole is completed. For perspective, however, a· review of the constellation of findings for this complex schema is needed. On this account therefore two aspects of the development will be summarized and discussed: its overall changes in form and the changing nature of object reference underlying the development of names in particular. Implications of the findings for developmental sociolinguistics will be included in the summaries, and considerations of their generalizability and theoretical implications will be touched upon briefly.

Structural Development

The origin of David's Attention to Object schema was not inferable from the playsession data. However, various considerations suggested that it might have originated in an association of object-contacting limb movements with the alveolar ridge articulation category. It was further speculated that while retaining their (as yet not understood) behavioral association, each category might then have differentiated into two or more subforms to produce pointing and showing gestures and the accompanying, essentially redundant, [l] and [d] vocalizations that appeared as phonetically distinctive forms in PS1. The observed [l] sounds, whose described development with that of the [d] sounds was from that point forward empirically founded, subsequently evolved into "look", pronounced consistently correctly by PS10 except when included in unusually long multiple-word utterances. The [d] sounds simultaneously evolved in a series of branching developments into "that", "there", "this", "the" and "these", each of which retained the initial [d] pronunciation as a prominent phonetic variant even at 2 years. The gestures, which at first were virtually inevitable accompaniments of the sounds, were seen with decreasing frequency over the year until by year end their co-occurrence seemed merely haphazard.

Between PS2 and 4 sounds were found from both the [l] and [d] categories which manifested a systematic type of ambiguity wherein they had the appearance and functioning of neither pure AO morphemes nor pure object names. This phenomenon, labeled pseudo-naming, was interpreted to mark for both sound classes a stepping stone in the evolution from AO morphemes to fully developed object names. During the first half of the year a large percentage of David's AO utterances were observed shifting away from their initial status as purely pragmatic, attention-directing, entities into the combined pragmatic-semantic level of usage exemplified in pseudo-names, and thence (while retaining their separate pragmatic aspects) to the conceptually autonomous or semantic level of usage of AO object naming nouns. Once this functional level had been reached, pointing or showing gestures were less necessary, since David's naming (together usually with direction of regard) seemed able to convey a particular object concept as well as his gestures. It was probably therefore as much as anything else the development of stable (and especially correct) names and multiple-word utterances which, in shifting the informativeness in AO acts to the vocalization, ultimately caused pointing and showing accompaniments to diminish in frequency over the year.

Later AO developmental products were forms that were well on their way to becoming verbs, adverbs, adjectives, etc. (e.g. "look"). Until year end virtually all of these potentially or actively semantic terms retained, like object names, their initial pragmatic status as AO directives. However, in PS9 the inclusion of some AO [d] variants in longer utterances with different overall functions implied for them a functional shift from the level of purely pragmatic usage toward that of usage as neutral non-naming object markers—i.e. either pronouns or the initially redundant object name affiliates which were later to become demonstrative adjectives—marking a change in focus in their case also (like that of object names a few months earlier) to semantic aspects of word signification. Finally in the last playsession 2 months later, the AO stream of development produced words whose appearance foreshadowed awareness of syntactic relationship, such as [dɪy] (for "the"), never uttered in isolation but only in a structure combination of words and without stress, and [dɪyz] (for "these") resembling a pluralization of one of David's previously developed forms, indicating perhaps his first glimmering of the possibility that plurality could be indicated by internal restructuring in pronouns. In line therefore with a widely demonstrated developmental pattern commented upon by Bates (1975) and others, this stream of David's communicative development can be approximately characterized as a weak ordering of three phases of linguistic emphasis corresponding respectively to the three levels of semiotic description, pragmatics, semantics and syntactics.

The transformation of David's sensori-motor morphemes into words resulted however from incremental changes not only in meaning but also in sound structure. With regard specifically to phonetic development, at 1 year, use distinctions for the C + V morphemes of all schemata, including AO, were determined by initial consonants (cf. Table 1), with the associated vowels, because of their vagueness and variability, appearing less significant. At the outset in fact, it often seemed that the trailing vowels were produced only as more or less unnoticed and unintended but inevitable concomitants of consonant production. The second phonetic refinement, usually occurring around mid-year, was for the vowel portion of the utterance to acquire greater stability and clarity, suggesting that both consonant and vowel were by then recognized and utilized in his perception and production of these sounds. The usual third step, seen in each case nearer the end of the year, was an increase in vowel refinement and/or the stable acquisition of a final consonant by the C + V form, creating by that time a highly refined third-order C + V + C approximation to the sound of an adult function word. In the case of "look", as of several words derived from other schemata (Carter, 1975a,b), a third order approximation was sufficient to produce the perfectly formed adult word. Each stage of phonetic refinement resulted in the possibility, and often the actuality, of an increase in the number of significant variants of the basic consonantal classes. Together with the resultant assimilation of new forms, this sequence of phonetic refinements, indicating a shifting focus from initial consonant in the first months to medial vowel in mid-year and then to final consonant toward year-end, described the gradual development of most non-substantive or function words, e.g. "look", "this" and "that", representing three of the four major AO strands of development (cf. Fig. 1). Early nouns, representing the fourth strand, were in sharp contrast initially learned in stable C + V or even C + V + C form, e.g. [ba] for bottle and [mɪyr] for mirror.

It is because of the slow and incremental nature of meaning and sound changes in their highly correlated and initially redundant sensori-motor morphemes that one could track the evolution of David's pragmatic attention-directing pointing and showing movements even into the symbolic levels of communication generally considered to represent language onset. As their thus demonstrated communicative antecedents in the AO schema, David's gestural pointing and showing acts therefore could be considered in his case formal precursors of those verbal acts that are also often, though figuratively, called pointing. From one perspective, it might seem strange to treat conventional vocal units as products of the altogether different modality of communication contained in gestures. In this regard, however, the findings for this child conform with suggestions advanced by Wundt in 1900 and underlined by Mead, Vygotsky, Piaget and others concerning the motoric origins of language in general. It should perhaps be stressed, however, that their ontogenic relationship was detected only through the connecting link of the co-occurring sensori-motor morphemes, or more specifically the shift through them of communicative development from the motor to vocal channel (cf. Fig. 2).

Referential Development

Viewed from its broadest perspective, such was the nature of David's Attention to Object schema development. However, it might be worthwhile to augment this broad and schematic synopsis by narrowing the focus for an inset rescan of the branch which provided the most detailed evidence of a very gradual transformation from pragmatic to semantic communication. Represented in Fig. 1 as Branch N, David's naming development passed through four main phases, excluding the early AO morpheme antecedents of pseudo-names: (1) the "[b] phenomenon", (2) pseudo-names, (3) overgeneralized names and (4) correctly differentiated names. In their longitudinal survey, these four phases of object indication were analyzed essentially only in terms of their distinguishing characteristics. In the following recapitulation of this

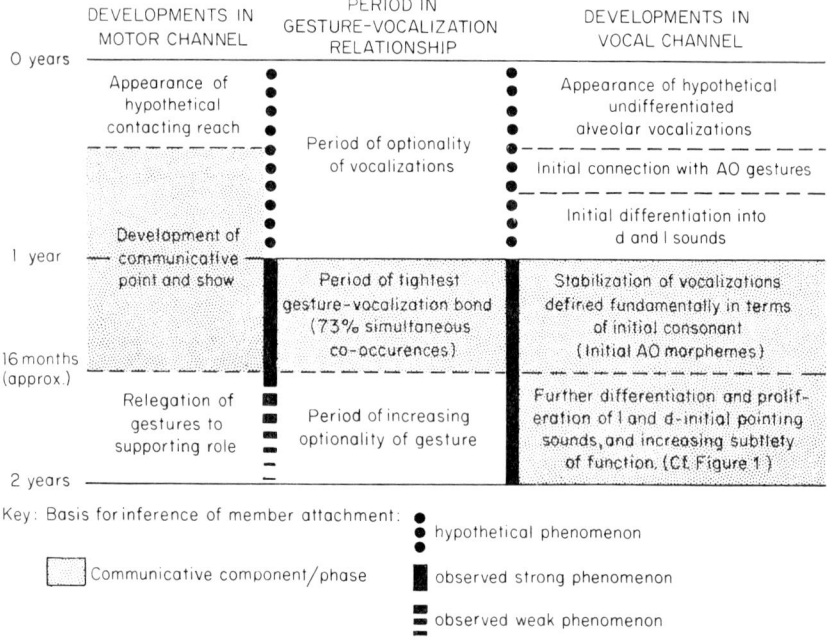

Fig. 2. Chronological developments in the AO schema gesture-vocalization relationship.

survey, however, a greater emphasis will be given to the possible social interactive processes which could have generated or triggered the interphase transitions.

1. *The "[b] Phenomenon"* (PS1, 2 and 3: 1;0(20)-1;2(16)). Along with regular AO morphemes and several possible naming sounds, David produced in the first three sessions a relatively large number of [b]-initial AO (pointing) utterances, many of which might reasonably be considered object names since the referent object had a name that began with [b] as well. One or two of these [b] utterances, however, in referring to an object that did not have a [b]-initial name, seemed to represent a phonetic over-extension. The structural significance of this phase was not clear.

2. *Pseudo-naming* PS2, 3 and 4: 1;1(22)-1;3(28)). PS2, and 4 produced numerous instances of the pseudo-name, a type of utterance which in exhibiting properties of both [l]- or [d]-initial AO morphemes and names of referent objects, could have represented a confusion or compromise between these two attention guiding utterance types. In the latter part of this phase

pseudo-names were extended to objects having very different sounding names. Because of its nature and location in the chronological sequence, this development seemed to mark an underlying transition from the level of *general referring* in which the nature of the referring sign is independent of the nature of the referent object (as in pointing), to the level of *particularized referring* in which the nature of the referring sign is by contrast determined by the nature of the referent object (as in naming). An infant's recognition of the logistics problems associated with the AO morpheme (because a co-occurring pointing gesture is necessary also in order to specify the referent object for the receiver, hence making it impossible, for example, to draw attention to distal things when one's hands are full of toys or refreshments) should provide him strong motivation for developing a new way to refer. It is also true, of course, that severe limitations on the number of objects that can without problems be denoted with an alveolar (in David's case, [l]- or [d]-initial) pseudo-name would seem equally to motivate his moving into the next phase of referring in which different names are developed for different categories of objects. In David's case, however, for whatever developmental reasons, pseudo-naming as a mode of referring represented an intermediate phase prior to naming.

The last observed pseudo-name occurred in PS4, the same playsession in which all *requested* objects were named (or requested by the regressive General Want Expresser ([ʔɜ;]) rather than requested by the more usual [m]-initial Request Object schema morpheme (Carter, 1975b). This playsession (at approximately 16 months) thus represented an important landmark in the transformation from general to particularized reference for both of the independently developing RO and AO schemata. If its interpretation is correct, the most important linguistic developmental significance of a pseudo-naming phase for David consists in its revelation of one infant's gradual awareness of the semantic level of signification, perceived initially in the recognition that different types of objects are more efficiently and effectively pointed out by various sounds that are in each case a function of the nature of the object itself instead merely of the act of pointing.

M. M. Lewis (1936) mentioned a phenomenon in the development of his child, K, that matches closely in both appearance and temporal sequencing David's development of extended pseudo-names. Lewis first noted for K an extended use of primitive sounds, corresponding probably to David's sensori-motor morpheme production. Later, when K began to use what appeared to be conventional words he tended to use them in precisely the same extended manner as he had previously been using the primitive or sensori-motor morpheme-like sounds. More infant data is clearly needed concerning this developmental nexus. If however as Lewis's example suggests, pseudo-naming is a generalizable phenomenon, one prediction which might be made as a result is that the infant's earliest names will tend to resemble his AO morphemes in at least the initial segment—assuming the generalizability of David's initial consonant emphasis; under this prediction infants exhibiting [d]-initial AO morphemes, such as Bubi Scupin's "da", would tend to produce [d]-initial "names" among their first words, like for example Bubi's "digda!" (for "ticktock", his name for clock) (Scupin, 1907). Testing this possibility on David's protocol, a rough tabulation reveals that in the first three playsessions David named correctly seven objects having [b]-initial names (representing the "[b] phenomenon"), four or five objects with [l]- or [d]-initial names, and only two or three objects having names beginning with any other consonant: [kɪ] ("kitty"), [pɪ] ("pitcher") and tentatively [klaeow] ("clown").

3. *Semantic Overgeneralization* (PS4 and 5: 1;3(28)-1;4(28)). In the concept and representation refinement process, a reasonable next step, and one which seems to have been observed for David, is manifested in the widely documented phenomenon wherein all (and only the) objects falling into a broad cognitive category are pointed out by the name of one member of the category, as in the application of the name "kitty" to all furry quadrupeds. This infant strategy could result in the correct labeling of category elements, as in the extrapolating application of the name "animal" to all such creatures. However, parents tend to teach particular names first, so that the infant's natural predisposition toward broad phonetic applicability together with an often idiosyncratic basis for distinguishing categories inevitably results in the type of mistakes designated labeling overgeneralizations. True semantic overgeneralization indicates the beginning of particularized referring, manifested in the child's early awkward attempts to either form or reflect separate referential categories through the assignment of distinct labels. However, the initial use of what appear to be overgeneralized names may at times actually indicate no more than *sound substitution*, with perhaps a somewhat reduced range of application, for either the AO morpheme or the pseudo-name, hence representing merely a slightly more complicated form of general referring (cf. e.g. David's use of "doggie" in PS4). Because the parent has no way to explain to the infant that he is using an inappropriate level of signification or type of categorization, he must correct the infant's utterances individually. It seems reasonable therefore that the infant would in the early stages interpret the adult's correction attempt as merely indicating a sound substitution for his utterance. This situation is perhaps more likely to obtain when the urged replacement sound resembles the sound being corrected. If the infant for example frequently points to an object and says [la], after which the parent says "glass"—or [da], after which the parent says "dog"—it seems probable that a quasi-permanent sound substitution would eventually be made; David's pseudo-names were presumably

engendered in this way. However, even though with less likelihood, the infant might in the same manner come to replace [da] with an altogether different sound, such as "book", and in so doing have developed what looks like an overgeneralized name but is actually no more than a new AO morpheme (that would, in resembling an adult word, tend to mystify parents attributing representational significance to it, like the parent in David's playgroup who said of her infant that "'book' is everything she points at".)

Sound substitution is a predisposition which would derive naturally from the general referring stage. However, it can be observed even after the level of semantic categorization has been reached, apparently demonstrating in the retention of earlier tendencies a transition to particularized referring which is piecewise rather than integral. The parent's correction of the infant's (truly) overgeneralized name is sometimes interpreted by the infant as a correction for the name not of the referent item, but of the larger category of which the referent item is but an instance. To illustrate anecdotally, I was told by one mother that having developed the name "doggie" in application to dogs, her infant then called a nearby cat "doggie", and then after being corrected, called the next dog she saw "kitty", upon which she was again corrected. This substitution and resubstitution of category names presumably recurred until the infant recognized that her mother's name correcting was intended to result in semantic recategorization rather than simply the renaming of a pre-existing category.

Sooner or later, however, the pseudo-naming and/or overgeneralizing infant will recognize that in general not only sound substitution but also a revised and substantially more restricted domain of application for his utterance is required when he is corrected since, among other things, his assumption of the applicability of one sound to an extremely large (or even universal) set of objects will have been shown so frequently unacceptable. Many factors undoubtedly can influence this change in awareness, moving him into the semantic level of utterance functioning. In David's case for example, the recognition was perhaps initially facilitated by the pre-existence of his two independently derived and phonetically distinct pseudo-names, predisposing him to divide referent classes into subcategories. As was glimpsed in the transformations from AO morphemes to pseudo-names, to overgeneralized names, and finally to differentiated names, repeated referential subcategorization was subsequently an important aspect of his gradual semanticization process. After an extended sequence of instructing, reinforcing and inhibiting social interactions, such as those parent-child interactions studied by Ninio and Bruner (1976), the infant will begin both to anticipate that newly encountered and different kinds of objects are likely to have new names (i.e. new sounds which are appropriate for pointing them out) and to have some sense of the kind and degree of differences between categories of objects having different names. Many other factors are involved in developing a full understanding of the nature of names, and even with this general understanding one can make labeling mistakes at any level of development. However, once the infant recognizes these two fundamental conditions on naming, entailing thereby a substantial reduction in the number of overgeneralizations, it is reasonable to say that he has in principle completed the referential transformation from pointing or showing acts to fully differentiated naming.

4. *Full Naming* (Beginning around PS5: 1;4(28). In line with these considerations, the fourth phase in David's naming development was characterized by a lack of labeling errors of the sort that result from semantic overgeneralization. Previously illustrated by naming events from later playsessions, in which the changes consisted essentially in an increased phonetic precision and vocabulary size and decreased frequency of gestural accompaniment, it will receive no additional comments at this time.

Final Observations

What overall conclusions can be drawn from our examination of David's second year Attention to Object communications? Although a thorough discussion of the observed trends must await a future report, a few general observations deserve immediate mention.

A. Because the sounds associated with AO acts tended to be restricted to a fairly narrow articulatory range, and because the development of David's AO schema could be described in an orderly manner in terms primarily of narrow phonetic differentiations of (or assimilations to) pre-existing forms, it may be inferred that there were internal phonetic constraints on the sequence of morpheme development at this early level that would probably preclude its predictability by any purely semantic theory. This inference, bolstered by the independent observation that his early sounds seemed to lack the semantic content which was perceptible in later utterances, would not of course apply to later vocabulary development on which phonetic constraints would no longer operate.

B. Corollary to this observation, because acquisition through assimilation of word forms into the pre-existing sound classes (or differentiation out of these classes) was in each case a function at least partially of phonetic similarity between the language-specific potential acquisition (or development) and the infant's pre-existing form, it would probably not be possible for the sequence of morpheme development observed of David to have perfect semantic parallels in all other language environments. In terms of the pattern of overt developments, at this very early level it may be only the nature of his vocal acquisition processes—such as those listed in the following subsection C—that could be potentially universal. As above, this observation would not apply to later semantic development. Evidence from other studies (Wundt, 1900; Stern, 1930; Lewis, 1936; Leopold, 1939; Werner and Kaplan, 1963) supports the possibility also that the specific initial connection between alveolar sounds and AO significance observed in David's morphemes might have generalizability.

C. In all branches of development the evolution of David's communication from the sensori-motor to semantic level appeared to be quasi-continuous, with the observed processes of sound and meaning development consisting of (1) *directed incremental changes,* (2) *schema differentiation* (resulting from either class subdivision or assimilation of some external model to produce a new variant), and (3) *schema integration* (resulting from mutual assimilation between pre-existing schemata). It should be emphasized that process (2) above seems to have been the means for the development not only of new demonstrative forms of the [d] class (Nodes 4 and 5 in Fig. 1), but for the interim development of pseudo-names out of AO morphemes as well (Nodes 1 and 2).

D. In attempting to assess whether in instances of any of these three kinds of development it was sound or meaning changes that occurred first, it became apparent in this analysis that one is heavily constrained by the nature of early prelinguistic vocalizations. Generally speaking, phonetic development, being much more salient than possible meaning shifts, is far easier to describe. Looking at David's early sessions, it was in fact difficult even to begin to assess whether he at any point entertained the possibility of two alternate meanings for a single form (such as for example, the meanings of "that" and "there" for [dæ] prior to its development of two stable [dæt] and [dær] subforms). It was as indicated practically impossible to find a basis for inferring any semantic meaning at all. However, when usages had in later sessions generally developed enough precision and stability to be analyzed, observed uses of clearly post-nodal or differentiated phonetic forms were usually virtually identical both mutually and to his previous uses of their undifferentiated precursors, with no more than a hint of any consistent shift in significance until subsequent playsessions, if then (cf. PS9 and 10 uses of [dæt] and [dær]). This evidence suggests that once his sound-meaning relations were capable of stabilization, phonetic distinctions derived from observing adult models were in general likely to be made before permanent or irreversible significance distinctions for his acquired forms in the second year (cf. previous discussion of the development of "this" vs. "the", and "that" vs. "this").

All of these observations speak to a level of description beyond that which characterizes a single schema. However, perhaps the most vivid disclosures of the present investigation concerned the developing AO schema in and of itself. The many contrasts and co-occurrences in David's interactions that allowed for the previous postulation of eight prelinguistic communicative schemata allowed also for tracing the development of this particular one of them as its representation transformed from gestures to words. In following this transformation several tasks were accomplished simultaneously. Among them was to trace the evolution of pointing and showing from actual to simply figurative acts; and provisionally, from figurative pointing acts (represented by the deictic adjective "this") into the use of a yet more abstract determinative ("the") having, when any, only a hint of pointing significance. The development of object names was also observed within this AO schema process, revealing their initial pointing significance in line with predictions by Werner and Kaplan (1963), Lyons (1973), Atkinson (1974), Bruner (1975) and others. Although descriptive of only a single case, the empirical support obtained for this developmental relationship conceivably helps to ground the characterization of reference acts involving the use of nouns or noun phrases as "pointing" in more than metaphor, since an epigenetic pointing origin for the first nouns might be considered in some sense residual or latent in the subsequent noun class of utterances as a whole. (This observation would apply with even more force to the other, more direct, AO schema derivatives: "this", "that", etc.) Finally, the tracing of his AO communication from physical to verbal, pragmatic to semantic and spatial to analytical brought the longitudinal analysis of this subject to the level wherein his vocal units of expression could be seen becoming conceptually autonomous, phonetically stable and semantically contrastive. It was to be the full acquisition of these three qualities which would allow his AO pointing vocalizations, already used in meaningful sequences, both to develop and to participate in the larger and more flexible structures of linguistic communication in which it was already apparent they would later figure centrally. The schema of drawing attention to an object is not only as previously indicated fundamental to communication in general—the starting form of David's AO schema development—and, as Peirce and others have stressed, crucial to formal language, the end-form of this development—but it can as demonstrated foster a complex component of linguistic awareness, manifesting a leading role also among the developmental processes that link prelinguistic communication to language. Although in this chapter it was isolated from other development for analytical purposes and its application was restricted to a single infant, the schema may prove to be an influential substratum of language development in general, with the infant's original Attention to Object movements and habit patterns serving as raw material with which to begin the development of language; his urgent desire to direct the attention of others with increasing certainty and precision, a dominant motivation for continuing this development; his orderly increase in attention to details of AO schema form and usage, a mediating mechanism with later phase ramifications; and the generation of several of the most essential syntactic categories, the ultimate contribution of this initially prelinguistic schema to formal linguistic competence.

ACKNOWLEDGEMENTS

Support for this study was received from Fellowship No. 1-F32-MH05743 from the National Institute of Health. My thanks go to Jim Lorentz for assistance with problems of phonetics, to Wanda Bronson for supplying the tapes for analysis, and to Leonard Seitz for many helpful suggestions.

14

Beyond Herodotus:
The Creation of Language by Linguistically Deprived Deaf Children

HEIDI FELDMAN, SUSAN GOLDIN-MEADOW
and LILA GLEITMAN

*University of California, San Diego, U.S.A., University of Chicago, U.S.A.
and University of Pennsylvania, U.S.A.*

CONTEXTS FOR LANGUAGE LEARNING

It is sometimes said that language is created by the young child, rather than merely learned. But if so, the creative act is massively contaminated by effects of the environment, with the outcome that some children come to speak English and others come to speak Tagalog. To understand what the child contributes to language learning from his own internal resources and dispositions, we ordinarily have to abstract away from the influences of a received, fully elaborated, natural language. In fact, there is a sizeable and growing literature that minimizes the child's contribution and seeks to account for language learning as a tight function of specifiable features of maternal and other caretaker speech (e.g. Snow, 1972; Levelt, 1975), on the plausible supposition that teachers or at least fluent users are required if language is to emerge in the novice. It does seem unlikely that a child deprived of this linguistic environment would come up with a communication system resembling a natural language (though, to be sure, *someone* must have, once upon a time). But so far there are not many conclusive answers from this literature about the requirement for a tutor or exemplar in the acquisition process. Could it be that a child would think to communicate even in the absence of this environment of communicators—is this a species characteristic of humans? Could this untutored novice design a system *de novo* for communicative purposes? And, most centrally, would that system look anything like the received language systems, rather than arbitrarily different from them—are there pre-given ways of organizing communicative intents, apart from the (perhaps fortuitous) likenesses that exist among the received natural languages?

We have been able to observe a number of children deprived of a catalyzing linguistic environment who allow us to address some of these questions, however tentatively. They are deaf children of hearing parents who, for reasons we shall discuss, have decided not to allow the children access to a manual language. If these children are to communicate, they must make a partly independent decision to do so, and they must largely create their own means. In this chapter, we report what we have surmised about the modes of communication these children have devised. We believe these findings bear on predispositions the child, any child, brings into the search for communication, and therefore bear derivatively on the allocation of internal and external resources for the normal language-acquisition process.

Evidence From Natural Language Acquisition for a Creative Component in the Learning Process

That language is responsive to external input requires no argument. But a number of inferential lines suggest a crucial role, as well, for species-specific endowments supporting language learning. That is, there is evidence of innate dispositions in humans to organize the linguistic environment in set ways. For example, a number of investigators have shown that the character of what is learned remains essentially the same, at least in early stages of acquisition, despite extreme differences in general intellectual capacity: Lenneberg (1967), Lackner (1976), and Morehead and Ingram (1976) have found that the order of acquisition of certain syntactic structures is the same, though slower, for feeble-minded children as it is for normal children. Lenneberg also showed that the language learning capacity early in life survives rather radical pathologies such as anarthria and organic damage to the speech centers in the brain, as well as other abnormalities (e.g. certain tracheotomies) which interfere with the ability to practice speech during the early learning period. These facets of the acquisition process (relative indifference to co-existing individual differences, relative immunity to pathology, and relative ineffectiveness of the opportunity to practice on the rate of skill development) are reminiscent of simpler behaviors in simpler creatures for which the evidence for a significant innate component is good (as a suitably distant example: swimming in tadpoles after lengthy immobilization; Carmichael, 1926).

Further evidence for this "inside out" rather than "outside in" component in acquisition comes from a look at the child's accomplishments under varying within-language input content and presentation conditions. While no one can doubt that facts about heard speech contribute to the course and outcome of the child's learning, still there are certain *non*-effects of adults on young language learners that would be puzzling on a strictly environmentalist interpretation. For instance, Newport *et al.* (1977) have shown that the rate of growth of selected syntactic structures is in many ways insensitive to a variety of individual differences in caretaker speech-style (e.g. the length and complexity of maternal speech does not predict the rate of growth in the child's MLU (mean length of utterance) nor in his tendency to express obligatory thematic relations). Similarly, enrichment of the input data does not appear to influence growth rates very dramatically, even when the procedures used are quite plausible as serving teaching functions. For example, Cazden (1965) systematically presented "expansions" (immediately presented adult versions of the child's utterances after he makes them) to learners over an extended training period. Such exemplars could reveal to the learner the appropriate linguistic renderings for concepts he has just tried to express. Yet these subjects showed no learning advantage over a group of control subjects. Thus, under diffuse and variable environmental conditions, there seems to be a maturational scheduling of language emergence that is hard to modify—a good argument in favor of species-specific endowments for language acquisition.

Finally, there is evidence that, in the presence of varying environmental influences, the child has narrowly defined pre-set ways of organizing these environments. This evidence comes from cross-cultural studies of language acquisition: despite significant differences in cultural ambiance and differences in the languages that are being learned, children seem to pass through very similar sequences of developmental accomplishments (Brown, 1973) within the same narrow development time frame (Lenneberg, 1967). Perhaps the most stunning fragment of evidence for a task-specific component in the acquisition process comes from Slobin (1973). He asserts, on the basis of cross-language studies, that among the earliest syntactic devices deployed systematically by young children is word-order—not only for acquirers of a word-order language such as English, but often for learners of highly inflected languages (e.g. Russian) with weak word-order constraints also. Slobin suggests that children may be biased to notice sequential properties of the speech-stream. The thrust of this finding is that language learning responds to internal specifications about the nature of human communication as well as to external specifications (i.e. characteristics of the input data).

Summarizing, there is emerging evidence that acquisition of the structure of language is unresponsive to large variations in non-linguistic endowment and linguistic environmental circumstances. Rather, language learning in its earliest stages seems to have a pre-set semantic and syntactic character, some of whose details are beginning to be discernible from descriptive, and particularly cross-cultural, studies of child development.

Communication in the Linguistic Isolate

In all of the settings just described, there has been an explicit, though varying, environment for the learner to organize mentally, and all these environments share critical properties. Natural languages are fundamentally alike, for whatever reasons. This fact restricts interpretation of most of these findings as arguments for innate structures: samenesses in acquisition can be viewed as effects of overriding environmental identities. What would happen if the child were given no language to learn? Is there a human "urge" to communicate which can manifest itself in the absence of a systematically communicating environment? Notice that the arguments in favor of a species-specific language endowment make no prediction on this further matter. (They assert only that a learner is disposed to organize language data in certain specific ways, if these data are in fact provided to him.) But if suitably circumstanced humans will "invent" a language when there is no presented language to be learned, this would allow us to ask more cleanly about possible task-specific properties of language functions: what if any, are the essential pre-given properties of any "allowable" human communication system (due, possibly, to conditions on acquisition)? These questions cannot even be raised in any humane situation we can devise, but surely in principle the kinds of inference that arise from the investigations we have cited would be materially enriched by use of an explicit deprivation paradigm—if only we could maroon some spare infants on a desert island to see if and how language develops on its own.

Classical cognoscenti will recall that this ultimate language learning experiment once was done. Herodotus (B.C. 460) reports that two infants were set apart from adults, but fed, and raised in an isolated cabin. No one was to speak to them on pain of death. The experimenters were an Egyptian and a Phrygian king. Their investigation was designed to resolve the question of which (Phrygian or Egyptian!) was the first of all languages on earth.

Appropriately enough for kings, the two appear to have been radical innatists, for they never considered the possibility that an uninstructed pair of children might not develop language at all. In the event, Herodotus tells us that these subjects began to speak Phrygian, and there the matter has rested for some millenia.

To be sure, tragedies of nature and circumstance have created more recent opportunities to observe language-deprived children. But in general the social and even nutritional deprivations of these individuals have been so extreme that nothing of value for the nature-nurture question can be gleaned from them. Examples are the feral children (summarized in an excellent discussion by Brown, 1958) who never could be taught language and who, to our knowledge, never created anything of the sort while in the wild. Similarly, socially isolated children (e.g. Davis, 1947; Fromkin, 1975; Rigler and Rigler, 1975) show variable capability for rehabilitation, but give no evidence of having developed any communicative skills while isolated. Of course not: if for no other reason, it would be pointless to externalize the language of the mind if there were no "other" to whom it could be addressed. For this and many other reasons, an interpretable deprivation experiment would require that the infant be raised in approximately normal social circumstances, with language being the sole, or at least the major, system of which the learner is deprived. In such circumstances, would human children —perhaps like the Egyptian children or perhaps like Marler and Tamura's white-crown sparrows (1964)—devise a skeletal species-specific variant of a human language? While the study we now report, of language-deprived deaf youngsters, is a very imperfect analogue of this situation, we believe it reproduces enough of its properties to suggest task-specific language endowments in the human learner.

A Study of Linguistically Isolated Deaf Children

Our observations of six deaf children not exposed to manual language, over a lengthy period during their early development, show that they do begin to use manual gestures of their own to reveal their thoughts and wishes to others. There is preliminary evidence that they—not we or their mothers—devise these gestures. They eventually begin to join pairs and even longer sequences (up to 13 "words") of these gestures into what we believe are manual equivalents of phrases and sentences. In both form and intent, in so far as we can make such inferences, these early communications look much like those of normally circumstanced language learners. Their communications are about the same topics discussed by hearing children of similar ages.

Moreover, these children follow a gesture-order rule for coding thematic roles within sentences, and they omit expression of certain roles as a function of the length and underlying structure of their sentences. All of this evidence points to systematicity in the deaf child's spontaneous communication. Despite many caveats owing to methodological limitations and thinness of comparable control data (studies of the acquisition of formal sign language are few), we believe we have suggestive evidence that these uninstructed novices, while severely limited in means, do have the internal wherewithal to develop a passable communication system. To the extent that it closely resembles early child speech, the self-generated deaf sign system may give us some insights about the properties of early normal utterances: in some degree, at least, it seems that the hearing child's "telegraphic speech" is what it is not solely because of what the learner takes from the linguistic surround, but also because of predetermined properties of "novice communication" in humans.

In what follows, we provide a description of early stages in the self-generated communication situation. The method of investigation, and particularly the bases for coding gestures and gesture sequences, are described in painful detail, for questions arise all along the line whether properties of communication by the subject or comprehension by the experimenter account for the structure of our findings.

SUBJECTS

Six congenitally deaf children, two girls and four boys, with no other apparent physical or cognitive problems, served as subjects. They ranged in age from 17 to 49 months at the first interview, and from 30 to 54 months at the last interview from which data are reported here (see Table I; continued interviewing of some subjects will be the basis for a forthcoming follow-up report). The children differed in family structure and in socio-economic background. The characteristic which they shared was their inability to rely on oral communication. The similarity in their circumstance was that none was exposed to formal sign language.

The children are moderately to profoundly deaf by their scores on standard audiometric tests, when measured with or without hearing aids. They were unable to acquire any verbal language naturally in the home. Under a program of oral education (see discussions below) they have shown only minimal progress in speech production and lip-reading. At the initial interview, Kathy, Dennis and Chris produced fewer than five words each.

David and Donald in their later sessions, and Tracy at both visits, could produce and lip-read a few single words, but primarily within structured situations, such as when they had to choose between flash-cards on which pictures were displayed. None of the children was able to use or understand the spoken words in the unstructured situations we introduced or in the daily activities we observed.

Why were these children not learning formal sign language? There is a controversy among educators of the deaf as to whether it is appropriate to teach a manual language. Some, including those at the schools through which we contacted these subjects, believe that profoundly deaf children can learn to lip-read and articulate English, if practice is frequent, formal, and begun early in life—but not so well if the child has an alternative means (sign language) of communication. Whether this is so, and whether it makes sense to withhold from the young deaf child a readily available communication system until "oralist" training can begin is a matter on which we will take no stand here. But this is the viewpoint of the school authorities in the metropolitan Philadelphia area who instructed parents of these subjects *not* to gesture to them formally or informally, lest this interfere with the motivation for acquiring spoken English. We have evidence (see pp. 376-378) that the families of these subjects followed the instructions rather well: they were observed to sign only in rather primitive and largely unconscious or unintentional ways. Sibling gesturing to the deaf children was similarly primitive. Overall, the manual effort by the family seemed to be unstructured, and responsive to the deaf child's gestures rather than the impetus for them.

PROCEDURE

We began this investigation without predetermined procedures, armed only with videotape machines and a collection of toys we thought might be enticing for children to communicate about. But we also had some serious hints that these subjects would make discernible contact with us. It is well known that deaf children educated in oralist schools often develop a set of idiosyncratic gestures which they use literally behind the teacher's back—of course it was the genesis of such gesturing that we were looking for. Fant (1972) has discussed these informal gestures, calling the mode "home sign". Tervoort (1961) has provided a most helpful description of their use by both Dutch and American children in oralist schools. On the basis of this prior evidence, and on the assumption that these "natural gestures" were at least partly self-generated by children (after all, the teachers clearly disapproved of them), we were primed to look for primitive iconic representations by our young subjects. Many long sessions of videotape peering were spent before we had any confidence that we could reliably extract the subjects' gestures from their wiggles and ear-scratchings. But as the subjects grew older, there was no longer room to doubt that they had begun to communicate by the use of manual signs. At this juncture, we settled into a regular schedule of visits with the subjects and tried to standardize these sessions and our analytic tools in useful ways.

Two investigators (S.G-M. and H.F.) visited each child in the home several times (Table I). The number of visits we were able to arrange varied across subjects. The interval between visits was from six to ten weeks, a span which allowed us to observe some developmental changes from visit to visit. The only major departure from this schedule was between the seventh and eighth visit to the subject we call Donald (all names used are fictitious). All sessions were videotaped.

Despite initial attempts to formalize the interactions, these sessions turned out to be simply relaxed play sessions, for the subjects were not amenable to more structured elicitation procedures. The toys we brought, the same for all subjects, served the purpose of narrowing the topic of conversation and keeping the children involved with us. Each toy had at least one of the following properties: it was multifaceted and detailed, such as a toy schoolhouse; it required skill and co-ordination to operate, such as a zoo from which the animals rolled out only when the proper key was fitted into a shape-matched keyhole; or it involved some dramatic event such as a bursting bubble. (The reader may now think he knows why most of the subjects' communications involved action and motion, as we will demonstrate, and perhaps he does. But, as with hearing children of the same ages, it is also probably significant that we could not engage the deaf children's interest with the Encyclopedia Brittanica or chess boards instead.)

Midway through the study, we stabilized the interview protocol to the extent possible. Each subject except Dennis was interviewed at least twice in the standardized way.*

---

*For details of this procedure, see Feldman (1975) and Goldin-Meadow (1975). These details are not reported here because, in the event, they had no relevant effect on the way the subjects behaved. For the same reason, data reported here come both from the informal and standardized interviews. Note particularly that none of the developmental changes we will report coincided with the changes in stimuli or procedures.

Table I

Subjects: ages at each session in years and months

Subject					Sessions						
	I	II	III	IV	V	VI	VII	VIII	IX	X	XI
Kathy	1;5	1;6	1;9	1;10	2;0	2;2	2;3	2;5	2;8		
Dennis	2;2	2;3	2;4	2;6							
Chris	3;2	3;3	3;6								
David	2;10	2;11	3;0	3;3	3;5	3;6	3;8	3;10			
Donald	2;5	2;5½	2;6½	2;7	2;8	2;10	3;0	3;11	4;0	4;2	4;6½
Tracy	4;1	4;3									

THEORETICAL BASIS OF THE ANALYSIS AND THE
DERIVATION OF CODING CATEGORIES

How can we get to the forms and meanings of the subjects' communications? Consider a typical event, at a session with the subject David. Mother is cooking lunch in the kitchen. David points toward a plate of food, puts his fist to his mouth and makes biting motions, and then points at one of us (Susan). Informally—and if David is behaving as *we* might behave in gesturing to a non-English speaker—we might claim that he was inviting us to lunch. Moreover, that in particular he was performing the signs FOOD-EAT-SUSAN. Further, that these signs had the syntactic properties of noun, verb, and noun respectively; and finally that a true rendering of the propositional intent was: *You-Susan will eat food.* But these decisions cannot really be made informally. Every one of them involves a strong claim about how the child's communicative acts relate to the relevant contents of his mind. For this reason, the description of findings (p. 375) hangs crucially on—is largely a consequence of—the coding decisions that preceded. Therefore the ideas behind the coding system are presented in detail; unless these are persuasive, there are no results to report.

Taxonomic decisions about the subjects' gestures and their meanings were arrived at on a kind of bootstrap basis. Neither the significant units nor their combinatorial and semantic properties were derivable on a prior theoretical basis. The criteria for segmentation of the gestures seem fairly straightforward, while the assignment of meanings to these gestures is distinctly more problematical.

On looking to the literature on the normal child's language acquisition for guidance, it is mildly dismaying to realize that almost all the very formidable problems we face in analyzing the deaf child's language arise for the hearing child's also, though they are not always explicitly discussed. The hearing child's use of our (adult) words sometimes gulls us into the assumption that he is using our language as well. For comparison, consider a hypothetical field observation of a hearing child in the setting just discussed. Mother is still in the kitchen, cooking lunch. The child points toward the plate of food and says "FOODEATSUSAN". It might be claimed the child was inviting us to lunch, that his utterance was segmentable into the words FOOD-EAT-SUSAN, categorizable as noun, verb, and noun, and semantically analyzable as *You-Susan will eat food.* For each decision about form, segmentation, and intent there is some question about whether the source is the utterance of the child or the language organization of the observer. Thus for the hearing child, approximately to the same extent as for the deaf subjects in this study, a number of features of the findings may be built into the coding procedures, and thus many of the outcomes are predetermined.

How to begin? Our mode of procedure is in part justified in terms of the limited goals of this research, as described in introductory comments: luckily these do not require us to get precisely at the contents of the deaf child's mind through his gestures. Our main aim is to ask whether communication develops similarly for the *deaf* child *without* linguistic input as for the *hearing* child *with* linguistic input. This commits us only to developing data for these subjects that are as directly as possible comparable to the data used to describe normal language learning. So wherever possible, we have leaned on the methodology of language-acquisition field studies in initial assignment of appropriate coding categories. In the next main section p. 375, which we have somewhat capriciously segregated from this one, and entitled "Results") we argue for the validity of the coding on quite different, retrospective, grounds: the subjects' behavior, over developmental time, coheres and is internally consistent when analyzed in terms of these coding categories.

Finally, we have taken care to establish the reproduceability and reliability of the coding, and the reliability scores are reported with the description of the coding categories below. The basis for deriving reliability scores was independent coding of a sample videotape (the eighth session with David; see Table I) by one of the authors and a trained coder who was not present at the videotaping session with the child. This tape lasted about 45 minutes and yielded about 400 codable gestures.

The discussion of coding categories proceeds in two steps: first, we describe methods for isolating the gestures from other motor acts and from each other, to determine the systematically functioning units of the manual system. Then we describe methods for assigning semantic/syntactic functions to these units.

The Isolation and Segmentation of Gestures

A good many of the child's actions can be interpreted meaningfully. For example, one can punch one's sister or grab her candy and the thoughts behind such acts are subject to easy inference—but that these acts are expressive and communicative is not evidence that they are symbolic or that they function within a language-like system. Analogously, the gurgles and coughs of English speakers are susceptible to meaningful interpretation— one is choking, one has a cold—but they are not "in English" (see the classic discussion of this issue by Sapir, 1968). The first task in this investigation, then, was to segment systematically functioning manual gestures from each other and from the stream of motor behaviors in which they are embedded.

(1) Extracting Communicative Gestures from the Stream of Motor Behavior

Two bases for recognizing a language-like *gesture* by our subjects seemed reasonable on the face of it: the motion should be an attempt at communication with another individual (henceforth: "the listener") and it should be an abstract representation of a communicative attempt, rather than a direct act; i.e. as remarked earlier, eating of candy may communicate that one is greedy, but it is not a "*greedy*-gesture". The criteria were considered to be satisfied if (1) the subject made an attempt to engage the listener by establishing eye contact with him; and (2) the gesture was not a direct motor act *on* the listener (e.g. pushing him, to convey "go") or on some object (e.g. throwing it away, to signify "no"). As a positive example, if the subject made a twisting motion of his fingers in the air, with his eye first on the listener's eye and then on a jar with a twist-top, we assumed a communicative gesture had been made. Ordinarily, auxiliary context supported these decision criteria. For example, there was often nodding and smiling if the listener then opened the jar, and there was often repetition of the gesture if he did not.

Once isolated, the gestures were described physically in terms of Stokoe's (1960) three dimensions, developed for description of American Sign Language: the shape of the hands, the location of the hands with respect to places on the body or in space, and the movement of the hand or body. Gestures were classified as different if they differed on any of these dimensions. Reliability scores were derived both for the isolation and description of the gestures. In the 45-minute sample videotape, 84% of gestures identified and described by either of the coders were identically identified and described by both coders, yielding 350 reliably coded gestures from this sample session.

(2) Segmenting Gestures: the Category *Sign*

The next job was to describe the gestures in terms of systematically functioning formatives of some kind. The task is similar to segmenting utterances of English, which have systematically functioning substructures (morphemes, phrases, etc.). Moreover, an utterance as a whole may be a systematically functioning unit (i.e. a sentence) or not (i.e. it may be half a sentence or two sentences long). Described here is derivation of the unit *sign*, analogous to morpheme or word, from the gestures.

When can we say that two gestures occurred in succession? For spoken language, this matter is partly approached on a distributional criterion (Bloomfield, 1933; Harris, 1951). Thus if a speaking child is heard to utter "booktable", an initial basis for claiming two units is not hard to find, if he also says "book" and "table" in other contexts, on other occasions. *Signs* were recognized within the gestured communications if they met this distributional criterion—if they had been observed to occur in isolation or within other combinations. While this criterion was considered sufficient, it could not be considered necessary (it is too much to expect every word to be used twice during the brief times we were with the subjects). There is another criterion, perhaps a better one, though it resists formalization: it is easy for an observer to perceive quite directly (presumably in terms of his own organization of motor acts) when there have been two signs as opposed to one within a gesture. There is a change or break in the flow of movement preceding and following the sign.

High inter-rater reliability scores were achieved by joint use of these two criteria: there were 335 cases (among the 350 gestures reliably isolated on the sample videotape) where sign boundary decisions could be made, and there was 93% agreement between the two coders on these decisions.

(3) On Defining a Sentence

Once it is determined that a string of signs has occurred, how can we decide whether they are *in construction* with one another, as in a spoken sentence? For English, there are intonational and junctural clues to sentence boundaries with which to begin (e.g. pre-pausal lengthening: Lehiste, 1970); then aspects of the emerging structural descriptions of the child's speech fill many gaps for questionable cases. Similar physical criteria exist for defining the manual sentence boundaries: (1) if two gestures appear to be uninterrupted by any appreciable time interval, they are candidates for being "within a sentence"; and (2) the hands must not return to the "neutral position" (hands relaxed in front of the body) between two gestures, if they are within a sentence.

The neutral position just described segments sentences in established manual languages (Stokoe, 1960). This same motor behavior is used consistently by our subjects, without teaching. The segmentations derived on the basis of our two criteria correspond to conceptual segmentations of propositions in natural languages; that is, pauses and the neutral position occur between sequences that we readily interpret as "complete thoughts". For 337 decisions about sign concatenation into sentences, inter-rater agreement was 93%.

Interpreting the Deaf Child's Communicative Intents

Moving now into the area of semantic imputations, coding matters become much more thorny, sufficiently so that decisions here are more conclusions than coding categories. It is hard—in fact it is the heart of the problem under study here—to know exactly what some sign or string of signs means to its user, even though our *subjects'* responses to *our* responses to *their* gestures often indicate that they are satisfied with our interpretations.

Glossing Signs by their Referents

Consider a subject making a small twisting motion of his fingers in the context of some interaction among him, us, and a jar of bubble soap. Is he referring to the "jarness" of the jar? To its "openness"? To the means, "twisting", by which it may be opened? The "act of opening"? All of the above? The problem of interpretation here is sobering, but it is in principle no different from problems of interpreting the single-word utterances of young speaking children.

Consider for comparison a hearing child saying "jar" under the same circumstances. If we knew the conditions under which he acquired use of this vocabulary item, we might be more secure about claiming it means *jar*. But vocabulary items are presumably acquired under rather diffuse extra-linguistic circumstances, i.e. within some complicated situation involving jars and other objects, and also involving motions and other events, so it is not easy to know what the child has picked out as the meaning of *jar*. (For instance, a child of one of us was often shown the picture of a baby on the baby-food jar, and also shown herself in the mirror. In both cases, the mother would say "See the baby . . ." The child also came to say "baby" in both circumstances. But later the child was observed to say "baby" also in response to roundish coffee stains on the kitchen floor, at which time it was realized that while the mother was looking at the baby, the child had been looking at the round picture and mirror frames.) Even if a gloss is specifically called for in a standardized situation, it remains something of a mystery how a unique concept is picked out. For instance, the child can point somewhere in the visible world and wait for an adult to provide a verbal label. But precisely what was pointed at when the adult responded, say, "jar"? Both interlocutor and speaker were seeing opening-of-jar in the visible world. The tendency of mothers and other English-speaking humans is to respond as though the child were querying the name of an object. This represents a strong implicit claim by the adult about the nature of the child's concepts, and about language acquisition (probably, but only probably, it is right). But if this is the condition under which lexical items are often acquired (points are responded to with noun labels) it is hardly surprising that an English speaker's first *words* are mainly nouns of English. But we do not know from this if English speakers' first expressed *concepts* are noun-like concepts.

The problem with lexical interpretation for the deaf subjects is approximately the same—only we are poignantly aware of it because we do not know the child's language and it is awesome even to impute knowledge of it to him. We suggest, however, that in so far as observations of the hearing child's usage are taken to provide evidence about his expressed concepts, the same evidence is available in the present study, and it requires only the same degree of scepticism.

Following the lead of most investigators of spoken language learning, we do provide isolated signs with tentative glosses, but we are wary. The first step is to guess at a probable referent on the basis of the extralinguistic context of use (cf. Bloom, 1970). The second step is one where we have rather an advantage over the investigator of spoken language: we gloss the item according to the form of the sign, for it is often iconic. Finally, the glosses are justified retrospectively in terms of the system as it becomes combinatorial.

The deaf subjects make reference in two ways: they point to objects, persons, and locations; and they "pantomime" properties of things and events in stylized ways.*

Glossing Points

The subjects very often point to things and people and places. We had a preliminary notion to exclude these pointings from analysis, because we were unsure whether they participated systematically in a language-like communication—after all, hearing people point also, but these pointings do not participate in the logical forms of their sentences. Two facts changed our minds. First, when the subjects' communications became combinatorial (more than one sign per sentence), it was clear that the points functioned systematically within these combinations: they had restricted privileges of occurrence relative to other signs within sentences (see pp. 383-401) and they showed constructionally sensitive physical deformations (i.e. points "flowed" into other gestures within, but not across, sentences, as described on p. 363). Second, the character of the deaf children's vocabularies is conceptually ludicrous, if points are excluded. This last needs some explanation. tion.

Clearly it is easier to pantomime an action than an object (a potentially fatal flaw in a manual language, if it requires a non-arbitrary relation

*The children produced a third kind of sign which served modulation functions. These *sign markers* were head-nods and side-to-side head shakes. Notionally, they are similar to the words *yes* and *no* in English. Clearly, these gestures were learned from the children's hearing caretakers.

between a thing and its name). An available instance of the nominal concept in mind (the real thing) is a reasonable *pro tem* way of rendering it, so the point serves a quite general function. If only motor-iconic signs, excluding pointing, are considered, these subjects' vocabularies, at various stages, are remarkable in excluding just the things that should be most obvious and salient to the subjects—most objects, particularly objects that are around whenever the child is around (his eyes, for example, or his nose) lack vocabulary items. Surely this is not because the gesturing child never refers to such matters, but rather because he has a kind of "universal morpheme" with which it is easy to make concrete reference to objects in the here and now.

For syntactic purposes, it is sufficient to treat the points to objects and people as pronominals or demonstratives, such as *this*. However, we have as a further ambition the analysis of these gestures in terms of the semantic intents of their users. These vary, though the pointing sign does not. For this reason, we provided a derivative gloss of points in terms of their presumed referents, based on the context in which they occurred. Each point was glossed as the object, person, place, etc., toward which the pointing was directed. One might think this methodological decision would yield enormously inflated nominal vocabularies for these subjects, compared to their hearing peers, for the latter are not usually granted a separate lexical item for each thing they refer to as "this". However, as will be demonstrated (pp. 379-381), the nominal vocabularies that result from this analysis are quite small, and highly restricted in semantic scope: the subjects do not point to everything they can see.

The context of use makes clear that points are also used to indicate some concepts that are not substantives. For instance, a subject responds to seeing a picture of his brother, by pointing first to the picture and then pointing toward the door—his brother is away at school. We classify the sign as *out* or *there*. Similarly, the subject makes successive downward points toward the floor to indicate that a shovel he has just been shown a picture of is stored downstairs, in the basement. We classify the sign as *down*. By similar means, the subjects can even gesture quite intelligibly about some perceptual attributes that are not directly representable in space or motion. For instance, they render *red* by pointing successively at various red objects in view.

In sum, the points can refer to objects and people (e.g. *duck* or *Mother*) to locative notions (*out* or *down*), and adjectival notions (*red*). Transparent aspects of the contexts of use lead us to these attributions of meaning.

Glossing Characterizing Signs

The subjects use a wide variety of signs more specific than pointing. These are essentially stylized pantomimes. Usually, there is no great difficulty or ambiguity in interpreting or classifying them. Thus we are confident that the subjects are able to gesture about actions. For example, hands jiggling on an imaginary steering wheel approximate a concept like *drive;* flapping arms approximate *fly*. In addition to the iconic properties of the signs, the contexts of their use strongly suggest verbal classifications of them. For instance, upon seeing a mechanical mouse beating a drum, the subject points to this object, and himself makes the *drumming* motion. This is action in response to action; it seems perspicuously verb-like in intent and we have no hesitation in making this classification. Similar contextual supports exist for interpreting certain gestures as adjectival in intent. For instance, as a toy tower is built higher and higher, the subject raises his arms (and eyebrows) and then points to it; he has indicated that the tower is *big*. In short, joint clues from the form of the sign and the context of its use are the basis for classifying characterizing signs as either verbal (*action*) or adjectival (*attribute*).

However, there are certain contexts in which action-based characterizing signs are used where an argument could be made that they are simple nominals, and not verbal at all, despite the fact that their derivational source in physical motions is verb-like. As an analogy from English, a word such as *walk* is basically a verb, but obviously this word functions as a noun in such sentences as *I swept the front walk yesterday*. The same issue sometimes arises for the deaf subjects: might they not have simple nominal intentions for characterizing signs, when the situation in which these are used is not expressly action-like? The clearest example of such a possibility is when the child uses characterizing signs in response to seeing pictures of objects. For instance, the *twist* motion of the fingers (relevant to jars and their openings) is made by a subject in response to seeing a picture of a jar in a book. The mouth is opened in a snarling expression in response to a picture of a lion. Open hands, palms forward, are held behind the ears and then flopped in response to seeing a floppy-eared Mickey-Mouse. Perhaps though these signs iconically recreate some typical shape or action of the object, they may be functioning as simple nouns. That is, maybe the *twist* in response to the jar picture is intended to convey the nominal notion *jar* and not the verb/adjective notion *twist* or *twistable*. We digress here to pursue this problem because the classificatory decision has systematic consequences for the semantic analysis of sentences in which such signs figure (p. 369).

The case we are considering is one in which the child first points at the noun referent, followed by the iconic sign, in non-action contexts. The interpretation we have made assumes that the point refers deictically to the noun referent and the characterizing sign refers to an action-based feature of that noun; hence roughly "jar (is that which is) twistable", "Mickey-Mouse (is the one with the) floppy ears", "Lion (is one who) snarls". But it is possible to assume, on the contrary, that the characterizing sign refers directly to the noun that it mimics, in which case the same sequence would be intepreted "This is a jar", "This is Mickey-Mouse", and "This is a lion". Notice that both interpretations fit the extralinguistic context, so this gives no guidance on this issue. Yet the fact that the subject has himself invented and used an action to describe this event seems to us to argue that action is involved in the mental intent. This argument is strengthened by a look at analogous innovative uses of language by speakers.

For the case of English, just as in the examples above, complex noun formation is often based on predicative sources. For example, etymologically speaking, a *cartwheel* is that *whose motion resembles the motion of the wheel of a cart*; hence, an *acrobatic trick*. But what is the psychological status of this item, etymology aside, for an English speaker as he says "We learned to do cartwheels in gym today?" Is there an implicit organization in terms of the etymological source, or only an unanalyzed two-syllable noun? This is essentially the same question being asked about the use of *twist* by the deaf subjects in non-action contexts. For English, the answer will be partly different depending both on the item and the speaker in question (for discussion, see Gleitman and Gleitman, 1970). Only a few philologists will be aware that a muscular cramp is called a *charley horse* because lame old family horses in England were typically named Charley. Only a minority of outdoorsmen, probably, will analyze *backlog* as a complex item and know just why it means a *reserve*. However, many compound words such as *birdhouse* are much more transparent, and these may be represented mentally as morphologically more complex than some of their synonyms (e.g. *cage*) by most fluent speakers.

There is one situation in which we can be sure that a lexical item has psychological substructure. Consider a child who has just received the unusual present of a pet aardvark and who names its cage the *aardvark-house* instead of, say, the *glip*. Both *aardvark-house* and *glip* are new forms, inventions. In the instance *aardvark-house*, the invention has the non-arbitrary, rule-governed, source *house for an aardvark*, so we must grant the inventor this complex mental representation.

The same arguments apply to the deaf subject's characterizing signs, for he is their inventor. That in conversation about Mickey-Mouse he creates a sign that looks like flopping mouse-ears is understandable only by acknowledging that he mentally conceives the mouse as the *one with floppy ears*. Then it is fair to grant him expressible knowledge of predicates of this sort. (For both hearing and deaf inventors, the psychological status of these words may change with time. After months of cleaning it, the aardvark house may be just a smelly box, and the action-iconic source of Mickey Mouse may be similarly submerged. These are often the historical facts both about spoken language (where *charley horse* is now a dead metaphor) and American Sign Language. For an excellent account of the loss of iconicity in formal sign languages, over historical time, see Frishberg, 1975.)

Summarizing, the etymological argument supports classification of items like *ear-flop* and *twist* in non-action contexts as having action-like substructure. We therefore classify them as describing the actions of things and people. We do not classify them, along with points, as nominals that refer directly to the things and people themselves.

Reliability of the Categorial Assignment of Signs

Whatever the merits of the taxonomic decisions we have made about points and characterizing signs, it is possible to provide reliable glosses of the subjects' gestures in terms of them. Reliability scores for assigning referents both to points and to characterizing signs were calculated. In the set of gestures identified, segmented, and similarly described by both coders from the videotape sample, there were 312 instances where decisions about a referent and a taxonomic categorization could be made. There was 93% agreement between the two coders on these decisions.

The Meanings of Signed Sentences

The problem here is to discover the semantic logic that holds signs together when they appear in construction with each other. This is hard to do even for an adult English speaker. A semantically perspicuous description of the English sentence is hard to come by. It is harder still to analyze the semantics of naturally occurring utterances, because of such problems as constructional ambiguity, production errors, and the like. The problems are measurably worse in analyzing the exotic productions of very young speakers who (presumably) express meaningful ideas, but do so in the absence of shared conventions about how these meanings are to be rendered linguistically. The same problems of course recur for the subjects in the present study. Because of their limited resources, both in lexical types and syntactic forms, all of their conversational intents are mapped onto only a few superficial structures: strings of two or a very few ordered signs. These only grossly limit inferences about what the child had in mind to express. As an aid, we have leaned on the situational context in which the signs occur. Let us illustrate with an example: Dennis is watching a toy mouse eat spaghetti. He looks at one of us, points to the mouse, produces the characterizing sign *eat*, and then returns his hands to the neutral position. The criteria for sentencehood have been met (see p. 363) but what does the child mean to express? Without context, the sign pair is as easily interpreted, say, as "Eat the mouse!" or as

"The mouse eats". But arguably, the context of use favors the latter inter-pretation. We conclude that Dennis has commented about an ongoing action, *"Mouse eats".*

Lois Bloom (1970), in a landmark study, was the first among recent students of language acquisition to make systematic use of situational contexts to enrich the possibilities of semantic interpretation. Although there is room for dispute about just how the extralinguistic situation can constrain inferences about what has been intended—since language encodes what the speaker happens to be thinking about a situation, rather than the situation itself—some plausible guesses appear possible. Bloom's method ultimately was justified retrospectively by aspects of her findings, particularly through the fact that the semantic-syntactic categories so derived elegantly described the subjects' emerging speech and made many acute longitudinal predictions about the acquisition of grammar. We have extended this method to the deaf subjects' sign sequences in order to develop data comparable to those currently appearing in the language acquisition literature. Details of this analysis and notation follow (but see Goldin-Meadow (1977) for a complete description).

Sentence Types: Action and Attribute

We separated the subjects' sentences into a group that seem to comment on or to request the actions of people and objects, and a group that seem to comment on the perceptual attributes of these people and objects. This division of the signed sentences follows from the prior division of the characterizing signs into a verb-like group (e.g. *eat, sleep*) and an adjectival group (e.g. *big*). Thus there are *action* sentences such as *"Mouse* (point) *eat* (biting motions)" and attribute sentences such as *"Drum* (point) *big* (raised arms)". The sentences whose elements were points only were assigned to these categories on the basis of the contextually derived meanings of the sentences. For example, the pair "hat-red", signed about a visible red hat (the subject points to the red hat, then points to other red objects in view), was assigned to the attribute category of sentences. But the pair "Susan-David", signed as a point first to Susan and then to David, after Susan gave a cookie to David, was reconstructed as an action sentence ("Susan gives a cookie to David").

---

*Simply for expositional clarity, we are adding appropriate inflectional suffixes and the like to the interpretation of sentences. But we are not claiming that the concordance *s* in our interpretation *Mouse eats* or the *the* in the interpretation *The mouse eats* is a property of the language of the subject. Use of these markers, we trust, simply disambiguates certain claims we do mean to make. That is, we interpret this sentence as noun-verb, not as, e.g. the compound nominal *mouse-eat*. For all instances cited henceforth, we never mean to imply that the subject has inflectional or derivational affixes in any of his sentences, nor determiners or quantifiers. None of these ever occur, or are inferrable, from anything the subjects do.

Reliability scores were established for classifying action and attribute sentences. Sixty-six such classification decisions were made in the videotape sample. There was 96% agreement between the two coders on these decisions.

The Semantic Analysis of Action Sentences

A detailed semantic coding of elements of the action sentences was now performed.* The coding categories roughly follow Fillmore's (1968) *case* and *predicate* analysis of the semantic logic of sentences. On this view, each sentence is viewed as a miniature drama whose scenario is given by the *predicate* (the verbal element, the characterizing sign) and whose *dramatis personnae*, in their various roles, are given by the *cases* (the nominal elements, the points). For example, the English sentence:

(1) Herod gives the head to Salome in the ballroom

expresses a semantic relation through its predicate (*give*) and the sensible connections of all its nominal phrases (*cases*) to each other and to this predicate. The example sentence (1) instantiates each of the cases we require for describing the deaf subject's relational meanings:

Actor: The object or person which performs an action to change its own state or location or to change the state or location of an external patient; *Herod*, in sentence (1).

Patient: The object or person which is acted upon or manipulated; *head*, in sentence (1)

Recipient: The locus or person toward which someone or something moves, either by transporting himself, or by being transferred by an actor; *Salome* in sentence (1).

Place: The locale where an action is carried out, but which is not the endpoint of a patient's or actor's change of location of an external patient; *ballroom* in sentence (1).†

*Excluded from this analysis are one-sign utterances and multi-sign utterances that consist solely of repetitions of a single sign, because the analysis of child "holophrases" in these relational terms may well be inappropriate (i.e. the one-word speaker or signer may have no relational meaning in mind; see Bloom, 1973, for discussion) and in any case, reconstruction of relational meaning on the basis of a single word would require too much guesswork. Multi-predicate utterances and attribute sentences are excluded on grounds of insufficiencies in the data base for the early stages of the deaf sign-language that we are reporting on in this chapter. The effect of these exclusions is that each sentence analyzed here contains at most one characterizing sign (which is always the predicate) and a maximum of three points (the cases).

†Obviously a variety of further cases have to be recognized to get at the semantic logic of English sentences as used by fluent adults. For some sentences there is an *instrumental* case (e.g. in "Herod tapped Salome with the *scepter*") and a *benefactive* case (e.g. in "Salome danced for *Herod*"), etc. Our subjects give little evidence of trying to express these additional relational meanings, so we discuss them no further in this section.

The usefulness of this analysis is that the same nouns can be identified as playing the same roles in quite different sentences, if these have about the same meaning. For example, in at least one version of a "case grammar", the nouns of:

(2) Salome receives the head from Herod in the ballroom

are assigned the same semantic roles that they had in (1); that is, *Salome* is still the recipient case, *Herod* is still the actor, and *head* is still the patient. In this way, the relational analysis explicates the semantic relatedness of sentences (1) and (2). For other sentences, the same nominals will play quite different roles. For example, in one version of a case grammar, the sentence:

(3) Salome takes the head from Herod in the ballroom

Yields *Salome*, not *Herod*, as the actor.* Thus on this (case) analysis, sentences (1) and (2) are alike, while (3) is different. In contrast, on any reasonable syntactic analysis (2) and (3) are alike while (1) is different: *Salome* is *subject* in (2) and (3) and *indirect object* in (1); *Herod* is *subject* in (1) and *indirect object* in (2) and (3).

It should be emphasized that nothing is implied in this discussion about the priority of either the syntactic or case descriptions. Both these analyses describe psychologically real representations of language, to the best of our belief. A serious goal in language description is to explicate how the presumed relational meanings are mapped onto the syntactic forms. Clearly, from our examples, the mappings are not one-to-one. But while the relation between these levels is to that extent complex, it is quite regular. There are fairly reliable clues in the syntax of English (both from word order and from such "case markers" as the prepositions) to the semantic roles. Consequently, the main argument that our subjects have a "language-like" communication system will come from the demonstration that the relational analysis of their gestures maps in regular ways onto a syntactic analysis of their gestures. Thus neither description can replace or supercede the other, if language description is to link sounds (or signs) to meanings.

We now describe how the subjects' sentences were coded in relational terms. There are two descriptive problems. First, we show how the context of

---

*It may appear to be an embarrassment to this kind of model that the semantic roles in sentences (2) and (3) are not treated identically, for on some accounts these sentences mean the same thing (i.e. if one is true, the other must be true; if the two are connected with *but*, a semantic anomaly results; a movie depicting the event would be the same for both sentences to be used appropriately, etc.). But it should be said in defense of this model that the subtle differences in vantagepoint between sentences with *take* (a quite active thing to do) vs. *receive* (a quite passive thing to do) is precisely captured by this difference in case labeling. Perhaps it is worth noting as well that we are not subscribing to the view that case grammars are the final solution to the problem of describing the semantics of natural language sentences. However, Bloom (1973), Brown (1973) and Bowerman (1975) have convincingly argued the value of this kind of analysis for representing the primitive semantics of child speech.

use of occurring sentences determines their analysis. Second, we show how certain labels are inferred on some occasions when they are not explicitly gestured.

(a) Rich interpretation and semantic coding. Consider the subject David, apparently wanting Susan to stay for lunch, and gesturing:

(4) *food* (point to food)—*eat* (bite motions)—*Susan* (point to Susan)

and then returning his hands to neutral position. By observing this sentence in context, we can assign predicate and case labels to the sequence. The deictic point to food is the *patient*; the deictic point to Susan is the *actor*; and the characterizing sign *eat* is the *predicate*. Moreover, the sequence in its entirety approximates the propositional meaning, or *semantic relation*, conveyed also by the English sentence:

(5) You, Susan, will eat food.

Had the context of use been different, the assignment of case labels might have been different also. Sentence (4) yields only a far-fetched example here: in the unlikely event that some food-substance was observed eroding the skin on Susan's hand, sentence (4) signed in response would have been coded as food (*actor*), Susan (*patient*), eat (*predicate*), and the semantic relation would have been coded as:

(6) Food will eat (at) you, Susan.

(b) Reconstruction of relational meaning when gestures are not explicit. What happens if the subject does not explicitly provide a sign for every one of the semantic elements we think he might have had in mind? After all, young speaking children are known to produce incomplete overt sentences due, arguably, to linguistic inadequacies, but they may have more complete thoughts in mind nevertheless. It is the essence of Bloom's method of "rich interpretation" that she tries to reconstruct the more complex meaning behind the incomplete utterance. (Later of course she attempts to relate this inferred thought to the actual linguistic formatives that are produced.) We have adopted the same strategy. As an illustration, suppose that in the same context presented for (4), the subject signed only:

(7) *Eat* (biting motions)—*Susan* (point at Susan)

We assume that (5) is still the semantic relation, rather than:

(8) You, Susan, *will* eat.

There are three grounds for this inference:

1. *Food* was part of the extralinguistic context in which both (4) and (7) were said, so *food* is the plausible candidate for fulfilling the *patient* role that is part of the logic of the predicate *eat*.

2. Enough overtly signed elements appeared in the sentence to lend plausibility to the analysis; that is, we excluded all one-word "sentences" from such analysis on grounds that they provide insufficient basis for inferences about relational meanings (see footnote, p. 371).

3. The case label that was inferred (did not occur overtly in the sentence under analysis) was one that had been overtly expressed by the same subject in some of his other sentences. That is, (7) is reconstructable as (5) rather than (8) only if the subject once said something like (4).

In further detail, we would not reconstruct, say, a *benefactive* case for sentence (4) or (7) even though one is logically possible and fits the context (e.g. "You, Susan, will eat food to please my mother") because the subject who signed (4) and (7) never was seen to sign a benefactive case. Yet we do reconstruct the *patient* case for (7) because we know from (4) that the subject conceives and sometimes expresses this relational meaning. The analysis rests on the supposition that there is a relational logic associated with specific predicates that we can reconstruct for the subjects, but only in so far as they express part of this logic in the utterance being analyzed and only in so far as they give prior evidence of deploying this logic in overt gesturing. (An exception here is the *place* case. Since the overt marking of this case is optional, we do not reconstruct it, but only score it when it is overtly signed.)

The descriptive outcome of this analysis is that the subjects' utterances are analyzed as containing predicates of different kinds, whose logic requires different case labeling and different numbers of case labels. For example, the predicate *sleep* requires only one case (*actor*) while *eat* requires two (*actor* and *patient*) and *give* requires three (*actor, patient* and *recipient*). Then in analyzing the gesture sequence:

(9) *sleep* (eyes shut, head down)—*dog* (point to dog)

we would argue that all cases logically required have been signed; but in

(10) *give* (palm up, hand extended)—*dog* (point to dog)

we would argue that two cases have been *omitted*. This supposition is implicated in the analysis of the subjects' syntax (p. 383).

Reliability scores were calculated for the assignment of semantic relations to sentences. There was 96% agreement between the two coders on the 66 relation assignment decisions that could be made in the videotape sample. Reliability scores for the assignment of semantic cases and predicates to the individual signs in sentences were comparable: there was 97% agreement between the two coders in the 115 case/predicate assignment decisions that could be made in the sample tape. All of the gestured sentences that were used for the syntactic analysis reported on pp. 384-398 were coded by two independent coders; disagreements were resolved by discussion, and sentences for which disagreements remained were discarded.

RESULTS AND DISCUSSION

All of the subjects we studied developed the ability to communicate with manual gestures. All began, like hearing children, simply by pointing to the people and things around them, engaging their listeners by eye contact (that is, they did not point if no one else was looking). These points continued to bear a heavy burden in the subjects' communications throughout our observation. In comparison, gesturing tends to decline for hearing children as speech emerges. As our subjects grew older, two striking changes in their communicative attempts took place. They began to use the points in combination, in ways that seemed clearly intended to convey semantic relations between the referents of the points. And they began to invent motor-iconic gestures that seemed to specify predicates of various kinds. These gestures, which we have called characterizing signs, soon came to be used in combination with the points in structured ways. Such extensive elaboration of the gestural mode is not typical for hearing children. As observers, we came inescapably to understand these signs and sign combinations as communicative acts—as comments about the world, queries, requests, and demands addressed to the listener. All in all, it is impossible to observe these subjects and deny seriously that they achieved considerable communicative skill in a gestural mode: each subject must be credited with an idiosyncratic "home sign" system that puts him into mental contact with those around him.

It is very difficult to convey in words the simultaneous pantomimic clarity and yet abstractness of the characterizing signs and their manifest constructional relations, when used within "sentences". They were iconic, certainly, but also highly stylized—just enough to render an intent, rather than an attempt to imitate veridically some scene or object in the visual world. We can do no more than give some examples that show the iconic content of the characterizing signs: a downward facing open palm moving back and forth signifies *cut;* flat palms bouncing on the floor designate *dance*; a point gliding diagonally upwards derives from tracing the *take-off* of an airplane; a point curling downwards from the nose derives from the *trunk* of an elephant: hands held in praying position denote the subject's (Catholic) *school*. Of course this last gesture is directly given in the environment. But the context for inferring its intent may help to concretize the nature of our own inferences about these subjects' meanings. In this instance, the subject was shown a picture of his older brother, who was at that moment at school, a Catholic school which the subject also attended. The subject pointed first to the photograph, then pointed to the door ("away"), then made the praying motion, then nodded most earnestly at us.

These are the kinds of interactions that lead us to claim that the subjects *undeniably* communicate, and they know they are doing so. This subject managed to convey to us that his brother was away at school.

A more detailed description and interpretation of our findings follows. It is organized in terms of the three questions raised in introductory comments: (1) does the deaf child manifest (successfully) an "urge to communicate" despite the poverty of his linguistic input? (2) is the communicative system of these subjects similar in character to natural languages? and (3) are the growth patterns in the deaf children's usages similar to the patterns observed in normal acquisition? We will give a qualified "yes" answer to all three questions in this section, and then comment more discursively in a final note (p. 408).*

Is There An Urge to Communicate in the Untutored Child?

The Egyptian isolated children on whom Herodotus reports were considered successfully tested when they ran to their caretakers shouting "bekos" (the Phrygian for *bread*), thus approximately demonstrating that (a) they, not their (Egyptian) caretakers had invented the language; and (b) their lexical items encoded about the same semantic notions as those of received languages. For our subjects, we take up these two topics separately.

The Child is Mother to the Sign

Certainly our subjects performed elaborate and structured gesturing, as will be demonstrated. But is it possible that the source was an *ad hoc* communication system unconsciously fashioned by their caretakers (unconsciously, because the subjects' parents were committed to oral

---

*Not all of the data and findings from this project are reported in the present chapter, but only sufficient to provide existential evidence on these three limited questions. The treatment will be more or less formal depending on the demands of each question for exhaustive statistical treatment; the effect is that the bulk of formal presentation concerns syntactic properties of these children's home sign. Much more detailed analysis of the early lexicons of these subjects appears in Feldman (1975). More complete syntactic/semantic description appears in Goldin-Meadow (1977). Summary accounts of some of these findings appeared in Goldin-Meadow and Feldman (1975, 1977). Data reported here are selections from that material. Finally, these subjects have progressed in their manual communication system well beyond the early data reported in this chapter. Very long (up to 13 morpheme) sentences can be identified in the productions of two subjects who we have continued to study (David and Donald). Analysis of this material is underway. Preliminary inspection of the advanced productions suggests the emergence of elaborate structures which—owing to their interaction with left-to-right production constraints—show an increasing disparity between deep and surface representations. These data will be described in a forthcoming report.

education)? Some of the mothers clearly did gesture to their children. To determine which member of the dyad bore the major responsibility for creating the system, we transcribed the gestures produced by Dennis' and David's mothers during the first four interviews. The same coding procedures were used for maternal and child gestures. Comparisons were made with respect both to lexicon and sentence form. There were no clear differences between mother and child in their tendency to point to objects. Since pointing is common in mother-child interactions, we might as well acknowledge that our subjects may have "learned to point" from speakers around them. But pointing does not exhaust the system. More interesting comparisons concern the use of the characterizing signs, and the embedding of signs in gesture combinations (sentences). Inspection of Table II reveals that the mothers did use approximately as many characterizing signs as the children, calculated either in types or tokens (columns 1 and 2 of Table II). However, there is a striking difference between mothers and children in the tendency to use characterizing signs within a sentence, as column 3 of Table II shows. There is no evidence here that the subjects were learning to integrate the characterizing signs into sentences from the mothers; if anything, the suggestion is the other way around. Moreover, the mothers produced few gesture combinations that were analyzable in propositional terms; that is, sentences that conveyed *semantic relations*, as we have defined these (pp. 371-375). Instead, most of their sentences consisted merely of, e.g. a head-nod followed by a point, or a repetition of a single point. Over the course of the four interviews, David and Dennis produced 127 and 42 sentences, respectively, that conveyed semantic relations, while their mothers produced 41 and 13. The mothers began production of these phrases later than their children. Both children produced a number of these sentences in session I. David's mother produced only three in session I compared to David's 27. Dennis' mother produced none until session II. Since the mothers *did* produce many one-sign gestures (see Table II), it is not possible to assume that the rarity of their combinations had to do with aspects of their conversational roles in these interviews. Rather, their gesturing is primitive and inept, compared to that of the children.

A number of further findings bolster the interpretation that the child's gesturing was independent, rather than learned by example from the mother. Only 25% of the children's characterizing signs were the same as the mothers'; each member of the dyad seems to create with some independence. Also, the children often created characterizing signs to refer to the toys we brought to the sessions, which neither they nor their mothers had ever seen. This is straightforward evidence that the children could create manual representations independent of a tutor.

Finally, there is a striking qualitative distinction in form between the signs

Table II
Mother-child comparison of number of characterizing signs
produced during sessions I-IV

| | Types[a] | | Tokens[b] | | | |
| | | | Alone | | In sentences | |
	Child	Mother	Child	Mother	Child	Mother
David	56	54	107	90	47	9
Dennis	25	23	50	58	18	3

[a]Types = Number of different characterizing signs.
[b]Tokens = Number of occurrences across types.

of mothers and children: the mothers depend heavily on objects in the world around them as props for their gestured communication—rather like people who cheat at Charades. For example, David's mother picked up a toy apple and poised it near her lips while performing an *eat* sign (biting motions). It is true that the child subjects also occasionally perform signs near appropriate objects in the world. However, in the bulk of the children's signing there is no such reliance on objects as props. Signing is their only means of communication and they use it analogously to the way we use spoken words. On the contrary, the mothers typically move, display, and wave real objects to hint at their meanings—the kind of desperate device we all employ in foreign places where we have no language to use.

Semantic Properties of the Lexicon

We find that the lexicons of the uninstructed deaf subjects are strikingly similar to the lexicons of young hearing children reared in normal language environments. This finding again suggests a powerful role for internal organizing principles in accounting for the acquisition of language in humans. We have acknowledged in earlier discussion the considerable hazards involved in inferring meaningful content from manifest forms, even with contextual support. Perhaps, then, it is worth reiterating here that field studies of the hearing child face the same problem: that the hearing child produces real words of English when he talks is no guarantee about the concepts behind them. We can do no more than develop data under similar assumptions, for comparative purposes. (Studies of the comprehension of speaker-hearers make clear that these difficulties are real. A number of investigations such as Clark, (1973c), Carson and Abrahamson (1976), Huttenlocher (1975), Thomson and Chapman (1975) suggest that a productive lexical item gives only the roughest clue to the child's concept in using it. We have not been successful at all in getting these subjects to participate in manipulative situations which would allow us to probe more directly for the meanings behind their signs.)

The Meaning of the Points

If clues from the context of use are accepted, it is apparent that the subjects' points express nominal concepts by making reference to actual instances of these concepts. The child points to a dog to refer to a dog and points to a cat to refer to a cat. That is, the point serves as a pronominal by means of which the deaf child can make reference to almost anything visible in the environment. The question here is whether these individuals chose to refer to the same things that hearing children choose to refer to, despite the fact that they were not provided with verbal labels for concepts.

One might well expect the outcomes to be quite different from those that have been reported for hearing children, owing to our coding decisions. We have glossed each point as its apparent referent (see p. 365). This means that a point is called *dog* if a dog is the salient object at the end of the line of regard of the point; but it is called *cat* if a cat sits there. In contrast, no one credits a speaking-hearing child with multiple lexical items just because he uses the word *this* deictically. Then it might be expected that the method of analysis would yield hugely inflated nominal vocabularies for the deaf subjects. Given this inflating factor, the *poverty* of the observed nominal vocabularies of our subjects is striking. They do not point to everything they can see. Rather, the semantic scope of their points is quite narrow, as can be seen from inspection of Table III. Table III is a content analysis of all the points that occurred within the subjects' two-sign sentences. (Isolated points were excluded, because their interpretation is subject to a good deal more ambiguity. The two-sign sentences were chosen because they are the most characteristic of these subjects' combinations, and because we could derive similar analyses from data for hearing children.) As the table shows, almost all of the points can be subsumed, in word meaning, under a few common superordinate categories: inanimate objects, people, animals, body-parts, food, clothing, vehicles, furniture and places. For comparison, we submitted data from Bloom's (1970: Appendices C, D, E, F, G; Katherine I, Gia I and II, Eric II and III) hearing subjects, all aged about 2 years, to the same analysis. Bloom's data are particularly useful for such a comparison, because the conditions for data collection were about the same as ours. Bloom too went to the children's houses armed with toys, which became topics of the conversation during those interviews. Thus, if the interview situation biases the sample vocabulary that is derived (and surely it does), very similar biases

Table III

Types of object lexical items used in sentences[a]

	Inanimate objects	People	Body parts	Animals	Food	Clothing	Vehicles	Furniture	Places	Total
Younger deaf subjects:										
Kathy I-IX	0·41	0·13	0·14	0·10	0·09	0·03	0·00	0·10	0·00	29
Dennis I-IV	0·53	0·12	0·00	0·00	0·12	0·00	0·06	0·00	0·18	17
Chris I-III	0·38	0·21	0·04	0·17	0·00	0·04	0·08	0·04	0·04	24
Older deaf subjects:										
David I-VIII	0·44	0·11	0·10	0·08	0·07	0·07	0·05	0·01	0·08	114
Donald I-XI	0·51	0·14	0·10	0·10	0·02	0·04	0·04	0·02	0·04	51
Tracy I-II	0·19	0·28	0·10	0·14	0·00	0·14	0·00	0·05	0·10	21
Bloom's hearing subjects:										
Kathryn I[b]	0·23	0·14	0·14	0·08	0·14	0·13	0·01	0·02	0·05	100
Gia I-II[b]	0·26	0·21	0·05	0·14	0·07	0·07	0·06	0·04	0·02	106
Eric II-III[b]	0·28	0·15	0·04	0·15	0·09	0·04	0·11	0·04	0·05	54

[a]Names for toys representing inanimate objects, people, animals, food, clothing and vehicles are included in their respective categories.
[b]Data are from Bloom (1970), Appendices C, D, E, F, G, lexical items in syntactic contexts. A small number of items did not fit in any of the categories: Kathryn, 0·06; Gia, 0·09; Eric, 0·05.

should have appeared in both her situation and ours. The content analysis of Bloom's lexical data shown in Table III was performed on items that occurred in the two-word sentences of her subjects, again for comparability with our own analysis, and is of course limited to the nouns, for comparison with the points. Approximately the same superordinate categories describe the hearing children's nominals as those that describe the deaf children's points, and the proportions of items appearing under each superordinate category are not strikingly different for the two populations, if we acknowledge that some biases arise because of the particulars of specific conversations.

A plausible interpretation of the similarities in expressed nominal meanings between the deaf and hearing subjects is simply that children converse about what interests them, a not so deep idea. But it is a sufficient one for what we set out to show here: the deaf child uses his communicative skills to express the same kinds of things as do hearing children just because he is about the same in interests and cognitive level, only he is deaf.

The Meaning of Characterizing Signs

Table IV shows similar effects for the characterizing signs, which we take to represent predicate notions. These usually pertain to simple actions—the motions of objects and persons and the transfer of objects among persons and across locations. For example, there are signs for *strum* (fingers strumming on the chest, an imaginary guitar); *hit* (hammering motions); *bike-ride* (rotating fists); *drive* (hands jiggling on an imaginary wheel); and the like. Rarer, and usually later in developmental appearance, are terms that describe perceptual attributes such as *big* (arms spread, open palm down) and *floppy eared* (open hands flapping, palms forward behind ears).

We can ask, as we did for the points, about the extent to which the medium of communication and the method of analysis predetermine the bias toward action verbs in the deaf communications. Surely it is easier to pantomime *eat* than, say, *ruminate*. But it is at least possible to conceive of pantomimes for bodily and mental states, e.g. *pain* by stomach-clutching or *sorrow* by tear-trickling. Yet the subjects do not attempt this. It is suggestive that the verb vocabularies of very young English speakers show the same bias toward action and motion verbs and a paucity of items expressing mental and bodily states. For comparison, we again analyzed Bloom's data (1970), this time her verb and adjective lists, in terms of the same categories used for the deaf children; the outcomes are shown in the bottom three rows of Table IV. Again the results for the two populations are roughly similar. The hearing children also speak much more often of actions than of mental states, attributes and the like. We conclude, as we did when considering the

Table IV
Types of action and attribute lexical items used in sentences

		Action[a]	Attribute	Total
Younger deaf subjects:				
Kathy	I-IX	0·92	0·08	12
Dennis	I-IV	1·00	0·00	9
Chris	I-III	0·92	0·08	13
Older deaf subjects:				
David	I-VIII	0·68	0·32	104
Donald	I-XI	0·68	0·32	38
Tracy	I-II	0·58	0·42	24
Hearing subjects:				
Kathryn	I[b]	0·68	0·32	66
Gia	I-II[b]	1·00	0·00	41
Eric	II-III[b]	1·00	0·00	45

[a]Action   = items marked + VB in Bloom's terminology.
Attribute = items marked + ADJ in Bloom's terminology.
[b]Data from Bloom (1970), lexical items in syntactic contexts in Appendices C, D, E, F, G.

nominal pointing, that the deaf children have a means of communication that enables them to traffic in the same matters, important to them, as do hearing children in contact with a received language.

Summarizing, the deaf lexicon is roughly comparable to the lexicon of young hearing children, despite the fact that the latter are exposed to proficient and mature models. Thus there is no evidence—for either group— that the nature of young children's vocabularies is in any direct sense a function of linguistic exposure and training.

Summary: Expressive Content Without Explicit Models

It has been suggested that the deaf subjects are the main creative forces in developing the "home sign" system for communicating their thoughts and wishes to others. They gestured sooner and in more complex ways than did the adults around them. Thus we have answered positively the first question raised by the Egyptian king for *his* isolated subjects: children raised apart from a fluent caretaker system *will* try to communicate and *can* do so; and they choose to express roughly the same lexical-semantic content as do children more fortunately circumstanced. Specifically, though they could have, the deaf subjects did not choose to discuss, say, their bodily states. Instead, like normal children everywhere, they communicated about ducks and food and hitting and running, and the semantic relations among these notions.

We tentatively conclude that much of the creative force for communication in humans, and the character of the concepts in which it traffics—at early stages, at least—comes from inside the novice himself. Though the same has been shown previously by Marler and Tamura for birds, those were merely birds. (And though the same has been shown by the Egyptians for humans, we had three times as many subjects as they did.) We claim these findings ought to bear seriously on the interpretation of correlational studies of the normal mother-child dyad in language acquisition. It seems that if the apparent "teacher" in this dyad is seriously deficient in the relevant language skills (as were the mothers of our deaf subjects) this does not seriously handcuff the apparent "pupil". Even if one considers the evidence that our mothers knew *less* than our child subjects to be weak, certainly there is no evidence that they knew *more*. Thus there is no evidence that the mothers could present the kinds of "graded lessons" or "miniaturized samples" often spoken of in this literature (cf. Levelt, 1975) as explanatory concepts in understanding the child's acquisition of language.

Is the Communication of the Deaf Children "Language-like?"

The ancient kings made a more radical supposition about language in isolation than any we have discussed so far: they presupposed that, in formal structural detail, their subjects' language would be just like that of naturally occurring languages. Specifically, it would be either Eguptian or Phrygian. Our findings allow us to approach this question more objectively than they did. We can ask whether the self-generated communication system shares structural features with natural language, as used by non-isolated hearing children of comparable ages. Throwing caution to the winds, we pursue an analogy made in our introductory remarks: white crown sparrow chicks that are isolated from birth will sing skeletal species-specific songs of their fore-birds nevertheless, approximating birds raised in the bosom of the family. At the same time, however, the songs of these isolated individuals lack the rich elaboration and detail characteristic of their socially reared peers (Marler and Tamura, 1965). To the extent that human language is similarly a species-specific characteristic, we might expect to find a skeletal resemblance between our subjects' communication and the hearing child's speech. But we would not expect this communication to be elaborate. That is, we are unlikely to replicate the finding that a language so sophisticated as Phrygian can be invented in one generation.

The question here is whether the categories and combinatorial devices of the home sign-system are like those of natural languages, when used by appropriately circumstanced novices. It has been demonstrated elsewhere that the forms and functions of sign languages such as ASL are so close to natural language that they should be accorded the same status (e.g. Bellugi and Fischer, 1972; Newport and Bellugi, 1977). Thus the fact that our subjects' communications are manual should not bar us from raising these structural questions. We will show now that the semantic intents of the subjects are encoded syntactically, in ways that resemble the speech of young speakers. These findings, in turn, will enable us to conclude that the subjects' gesturing takes place in terms of the same hierarchy of category levels (phonological element, morpheme and sentence) that universally characterize natural languages. The major quantitative treatment is expended on this issue for, in our view, the essence of a language-like communication system is its mapping of meaningful relations onto organized output structures. It is this *syntactic* property of natural languages that enables their users to make infinite use of finite (phonological and lexical) means, and distinguishes them most clearly from the expressive and semantically non-trivial communications of other beasts, even including college-educated primates.

Structure in the Representation of Semantic Relations: Reduction Rules

We find that the gestured sentences of these subjects are very short, just like the sentences of young speakers. However, we will present evidence that the underlying semantic representations associated with these gestured sentences are neither so simple nor so short as the overt sentences themselves. That is, the subjects map relatively complicated thoughts onto relatively simple output structures. We will demonstrate that there are regularities in the ways the long semantic representations are mapped onto the short overt sentences. This orderly, but not one-to-one, mapping of meanings onto surface structures is tantamount to a rule of syntax, a *reduction* rule.

The Gestured Sentences of the Deaf Subjects are Short

Our subjects, like young children everywhere, tend to produce very short sentences. Throughout the period of observation, the majority of gestures by each subject consisted of a single sign (76%, pooled over all subjects and all sessions; see Table V). Moreover, 69% of the remainder of utterances (pooled over all subjects and all sessions) consisted of two signs only. Thus the "MLG" (mean length of gestured sentence, in signs) is in the range from 1·0 to 1·5 throughout the course of observation. This is rather surprising. After all, it is not as if our subjects, like hearing children, have to acquire a

Table V
Number of strings produced by each subject classified according to length

| | Number of signs per sentence | | | | | | | | |
	1	2	3	4	5	6	7	8	9+
Younger subjects:									
Kathy I-IX	672	62	13	5	0	1			
Dennis I-IV	290	40	5						
Chris I-III	378	50	9	4					
Older subjects:									
David I-VIII	1,550	530	164	87	26	14	6	6	6
Donald I-XI	1,006	151	25	5					
Tracy I-II	348	67	14	3	1	1			

new and arbitrary representation for each word they want to say. Recall we have been content to give them credit for a lexical item if only they will point at something; and we call two successive points, even in the absence of a characterizing sign, "a sentence". On this evidently generous criterion, would it not seem an easy matter to produce long sentences in developmental advance of hearing children at the two-word stage of production? For instance, the subjects could just point successively to five different people in the room or to ten peas in a pod. But the fact is they do not do this. The deaf children are limited in the number of points and other signs in a sentence, just as hearing children are limited in the number of words in a sentence. (As the subjects grow older, they do produce some longer sentences, as we will demonstrate when we look at their developmental progress; see Table XI). We suspect this close synchrony in superficial structures of the deaf and hearing subjects, despite specifiable differences in the demands of the expressive medium and the context of learning, suggests that the same organizing principles are at work in both populations.

The Semantic Representations of the Signed Sentences are Long

We have just shown that the signed sentences are short. Here we show that their underlying representations, in terms of semantic elements, are longer; i.e. the semantic elements are not mapped one-to-one onto signs in the output sentences.

Recall from the methodological discussion (p. 370) that each sign within a sentence was coded for its relational meaning (act or attribute) on the basis of its form and the context in which the sentence was uttered; and that high inter-rater reliability was achieved for this coding. Each child exhibited the ability to sign both act and attribute semantic relations, but the acts far outnumbered the attributes for each subject. (This outcome is taken up later,

p. 402, see Table XII, when we discuss the results in developmental terms.) The action sentences, for which we had substantial amounts of data, were submitted to a case analysis, whose results are shown in Table VI. This table shows the percentages of each semantic element type in the subjects' action sentences (for the two-sign sentences that were most characteristic of these subjects). Inspection of this table reveals that each child exhibited the ability

Table VI
Semantic elements in action sentences[a]

| | Act predicate | Cases | | | | Total one-relation action sentences |
		Patient	Recipient	Actor	Place	
Younger subjects:						
Kathy	0·81[a]	0·57[a]	0·33	0·33	0·00	33
Dennis	0·62	0·88	0·40	0·19	0·00	27
Chris	0·85	0·62	0·41	0·20	0·00	29
Older subjects:						
David	0·74	0·62	0·32	0·34	0·05	248
Donald	0·85	0·64	0·28	0·21	0·02	84
Tracy	0·87	0·53	0·00	0·54	0·08	24

[a]Each cell represents the proportion of times each semantic element occurs in one-relation action sentences, for each subject. Thus, for example, an *act* predicate appeared in 0·81 of Kathy's sentences and a *patient* appeared in 0·57 of her sentences.

to sign the *patient, recipient* and *actor* cases, just those that are most salient to action semantic relations, a finding that has also been reported for young hearing children (Brown, 1973). The *place* case, which serves to modulate certain action relations, was much rarer. Further modulating cases (such as *instrumental, benefactive* and *source*) are rarely explicitly signed by these subjects, a result that again reproduces the findings in the literature on early stages in first language acquisition (Brown, 1973).

If the coding procedures are taken to be valid, then, we have demonstrated that the subjects' overt gestures refer primarily to *action* semantic relations which are conveyed by expressing an *act* predicate and the *patient, recipient* and *actor* cases. Despite the fact that certain semantic elements appear much more often than others (e.g. the percentage of signs that are *patients* is far greater than the percentage of signs that are *actors*), each subject does exhibit the ability to gesture each of these relational meanings, within two and three-sign sentences.

How shall we represent the semantic structure of the signed sentences? It would seem most straightforward to claim for each overt sentence only the relational meanings that were expressly gestured. That is, if the subject gestures "cookie—give" when his sister is giving him a cookie, we might code the semantic intent as *patient-act*. It will be recalled, however, from the methodological discussion (p. 371) that we inferred the existence of further semantic elements that were not at all represented in the gesture, but which seemed to be implied by the extralinguistic context of use. That is, for the present example, we would reconstruct the semantics as "sister (*actor*)—give (*act*)—cookie (*patient*)—David (*recipient*)". (In this notation, nothing is claimed about the order of occurrence of the elements either in underlying or surface representations.)

The results presented in Table VI already lend some plausibility to this kind of reconstruction: each subject did, though on separate occasions, exhibit the ability to gesture each of these cases, and thus we can be sure that he could conceive of all of them. Table VII presents a further sample result that considerably bolsters the argument in favor of such reconstructions: though few of the subjects ever explicitly gestured all of the semantic elements required for three-case predicates such as *give* within a single sentence, they did often sign all of these required elements if we pool the case labels over all of the sentences containing *give*. Table VII shows such productions from David. He exhibits knowledge that *actor*, *patient* and *recipient* are associated with this predicate, and he exhibits the ability overtly to express each of them in this predicate context. On this basis, we suggest that the full logic of *give* is mentally involved whenever this predicate is involved; i.e. the semantic intent is reconstructed as shown in the final column of Table VII. The effect of this decision is that the five syntactically and lexically distinct sentences of column 1 of Table VII are claimed to be identical in underlying semantic structural typology. (Obviously, we were not able to elicit the whole range of case labels for each predicate for each subject, since the children would not submit to formal elicitation procedures in the manner of linguistic informants. They would not produce gestured sentences just because we needed them for complete analysis. The data of Table VII provide only existential evidence supporting reconstruction of "omitted" case labels. However, by extrapolating from this kind of evidence, we reconstructed the case labels for all predicates for all subjects in the same way.)

Short Sentences from Long Thoughts: Reduction at the Surface

We presented evidence on p. 384 that the subjects' signed sentences were short, generally only two signs long. A first guess in explaining this brevity is

Table VII

Sample of David's signed sentences with the predicate *give*[a]

Actual signed utterances	Coding of overt signs according to semantic element type
(1) cookie—give	patient—act
(2) sister—David	actor—recipient
(3) give—David	act—recipient
(4) Duck—Susan	patient—recipient
(5) book—give—David—book	patient—act—recipient—patient
(6) crackers—give—David—give— crackers—give	patient—act—recipient—act—patient— act
(7) give—gum—mouth	act—patient—recipient
(8) give—hole	act—recipient

Situational context of use	Inferred propositional intent[b]
(1) Sister just gave cookie to David	You—sister give cookie to David
(2) David wants sister to give him a toy motorcycle	You—sister give motorcycle to David
(3) David wants Heidi to give him a mask	You—Heidi give mask to David
(4) David wants sister to give the duck to Susan	You—sister give duck to Susan
(5) David wants mother to give him the book	You—mother give book to David
(6) David wants mother to give him crackers	You—mother give crackers to David
(7) David wants Heidi to put gum in his mouth	You—Heidi give gum to mouth
(8) David wants Heidi to put key in keyhole	You—Heidi give key to keyhole

[a]The predicate *give* is an open palm, facing upward, with an arm extending toward listener. The nominals are always points.
[b]Since David is appropriately greedy, almost all uses of *give* have himself as the recipient. Example (7) is not an exception, because here he wants the gum in his own mouth. Examples (4) and (8) are the only ones in the sample where David is not the recipient. Notice that our own interpretation of the predicate in (7) and (8) is *put*. But David makes the *give* sign (see [a] above) so there is no indication that he distinguishes between these two concepts. Thus while we use the word *put* to describe our interpretation of the situation (column 3), we use the word *give* to describe the propositional intent (column 4).

that the subjects' semantic intents were so simple that it took only two words to express them. But in the last section we presented evidence that this is not so: the children were able to conceive of and express semantic relations in terms of a substantial number of case and predicate notions. Only they did this, generally, two signs at a time. These outcomes raise two questions: why are the signed sentences so short; and what is the basis on which the short sentences are related to the long thoughts?

We suggest that the same hypotheses generally put forward to describe the brevity of hearing children's sentences fit the deaf children's as well. Presumably the young child has memorial and information handling inadequacies that limit the character of his outputs, whatever the complexity of his intents. If there are such output constraints, there is a "cost" to every word and so the child must "telegraph" his intents with as few of them as possible, omitting others (Bloom, 1970). Put another way, the semantic elements are in competition with each other for space in the output sentence. Our question now is which (among the semantic elements) will be the winner and which the loser in this struggle for overt expression.

We have seen from Table VI that some semantic elements are signed more frequently than others. The *act* and *patient* are signed very often, compared to the *actor* and *recipient*. Table VIII shows the pairwise co-occurrence of these semantic elements (disregarding order) for the two-sign sentences that are most characteristic of these subjects. Again the frequencies of the various pairs are quite different. For instance the pairing of *act-patient* is quite common (39% of all pairs of semantic elements, over subjects) while the pairing of *actor-patient* is rarer (5% of all pairs of semantic elements, over subjects). We might examine these frequency distributions to determine which semantic elements the children are biased to express overtly. But these data displays may well be misleading. We already know that there are in the subjects' repertoires one-case predicates such as *sleep* (which requires only the *actor* case), two-case predicates such as *hit* (which requires *actor* and *patient*) and three-case predicates such as *put* (which requires *actor*, *patient* and *recipient*).* For this reason alone, the frequency of appearance of the semantic elements should differ since, e.g. *actor* and *act* are logically required in all the action sentences, but *patient* is logically disallowed for some of them (for instance, *sleep*). On these grounds, one would expect more *actors* and *acts* to be signed than *patients*. A more realistic measure of the frequency of explicit signing of the various semantic elements, then, takes into account whether they are allowable, given the logic

---

*Analysis here is again for the action sentences (those with *act* rather than *attribute* predicates). Excluded from further analysis are two-case predicates such as *go*, in "You go there" which require the *actor* and *recipient* cases. Though these do occur in our corpora, they are rare, making quantitative treatment of them problematical. A more fine-grained syntactic analysis, distinguishing between transitive and intransitive *actors*, does allow further interpretation of this rarer kind of two-case predicate. In fact a good deal more structure than will be reported here falls out of this further atomization of sign types. These results are reported in Goldin-Meadow (1977). The scope of discussion here is narrower. We simply demonstrate that the subjects' overt sentences are orderly, but significantly reduced, mappings of the semantic elements defined on pp. 371-374. For a complete syntactic description of the signed utterances, see Goldin-Meadow (1977).

Table VIII
Pairwise occurrence of semantic elements in action sentences with two
signed elements (in proportions)[a]

	PA[b]	PR	AR	A Actor	P Actor	R Actor	Total action sentences
Kathy	0·36	0·06	0·18	0·21	0·09	0·03	33
Dennis	0·44	0·22	0·07	0·00	0·11	0·04	27
Chris	0·41	0·14	0·17	0·17	0·00	0·00	29
David	0·34	0·18	0·08	0·22	0·05	0·02	248[c]
Donald	0·50	0·08	0·17	0·14	0·04	0·02	84[c]
Tracy	0·45	0·00	0·00	0·38	0·08	0·00	24[c]

[a]This table includes all two-element action sentences regardless of the order of the elements in the sentence. For example, the column marked "PA" includes sentences in which patients precede acts, acts precede patients, patients and acts are signed simultaneously, and also sentences in which one or both elements are repeated. The proportions do not sum to one because from 5 to 10% of the sentences combined three elementrs, and so are excluded here (see also footnote[c]).
[b]P = Patient, A = Act, R = Recipient.
[c]David and Donald produced a few Act-Place sentences (3% and 2% of their action sentences, respectively) and Tracy produced one Actor-Place sentence (4% of her action sentences).

of the predicate. Table IX shows these conditional probabilities of the appearance of semantic elements in the two-sign sentences: the entry for each semantic element is given as a proportion of the times it *could* have appeared, treating separately the one-case, two-case, and three-case predicate types.

It is clear from Table IX that the frequency of explicit occurrence of each semantic element, as a proportion of the time it could logically have occurred, diminishes as we move from predicates requiring fewer cases to predicates requiring more cases (moving from left to right across the rows of the table). This outcome is anticipated on the hypothesis stated earlier: there is a constraint toward brevity in the output sentences. Since the more complex predicates logically involve more semantic elements, this brevity constraint will lead to more frequent omission of explicit signs in the longer predicates. Notice, for example, that the *actor* is always expressed in a one-case predicate (conditional probability of 1·00) but more rarely (conditional probability of 0·24) in a two-case predicate, and almost never (conditional probability of 0·06) in a three-case predicate.*

It remains now to ask how the subject chooses semantic elements for expression, when the bias toward short sequences disallows him to choose all that are logically required. It is possible to suppose that the subject will omit semantic elements haphazardly. On this hypothesis, we can estimate the conditional probability that each semantic element will occur in each sentence type. These chance expectations are shown in the bottom row of Table IX: if the sentence length is two, both semantic elements (*actor* and *act*) have a conditional probability of 1·00 in a one-case predicate; but one of the required semantic elements (*actor*, *act* or *patient*) must be omitted from a two-case predicate, yielding a conditional probability of occurrence of 0·67 for each of them; and two of the semantic elements (*actor*, *act*, *patient*, *recipient*) must be dropped from the three-case predicate, yielding a conditional probability of occurrence of 0·50 for each of them. We have already looked at support for this hypothesis: the conditional probability of appearance of each semantic element does diminish moving from left to right in Table IX.

But notice that the fit of the findings with this "haphazard omission" hypothesis is rather poor. For example, the expected values for the *actor* case (leaving aside the one-case predicates, for reasons described in the footnote) are 0·67 and 0·50 but the obtained values (row 8 of Table IX) are 0·24 and 0·06. That is, the *actor* is omitted much more often than would be expected by chance. In contrast, the *act* predicate resists omission much more strenuously: while the expected values are again 0·67 and 0·50, the obtained values are 0·87 and 0·59. Similarly, the *patient* case has expected occurrence values of 0·67 and 0·50, but obtained values of 0·86 and 0·73. It appears, then, that the *actor* case is being singled out for omission as the semantic logic of the sentence becomes more complex, for its appearance is dramatically less frequent than would be expected by chance. Consequently, the *act* and the other cases are explicitly signed somewhat more often than would be expected by chance, the selective omission of the *actor* having left space for them in the surface sentence.

The facts for three-sign sentences produced by these subjects at the same developmental period (often within the same interview session) support the notion that the *actor* is part of the underlying semantic structure of the children's sentences, but has a low priority for overt expression. Table X displays the expected and obtained conditional probabilities for the semantic

*It is almost, but not quite, a tautological outcome of the coding procedure that both *act* and *actor* are always explicitly signed in one-case sentences. Recall that one-sign utterances were excluded from sentence status (p. 371). Then we report no instances of a one-case predicate (e.g. *sleep*) from which one of the two elements (*act* or *actor*) is presumed to be omitted. It is just possible, under our coding scheme, that this situation could have occurred, just when the optional *place* case was explicitly signed with a one-case predicate, e.g. the subject could have gestured "sleep in bed" or "baby in bed" as ways of indicating "baby sleeps in bed". But this never happened, so the appearance of both *actor* and *act* in one-case predicates is 100% (see Table IX). Given the dependence of this fact on the coding procedure, we cannot dignify the outcome for one-case predicates by calling them "findings". The interest of Table IX lies in the effects for two-case and three-case predicates, as well as in the relations between the entries in this table compared to Table X.

Table IX
Conditional probability of case and predicate production in sentences with two signed elements

	One-case			Two-case				Three-case				
	Actor	A[a]	Total	Actor	A	P	Total	Actor	A	P	R	Total
Kathy	1·00	1·00	3	0·44	0·77	0·77	9	0·13	0·81	0·63	0·44	16
Dennis		1·00	0	0·20	0·80	1·00	10	0·08	0·46	0·85	0·62	13
Chris	1·00	1·00	4	0·00	1·00	1·00	7	0·00	0·71	0·64	0·64	14
David	1·00	1·00	17	0·28	0·85	0·83	88	0·02	0·47	0·78	0·73	88
Donald	1·00	1·00	5	0·10	0·93	0·90	29	0·08	0·75	0·53	0·53	40
Tracy	1·00	1·00	6	0·30	0·85	0·85	13	0·00	1·00	1·00	0·00	2
Summed over subjects	1·00	1·00		0·21	0·88	0·89		0·05	0·70	0·74	0·49	
Summed over instances	1·00	1·00	35	0·24	0·87	0·86	156	0·06	0·59	0·73	0·63	173
Chance expected values	1·00	1·00		0·67	0·67	0·67		0·50	0·50	0·50	0·50	

[a] A = Act, P = Patient, R = Recipient.

Table X

Conditional probability of case and predicate production in sentences with three signed elements

	One-case[b]			Two-case				Three-case				
	Actor	A[a]	Total	Actor	A	P	Total	Actor	A	P	R	Total
obtained	1·00	1·00	1	1·00	1·00	0·75[b]	8	0·07	1·00	1·00	0·93	15
expected	1·00	1·00		1·00	1·00	1·00		0·75	0·75	0·75	0·75	

[a] A = Act, P = Patient, R = Recipient.

[b] A three-sign sentence can occur for a one-case predicate if the *place* case, in addition to *act* and *actor*, is explicitly signed. There is only a single instance of this in our data. Similarly, a three-sign sentence for a two-case predicate can have an "omitted" case label just when the optional *place* case occupies the third "slot" in the surface. For two of the eight instances in the data, *place* was signed, and *patient* was omitted.

elements in three-sign sentences (here the data are pooled, for the number of instances is small). We assume these longer sentences occur as relaxations of the constraint toward brevity. Thus there are now three surface "slots", each of which can be filled with a semantic element. We should now expect no omissions of semantic elements in sentences with either one-case or two-case predicates, for there are three slots in the surface and only two or three semantic elements to fill them. This is essentially the finding (but in two instances, a subject signs the *place* case, accounting for the two deleted *patients*). But for three-case predicates, which involve four semantic elements, there is again one slot too few, so we should expect each of the required elements to appear with a conditional probability of 0·75. But instead, *act* and *patient* were always signed (conditional probability of 1·00), and the *recipient* in 0·93 of all instances. The *actor* is again singled out for omission from such three-word sentences, appearing for only 0·07 of the three-case predicates where it was logically involved.

This finding certainly tells us something about the priority of expression of the various semantic elements. But more than this, the variable appearance of the *actor* (conditional on the number of other semantic elements) bolsters reconstruction of the *actor* case in the many instances where it was omitted. The structure of this argument is analogous to that of Bloom (1970) who reconstructed missing *subjects* in negative sentences on grounds that (1) the *subjects* were there in corresponding positive sentences and (2) the length (in morphemes) added by the negative element was sufficient reason for *subject* omission in these, if there really was a length constraint on sentences used by novices. Similarly, we have shown that the *actor* case is part of the underlying representation of these subjects' intents, for its non-appearance is a regular function of the length (in signs, and also in semantic elements) of sentences in which it could occur. Summarizing, the results cohere on the view that the children have an output constraint on their signed productions that interacts with the underlying semantic structure of the sentences and with the priority assignment of elements within the underlying structure. The outcome is short sentences with the *actor* omitted.

Let us now describe how the deletion of *actors* takes place. So far we have concluded that the utterances can be coded as semantic relations consisting in a set of semantic elements (the *act* predicates and the cases). They can also be coded syntactically, as a set of output structures, and these are primarily two-sign utterances. The linguistic descriptive question is whether there are regularities in the ways the internal (semantic) representations are mapped onto the external signed sequences, i.e. whether there are syntactic rules in this system. The finding for *actor*-omission suggests that there are. Roughly, there appears to be a rule that maps internal representations of any length onto superficial structures of preferred length two. The rule operates by omitting *actors* as a function of the number of underlying semantic elements. Once the actor is omitted, if the output string still exceeds length two, then one of the remaining semantic elements is omitted at random. In so far as the length constraint is relaxed (i.e. there are sequences of length three) the same rule holds: the *actor* is omitted if the internal representation exceeds length three, and there should never be occasion to omit anything else.

It should be acknowledged that these principles do not operate categorically, but rather are only statistically discernible. To this extent it may be over-exuberant to grant them the status of "rules", but regularities they certainly are. (Similar caveats apply, at any rate, to regularities in the output structures of speaking-hearing children at early stages.)*

Why should the *actor* be selected for omission when there is competition for space in the signed sentences? Quite possibly, there are semantic grounds. The child seems to be more interested in what got done to whom or what, and less interested in who the culprit was who did it. One obvious hypothesis about why is that the *actor* might have been, most often, the subject himself and if so, any appropriately egocentric youngster might assume this is self-evident and thus unworthy of mention. But the findings are otherwise: 7% of *actors* and 17% of *recipients* that are overtly signed represent the subject himself; 11% of *actors* and 34% of *recipients* that are omitted (and that we reconstruct) represent the subject himself. (The *patient* is almost invariably an inanimate object, so this category has no relevance here). These findings do not fit with the explanation either (1) that the *actor* is omitted most often because it is primarily the case-label for oneself, or (2) that the *actor* is omitted the more often *when* it is oneself than when it is someone else.

The number of alternative semantic hypotheses one could develop (about "cognitive salience" and similar vague notions) to describe *actor* omission are practically infinite, so we will not go on developing them. Anyhow, the explanation may turn out to be internal to the subjects' syntax (i.e. it could turn out to be related to sentence-functional notions such as "subject of" rather than to semantic notions such as "self" or pragmatic notions such as "addressee", "topic" or "new information"). Whatever the explanation, the descriptive facts turn out to be about the same as those for the hearing child. Bloom (1970) has shown the same selective omission of transitive actors in

*The regularities are discernible in terms of a sign classification based on case notions. There may be better classifications (for all we know) of the signs and sentence forms that would account for yet more of the variance in omission. A good candidate is a topic-comment analysis, one that has been useful in the description of ASL (Fischer, 1974; Friedman, 1976). That is, there may be a deeper generalization underlying *actor* omission which artifactually yields significant results under a case analysis (i.e. because *actors* are often *topics*). But whatever the "best" units and the best analysis, it clearly involves a non one-to-one mapping of semantic entities onto surface structures: a syntactic mapping of meanings onto external forms. This was what we set out to demonstrate.

the two-word sentences of hearing children (for a comparative discussion of these data, see Goldin-Meadow, 1977). So again we have suggestive evidence that the same organizational principles are guiding the deaf children without linguistic input as guide the hearing children with linguistic input.

Structure in the Representation of Semantic Relations: Gesture Order

In the previous analyses, we disregarded the order in which the signs appeared within sentences. Figure 1 presents the two-sign sentences once again, now classified according to the temporal order of appearance of each semantic element in the sentence. As the figure shows, the subjects seem to have preferred orders among some of the semantic elements, though not all orderings reach statistical significance for all subjects.* All of the children always produced *patients* before *recipients*. Certain of the children tended to produce *patients* before *acts* (David $X^2 = 5.48$, p<0·02; Dennis $X^2 = 7.36$, p<0·01). In addition, David always produced *acts* before *recipients* and Donald showed a strong tendency in the same direction ($X^2 = 10.28$, p<0·001). Note that not all the children showed ordering tendencies for all pairs of these three elements, but those who did show ordering tendencies all showed them in the same direction. Kathy's productions provided too few examples for statistical evaluation of ordering tendencies, though her data show trends in the expected direction both for *patient-recipient* and for *act-recipient* sentences. Chris does not show any ordering tendencies in terms of the semantic elements.

Overall, a tendency to deploy temporal order as an organizing device seems to emerge in some deaf subjects without instruction, as it does in hearing subjects with instruction (i.e. in speakers learning English), and as it sometimes does also in hearing subjects without instruction (i.e. in certain speakers learning languages such as Russian, which does not have strong word-order constraints; Slobin, 1973). To summarize the constraints on gesture order that characterize the corpora of (at least) David, Dennis and Donald, we can write:†

---

*All sentences containing points at pictures are excluded from this analysis, because the subjects tended to point at pictures they were shown before producing other signs. The pictures pointed at were most often facsimiles of objects playing the *patient* role. Thus the *patient*-first orderings would have been inflated, perhaps wrongly, had we included these sentences. As a result, data from Tracy are excluded from this analysis because she produced very few sentences conveying action semantic relations which did not contain points at pictures. It is worth noting that the data reported in the text were also analyzed to discover whether gesture order might be explainable as a function of sign form (points vs. characterizing signs), and that this analysis failed (for details, see Goldin-Meadow, 1977).

†The notation follows the usual in linguistic description. The brackets indicate that a single selection is required from the options listed within those brackets.

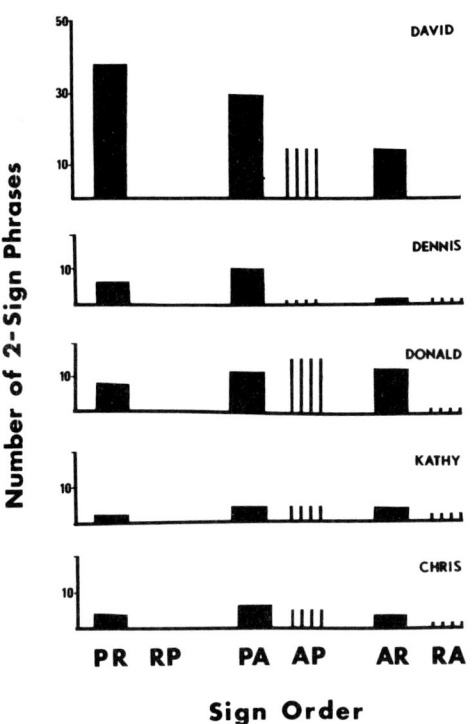

Fig. 1. Number of two-sign sentences classified according to the order of each element in the sentence. P = Patient, A = Act, R = Recipient.

(a) sentence → patient—act—recipient.

Now the brevity constraint operates to reduce the number of overt elements to two, in most instances. The resulting surface structure can be described:

$$(b) \text{ sentence} \rightarrow \left\{ \begin{array}{l} \text{patient} - \left\{ \begin{array}{l} \text{act} \\ \text{recipient} \end{array} \right\} \\ \text{act} - \qquad \text{recipient} \end{array} \right\}$$

That is, a two-word sentence consists either of a *patient* followed by either *act* or *recipient*; or of *act* followed by *recipient*. As for the *place* and *actor* cases, we have previously noted that they are relatively rare in appearance (p. 384). Now we find that these same infrequent elements are not restricted according to any clear ordering principle. (but see Goldin-Meadow (1977) for a suggestion that intransitive and transitive actors may be treated differently in this system; the manual language may be ergative). Both these facts suggest that, syntactically, both *actor* and *place* are freely occurring optional category types that lie outside the core obligatory syntax. They behave syntactically like, say, sentential adverbs in English sentences.

Levels of Linguistic Representation

All natural languages that we know of are organized in terms of formatives at at least three levels: phonological elements, morphemes and sentences. The levels are organized hierarchically: each level, roughly, consists of integral sequences of formatives from the level below. That is, morphemes roughly are sequences of phonological segments; and sentences roughly are sequences of morphemes. If the deaf subjects' signed communications display these levels of representation, they share one more important formal linguistic universal with natural languages (see Hockett (1966) and Greenberg (1966) for discussion of linguistic levels in approximately this sense; but see also Fischer (1974) for a suggestion that some of these putative universals may be modality-specific). Evidence for these levels of representation in the deaf corpora has been presented already. That is, all the analyses presented rest on a series of coding decisions that isolated physical ("phonological"), sign (morphemic) and sentence units in the subjects' gesturing. To the extent that the findings were non-random, this is retrospective justification for the descriptive classifications themselves. The relevant facts are briefly reviewed here.

Evidence for Phonological Elements

Discussed earlier (p. 362, (1)) was the physical taxonomy of formal sign languages developed by Stokoe (1960), in terms of hand-shape, movement, and position of the hands on the body and in space (see also Lane *et al.*, 1976). It would not be surprising if the gestures of our subjects were physically organized in similar ways, for the historical sources of formal sign languages (excluding importations such as finger-spelling) were apparently motor-iconic pantomiming of the same sort whose genesis we are observing in this study (Frishberg, 1975; Battison, 1974). Further, the motor movements of any sign language must be at least in part consequences of limiting manual-visual organization in humans, just as natural language phonology is in part a consequence of articulatory-acoustic organization (Lieberman, 1969; Liberman, 1970). For these reasons, the outcome that our subjects' gestures were exhaustively and fairly reliably codable in terms of Stokoe's system was expectable: 84% of putative gestures were identically coded on these physical dimensions by both coders. However, the reliability of this coding is at best an indirect argument that there is a kind of phonological substrate in terms of which the subjects' signs are mentally organized. Unfortunately, we do not have a formal physical taxonomy available at the time of writing.

However, we do have evidence at this level for sign and sentence boundary effects. The change in "flow of movement" at morpheme boundaries was readily observable and was reliably codable (93%; see p. 362). Further, all of the sentences on which the analyses on pp. 375-398 rest were isolated in terms of the appearance of a phonological sentence-boundary symbol: the return of the hands to neutral position in front of the body (p. 363). That is, to the extent that the boundary symbol picked out long forms that were susceptible to independent semantic and syntactic analysis, we can conclude that it functions to mark divisions at a higher level of linguistic organization.

Evidence of Morphemes

The distinction between morpheme and sentence is often cloudy in the speech of young children, and the same vagueness appears in our data. To some extent, the young subjects seem to use signs "holistically" (possibly: with sentential intent) rather than embedding them in longer structures that express semantic relations overtly. That is, the modal utterance of all our subjects was one sign long. Nonetheless, evidence for a distinction between sign (morpheme) and sentence in these data is very strong.

First, on physical grounds, coding of signs within putative sentences is reliable (p. 362, (2)).* Second, a distributional criterion for the morpheme is met: in 74% of sample instances, gestures characterized as signs within sentences were observed to occur either in isolation or within different sequences used by the same subject. Third, the semantic and syntactic analyses presented earlier cohere only on the assumption that the long gestures observed consist of formatives at approximately morpheme level. And finally the apparent referents of the individual signs (p. 381) are closely analogous to referents of concrete nouns and verbs in English.

Evidence for Sentences

Again, the evidence that the subjects organize their communications in terms of a level of representation above the sign is overwhelming. To deny this, one would have to claim that the findings for sign order and reduction of semantic roles were coincidences, or that similar findings would derive from

*This analysis was performed for David, session IV. Nineteen types of signs occurred during this session. Fourteen of those signs occurred in more than one context, either during the same session or in the previous sessions I-III. Notice that the percentage of signs that occurred in more than one context is very high (74%). It should not be expected that the subject will gesture every sign in his repertoire twice, as this analysis requires, during a few interview sessions. Thus the outcome suggests that the signs we isolated were systematically recurring units, and that they participated in varying sign combinations.

arbitrary sign groupings (different from the groupings obtained by use of the sentence boundary symbol). The systematicity of the semantic and syntactic descriptions argue instead that these subjects mentally organized sequences (usually pairs) of signs within a larger framework, closely analogous to the "telegraphic" sentences of young hearing children.

Summary: Syntactic Patterning without Explicit Models

The home sign system of the deaf subjects displays many of the structural organizing principles that also characterize the early speech of hearing children who receive a language model from the adults around them. The subjects use both gesture-order and reduction devices in externalizing their thoughts. As is true for spoken languages, and perhaps most true of all for languages as spoken by very inexperienced practitioners (little children and foreigners), the syntactic patterns are closely associated with relational semantic entities. The sign types (point and characterizing sign) approximately accord with a dichotomy between nominal and predicate (including predicate adjective) notions. Gesture order and reduction function in terms of relational semantic meanings. Similarly, though imperfectly, the categorial and syntactic patternings of English are also semantically relevant, so it is almost true that a noun is a person, place, or thing, and a verb is an action; and it is almost, but imperfectly, true that predicates of like meaning participate in like transformational manipulations. The fact that syntactic categories reflect semantic categories does not, of course, make the former non-syntactic nor the latter non-semantic.

Syntactic patterns in these subjects' gesturing apparently arise as a consequence of perceptual and production constraints found also in the instance of spoken language. Though the semantic elements of a propositional idea may be unordered in mental conception, still they must be temporally ordered in the sound stream or in the flow of manual gestures. This physically imposed sequencing comes to be exploited in systematic ways, by speakers of word-order languages and by at least some of our deaf subjects inventing their own gestured language. Also, problems in handling long sequences are apparently responsible for the patterned omission of certain aspects of the proposition. Thus we find the same forshortened rendering of propositions in the gesturing of deaf subjects as in hearing acquirers of spoken languages.

Finally, the formatives of the manual system of the deaf subjects are at three distinguishable levels of representation (phonological, morphological, sentential), hierarchically related to each other, similar again to the structural facts about spoken languages.

We concluded earlier (p. 376) that these subjects had successfully manifested an urge to communicate, and about the same matters talked about by hearing children of like ages. We believe the evidence just presented suggests that in structure also the home sign system looks suspiciously like familiar instances of novice language use. This outcome is surprising in part because the physical means of expression (hands and eyes) is different from the usual (mouth and ears) in language use. It is the more surprising because the context of learning is radically different from the usual. There is no fluent listener accurately comprehending the child's attempts, and there is probably not even an enthusiastically approving caretaker applauding the emergence of this gestural system. The parents of these subjects have serious commitments to the child's acquisition of spoken English, not home sign.

These results deserve to be considered in evaluating correlational studies that claim syntax acquisition can be accounted for as reflections of caretaker speech (see e.g. the collection of articles on this topic in Snow and Ferguson, 1977). It seems to us, based on the findings here (and many other studies, e.g. Bever, 1970; Slobin, 1975), that syntactic organization of language materials arises partly because of the interaction of semantic representations with the perceptual and memorial activities that are required to render these in modes (acoustic or visual) that are observable to listeners. In sum, we claim that the task of rendering propositions in real time to a communicative partner is an internal impetus for the appearance of syntax in child speech. We do not deny that the conventional use of word-order (and deletion) by one's mother is also an impetus for the use of such devices by the learner of English. But we hold that prior convention is not the whole story in understanding the formal nature of child language.

Developmental Patterns

We have so far seen that the home sign system of the deaf subjects is in content and syntactic form rather similar to the speech of hearing children. Here we ask whether there are similarities in developmental patterns as well. While there are some developmental changes in the manual system, these are neither neat nor very rousing. Some of the reasons for this are methodological, but some seem to be substantive.

Constraints on the Subject Population

It was not possible to find subjects at the very beginning of development. This is because it is hard to identify deafness in children at young ages, and even harder to measure how profound the hearing loss is, owing to difficulties young children have in understanding and following instructions in audiometric tests. Usually, parents do not suspect that their children are deaf until it is clear that their language learning is delayed, and by that time they are usually over 2 years old. Only one of our subjects (Kathy, 17 months at the first interview) was identified to us earlier in life than this.

A partly symmetrical problem arises in finding usable subjects older than the ones we studied. Oral instruction begins for these subjects when they are about three. Our subjects in the older age ranges were already receiving such instruction (though none had yet made much progress with it; see p. 357), and they were coming into contact with other deaf youngsters. Assessment of the independent development of gesturing becomes progressively more contaminated by these factors as developmental time passes. Further, the exposure to English, through oralist training, can be expected to interfere with progress with the little-reinforced gestural system. Only two of the six original subjects (David and Donald) are continuing to show significant advances in manual language that seem on the face of it to be relatively uncontaminated by the competing system.

Nevertheless, within the age range we could observe, there was growth in the home sign system. But there were also some clear differences in the rate of development and in achievement level between these subjects and hearing children acquiring speech.

Syntactic Development: Increases in Sentence Length

All of the subjects except the youngest (Kathy, 17 months) gestured in two-sign sentences the first time we saw them, so we cannot document a pure "hologesture" stage directly. Kathy produced one two-sign sentence at interview II, when she was 18 months old. Donald was 24 months, Dennis 26 months, and David 34 months when first observed, and all already gestured in two-sign sentences. (Chris and Tracy were too old when first interviewed to contribute relevant data here.) Based on these observations, we can guess that the two-sign gesture emerges in these subjects late in the second year of life or early in the third. The facts are similar for hearing children. Lenneberg (1967, p. 130) reports the appearance of two-word sentences between 24 and 30 months, and many children begin to produce them as early as 18 months or so (see also Bloom, 1970, and many other sources).

However, once the deaf children come to convey semantic relations two signs at a time, they do not come to favor these two-sign forms. They still continue to gesture one sign at a time in the preponderance of instances, even at 4 years of age.* As a consequence, the mean length of their gestures, in signs (the "MLG") remains very low (see p. 385). Only David (at 40 months) achieved an MLG above 1·5 during the course of study. This contrasts with the facts about hearing children. Bowerman (1975, p. 270) presents MLU data for seven hearing children (interviewed by herself or other investigators) speaking a variety of languages, who were at the two-word stage. Their ages were between 19 and 30 months. The MLUs of these subjects ranged from 1·30 to 1·50, already higher than that of the deaf subjects at similar ages. But moreover, Bowerman presents data for six youngsters who were even more advanced on the MLU measure (ranging from 1·60 to 2·00; some are the same children, now older, and some are not). Overall, these subjects fell into the same age ranges (between 18 and 28 months) and they characteristically used many three-word sentences. None of our deaf subjects' MLG falls into this higher range, even though some of them were 4 years old.

This comparative lack of growth in MLG should not be interpreted, however, to suggest that the subjects' sentence forms did not change with age. The upper bound on the deaf subjects' sentence length does increase as they grow older, as shown in Table XI. The upper bound for the children when younger was from one to four, but it was from four to seven for the older children, and David's was thirteen. But even so the one-sign utterance is still the most frequent, so MLG hardly rises.

Summarizing, the normal and deaf populations are similar in the developmental moment at which two-unit sentences emerge, and probably not too different in the moment at which even longer sentences are first produced. But the two populations are different in the *characteristic* length of sentences at all ranges, and this difference increases with increasing age.

Semantic Development

Table XII displays the proportion of *act* and *attribute* semantic relations conveyed by the sentences of each subject. The table documents a fact mentioned earlier (p. 383), that *action* semantic relations predominate for each subject. Similar findings appear in the literature for hearing children. Brown (1973, p. 174) reports that 12 children (interviewed by himself or other investigators, and ranging from 1·10 to 2·06 in MLU) from different cultures all conveyed action and attribute relations in their communications, but that the action relations predominated. Bloom *et al.* (1975) report that

*Differences in coding magnify some of the differences between MLGs and MLUs, as usually measured. We did not exclude single-point responses to pictures (which are very similar, in conversation, to one-noun responses to queries). Nonetheless, the MLGs are clearly depressed, compared to MLUs for children of this age. Lenneberg (1967, p. 130) reports that the grammatical complexity of speech from 4-year-old normals is roughly adult.

Table XI
Upper bound on sentence length, in signs[a]

	Age in months						
	15-20	21-26	27-32	33-38	39-44	45-50	51-53
Younger subjects:							
Kathy	1	4	4				
Dennis		2	3				
Chris		3	4				
Older subjects:							
David				3	9+	9+	9+
Donald			2	3		4	3
Tracy						4	5

[a]Single instances of a longer sentence were excluded (e.g. Kathy produced a single two-sign utterance at 18 months and David produced a single six-sign utterance at 35 months; and these were excluded from this table).

their subjects, aged 19 to 25 months (MLUs from 1·0 to 2·5), all expressed action relations well before they expressed attribute relations. Since our subjects were interviewed at quite different ages, we can give no strong documentation of a similar effect for them. However, in so far as the data of Table XII, which pools over all sessions, can be interpreted as revealing age effects, the results are similar: the three subjects (Kathy, Chris and Dennis) all of whose data come at ages under 3·6 years produce proportionally more action semantic relations than the three subjects (David, Donald and Tracy) whose age was over 3·6 sometime during testing.

In sum, there is weak evidence supporting the view that these subjects, like normal youngsters, talk mainly about action at early ages, but begin to express attribute concepts increasingly with increasing age.

Is Development of the Home Sign System "Normal"?

We have commented on a number of developmental similarities between the deaf subjects and young speakers. The semantic relations they express first are the same (*actions* before *attributes*, previous section) and they express these in terms of the same case relations (e.g. *patients* and *recipients*, but not *instruments*, pp. 386-387), and similar lexical categories (concrete nouns and motion verbs, p. 378). The first-used syntactic devices also seem to be the same as those reported for children learning English. Word-order is an early deployed device (p. 376) as is the omission of transitive *actors* in sentences whose predicate structure is complex (pp. 387-396). Sentences tend to be very

Table XII
Action and attribute sentences

	Action sentences	Attribute sentences	Static sentences[a]	Total one-relation sentences
Younger subjects:				
Kathy	0·86	0·09	0·05	42
Dennis	0·87	0·10	0·03	31
Chris	0·70	0·26	0·04	43
Older subjects:				
David	0·58	0·37	0·05	438
Donald	0·63	0·36	0·01	145
Tracy	0·38	0·57	0·05	65

[a]The sentences labeled "static" could not be classified as either action or attribute. A sentence was considered to be static if it could potentially be a comment on the static location or possession of an object. For example, consider a child who points at a picture of his brother and then points out the door. The child could either be commenting on the fact that his brother went outside (an action) or on the fact that his brother is now outside (static location). Similarly, a point at his own Halloween costume and then at himself could either be a comment on his having received the costume at one time (an action), or on his current possession of the costume (static possession). Because of these problems of interpretation, these sentences were classified separately. Note, however, that static sentences make up a small proportion of the total sentences produced by the children.

short (p. 384) and show increasing length, when measured in terms of upper bound, with increasing age (p. 402). Thus developmental orders for various contents and structures seem to be roughly similar without input as with input.

These parallels between our population and normal language learners seem somewhat odd on the face of it. There are four obvious reasons to expect differences in developmental patterns. First, the visual-manual modality may impose acquisition constraints different from those that characterize auditory-acoustic systems (though early results from an ongoing study by Newport and Ashbrook at San Diego, on the acquisition of ASL by deaf children of deaf parents, suggest many parallels between learning sign languages and spoken languages). Second, our subjects have no richly elaborated language system to learn; they must *create*, as well as *acquire*, a means of communication. Third, in so far as an actively teaching individual is implicated in the acquisition process (as suggested by Snow (1972) and others), one is lacking in this situation: though the caretakers are cognitively mature they are no more fluent than the children in the manual system. Finally, and probably most important, there is no clearly *co-operating* communicative partner. The adults around our subjects do not accept the manual communicative mode in ways that would seem to be conducive to joint, active, attempts to specify and enrich the system. No conventions for expression seem to be adopted by mutual agreement. If the child makes a gesture, we do not observe the mother gesturing it in return. Even to the extent that the adults do gesture, they are quite inept, dependent on props, and often unaware that they are being expressive. If humans have the capacity to create communication systems on their own, this hardly seems the ideal situation in which to try to do so.

Given all these reasons to expect developmental differences, it is almost reassuring to discover that there are some. The developmental parallels between the deaf subjects and normals are not at all perfect. The similarities are at the beginning of development, but differences crop up increasingly later on. Primarily, the MLG of our older subjects is clearly depressed. Four-year-old hearing children with an MLU below 1·5 (like Tracy and Donald) are rare indeed; this attenuated growth is reason enough, in a hearing population, to suspect a long-term language or thought abnormality.

There is another apparent delay in language growth. We take it as obvious that 4-year-old hearing children express a variety of new case notions, such as the *instrument*. They talk of eating with spoons and hitting with hammers, and they do so in ways that conform to the rather complicated structural requirements for such expressions in English. Even Brown's (1973) much younger subjects produce a few instruments. But among our subjects, we have observed only David begin to gesture of such matters (he gestures, e.g., about digging with a shovel); and we cannot be sure that even he encodes this notion in structurally distinct ways (for further discussion, see following section). Again—similar to the instance of MLU—the onset time for certain basic notions is about the same in both populations, but the deaf subjects advance much more slowly, and not as far.

We have left aside discussion of a number of further properties of these children's gesturing, because the data were not presented in this chapter (see Goldin-Meadow (1977) and forthcoming reports on advanced stages of the home sign system). For completeness, further parallels can be found. For instance, our subjects show increasing tendencies, over time, to conjoin propositions within a single gestured sentence, though they have no overt morpheme of conjunction. There are also other non-parallels. For instance, these subjects never develop any means for creating complex morphemes from simple ones (there are no derivational devices) or marking tense, aspect, or case (there are no inflectional affixes, prepositions, etc.). This latter fact may be artificially magnifying the morpheme-length difference (MLU to MLG difference) between the deaf subjects and speakers of inflected languages. Highly inflected languages clearly yield inflated MLU counts, unless some way is found to make corrections for this (i.e. every adjective, noun, etc. has an associated case-affix—even if the young speaker chooses the wrong one—so that each such lexical item consists of a minimum of two morphemes; see Williamson, forthcoming, on such problems in analyzing for MLU in children learning Malasian Tamil). Strict word-order languages will have comparatively lower MLUs, it would appear. At the extreme, pidgins (which are almost totally uninflected, a fact to which we will return) ought to show very depressed MLUs. There is little doubt that the home sign system is very like a pidgin (see discussion p. 408), and so yields comparatively low MLG counts. (But this cause is not, in our opinion, large enough to account for the magnitude of difference between our subjects' MLGs and hearing children's MLUs: there is a degree of pidginization, it seems, in all child language (Smith, 1973).)

A Note about David

We have so far claimed that parallels between the deaf and hearing populations are close at the beginning and less close at later stages of language development. But the subject David is very likely an exception to the rule that the home sign system must increasingly lag behind the emerging language system of children exposed to a culturally elaborated language. We do not know why David has gone so far. Perhaps he is the smartest of all our subjects, the William Shakespeare of the home sign system. Perhaps even though his caretakers are not fluent in the manual system, they may be more amenable to taking the role of communicative partners in manual gesturing. Whatever the reason, there is no doubt that David at the later observations could express himself very fluently about matters that interested him. Below we give an example of how David responded after being shown a picture of a snow-shovel. He gestured:*

(1) shovel[a]—dig[b]
(2) shovel—put-on-boots[c]—outside[d]—downstairs[e]—shovel—dig—put-on-boots
(3) David[f]
(4) dig—outside—snow[g]—shovel—snow
(5) dig—yes[h]
(6) shovel—downstairs—dig—downstairs

There is no difficulty in understanding David when one actually sees this

---

*David here produces a sequence of six sentences (each of which ends with the return of the hands to neutral position). The superscript on each sign type that we gloss in this example is actually rendered by the following gestures: (a) point to the picture of a shovel; (b) digging motions, hands holding an imaginary shovel; (c) hands pulling upward from toe to middle of leg; (d) point toward the door of the room; (e) jabbing points toward the floor—toward the basement where the shovel is stored; (f) point to his own chest; (g) arms held parallel, flat hands, palm downward; fingers flutter, as arms are gradually lowered to the sides; (h) nod: a sign-marker.

scene. He said that "The shovel is to dig with. I put on my boots and take the shovel from the basement and go outside and dig. Me! I dig when it snows outside and I shovel the snow. Yes, I dig. The shovel is kept in the basement, what I dig with is kept down in the basement." This 4-year old does not have much trouble in expressing himself.

Despite David's expressive capacities, we do not seek to claim (pending further analysis) that David's *language* has become as complex as the language of a hearing 4-year-old, but only that his expressible thoughts are growing more complex. This caveat simply reiterates the stance we have assumed all through this discussion. We are chary of calling these expressive gestures "language-like" unless it can be shown that they take place within a structured system. We have shown this structure in the two- and three-word sentence system of all the deaf subjects. Sufficient data on complex sentences by David (and Donald) are only now beginning to come in quantities sufficient to allow similar analysis. Possibly David has elaborated his structures to accommodate his now elaborate expressed thoughts. But possibly he has not: the lexical items in the example above may be simply strung along in a row; he may have run out of syntactic means. So, pending further analysis, we claim only that David's sentences have become longer and meatier, but not necessarily more complexly organized. Still, here is at least one child who is communicating in very human ways, in the absence of someone who is systematically showing him how to do so. What stronger evidence could be asked for in answer to the question whether there are significant internal predispositions in humans that are relevant to the emergence of language?

SUMMARY AND CONCLUSIONS

We have studied the communicative system developed by young children who are as radically deprived of language input as can be imagined, this side of feral children. We have found that these linguistically isolated individuals display communicative skills that are language-like, despite their deprivations. We conclude that there are significant internal dispositions in humans that guide the language acquisition process.

Surely some of these guides are quite general, and do not apply to language in particular. For example, the mental contents that are communicated about at various stages in the young child's life (e.g. the actions and motions of things and people, as opposed to perceptual attributes of those things and people) are surely consequences of general cognitive functioning, and not consequences of language-specific properties of mental organization. In contrast, the exploitation of sequence, the representation of content in terms of a hierarchically organized set of levels, and the adoption of regular principles for the selective omission of some material—all observed in the deaf subjects—seem to be specifically language-like, not variants of organization common to all higher-order mental functions. The emergence of these language-like formal means of representing thought by the deaf subjects without models suggests the existence of language organizing principles that account for the structure of their gesturing.

It is worth noting that many of the effects we have reported fit naturally with other demonstrations that language grows out of the construction of the human mind, rather than being solely an arbitrary system that is acquired "from without" by such minds. Newport *et al.* (1977) performed a correlational study to determine aspects of language learning that were more and less sensitive to the nature of external input (in their study, the properties of maternal speech). They found that the young child's tendency, over a 6-month interval, to express more and more of the content of thought in the speech-stream (i.e. the appearance of explicit lexical items conveying increasingly more of the required logic of sentences) was insensitive to aspects of the speech of different mothers at the beginning of the 6-month interval. For example, the elaboration of the child's sentence content was not correlated with the mother's MLU or sentence complexity when talking to the child, nor with her tendency to repeat, expand, etc. The parallel finding in the present study is that the subjects came to say longer and longer sentences with increasing age, expressing progressively more of the sentential logic, even though there was no model language user at all who they could copy.

Newport *et al.* found a different result for the rate of development in the inflectional structure of English (verbal auxiliary and plural formation). In this regard, the children's growth rate was evidently sensitive to properties of maternal speech. Specifically, children whose mothers had strong tendencies to front the verbal auxiliary (by asking yes/no questions) had children who acquired the auxiliary structure most rapidly. Here, where there seems to be a very specific and powerful effect of the language environment on language learning, there is no progress at all among the deaf subjects: they never "think of" such devices as inflectional affixes to mark number or time in their gesturing.

The results of this study were quite different from those reported in other studies of the effects of maternal speech on language learning. Most prior studies really do not measure child language growth as a function of caretaker speech. Rather, they simply describe mother-speech and child-speech at various developmental moments, and argue inferentially from properties of these corpora tht the mother-style must have influenced the child-style. This kind of argumentation is not too convincing. There have been a few studies which were correlational in method. But again the findings of Newport *et al.* differ seriously from those achieved in other correlational studies. These differences derive chiefly from a difference in the method of analysis. Most of the studies in the literature report simple correlations between aspects of mothers' speech and aspects of children's speech, either at the same time, or measured some months later. Many such correlations can be found (Newport *et al.* found the same ones that are usually reported). The trouble is that cause and effect cannot be disentangled from these simple correlations: the nature of the child's speech might be the "cause" of the mother speaking in such-and-such a way to him, as easily as the nature of the mother's speech might be the "cause" of the child's learning to speak in such-and-such a way. (By analogy, one might measure the mother's angle of regard when she looks down at her tiny child. Then one could measure his growth during some succeeding interval. One will find (a) that the child grows; and (b) that the farther down the mother looked at time one, the more the child was likely to grow by time two. The reason is not that the looking down caused the child to grow. The reason is that the baseline size of various children differed at the first measurement and, the smaller you are—on the average—the faster you grow, for growth curves decelerate over time.) Newport *et al.* made a statistical correction for this problem. They partialled out differences in the age and stage (on each linguistic measure) of the subject children; simple correlations were then performed, using these double-partialled data, between the mother's speech style at time one and the child's growth rate between time one and time two. There were now many fewer correlations. Generally, the result was that language-universal aspects of child language (i.e. its marking of substantive content) were insensitive to the observed differences in maternal speech style; but language-specific aspects of inflectional morphology (i.e. the verbal auxiliary and nominal inflection structures) were sensitive to differences in maternal speech style.

Summarizing, where Newport *et al.* were able to show a significant role played by properties of the external model, the present study shows a non-effect: no learning without the external model. In contrast, where Newport *et al.* found insensitivity to the maternal environment, we find progress among the deaf subjects (though, to be sure, it is sometimes slow). The two studies taken together, then, begin to disentangle two kinds of factor in language learning: those that are direct consequences of the input and those that seem to come from inside the novice himself.

Some supporting evidence for the distinction just made comes from studies that at first seem far afield. Labov (1971) and Sankoff and Laberge (1973) have reported on some expressive and structural properties of Tok Pisin, a New Guinea pidgin now becoming creolized. Roughly, a *pidgin* is a contact-vernacular which is nobody's native language; it is called a *creole* at the point when its use becomes general, and it acquires native speakers. Pidgins emerge, often among adults, in a setting where the speaker's own language does not serve the purposes of communication, for the listener speaks a different language. To handle this problem (under circumstances where contact is not general enough to motivate acquiring the other language) the two parties devise a "simplified" expressive means—the pidgin. It seems fair to call this setting, like the one in the present study, a situation in which language is being created, though here certainly not from scratch. It is curious that Tok Pisin is characterized by the use of word-order as the preferred device for marking the semantic roles, by a relative absence of multi-propositional sentences, and by relative simplicity of inflectional apparatus; and the process of creolization in Tok Pisin is marked by the development of devices for sentence embedding, and a change from optional adverbial marking of time toward obligatory tense marking within the verb-phase.

The analogy between development in Tok Pisin and in child speech is quite clear, and it was noted and discussed in a very important seminal paper by Slobin (1975). The analogy to the deaf subjects' gesturing is also transparent: in *their* language-like creation too, the semantic roles are marked by word-order and there is an absence of inflectional apparatus and multi-propositional sentences.

Slobin (1975, based on data from Broch 1927), provides the even stronger example of Russenorsk, a minimal pidgin spoken by Norwegian fishermen to the Russian merchants with whom they trade (on the relatively rare occasions when the ice melts on the Norwegian Sea). Even though one of the parent languages, Russian, is highly inflected, Russenorsk, a primitive system with novice (though adult) speakers, has almost no inflectional apparatus. There is one major exception, an affix on verbs which distinguishes them from nouns. Slobin comments that a clear distinction between noun and verb may be a minimal structural requirement, if a language is to be efficiently expressive. Russenorsk also marks the basic distinction among the semantic roles by a syntactic device, word-order. Again, Slobin suggests an analogy to first-language acquisition, where word-order is commonly deployed early, and where the more complex aspects of inflection are learned relatively late. The analogy to the deaf subjects' home sign system is also suggestively close. These subjects too mark the semantic roles in terms of word-order restrictions. Furthermore, they too differentiate the forms of nouns (points) from the forms of verbs (characterizing signs, pantomimes). Thus similar means for encoding meaning are adopted by speakers of pidgins, young first-language learners, and the deaf signers in the manifest absence of relevant input data. Novice communication seems to have well-defined formal properties, under a variety of circumstances, despite differences in users (adult vs. child), and differences in modality and environment (deaf vs. speaking children).

Now looking at studies yet farther afield, it is interesting to ask what happens where a fully-known language is rendered in a new modality. The history of writing affords some hints about what happens to language when its users are cast rather into the role of novices, this time because a system which they have fully elaborated and controlled is recast in a visual, rather than acoustic modality. It is at the least a curiosity that early writing systems rarely rendered the inflectional aspects of the spoken languages which they transcribed, but left them out (Gelb, 1952; and see Gleitman and Rozin, 1977, for discussion in a similar context). In contrast, the early writing systems pretty well marked word-order constraints by convention (i.e. by mapping them onto left-to-right or some other visual order). Similarly, it appears that novice readers of English have great trouble getting meaning out of the forms that render inflectional material (e.g. the -*ed* that marks the past tense; Labov, 1970). In contrast, they have significantly less trouble in getting the meaning out of formal devices that render word-order (i.e. they easily understand that left-to-right order on the page is a mapping of temporal order in the speech stream; Rozin *et al.*, 1971; Rozin and Gleitman, 1977) and substantive content (e.g. the visual forms that mark words like *dog* or *run*; Labov, 1970; Rozin and Gleitman, 1977). These novice readers are experts in all these matters (inflections, word-order, substantives) in the context of speech and hearing. But when cast into the role of novices learning visual language, they have special difficulties with the inflectional materials again. Once more, we note the parallel here with home sign: the novice deaf subjects make progress in creating signs for substantive and verbal notions (the points and characterizing signs) and in deploying word-order, but their gesturing is uninflected.

Summarizing, a number of lines of evidence suggest a significant role in novice communication of dispositions to organize language materials in certain ways.

A final point lest we be misunderstood. To say that the character of language is affected by internal predispositions, as we do based on the evidence of the deaf children and other studies just cited, is not to deny a significant role also for structured properties of the input data and properties (affective and communicative) of caretakers. It is good to have a mother. Language learning will differ, depending on how that mother talks, a fact which has not been in doubt at least since the incident at the tower of Babel.

The findings presented here conflict only with claims that have appeared in the literature to the effect that the contributions to language learning from internal dispositions in the learner are minimal and nonspecific.

We believe that progress in understanding the language learning feat depends seriously on disentangling two kinds of descriptive facts: those that are accountable on an "inside-out" view and those that are "outside-in". There is every reason to suppose that the laws underlying learning new and arbitrary materials (such as lists of nonsense syllables or The Pledge of Allegiance) differ materially from the laws underlying learning that which is prefigured in internal representations (such as mathematical relations, and universal aspects of the structure of language). This point is reminiscent of some recent findings in the field of animal learning. It appears that, the clamor of 70 years of behaviorism notwithstanding, different species of animals are biologically "prepared" to learn certain associations much more readily than others (Seligman, 1970). Thus pigeons rapidly learn to hop from one perch to another so as to avoid a shock but will take just about forever if the required avoidance response is to peck at a key (Bolles, 1975). Some kinds of preparedness, to learn certain things and not others, may be built into humans just as it is wired into pigeons, with language-use as natural to the one species as hopping-off-perches is to the other.

With the aim of contributing to an unraveling of these components in language acquisition, we have tried to resurrect the deprivation paradigm described by Herodotus, and perhaps to take a step beyond.

ACKNOWLEDGMENTS

We are much indebted to Henry Gleitman for his very extensive and generous contributions both to the theoretical foundations of this work and to the writing of this chapter. Many times we would have been mired down without him, both in understanding and organizing the findings. We are indebted to Elissa Newport, who offered invaluable guidance on coding and analyzing the data, as well as contributing many ideas expressed in this chapter. We owe a debt also to Rochel Gelman, who was deeply involved in the original design and analysis of the study, and in its overall conception. Specific citations to these colleagues do not appear in the text, just because their influence in this investigation is too broad to be pinned to any specific remark or section in the chapter. We acknowledge also a deep intellectual debt to Noam Chomsky, whose writings on the formal nature of language and on language acquisition quite obviously provide the general framework within which we thought about our subjects' communications (see particularly Chomsky, 1965; 1968). A number of sponsoring agencies are thanked for supporting this work: Grant No.

MD23505 from the National Institutes of Health and a grant from the William T. Carter Foundation (to Gleitman), Grant 5-T01HD00337 (to R. Gelman), a Spencer Foundation grant through the University of Pennsylvania (to Feldman and Goldin-Meadow), and a Spencer Foundation grant and a Social Sciences Division Research grant both through the University of Chicago (to Goldin-Meadow). We thank also Marion Gilbert, who heroically typed numerous versions of this manuscript, and also Lisette Tefo, Barbara Gray, and Lorraine Stepneski, who helped in coding and transcribing the videotapes, and also our subjects and their families who graciously donated their time.

15

Structural Parallels between Language and Action in Development

PATRICIA MARKS GREENFIELD

University of California, Los Angeles, U.S.A.

Are there organizing principles underlying linguistic functioning which also underlie cognition in other modes, for example, action? If so, what are they? These are the basic questions to which this chapter is addressed.

The historical background to these questions lies in linguistics and psycholinguistics. Chomsky's formulation of transformational grammar (e.g. 1965) led to a psychological hypothesis of universal linguistic capacities—that is, cognitive capacities *specific* to language. There is, however, an alternative formulation concerning universals, originating with Piaget (e.g. 1962), which has become increasingly popular in recent years. This view posits universal cognitive capacities which are *not* specific to language, but which also structure cognition in other modes. My chapter explores this second alternative. In terms of linguistic theory, this formulation is compatible with the post-Chomskyan development of generative semantics (e.g. McCawley, 1968; Lakoff, 1971). Because generative semantics sees grammar as having a semantic aspect as well as a syntactic one, grammatical structure is no longer isolated in principle from perceptual and cognitive experience of the world.

This theoretical point of view is consonant with that of Piaget, who relates linguistic structure and its development to an underlying cognitive organization. Piaget's perspective on the relation between language and thought has been most fully elaborated by Sinclair (e.g. 1971). Whereas the point of departure for Piaget and Sinclair is the infant's preverbal cognitive structures, the point of departure for this chapter is linguistic structure. I begin with structural features of language—e.g. hierarchical organization—

and look for parallel structures in action. What is already known about the course of development of the language structure is compared with the course of development of the corresponding action structure.

In looking for parallels between language and action, I have begun with the fact that language is a combinatorial activity—combinatorial on all levels, the phonological, syntactic, and semantic—and have sought out combinatorial activity on the physical plane. One such domain is construction activity, for it involves combining objects into physical structures, just as linguistic units (e.g. phonemes) are combined to form language structures. Another combinatorial activity is drawing, for it involves combining lines to form two-dimensional structures. Vereeken (1961) has applied Piaget's theoretical perspective to account specifically for the development of complex "constructive-praxic" behaviors (i.e. blockbuilding, drawing, copying spatial arrays, etc.). The facts presented by Vereeken support our analysis at a number of points and will be presented where relevant.

In concentrating on object manipulation and drawing, I do not intend to exclude other forms of activity, particularly perceptual, from the structural analogy with language. I am simply exploring domains where the child constructs structures which have an external form. Construction activity and drawing are also areas which are important in the everyday play of the child and therefore have interest in their own right.

PARALLELS TO REFERENTIALITY AND SEMANTIC ROLES IN OBJECT COMBINATION

Correspondence

In all types of representation, one element—the signifier—stands for another —the signified. In language, the signifier has some additional characteristics: it does not resemble what is signified in any way, and its significance or meaning, therefore, is a matter of social convention. The most basic aspect of all types of representation, however, is *correspondence* between two elements —signifier and signified. Such correspondence is a feature of the earliest type of object manipulation. Its origins appear to lie in the bilateral symmetry of human beings. Typically in the fourth month of life the infant begins to play with her hands; she discovers that one hand corresponds to the other. Forman (1971, 1973, 1975) sees the bilateral symmetry of the human body as the origin of the similarity relation, in which two things are perceived as alike yet different from each other. For instance, the child discovers her two hands which are the same, yet distinct. Such similarity can be considered a basic type of correspondence. The earliest form of object combination is a symmetrical one: the infant, holding one object in each hand, bangs them together at the midline. This probably occurs as early as the seventh month of life. In bringing the objects together, the infant places them in correspondence. Through the objects' connection to the hands, experienced as alike yet distinct, the infant constructs this relation of correspondence between the two objects (Forman, 1975). At this point, object correspondence is very much on the action plane, tied to the infant's own body. Forman (1975) has observed infants' spontaneous play with groups of five blocks, some identical, some different in shape and size. Whereas the 7- to 8-month-old infants show no particular preference for banging similar or different blocks, there is a clear preference for similar blocks by 11 to 12 months, the next age level in this study. In banging identical blocks together at the midline, the infant is revealing a capacity to produce not only action correspondence as in the earliest stage, but also a primitive sort of *formal* correspondence between two elements, the basis of the referential act.*

The Growth of Asymmetric Relations

Up to about the eighth month, the infant is limited to symmetrical combination of objects. Yet linguistic structure on the grammatical level involves asymmetrical combination—asymmetry in the sense that grammatical elements play different yet complementary roles in the overall structure of a sentence.†

Asymmetry also develops on the plane of action. Around the eighth month the infant makes her first asymmetrical combination of objects when she bangs some object, e.g. a spoon, a block, against a table top (Cattell, 1940; Forman, 1975). Translating Chafe's grammatical terminology to refer directly to situational structure, one could say that the spoon functions as an instrument—something which the agent uses—in this situation. Because,

---

*Harris (1972) presents the idea of a non-verbal form of referencing in her thesis. Her test of referencing is a formboard in which the shape of a piece must be matched to the shape of a hole. This more complex form of referencing does not appear until 25 to 31 months of age. Because this form occurs so much later and because it occurs long after most children have begun to use words referentially, it cannot be considered the non-verbal *origin* of referencing behavior.

†The grammatical model to be used in this chapter will be a semantically based case model like that proposed by Fillmore (1968) or Chafe (1970). These models see deep grammatical structure in the meaning relations expressed by a sentence, relations among elements like agent, action, object (Fillmore's term) or patient (Chafe's term), and so forth. Take for example the sentence *John closes the door*. Here *closes* expresses a process undergone by the patient *door*; *John* functions as agent, the instigator of the process.

however, the ability to release an object voluntarily has not yet developed, the object is identified with the instigating hand itself. It therefore functions, psychologically, more in the role of agent than instrument. In the same object-table relation the table has the characteristics of a patient *par excellence*—immobility and passivity. These characteristics contrast sharply with those of the mobile, active spoon. Hence, at the outset of asymmetrical object combination, the infant's behavior reveals a correlation between role and physical form.

In the next stage action role begins to be dissociated from physical form: two similar or identical objects play distinct roles. With blocks this means that one block is used to strike another without being released.

At the next stage, location is differentiated from the patient role. With the new ability to release the moving block, the table or block, earlier in the role of patient, is transformed into a location and the agent block becomes an instrument in relation to the child's hand as agent. (The stage just described is the result of further analysis of Forman's (1975) data.)

An observation by Forman (personal communication, 1974) also shows the progression away from defining action role in terms of physical characteristics. He found that babies will place an object inside a ring at an earlier age than they can place a ring over an object. Apparently the ring looks like an immobile location in relation to the object and is initially treated as such. Later babies discover the reversibility of roles. Whereas Piaget has stressed reversibility in the growth of cognitive organization, I wish to point out another aspect of the earlier stage: that role assignment is not random, but is based on the physical qualities of the two objects, perceived in relation to each other. The dual role possibility for the blocks (active and passive), reflects the same accomplishment as the dual role possibility for the small object and large ring.

The emergence of object roles just described appears to mirror the development of semantic functions in early language (Greenfield and Smith, 1976). That is to say, children are able to express agent (e.g. *daddy*, hearing father come in door and start up steps) before instrument (e.g. *button* after pushing button which makes record turntable revolve); patient (e.g. *ball*, catching a ball) before location (e.g. *box*, putting crayon in box).*

---

*Harris (1972) approached this same question of parallels between action and language through a study of development in both modes. One hypothesis was that common structural features in the verbal structures and non-verbal object manipulation tasks would produce the same order of acquisition in each mode. The hypothesis was confirmed for a limited subset of the tasks and language structures. One problem was that the materials for the non-verbal tasks were so heterogeneous and the criteria for mastery so diverse that they differed along many dimensions besides the strictly structural ones defined by Harris. One would not expect the resultant order of acquisition to reflect these structural factors alone. Another problem lay in the classification of the tasks. For instance, the task representing interaction (of distinct semantic roles) consisted

Another important aspect of the development of asymmetric object combination is the development of asymmetric use of the two hands. If infants are presented successively with small graspable objects, the typical six- to eight-month old will keep taking objects, first with one hand then the other. Around a year, however, the infant typically passes the toy from one hand to another, freeing the first hand to accept the next toy (Bruner, 1971). Here one hand takes the more active agentive role, the other serves a more passive, locative role. This differentiation is stabilized with brain lateralization, a developmental process in which the two sides of the brain begin to take on more specialized functions. Lateralization results in handedness. Forman (1972) points out that between 18 and 24 months of age the right-handed child begins to initiate most instrumental behavior with her right hand, while the left hand performs support functions such as stabilization, etc. In this way, the child creates differentiated roles not only for objects but also for herself. The conceptualization of persons in both active and passive roles is also prerequisite to later developing grammatical structure, which involves a contrast, for example, between the active agent and the passive beneficiary: for instance, in the sentence *Mary gave John a Cookie, John* plays the role of beneficiary, *Mary* of agent. (Edwards (1973) sees the origins of the child as object in some of Piaget's (1954) observations of his own children. The problem with all of his examples, however, is that because the child instigates an action in each case, it seems impossible to separate child as agent from child as patient.)

Co-ordinating Asymmetric Relations in Action and Language

As far as the psychological significance of structural parallels between language and action is concerned, such parallels should make possible the co-ordination of language and action; responding to verbal commands for action is an example of such co-ordination. If this is the case, then one would expect that the more concordant the structure of the command with the structure of the desired action, the easier it should be to carry out the command. Huttenlocher and her colleagues (Huttenlocher and Strauss, 1968; Huttenlocher *et al.*, 1968) have tested this question with respect to the relation between active and passive object roles. For example, they compared

of linking three pieces of a boat in correct order. This task seems to reflect cognizance of order and the total boat Gestalt as much as simple interaction of roles. Finally, there were many problems in Harris' classification of linguistic structures. For one, structural types were, to some extent, defined in terms of utterance length, thus confounding structure and length. It is for these reasons that this thesis is not discussed at length in this chapter.

fourth grade children's responses to the following sentences; in each case the child was asked to position the red truck relative to the green truck, which was fixed in place:

The red truck is pushing the green truck.

The green truck is pushing the red truck.

Children made fewer errors and responded more quickly when the mobile truck in the action had the role of agent in the sentence. In such a case the stationary or passive truck in the action would have the role of patient in the sentence. Thus, in the first sentence grammatical roles are in accord with action roles; in the second in contrast they are in conflict. And comprehension of the first sentence is correspondingly more difficult.

SEQUENTIAL OBJECT COMBINATION

The Development of Basic Strategies

After the basic binary role relations have emerged as described, they may be combined in various ways to form more complex structures. This development has been traced in a situation where children are given a set of five seriated nesting cups to manipulate (Greenfield *et al.*, 1972). Figure 1 depicts the three strategies in the developmental order in which they emerged. Figure 2 shows the ages at which each strategy became dominant. Strategy 1 (Fig. 1) is of course the creation of a binary relation between active and passive cups (instrument and location, in terms of Chafe's terminology). A possible linguistic parallel, a simple sentence, is presented in Fig. 3.

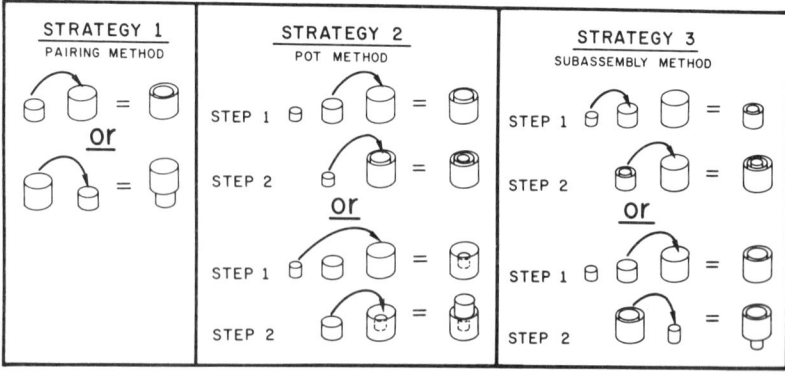

Fig. 1.

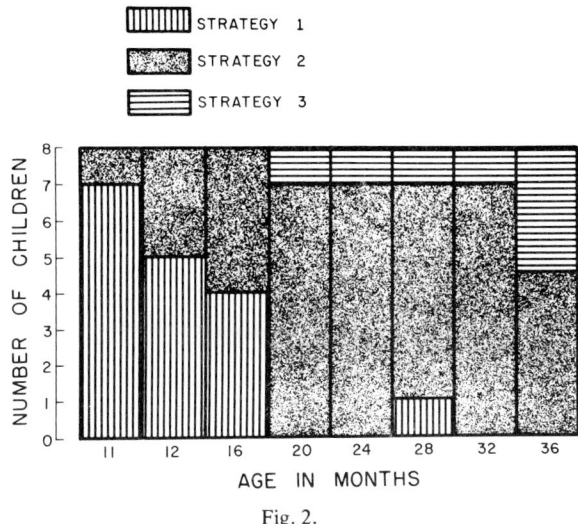

Fig. 2.

In the second strategy, the pot method illustrated in Fig. 1, two or more cups are placed in or on another cup. Thus, a single structure consisting of three or more cups is formed. This strategy can yield an ordered series or a "pile" as Fig. 1 shows. In this strategy, the child successively holds a number of cups which move into or onto a single stationary cup. This stationary cup thus functions as a pot, holding the mobile cups. With respect to the stationary cup, each moving or acting cup bears the same relationship of actor to acted upon, instrument to location.

Clearly, the first move in making such a structure conforms to the definition of Strategy 1. The strategy producing the *final* structure is what is of interest, however. Strategies therefore describe certain formal properties of *complete sequences* of cup combinations rather than *individual moves*. Figure 3 depicts the linguistic parallel as a compound sentence with multiple instruments (deep structure).

The third strategy is distinguished by the fact that a previously constructed structure consisting of two or more cups is moved *as a unit* into or onto another cup or cup structure. This strategy, applied to the cups, has a number of variants. Figure 1 illustrates a "pure" form in which a two-cup unit is place in or on a third cup. If the child continued to employ this strategy to build a larger structure, the resulting three-cup unit would be placed in or on a fourth cup, and so on. Again, this may yield either a seriated or "piled" final structure. In terms of individual cups, the distinctive feature of this strategy is that the stationary cup that is acted upon in the first move becomes the acting cup in the second move. Thus, one or more cups

STRATEGY 1 : PAIRING METHOD

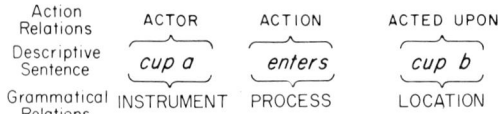

STRATEGY 2 : POT METHOD

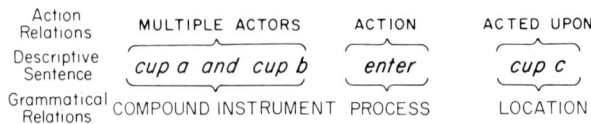

STRATEGY 3 : SUBASSEMBLY METHOD

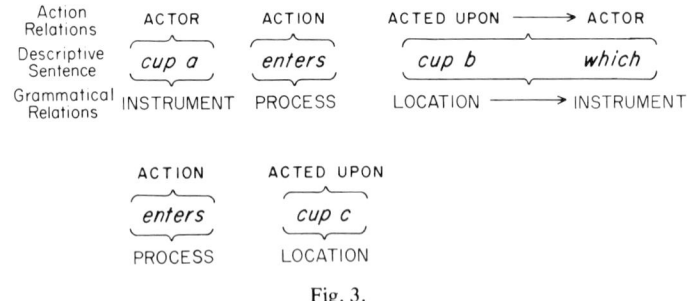

Fig. 3.

has a double role: it makes the transition from being acted upon to acting. In terms of the multi-cup units or subassemblies, the defining feature is that each multi-cup unit functions as a single moving or acting cup.

Figure 3 depicts a possible linguistic parallel to the subassembly strategy; a relative clause sentence in which location in the first clause switches roles to become instrument in the second clause. From what is known of the emergence of the sentence types shown in Fig. 3 in children's language, the developmental sequence parallels that of the manipulative strategies.

Just as one could see instrument originating in the agent role at 11 months when moving cup is treated as if an extension of acting hand, so the instrumental role in grammar may well originate in the grammatical agent (Schlesinger, 1973). This possibility of a common origin could also hold for other pairs of related grammatical functions like patient and location.

The generality of these strategies has been confirmed by their appearance when children aged 2 to 6 were asked to construct two models—a bench and a propeller—using nuts, bolts, blocks and sticks (Goodson and Greenfield, 1975). Each model could be built by two different methods. The two methods for constructing the propeller are shown in Figs 4 and 5. The piling method is

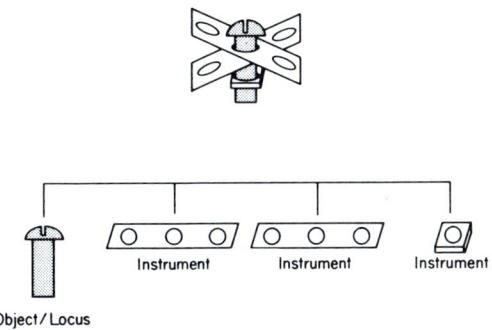

Fig. 4. Piling strategy for constructing a propeller.

parallel to the pot method for the cups: multiple instruments are placed one at a time on a single locus. The second method parallels the subassembly with the nesting cups: the two sticks are first combined to form a sub-assembly which then functions as a single unit in the next combination. That

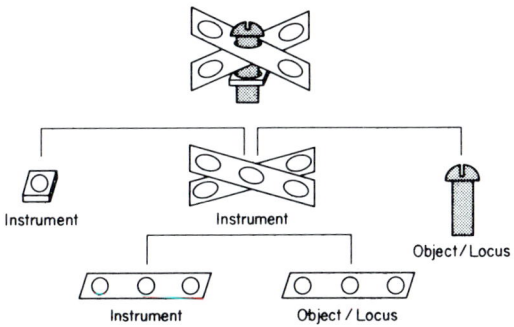

Fig. 5. Subassembly strategy for constructing a propeller.

move also involves a role change for the locus of the first move, as Fig. 5 shows. Just as the pot strategy preceded the subassembly with the nesting cups, so the piling strategy precedes the subassembly method for constructing the propeller.

Co-ordinating Role Change in Action and Language

At a certain point in development, grammatical role change poses difficulties in sentence comprehension, just as it does in construction behavior (Sheldon, 1973). Using small animal figures, 3- and 4-year-olds were asked to act out the four sentence types represented below:

1. The dog bit the *cat* that chased the rabbit.
2. The *dog* that chased the rabbit bit the cat.
3. The *dog* that the rabbit chased bit the cat.
4. The dog bit the *cat* that the rabbit chased.

Each sentence has a co-referential noun (in italics), that is, a noun to which the pronoun *that* also refers. Relative clause sentences where the co-referential nominal has the same grammatical function in both clauses (sentences 2 and 4) involve no role change. Where the co-referential nominal acts as the agent of one clause and the patient of the other, the sentence involves role change (sentences 1 and 3).

If role change creates processing difficulty, then children should make fewer errors in carrying out sentences 2 and 4, and this is precisely what happened. Thus, role change creates the same difficulty in sentence comprehension that it does in object combination.

Basic Strategies Applied to the Development of Block Building

Parallel in structure to the pot or piling strategy is stacking blocks one at a time. Thus the child who can place one block on another soon learns to make a stack of multiple blocks. According to Gesell and Amatruda (1947), the child given ten blocks, progresses from a two-block tower at 15 months to an eight-block at 30 months. A row of blocks involves the same basic strategy (the table now being the "pot" or common location) except that the child must relate each successive block not to one location, as in the stack, but to two—table and preceding block. Hence, it requires consideration of a double relation (Forman, personal communication, 1974). The row involves the pot strategy in two dimensions and should therefore be later to appear than the stack. Numerous investigators (e.g. Guanella, 1934; Cattell, 1940; Forman, 1975) have found this to be the case. It is interesting that early attempts at constructing rows are an attempt to reduce the problem to a single relation. According to Vereeken's (1961) account of some German work by Brandner, before 22 months of age, "horizontal row-building is the result of the symmetrical action of the hands: the child takes a block in each hand and places them beside each other" (p. 23). In this way the child relates the blocks directly to each other, cognitively by-passing their relation to table top. After 22 months of age, brandner noted the first non-symmetrical row-building, carried out with one hand and progressing in one direction. Thus, the development of row building also repeats the earlier progression from symmetrical to asymmetrical relations.

The subassembly strategy involves an extra hierarchical level of structure in comparison with the pot strategy because a multi-cup unit functions as a single element. With blocks, a simple bridge (Fig. 6) has this same structural characteristic; the superordinate block functions in relation to a unit

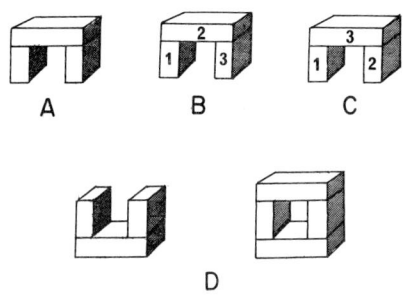

Fig. 6. The block bridge and strategies for constructing it.
A, Bridge. B, Chain method: 1 goes on the table, 2 touches 1, 3 touches 2. C, Hierarchical method: 1 goes on the table, 2 goes on the table, 3 touches 1 and 2. D, Attempts to reduce degrees of freedom.

composed of the two subordinate blocks. There have been many reports that children are able to construct bridges only after stacks and rows (e.g. Cattell, 1940; Forman, 1975). There are in fact two methods of constructing the bridge. One is a chain method (Fig. 6) in which the end of each block becomes the point of departure for the next block. The other is a hierarchical method in which the two support blocks are placed first, one at a time, and then linked by the superordinate bridge block. In this second method the two support blocks function as a subassembly in relation to the bridge block. If the child is gradually acquiring a capacity to construct added hierarchical complexity, then this chain strategy should be the first one used to construct a bridge, exactly what Forman (personal communication, 1974) finds. Note that the younger children who use the chain method rather than the hierarchical method are in effect choosing added *manipulative* complexity (the problem of balancing or securing the bridge block) in order to avoid added *cognitive* complexity (hierarchical organization).

Another quality of the chain strategy is that it reduces the degrees of freedom for placement of the next block. Degrees of freedom is a concept developed by Bernstein (1967) and Bruner (1971) to describe the early stages in the acquisition of motor skills. Ninio and Lieblich (1976) have adapted this concept for a representational task involving drawing. If an earlier line can be used to establish a point of departure for the succeeding line, then, according to Ninio and Lieblich, the number of degrees of freedom are minimized. The chain strategy (Fig. 6) conforms to this requirement whereas the superordinate strategy does not. Hubner and Greenfield (unpublished data) had children aged 3 to 6 copy a block bridge. The strategy of some of the children who failed is most instructive here. Figure 6 presents two instances in which the children appear to be making an attempt to minimize degrees of freedom by using the first block to define points of departure for later blocks. These children not only minimize degrees of freedom; they also avoid the manipulative complications of the chain strategy introduced by the forces of gravity. It is this adaptation to gravity which leads them astray. What these two children (ages 3 and 4) appear to be doing is using a base block to determine the position of the two uprights. Among the children who successfully complete the bridge, the overwhelming preference is for the hierarchical method. Using Ninio and Lieblich's way of computing degrees of freedom, the hierarchical method presents two degrees of freedom for placement of the second (support) block. (This calculation is based on the fact that the block's position is determined in one dimension by the table surface, but is indeterminate in the other two dimensions.) This contrasts with zero degrees of freedom for placement of the second block in the chain method, for the first block determines the second block's position in all three dimensions. (Under either method, there are zero degrees of freedom for the third block.)

Thus, there is a development from lesser to greater hierarchical structure, from fewer to more degrees of freedom. In terms of possible linguistic parallels, one can think in terms of the linguistic descriptions of the construction process presented in Fig. 6. One thing to note is that the hierarchical method involves a compound structure (compound object, to be exact) whereas the chain method does not. Although one would need to know more about the development of discourse structures in children's language to know for sure which linguistic description would have developmental priority, existing knowledge would indicate that a child would be able to produce a series of simple sentences before producing a compound sentence. Hence, there is reason to believe that the development of alternative strategies for construction of a block structure—the bridge in this case—mirrors the development of corresponding forms in language.

THE DEVELOPMENT OF COMPLEX
HIERARCHICAL ORGANIZATION

Hierarchy is organization by levels, in which lower level units combine to form higher level ones. The subassembly constructions with cups, or nuts, bolts and boards are examples of simple hierarchical structure, as is the arch constructed of blocks. Language is hierarchically organized in many ways. For instance phonemes combine to form morphemes and morphemes combine to form sentences. In language development, hierarchical structure proceeds from lesser to greater complexity in a number of different ways. One simple illustration is the fact that the earliest phonological units precede the first morphological ones developmentally, which, in turn, precede the first syntactic ones. Put non-technically: babbling precedes the first word, while single-word utterances precede the first sentential word combinations. Levels of hierarchy of course go even further in language: for instance, simple sentences precede compound ones, as has already been mentioned. The point is that language structure encompasses many levels of hierarchy and that the capacity to deal with progressively greater hierarchical complexity appears to develop with age. Thus far I have traced the emergence of the ability to construct simple sorts of hierarchical structures with a number of different kinds of material. Now, however, I should like to turn to the development of more complex types of hierarchical structure.

Complex Hierarchies in Block Construction

Would the ability to create hierarchical structure develop systematically from lesser to greater complexity in construction activity as well as language? The study with Hubner was designed to answer this question by observing how children of different ages (from 3 to 6) reproduced three block models varying in hierarchical complexity. The models are shown at the top of Fig. 7. Model I is of course the simplest—the now familiar arch consisting of two subordinate blocks joined by a superordinate block. Model II is of greater complexity: a hierarchy of hierarchies in which two subordinate arches, each a hierarchy in itself, is joined by a superordinate arch. Finally, model III on the right has the greatest hierarchical complexity of all, for it consists basically of two model IIs (although the arches differ in orientation) joined by a superordinate arch.

Systematic development of hierarchical complexity was manifest in a number of ways. In the first place, there was a developmental progression

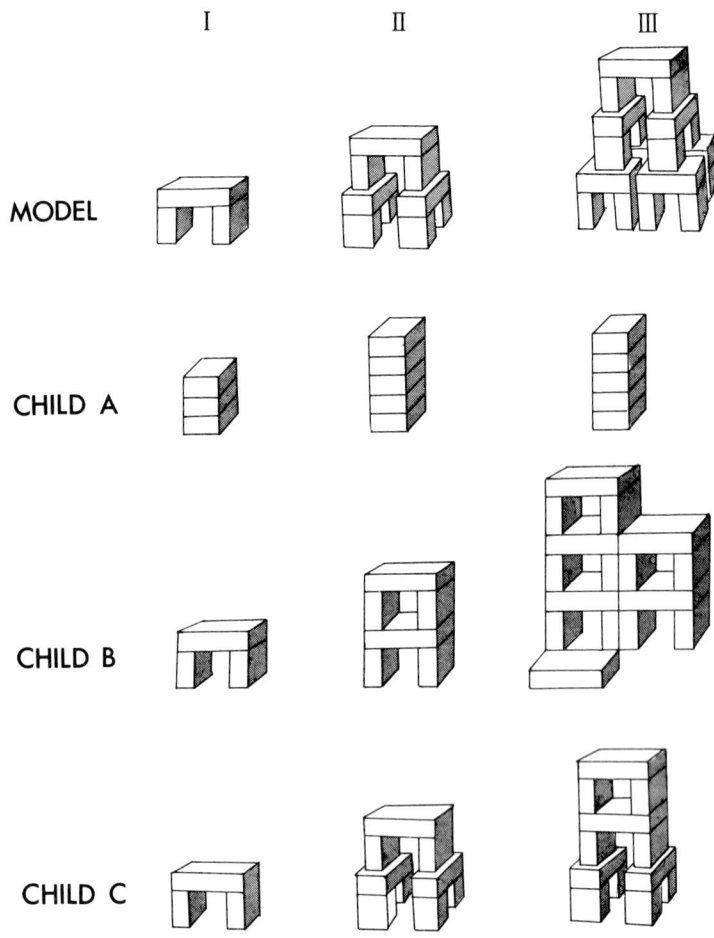

Fig. 7. Block models, three stages of hierarchical development.

from model I to model II to model III. Thus, with one exception, all children who successfully copied model III, the most complex, also successfully copied model II and model I; while all children who successfully copied model II also succeeded with model I. The older the child, the more models successfully completed. Thus, 3-year-olds were, at best, able to complete only model I accurately; the limit of 4-year-old competence was model II; for 5-year-olds it was III; but not until age 6½ could virtually all children complete all three models perfectly.

Another aspect of the systematic development of hierarchical organization was the internal consistency of each child in his or her qualitative approach to different models. The three bottom rows in Fig. 7 illustrate this point with three subjects' constructions. Child A is unable to achieve the hierarchical organization required for even a single arch. Note the consistent structural approach across all three models, partially preserving the feature of relative height. Single arches are the limit to the second child's ability to organize hierarchically. Thus, this child accurately reproduces model I, but is unable to reproduce the basic structure of models II and III. Note that although this child correctly increases the number of arches and the height of each successive model, she is unable to achieve that degree of hierarchical complexity whereby subordinate arches are united by a superordinate one. Because this child shows herself able to construct as many as five arches at a time, she also illustrates the point that, psychologically, hierarchical organization is not merely a question of producing more constituent elements, but also involves an understanding of the *relations* among these elements, specifically hierarchical integration of lower order units. The third child is able to complete models I and II, but not III. Note that his approximation to model III involves the same degree of hierarchical diversification or complexity as model II. His version of III differs from II in a repetition of the top bridging arch; the feature of relative height has been maintained without the feature of hierarchical diversification. This kind of consistency provides evidence that this task is tapping underlying structural competence rather than more superficial and variable aspects of performance. These three childrens' constructions also show that hierarchical complexity is a psychologically meaningful variable.

Generality of Hierarchical Development

Is the ability to construct a certain degree of hierarchical complexity a general one which can be applied to various tasks? A study with Schneider (Greenfield and Schneider, in press), investigated this ability with another set of materials. Children aged 3 to 11 were asked to reproduce a mobile made of plastic construction straws, shown schematically in Fig. 8. In terms of formal structure, the mobile resembles block model II, the arch-of-arches, with the addition of a second level in each of the two arches. Children's attempts to reproduce the mobile revealed a number of parallels to the development of hierarchical structure in the block tasks. Just as 3-year-olds were unable to complete block model II, the double-branched arch-of-arches, they were generally unable to create a double branched mobile. In terms of hierarchical structures, the most complex constructed by a 3-year-old was a simple arch (see Fig. 9). Another parallel stems from the fact that 4-year-olds often built reiterative structures in chainlike fashion (see Fig. 9) but almost never made a double branching structure. Recall that in the block construction task children who could not configure arches in a hierarchical branching structure were able to repeat them in linear arrangement (Fig. 7,

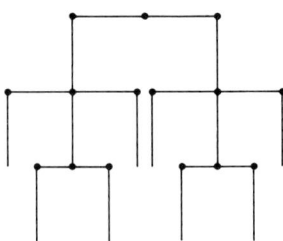

Fig. 8. Mobile model.

Child B). Five-year-olds, able to reproduce a double-branched arch-of-arches with blocks, usually created the corresponding mobile structure—a two-branched hierarchy with but a single level in each branch. These are shown in Fig. 9. Thus, both materials revealed that the ability to construct a chain structure precedes the ability to use the same elements in a hierarchical tree structure. The 6-year-olds added the second level, correctly reproducing the model for the most part; this group is not directly comparable to the 6-year-olds in the block construction study because block model III involved more branching. Yet parallel stages at particular ages with the two materials are striking as far as the tasks permit comparison.

Children's spontaneous drawings also show structural development in the direction of greater hierarchical complexity (Kellogg, 1969; Alaniz, 1973). First the child draws single lines (scribbles). Next these lines are combined to form a diagram. Finally, diagrams are combined two or three at a time (combines and aggregates). Examples of each stage are shown in Fig. 10. Thus, the developmental progression in spontaneous drawing is from individual elements to combination of elements to "combinations of combinations"—progressively more complex hierarchical organization. The evidence indicates that stages of hierarchical complexity may indeed have some generality across materials and superficial differences in task structure.

There is other evidence that confirms this point. Wood and Ross (1972) investigated the development of construction routines for assembling a hierarchically structured puzzle toy consisting of five pyramidal levels. Each of the first four was constructed by joining two subunits, consisting in turn of

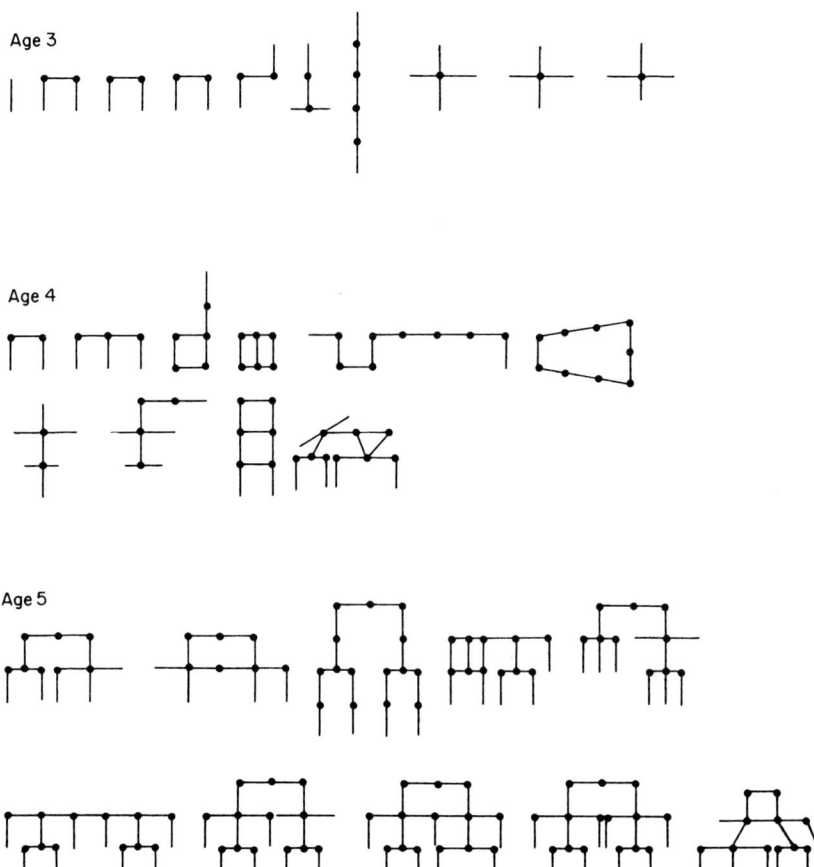

Fig. 9. Mobiles constructed at ages of 3, 4 and 5. If a child constructed two or more separate structures, his or her most complex one is shown in the figure.

two individual pieces. The hierarchical structure required by this puzzle developed gradually with age. The results presented support the notion that development involves increasingly complex hierarchical organization. Forman *et al.* (1973) found evidence of this same type of development using a jigsaw puzzle task.

A study by Miller *et al.* (1970) demonstrates that the principle of increasing hierarchization could account for development in another cognitive domain. Children in grades 1 to 6 were asked to describe cartoon-like drawings that differed in whether or not recursive thought was pictured and in the number of such hierarchical embeddings. Fewest errors appeared on the simplest type of embedding: a boy thinking of people, X and Y; the most errors on the most complex type: a boy thinking that X is thinking of Y thinking of Z. The results suggested a developmental progression in the ability to deal with embedded or recursive thought.

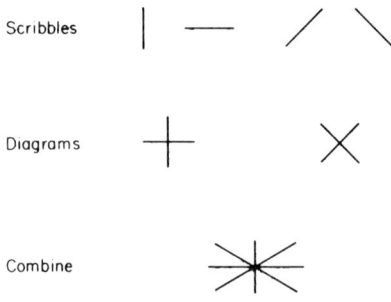

Scribbles

Diagrams

Combine

Fig. 10. Three stages in children's drawing.

Theoretical Views

These empirical studies illustrate the general principle formulated by H. Werner (1948) that developmental change is characterized by increasing differentiation and hierarchical integration—i.e. increasingly complex hierarchical organization. Newell *et al.* (1958) and Miller *et al.* (1960) took hierarchical structure as central to their analyses of the organization of behavior. Newell *et al.* were using computers to simulate adult problem solving, while Miller, *et al.* were concerned with many levels of behavior, from reflexes to motor skills to language. Neither group dealt with the ontogenetic development of these hierarchies. Miller and his colleagues were, however, concerned with the microdevelopment of hierarchical structure as adult learners acquired new motor skills.

Bruner (1968; Bruner and Bruner, 1968) has recently put forth evidence for an ontogenetic theory of skill involving progressive hierachical complexity. Perfection of individual acts paves the way for their inclusion in a larger sequence of skilled activity. Bruner bases his ideas in part on Lashley (1951). Lashley rejected associationistic chaining in favor of syntax as a basis for the organization of serial skilled action. Our analysis in contrast investigates chaining and syntax (more complex hierarchical organization) as two points in a developmental progression.

THE SURFACE STRUCTURE OF ACTION:
ORDER OF ELEMENTS

It is necessary to make a distinction between variations in object combination which yield different structures and those which do not. The former are analogous to semantic relations—the base structure of language; the latter to the temporal ordering of words—the surface structure of language. Surface structure can be thought of as the temporally ordered syntactic means used to realize semantic or meaning relations that comprise deep structure.

The Surface Structures of a Line Drawing

The concept of the development of alternative surface, or real-time realizations of a given deep structure can be applied to line drawing, as a study by Ninio and Lieblich (1976) shows. They had children aged 3;11 to 4;10 copy an inverted T form. Fig. 11 shows an example of each of the three strategies

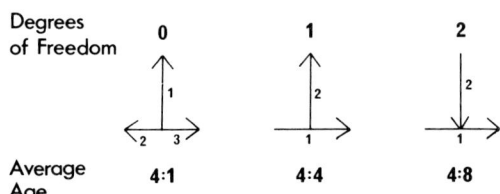

Fig. 11. Three strategies for drawing an inverted T.

which can be used to copy the design successfully. Again, degrees of freedom assess the number of dimensions that need to be mentally represented in order to determine the point of departure of all lines after the first one. The strategy shown at the far left of Fig. 11 has zero degrees of freedom because one end of line No. 1 specifies the point of departure for all subsequent lines; hence, mental representation of the point of departure is not required. As predicted, this strategy is most frequent among the youngest children. The middle strategy has one degree of freedom because the point of departure of the second line is specified in one dimension (vertical) but not the other (horizontal); this strategy is the next one to develop. Note that in purely *motor* terms this strategy is simpler than the developmentally prior one: it involves only two straight lines going in two directions, whereas the other involves three. Thus construction or representational strategies cannot be reduced to a matter of motor skill. Once again a more complex motor pattern is used before a simpler one when it achieves greater *cognitive* simplicity.

The last method of drawing the inverted T is exemplified at the far right of Fig. 5; this is a variant of the "adult" way. This method has two degrees of freedom because the child must use mental representation to specify both dimensions of the point of departure of the second stroke. If one assumes that children are becoming more skilled with age, then this progression of strategies shows that the degrees of freedom for motor movements expand as proficiency increases. (Vereeken (1961, pp. 104-105) has noted related phenomena in the development of the cross figure in children's drawing.)

Surface Realizations for Building a Tree Structure

This same pattern of development emerges if we examine strategies for successfully replicating the mobile, shown in Fig. 8. Because 6-year-olds were the youngest group generally able to succeed with this task, we looked at the development of strategies between 6 and 11, the oldest age in our sample.

The striking feature of the typical 6-year-old strategy was that it involved starting at the bottom of the mobile and working upwards. Six out of ten used this chain strategy, working up one side, across the top, and down the other side. Specific examples are shown at the top of Fig. 12. The dominant starting point for the older three groups was the superordinate connecting level. This starting point implies that the mobile is being conceptually organized as a hierarchy—in terms of the superordinate and subordinate parts. The chain strategy, in contrast, does not—it violates hierarchical organization by failing to progress systematically either from subordinate to superordinate parts or vice versa. Hence our examination of strategy reveals one additional stage after age 6 in the development of hierarchical organization: awareness of the total hierarchical structure at age 7. Vereeken (1961) considers this awareness of the structure of the whole to mark an operational level in the development of spatial representation: When the child constructs a part, he or she remains aware of the total structure of which it forms a component part.

The chain strategy also involves fewer degrees of freedom than a strategy that starts at the top of the mobile, for the chain method restricts placement of the next straw to a single branch, whereas a superordinate strategy does not. Thus, progression from chain to superordinate organization parallels the progression in arch-building methods, but at a more complex level of hierarchical structure.

Another surface structure variable is interruption. Subordinate clauses (embedding) in language can result in the interruption of one constituent unit by another. For example, compare these two sentences.

1. *The man is eating the fish.*
2. *The man is wearing a hat.*

with a third:

3. *The man wearing a hat is eating the fish.*

Sentence 3 contains the underlying propositions of 1 and 2; but the transformation by which sentence 2 has been embedded in sentence 1 has left an interrupted constituent in the surface structure. That is, *The man is*

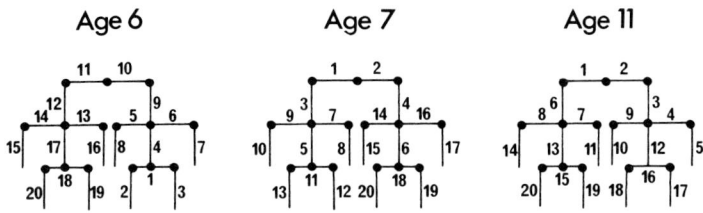

Fig. 12. Typical strategies for constructing a mobile at different ages.

eating the fish is interrupted after *man* by the phrase *wearing a hat*. Psycholinguistic research has indicated that interrupted forms are more difficult to process than uninterrupted ones (Bever, 1970). The reason posited for this is tht interrupted forms increase memory load because the first constituent must be stored while producing or processing the second so that it may be later completed. In the process of acquiring language, moreover, younger children avoid interrupted forms more than do older ones.

The principle of interruption operates at the surface structure level in language. Interrupted vs. non-interrupted sentences differ in their temporal relationships between units, not necessarily in their underlying semantic relationships. Analogous to language, interruption in action was considered to be a surface structure dimension.

The mobile construction task already described also explored whether interrupted strategies would also develop with age in the domain of construction activity. Conceiving of the mobile's structure in terms of its constituent parts—branches and levels—we conceptualized strategies as differing in the degree to which these constituent parts would be interrupted. Our hypothesis that strategies would become increasingly interrupted with age was confirmed by the results. In addition to the chain strategy of the 6-year-olds, Fig. 12 shows two different degrees of interruption common in the

7- and 11-year-olds. Note that in the two younger groups each constituent part—superordinate level, branch, and within-branch tier—is completed before going on to the next constituent unit. This is not true for the 11-year-old, who often interrupts one constituent to begin another and then comes back to complete the first one. We developed a measure of how much interruption occurred by quantifying the extent to which children skipped from one part of the structure to another in the construction process. This measure revealed a steady increase in degree of interruptedness at each successive age level from 6 to 11 (except that 7- and 9-year-olds did not differ from each other).

An auxiliary procedure uncovered a tendency for children to avoid interrupted strategies even though capable of them: after a child had completed the mobile, he or she was asked to do it a "harder" way and then given a demonstration of a maximally interrupted strategy if necessary. Many of the older children were, when probed in this way, able to construct the mobile using a more interrupted strategy than they had preferred in their original construction. In summary, we found that competence in using interrupted strategies increases with age, but use of less interrupted forms persists even among the oldest children.

Generality in the Development of Interrupted Strategies

Again, though, the question of the generality of this principle in the development of construction activity presents itself. Performance with another set of materials—the nuts, bolts, blocks and sticks described before—sheds light on this question (Goodson and Greenfield, 1975). Children from 3 to 6 were asked to construct a bench (with the model present) using methods differing in interruptedness. The two methods are shown in Fig. 13. A difference in the order in which pieces are combined introduces interruption into the second strategy: the child begins one side or subunit of the bench then leaves it to work on the other side. In the end, he or she must remember to return to the first side to complete it. This process is depicted in the right column of Fig. 13; Step 2 shows the point of interruption. Subassembly with Interruption contrasts with Simple Subassembly, shown in the left column of the figure. In that method, one side or subunit (subassembly) of the bench is completed (Step 3) before the second one is begun. Although more children were able to complete the bench without interrupting a subassembly than with interruption, this difference was slight. There was, however, a decided preference for the uninterrupted method: 18 out of the 21 children who showed themselves capable of both methods used the less interrupted rather than the interrupted one spontaneously.* Thus, although there was less developmental lag between competence with the uninterrupted and interrupted methods of constructing the bench than there had been with the mobile, the tendency to use an uninterrupted strategy, even when capable of using an interrupted method, manifested itself just as strongly.

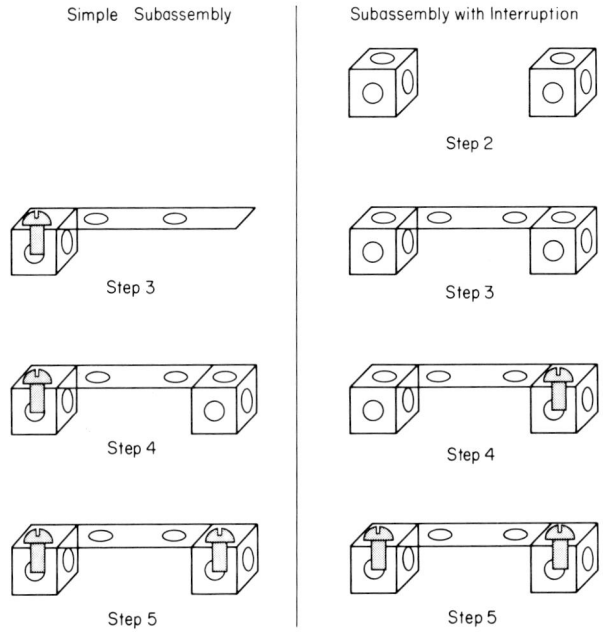

Fig. 13. Two strategies for constructing a bench.

It is also possible to look at the bench as a complex sort of arch. Forman (personal communication, 1974) points out that the simple subassembly method resembles the chain method of constructing a block arch, while the subassembly with interruption resembles the hierarchical method. These parallels stem from the fact that the bench is, in fact, an arch with complex rather than simple supports. Just as the chain method for building the arch minimizes degrees of freedom, so does the uninterrupted subassembly method for building the bench. The developmental sequence is parallel in both cases: degrees of freedom are minimized at the initial stages of mastery. Here interruptedness is equivalent to degrees of freedom but at a higher level of hierarchical complexity.

*Again, children were initially shown a completed model. If they used one of the two possible strategies for completing it, then the alternative method was modeled for them and they were asked to copy it. The children who demonstrated a capacity to use both methods ranged in age from 2;11 upwards.

By looking at methods for building the more complex block structures, models II and III (Fig. 7), it is possible to examine the development toward expanded degrees of freedom at this more complex level. The progression is very clear for model II, the arch-of-arches. The youngest children to succeed in building it are 4 years old. Almost all of these children use a method in which each arch is completed before a later one is begun (Fig. 14). Most of the older children (5 and 6½) in contrast use a layer-by-layer method (Fig. 14) in which both bottom arches are begun before either is completed. It is possible to argue that the layer-by-layer method is not more interrupted; rather the child is representing the structure in terms of different units:

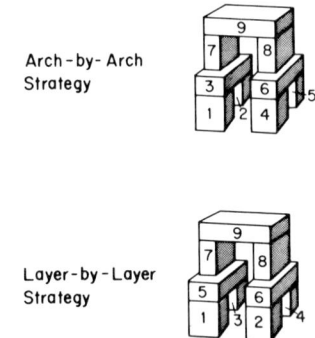

Arch-by-Arch
Strategy

Layer-by-Layer
Strategy

Fig. 14. Two strategies for constructing an arch-of-arches.

layers rather than arches. If, however, one thinks in terms of degrees of freedom rather than interruption, then it is clear that the layer-by-layer method creates more degrees of freedom than the arch-by-arch method.

The force of gravity is a factor in block models whereas it is not in building the mobile, for the children lay out and connect the straws on a table top while it is in process of construction. The gravity constraint on block construction produces a different sort of hierarchically organized construction method with the two materials: (1) gravity prevents the chain method, used by 6-year-olds to build the mobile, from being applied to the more complex block models; (2) older children build the straw mobile from the highest hierarchical level down, whereas everyone must build the block models from the ground up. Hence, the construction of representational strategies is not a given; rather it takes place through the interaction of the child's cognitive capacities with the real possibilities of the physical world. Nevertheless, across a wide variety of materials it appears that competence with interrupted strategies develops with age, and that there is a tendency to avoid interrupted strategies even when such competence has already developed. This course is paralleled in language development. Whereas children may comprehend interrupted forms almost as well as uninterrupted ones (Sheldon, 1973), they avoid them where possible in production (e.g. Slobin and Welsh, 1973).

A THEORETICAL PERSPECTIVE: STRUCTURALISM

Implicit in the foregoing discussion of structural parallels between language and action in development is the theoretical perspective of structuralism. Piaget, in his book *Structuralism* (1971), states that it is the construction of relations among constituent elements that is basic to a structure. In describing the development of construction activity in different media, I have used the external physical structures as an index to cognitive structure. Just as the physical structure emerges gradually, through the construction process, so mental structure is constructed out of the child's potential organizational capabilities in interaction with requirements of the task and the possibilities of the medium.

Piaget contrasts "*structures* and *aggregates*, the former being wholes, the latter composites formed by elements that are independent of the complexes into which they enter" (1971, p. 7). It is this quality of wholeness that makes a structural perspective necessary for the psychological analysis of complex behavior. The physical organization of the arch cannot be reduced to an aggregate of three blocks; nor can the arch-of-arches be reduced to an aggregate of three arches (see Fig. 7).

These facts imply that the mental organization needed to produce the arch cannot be reduced to that required for an aggregate of blocks. Similarly, the mental organization needed to build the more complex structure cannot be reduced to that required for the simpler. In order to analyse the cognitive organization required in each case, it is necessary to analyse the inter-relations of elements and specify them for that particular structure. Although simpler structures may be a subsystem of more complex ones, complex structures cannot be extrapolated from simpler ones; the interrelations of the component subsystems remain unspecified. Similarly, although each block model has common elements and even common substructures with the other models, the more complex ones are more than aggregates of the simpler. The evidence from our study of children's block building shows that an ability to construct aggregates of constituent elements is not sufficient to construct a complex hierarchical model.

A fundamental assumption of behaviorism is that the analysis of simple behavior leads to an understanding of complex behavior, for complex behavior is seen as an additive function of its simple components. Structuralism, in effect, says the reverse: analysis of a complex behavior may imply understanding of its simpler subsystems, but understanding the subsystems or components is not sufficient to understand the complex behavior of which they form a part. A corollary of this is that one cannot understand a simple element of behavior (construction behavior in this case) without understanding its role in the total structure. It is for this reason that replication of models is a good method for studying structural development. The model provides definition of the "whole" in relation to which the child's partial contruction can be understood, not in terms of success or failure but structurally. Because an imitation reflects the cognitive organization of the imitator as much as the structure of the model (Piaget, 1954), it is an excellent experimental tool for the study of structural development.

The block construction task provides evidence that "parts" can be analyzed, psychologically, only in relation to the "wholes" of which they are components. No understanding of the process of arch construction could lead to an understanding of why a child can build individual arches, but cannot place one so that it bridges two previously constructed arches. The behavioristic assumption that the whole is equal to the sum of its parts has been one of the most resistant to change in American psychology and still permeates much of American cognitive psychology. The approach in this chapter has not been to talk of vague "wholes" in the manner of gestalt psychology but to analyse the nature of relations among the parts.

Piaget (1970) sees behavior of the sensori-motor period as containing three general structural elements—*order* relations, *subordination schemes*, and *correspondences*. Each type of structural element has come into play in what has preceded—*order* relates to what I have called the surface structure of action, *subordination* to its hierarchical organization, and *correspondence* to the enactive recognition of similarity. This latter, touched upon only briefly, is crucial to the child's ability to replicate a model, for the child must of course recognize points of correspondence between the model and her own attempt. Correspondence is key to the whole notion of representation and the ability of a structure in one medium to stand for a structure in another.

Goodnow and Levine (1973) first suggested that design copying could be described in terms of grammatical rules. While this was a valuable contribution to theory, Ninio and Lieblich (1976) point out that Goodnow and Levine's ordering rules failed to take into account deep structure, the overall structure of the design being copied (semantic structure in their terminology), and therefore led to errors. Goodnow and Levine tried to develop ordering rules for lines (e.g. start at left and drawn to the right; start at top and draw downwards) that would hold across designs with different structural characteristics. Clearly the principles behind the three strategies shown in Fig. 11 would lead to different directions of movement with, for example, different orientations of the T or with a ⌊＿⌋ design. Goodnow and Levine were considering surface structure, the temporal order of elements, without taking into account the deep structure from which they were generated.

The conceptualization of surface and deep structure in action bears a close relation to the difference between aggregates and structures. Surface structure is very close to an aggregate in that elements are produced one at a time in a linear sequence. The concept of base structure implies that, though production requires linear temporal ordering of individual elements, this ordering cannot be understood without knowledge of the underlying semantic structure from which it was generated. The *aggregate* or chain of elements in temporal production is a function of the *structure* which is being brought into existence. The possibility of alternative surface realizations of a given base structure marks cognitive reversibility in Vereeken's (1961) extension of Piaget to construction activity. Such reversibility is one of the hallmarks of an operational level.

Because structures are systems of relations, they can apply to different content areas. Thus, language and action, two separate domains, can be governed in their function and development by the same organizational principles. The level of analogy suggested is that of structural principles operating in both language and action, but not originating in either, which determine relative cognitive complexity within each domain. An attempt was made to demonstrate that inter-element relationships previously described for language also apply to construction in different media without assuming equivalence of the individual elements across domains. The pieces or lines used in construction are not considered to be analogous to specific words in sentences, nor are the final products assumed to be equivalent to specific sentences or linguistic structures.

Principles of structural organization in development must represent neural capacities which generate linguistic behavior, as well as behavior in other modes. Such a formulation seems to fit neural facts like the specificity of various cerebral brain areas, connections between the hemispheres, and Pribram's (1971) hypothesis that the brain functions like a hologram. From the point of view of behavior, this type of general, and therefore amodal, organization on the neural level is implied by the earliest infant behavior (Bower, 1974), early language development (Greenfield and Smith, 1976) and the co-ordination of language and action in adult behavior.

A study was carried out to see if the isomorphism between language structures and action structures identified for the combination of seriated

cups (Fig. 3) was in fact used by adults to carry out verbal commands
(Greenfield and Westerman, in press). Participants were given commands
such as are shown in Fig. 15. Instructions having the form of an embedded
sentence in fact generally led to the subassembly strategy as shown in the
bottom of Fig. 15, while instructions having the form of a conjoined sentence
often led to some form of the pot strategy (top of Fig. 15). The exact
sentences are shown in Fig. 16. Another finding was that explicit syntactic
embedding (the "complex" forms in the embedded sentences of Fig. 16)

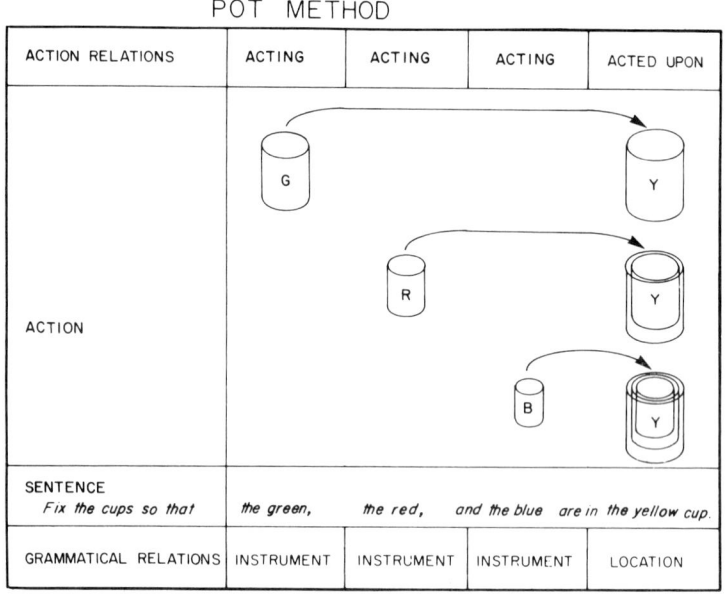

Fig. 15.

EMBEDDED SENTENCES

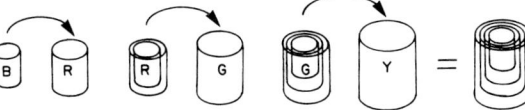

PAIR I

SIMPLEX ... *blue is in red, red is in green, green is in yellow.*

COMPLEX ... *blue is in red, which is in green, which is in yellow.*

SERIATED

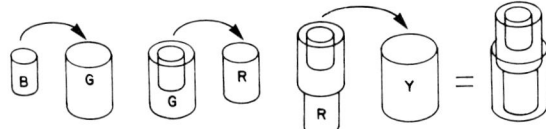

PAIR II

SIMPLEX ... *blue is in green, green is on red, red is in yellow.*

COMPLEX ... *blue is in green, which is on red, which is in yellow.*

NONSERIATED

CONJOINED SENTENCES

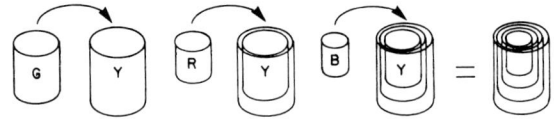

PAIR III

SIMPLEX ... *green is in yellow, red is in yellow, blue is in yellow.*

COMPLEX ... *the green, the red, and the blue are in the yellow cup.*

SERIATED

PAIR IV

SIMPLEX ... *blue is in yellow, red is in yellow, green is in yellow.*

COMPLEX ... *the blue, the red, and the green are in the yellow cup.*

NONSERIATED

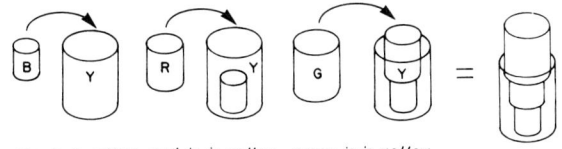

PAIR V

SIMPLEX ... *blue is in yellow, green is in yellow, red is in yellow.*

COMPLEX ... *the blue, the green, and the red are in the yellow cup.*

NONSERIATED

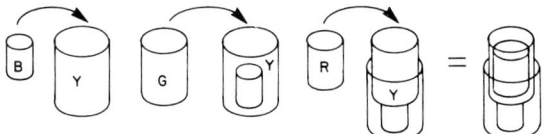

PAIR VI

SIMPLEX ... *green is on red, yellow is on red, blue is on red.*

COMPLEX ... *the green, the yellow, and the blue are on the red cup.*

NONSERIATED

Fig. 16.

facilitated processing of the commands (i.e. reduced response time) where the course of action was not obvious from non-verbal aspects of the situation (specifically, pair II where the verbal command required the person to violate the seriated structure of the cups in a specific way). These findings seem to indicate that the common organization of language and action has discernible behavioral consequences in the co-ordination of the two modes in adult behavior.

This theoretical formulation has been in terms of common structural features in more than one domain rather than specific parallels between sentences and action patterns. A major reason for this is that, while any two domains may have similar principles of operation, the actual combinatorial possibilities may be quite different due to design features of the two media.

For instance, with the construction of the mobile, an analogue to the most interrupted strategies (Age 11, in Fig. 12) could never occur in language because it would involve shifting back and forth several times between clauses, sometimes after but a single word! The more complex the behavior the more this sort of divergence between media and modes seems to occur. Thus, parallel sentences could be constructed for the cup strategies and the single arch, but not for the more complex block constructions. Hence it seems that an approach to the relationships between language and action in terms of structural principles rather than specific sentence parallels will ultimately prove applicable to much wider ranges of behavior.

Because these principles of cognitive organization are so general they guide development over and over again in many specific acquisitions. For instance, hierarchy in language has many different meanings and, at different times, many different developmental increases in hierarchical complexity occur. It is the same for action. Thus subassembly with role change occurred at age 3 with seriated cups (Greenfield et al., 1972) and at age 6 in using nuts and bolts to build a propeller (Goodson and Greenfield, 1975). What is common in both contexts, however, is the structural progression of activity within that particular context: from a piling or pot method to a subassembly strategy.

What we can conclude is that in so far as the character of the materials permits the expression of the same strategies in two different contexts, the progression of stages will be the same, although often occurring at different times. This would be an example of horizontal décalage as Piaget defined it: a child operating at different levels of the same sequence of cognitive development with different materials, due to different tasks. As Fischer (1974) has pointed out, Piaget's notion of the construction of cognitive structures (as opposed to simple preformation) implies that such a developmental process occurs with each new problem. Pre-existing abilities, themselves a product of past interaction of maturational level and problems presented by the environment, are of course a limiting factor, both qualitatively and quantitatively in this construction process. Thus, *décalage* is to be expected. The more similar two problems, the more level of skill with one will predict performance with another. Although action in different modes and media may rest on the same basic organizational capacities, each mode and medium also has its own distinctive properties (Olson, 1970). For instance, speaking demands certain vocal skills while building with blocks demands certain manual skills. Speaking also requires a certain representational level not necessary for construction activity. In so far as these requirements vary among modes and media, the rate and timing of development in one would not necessarily be the same as in another. The rate of structural development in a particular medium would vary as a function of experience with its particular features (e.g. opportunities for manipulative activity) as well as experience in using the general organizational skills that are the focus of this chapter. Hence, correlations between behavioral indices of structural development in two domains, e.g. grammar and blockbuilding, are not presupposed or predicted by language-action parallels.

EDUCATIONAL IMPLICATIONS

Much current theory and practice in early education stresses children learning through spontaneous interaction with materials. But what exactly do children learn from such interaction? The developmental sequences described provide a tool for assessing where, developmentally, a child is with her use of particular materials. Although many of the findings reported have emerged from structured situations in which the child was given a model to imitate or replicate, the structural descriptions can now be used to analyse children's *spontaneous* play. Knowledge of developmental stages in the use of representational media can also provide a basis for testing various ways of presenting materials: is a model a stimulus or a damper for the child's spontaneous activity with different materials? What role do verbal instructions have? And so forth. An understanding of structural stages can, in addition, provide a basis for measuring creativity: not only originality, but also structural level can be taken into account in defining the creative use of different media. For the first time there exist conceptual tools for the psychologist to accord as much cognitive significance to children's everyday play activities as children do themselves.

Section 6

Symbols and Society

16

Social Relations and Early Language

DEREK EDWARDS

Loughborough University, England

This chapter examines aspects of the social-relational basis of early language development in children. Language develops in a richly social-relational context, and this is no passive context serving merely to provide appropriate (grammatical) linguistic input to some language acquisition device. Rather, the "context" is itself the central nexus of interactions, meanings and messages which determines the semantic and pragmatic nature of children's early language. Moreover, we are concerned not merely with the "situational context" of particular individual utterances, as recorded by an outside observer. The context is cognitive- and social-psychological; it is the child's own growing social-relational competence, involving some implicit understanding of the structure and function of interactions and messages in which she or he is involved. The context of early language development is the context as perceived and interpreted by the child—the child's own understanding of his world and of his social relationships.

Thus, early social relations structure early language only through the mediation of the child's own cognitions. Adults' use of language becomes children's use of language only via the child's processes of comprehension cf. McNeill, 1966a; MacNamara, 1972) and these processes involve both knowledge of the structure and workings of the physical world, and also competence in the kinds of face-to-face social relationships with adults in which adults constantly use language to express meanings and messages (Edwards, 1973; in press). Clearly, in order to understand such processes, we need to have records which describe in some detail the situational and communicational contexts of early language, not only for each isolated utterance but for a variety of similar utterances, and indeed for interactions in which the child may utter nothing recognizably linguistic, and we need to consider the kinds of meanings that the child does not express as well as those that he does. Moreover, we have to consider the language and behaviour of those with whom the child interacts, and how and by whom such interactions are structured and initiated. All of these data are essential to our understanding of how children first come to express meanings through language.

In the first three sections below we shall discuss three kinds of social relationships in which early linguistic meanings are forged: those involving requests (soliciting the agency of others), constraints on actions (involving physical constraints and social prohibitions on the child's own agency), and what Bruner (1976) describes as the co-ordination of joint activities involving mutual direction of attention. These three areas overlap, and the latter is in principle especially large, to some extent superordinate to the others.

The discussion of early language in terms of the child's involvement in these three kinds of social relationship enriches our understanding of what early utterances might really mean. Expressions which we shall discuss in terms of requests and constraints were described by Guillaume (1927) as

> the language of the will . . . that is, the verbal element in reactions of negation (rejection of caretaking, of objects, aversion to certain activities or attentions) and positive reactions of desire (desire for an object, an action, its continuation or recurrence) (translated by Bloom, 1973, p. 96 fn).

Guillaume describes these meanings psychologically, indeed experientially, as expressions of "the will". In fact, we shall see that they are basically social-psychological, formed out of and communicating messages within the socializing nexus of interpersonal child-caretaker relations. Indeed, we shall argue that the child's first linguistic expressions of "wanting" are not descriptions of any experiential state of desiring, but rather are requests for others to perform actions. Constraints and prohibitions involve the child's burgeoning selfhood in relation to others; the child is becoming a socialized and individuated person, with a growing understanding of the kinds of things he may and may not do, the extent of his freedom of action and his powers to impose constraints on others; such processes underlie early language.

Brown (1956) described the procedure whereby children learn from adults the names of things, as "the Original Word Game". Again, we shall examine the richness of such games in terms of interaction, meanings and messages, and show how they go well beyond the mere learning of object labels. They are part of a very broad range of joint activities, often ostensibly playful, in which mother and child locate, name and describe aspects of the world around them (Bruner, 1976).

JOINT ORIENTATIONS

In this section we examine how the familiar early vocabulary and syntax of deixis and reference, including demonstratives, object labels, locative questions, ostensibly experiential "verbs" such as *see* and *look*, and also the sequencing of dialogue itself, obtain their conversational, semantic and pragmatic natures from the child's competence in the co-ordinated and reciprocal direction of each other's attention and actions which she and her mother have been developing together since birth.

By the time children come to utter their first linguistic messages, generally by 18 months of age, they have already developed the sort of knowledge of the nature and workings of their immediate physical world which is prerequisite to their understanding how language codes, classifies and describes that world (Edwards, 1973). They will also have developed a sophisticated pre-linguistic competence in face-to-face communication with their caretakers, in such contexts as playing with toys, looking at pictures, as well as the more obvious foci of early socialization (feeding, toilet training, etc.). While the child is still unable to produce words and sentences, the mother nevertheless continually talks to her child, integrating her words and meanings with the pattern of interaction and with the child's structured behaviour *vis-à-vis* objects of mutual attention. Children learn language in such interactions through their comprehension of the semantic and pragmatic functions served by the adults' words.

Part of what is learned is simply the sequencing of vocalizations in dialogue, even in the absence of meaningful verbal communication. For example, Mark (Mk) at 17½ months, still unable to utter a single clear word, initiates and conducts a "telephone conversation" with his mother (M):

(1) MARK at 1;5(14)

Mk pulls his toy telephone out of a large box of toys and brings it to M, offers it to her looking at her face; M reaches out and accepts it.

(M: Oh great. We can have a telephone conversation. Who are you going to ring up Mark?)

Mk lifting receiver to his ear, looking into M's eyes.

(M: Hello Mark)
Mk: [2ɛːˈ2ɛ]

Mk talking into mouthpiece.

(M: Hello, How are you today?)
    (Hello Mark)
Mk: [həː]

(M: How are you?)

Mk replaces the receiver.

(M: That's very rude. You've hung up)

Mk lifts receiver to ear again.

(M: Hello. Have you had your dinner?)
   Mk: [2ə˙2ə:]

Mk talking into mouthpiece, eye contact with M.

(M: Was it good? Was it a good dinner?)
   Mk: [2ə˙2ə2ə2ə:]
(M: It was?)
   Mk: [2ə˙ə:]

What is remarkable here, and the sound recording itself is in this respect even more impressive than the transcription, is the way Mark's utterances begin immediately after his mother's. He has a clear conception of conversation as a properly ordered sequence of vocalizations in which he and his mother take turns, the "speaking" being sequenced in relation to the other's speech, probably involving processing of pitch contour (Kaplan, 1969, showed discrimination of intonation contours at 8 months), facial expression and eye contact. Surprisingly perhaps, some basic competence in how to hold a conversation precedes having something to say.

A common context for such sequenced joint behaviour is the object-labelling game. Again, at 17½ months Mark shows some competence at the game despite being unable to provide any object labels:

(2) MARK at 1;5(14)
(M: That's your hair)
   Where's your nose?)
   Where's your nose?)

Mk standing pulling his hair with one hand.

Mk touches his right eye with his right forefinger, looking at M.

(M: That's not your nose)
   Nose.)

M putting her finger on Mk's nose. Mk's attention switches to a picture of Hitler as a baby, on the cover of a magazine.

   Mk: [æidi]
(M: There's a baby)
   Mk: [2ə:]
(M: Baby)
   Mk: [ɛiŋ:]
(M: Baby)
   Mk: [dədə]
    [endede]

Mk picking up the magazine, plus another which was underneath it.

(M: You have that one Mark)
   You have that one with the baby in)

M taking second magazine from Mk, leaving Mk with the "baby" one.

Mark, before he can produce words, is able to engage in co-ordinated interaction with his mother, involving the sequencing of utterances and gestures by both, in which objects are being gesturally and perceptually selected and also named. In anticipation of the fourth section below, p. 464, notice here how Mark's mother begins the sequence by tuning in to Mark's own ongoing actions and focused attention—his holding his hair. She provides a label, and succeeds through words and actions to redirect his attention to the other parts of his body. When Mark's attention shifts to the picture of baby Hitler, his mother follows, "replies" to his "utterance" as if it were an initiation of dialogue, and so engages in an exchange of utterances in relation to the objects of their shared attention. Mark is learning how to play the "Original Word Game".

Let us now examine how the game is played by a child who has started to talk. Alice (A) is 18 months and 21 days old; Sheila (S) is her regular daytime caretaker.

(3) ALICE at 1;6(21)

	A and S looking at picture book.
A: horse ↑	
horse ↑	A pointing to picture of a goat
	A still pointing at goat, now looking up at S's face.
(S: No, no, that's not a horse)	
A: cats ↑	A looking at the picture (goat).
cats ↑	
(S: No)	
A: what's [æt]	
(S: What is it?)	
A: [ʔɪsæt]	
(S: That's a goat. Alice say goat)	
Goat.)	S tapping goat with forefinger.
A: [ʔɪsæt]	A looking and pointing at picture
[ʔɪsæ:t]	of cow (on the end of a row of
[sæt]	pictures).
(S: Oh you know the end one)	
A: moo	
(S: Moo (laughing). That's a cow)	
	(several minutes of interaction)
	A and S looking at large circus picture containing many animals.
A: monkey	A pointing at monkey.
see monkey ↑	
(S: Yes that's the monkey)	
Where are the penguins?)	(Two penguins are visible in the large picture).
(S: Alice find the penguins. Where are they?)	

A: [?ɪz] gone	A looking at picture.
(S: (laughing) Where's it gone?)	
Where's the penguins?)	
A: see	A suddenly pointing to one of the penguins.
(S: Yes. There's one, two)	S pointing to the two penguins in turn.
A: [?əz] that	A pointing to same penguin again.
(S: The penguins)	(S does not point)
Two. One two)	
Where's the clown?)	
A: see clown	A looking (not pointing) directly at clown.
(S: Where is the clown?)	
(5 secs)	
(S: Alice touch the clown)	
A: touch↑ clown↑	A looking at clown; no hand movements.
(S: Touch the clown)	
(7 secs)	
(S: Alice touch the clown)	
A: touch↑ clown↑	
(S: Where is the clown?)	
A: see	A brusquely prodding right forefinger down on clown's face.

Alice's *whats* [æt], [?ɪsæt], etc. are clearly derived from the adults' questions "what's that?". However, it is unlikely that Alice is in any sense asking questions. Rather, she understands this as the kind of thing to say at appropriate points in the sequence of words, orientations and gestures that constitute the game. These utterances function for Alice as deictic-locatives in the co-ordination of joint attention towards things to be named. Indeed, as "questions" they would often be presuppositionally inappropriate in both child and adult usage, since both often know the name already. Alice was even capable, somewhat earlier at 17 months 7 days, of sequencing the words and playing the game by herself:

(4) ALICE at 1;5(7)

	S has left the room and closed the door behind her.
A: [ə] shut ↑	
(D: Sheila's shut the door, yes)	(D is myself)
A: door ↓	A pointing at the door.
[əz] that ↑	
door ↓	
[?uz] that ↑	

door ↓
[2uz] that ↑
door ↓

There is always a danger, if one does not examine the detailed and various contexts of early words, of misclassifying early language by the criteria of adult grammar (cf. Edwards, 1973; in press). Apart from the apparent "question" *what's that*, the object naming game provides a rich source of other possible misclassifications, including the other commonly described early "question", *where's X*. In example 3 above, Sheila uses this locative question in order to introduce an object label ("X") for which Alice is required to indicate or find the situational referent. Children's responses to such questions are typically actions rather than answers—they look for, pick up, show or indicate the object concerned. Indeed, the "question" as used by children (and sometimes adults!) is often not even addressed to a listener, but having been acquired in the context of jointly regulated interaction, may subsequently be uttered as a kind of self-directive when looking for some object. As Lock (this volume) points out, Vygotsky's (1966) description of the process whereby "intermental" categories become "intramental" ones can be applied to this kind of development of symbols and meanings out of social interaction, in this case words for the guidance of thought and action (Vygotsky, 1962).

Alice's word *see* functions not as a label for visual perception, but as a deictic-locative word for indicating the location of a named object. Her use of *see* is clearly similar to that described by Gruber (1967):

> whenever *see* is uttered . . . Dory is either reaching for the object . . . pointing to it, or showing it to her mother. This is amazingly consistent throughout the filmed and taped observations . . . *see* consistently has the performative meaning of "I indicate to you", and it is possible to claim that this word has no other meaning.

Alice, typically of many young children, first learns words like *look see*, *whats*, *wheres*, and *that*, as deictically functional words in the context of an object-labelling procedure wherein child and caretaker are engaged in reciprocal and co-ordinated actions, gestures and utterances *vis-à-vis* sequentially attended aspects of the immediate perceived world. And it is to the child's competence in and understanding of such procedures that her comprehension and use of these words is assimilated (in the Piagetian sense), since these are the very words that caretakers themselves use in what are, for children, sequences of deictic object labelling. Their adult functions as questions and experiential verbs are probably not assimilated, and so do not become part of the child's early linguistic competence. Indeed, S seems to be aware of this; her response to Alice's *see monkey* is "yes, that's the monkey", rather than an acknowledgement that the monkey is visible and that Alice is looking at it.

However, it should not be thought that the procedures established by mother and child for "regulating joint activity and joint attention" (Bruner, 1976) are limited to the deictic-locative meanings underlying the Original Word Game. As Bruner stresses, such procedures are an important context for the child's acquisition of much descriptive and pragmatic language. Having engaged the child's attention, typically in some game, mothers will frequently waste no opportunity of describing the motions, actions and attributes of the things attended. We shall consider the role of mothers' (or caretakers') understanding and even tuition of children in children's language development more explicitly in the fourth section below (p. 464).

REQUESTS: SOLICITING THE AGENCY OF OTHERS

One aspect of the developing non-linguistic knowledge of infants (Piaget, 1952, 1954; Edwards, 1973) is that persons are agents as well as objects, having a special capability of self-initiated actions. Moreover, they are social-relational; they can be interacted with, and their agency can be solicited. All of this is understood before the infant is able to comprehend or express requests through language alone. In this section we examine how children's early linguistic expressions of requests derive from their assimilation of adults' use of language in contexts in which, again since early infancy, they have developed an essentially prelinguistic communicative competence in soliciting the agency of others. This is a process of development which demonstrates rather clearly the transition from interpreted actions through communicative gestures to the semantics and pragmatics of early language.

For several months of my daughter Helen's "Stage 1" language (Brown, 1973) she used a peculiar word which had several allomorphs (conditioned by the phonology of the subsequent word) all of which I shall represent as *dr*. This functioned as a word for requesting things, and occurred invariably in sentence initial position. Here are some examples:

HELEN at 2;1

(5) H: dr jelly   H looking at D (myself); there is a
        dr jelly daddy   packet of jelly sweets on a shelf out
                                           of H's reach—she has to ask D or
                                           her mother for one.

(6) H: dr biscuit   H looking at M (her mother), both
        dr biscuit   in living room. Biscuits are in
     (M: No, you'll get your dinner soon) kitchen.

(7)   M putting H to bed. H always takes
                                        "bunny" to bed, but this time bunny
                                        is absent.
H: dr bunny   H looking into M's eyes, as M adjusts
   dr bunny   the blankets.
   dr bunny
(M: Wait a minute)   M goes and gets bunny.
H: bunny   M gives it to H. H laughing.

(8)   H: dr nappy   H looking into M's eyes.
         dr nappy
(M: Do you want your nappy changed?)
     OK)   M reaching behind her chair, pulls
H: nappy   out a clean nappy.
   nappy

(9)   H sitting with D who is reading
                                        his own book. H pointing at (written)
H: words   page of D's book.
(D: Yes. This is daddy's)   (H has her own collection of "Noddy"
H: Helen dr noddy   books, which are presently on a
   noddy   table beyond her reach.)
   noddy book   H and D eyes, and at Noddy books.
(D: Do you want your Noddy book?)
H: dr noddy book   H laughing.
   where's ə noddy book   D fetches a Noddy book for H.

(10) Age 2;1(7)
                                        H tries to get down off a chair but
                                        cannot.
(D: Do you want to get down?)
H: dr get down   H smiles, looking at D.
                                        D lifts H down.

Helen is clearly able to make linguistic requests for persons to do things for
her—get a sweet, get dinner, change her nappy (diaper), lift her down. With
words she can even *ask* for things not visually present (the biscuit in the
kitchen; the bunny), though it is not the word itself that allows her to
conceive of such spatially displaced objects (cf. Piaget's "object concept",
and examples below of non-linguistic requests). The word *dr* seems to have
derived from her assimilation of her parents' "do you want (to, a, . . .)" to a
single-word scheme for asking for things; this certainly seems plausible from
the protocols above, and would account for its invariant initial position.
Moreover, although the convention is followed here of writing parental
speech in the full conventional orthography of "Do you want a/to . . .", a
phonetically more accurate transcription would be something like a slurred
[dʒuwanə . . .]—much closer to Helen's *dr*. (Similarly, Sheila's "what's that"
was a lot closer to Alice's [ʔəsæʔ] than the transcription suggests.)

So Helen had a word for requesting things. She also had another: *want*. This is a word typically found in the early language of English speaking children, and taken on face value looks like an expression of an experiential state of desire. However, it seems likely that children first learn this word in a restricted aspect of its adult usage—for getting people to do things. In Helen's early usage, this word was even more restricted, to requesting that objects be handed to her (causative transitory possession—see Edwards, 1973). Children who do not have *dr*, however, probably use *want* to request all kinds of things. Again, Gruber (1967) recorded a similar "requesting" usage of *want* in Dory:

> From the context it was clear that the performative "I demand" was intended, and not the reportative statement expressed by the adult form "I want". The difference between the two should be made clear. For the performative it is obligatorily the addressee that something is wanted of. This is not so for the reportative.

There are two aspects of this analysis which we might bear in mind when examining infants' growing competence in making requests non-verbally. Firstly, there is the structured situational context of these verbalized requests. They occur in the context of face-to-face non-linguistic interpersonal communication, and presuppose an intersubjectively shared cognitive and social-relational framework in child and adult including an understanding of the objects, their spatial locativity, their differential accessibility by self and other, the capacity of persons to do particular actions (agency) and an understanding of how to engage the other's attention and solicit that agency within that conceptually structured world. Secondly, there is the distinction between index and intended message (cf. MacKay's (1972) discussion of "index" and intentional "communication"). Although the word "want" may be used by an adult to report his experiential state, and the child's word *want* may *indicate* (quite accurately) to the adult that the child is in a state of desire, the child's intended *message* is probably restricted to the performative message of requesting that the addressee do something. Similarly, infants' noises and actions may be indexical of (i.e. perceived by adults as evidence of) states and desires, but when such noises and actions become meaningful messages, the intended message is probably of the order "you do this" rather than "I experience this". We shall return to this distinction after looking again at Mark and Alice.

MARK at 1;5(2)

(11)   M sitting on floor. Mk starts climbing
  (M: You want a ride?)   onto M's back.
    Come on, up you get.)   M getting to her feet, with Mk
    Up↑   Up↑)   holding on to her back.

(12)

Mk: [ʔidɛidɛi]
    [ʔiʔi]

Mk follows M into living room, starts stamping up and down, in an agitated manner, looking all around.
Mk running out and into the kitchen
Mk returns, standing in living room doorway looking at M.

(M: Are you hungry?)
    Are you hungry?)
Mk: [ʔɔː]
    [ʔɔgɔgə]

Mk laughs wildly, stamps about again.

Mk looking at M, whining.
M goes into kitchen and brings Mk a cup of milk, which Mk accepts and drinks.

(13)   Age 1;6(14)

Mk: [ʔəː]
(M: You want me to open it?)

Mk holding the closed box which normally holds D's microphone.
Tries and fails to pull it open.
Mk offering box to M.
M accepting box.
M opens it and hands the two halves to Mk.
Mk shuts box, hands it back to M.
M opens box and hands to Mk again.

(14) Age 1;9 (Mk now capable of a few single word utterances)

(M: What do you want?)

Mk: [ʔəː]
    [ʔajə]
(M: This?)

Mk stands looking up at mantelpiece on which, well out of Mk's reach, is the formboard-top of his postbox.
Mk runs to M, grasps and pulls her hand.
M getting up from chair,
Mk pulls M, by the hand, to the mantelpiece.
Mk pointing and looking at postbox top.
M grasping postbox top, puts it into Mk's two uplifted hands.
Mk sits on floor and plays with postbox top and shaped blocks.

Examples 12, 13 and 14 demonstrate quite clearly that Mark, though unable to encode his messages in words, nevertheless has a thorough non-linguistic understanding of the conceptual and social-relational prerequisites to making the kind of linguistic requests that Helen could. He looks at his mother, gains her attention, gives her objects to open and points at objects to be given him. He shows an understanding of all aspects of the shared cognitive and social-relational framework identified as underlying Helen's competence. He is even able to get spatially displaced objects brought to him (sustenance from the kitchen), though his lack of a verbal language prevents him from making a direct explicit reference in this case, and for some time he stamps and whines in apparent frustration.

Example 11 is important in exemplifying how such non-linguistic communicative competence probably arises. Mark is making no ostensible communicative gesture; he is trying to climb onto his mother's back. His mother treats this as indicating that Mark wants to "go for a ride" and off they go. In a later transcription (at 1;6(14)) Mark stands behind his mother and, without trying to climb up, merely raises his arms. An action, once merely indexical to the mother of something Mark was trying to do, became a ritualized gesture functioning for Mark as an intended request to "go for a ride". This is of course the very process described by Lock (this volume) whose analysis drew my attention to its importance.

Finally, we can see in Alice how the whole process probably develops from interpreted action, to non-linguistic gesture, to the assimilation and use of language:

(15) ALICE at 1;4(7)
      (A capable of some one-word speech).   A reaching towards and looking at a
(S: Do you want bunny?)   slightly out of reach toy "bunny".
                                      S walks across room, gets and gives
                                      bunny to A.

(16)   S has already peeled and sliced an
                                      apple and given it to A.
                                      A has eaten it piece by piece.
                                      A holds hand out towards more
                                      pieces of apple on edge of table
                                      near S. Looks at apple, then
                                      into S's eyes, still reaching.
(S: More? more?)   S puts another piece in A's hand and
                                      A eats it.

(17) Age 1;5(7)
                              A looks at teddy in A's cot, beyond
                                      the rails; tries and fails to reach
                                      teddy.
  A: teddy   A holding on to cot rails, looking at S.
(S: There's teddy)   S picks up the bear; giving it to A.
(18) Age 1;5(21)

                              A is having some difficulty holding
                                      the neck of a cloth bag open while
                                    she drops plastic bricks into it.
                                    A moans as a brick falls to floor.

(S: What's the matter?)	A looks at S, holding up the bag, facing S, offers bag to S.
(S: I've got to hold it s'pose)	S accepting bag. S sits holding bag open while A drops bricks into it.

(19)

	A sitting in high-chair after dinner.
A: down ↑	A holding her arms up, looking into S's eyes.
(S: Please. Please.)	
	A maintains posture. S lifts A out of chair and onto floor.

(20)   Age 1;6(21)

	A tries in vain to climb up onto sofa. With arms on seat and one leg reaching up towards seat, A looking
A: please ↑ please ↑	towards S.
(S: Please?)	
Up, up, up, up)	S helping A up onto sofa seat.

In the first description, as in Mark's attempt to climb onto his mother's back, Alice's action is non-"communicative". It is not an intended message, and is probably not even interpreted anthropomorphically by S as a message. Sheila is able to understand Alice's action as indexical of an attempt to grasp the toy rabbit, and so walks across to her and gives her the rabbit. This is probably exactly the kind of social feedback from intended actions that converts actions into gestures and messages (cf. Lock, 1976). In fact, Alice was already at this age capable of making non-verbalized intended requests, as example 16 shows. Examples 19 and 20 capture part of the process wherein Alice learned how to encode the request function with the word *please*. In 19, Sheila was ostensibly teaching Alice some etiquette. Alice's subsequent usage of *please* suggests that this word was assimilated by her to her understanding of the more basic social-relational process of soliciting the agency of others. It became used, as in 20, as a request word. Alice of course knew nothing about decorum.

It should be noted that although we have concentrated in this section on utterances which encode the request function itself, young children also make requests when uttering words related to other aspects of the situational context. Perhaps the most common of these is the word *more*, early uses of which Brown (1973) characterizes as a linguistic extension of Piaget's "procedures for making interesting sights last", becoming used for requesting from someone a "recurrence" or "another instance" of some object, action or event.

CONSTRAINTS ON INTENDED ACTIONS

The third nexus of social relations in which language is acquired is that which involves the socialization of the child through constraints upon his freedom of intended action. This particular source of early meanings is dealt with in some detail in Edwards (in press) so I shall first merely summarize here some of its salient features. Parental use of language in the context of constraints or prohibitions on the child's freedom of actions apparently give rise to a variety of early linguistically coded meanings, including children's "rejection" sense of negation (Bloom, 1970), persons' "possession" of objects in terms of persons' differential privileges of access to and use of such objects, and also some idiosyncratic uses of various adult verbs and adjectives, including *hot*, *sticky*, *sharp*, *careful*, *tired*, *leave* and *busy*. For some of these expressions (though not for "possession"), children may make no functional semantic distinction between constraints imposed by the nature of the physical world, and constraints imposed only by social prohibitions. Some uses of negation, possession and the word *leave* can be illustrated by some selections from my transcript of Alice at 19 months:

ALICE at 1;7(7)

(21) A: no touch (S: No touch) No that's correct)	A standing looking at D's tape recorder.
A: mummy's tape	A pointing and looking at tape recorder.
(22) A: don't ↑ mummys watch (S: Mummy's. No touch) A: don't touch	A looking at her mother's watch on table and out of A's reach.
(23)	S absent. A starts pulling a (parents') book down off a shelf).
(D: Hey, Alice) A: daddy's daddy's book (D: Daddy's book is it?)	(D is myself) A pushing the book back.
A: doggie ↑ my doggie	A walks into centre of room, looking at the toys on the floor. A pushing a toy dog-on-wheels out of her path.
A: toys ↑	A carrying a small wooden xylophone to D, puts it in D's lap.
my toys ↑ my: toys ↑ (D: Oh, thank you)	

	S enters.
	A takes xylophone off D's lap.
A: my toy	A handing it to S.
(24)	
(S: Leave)	A pulling at zip on parent's brief-case.
A: leave	A letting go of zip.
no: Alice ↑	A and S eye contact.
(S: Hm?)	
A: no Alice ↑ can't ↑	

Example 21 is instructive. It seems that the tape recorder, as an object not to be touched, was assimilated by Alice to her general understanding of objects "possessed" by her mother. In fact, Alice's parents did not own a tape-recorder and had never attended a recording session, so that Alice could have had no opportunity to learn directly that this machine belonged to her mother. In 23 we see Alice, having been thwarted in her efforts to handle a parent's book, encoding the constrained-action possessive. But note how she goes on in subsequent utterances to assert, in contrast, her "possession" of her own toys, the things she *can* play with. Social prohibitions have created for Alice a cognitive category by which objects can be classified and related to persons. In 24, the force of Sheila's word "leave" is clearly comprehended; Alice acknowledges its force as a prohibition on her actions by letting go of the forbidden object (she might well have called it *daddy's* or *mummy's*), and by recoding the prohibition with some negations.

Thus Alice's use of possession, as with her uses of negation and of *leave*, were from an adult perspective over-restricted, though typical of reported uses by young children. These restricted uses derive partly from the special ways in which adults talk to children (see below, and in the next section, p. 464), although it should be noted that Sheila used negations also to encode denials of propositions. However, they derive most crucially from children's own processes of comprehension—from how they make sense of adult language in terms of its uses and functions in situations as understood by the child. Such situations include those described here, where the child's freedom of intended action is, or has been, constrained. (For a more thorough discussion of negation, possession and other expressions, see Edwards, in press.)

That such uses derive, through comprehension, from those of adults in similar contexts is supported by some of Sheila's own uses of negation and of words like *dirty* and *hot* in the context of constraints on Alice's actions:

ALICE at 1;4(7)

(25)	A handing to S a sheet that S has already removed from A's cot to wash. The sheet is not visibly stained or dirty.

(S: This one's dirty. Dirty)	
A: dirty	S takes sheet from A and puts it
(S: Dirty, yes)	back on the washing pile.
(26)	A puts the end of her toy mop up
	to her mouth.
(S: Don't eat it. That's dirty)	S and A direct eye contact: S's
Dirty. Mustn't eat it)	voice stern.
	A lowers the mop.
(27)	
(S: It's too hot now, Alice)	S breaks a boiled egg onto a
Too hot)	saucer, out of A's reach.
A: hot	A looking at egg on saucer.
(S: Yes, it's hot)	
	A moans anxiously, high-pitched.
(S: Wait a minute)	
(28) Age 1;4(7)	
(S: No. Not up there. No)	A starts climbing up stairs in hallway.
	S speaking loud and firmly, looking
	at A. A hurriedly steps down and
	falls over.

Such adult uses of words as these pose problems for the child's language learning. What might the words mean? Sheila's word "dirty" was used in the context of Alice holding and offering a quite unremarkable cot sheet. It is unlikely in either 25 or 26 that Alice could have comprehended the attributive "dirty". However, particularly in 26, it was used quite clearly in the perfectly understandable context of Alice's being told off and prohibited. It is in such processes of comprehending the uses of adult words in terms of their social and referential functions that children's early linguistic meanings are made. Another example is Alice's word *careful*, which came to be uttered by her in situations where care was irrelevant, but her ongoing actions were fraught with difficulty. While Sheila had used the word endeavouring to restrain Alice's behaviour in situations such as climbing on chairs, carrying or playing with delicate objects, foreseeing possible consequences and the need for care, Alice assimilated the meaning to her own understanding of those same situations—i.e. that they involved some difficulty of execution.

MATERNAL LANGUAGE AND BEHAVIOUR: IMPLICIT TUITION

Having defined three broad contexts in which early language has meaning and function, in which the child is seen as assimilating adult meanings to his cognitive and communicative competence, we turn now to a brief examination of the active contribution of caretakers to early language learning. Implicit in the foregoing descriptions of caretaker-child interaction is the active role played in early language learning by the caretaker, not only as a source of language input, even of specially adapted language input (Drach *et al.*, 1969; Snow, 1972), but as a person who is able to take account of the child's intentions, read significance into his actions, anticipate him, and engage with him in reciprocal interactions out of which the child is able to learn how language codes messages. Although it is very likely that cultural, social class and individual differences will prove to be important, it may be useful to look at some aspects of Sheila's and Mark's mother's behaviour in order to highlight some important parameters. Much of the behaviour of Mark's mother, in particular, seems implicitly designed to teach him language. Let us begin with a sequence of interaction between Mark and his mother.

(29) MARK at 21:0

	Mk sitting on floor with M, trying to put shaped blocks through appropriate holes in the formboard lid of his toy post box.
Mk: there ↓	Mk trying to push square block into triangular hole.
(M: No)	
That's right)	Mk sliding square block to square hole.
Mk: there ↓	Mk pushing block and it drops in. Mk tries to force spherical block into triangular hole.
(M: No. The other one)	
Mk: [2ɪ] there	Mk offering the block to M, looking at M's face. (M makes no gesture.)
(M: No, you do it)	
The other one)	Mk trying to push sphere into square hole.
Mk: [2æ:]	
(M: That's right)	Mk drops it through round hole.
Mk: there there	(immediately after it drops in)
(M: Where's that one go?)	M pointing to triangular block on floor. Mk picks it up, dropping
Mk: there	it through correct hole.
(M: That's right)	
Where does that one go?)	M handing a square block to Mk.
Mk: [2ɪ:]	Mk trying to force it through triangular hole.
(M: That's right)	Mk pushing it through square hole.
(M: No. It won't go there)	Mk trying to push a square block
Really. No no. There's no point in struggling.)	through the round hole.

                                          Mk switches to triangular hole.

(M: (laughs) No, the other one)
    The other one)
    No, the other one)   Mk reverting to the round hole.
    Mk: [2ɛ:]   Mk switching to square hole.
(M: That's right)

His mother's language is closely synchronized with Mark's utterances and actions, commenting on his actions and their consequences, providing linguistic expressions to code these and the objects of his attention. She participates in the actions, handing Mark shaped blocks and using deictic-locative language integrated with looks and gestures which both follow and guide Mark's actions and visual attention. And note the kind of language she uses—phrases and short sentences, sometimes single words, negatives that express constraints on actions, "where's?" questions to structure Mark's searching and location-finding, deictic words in conjunction with deictic gestures and located objects. Mark and his mother are merely playing, and M is concentrating on Mark's ability to put the various blocks through the appropriate holes. But the interaction is rich in communication and it is difficult not to describe M's activity as language-*tuitional*. Implicitly, probably unconsciously, her speech and behaviour constitute an intricately structured attempt, guided by her understanding of Mark's linguistic and communicative competence, to teach Mark some language.

Sometimes, of course, mothers teach language to their children in a quite explicit fashion; the "Original Word Game" is the obvious example. But even here, as we saw above in the first section (p. 453), while the caretaker is explicitly teaching object labels, implicitly she is teaching deixis and locativity, the synchronization of dialogue, and the general communicative competence of co-ordinating joint action and attention through an integrated use of language and gesture. Indeed, *implicit* language tuition is the richer and the more pervasive. Mark's mother tended to use the Original Word Game as a kind of test of Mark's vocabulary, often not even telling him the "answer" when he failed to produce the word.

Let us examine the process more closely. Both M and S were observed to make sure of the child's comprehension of their language by actively manipulating the physical environment in order to focus the child's attention onto referents. Here is an example from each:

(30) MARK at 1;6(14)
(M: Come and sit in your chair)   M looking at Mk with one hand on
                                  back of Mk's chair, pushing it
                                  slightly towards him.
                                  Mk looks at the chair, walks towards
                                  it looking at the cup of milk in M's
                                  other hand; sits in chair.

(31) ALICE at 1;8(7)

	A hugging toy dog "wuff-wuff",
A: wuff-wuff	looking at S.
love wuff-wuff	
(S: Alice love wuff-wuff)	
(S: There's wuff-wuff's tail)	S getting hold of dog's tail,
	waggles it to and fro, lets go.
A: wuff-wuff tail	A looking at and then waggling
	dog's tail.

By holding the chair and pushing it toward Mark, his mother drew his attention to it, as a referent object. Similarly, Sheila, in waggling the dog's tail, encoded it as the dog's "inalienable possession" while actively directing Alice's attention to it as a perceptually and kinetically discrete object attached to the dog (cf. discussion in Edwards, 1973). Thus both Mark's mother and Sheila were able to aid the children's comprehension of their language by simultaneously orienting and structuring the children's perception of the referents.

Another important way in which caretakers can be implicitly tuitional is by informing the child of something he patently already knows, or by instructing him to do something he is clearly about to do or is already doing.

(32) ALICE at 1;7(21)

	Alice has just completed a jig-saw
	puzzle, and is standing looking at it.
(S: That one's finished Alice)	
You going to do the other one?)	

MARK at 1;5(14)

(33)	M and Mk have been looking through
	a picture book, naming pictures;
	book now open at picture of a
	baby's cot.
	Mk turns and carries open book
	towards D.
(M: Show the cot to Derek)	
Mk: [ʒəʒəː]	Mk holds the book open in front
(D: It's a cot isn't it)	of D (picture facing Mk).
(34)	Mk picks up formboard lid, putting
(M: You're going to put the lid on?)	it onto the postbox, already pressing
Press it down. That's it.)	it down tight.

In the first example (32) Sheila is ostensibly telling Alice something—informing her that the jig-saw is complete. But Alice has herself just completed it and is standing looking at it. It seems more likely that the important (perlocutionary) function of Sheila's statement is the implicitly tuitional one—to 'take advantage of Alice's comprehension of what she has done and can see in order to teach her the word "finished". (Sheila's intonation gave emphasis and rising pitch to the first syllable of "finished".) Mark's mother similarly encodes for him actions he is already doing, or which she can see he is already about to do. Her sentences embody in language the linguistic code for describing the structured relations and elements that constitute Mark's probable sensory-motor conception of his current actions and environment (cf. Edwards, 1973). Mark's mother is also likely to verbalise for Mark the content of his own non-verbal message:

(35) MARK at 1;11

Mk: [2iː ˈbədəː2]   Mk holding door handle (door
                                            closed; Mk not pulling at handle),
                                            looking back towards M.

(M: You want me to open the door?)
Open the door)   M gets up and opens the door.

Here Mark's mother shows him how to ask her to open the door, and ostensibly instructs herself to do it in the act of opening it. In so doing, as in telling him to do what he himself is doing already, M sacrifices the subtleties of adult presuppositional appropriateness for the sake of coding for Mark what she can safely assume he is currently attending to and thinking about. This is all a far cry indeed from earlier notions of infants' "immersion" into a speech community, in which they "overhear" (McNeill, 1966b) a degraded speech input.

CONCLUSION

Early language development takes place in a richly social-interactional context in which the child's acquisition of linguistic meanings is structured and constrained by his current processes of comprehension—by his efforts to make sense of adult language in terms of its referential and pragmatic functions. This comprehension process is itself a function of the child's current cognitions about the referent world, and of his own understanding of the social interactions in which language is addressed to him.

We have approached an understanding of this process by selecting, more or less arbitrarily, three kinds of early face-to-face interactions: those involving the child's and caretaker's mutual co-ordination of attention towards actions, objects and events; those in which the child is attempting to solicit on his behalf the agency of another person; and those involving the imposition of constraints upon the child's freedom of voluntary action. In looking at language development in terms of its basis in social interactions, we have discovered a variety of linguistic forms and meanings for each nexus of social relations. Another approach (e.g. Halliday, 1976) has been to select a variety of linguistic forms and functions and look for their emergence in early language. I believe this latter approach to be in danger of over-interpreting early utterances in terms of distinct functional classifications which anticipate perhaps unjustifiably early their development into the adult grammatical system. The child brings with him essentially non-linguistic processes of comprehension and communicative competence which impose their own structure on child language. For example, while Halliday claims that, in contrast to adult language, utterances in child language have singular and distinct "instrumental", "regulatory", "interactional" (etc.) functions, it seems to the present author that even in early child language these functions are not easily defined, whether on formal, semantic or pragmatic grounds. The discussion of requests in the second section (p. 456) above, for example, rather undermines the "instrumental-regulatory" distinction. The child instrumentally "gets what he wants" by attempting to regulate the behaviour of others.

In contrast, other studies are coming to fruition (e.g. Bruner, 1975, 1976) which approach the process by tracing the child's social-interactional development from birth into his early use of language, via the development of essentially non-linguistic communicative competence. Although we have yet to see the outcomes of this exciting research, its basic approach may leave us with a beautiful description of the growth of communicative competence in which we have a good understanding of how early words function in referential and interactional communication, leaving us wondering how they are ever organized into the complex system of adult grammar. Although Bruner might now hesitate to emphasize the gap so strongly, this approach has yet to suggest that it might bridge "the enormous discontinuity between mere 'gestural vocalizations' and the complex and highly constrained grammar of language" (Bruner, 1966).

It is apparent that looking back from adult linguistic competence towards an explanation of its origins in early cognition and communication, and looking forward from the birth of neonates towards their eventual communicative and linguistic competence, are two complementary perspectives that need to be borne in the minds of the same investigators, lest our understanding of the process falls between two schools. This chapter has erred perhaps on the side of the latter.

17

Word, Context and Imitation

LINDA FERRIER

Jaffrey, New Hampshire, U.S.A.

The present volume appears to represent a consensus of opinion that a focus of research is overdue on the social abilities of the young child and that his interactions with other social beings are critical prerequisites to his subsequent linguistic and cognitive development. The work of Bruner (1975), Trevarthan (1976) and Newson (1974) suggests that the child is biologically equipped to entune with another human being virtually as soon as he is born, in the context of the everyday routine interactions in which mother and child are monotonously involved. Further, that the mother imposes meaning on these routine interactions, marks their temporal limits, both gesturally and verbally, and punctuates the naturally occurring junctures within them. It is against the theoretical background of the early mutual involvement of the mother-child pair in the innumerable repetitive events of child-rearing that the child's emergence as a language user has to be set. By the time the child utters his first word, he and his mother have negotiated a common repertoire of meanings, whether realized verbally or gesturally, and a host of expectancies about each others behaviour.

Since the tide has turned from the exclusive study of syntax which occupied the 1960s, it seems that the time has come to consider the "given" components of language, i.e. the elements which the child lifts from his verbal environment before the combinatorial or "new" possibilities of syntax are at his disposal. Several changes of focus have ushered in this alteration in research interest: first the movement towards the study of speech acts as epitomized by Searle (1969) and secondly the awareness of gesture as the symbolic precurser of language (Lock, Clark, this volume).

"Imitation", defined as the repetition of the whole or part of a preceding utterance, has been much discussed as a possible process involved in the advancement of syntactic competence, with opinion divided as to whether it advances productivity (Ryan, 1973). The previously mentioned change of focus away from syntax allows imitation to be reconsidered as a process important at the one-word utterance stage and perhaps beyond.

The topics covered in this chapter will be as follows:

1. The development of shared meanings in the context of social inter-actions realized by gesture.
2. The move from the realization of these meanings by gesture to their realization by verbal, though idiosyncratic, means, with data on the imitative stratagem of my own child.
3. The subsequent overgeneralization of these shared meanings.
4. The child's initial errors as a result of the complexity of the socio-physical setting of his early language encounters.
5. The early ability to retain the intonational contour of routine utterances and to reproduce them on strings of items interspersed with jargon with little or no semantic content.
6. The later incorporation of whole fragments of imitated material into syntactically composed utterances.
7. Finally, the theoretical status of imitation is considered.

GESTURE IN CONTEXT

It does not need to be brought to the attention of parents, but perhaps to those less closely concerned with child-rearing, that a baby in the first year of life probably averages three nappy changes per day (conservative estimate), three snoozes and three meals. Which means that by the time he is ready to produce his first word he has entered into approximately 2,000 of each of these everyday child-rearing routines. Each of these occasions is an opportunity for mother and child to build up a set of expectancies about the behaviour of the other which is the foundation for later communication. So, when my 15-month-old daughter handed me the soap while in the bath I could unerringly read off from this behaviour a request that I should blow bubbles since we had probably engaged in this behaviour 50 times before.

The very exclusive relationship of mother and child in the first 2 years, allows for the development of sometimes bizarre and idiosyncratic signals. However, as Newson points out (1977), almost anything can be given meaning, as long as it is mutually agreed upon. So, at 13 months, when my daughter wanted a drink she walked to the corner of the kitchen where the electric kettle stood and put her finger in the hole which served to open the drawer beneath. This particular gesture I understood perfectly and it survived for several months before a verbal demand superceded it. It had its history in the fact that my daughter had seen me walk to that corner to fill up her bottles from the kettle innumerable times in the preceding months. It continued as a successful demand even after I had ceased to fill her bottles from the kettle and used tap water instead.

So both mother and child used the predictability of each others behaviour to manufacture mutually understandable symbols.

LANGUAGE IN CONTEXT

To move from the behavioural contexts routinely entered into by mother and child, to the language embedded in them; contrary to Chomsky's oft-stated view that language is constantly created anew, the language of mothers to small children is highly repetitive, context bound and predictable. Chomsky asserts that the vast majority of sentences in any representative corpus of recorded utterances will be "new" sentences in the sense that they will occur once and once only. However, observing my own behaviour with my 15-month-old, I noted that whenever my daughter sneezed I said "Atchoo", whenever she fell down (at this point in time at almost half hourly intervals) I said "Upsadaisy", whenever I picked her up out of her cot I said, "Hello my love. Where's my nice girl?" It in fact requires an enormous effort of will *not* to respond to ones child's behaviour with these various ritual formulae. It is not unusual for mothers, after several years of child-rearing, to employ them unappropriately and embarrassingly to other adults. It is perhaps the fact that mothers' language to their children is both repetitious and context-tied which allows the child to get his foot in the door and make his initial attempts at breaking the linguistic code.

However, at this early stage, mother and child are wrapped in an exclusive child-caring relationship and the meanings forged within it are often idiosyncratic and only distantly linked to the language of the larger social world. The idiosyncracy of the child's early utterances is based on two facts. First, that the mother-child pair evolve a system of meanings which is the result of their constant adaptation to each other's needs and interests. So my daughter's first demand to be allowed to draw was "Pussy" since I constantly drew cats for her, a dominant interest at this point. The mother must alter her child-rearing practices to accommodate the changing capacities of the child. This adjustment brings into the relationships new verbal items. His activities, in turn, are constrained by the values and plans operated by the mother and into which she must fit her child-rearing activities. So at one point my 13-month-old daughter's newly acquired interest in maintaining a vertical position made it virtually impossible to change her nappy lying down. Consequently, I employed the alternative stratagem of changing her standing up on the window sill. This distractive device brought into conversation the birds on the roof top opposite. After about a week the item "birds" appeared in my daughter's repertoire.

The second source of this idiosyncracy lies in the complexity of the relationship of language to the socio-physical world. The child picks out items from a ritualized set of social encounters which he then turns to his own use and generalizes, often inappropriately beyond those initial learning contexts.

I made a collection of these idiosyncratic productions when studying my own daughter's one-word utterances. Analysis of these allowed a diagnosis of the stratagems she was employing in selecting items for use from my utterances.

1. "Look": At the age of 16 months one typical and repeated demand made by my subject was for drawers and doors to be opened for her. Before this age her demands were transmitted by gesture (pulling at the the drawer or door) accompanied by an item "25" from her "proto-language" (Halliday, 1975). At this point I observed that my typical reaction to such a demand was to check my interpretation of her utterance by asking "Do you want to look?" She shortly afterwards produced "Look" in exactly those same physical contexts, but as a demand form replacing her protolanguage term.

2. "Out": Shortly after the development of "Look", "Out" appeared in a similar manner. Till this time she communicated a desire to get out of her feeding chair by making efforts to get out accompanied by her protolanguage demand. I would once again check her message by saying "Do you want to get out?" She subsequently used "Out" as her demand form. It was used appropriately in that specific physical context, but when a week later she needed assistance to climb *into* a high chair, she generalized "Out" to that situation.

3. "This" and "That": These were used in free variation as demands for objects out of reach and their acquisition had a similar history. The context of their first use was the bath where there is a large basket of toys suspended from the shower for use in the bath. Her gestural demand was replaced by "This" and later "That" which were again lifted from my check utterances "Do you want this/that?" "This" and "That" were subsequently extended to any situations in which she wanted an object out of reach and were used appropriately.

Shortly afterwards she lifted "Up" from my check "Do you want to get up?" which was then generalized to situations in which she wanted to get down. She also employed "Chair" from my check "Do you want to get on the chair?" She then used it as a request for help to get onto tricycles, window sills and a rocking horse.

It appeared, then, that many of her early utterances were tied to repeated family routines of the sort described, in which my language was notably repetitious. But the very invariance of those routines and of my language within them allowed my daughter to hit on the productive stratagem of utilizing the last word of my utterance by transforming its function to that of a demand for goods or services. The perceptual salience of sentence final position has been noted elsewhere (Slobin, 1973). Almost immediately the term had been acquired in those social/physical contexts in which my source utterance was embedded, she immediately generalized it to other similar situations, sometimes appropriately and sometimes not.

Generalization

There is evidence from other researchers that children may use pairs of antonymic adjectives with the same meaning (Clerk et al., 1974; Donaldson and Balfour, 1968). At the very early stage which I am documenting, the reason appears to be that the child is involved in language as "process" and not as "content" (Newson, 1977), i.e. he has hit on the notion of language as a social tool, but has not yet reached the level of acquiring semantic boundaries. The terms within his semantic system are as yet not contrastive because he is not yet using language to construct abstract representations of the world. As a consequence of this his utterances have no true propositional content. As described by Dore (1975) they have merely "primitive force" and "primitive reference". The small child is not concerned with truth or falsity. As further evidence for this, at 19 months my daughter would always respond to yes/no questions but only with the response "no", even when the negative was obviously inappropriate. For example:

Mother: "Do you want a cherry?"
Child: "No."

When offered cherries, she gobbled them up and demanded more. It was not until 2 months later that she started to use "yes" as an alternative response. (I deduced that her cue to yes/no questions was largely intonational since yes/no interrogatives have rising tonic as neutral term while all other clauses types have falling tonic.) It was not that at this point she was unclear about her *intentions*. She was very certain she wanted cherries when offered them.

Nor was she ignorant of the referent of the word "cherries". It was rather that her linguistic system was just not sophisticated enough to allow her the possibility of stating her intentions in truth value terms.

Other researchers have reported that early "wh" questions appear to be learned off as whole units and that it is their force which is responded to (Brown, 1698; Holzman, 1972). To present yet more anecdotal evidence from my own child, at 26 months my daughter was very well-versed in the social niceties of meeting strangers. From my observations, when people meet a small child they generally ask one of two questions, "What is your name?" or "How old are you?" Whenever my daughter was asked the first, I usually chimed in with the response, "Antonia". On one particular occasion a stranger asked her "Are you going out?" to which she responded, as if it had being the predicted question, "Antonia".

The ability to generalize is obviously of enormous importance to the human species. It is what has allowed man to predict the events of the future from the patterning of events he has met in the past. At this early stage, when the language learner is flexing his generalizing wings, it seems he often strays over adult conceptual boundaries, perhaps because initially language is a social device and only secondarily and later the embodiment of semantic distinctions.

Errors of Reference and Segmentation

Further analysis of my daughter's "odd" utterances suggests two more dimensions of error. First, the child is faced with the problem of analysing which items of verbal material attach to which real objects or attributes of real objects. Because "things" are referentially complex, problems may arise.

To consider the ontogenesis of some other of my daughter's utterances:

1. "ϕ" (phew!): An item which I systematically used for a while when I entered my daughter's bedroom each morning to be greeted by a rather offensive smell. My utterance was an exclamation and its "application" (Lyons, 1968, p. 434) was the smell. My daughter, after a couple of days, produced it in the same setting, i.e. her cot in the morning but when in fact the smell was absent. For her it was a form of greeting and tied initially to that particular routine.

2. At 22 months she referred to her nappy as a "soggy", e.g. "Put another soggy on", the confusion arising from my frequent remarks as to her wet state. She had simply confused an attribute of her nappies with a name.

Finally, as noted by other observers (Brown, 1973) the stream of maternal language is often mis-segmented by the infant resulting in some strange productions:

1. Hat on off. (Request for hat to be taken off.)
2. Bye-bye shoes on. (Remark addressed to shoes as walked past them.)

Here "hat on" and "shoe on" are terms lifted from previous maternal productions accompanying the activity of dressing.

At the morphological level, mis-segmentation results in such items as "two noranges" and "two napples" where the nouns have acquired the final /n/ of the indefinite article which precedes in such routine utterances as "Do you want an apple/orange?"

MUTUAL MUSIC

At about the age of 20 months and simultaneous with early syntactic productions, a new capacity appears, the ability to retain the prosodic contour of utterances in the environment, with minimal lexical content but where the functional label is quite clear. In Bruner's words (1975)

> A fourth process is puzzling. It consists of the child learning phonological patterns almost as place holders imitatively. They constitute even pre-verbally a kind of prosodic envelope into which the child "knows" that morphemes go— an interrogative and vocative/demand contour, and possibly an indicative. It is as if a mode were being inferred, a place holding matrix established and lexis then added.

For example, at 21 months my daughter produced the utterance:

1. "Ursie, xxxxx bath." (An imitation of my utterance "Ursie, are you going to come and have a bath?") Similarly
2. "/ə/ peel it xx like." (A demand to be allowed to peel her own apple and an imitation of my offers in previous apple-peeling situations: "I'll peel it if you like.")

The notation xx represents place marking jargon, i.e. babbled strings of sounds with no semantic content.

In both cases the link to the previous learning context were clear and the social function obvious. The melody had been retained while much of the lexis and syntax was still beyond her. It, in fact, appears very common at this stage for emerging word classes, e.g. articles, personal pronouns, prepositions to be initially marked in the linear string by a shwa sound /ə/ , as in 2 above, which is later replaced by the adult morpheme.

Also, at about this time, my daughter learned to respond to stereotyped "frame plus filter questions" (Wells, 1973) of the type:

    1. Mother: "Where has daddy gone? Daddy has gone to _____?"
        Child: "Work."
    2. Mother: "Half a pound of two-penny _____?"
        Child: "Rice."
    3. Mother: "Antonia has gone down the _____?"
        Child: "Plug hole."

where the pause and rising intonation request the ritualized responses, but where the lexical content for the child was quite empty.

This appears to be a move beyond the previous stage in which only the final word of my utterance was responded to. Her attentional range seemed to now include intonational contour and utterance length plus some primitive awareness of the places to be later occupied by morphological classes. It appears, in fact, that this awareness of places in the linear sequence exerts a powerful force. At 20 months a rather odd phenomenon occurred in my daughter's verbalizations, similar to that recorded by Lois Bloom (1973). She had initially learned to say "Bye-bye" in the social context of leaving someone and would produce two-word utterances, e.g. "Bye-bye, Daddy". She then generalized this utterance to all occasions when I carried her out of a room into another. However, in this situation there was no lexical item to fill the slot previously filled by known persons, e.g. Daddy. Consequently, she produced the routine "Bye-bye /dɛ/ /dɛ/" where "/dɛ/ /dɛ/" was an empty form which appeared to fill the vacant place in the sequence. This form survived for about 4 weeks before it disappeared.

So, early syntactic processes are accompanied by the development of the ability to retain unanalysed strings of lexical items (e.g. nursery rhymes, television jingles, stereotyped family routines) sometimes interspersed with jargon, with the prosodic contour intact.

SYNTAX FREES FROM CONTEXT

With the gradual abstraction of syntactic patterns from his environment the child begins to shed his verbal ties to previous contexts. Syntax allows for the coding of new thoughts in new unritualized situations. However, the change is a gradual one and initially many complex utterances incorporate unanalysed chunks lifted from pervious routeins. For example, "more pudding left." (a demand for more pudding) where the final elements in my previous rejection "No more pudding left" were utilized whole-sale.

At 26 months my subject hit on the device of using a routine formula to encode the demand force of her utterance combined with a final word realizing a "primitive proposition" (Dore, 1975).

e.g. 1. "I do it head." (Demand to be placed on father's head.)
    2. "I do it see-saw." (Demand to be bounced on father's knee.)
    3. "I do it nappy on." (Demand to put own nappy on.)

About a month later she produced, for about 2 weeks, a strange compound
        "I have a do it." (e.g. as a demand to clean her own shoes)
which appeared to be an amalgam of the two forms "I have a go" and "I do it". Another compound utilizing two previous one word functions was "last more" which was a request to walk in the snow again after being prohibited from doing so. Both these examples were instances of two previous individual functions being combined, it seems to me, merely to add extra social force. Clerk (in preparation) has produced similar data from her own child of the tendency to produce compounds made up of previously practiced fragments.

However, it is in the first use of personal pronouns that contextual links to the past are still obvious.

e.g. 1. "On my knee." (Request to be put onto mother's knee and lifted from my previous check utterance "Do you want to get on my knee?")
    2. "Don't bite you pup." (Prohibition addressed to the dog meaning "Don't bite me" and lifted from my utterance "Did the pup bite you?")
    3. "I help you." (Demand meaning "You help me" from my offer "Shall I help you?")
    4. "Do egg for you." (Demand that mother should open her egg taken from my offer "Shall I do your egg for you?")
    5. "Pussy scratch you." (Statement that pussy had scratched her lifted from my utterance "Did pussy scratch you?")

It will be noticed that in all these examples her stratagem was exactly the same as at the previous one-word utterance stage, with only an increase in utterance length, i.e. she reproduced the final items from my preceding check utterances in which I frequently interpreted her gestures, noises or facial expressions. Note again that my utterances did not usually immediately precede hers in time, but were uttered in other similar routine contexts. Mastery of the personal pronoun system I take to be a new step towards the final realization of the arbitrary relationship between language and the world. Since the reference of personal pronouns is always relative to the speaker-hearer, my daughter's previous stratagem of using items unaltered from the utterances of another speaker-hearer failed to account for the deictic notions inherent in correct pronoun use.

Further, alongside the elaboration of syntactic processes at this point, my daughter was still acquiring new unanalysed but situationally appropriate routines. In fact, while at the earlier one-word utterance stage the necessary prerequisite for a new verbal item was a long history of social use, at this point one or two exposures sufficed for learning to occur.

> e.g. 1. "Home, James." (Uttered appropriately when getting into the car after a shopping expedition.)
> 2. "I /ə/ go berserk." (Uttered after new puppy had piddled on carpet, yet again, and obviously an imitation of my exclamation "I shall go berserk!")
> 3. "Ye gods!" (Uttered appropriately while driving in the car and hit a large bump in the road.)

While sometimes the strategy of incorporating unanalysed chunks from the verbal environment into complex sentences produces rather strange utterances there would seem to be certain processing advantages inherent in this device. While learners of English as a second language generally use a syntactic approach involving the learning of individual word classes, they almost always have problems memorizing which verbal particles attach to which verbs, a problem which native language learners rarely seem to encounter. This, I assume, is because small children initially learn verb and particle as part of one indivisible unit, often with "it" as complement, which only much later becomes subdivided, e.g. "Eat it up. Chop it up."

So at this stage, simultaneous with the development of syntactic processes, there continues the learning of new unstructured routines and also the incorporation of previously learned strings within syntactic utterances.

IMITATION RECONSIDERED

Imitation is obviously the method by which children acquire items at the one-word utterance stage. There is, however, still some dispute as to its status at the subsequent syntactic stage of development. Clerk *et al.* (1972) who emphasize strongly the imitated component of early productions, consider *all* early two-word utterances to be "accidental collocations of single words each being separately occasioned by the situation". Dore *et al.* (1976), on the other hand, consider some of the "rote productions" I have been describing as merely transitional and preceding truly syntactic productions. However, they do not consider the later incorporation of such rote items into larger structures, suggesting that rote learning not only precedes but accompanies early syntactic processes. So at 21 months my daughter produced:

1. "Bye-bye airplane sky."
2. "Wheresa airplane sky gone?"

3. "Wheresa Mummy shoe?"
4. "Theresa Mummy shoe?"
5. "Theresa Boodgums."

In 1 and 2 "airplane sky" was functioning as one unit, both on distributional and intonational grounds. In 3 and 4 "wheresa" was operating as one rote-learned unit as was "theresa" in 4 and 5.

While much of the data adduced by Clerk (in preparation) is very similar to mine, it seems unlikely that *all* two-word utterances are *accidental* collocations of single words. It seems to me, that if there is some principle of organization underlying the production of two-word utterances, which allows for the creation of further similarly patterned utterances (which has, I think, been amply demonstrated by Brown, 1973) then that principle is by definition syntactic. On the other hand, what Dore *et al.* consider (1976) to be transitional devices appear to function over a considerable period of time and co-occur with syntactic processes and perhaps only longitudinal data can reveal their significance. Moreover, my data, like Clerk's, suggest that rote-learned items are frequently incorporated into syntactically structured ones.

However, at this stage in development it seems quite possible that there may exist large individual differences in the reliance of particular children on stereotyped sentences as opposed to syntactically productive ones. Even as adults we operate with a proportion of "frozen routines" so it is a capacity which we never completely abandon. It seems, therefore, reasonable to suppose that for some children it is an important stratagem whereby the child can operate in his social world and manipulate the people and objects in his environment, when he has only minimal syntactic capacities for constructing new utterances. More work certainly needs to be done on how and where children incorporate rote-learned items into their syntactic productions.

Having allowed imitation to re-enter the scene as a respectable theoretical process underlying early language development we must consider further the capacities it rests on. Many advances in the study of child language seem to consist in the recognition of areas of competence previously ruled out by self-imposed theoretical constraints. Study of my own child leads me to suggest two capacities, which the child possesses and which are necessary for imitation to occur, deserving further study. Both precede and accompany the syntactic processes; first, the capacity to categorize and recognize patterns in the social interaction of his everyday life. The child is born into a patterned social setting where each day presents him with a similar sequence of child-caring routines to the day before. He in turn appears genetically wired to perceive similarities between social situations and expects the world to present him with a sequence of similar events. With time this ability improves and he can perceive patterns after only one or two repetitions while earlier it required a long build-up of instances. On this capacity rests the later one to produce "felicitous" (Austin, 1961) utterances, i.e. to use language in a socially appropriate manner, transgressing none of our conventional context-dependent rules of usage. The second but related capacity the child possesses is that of being able to reproduce large verbal fragments lifted from his verbal environment with prosodic contour intact but with minimal syntactic or semantic analysis. At this time, like at no other, the child can produce long strings of socially appropriate nonsense (*vide* small children's very plausible sounding, but nonsensical telephone conversations in which they can appropriately imitate sequence initiators and terminators, e.g. "Hi" "How are you?" "Okay then" "Bye" plus expressive devices such as laughter, but with very little lexical content). This ability to produce unanalysed chunks of verbal material in the appropriate social context gives the child the social tools to create his own social space within the family, to get his needs met, before he has constructed any abstract scheme of word meanings and word relations. (Consider some early social space-makers: "And me" "Don't" "Give me" "Get off" "Stop it" which may be used unanalysed for a long period of time.) It also seems to be the means by which the child marks the place in linear sequence later to be occupied by morphological classes.

There is a need to study more carefully the early "mutual-music" entered into by mother and child. In the very early months of the child's life the mother provides the child with language productions which differ markedly from those she employs to other adults. They are characterized by exaggerated pitch range (Philips, 1970) and changes in voice characteristics, e.g. whispering, singing. Mother's also produce frequent vocalizations imitating the intonation contour of the baby's previous noises including crying (Holzman, unpublished data). The baby is introduced to this prosodic dimension of language long before the content has any meaning to him at all. It would not, therefore, be surprising if it were the prosodic features of utterances, set in the patterns of repeated social contexts which helped in the recognition of early utterance functions.

One final note on the methodology of imitation collection. One reason why imitation has not achieved the theoretical status it deserves as a process involved in early language development is that delayed imitations, which in my data are the crucial ones, do not generally turn up using the classical research method of running a tape-recorder for a give length of time and treating all utterances within that period as a text. Given that this method also ignores the context of occurrence of the utterances being studied and frequently also the maternal language in the dialogue, it is not surprising that the creative aspect of language has been given so much weight. There remains the theoretical problem of how to establish the links between the child utterances and the maternal ones of which they are an imitation, but which may have preceded them by several days. Hope lies in the fact that, at least in the early days of language production, children do not appear to imitate "one off" maternal productions, but only those which have a long history of occurrence in repeated social contexts. Proof of the relatedness of child and maternal utterances requires longitudinal and contextual data. Any validity that my data may have rests on the following facts; that my utterances were virtually the only input for my daughter; that at any point in time I could check with my current routines to establish the link with my daughter's utterances; and that I could follow each of her productions from its first appearance through all its subsequent history of occurrence.

CONCLUSION

The insights gathered from the constant, everyday involvement with my own small daughter lead me to the following conclusions: that small children employ two features of their environment to break the linguistic code; (1) the repeated patterning of child-caring events and (2) the ritualized nature of maternal language within those events. They lift items from these original learning contexts which they then generalize, sometimes inappropriately to new contexts. Due to the complexity of the sociophysical world in which language is embedded they may misconstrue the referential links of language to the real world or the functions it serves in the social one. There are two capacities on which the child's ability to imitate appears to rest which are deserving of further attention; first the ability to recognize the patterns in the social sequence of events in which he is constantly involved and secondly the ability to attend to and reproduce the prosodic patterns to which he is exposed before meaning or syntax are at his disposal.

18

Context, Word and Meaning:

Toward a Communicational Analysis
of Lexical Acquisition

SUSAN R. BRAUNWALD

University of California, Los Angeles, U.S.A.

This chapter traces the daily acquisition and evolution of the *meanings* of a child's first 50 words as they communicate in situational contexts. The problem of reference is approached from a pragmatic perspective, and new factual data from a diary source are introduced to support an interaction model of lexical acquisition (MacNamara, 1972; Nelson, 1973, 1974) and a cognitive theory of semantics (Olson, 1970). Lexical acquisition is thus considered as a function of an inclusive process of communication rather than as a separable component of language development. It is hypothesized that the child's communicative intentions in interaction with environmental variables influence the acquisition, extension and differentiation of her first words.

My thesis in this chapter is that the course of lexical acquisition must be understood in terms of the child's overall system of communication at a given moment in time. Hence, it is necessary to describe the context-specific communicative functions of a child's words before it is possible to determine the underlying mental representation of her meanings. For this reason, *I re-evaluate a number of controversial issues*, which crop up in the theoretical debate over the structure of early word meaning (cf. Bloom, 1973; Bowerman, in press, 1975; E. Clark, 1973a, 1973c; MacNamara, 1972; Nelson, 1973, 1974), *in terms of the situation-specific communicative purpose of the child's utterance.*

By communicative purpose I mean: in so far as the situational context allows of judgement, what is the discernible reason for the child's utterance? Does she want to be picked up, have a diaper changed, or call her mother's attention to an exciting event in the environment? Perhaps she is whining for her bottle or cajoling her mother into giving her a second cookie. In other words, a first question to ask in evaluating the meaning of a child's word is: for what context-specific reason is the child communicating at this moment?

Once the child's apparent reason for communicating in a given context is defined, the second question to ask is: Why has she selected one word rather than another to encode her intention? If the totality of her communicative repertoire is considered, what are the alternative possibilities available to the child for conveying her context-specific meaning to an interlocutor? Does she have a communicative choice among words in her lexicon, or is she perforce limited to using a single word to encode her intentions and meanings in a variety of situations? If she is, in fact, limited to using a single word in her repertoire in a range of situations, on what basis has she selected this particular word, rather than any of the other words in her lexicon, to serve a given communicative function? Certain facts about the process of lexical acquisition, for example, semantic extension, appear to be quite logical from the child's communicative perspective when questions such as these are considered.

This chapter is organized in such a way that it is possible for the reader to evaluate the same data from multiple theoretical perspectives. The first section is devoted to an overview of the process of lexical acquisition. I briefly trace the acquisition, evolution and differentiation of my daughter, Laura's, first 50 words so that the reader has some overall impression of the idiosyncratic form of many of her words and the scope of the meanings which she can convey. In this section, the word—that is to say any arbitrary union of a consistently used phonetic form with a meaning—is the theoretical unit of analysis. Thus, examples of developmental processes such as semantic extension and underinclusion from Laura's lexicon can be easily compared to data from other diary sources (Bloom, 1973; Bowerman, in press, 1975; Clark, 1973a; Ferrier, 1975; Nelson, 1973).

In the second part of this chapter, the theoretical unit of analysis is the situation-specific social interaction in which the meaning of a word is acquired, extended and differentiated (cf. Ferrier, this volume). I conceptualize the process of lexical acquisition in terms of a self-contained but dynamic communicative system for conveying situated meaning. The detailed developmental histories of three words: (1) *ba*—ball, round objects, milk, and liquid served in a cup; (2) *bow-wow*—initially the sight of dogs and doglike toys, miscellaneous animals and cars as well as the sound of barking, car engines, airplanes, birds' chirping and noises from the outside which are audible in the house; and (3) *tree*—trees, shoes and briefly socks are presented. Each of these words illustrates a different developmental process, which, if analyzed apart from the totality of the child's communicative system, could easily be mistaken for a single process, semantic extension. The process of semantic extension, as exemplified by the word *tree* is distinguished from: (1) the pragmatic manipulation of a word with a specific referent as a situation-specific attention getting device, *ba*; and (2) the cognitive mismatch between a concept, a word and the real-world referent to which the word refers, *bow-wow*.

To avoid any confusion, it should be made clear from the outset that my purpose in this chapter is a descriptive one. In emphasizing the methodological importance of a situational analysis of the child's communicative intention to a theory of lexical acquisition, I have deliberately sidestepped a number of complicated philosophical and linguistic issues. Moreover, I make no claim to define the underlying mental representation of word meaning. Rather, the goal of this chapter is to delineate the outward manifestations of the interaction of linguistic and non-linguistic processes in one child's solution to the problem of meaning. In this manner, it may be possible to begin to clarify the nature of the problems which all children must solve in order to discover and use language as an effective communicative tool.

DATA BASE

The data for this study come from a daily record of the language acquisition of a female child, Laura. Laura is the second child of professional parents. There is a 2 years and 9 months age difference between Laura and her older sister, Joanna. The record was begun when Laura was born and continues in detail to age 3½. Utterances were recorded on the basis of emergent structure, and each entry includes the linguistic and non-linguistic context of the speech event. The record was kept by the author, Laura's mother, who was the full-time caretaker throughout this period.

Throughout the period from 8 months to 2 years, a daily record of Laura's lexical acquisition was kept. The present study is based on the data covering a 1-year period from 8 to 20 months. (Due to unavoidable circumstances, there is no record from 10 to 11 months). At 8 months, there is no evidence of a receptive or productive lexicon. Twenty months was selected as an arbitrary cut-off point far enough into language development so that the effects of the emergence of syntax on the differentiation of the meanings of Laura's early words could be examined. At 20 months, Laura's lexicon contained approximately 391 words and her word combinations conformed to Brown's (1973) description of Stage 1.

Words which were imitated from the speech of others as well as spontaneously produced words were recorded in the diary. However, a word was not entered in the record of Laura's cumulative lexicon until it was spontaneously produced. It was also possible in hindsight to discover the probable source of some of her spontaneously produced words. In these instances, presumed sources of a word were recorded at the time of spontaneous production. It is, therefore, possible to trace the etiology of some of Laura's lexicon to an ostensible source of input. Reappearances of a given word were recorded until its meaning was definitely a stable or "established" part of Laura's repertoire. "Established" or "stable" in this context is defined in terms of efficacy of communication. When Laura used a given "word" repeatedly and consistently over a number of days to refer to a discernible object, need or situation, the meaning was considered "established" for purposes of intra-family communication.

Two kinds of problems of meaning arose in the recording of the data. In some cases, it was not possible to discern a meaning for a word in which situational factors indicated the child's communicative intent. When this happened, all instances of the word were recorded until a probable meaning became apparent from repeated usage or the word disappeared altogether. In other cases, the problem was to be certain that it was the child who ascribed meaning to a given utterance rather than the adult-participant anticipating or reading in a meaning to a "baby-talk" word. In these cases, the word was recorded with the note that its actual meaning to the child was unclear. Such a word was watched over time until repeated usage established it as belonging to Laura's repertoire of meaningful words.

Any changes in an "established" word in the repertoire were noted. Changes involved: (1) the disappearance of a word with the reappearance of the same meaning in a different phonetic form; (2) complete disappearance of a word; (3) disappearance and reappearance of a word in the same phonetic form and (4) over-extensions with subsequent differentiation.

New lexicon was reviewed on the month birthdate, and each month birthdate contains a listing of the new acquisitions for the immediately preceding month. Any changes in the status of previously acquired vocabulary are also summarized at this time. Finally, as a control, running samples of: (1) all vocalizations and (2) comprehensible speech were hand recorded at alternate two week intervals from 13 to 16 months. In addition, for the period from 16 to 20 months, two hours of tape-recorded data were selected at random from an extensive audio record which serves as a control sample of Laura's ordinary or "average" speech.

THE THEORETICAL AND METHODOLOGICAL
IMPORTANCE OF CONTEXT

Since a primary virtue of a daily diary study is the possibility of documenting subtle change, it was decided to trace in detail the developmental histories of several representative words, *ba*, *bow-wow*, and *tree*. It was also decided that the mechanism underlying the acquisition, evolution and differentiation of these words might be better understood if each word were traced in its communicative context rather than as an abstract, context-free meaning in a lexical entry. The reason for this methodological emphasis on context is that the child is, in fact, trying to figure out and to convey meanings which are anchored in a real-world setting and which are part of an active process of social interaction between speaker and hearer.

The Discovery of Situated Meanings

The child's first and foremost task in acquiring a lexicon is to discover how to comprehend and to convey situated meanings. Olson's (1970) cognitive theory of semantics provides an extremely useful theoretical framework for conceptualizing the problem which confronts the child. According to Olson, the speaker's choice of a word, or words, to refer to a perceptually salient object in the environment depends upon the other alternative referents in the situational context. The speaker, who already knows what she is talking about, chooses words which provide the listener with sufficient information to partition the real-world situational alternatives and, hence, to select the appropriate referent (cf. also Brown, 1958). For instance, assuming that the speaker and listener share the same real-world referent for the word *bow-wow*, a mother's utterance "Look at the bow-wow!" in the presence of a car and a dog should unambiguously eliminate the car as a focus of interest and call the child's attention to the dog.

The developmental task confronting a child, who is learning the meaning of a word, should be transparent from the example of the mother who is ambiguously labeling the referent dog with the word *bow-wow* in the presence of *both* a dog and a car. In fact, this example raises the theoretical problem of defining *how* the child and her interlocutors come to a social agreement about the range of referents for which a given word may be used. Obviously, it is not an easy task for a young child to discover the arbitrary, conventional link between a word, its real-world referent and her own concurrently developing conceptual schema for that referent. As will be seen in the discussion of the history of the word *bow-wow*, Laura initially experiences difficulty in figuring out the referent of a word when the labeling event is ambiguous.

In order to understand the language which she hears, the child must be able to discern correctly the relationship of words in the speech of others to their real-world referents in the situation. From the perspective of comprehension, her developmental task is to discover the match between a word which she hears and its real-world referent (MacNamara, 1972). Recognition of a word must lead her to recall one particular object rather than another (Huttenlocher, 1974).

The child's task in speaking is just the reverse of her task in comprehension. In terms of production, the child must make her own words partition the situational alternatives for her interlocutor. As will be seen later in this chapter, Laura initially invented her own idiosyncratic but effective system of communication in which a minimum number of monosyllables and words refer to a wide range of referents. Her idiosyncratic system worked well because her homonymous "words" were uttered in non-overlapping contexts. As a rule, there was only one possible referent for her homonymous word in the situation. Werner and Kaplan (1963) have also noted this phenomenon of plurisignificance. Unfortunately, it is impossible to know if Laura's child-invented system for partitioning a maximum number of situations with a minimum number of words was fortuitous or deliberate. In any case, her communicative system was remarkably consistent and effective (cf. Feldman *et al.*, this volume, for a parallel example of child-invented systems of communication).

Intentionality as a Key to Referential Meaning

A second reason for emphasizing the situational context is that a pragmatic analysis of the intention of the child's utterance is crucial to defining the relationship between a word and its referent. It is theoretically important to differentiate between (1) babbling and (2) "baby-talk" words, many of which use the same monosyllables and reduplicated syllables as babbling. The distinction between (1) a speech act (Searle, 1969) involving an unchanged relationship between word and referent and (2) a shift in referent, and, hence, word meaning must also be made.

Babble or word? A fundamental problem in the analysis of early lexical acquisition is when to ascribe word status to the child's utterance. By what cues are the meaningful words *ba* and *dada* to be differentiated from the countless other "bas" and "dadas" babbled in the course of a day? A pragmatic analysis is helpful in marking the distinction between word and babble. Indeed, the notion of a speech act (Searle, 1969) has been investigated developmentally (Bates, 1976; Bruner, 1975; Dore, 1975), and there is evidence to support the assumption of purposeful communication from the onset of lexical acquisition. Thus, in most instances, behavioral cues in situational context permit the listener to distinguish vocalizations with referential meaning and communicative intent from babbling. For example, when Laura at 1;0(18) uttered the syllable "ba" while looking at a neighbor's dog's ball in the ivy and then picked up the ball and repeated "ba", as she did so, her mother ascribed referential meaning and word status to the syllable. However, when at 1;1(0) Laura uttered "ba, ma, ba, ba", while playing quietly alone with the garbage on her highchair tray, her mother interpreted the vocalization as a semantically empty babbled accompaniment to play.

Multiple meanings or speech acts? Not only must an interlocutor determine the difference between babble and meaningful utterances, she must also distinguish among the multiple meanings and intentions which may be expressed by a single phonetic form. An "educated guess" as to the situation-specific intention of the child's utterance is an important first step in distinguishing between semantic and pragmatic processes in the child's use of a word. The pragmatic manipulation of a word with a single, defined referent should not inadvertently be classifed as a semantic extension of the referential meaning.

An example makes the distinction between semantic and pragmatic processes clear. When Laura (1;5(1)) says "bow-wow" as she is pointing to a llama on a decorated wooden chest, she is extending the referential meaning of the word to an inappropriate, although obviously perceptually similar referent. However, when at 1;0(7) she says "bow-wow" as she is standing at the front door, she is pragmatically manipulating the word *bow-wow* as a request to be taken outside to see the neighbor's dog. *Bow-wow* has no immediate contextual referent and obviously is not an extension of the meaning of the word *dog* to the front door!

THE FIRST FIFTY WORDS

Before turning to a detailed discussion of *ba, bow-wow* and *tree,* a brief overview of the acquisition of Laura's first 50 words is presented in order to place the ensuing analysis in a developmental perspective. The first 50 words were selected as a developmental cadre in order to keep the present study parallel to Nelson's (1973) longitudinal survey of the lexical acquisition of 18 American toddlers.

When Laura was 15 months and 12 days old, she uttered her fiftieth spontaneously produced meaningful word, the syllable "pay", to request Joanna's lunch pail. By 16 months her lexicon contained 52 actively used words, 39 of which were among her original first 50 spontaneously produced words. For this reason, the overview of Laura's lexical acquisition concentrates on the period of development from 0;9(8), when Laura, in response to a photograph of her father uttered her first meaningful words "ah dada", to 1;4(0) when there is no doubt that she knows and uses 50 words.

The striking feature of Laura's lexical acquisition throughout the 7-month period from the utterance of her first word to the end of her sixteenth month is that the process of vocabulary growth is inseparable from the development of her communicative competence as a whole. While for research purposes it is possible to speak of a process of lexical acquisition and to roughly assign meanings to Laura's words, the fact of the matter is that she gradually invented her own system of communication. In effect, she discovered a way to use a minimum number of words in conjunction with the situational context to convey a variety of highly meaningful messages to her listener. Laura's system of communication was effective as long as her listener could use situational context to figure out the referent of her word and the intention of her utterance. The important point to note is that by the end of her sixteenth month Laura could communicate in a wide range of day-to-day situations. However, if her language were to be measured against the standard of conventional English, she could barely talk. The reality of this larger communicative process is unavoidably and unfortunately obscured in the following summary of her lexical acquisition. It should nevertheless be kept in mind.

The Form of Laura's Words

One possible way to conceptualize the acquisition, evolution and differentiation of Laura's first 50 words is to emphasize the form of the word as the unit of analysis. The emergence and disappearance of Laura's words can be charted as well as any changes in the meanings expressed by her stable words. Table I presents Laura's first 50 spontaneously produced "words" in their order of acquisition. As can be seen, the term word is being used rather liberally to refer to any recognizable union of a phonetic form and a meaning.

Table I
The form and meaning of Laura's first 50 spontaneously produced words

	Child's word	Adult's word	Context of first use	Range of use in order of occurrence	Range of use at 16 months
1.	Dada/daddy 0;9(8)	Father	L noticed a photograph of Father.	Father; doll; baby in a photograph; Laura herself in a mirror; to M in a photograph; to people in general; to J specifically; to call attention to herself; occasionally to any man.	Father, sometimes is used to designate any man.
2.	Ma/um-ma 0;9(8)	Milk	To request a cup of milk.	Milk only	Discontinued. Replaced by ba, 1;1(11).
3.	Bye 0;9(29)	Bye/bye-bye	In response to the gesture of waving.	Social routine to mark departure; non-existence.	From 1;1(9) to 1;3(8) the word was discontinued but the gesture was retained. Productive from 1;3(8) onward.
4.	Hi 0;11(4)	Hi	L is talking on a toy telephone.	Greeting; a way to call attention to herself; notice.	Hi + noun frequently used as greeting, attention getting device and expression of notice.
5.	Dat 0;11(4)	That?	Request for food from the table which L cannot reach from her high chair.	Request for the name of an unknown object (a) which L is holding (b) to which L is pointing.	Discontinued as a request for food. Infrequently used as a request for information.
6.	Oh-oh 0;11(7)	Oh-oh	As L's doll fell out of the stroller.	To falling objects whether accidentally or deliberately dropped, to express notice of perceptually unexpected events; to spills; to indicate that J has hit her.	The entire range of use remains productive.

Table I *continued*

	Child's word	Adult's word	Context of first use	Range of use in order of occurrence	Range of use at 16 months
7.	Mama/Mommy 0;11(10)	Mother	In response to the sound of M's voice coming from another room.	Mother; request for care. Discontinued 1;1(0)-1;1(28)	Mother.
8.	Irma 0;11(13)	Irma (temporary housekeeper)	As L watched Irma make the bed.	Irma; mother; 1;1(0) possible meaning = caretaker.	Discontinued c. 1;2(0) when Irma left the household.
9.	Bow-wow 0;11(17)	Dog	L is sitting by an open window. A dog is barking but not visible.	To the sound of (a) barking, (b) an airplane, (c) car engine, (d) birds, (e) any outside noise audible in the house; to a toy dog; to sight of car; to sight of dog.	Dogs and barking only.
10.	Twee 1;0(7)	Tree	As L touched the bark of a tree in a botanical garden.	Trees; the sole of L's orthopedic shoe; shoes; sock.	Trees. Shoes. L will not substitute the word shoe for this second meaning.
11.	Hikee/Hi kee 1;0(9)	Hi, kitty	To the family's cat as he entered the room.	To express notice of the cat; to greet M first thing in the morning; to express notice of dogs (Bow-wow. Hi kee).	To greet cats; to express notice of cats.
12.	Ch/chee 1;0(9)	Cheese	As M handed J a piece of cheese.	To request first and second servings of cheese at the table or from the refrigerator.	The entire range of use remains productive.
13.	Ba 1;0(9)	Ball	To identify a picture of a ball in her baby book.	Ball; round objects including a grapefruit, an orange, a seedpod and the doorbell buzzer; to request first and second servings of liquid in a cup.	The entire range of use remains productive.

No.	Child form	Gloss	Situation	Usage	Notes
14.	Hikoo 1;0(12)	?	As M came to get L from the crib.	Greeting routine for several days.	Discontinued.
15.	Hidee/ Hi dee 1;0(13)	Hi, daddy Hi, Joanna	To F as she snuggled in our bed early in the morning.	To greet F; to greet J.	Discontinued as a greeting to F. Developed into Hi, Dee-Dee as a way to greet J.
16.	Da 1;0(23)	Down	As a request to get down from her high chair.	To request locational or positional change. Used where the words up, out and in would be situationally appropriate.	Specifically used for request to get down from her high chair or in other situations where down is the appropriate request for positional change.
17.	Cookie 1;0(23)	Cookie	L is eating a cookie. L showed it to M.	Cookies; novel round foods; music on the hi-fi or car radio; rocking in the rocking chair; ice cream; the rocking chair.	The entire range of use remains productive.
18.	More 1;0(23)	More	To request a second cup of milk.	Used only once.	Discontinued until 1;5(7).
19.	Baba 1;0(23)	Banana	L is eating a banana.	Bananas.	Bananas. The form baba is also used for L's nursing bottle.
20.	Bot/Bobbie, Bobble, Baba 1;0(23)	Nursing bottle	As L noticed her nursing bottle in the sink.	To her own and other babies' nursing bottles; to baby oil bottle; to milk bottle.	Baba = nursing bottle. Bobble = other kinds of bottles.
21.	Dee-dee Tee-tee Tidee 1;0(23)	Thank you	In response to being given something. M answers "you're welcome".	Response to receiving something; response to assistance.	Very rarely used around 1;4(0). (Reappeared 1;4(18) as Tatu and used actively thereafter.)

Table I *continued*

	Child's word	Adult's word	Context of first use	Range of use in order of occurrence	Range of use at 16 months
22.	Caca 1;0(24)	Cracker	L is showing M a graham cracker.	Non-productive.	Discontinued. Meaning subsumed under cookie 1;2(0).
23.	Bur 1;0(24)	Bird	As L noticed a robin on the lawn.	The sight of birds; plastic hen in barnyard set; pictures of birds; birdsong.	The entire range of use remains productive.
24.	Z/C 1;1	Horsie (toy bouncing horse)	As L tried to climb onto her rocking horse.	L's rocking horse; a friend's wheel toy horse; to request help in getting on her horse.	The entire range of use remains active, but the form is changed from Z to C.
25.	Kee/kitty 1;1(1)	Kitty/cat	Differentiated from the fusion hikee.	To express notice of, greet, or talk about the family cat and cats in general.	The entire range of use remains productive.
26.	Dee-dee 1;1(5)	Bell; ring	To request that M make the bell on an old alarm clock ring.	Discontinued 1;1(11) when L broke the clock.	Discontinued.
27.	Um-mm 1;1(11)	Umm good	To initiate a game in which M pretends to eat. M says "Umm good!"	To initiate food game; to the taste of foods which L likes.	The entire range of use remains productive.
28.	Pooh 1;1(15)	Pooh	As L is in the act of defecating.	To call attention to bowel movement, urine and flatulence; to request a diaper change; to J's bare bottom; to spills of any kind which must be cleaned with a paper towel.	Bowel movement.

#	Word	Age	Form	Context	Function	Productivity
29.	Lolo/Lola	1;1(20)	Pacifier	L's pacifier was sitting in front of her high chair. L repeated lolo lolo until M gave it to her.	To request and talk about pacifiers.	Pacifiers.
30.	Broo	1;1(21)	Broom	L said "oh-oh broo" as a broom which she was dragging crashed to the floor.	As L notices or plays with the broom or dust mop; to request either item.	The entire range of use remains productive.
31.	Aw	1;1(22)	Off	L is trying to pull her bathrobe off.	To request assistance in taking off clothing and shoes.	Used infrequently but appropriately.
32.	Key	1;1(24)	Key	L noticed M's keys on the kitchen counter and asked to have them.	To request M's keys both when they are visible and when they are in M's purse; to photograph of keys.	The entire range of use remains productive.
33.	But	1;1(16)	Button	L is pulling at F's pajama button. F: "Oh-oh, what are you doing?" L: "But."	To buttons on shirts only.	Very rarely used.
34.	Ah	1;1(29)	Up	L is holding M's legs and begging to be picked up.	To be picked up; to be put into the high chair or the stroller.	The entire range of use remains productive. Most frequently used as a request to be held.
35.	Dee-Dee	1;2(0)–1;3(3)	Joanna	J is annoying L.	Two forms of referring to J, dada and Dee-Dee coexist until 1;3(3).	1;3(3) onward Dee-Dee is L's name for J.
36.	Boo	1;2(10)	Spoon	L is banging her spoon in her bowl.	To identify her spoon; to request a second portion of whatever food she was eating; fork.	The entire range of use remains productive.

Table 1 *continued*

	Child's word	Adult's word	Context of first use	Range of use in order of occurrence	Range of use at 16 months
37.	Powba 1;2(14)	Powder	L said "powba" repeatedly until M put talcum powder on her stomach.	Non-productive.	Discontinued until 1;5(7) when it reappeared as "power".
38.	Gen 1;2(14)	Again	To request that M continue tickling her.	To request repetition of an action.	To request repetition of an action.
39.	Ooo/hoo-oo 1;2(18)	Hot	To her food which is hot.	To hot food; to hot car seat; to hot pavement; to cold car seat; to ice cubes; to the oven.	To things which are hot; to the oven.
40.	Papu 1;2(20)	Newspaper	L is carrying a throwaway newspaper which comes once a week.	To L's specific newspaper; to newspapers; to paper.	The entire range of use remains productive.
41.	C 1;2(20)	Swing	To request that M swing her on her swing.	To request that M swing her; to the sound of the telephone; to toy telephone; to photograph of telephone; to a hairbrush; to a sock; to her rocking horse.	Discontinued for sock. Otherwise the entire range of use remains productive.
42.	Baby 1;2(22)	Baby/baby doll	As L noticed a rubber doll which her swimming teacher uses.	Used interchangeably with "dada" to refer to dolls; to babies and to Laura herself.	The entire range of use remains productive. "Dada" is discontinued and replaced completely by baby.
43.	Car 1;2(22)	Car	As L noticed a passing car.	To the sight and sound of cars; truck; bus.	The entire range of use remains productive.

44.	Me 1;2(26)	Me?	L is angry and wants M to hold her.	To call attention to Laura. Often volitional and accompanied by whining.	Very rare. It is not clear whether *me* is a pronoun *per se* or an attention-getting device.
45.	Guckie 1;2(28)	Duckie	To ducks on a toy block.	To ducks on a toy block.	Discontinued. (L no longer plays with the blocks.)
46.	Goggie 1;2(28)	Doggie	To dog on a toy block.	To dog on a toy block.	Discontinued. (L no longer plays with the blocks.)
47.	Hay 1;3(8)	Hair	As L touches people's hair.	To identify hair.	Hair.
48.	Out 1;3(9)	Out	To request that M help her out of a wading pool.	To get out of pool or bathtub; to get out of her high chair or crib.	The entire range of use remains productive.
49.	Beh 1;3(12)	Bread	To request more bread.	To request bread.	Requests for bread.
50.	Pay 1;3(12)	Pail	To request J's lunch pail.	J's lunch pail.	J's lunch pail.

A quick glance at Table I reveals a number of interesting facts about Laura's lexical acquisition. In the first place, Laura's lexicon is a *context-dependent* system. ,Forty-one of her first 50 words depend upon the social interaction between the child and her interlocutor within the framework of specific situational contexts in order for Laura's word to function as meaningful communication. In fact, an interlocutor is able to understand the meaning of Laura's utterances to the extent that she is privy to and aware of the specific developmental histories of individual words. Perhaps, because Laura's mother was actively recording daily notes, she became aware of the consistency of Laura's "words" in recurrent settings and recognized them as a purposeful attempt to convey meaning with language.

Twenty-one of Laura's first 50 words (daddy, hi, bye, oh-oh, mommy, Irma, bow-wow, tree, cookie, more, pooh, off, key, up, again, baby, car, out, me, duckie and doggie) are plainly recognizable words in the English language. However, of these 21 words, only eight (bye, hi, off, key, again, oh-oh, mommy and out) are used with essentially the same range of reference, and, hence, meaning as the standard adult word. The remaining 13 words are either: (1) heard once only (more); (2) briefly used and subsequently non-productive (Irma, doggie, duckie); (3) idiosyncratically extended after a period of conventionalized use (daddy, Irma, tree, cookie, up, car, pooh); (4) underinclusions with a specific referent (doggie, duckie); or (5) initially unmatched with a specific referent so that the scope of Laura's meaning is unclear (bow-wow, baby, me).

Twenty-three of Laura's words are partial phonetically incomplete imitations of adult words. It is difficult to understand the meaning of these words unless the original source of the partial imitation is known. Another four words are obviously child-invented. Indeed, onomatopoeia (dee-dee—the sound of the alarm clock bell ringing; lolo—the sound which Laura makes when she sucks her pacifier; and C—the sound of the swing whizzing and the telephone ringing) is probably the basis of three out of four of these self-invented words. The meanings of two of Laura's words (dat?—a labeling routine and um-mm—a food game) are completely embedded in the social interaction.

Three of Laura's first 50 words (thank you, hi and bye) are best described as social routines. By social routine I mean that the child is acquiring more than a word. She is learning the culturally appropriate social ritual in which the word is embedded. For example, Laura (0;11(4)) learned the word *hi* in relationship to the telephone. A favorite activity was to pick up the receiver of both toy and real phone, put the receiver to her ear, announce "hi" and then continue to babble. *Hi* definitely functioned as a social routine in which Laura was learning a ritualized cultural expectation as is indicated by her insistence upon a reciprocal greeting in response to her own "hi".

*L,0;11(23)
L's grandfather and uncle came to visit. L sat across from them on the sofa and said "hi, hi, hi", until they stopped their conversation and said "hi" back.

L,0;11(25)
The babysitter's boyfriend came over. L persistently said "hi, hi" to him and smiled in delight when he answered. This became a game between them.

This socially reciprocal function was developmentally prior to the very productive use of *hi* as a means to express notice of both animate and inanimate objects.

The Meanings of Laura's Words

The meanings of Laura's first 50 words reflect what is important in a toddler's world in general (cf. Nelson, 1973), but they also reflect the routines and structure of her own particular household. Thus, among Laura's first 50 words there are many meanings which are common to the lexicons of other toddlers as well as a few unusual ones (i.e. lunch pail, pacifier, strawberry, etc.). Table II summarizes the range of meanings which Laura was able to express by the end of her sixteenth month. The 52 words in Table II were all in active use at 16 months, although some words were used more frequently than others.

From Table II it can be seen that Laura's 52 actively used words permit her to communicate about the important people, salient objects and repetitive routines in her daily life. She can request first and second servings of her favorite foods (cheese, cookies, crackers, bananas, eggs and favorite small round fruits which are kept in the refrigerator). She has clearly differentiated her word for nursing bottle, *baba*, from her word for other kinds of bottles, *bobble*, so that there can be no mistake about which kind of bottle her mother should give her. She can indicate her desire for a diaper change or to have her shoes or clothing removed. She can inform her parents of accidents of all kinds including tattling on her older sister, Joanna, by announcing "Oh-oh Dee-Dee". She can request locational and/or positional changes as well as express notice of an ever increasing number of events which occur in her environment. In effect, Laura's first 52 actively used words form the basis of a self-contained system which permits her to com-municate with the members of her immediate household. Although many of her words were idiosyncratic, there can be little doubt that Laura has discovered the arbitrariness of the link between word, situation and meaning.

*In the examples L = Laura; J = Joanna, Laura's older sister; M = mother, and F = father.

Table II
Laura's actively used lexicon at 16 months*

NOMINALS

Specific

Dada, Daddy	Father
Mama, Mommy	Mother
Dee-Dee	Joanna (sister)
Baby	Laura, herself
pay	Joanna's lunch pail
*Pea	Peanuts, the family cat
*Nana	M's grandmother
but	button on shirts only

General

Dada	man
baby	babies
*doll	dolls
bow-wow	dogs
tree	tree
kee	shoe
kitty	cats
ba	ball, doorbell, round objects, liquid in cup
chee	cheese
cookie	cookies, crackers, novel round foods, rocking, rocking chair, music on radio or record player
bur	birds
baba	nursing bottles
bobble	milk bottles
pooh	feces
*eye	eye

General

baba	bananas
lolo	pacifiers
key	keys
broo	broom or mop
hoo (hot)	oven
boo	spoon, fork
papu	newspapers, paper
C (cee)	swing, telephone, hairbrush, rocking horse, cars
car	trucks, buses
*ahlbee (strawberry)	small round fruits and vegetables
*eh	egg
*potty	L's small potty toilet
*pee-pee	urine
*sa	sock
*fower	flowers

ACTION WORDS

Notice

oh-oh — to express notice of perceptually unexpected events

Hi + nominal — to call attention to herself, i.e. "Hi, baby".

Pragmatic manipulation of nominals to express notice of events in the environment, i.e. "bow-wow" to call attention to barking.

Demand

gen — again (repetition of action only)

out

*e (in)
da (down)
uh (up) — to request locational or positional change

Pragmatic manipulation of nominals, i.e. "boo" to request more food; "pooh" to request a diaper change, etc.

Descriptive

Bye — describes the action of a person or object which is passing L.

Pragmatic manipulation of nominals, i.e. "broo" as L is dragging a broom, "ba" as L is bouncing a ball, etc.

MODIFIERS

States		*Locatives*	*Attributes*
hoo (hot)	hot	Pragmatic manipulation of nominals to express location, i.e. "tree"	
bye	all gone	to go outside and visit the tree; "bow-wow" to ask to visit the neighbor's dog, etc.	*Possessive*

PERSONAL SOCIAL

Assertions		*Social expressive*	
me	a whining, volational word which functions to make the listener aware that L is unhappy about something.	um-mm hi tidee *ow dat	food game reciprocal greeting thank you ouch routine for getting M to label an unknown
*un-un	rejection (rarely used)		item

*This table follows Nelson's 1973 format of classifying the development of the first 50 words. The asterisk preceding a word indicates that it was not among Laura's first 50 spontaneously produced words (see Table I).

Thirteen of Laura's first 50 spontaneously produced words were extended to new referents. In every case of a true extension, as opposed to a mismatch between word and referent, there was evidence of a single referential meaning prior to the extension. Table III presents the data on the temporal relationship of Laura's extensions to the first referential use of the word. The stable system of homonyms which Laura invented by extending the meanings of existing forms to create "new" words as well as her "temporary" extensions to cover a single novel instance support the hypothesis that she used her own arbitrary system of communication.

The examples of extension in Laura's early lexicon suggest that her initial strategy for increasing her vocabulary involved the creation of new meanings for some of her existing words. In fact, by 16 months, her 52 actively used words conveyed approximately 71 different meanings. Moreover, the rate of her vocabulary growth was slow in contrast to a few months later when she acquired many new words. Table IV summarizes the monthly rate of Laura's lexical acquisition from 9 to 16 months.

Table III
The temporal relationship of an extension to the first use of a word

Word	First referent	First extension	Dimension
dada 0;9(8)	Father in a photograph; Father	doll 1;1(23)	human likeness?
Irma 0;11(13)	Irma—temporary housekeeper	Mother c. 1;1(0)	caretaker?
bow-wow 0;11(13)	when used to refer to sight of dog.	picture of monkey 1;0(3)	prototypical exemplar?
tree 1;0(7)	trees	sole of shoe shoe 1;0(19)	texture
ba 1;0(9)	ball	grapefruit 1;1(1)	roundness
da 1;0(23)	to get down from high chair	to get out of the bathtub and the swing 1;1(0)	positional change
cookie 1;0(23)	cookie	bagel 1;3(0)	round shape, edibility
pooh 1;1(15)	in the act of defecating	urine; breaking wind 1;1(20)	function
broo 1;1(21)	broom	dust mop 1;2(13)	function? prototypical exemplar?
boo 1;2(10)	spoon	fork 1;3(24)	function? prototypical exemplar?
oo/hoo 1;2(18)	hot	(a) to cold car seat (b) while sucking ice cubes 1;3(0)	perception of an extreme in the range of the expected temperature.
car 1;2(22)	car	mailtruck or bus 1;4(0)	function
ah 1;1(29)	up	to go outside May not be extension but a phonetic process from which the word "out" emerges.	

Table IV
The rate of acquisition of Laura's first 50 spontaneously produced words

Age	Number of new words	Number of discontinued words	Number of discontinued words which reappear	Number of prior words remaining in use	Total number of actively used words
8-12 months	9	1	—	—	8
12-13 months	14	2	—	6	20
13-14 months	11	3	—	17	28
14-15 months	12	1	1	26	39
15-16 months	19[a]	5[a]	—	34	52

[a]One of L's new words was discontinued and replaced with a different word. It is, therefore, counted twice, once in each form, under the column number of new words. The discontinued form is counted under the column discontinued words.

The rate of lexical acquisition began to accelerate between 16 and 17 months when Laura acquired 35 new words. However, the dramatic increase in her vocabulary, which suggests a new strategy toward the problem of conveying meaning with words, occurred between 17 and 18 months. During this interval, Laura added 80 new words to her cumulative lexicon. For whatever developmental reasons, she was suddenly able to increase rapidly the number of words in her vocabulary. From 17 months onward, her earlier strategy of extending the meanings of her existing words became much less essential to her ability to communicate.

During the early period of lexical acquisition (0;9(8)-1;4(0)), semantic extensions functioned as a means to expand the range of situations about which Laura could talk in the absence of specific lexical items. Her extensions of a word with a defined referent to a new object or event were based on some similarity which Laura perceived between the extended referent and her first referent. This similarity could be a subjective, affective state experienced by Laura as well as a perceptually objective and/or functional feature of the referent.

The word *cookie* illustrates clearly the distinction between an extension based on a perceptual and/or functional feature of the referent and one based on a subjective, affective similarity experienced by the child. Extensions of the meaning of *cookie* involve both processes contemporaneously. The word *cookie* entered Laura's lexicon at 1;0(23) through a process of comprehension (0;9(8)) and imitation (1;0(22)). It was used for over 2 months with a clear reference to cookies and crackers (1;2(0)) prior to being extended on the basis of perceptual and perhaps functional features of the referent to other round edible things including: (1) a bagel (1;3(0)), (2) cheerios, a donut shaped cereal which Laura had never seen or eaten before (1;3(17)), and (3) a round slice of cucumber (1;3(30)). It is noteworthy that these extensions permit Laura to ask for unusual foods which were novel and not regularly served to her in our household.

Concurrent with the perceptually based extensions of *cookie* is a second subjective or affective extension of the word ostensibly on the basis of a dimension of pleasure to three separate kinds of situations: (1) to request music on the hi-fi or the car radio and to identify the sound of music (1;3(13)); (2) to request that someone rock her, to describe the act of rocking and to identify the rocking chair (1;3(19)); and (3) to talk about ice cream (1;3(21)). Unfortunately, in each of these cases there is an element of roundness. Records are round. The seat of the rocking chair is round. Ice cream whether in a bowl or a cone is round. Nevertheless, my distinct impression is that the affective state of being happy is the basis of these extensions. Music, rocking and ice cream were three of Laura's favorite things. Moreover, at a later stage the word "ka-king" became Laura's word for both ice cream (1;6(1)) and rocking (1;6(22)).

Although the etiology of Laura's extensions is not always transparent, their communicative function appears to follow an orderly pattern. It is hypothesized that Laura's extensions reflect the generalization of a known means of communication to new situations. This was an important strategy during the early stage (0;9(8)-1;4(0)) of lexical acquisition when Laura had to make her needs understood on the basis of a limited lexicon. Data in support of this hypothesis are presented in the discussion of the word *tree*.

As pointed out at the beginning of this section, the reality of Laura's communicative system is unavoidably obscured in a discussion which emphasizes the word as the theoretical unit of analysis. The next section of this chapter focuses more specifically on the place of Laura's early words in a communicative system.

BA—THE DEVELOPMENT OF COMMUNICATIVE EXPLICITNESS

A detailed consideration of the acquisition and evolution of the meanings subsumed by the syllable "ba" reveals the ingenuity with which Laura purposefully and consistently employed even such limited expressive means as a monosyllable to achieve multiple communicative ends within a defined range of situations. Two kinds of situations were encoded with the monosyllable "ba": (1) a situation involving balls or round objects and (2) a drinking event involving milk or other liquid served in a cup. The gradual recoding of the meanings expressed by *ba* in the drinking event into communicatively explicit messages which differ from one another on the basis of subtle variations in an essentially recurrent and stable situation is discussed in this section.

The Acquisition of the Meanings of *Ba*

Ba *meaning ball.* Laura acquired the word *ba* with an initial meaning of ball through a process of imitation (0;11(25)-1;0(7)) and comprehension (1;0(4)). From 12 to 13 months *ba* meaning ball was a spontaneously produced and stable word in her lexicon whether it be in response to recognition of a picture of a ball in her baby book (1;0(10)) or to a markedly different ball such as the dog's ball she noticed in the ivy (1;0(18)). During this same period, Laura played frequently with the ball both alone and with others. There is thus evidence from her non-verbal behavior as well as from her linguistic production and comprehension to support the assumption that Laura had a concept of an object ball which she referred to as "ba" in her own speech although she understood the word ball *per se* in the speech of others.

It is important to establish the fact that Laura used *ba* with a stable reference for a period of time prior to extending its meaning in order to appreciate her arbitrary inventiveness in the next step of the development of its meanings. This next step in the evolution of the meanings of *ba* actually involves two separate processes which might easily be mistaken for one, that of semantic extension. One of these processes is in fact an obvious extension (E. Clark, 1973a) on the basis of shape—roundness—to other round objects such as a grapefruit (1;1(1)), a round seed pod (1;1(2)), and requests to push the round buzzer to the doorbell (1;3(0)). However, the second process introduces a clearly pragmatic dimension to the development of *ba* and illustrates Ryan's (1974) contention that ostensible fluctuations in early meanings may actually represent different kinds of utterances or speech acts (cf. Greenfield and Smith (1976) for an analysis of the relationship between word and referent that emphasizes the semantic function of one-word utterances).

Ba *meaning milk.* At the same time that Laura began to extend *ba* meaning ball to other round objects, she also began to use *ba* to request milk (1;1(6)-1;1(11)). Shortly thereafter, this second usage was generalized to request juice and then anything to drink in a cup. *Ba* was used to request first and second servings of liquid in a cup only and to comment on activities in the drinking situation. In other words, while it is possible that Laura initially extended the meaning of *ba* to milk because she noticed the round mouth of her cup, the important issue is not the etiology of this second usage but its subsequent function as a multi-purpose homonym in her speech. Laura consistently uttered "ba" either in situations involving balls and other obviously round objects or in situations referring to milk and more globally to various aspects of a drinking event involving liquid in a cup. For example, these two instances of *ba* were recorded ten minutes apart, and each has a different meaning.

L,1;3(0)
Ba = milk
L is watching J drink milk. L then demands milk for herself.
L: Ba, ba, ba, ba. (A series until M filled L's cup.)

Ba = ball
L is playing with a ball. This is a series of separate one word utterances.
L: Ba. (L is throwing the ball.)
L: Ba. (L is running to the ball.)
L: Ba. (L is putting the ball in a basket.)
(There are another 12 references to ball in this series before L ceases to talk about the ball!)

Notice that the participant must depend exclusively upon shared real-world possibilities in relation to situational context in order to disambiguate the referential meaning of *ba* since there is no linguistic context. Moreover, in the first example, the participant must also understand the intention of the child's utterance in order for effective communication to take place.

The differentiation of the meaning of ba *in the drinking event.* It will now be argued that the evolution of the meanings of the second usage of *ba* differs systematically in relation to Laura's communicative intention in a situational context and exemplifies developmentally Olson's (1970) cognitive theory of semantics. Extending the idea of nameless concepts (Nelson, 1974) or cognitive meaning in advance of language (Bloom, 1973; E. Clark, 1973a, c; Greenfield and Smith, 1976; Huttenlocher, 1974; MacNamara, 1970; Nelson, 1973, 1974; Piaget, 1962; Sinclair, 1973; Slobin, 1973) to the present problem, it is hypothesized that Laura discriminates conceptually among aspects of the drinking event during the period when *ba* is a multi-functional word in this context. For example, it is obvious from her behavior that she knows the difference between a full cup and an empty one or between the taste of milk and the taste of juice. However, for lack of terminology, she applies her one word relevant to drinking with ostensibly global reference. Initially, *ba* is the only word in Laura's lexicon which refers to a drinking event in which liquid of some kind is served in a cup. The words *water, cup, juice*, *more*, *all gone*, *pour* and *drink* are non-existent in the first 50 words of her productive lexicon as linguistic means to "partition the alternatives" (Olson, 1970) of this drinking event. Lacking differentiated linguistic means to communicate in this drinking situation, Laura relies upon the pragmatic manipulation of the only word she knows which successfully calls the participant's attention to the needs, items and actions in this setting.

If this pragmatic interpretation of the multiple meanings of *ba* is justified, its differentiation into the more conventional linguistic forms used to encode aspects of the drinking event should follow a predictable pattern. When specific aspects of the larger drinking event are held constant and analyzed longitudinally, the replacement of *ba* with vocabulary growth and syntactic development should differ systematically in relation to the child's focus of attention and communicative intention. Therefore, in order to discover the interrelationship between pragmatic factors and lexical acquisition, the drinking situation *per se* was classified on the basis of contextual information into more specific events and traced longitudinally over a one-year period from 0;8(0) to 1;8(0).

The Encoding of Initial Requests for Liquid in a Cup

One recurrent event in the drinking situation involves *initial* requests for liquid in a cup both with and without situational supports to elicit the utterance. On the basis of a situational analysis of this context, it was discovered that Laura had a stable schema with reference to requests for milk *only* prior to the extension of *ba*. From 0;9(8) to 1;1(0) Laura encoded requests for milk with the syllables "um-ma" and/or "ma".

L, 0;9(8)
If M says to L, "milk, Laura, milk", L will say "ma". M then goes to get L a cup of milk. L does not always respond "ma", but her response is frequent and consistent. L seems to comprehend the word milk.

L,0;11(17)
L says "ma" and also "um-ma" when she wants a cup of milk. This is an established routine, and the milk does not have to be visible in the situation. For example, today at lunch L was eating a peanut butter sandwich, and, in the absence of milk or a cup to serve as a cue, she asked "ma, ma, ma" until M brought her a cup of milk.

At 1;1(0), "um-ma" and "ma" disappeared as a means to request milk, and for a ten-day period this situation was not encoded linguistically. Apparently at 1;1(9) Laura had not yet extended *ba* to milk since she uses her labeling word *dat* in response to the world *milk*.

L,1;1(9)
L has finished drinking her milk.

M: Bye-bye milk? Want more milk?
L: Bye-bye dat. (As L handed M the empty cup.)

At 1;1(11), Laura began to substitute the word *ba* as a request for milk in a comparable situation. Although the phonetic form of the word used to request milk fluctuated, there is an underlying orderliness and stability in Laura's communicative intention and a continuity in the situational context between the last use of "um-ma" and the first use of "ba".

Shouts of "ba" to request first servings of milk and later other liquids as well were a remarkably stable communicative routine in Laura's repertoire throughout the entire holophrastic stage of development. Indeed, no amount of adult labeling could persuade her to substitute another monosyllable such as her original "ma" in this context.

L,1;4(14)
(From tape transcription) L is in her highchair in the dinking room. M is making breakfast and is going back and forth from the kitchen to the dining room.

(a) L: Ba/ (2·6)*
     M: No/ = We don't have milk yet/ (0·1)
          Just a minute, Laura/
     (148 seconds intervene during which food is served and the family begins to eat. L calls M's attention to the fact that she has no spoon. M brings her a spoon but still fails to bring milk.)

(b) L: BA!/ (loud shout) (1)
     M: Oh, I forgot milk/ (0·2) Just a minute I'll// get the milk]
     F: // I'll get] the milk/
     (233·6 seconds intervene during which L eats her egg and engages in a conversation with M and J. She finishes her milk and requests more.)

(c) L: Ba/ (1) Ba/ (1·2)
     M: Can// you] say Ma?/ (1·1)
     L: //Ba] (0·2) Dada/ (0·8)
     M: You want Daddy ta give ya the milk?/ (1·4)
          Here/ = Mommy'll give ya the milk/ (0·3) Can you say "ma"?/ (0·2)
     L: Ma/ (0·2)
     M: Milk/ (0·8)
     L: Ba/ (softly)

It is worth noting that Laura's loudly shouted "ba!" in the second example is a felicitous speech act which appears to fulfil all of Searle's (1969, p. 66) conditions for the successful performance of the illocutionary act, request (Table V). What is missing from Laura's utterance are the arbitrary, culturally defined linguistic and social conventions for encoding a request but not the actual intention of requesting.

*Time is in seconds; = = latching; //] = overlap; / = end of utterance.

Table V

Propositional content	Future act A of H	M is to bring milk
Preparatory	1. H is able to do A. S believes H is able to do A.	1. M is able to bring milk. From prior experience L believes that M can bring milk.
	2. It is not obvious to both S and H that H will do A in the course of normal events of his own accord.	2. Since M has failed to bring milk as she normally does, it is not obvious to L or to M that M will bring milk on this occasion.
Sincerity	S wants H to do A.	L wants M to bring milk.
Essential	Counts as an attempt to get H to do A.	M interprets L's utterance as an attempt to get M to bring milk.

At 16½ months, Laura began to encode her initial request for milk more conventionally on the basis of the incorrect application of a previously acquired social routine, "thank you".

L,1;4(19)
L is eating breakfast. This routine was repeated four times in the course of the meal in order to request milk. The *thank you* precedes rather than follows servings of milk.
L: Ba. Tatu. (Milk. Thank you.)

Although she has the wrong social routine, she does have the right idea. One month later (1;5(16)) the word *please* enters Laura's lexicon and is heard for the first time not as an isolated word but in combination with *ba*.

L,1;5(16)
L wants a cup of milk.
L: Ba, pea. (Milk, please.)

The addition of the social routine, "please", unambiguously marked the intention of "ba" in this situation as a request for milk. In fact, the word *please* was immediately generalized to mark requests in other settings as well (1;5(17)-1;5(19)).

The imperative of the verb to pour in the presence of a bottle of milk, an empty cup and an agent to do the pouring also appeared, on the same day as "ba, pea", as an unambiguous request for an initial serving of milk.

L,1;5(16)
L is not actually pouring milk but wants her sister to do so.
L: Pour, pour.

The verb *pour* was first heard two weeks earlier (1;5(1)) as Laura was actually an agent in the act of pouring.

    L,1;5(1)
    L is pouring juice from her cup into a can.
    L: Pour.

and subsequently thereafter (1;5(12)-1;5(14)). There is, therefore, little doubt that Laura intends *pour* as an imperative in this context. At 1;6(14), the imperative and Laura's social routine were combined in "ba, pea, pour" (milk, please, pour) to request a glass of milk.

Three weeks after the appearance of *please* and *pour*, Laura began to encode differentially an initial request in the drinking event in which others have been served and she herself, or her sister, Joanna, have apparently been overlooked. She unambiguously refers to the forgotten person as opposed to the liquid in the cup or the act of pouring.

    (a) L,1;5(29)
        M had given L a glass of milk but had neglected to serve J.
        L: Dee-Dee, ba please.
        M: Oh milk for Joanna's cup. (As M poured milk for J.)
    (b) L,1;6(1)
        M had just poured J a glass of juice.
        L: Laura. Laura. Laura.

Example (b) illustrates a clear cut and real communicative choice on Laura's part since the words *juice* (1;4(3)), *pour* (1;5(1)), *cup* (1;3(17)), *please* (1;5(16)) and *Mama* (0;11(10)) are available as alternative words in her lexicon for calling her mother's attention to her oversight. At 1;7(22) the word *milk* is finally used in an initial request for a glass of milk.

    L,1;7(22)
    M had just poured milk for two other children.
    L: Laura milk too.

Notice that in the context of an initial request for milk, the word *milk* is first heard in the same situation in which Laura initially relied upon naming the person in need as opposed to the substance in the cup.

In the recurrent event of requesting an initial serving of milk or something to drink, the monosyllable "ba" was differentiated into: (1) a social routine "milk, please"; (2) the verb *pour* used imperatively and (3) references to Laura, herself, or Joanna, as the person in need. Each of these alternatives to *ba* now partitions a limited aspect of the drinking event in such a way that the linguistic encoding of Laura's request is more informative to her interlocutor. My point is that Laura seems to be sensitive to subtle distinctions in the situation and to encode this awareness linguistically. She is no longer limited to shouting "ba" no matter what the variation in the basic situation in which she is requesting milk. For this reason the encoding of her request is less ambiguous and context-dependent.

The Encoding of Requests for "more" Liquid in a Cup

A second recurrent situation involving the differentiation of *ba* involves requests for additional servings of milk or other drinks. Normally, such a request can be encoded by the one word utterance "more". However, the word *more* failed to develop productively in Laura's lexicon during the holophrastic stage. "More" was clearly uttered once at 1;0(23) after Laura had finished her milk and was not heard again in any context for almost 5 months. At 1;5(7), Laura again uttered the word *more* as she climbed up onto the coffee table in order to help herself to some additional lemonade. It is not until 1;5(11) that *more* is first heard to request additional milk.

In order to request additional servings in the drinking event, Laura extends her initial request form, *ba*, often accompanied by the gesture of holding out her empty cup, to this similar situation. From 1;1(13) onward, *ba* is a highly persistent means of requesting more milk. For example,

> L,1;2(0)
> L is holding out her cup for more milk.
> L: Ba. — Ba.

Notice that in this setting Laura's attention is frequently focused on her empty cup, a focus which she will begin to encode linguistically with the addition of the word *cup* to her lexicon.

> L,1;3(17)
> L wants more milk in her cup.
> L: Ca ba, ba. (Cup milk, milk. Ca = L's temporary word for cup.)

> L,1;5(27)
> L wants more milk in her cup
> L: Ba, pea. Bowl, pea. (Milk, please. Cup please. Bowl = L's temporary word for cup.)

From 1;5(11) onward, *more* is used on occasion to request additional milk. What is interesting is that in terms of emergent structure *more* is first combined not with the word *milk* but with the word *cup* in these early two word requests.

> L,1;6(6)
> As L handed M her empty cup for more milk.
> L: More. More cup.

In time, *please* is added to this request.

L,1;6(15)
L wants more milk in her cup.
L: More cup, please.

An alternative differentiation of *ba* as a request for seconds is, as with initial requests, the imperative of the verb *pour*.

L,1;6
L is handing M her empty cup.
L: Here mommy, pour.

In contrast to the word *more*, *pour* is at first only combined with *ba*.*

L,1;6(14)
L is asking for more milk.
L: Ba pour, pour it.

L,1;7(4)
L is yelling and holding up her cup for J to refill it.
L: Ba pea, ba pea. Dee-Dee pour it pea. (Milk please, milk please. Joanna pour it please.)

The pragmatic extension of *ba* to request second servings and its subsequent differentiation into *more* which initially combines with *cup* and *pour* which combines with *ba* invalidates the notion that a child's early lexicon can be readily classified into substantive words such as *milk* and function words such as *more* (Bloom, 1973). The word *more* in the drinking event is non-existent from 1;0(23) until 1;5(7). Nevertheless, Laura clearly has a notion of recurrence and an intention to have her cup refilled which she regularly encodes linguistically. Prior to the acquisition of *more*, which is immediately generalized to multiple contexts, Laura relies upon *ba*, often coupled with a physical gesture, the extension of her empty cup to request the recurrence of milk. It is doubtful, however, that Laura actually thinks that *ba* means "more" or "cup". It is more likely that she uses her word *ba* meaning milk to call the participant's attention to the condition of her empty cup. In this case, pragmatic manipulation of a substantive word serves the same communicative purpose as a function word, *more*.

The Non-volitional Uses of *Ba*

A third context in which *ba* was not used for requests was analyzed in order to be certain that *ba* was not merely some kind of context specific volitional

---

*These examples refer to emergent structure. This does not mean that *more* and *milk* and *pour* and *cup* are not eventually combined at a later point in development.

marker such as Piaget's "panana" (1962, p. 219). From 1;1(14) onward, it is possible to demonstrate a stable reference to milk *per se* as a separable, unique entity which can be noticed, acted upon and used up.

L,1;1(14)
L is watching M carry a milk bottle.
L: Ba.

L,1;2(0)
As L poured her milk into her bowl and splashed it around.
L: Ba, ba, ba.

L,1;2(13)
L wants to have the milk bottle lid. M gave it to her.
L: Ba, ba, (scream, babble.)

L,1;2(13)
The milk in L's cup is finished.
L: Oh-oh, ba, ba.

L,1;3(15)
L is blowing in her milk.
L: Ba, ba, ba.

L,1;3(15)
L noticed a milk carton which was across from her on the table.
L: Ba, ba, hi ba.

L,1;4(8)
L dunked her cookie by pouring the glass of milk over it!
L: Cookie. Ba.
M: There's the milk right there.
L: Oh-oh.

In addition, Table VI presents paired examples so that the reader can easily compare the initial situations, all of which were encoded with "ba", to the subsequent differentiation of the linguistic encoding of a similar situation. Finally, the fact that *ba* persists with reference to milk long after the lexical differentiation of other words in the drinking event such as *cup* (1;3(17)), *bubble* (1;4(8)), *juice* (1;4(3)), *coffee* (1;5(15)), *water* (1;6(27)), *straw* (1;4(29)), *more* (1;5(7)), *cold* (1;6(2)), *blow* (1;4(31)), *pour* (1;5(1)), and *drink* (1;5(27)) suggests that *ba* is indeed Laura's specific word for milk. In fact, the word *milk* is first produced not in a volitional context but in a potential action situation.

L,1;7(19)
As L reached for the milk carton apparently in order to serve her sister some milk.
L: Pour Dee-Dee milk. (Pour Joanna's milk.)
M: No, that's not your job.

Table VI
Differentiation of "ba" in non-request contexts

Context of "ba"	Context of differentiated word	Etiology of differentiated word
Ba—act of drinking. L,1;1(14) (At intervals as L is drinking milk.) L: Ba	*Drink* ←←←←*Drink*—symbolic play. L,1;5(28) (As L finished swallowing her milk.) M: Drink the milk please. L: Drink.[a]	*Drink*—symbolic play. L,1;5(27) (L and J are playing tea party. L is pretending to drink coffee from a small tea set cup.) L: Cakey. Cakey. Drink. Drink.
Ba—act of spilling. L,1;1(14) (L is dumping her milk.) L: Ba. L,1;3(14) (As L saw J spill a bottle of milk.) L: Oh-oh ba, oh-oh, oh-oh ba.	*Spill* →→→→*Spill*—drinking event. L,1;7(21) (As L spilt milk.) 1;7(21) L: Oh-oh spill milk. M: What happened? L: Spill milk.	*Spill*—drinking event. 1;7(21)
Ba—focus on the result of spilling. L,1;4(1) (L spilt keifer drink on her high chair tray.) L: Bye-bye ba. Un-un ba.	*Laura do* ←←←←*Laura do.*—L as the source of verboten action. L,1;6(14) (As L viewed a huge puddle of milk she had spilt.) L: Laura do.	*Laura do.*—L as the source of verboten action. L,1;6(10) (As L took the phone off the hook.) L: Laura do.
	Spill ←←→→*Spill*—drinking event. L,1;7(28) (L's milk was spilt.) 1;7(21) L: Laura spill milk.	*Spill*—drinking event. 1;7(21)
Ba—act of pouring L,1;2(0) (As L poured milk from her cup into her bowl.) L: Ba. Ba. Ba.	*Pour* →→→→*Pour*—drinking event. L,1;5(1) (As L poured juice from one cup to another.) 1;5(1) L: Pour juice. L,1;5(13) (As L poured milk onto the high chair tray.) L: Pour, pour, pour.	*Pour*—drinking event. 1;5(1)
Ba—act of blowing bubbles in the milk. L,1;3(15) (As L is blowing in her milk.) L: Ba, ba, ba.	*Bubble* ←←←←*Bubble*—swimming L,1;4(8) (As L is blowing bubbles in her milk.) L: Bubble, bubble.	*Bubble*—swimming lessons> blowing bubbles in any body of water. L,1;4(5) (As L is blowing a bubble in her wading pool.) L: Bubble

Context of "ba"	Context of differentiated word	Etiology of differentiated word
	Straw →→→→*Straw*—drinking event.	1;4(29)
	L,1;4(29) (As L is blowing bubbles in her milk with a straw.)	
	L: Straw.	
	Blow	*Blow*—drinking event.
	L,1;4(31) (As L put her straw in her milk glass and began to blow.)	1;4(31)
	L: Mama, straw blow. Blow.	
Ba—empty cup; finished milk.	*All gone* →→→→*All gone*—drinking	
L,1;1(14) (As L handed M her empty cup.)	L,1;7(28) (L spilt her milk on the floor and is waving her empty cup.)	event. 1;7(28)
L: Ba.	L: All gone.	
Ba—focus on taste	*Cold* ←←←←*Cold*—differentiated	
L,1;4(17) (As L is drinking milk.)	L,1;6(2) (After L had tasted her cold juice.)	from hot as signal of extreme temperature.
L: Ba um good (um good = food routine).	L: Cold, cold.	L,1;5(9) (It is a very hot
	M: What's cold?	day; as L ran to the air
	L: Cup.	conditioner.)
	L,1;7(21) (No cue as L is riding in a very hot car.)	
	L: Cold milk. Cold milk.	
Ba—items associated with milk.	*Bottle* ←←←←*Bottle*—differentiated	
L,1;1(14) (As L noticed a milk bottle on the counter.)	L,1;4(0) L occasionally calls the milk bottle "bobble".	from L's word for baby bottle.
L: Ba.		
L,1;3(26) (L is watching J take cups to the table.)	*Nestor cup* (L's ←←→→*Nestor cup*—identifying	
L: Ba, ba, ba.	name for her special milk cup. Nestor is a little boy whom L knows. Her cup has a picture of a boy on it.)	milk cup.
		L,1;7(15) (As L noticed
		her milk cup.)
	L,1;7(25) (L has just handed her special cup to M)	L: Nestor cup.
	L: Nestor cup. Nestor cup.	
	M: Yes, I see the Nestor cup.	
	L: Pretty Nestor cup.	

[a]Not imitation. L has already used the word *drink* spontaneously.

While Laura's initial utterances of "ba" in the drinking event are clearly intelligent social acts with communicative intent (Vygotsky, 1962) her linguistic encoding is idiosyncratic. Nevertheless, the participant is able to understand what Laura is trying to say. It is likely, therefore, that the participant in interpreting Laura's utterance perceives a mismatch between the literal meaning of the word and the situational context and mentally fills in her own word for encoding the intention of the utterance. In a sense, the participant automatically attributes these meanings to the child's monosyllable. For example, when Laura shouts "ba" as she holds out her empty cup for a second serving, the participant interprets the child's word *milk* as if it were her own word *more* and refills the cup. As has recently been shown experimentally (Clark and Lucy, 1975), when the literal linguistic meaning and the conversationally conveyed intention of the speech act do not coincide, it is the pragmatic intention which is understood and remembered. This finding seems especially relevant to the problem of interpreting early word meanings in that the participant regularly responds to the intention of the child's utterance even though it is not as yet encoded in a conventional linguistic form. In other words, the participant's interpretive processes of comprehension must not be mistaken for the literal referential meanings of the child's word.

While it is possible for heuristic purposes to create a dichotomy between an abstract semantic meaning and the *actual* use of word meaning in a situational and communicative context, to do so obscures the reality of the developmental process. In adding new words to her lexicon in the drinking event, Laura is not just adding semantic information to a lexical entry. She is learning important social and cognitive information about when to use which word. This information must somehow be available to Laura as she refines her linguistic encoding of the drinking event, and lexical acquisition is in reality inseparable from the broader issue of communicative competence. In conclusion, the differentiation of *ba* in the drinking event can best be described as the progressive recoding of comparable repeating situations into increasingly more explicit and informative terms.

BOW-WOW AND *TREE*: THE DISTINCTION BETWEEN A COGNITIVE MISMATCH AND A SEMANTIC EXTENSION

The example of the acquisition, evolution and differentiation of the meanings of *ba* focuses nicely the dimensions of the problem of defining when and how a child's first words become meaningful communication. As this example illustrates, meaning is contingent upon the sensitivity and problem solving abilities of both the participant and the child. Thus, when the acquisition of first words is considered in *actual* communication, the problem of meaning can be posed from two perspectives. The problem of the match exists for the adult-participant as well as for the child.

Not only is the child learning the adult's culture and language, the adult is learning to adjust her behavior to the child's world. In fact, subtle communicative interactions and adjustments between parents and children have been documented from earliest infancy on (Lewis and Rosenblum, 1974). As the child begins to acquire language, the adult's modification of her behavior is potentially significant for the course of the child's lexical acquisition. Both the clarity and consistency with which the adult partitions and labels the environment and her ability to figure out and accept the child's first word approximations have consequences for the child's strategy of lexical acquisition (Nelson, 1973).

The problem of the match from the adult's perspective is to infer the meanings of the child's first words from situational contexts in which shared real-world possibilities clarify the child's communicative intent. Moreover, because of the child's developmental level, these real-world possibilities are limited in scope. For example, although the participant may have to figure out if "ba" means milk or ball, it never even occurs to her to look for an analytic meaning. In Laura's world the participant may have to decipher the relationship of the word *milk* to the pragmatic intention of the speech act, but "ba" couldn't conceivably refer to an "unmarried man"! Having inferred meanings to Laura's words, many of which are idiosyncratic, the participant temporarily adds them to her own lexicon. In effect, the participant is temporarily bilingual to the extent that she is willing to learn to understand the child's language and modify her own in order to communicate in return. This is a subtle and continuous process (Braunwald, in press).

Like the adult, the child infers the meanings of words from real-world possibilities in a situational context. However, the child's task is infinitely more complex for she must discover the link between situation and word meaning for the first time. In essence, she must discover the match between the real-world objects, actions and states encountered in her environment, her mental schema or concepts and the words in the language which she hears.

The acquisition and evolution of two early words, *bow-wow* (0;11(17)) and *tree* (1;0(7)) will be contrasted in order to illustrate the problem of the match confronting Laura in discovering the reference of a word and incorporating it meaningfully into her own lexicon. These two words demonstrate how the clarity, consistency and circumstances of adult labeling and the salience of the object in the child's daily environment relate to the child's comprehension of the match between word, concept and object. The outward manifestations of this problem, raised theoretically by MacNamara (1972) and Nelson (1973, 1974) are clearly exemplified in the data on Laura.

Bow-wow — Mismatch

Initially, *bow-wow* enters Laura's lexicon (0;11(17)) as a multi-purpose word referring to the sound of barking, birds chirping, car and airplane engines or any noise audible in the house from the outside as well as to the sight of dogs and cars. Superficially, *bow-wow* is an inexplicable semantic extension based on sound and/or movement. However, when the etiology and evolution of *bow-wow* are considered, Laura's global reference is neither a semantic extension based on a criterial feature of dogs nor an example of the early overinclusions cited by Bloom (1973) as instances of chained concepts (Vygotsky, 1962). Rather it is symptomatic of the problem of the match which Laura must solve.

Laura's parents repeatedly labeled "bow-wow" in two specific situations. In one situation, the barking of a neighbor's dog was labeled in the room of the house in which it was most audible. The sounds of car and airplane engines, birds in the garden and many other outside noises were also audible in this room. In the absence of visual cues, it is highly doubtful that an 11½-month-old infant had the concepts to relate each of these sounds to its physical source and so she did not realize that *bow-wow* only referred to barking. In fact, Laura continued to use *bow-wow* to refer to the sound of cars after she had discontinued its use to refer to the sight of cars (1;0(4)). Indeed, this example raises the interesting issue of how the child integrates perceptual input from various modalities into a unified schema with relation to a word.

In the other situation, a dog was labeled "bow-wow" in a neighbor's driveway and a car was always also present. How was Laura to know which item was "bow-wow"? Apparently, she concluded that both objects were "bow-wow" since her use of the word is not situation specific with respect to either dogs or cars. When *bow-wow* refers to dogs it is extended to other dog-like animals and toys including a bright orange toy dog (0;11(20)), a picture of a monkey (1;0(3)), a toy monkey (1;0(14)), a lion puppet on television (1;0(15)), and a large longhaired cat (1;0(19)). For a brief period (0;11(19)-1;1(10)), *bow-wow* is also frequently used to refer to cars under diverse circumstances. Figure 1 illustrates the ambiguity of the labeling event from Laura's perspective and presents evidence of her confusion as to the referent of the word *bow-wow*. The fact that Laura labels cars as "bow-wow" in

Fig. 1. The labeling event from the child's perspective in a mismatch.

completely unrelated settings suggests that she has indeed misconstrued the adult reference. From 1;1(0) onward, *bow-wow* is discontinued for cars and other mechanical noises and is used to refer to dogs and barking only. During the time lapse (1;1(10)-1;2(22)) between the comprehension of the word *car* in the speech of others and the appearance of the word *car* in her own speech, in the identical circumstances which initially elicited "bow-wow", Laura fails to comment about seeing and hearing cars.

Figure 2 illustrates hypothetically one possible reason why Laura initially experienced difficulty in matching *bow-wow* to its real-world referent. It is hypothesized that initially Laura is matching the word *bow-wow* to separate visual and auditory schema. Instead of matching the word to one referent which can be known both visually and auditorily, she is initially matching it to two separate and ill-defined referents: (1) an auditory schema—noises from the outside which I can hear in the house; and (2) a visual schema—items which are similar to the two objects which I see in the neighbor's driveway.

The meaning of the word *bow-wow* is nebulous because Laura's cognitive schema for the real-world animal dog does not initially unify information about the sight and sound of dogs. In fact, in the process of trying to match the word *bow-wow* to a referent she may actually begin to discover how the sight of a dog and the source of the noise which she hears are related. My

(1.)   A WORD MATCHED TO SEPARATE PERCEPTUAL SCHEMA.

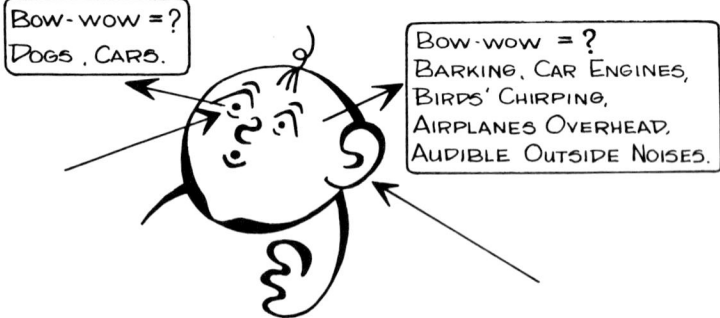

(2.)   THE SAME WORD MATCHED TO A UNIFIED SCHEMA.

Fig. 2. The child's use of a word as evidence of the unification of a perceptually based cognitive schema.

point is that the child's problem is not always one of matching a word to an existing cognitive schema. Sometimes the process is reversed. The child acquires a word and then builds a meaning on the basis of whatever generalizations she can make as a consequence of repeated exposure to that word in a situational context. Similar examples in which the child misconstrues the meaning of an adult's word have been discussed in the literature on lexical acquisition (cf. Bowerman, in press; Ferrier, 1975). The important point to keep in mind is that in a mismatch the child's word use is idiosyncratic because she has not yet discovered the relationship of a word to its real-world referent. As soon as this relationship is perceived, the idiosyncratic use is discontinued.

Tree — Semantic Extension

In contrast to *bow-wow*, the relationship of the word *tree* to its real-world referent was readily perceived by Laura. In this case, a large tree in the front yard was consistently so labeled with word and pointing gesture by Laura's babysitter. Figure 3 illustrates the clarity of the labeling event from Laura's perspective and the basis for the semantic extension of *tree* to mean shoe. As can be seen from Fig. 3, the word *tree* unequivocally entered Laura's lexicon with a specific reference to the real-world object and was clearly generalized to trees in many situational contexts.

Laura's extension of *tree* to shoe (1;0(19)) as she was examining the sole of her orthopedic shoe is an interesting one from the perspective of communicative need leading to linguistic creativity. If viewed in terms of the problem confronting Laura, the extension of *tree* to the wood-like sole of her shoe, rather than to any other wooden objects in the household to which *tree* never referred, is explicable as the result of an immediate communicative need. With a lexicon of only 12 words (Dada, ma—milk, bye, hi, oh-oh, Mama, Ch—cheese, Irma, ba—ball, bow-wow, that? and tree), Laura was hard pressed to discover a linguistic means to call attention to a highly annoying pair of orthopedic shoes. While she might have used her labeling word "that?" to request a name for shoes, *tree* is actually the only word in her existent lexicon which refers to an object with any kind of attribute in common with her shoe. In this sense, the extension of *tree* to shoe demonstrated an intelligent recognition of a hard substance, wood, in two very unlike contexts. The fact that "tree off" (1;1(23)) was one of Laura's earliest and most persistent word combinations is additional support for the contention that communicative need influences the discovery of linguistic means.

RECOGNITION OF THE MATCH BETWEEN
A WORD AND ITS REAL-WORLD REFERENT

1; 0(7)

AS L. FELT THE BARK OF A TREE
IN A BOTANICAL GARDEN.

L: TREE.
(AFTER M. HAD MOVED AWAY FROM
THE TREE.)

M: TAKE MAMA TO THE TREE.
(L. TOOK M. TO THE NEAREST TREE.)

SEMANTIC EXTENSION

L. CALLED HER SHOE SOLE, WHICH
IS HARD AND WOOD-LIKE, "TREE."

TREE BECAME L.'S WORD FOR SHOE
FROM 1; 0(19) UNTIL 1; 4(16)

Fig. 3. The labeling event from the child's perspective in a semantic extension.

As with other of Laura's extensions, *tree* became in effect a homonym in which situational context and behavioral cues clearly disambiguated the reference. *Tree* persisted as Laura's word for shoe from 1;0(19) to 1;4(16) and was briefly extended to socks as well (1;2(9) to 1;3(22)). During this period, it was also possible to demonstrate that Laura understood the word *shoe* in the speech of others although she consistently used *tree* in her own speech.

L,1;3(22)

We are curious to know if we can elicit the word *shoe*, regardless of meaning, in order to know if Laura uses "tree" for shoes although she could say "shoe". We, therefore, said to Laura, "Laura, say 'shoe', say 'shoe' " on four separate occasions.

(a) L is lying on the changing table.

M: Say shoe, Laura, say shoe.

L: Tree.

(b) L is lying on the changing table. M said "shoe" and rubbed noses with L. M repeated this game several times, and then waited for L to say "shoe" as a nonsense sound in order to reinitiate the game. L plays this game with the sound "R" and readily says "rrr" in order to get M to keep on rubbing noses.

(c) L and M are in the kitchen.

M: Say shoe, Laura, say shoe.

L did not respond but definitely looked down at her shoes.

(d) L and M are in the kitchen.

M: Say shoe, Laura.

L after looking at her shoe looked up and said "tree".

Tree was discontinued in an all-or-none fashion with the substitution of *shoe* in Laura's productive lexicon.

L,1;4(16)

L is lying on her changing table and picked up her orthopedic shoe.

L: Hi shoe. Hi shoe.

M: What's that! Say shoe.

L: Tree.

"Tree" was not heard again for shoe subsequent to this utterance.

As the histories of the words *bow-wow* and *tree* illustrate, there is an important difference from the point of view of communication between a mismatch of word and referent and a semantic extension. Superficially, a mismatch resembles an extension in that the child uses a word idiosyncratically with respect to the conventional adult meaning. However, the underlying developmental processes differ. A mismatch is a failure to differentiate the alternatives partitioned by a given word as is the case for *bow-wow* meaning car. When Laura uses "bow-wow" for cars, she has failed to perceive the relationship of a word to the real-world alternatives within a situation. As soon as she does so, this usage disappears. An extension, on the other hand, is a generalization of a word with a clearly defined referent for purposes of expanding the range of situations about which the child can talk. When Laura uses the word *bow-wow* for the visually cued nameless items which are doglike, she is extending or generalizing. Extensions of *bow-wow* to nameless, unfamiliar animals continue for many months.

CONCLUSION

Timeless controversies about the nature of Man are implicit in any attempt to describe the system of mental representation which underlies the acquisition and evolution of a child's first words. Thus, one turns to a study of the ontogenetic beginnings of language in the hopes of gaining some small glimmer of insight into fundamental issues relating to the origin, form and function of human communication. What one discovers instead is that the system of mental representation underlying the acquisition of language must be complex even at the stage of "dada", "mama" and "bow-wow". In fact, when the acquisition of meaning is analyzed in a situational context as words emerge and change, one finds factual evidence to suggest that the process is subtle and diffuse. In lieu of substantive answers, one uncovers a complex network of interacting cognitive, social and linguistic processes which indicates that the problem of defining the underlying mental representation of a child's first meaningful words may be incredibly difficult.

It is also difficult to draw theoretical conclusions about the system underlying a child's meaningful use of first words for a serious methodological reason which is unavoidable in the study of child language. In analyzing the child's early language, the adult searches for order and imposes a structure upon the data which makes organizational sense to her. It cannot be said with assurance that the same organizational structure underlies the child's system. All the adult may be describing is her own abstract, theoretical knowledge superimposed upon the corpus collected from the child. Nevertheless, what does emerge clearly from this study is the fact that lexical acquisition is in reality inseparable from the larger process of communication. Other processes such as the pragmatic extension of a word with a single referent or a mismatch between object, concept and word must not be mistaken for semantic extensions.

Above all, it is obvious that from its inception language is a powerful communicative tool. Cognitive, social and linguistic knowledge must somehow dovetail together to permit Laura to discover the linguistic and social conventions used by her speech community for encoding informatively a given intention in a given setting. To study the beginnings of this process fills one with enormous admiration for the ingenuity, intelligence and tenacity of a cherubic toddler who with a system of "mas" and "bas" and physical gestures manages to hold her own in a social, talkative world.

ACKNOWLEDGEMENTS

I would like to thank P. M. Greenfield, E. O. Keenan and K. Roberts for reading an earlier version of this paper, and H. A. Patterson for preparing the manuscript. I especially want to thank my own family for their loving patience and encouragement during the years of diary keeping which made this chapter possible.

19

The Child as Psychologist:

Construing the Social World

M. M. SHIELDS

University of London Institute of Education, England

This paper probes the implications for psychology of recent advances in the study of young children acquiring communication skills. Traditional ways of thinking about cognitive and social development provide too tenuous a base for developmental psycholinguistics, and in particular they give little account of the basic cognitive schemes which organize the child's construction of human persons as distinct from inanimate objects. It is argued that an attempt should be made to combine the basic Piagetian methodology of analysing the logical implicature of behaviour with recent advances in the pragmatics of natural language to tackle the logical implicature of basic communication skills. Features of the linguistic communication skills of 3- and 4-year-old children are examined to uncover what they reveal about the presuppositional and pragmatic base of childrens utterances. It is suggested that they show the beginnings of a model of human beings acting in a rule-governed social world. This model has abstract generalizable features of a far more complicated kind than those quantifiable characteristics of objects which govern our actions in the material world. These generalizable features form the basis of the differentiated personal constructs which gradually build up from childhood onwards. The mapping of these constructs would build up a more rich and credible picture of the development of human thinking and human behaviour than the study of cognitive development has hitherto been able to provide.

There is a curious asymmetry in the literature concerned with child development between those studies which take as their field the cognitive development of the child, and those which are concerned with the development of his relationships with persons and his knowledge of the complex web of social connections within which he lives. In traditional studies of cognition, the child and the researcher are both seen to be operating with a system of concepts which, though different in focus and in degree of elaboration, are within the same domain—the domain of objective knowledge—and within this domain the cognitive psychologist and his child subjects are, in a sense, fellow workers. Turn to the work on social or emotional development and the picture changes. For one thing, a new vocabulary emerges which deals less with perceptions, memory and operations and more with psychological entities such as attachment, dependency, affiliation and aggression. Whatever vocabulary he uses, however, the student of emotional and social development is doing the same kind of job that the student of cognitive development is doing, he is developing classifications, measuring constants, creating conceptual systems and theories about personal and interpersonal behaviour. He does not usually, however, regard his subject as engaged in the same activity at all. While the researcher is developing concepts about affiliation, his subject is affiliating, while the researcher is evolving categorical systems for observing interactions, his subject is interacting. The developmental psychologist does not appear to think that any of this behaviour does or could result from his subjects doing what he himself is doing; that is, forming a reasoned model of the social and personal world, using inference and deduction, deriving logical models from his own and other peoples social actions and elaborating hypotheses, expectations and rules.

The impact of the personal and social world on the child is almost always described in terms of affective rather than cognitive consequences. Yet Schaffer (1971) has shown that attachment, that most powerful manifestation of affect, must be closely tied up with perception and the development of stable representations of identity for the caretaker and other familiar family figures. Such representations are of course soaked with emotional meaning, and this makes them more significant and powerful, but in what way does this make them less cognitive than the representations of physical objects? Furthermore, as Bromley (1975) has pointed out, the child acquiring language develops a whole repertory of verbal labels and speech acts concerned with the activities and feelings of persons. There are words about thinking, wanting, liking, being friends. There are claims for possession, assignments of roles, words for sharing play proposals, threats, protests, appeals to social rules. In so far as children can use this repertory, it appears reasonable that the terms of it refer to internal representations of behaviour as much as words like *mug* and *chair* refer to representations of experienced objects. Furthermore, if they can use these words in talking to other people, there is a presumption that they assume that other people share these representations in a way which will allow them to understand to what the speaker is referring in using a word like *friend*, or in assigning roles such as *mummy* or *daddy* whether in earnest or in play.

THE INADEQUACIES OF TRADITIONAL APPROACHES TO CHILDRENS SOCIAL LEARNING

Why has the term *cognitive* come to be associated almost exclusively with knowledge of the inanimate world? One reason is the division of labour between psychologists where boundaries have developed between learning theory, social psychology, psychology of the emotions and developmental psychology. Another is the tradition of scientific work within psychology with its emphasis on laboratory experiment. Experiments in learning, whatever their theoretical base, tend to use simple overt responses to simple sensory inputs, or operations on carefully selected manipulanda in order to control the variables in the experimental design. Complex inputs from human beings make for messy experiments, or suspect confederacies between the psychologist and his human tools. A third factor which cannot be over-estimated is the impact of Piaget's work both on cognitive psychology and child development. His attempt to establish a synthesis between biological function and adaptation and the logical properties of thought has remained within the traditional boundaries of epistemology with its concentration on space, time and substance. In accounting for the unique and powerful fit which has developed between man's thinking and the objective world, Piaget has concentrated on operations on the inanimate environment and the mathematical logical schemes which develop from them. Only in his early work on moral thinking did he deal at length with some of the cognitive rules governing social behaviour (Piaget, 1932).

CHILDREN—SELF ORIENTED OR SOCIALLY ORIENTED?

Piaget also contributed to another group of theories usually gathered under the heading of early childhood egocentricity, which have been extremely pervasive in developmental studies, and which have tended to block investigation of children's social understanding. Theories of childhood ego-centricity fall roughly into two groups: those which are "instinct" based and which assume that the child's thinking is dominated by internal dynamic states, and those which are cognitively based and hold that the child's perception of reality is biased by an original monocentric viewpoint which does not allow for differences in perspective between the child and others.

The instinct based group is very diverse and unfortunately this endows the term "egocentricity" with a confusing range of meanings which are com-plicated and semantically infected by the common-language use of ego-centricity as a synonym for selfishness. Not only is the term used in psycho-dynamic research where it is loosely identified with the orientation of the instinctual self or "id", it is also used in behavioural research which bases the study of socialization on the acquisition of secondary motivations derived from primary biological drives. It has also been employed in sociological investigations in the tradition of Durkheim and G. H. Mead which make the assumption that the child is a kind of animal or savage who is tamed into humanity by the modification of his primitive, instinctual, egocentric needs by socializing agencies. This assumption of original egocentricity sometimes appears very like a scientific version of the doctrine of original sin! However, both instinct based egocentrism and cognitive egocentrism have recently come under fire.

The theory that the young child is dominated by organismic drives has now begun to cede before a more ecological model of constant interaction between the child and his environment, above all his social environment. Bowlby's monumental study of attachment has indicated a genetic base for social processes, and the mounting number of close studies of mother-child interaction are outlining a picture of the baby as a social interactor from the outset (Bowlby, 1969; Trevarthen, 1974).

There is now ample research to attest the disposition of young babies to prefer human voices to other forms of noise (Eimas et al., 1971; Eimas, 1976). There is also much evidence that they attend preferentially to human faces and that the attachment to specific human beings is based on the development of a differentiated perception of persons (Bowlby, 1969; Schaffer, 1971; Carpenter, 1974). The cross-modal association of auditory and visual inputs at an extremely early age is suggested by the work of Aronson and Bower (1974) which appears to indicate that the young baby of 3 weeks expects the human voice to appear in the same orientation as the human face. Furthermore, the fine-grained studies of young babies which have been made possible by the development of audio/visual recording technology are now revealing the delicate interchange of attention and imitation between mother and infant, and some of these have also suggested that there appears to be some innate mechanism which allows visual inputs to elicit isomorphic motor outputs, i.e. that there is a neural foundation for imitation (Bower, 1975). The early operation of this mechanism in the first weeks of life fades in the same way that the stepping reflex fades, and provides further evidence that the prewired dispositions of the human nervous system have to be modified by various kinds of learning before the sketched in connections can become the basis of voluntary action (Bower, 1975). The mounting evidence that there is an extensive and powerful genetic base for man's social propensities does not mean that social knowledge is innate. To count as knowledgeable, innately programmed behaviours must be adapted to the world outside the organism by the processing of information from the environment, including feedback from the behaviour itself. Knowledge, whether "know how" or "know that" is essentially adapted and therefore interactional in origin, whatever the contribution of the innate component. The recent controversies about the hypothesis of an innate language acquisition device are a warning against attributing too much of the skill acquired interactionally to a genetic base.

If the hypothesis of endogenous egocentricity has begun to melt in the light of recent research on young babies, so too has the hypothesis of cognitive egocentricity. Until recently it was one of the major paradigms used in research on the development of social perception in children. Almost half the work cited by Schantz in her recent review of social cognition was work on role-taking which explored the development of skill in allowing for the different perspectives of others (Schantz, 1975).

Flavell, who has been a leading worker in this field has, however, recently urged a more careful look at the component ideas behind egocentrism (Flavell et al., 1968, 1974). His own work and that of his team have shown that if the task is made sufficiently simple quite young children are capable of taking account of the viewpoint of others (Masangky et al., 1974). In his analysis of the child's role-taking skill. Flavell counts as the first stage, the child's understanding that an object can look different from different orientations and yet be the same object. He then postulates the child's knowledge that other people may be seeing a different aspect of the same object as the next stage (Flavell, 1974). However, there must surely be an intervening stage, one in which the child credits other people with the same ability to construct one object from different appearances that he has himself achieved. Indeed the hypothesis that the object appearing in the perception of two different people is the same object is the foundation of the entire system of linguistic reference without which communication would not be possible. Hence it is a far more fundamental and wide ranging achievement than the differentiation of other points of view, important though that is. Indeed the child's hypothesis that other people also attend to conceptually constructed objects and not to phenomenal appearances should be recognized as the astonishing cognitive achievement that it is, instead of being dismissed as the source of "egocentric" error.

BUILDING A MODEL OF SOCIAL INTERACTION

The child, however, not only understands the idea that there is a perceptual and conceptual field which is shared, he also learns to share a world of action and interaction in which the behaviour of others must be perceived and in which others must perceive his behaviour. If actions are to be co-ordinated reciprocally expectations must be built up as to what actions go with what, and Garvey (1976) and Bruner (1975, 1977) have traced the development of what Garvey calls action "formats" which can be linked into more elaborated sequences and which themselves can be objects of reference, although they are not "out there" like spatial objects.

It would be reasonable to expect the representations of his own and other people's behaviour to give rise to generalizable features in the same way as do representations of the impersonal world, and that these generalizable schemes would give rise to cognitive models. Unfortunately longstanding traditions in the social psychology of childhood have tended to divert attention from the nature of the models the child makes use of and to focus almost exclusively on his motivation. Thus processes such as modelling and identification are usually considered in terms of the rewardingness of the persons modelled, the child's dependence on them for satisfaction of his basic needs and his conception of their power and status. Rarely, if ever, is there any theoretical consideration of the basic cognitive content of such a model, how it is organized, retained in memory and elaborated, and what parts of it are selected to form schemes which can provide plans for imitative behaviour. Still less considered and investigated are the constants of such a model, i.e. those parts of it which are generalizable to all the many human beings whom the child encounters from an early age who neither nurture him, reward him, nor necessarily differ from him very much in power and status, and whom yet he may imitate, as Piaget's daughter Jacqueline imitated a small visitor who had flown into a rage, screaming and stamping and pushing the playpen (Piaget, 1962). If these processes of modelling, imitation and identification are going to be given cognitive structure, there will obviously have to be considerably more work on the intellectual aspects of the child's model of a human being.

CONSTRUCTING A NEW MODEL OF CHILDRENS SOCIAL THINKING

Adult social psychology has undergone great changes in the last 20 years, and has developed theoretical systems which allow for the fact that social behaviour is mutually represented in the minds of persons who are conducting relations with each other. This notion was formulated by Asch in 1952, and Heider (1958) began the link with European social phenomenologists such as Schutz (1967) which has proved increasingly influential in social psychology and socio-linguistics. These advances have till the present made virtually no impact on the social psychology of childhood, a fact complained about by Schantz in her review of the field (1975). It is only in the study of prelinguistic and protolinguistic communication that new ideas are beginning to make themselves felt, and this is partially because new observational technologies are revealing complicated networks of behaviour that make the traditional theories of child socialization look simplistic or plain wrong.

Advances in theory are often closely linked to advances in technology which give a closer view of the phenomena to be studied, and one of the delaying factors in building up a richer model of children's grasp of social processes has been lack of a methodology of study which is appropriate to the task. Interpersonal communication can now be recorded by audio-visual means, though there are still difficulties in recording in natural settings, and these recordings show that the study of communication is the key to opening up this field of investigation. The fine-grained studies of prelinguistic and protolinguistic communication, several of which appear in this volume, are a mine of fascinating information, but it is possible that they might yield even more information, and be more closely integrated with the later stages of development when language begins to play a dominating role, if a detailed examination of the cognitive implications of communication is put in hand. The question is, how to go about it?

BUILDING A MODEL OF THE COMMUNICATION PROCESS

When one is attempting to build up a new cognitive model, it is natural that one should take note of the ways that existing cognitive models have been built. Inevitably Piaget's work comes into mind, and there have been many attempts to align developments in communication with stages in sensory-motor and intuitive development (Edwards, 1973; Morehead and Morehead, 1974; Bates, 1976a). Interesting and important though some of this work is it suffers from the 'fact that Piaget's work is based on a different epistemological domain—the domain of thinking which relates to the inanimate world. Piaget once said that children learn about persons as they learn about things. If he meant by this that they form representational schemes both of other persons and of their interactions with them and that these schemes assimilate new instances, and accommodate and elaborate as new experiences cease to fit the previous structure, then he is certainly right. The question then arises as to the logical nature of these schemes for he surely cannot mean that they are of exactly the same logical kind as those which govern encounters with the spatio/temporal world. The constancy of objects in space can be stretched to cover constancy of identity of persons which is a necessary preliminary for the development of specific attachments, but what of reversibility which, according to Piaget, originates in the grouping of spatial displacements which allows the child to back track and make detours by compensating movements in one direction by moving in another? Time, and human action in it, is irreversible and what has gone before is retained and reconstructed only in the minds of persons. Likewise, what is to come is unfolded in human intentions. Encounters with persons must consider the experience rolled up inside each and the potential unrolling of future activity in the consciousness of both those involved. Things in space which are the manipulanda of operations have neither quality, and operations upon them produces a different cognitive outcome— a mathematical logical outcome.

Piaget, of course, acknowledges interpersonal interaction as a major force in establishing the grouping of actions into logical structures, and also postulates that the logical organization of structures of thought is a necessary prerequisite for the co-ordination of interactions with other people on an agreed programme (Piaget, 1951). Naturally mutual understanding between persons in communication and action depends in part on the sharing of certain logical schemes, but this is not to say that the logical schemes that persons share about the object world are of the same kind as the schemes they share about the world of persons.

It is suggested here that a close look at the logical implicature of acts of communication might illuminate the field and, fortunately, work on semantics and pragmatics which originated in linguistic philosophy has now begun to seep through into studies of natural language in a way that concentrates on just those features which make communication effective. There is not only the work by Austin and Searle on illocutionary acts, and conditions for their successful performance (Austin, 1962; Searle, 1969), there is also work in pragmatics which is picking out presuppositions and postulates which have to be considered if the relation between utterances and their contexts are to be fully understood (Grice, 1968; Apostel, 1971).

Charles Morris made the tripartite distinction between *syntax*, or the study of the relations of signs among themselves, *semantics*, or the relation between signs and their designata, and *pragmatics* as the study of signs within the total behaviour of sign interpreters (Morris, 1938, 1946). While Morris focused on the interpretations of hearers Carnap defined pragmatics as any investigation of language containing explicit reference to a speaker (Carnap, 1942). Whether the experiences of interpreters are the same as the experiences and behaviours of speakers, is, of course, a further question. Grice argued for the possibility that the speaker's intended meaning should be distinguished from the meaning of his utterances as interpreted by listeners, and also from the "timeless" interpretation which could be placed on utterances in which words had a range of conventional dictionary meanings. Furthermore, utterances were interpreted in specific contexts, and, because of the wide range of meaning possible for the majority of common expressions, only the context could add sufficient precision by the constraints it placed on use to allow of reliable interpretation by a listener. This implies that the listener must bring his own experience to the aid of his understanding, and even so speaker's meaning and listener's intepretation might not completely match. For this reason words taken out of context cannot be interpreted with the precision which they have when uttered in context, and with some specific intention, by a particular speaker (Grice, 1968). The difference, as many critics point out, is severely constrained by convention: if the speaker chooses a certain utterance to convey a meaning other than the face interpretation of the words he uses, he must make use of additional conventions or frames which allow him to use it in this way and also allow the person who is the target of his message to interpret it in the way he intended. These conventions may reside outside the specifically linguistic part of the utterance in common interpretations of the shared field of meaning on the occasion of the utterance. In short, even for mature speakers with an extensive grasp of language, the exchange of meaning through speech is dependent on the sharing of an intersubjective field in which the intentions and perceptions of each partner together with a world of shared meanings must be represented both in the speaker and hearer for any exchange of meaning to be successful.

THE LOGICAL AND PSYCHOLOGICAL IMPLICATURE OF COMMUNICATIVE ACTS

This highlights the kind of problem that the young child is called upon to solve in learning to communicate. He must not only himself have representations of the world which forms the context of communication, he must also develop representations about the internal representations of others. What could be the minimum, the basic skeleton of such representations logically implied in a successful act of communication? We take so much of the immense complexity of human skill for granted that when it is spelt out in detail it can look like a tedious statement of the obvious. Take the minimum pragmatic implicature of the following speech exchange between two small children playing, one in which the intentions and meanings of one person are successfully signalled to another. There are two little girls in the nursery home corner, Michèle (3;8) and Lisa (3;9) and Freddie, a boy (4;2) attempts to join in. He addresses Michèle who is apparently organizing the play sequence:

Example 1
(1) Fre to Mic: I can be dad, can't I?
(2) Mic to Fre: You can be dad;
        to Lis: and we can be two mums.

In this ordinary little exchange, there are two speaker/hearers and one listener who does not speak and two utterance tokens, both of them complex. Stripping the situation down to its barest communicational bones and ignoring the context and the implied rules about roles, what can be said about Freddie's locution from the point of view of his implied beliefs and intentions?

(1)   He apparently believes that Mic will hear his utterance.
(2)   He apparently believes or expects that she will attach a specific meaning to what she hears.
(3)   He intends that she should attach a meaning to it.
(4)   He believes that this meaning is a possible meaning of his utterance in his language (English, nursery dialect).
(5)   He believes that Mic shares this language.
(6)   He believes that if Mic attaches his intended meaning to his utterance, she will know that he is the source of it.
(7)   He expects or hopes that as a result of attaching meaning to his utterance Mic will also perform some action by gesture or word which will allow him to play the role which was specified by the meaning of of his utterance.

Then there is Mic's side of this communication transaction; to count it as successful we must conclude:

(8)   Mic does in fact hear Fre's utterance.
(9)   She recognizes it as having a possible meaning X in the language she understands.
(10) She in fact attaches this meaning to it.
(11) Mic believes that Fre was the source of the message.

(12) She believes that Fre intended the interpretation she attached and not another.

(13) She believes that Fre also intended that she should perform some action as a result of her interpretation of his utterance.

(14) Mic then utters (2) above with the full implicature laid out in (1) to (8) and immediately conjoins a remark to a second addressee with a similar implicature.

With all this, nothing as yet has been said of the web of shared meanings about the world which underly the content of the exchange, only the implicature of linguistic communication as a process has been studied. This appears to show that, at a minimum, the speaker must have an image of his interlocutor as (a) having auditory perception, (b) possessing speaker/hearer competence in a shared code of signals, (c) having the ability to identify the source of a message, (d) being able to interpret a message with regard to its frame of reference, (e) being able to interpret the message with regard to intentions of the source and (f) being able to act or react to the message in some way corresponding to the tentative expectations of the speaker.

If we look at the content of the messages, we can unpack the implicature of (d), (e) and (f) more thoroughly. Take Freddie's utterance first:

I can be dad, can't I?

Considered as a speech act, this is a tentative role claim within a set of roles appropriate to a game which is assumed to be known by both speaker and hearer. It is couched in a request form, consisting of a sentence with interrogative tag, the sentence bearing the content of the request and the tag functioning as response elicitor. The utterance begins with the discourse deictic *I* which contrasts speaker role to that of addressee and others present, and also identifies the claimant role with the speaker role. This is followed by the modal auxiliary *can* which, like all modal expressions, has a complex range of meaning. Part of the meaning relates to possibility, i.e. *dad* is a possible role within the game which is the shared field of reference, it is also the most probable role for a boy to claim in house play where there are already two role playing girls. *Can*, however, is also used to signal permission, i.e. social possibility, and so it is linked with a set of social relations, part of which inheres in the specific context but part of which is more general, belonging to rules for entry into groups. The modal auxiliary implicitly acknowledges the organizing role of Michèle and her prior right to distribute roles in "her" game. If a group of fairly equal friends were picking up roles in a game, the role claims would be more likely to use the modal *will* and be expressed as intentions, e.g. *I'll be the dad* or *I'll be father Christmas*, or collectively, *Let's be policemen*. Sometimes uncertainty may cause a change of focus between sentence and tag, e.g. *I'll be the nurse, can I?*

The remainder of the predicate *be dad* consists grammatically of a non-finite *be* which has a rather stronger function than merely coupling the subject and complement and carries the meaning of "play the part of" and *dad* which is a specific reference to an abstract object "the role of dad" which is part of the shared meaning. The tag, *can't I*, is a response elicitor couched in the interrogative form, syntactically expressed by fronting the auxiliary which carries the main semantic load. The negative post-positioned on *can* is an implicit acknowledgement that Michèle might negative the request, though the hope and expectation is that she won't. Nothing has so far been said about intonation. The tonic stress in fact falls on *dad*, but if it had fallen on *can* the nature of the speech act would be different, e.g.

I can be DAD, can't I   (tentative role claim)
I CAN be dad, CAN'T I   (protest or appeal against
                                       rejection of role claim).

So much for Freddie's attempt to join the game, now let us look in detail at the interlocking piece of discourse, Michèle's response:

Mic to Fre: You can be dad,
        to Lis: and we can be two mums.

Michèle's utterance is complex, consisting of two remarks with separate addressees conjoined by *and*. The *you* coheres with the *I* of the previous utterance with the appropriate shift of person and carries a contrastive tonic stress referring forward to *we* in the next part of the utterance. Michèle does not need to nominate herself until she includes herself in this contrastive *we*. *Can be dad* picks up and concedes the role claim, and would probably have been elipted rather than spelt out if it had not been in distributive contrast with the second part of the utterance. Otherwise, the response would have been *Yes*, or *yes, you can*. Michèle then uses *and* to conjoin a remark to a different addressee, and uses *we* to join speaker and addressee in a single set. The inclusive *we* seems to emphasize possibility rather than permission in the semantic field of *can*. The rest of the predicate *be two mums* carefully distributes the roles with the quantifier *two* which coheres both with the *we* and with the pluralization of *mums*, which refers to a complementary abstraction to the role of dad claimed by Freddie.

It is not claimed that this analysis is in any way exhaustive, but it does attempt to consider together both the pragmatic, semantic and syntactic elements within a snippet of interpersonal discourse so that the full psychological complexity stands revealed. The reference, or what Halliday might call the ideational element, is concerned with a game in which the roles and rules are represented in the minds of the two children speaking. The game of mums and dads is not a concrete existent which can be pointed out like a table or chair, it is a set of roles, rules and expectations which allow some latitude of interpretation, but are distinct from the set governing "doctors and nurses" or "policemen", and even more distinct from roles played in real life. It takes some time for children to learn and elaborate these rules though they begin very early (Bruner and Sherwood, 1976). They appear, however, to find no difficulty in representing them as being shared, for although there may be frequent arguments about the rules, these could only take place on the presupposition that other persons understand and follow rules, even if they are the wrong rules.

These rules are part of the latent frame of reference which is presupposed in interaction, the immediate or manifest frame of reference is each child's perception of what they and the others are doing at the time of utterance and an interpretation of the immediate environmental setting. This immediate frame of reference contains both the direct reflection of what is going on in the mind of each participant, and inferences about how these events are reflected in the mind of others. This double focus is made possible by the construction of a system of rules and probabilities based on previous experiences of persons and interpersonal interaction. It seems probable that this system of rules and probabilities has constant features which are as generalized and powerful as those which govern interactions with things in space which have hitherto tended to dominate thinking about cognition. This chapter suggests that basic structural features of language provide clues to the structural features of social cognition, but only if these linguistic features are considered in the light of their place in interpersonal interaction.

LANGUAGE CONSIDERED AS AN INTERACTIVE SYSTEM

If one examines sequential dialogue, and not individual utterances, there appear to be three main dimensions of attention and organization in the linguistic behaviour of speakers: (a) that which organizes and acknowledges the relation between the participants; (b) that which picks out the mutual field of attention; and (c) that which expresses what the speaker is doing in speaking. These are closely interwoven parts of the meaning system, each affecting the other, and they are distinguished for the convenience of the onlooker's attempt to understand without any implication that they can be separated in performance.

The speech act element, that which indicates what the speaker is doing in speaking, is embedded in the other two and is affected by the speaker's beliefs about the other person's perceptual field, and also about his probable response as constrained both by his current activity and by behavioural constants derived from his range of predictable responses inferred from previous encounters. It also includes hypotheses about the latent frame of possible previous experience, at least some of which is expected to be similarly conceptualized and shared. In particular, the speaker will have inferences about the listener's social experience which will be expected to result in rule-like generalizations, some of which are also expected to be held in common. The common element in experience is a necessity for efficient communication, but without some diversity of viewpoint, intention, experience or rules, communication in the sense of giving new information or stimulating new action would be unnecessary or even impossible. Both commonality and diversity are essential for the reciprocal creation of the future which lies at the heart of social interaction. When language is considered from this point of view, many features which have either been neglected or misinterpreted begin to form part of a coherent whole and many elements which have already been extensively studied acquire new richness.

Take first the dimension of language which serves to set up and maintain the relationship between speaker and hearer. This contains devices to set up a mutual field of attention, such as summons and address, devices to maintain reciprocity such as turn-taking, acknowledgements such as *yes* and *no* which also double up as answers, tags, and other requests for response and acknowledgements. These all appear very early in language. Mutual acknowledgement and turn-taking are such primitive features of the communication system that they are among the first manifest signs that communication is taking place at all (Lewis and Freedle, 1973).

Prelinguistically the young baby has a repertory of devices for creating a mutual field of attention, but among the first acquisition of actual language are the vocative use of names and titles, *Anna! Mummy!*, greetings and summons such as *Hi* or *Hey*. Slightly later, but rapidly reaching a high frequency are words such as *look* which are specifically directed at securing visual attention. *Look* was by far the most common verb in the nursery language records collected by the author, being more than twice as frequent as the runners up, *come*, *get* and *put* and their compounds.

Having set the field up, the child often works to maintain it by using the alternation of dialogue turns by which he signals that the field is still mutually shared. This is not at first a closely knit series of exchanges unless the mother/caretaker attempts to organize it thus. The echoic and imitative vocalizations of young children, their tendency to pick up and feed back the terminal part of the vocalizations of adults may operate as much as a channel-holding device as a check on the negotiation of meaning. This echoic, running commentary type of language instanced by Bloom's study of her own daughter (Bloom, 1973) appears to resemble in many ways the repetitious running commentary of the mothers in the dialogues examined by

Snow (1975, 1976). The child may be doing what the mother is reported by Snow to be doing, i.e. attempting to maintain contact and/or to explore the possibility of interpersonal meaning rather than specify particular meanings. For the child this mere possibility of an intersubjective field may be sufficiently satisfying. The reciprocal utterance/response form is a function of face-to-face communication, and the young child may move about playing and uttering odd words, content to be within contact range, accepting the minimal response of the mother or caretaker as a sign that the field is still "live". If she should fail to respond the child will usually approach and make attempts to restore the field.

In more intensive communicative episodes which have the turn-taking character mentioned previously, the child will learn devices such as discourse deictics for naming and claiming the speaker role, (own name, or *I*) for designating the listener role (name, status name, or *you*) and for referring to "third persons" (*he, she, they*) or things (*it, they*). Around the speaker/listener pair will begin to grow a penumbra of interpersonal meanings defining discourse and action roles. These roles will also come to reflect the asymmetries of status and initiative inbuilt in the age and power relationships within the family and later still the specific address forms which specify these differences within society. Names, and role names such as *mummy* and *daddy* begin to develop complex functions and rules for usage which are certainly visible by the time the child is 3. Their use as calls or summonses branches out into their use as address forms, especially at the initial stages of an interaction sequence, in making formal requests, and also in terminal sequences where some breach of interpersonal frame has caused distancing, as in examples *B* 1 and 2 below. In such sequences they are frequently accompanied by modulation of the verb phrase as the child grows older.

THE MODULATION OF SPEECH ACTS TO TAKE ACCOUNT OF THE LISTENER

This sophisticated device of using auxiliary modal verbs for the modulation of speech acts to suit the intentionality, status and relative interpersonal distance of speaker and hearer comes at the end of the second year and beginning of the third year of life (Wall, 1974). It depends on the acquisition of a series of rule-like constraints on behaviour and regularities in the outcome of events which begin to peg out the complex and overlapping field of objective possibility and probability and social permissibility. An early

stage of acquiring these rule-like social constraints is charted by Derek
Edwards in this volume. Negative and interrogative forms are the first
modulations, and they are followed by modal auxiliaries and other modal
expressions. Their elaboration and interweaving with language is a
continuous developing process. The use of modal expressions is one of the
main features to show rapid increase in incidence in the language of children
between 3 and 5, and the connection with the social rule system is their
dominant feature (Shields, 1974). There is no doubt that the system grows
more refined and complex for many years as experience of both the
impersonal and personal world accumulates and becomes more
differentiated, but even preschool children use modulated forms which bear
witness to the development of some consideration for the voluntary nature of
human activity, the need to consider the status and views of others and
negotiate interpersonal activity.

Here are some examples of social overture which not only use modal
auxiliaries, *shall, will, can*, but also use direct address by names as well as
discourse deixis by pronominals indicating the importance of the
interpersonal frame:

A 1. girl (3;7):   Shall we play with something else, Andrew?
   2. boy (3;7):   Will you come and play with me if I don't hit you?
   3. boy (3;11): There you are Steve, everytime, you know, I'll sit near you and
                   I'll play with you.
   4. girl (4;5):   Michèle can I play with you, and can I be the sister or the other
                   girl?

and here are some examples of brush off and territorial defence, which again
exhibit modulation and contrastive role:

B 1. boy (4;9):   No, I won't be your friend.
   2. girl (4;2):   Don't be silly Anne or I really won't play with you.

ORGANIZING THE SHARED FIELD OF REFERENCE

The elements of language which connect the utterances of speakers with a
shared field of reference can be divided into three groups, those which plot
the immediate field of attention and activity around the speaking pair, those
which connect the utterance with what has already been said, and those
which place the utterance against a latent frame of meaning which all
members of the communicating set bring into the interaction with them. The
analysis of this set of features has usually been dominated by consideration of

the most powerful member: specific labelling, whether of persons, events, environments or things. This has diverted attention from the important role of other features such as deixis which serve to point out the focus of attention within a shared field which is organized by co-ordinates expressing proximity to the speakers standpoint.

There is evidence of prelinguistic deixis in work on young babies (Edwards, this volume; Bruner, 1975) and among the first functors which appear in nearly all the protocols of initial language acquisition are a number which seem to act as primary field organizers noting the appearance and disappearance, accumulation, and iteration and absence from the field of persons and objects. These are words such as *Hi, more, allgone, away, no, another* and *again* (Brown, 1973; Schaerlaekens, 1974; Bloom, 1973). Most of these double as performatives in demand and request forms, and even in their referential role appear to pick out aspectual features of shared activity, its ongoingness and its termination. The combination of these primary functors with specific referents is what gives the early two-word utterances their "pivot look".

Very soon the list of functors is extended by the field deictics such as *this* and *that* and *here* and *there*, placing the referential material in relation to the immediate or distal focus of the speaker. Pronouns which organize objects and persons in the "third place" in relation to the speaking pair such as *he, she, it* and *they*, begin to appear together with words which associate persons and things such as *my* and *mine* which supplement the device of juxtaposing the referents as in *daddy chair, mummy book*. The focus of organization is the speaker/hearer relationship, and deictic devices plot the field of reference from this central point, all else being in third person or third place. Soon this intersubjective space will be further organized by locative expressions which relate objects in it one to another. The first prepositions, *in* and *on*, pick out containment and juxtaposition, and they are soon joined by many other locating expressions. Indeed locatives are the most frequent adjuncts in the speech of children before school. Nevertheless, space continues to be plotted from what Herbert Clark calls the cononical encounter, face-to-face interaction (H. H. Clark, 1973).

The emphasis on specific naming as the main feature of reference has helped to conceal the role of intersubjectivity. Reference has been treated as though it expressed a direct connection between a word and a thing within a single mind, or even between a word and a thing "out there". This is to confuse at least three separate dimensions of meaning. First, there is the connection between the mind and what lies outside it which is mediated by the afferent nervous system, and has the effect of building up a representation of that world within the mind. This is what Pavlov called the first signalling system, and, although human communication will profoundly affect some aspects, other aspects are objective in the sense of providing a good fit with material realities. Secondly, there is the linguistic system of reference which is a social device which maps arbitrary vocal signals onto this representation and allows us to communicate about it, and thirdly there is the act of reference which depends on mastering the linguistic system, but is not aimed at the connection between words and referents. Its aim is to use the system to call up representations in another mind. What is important is not that the referent should be present, but that it should be perceived, recalled or attended to. An act of reference is successful, not by means of the connection between word and event in the mind of the speaker, but by the speakers success in evoking a similar representation in the mind of the listener.

THE INTERPERSONAL NATURE OF THE ACT OF REFERENCE

The fact that the reference system is a social product, existing as a shared complex in the minds of members of the speech community into which the child is born, does not make the system into an object for the child. The child has to undergo an extensive apprenticeship in acts of reference in which he attends to the focus of attention of another person, and in which that other attends to his, before he can grasp the signals which form the vocal articulation of this shared focus. Much has been made of the arbitrary connection between the vocal signals and their significates, but there is nothing arbitrary about the structure of an act of reference which requires a joint focus of attention and an index for what is attended to which can be relied upon to create this focus between speaker and hearer through perception or recall.

The index may be a specific nominal, or it may be a deictic device, more often the latter. The use of such non-specific referents is wholly dependent on the hypotheses of both parties in the interaction about what the other is attending to. This process is seen at work in the language of nursery children in the following extract from a series of 61 exchanges. The specific nominals are nearly all employed to give privileged information in answer to questions. Apart from the initial remark in the conversation, the sea-shells which are the focus of attention are indexed by *this*, or *that*, or *them*, or *this one, that one* or *those ones, some. One* is an extremely abstract index referring only by countability. In remark 9 the specific referent *shell* is probably used in contrast to *stone* in remark 8, the focus on shells having to be reinstated after the discovery of a stone. In remark 11, shell is again specified, possibly in contrast to *those ones*. Both mentions are in object position. In the 47 nominal groups in subject position in the total of 61 exchanges, only four are expounded by specific nouns.

Example 2: Sample of Elicited Conversation
Ch/NS No. 5,6/2/70. A student teacher half empties a large collection of shells onto a table. Anna (4;11), Ann (4;7) and Teresa (4;10) come up to look at them.

	1. S.T.:	(to all) I've brought these shells from the sea-side.
Anna turns several shells over.	2. Anna:	(to S.T.) I haven't seen them at the sea-side.
Ann picks out three periwinkles, and picks one up to examine.	3. Ann:	(to all) Some are small. That's small.
Ter shows a shell.	4. Ter:	(to all) Look!
Ann sorts out a collection of periwinkles.	5. Ann:	(to S.T.) That one's small and this one is.
Picks up a marble pebble and holds it out to Ter.	6. Anna:	(to Ann) That's a round one.
	7. Anna:	(to Ter.) What's that?
	8. Ter:	That's a stone.
Anna goes to fetch a large conch shell from the nature table.	9. Anna:	(to S.T.) We have a shell over here.
Ter is holding a large whelk to her ear.		(to Ter) What can you hear in your shell?
Ter puts the shell down and tries another.	10. Ter:	A noise.
Anna returns with the conch weighing it up and down in two hands.	11. Anna:	(to all) This is a bigger shell than those ones. I can carry this one.
Ter sings into her shell. Anna puts her conch shell to her ear.	12. Ter:	Can you hear anything, Anna?
	13. Anna:	The sea.

(Conversation continues for 61 exchanges.)

In the sample of the language of nursery school children collected by the author of which this example is an extract, no less than 93% of the nominal groups in subject position were expounded by pronouns. What is not always realized, however, is the sheer pervasiveness of this system in the English language as a whole. The collection of written and spoken material on which Quirk and his colleagues based their *Grammar of Contemporary English* (Quirk *et al.*, 1972) has been examined by Aarts for features of the nominal group, and he found that in adult informal speech 87% of the subject groups were represented by pronominals, this dropped to 79% in light fiction and to 70% in formal written and spoken English (Aarts, 1971). Only in scientific

English did the proportion reduce to 39% and this was probably due to the linguistic effects of the scientific posture of impersonality which tries to eliminate human agency by jacking up the number of passive sentences, e.g. *Correlations were calculated* rather than *I calculated correlations.*

THE INTERPERSONAL STRUCTURE OF TIME REFERENCE

Time reference is even more dependent on hypotheses about the experiences of others. It is always plotted from the *now* of the time of utterance. Events in the past and events in the future are not immediately perceptible at the time of speaking, they are wrapped up in memory or about to unfold in predicted happening or intended action. To refer to events in the past or future successfully, the speaker must rely on the ability of others to bring into the present, i.e. the time of utterance, events which have been experienced in the past, and to understand others when they do the same. The speaker also relies on them to be able to unfold future events from the time of utterance either as prediction or intention.

As has already been pointed out, the early devices for organizing the shared field appear already to have a time element or aspect which is close to the "now" focus. This gradually extends into the past and progresses into the future, but for the young child it is nearly always closely linked to current human activity. According to Roger Brown, the past tense begins to be marked on to the children's verb phrases at an MLU of under 3·0 morphemes and follows very shortly after the marking of progressive aspect (Brown, 1973, p. 271). Roger Brown also notes the fact that before the children he studied showed any marked form of the verb, the parents regularly glossed for progressive, past, intentional and imperative senses thus scaffolding the development of an idea of shared past and intended future differentiated from the now ongoing field of activity. The elaboration of these forms is cultivated by gambits of the *tell daddy what we did today* variety. The future is stretched and sequenced by interactions such as:

Example 3
E. (2;16):   Go swings?
Mother: In a minute, when I have finished washing up.

From the now and immediately after now of *going to*, time is matched to the sequence of activities by *in a minute, later, when we have had dinner, when daddy comes home, tomorrow, next week*, and so on. Finally, well on into school life, the succession of past or projected events can be matched to an objective calendar, but the use of that calendar remains the same as the use of the early time markers—the matching and co-ordination of human actions in the past and in the future.

THE CO-ORDINATION OF UTTERANCES IN DISCOURSE

The ability of the child to take account of the sequence of events leading up to the present is witnessed by his capacity to fit his actions and words to the previous actions and words of himself and others in a series of interactions lasting over several turns. The careful carpentry whereby remarks are fitted one with another, taking account of what has previously been transacted can be seen not only grammatically in ellipses and pronominal reference but also semantically in the ability to recognize the hypotheses contained in yes/no questions, and confirm or negate them, and the proposals contained in demands, commands, suggestions and pleas, and assent to or refuse them. There is skill even in using such minimal responses as *yes* and *no* (Shields, 1975). Ellipsis or grammatical abbreviation which also fits responses in with questions matching both for grammatical form and propositional content and avoiding the redundancy of repetition is present very early but has too often been glossed over in the obsession with the grammar of the sentence. (Brown, 1973, p. 239; Shields, 1972). Ellipsis is part of the grammar of discourse, not part of the grammar of sentences.

Dore (in preparation) has shown that even responses which initially appear not to be answers to the previous utterance are often related to another part of the shared field of attention which could be relevant, and Garvey maintains that many responses which are not immediate responses to previous questions are often probes for further specification of the questioners intent or field of reference (Garvey, 1976). Remarks which have no ascertainable connection with previous utterances in a discourse are the exception rather than the rule, unless the speaker is introducing a new topic, or making a new initiative in action.

The fit between speakers' remarks is maintained on several different levels. There is the level of textual cohesion which is carried not only by devices such as ellipses which have already been mentioned but also by definite and indefinite reference. Maratsos' work shows that very young children begin to distinguish between *a* and *the* as markers of the new and old material in discourse (Maratsos, 1976). Secondly there is cohesion between speech acts, so that answers cohere with questions, consents or refusals with demands, suggestions, pleas and complaints. In this way the active intent of one speaker is interlaced with the intent of others in the communicating group. Thirdly there is thematic cohesion in which the topic of reference is held and elaborated. This may relate to the immediate field of perception and activity, or the latent field which the speakers bring with them into the action in the shape of previous experiences, concepts and rules. Both the immediate field and the latent field form part of the presupposed or taken for granted background, usually specified only for the purposes of directing attention, changing the focus of attention or where misunderstanding must be repaired. Garnica has suggested that even speakers under 2 may make attempts to repair misunderstanding by varying intonation to highlight semantically important material (Garnica, personal communication). Lee (1974) showed 4-year-olds becoming quite adept at seeking direct clarification of the utterances of others by questions. These are both exercises in efficiently holding a joint focus of attention which may inhere in current activity, past recollections, or future plans or in the systems of behavioural roles and rules which begin to elaborate very early.

THE MANIFESTATION OF PRESUPPOSED RULE SYSTEMS

The powerful and largely tacit networks of shared rules and meanings which structure our fields of social action have, with the possible exception of those defining sex role, not yet been fully traced to their childhood origins. We now know that socialization begins from birth, the structure of the rule systems acquired have yet to be systematically explored. Indeed the idea that rule systems rather than affective bonds underly social relationship has still to gain acceptance (Hafré, 1974b). Edwards, however, points out elsewhere in this volume the importance of the early learning of constraints on behaviour as an introduction to a shared meaning system. The scrap of conversation between Freddie and Michèle analysed at length earlier on showed that 3- and 4-year-old children take such systems of rules for granted within a play setting, but the system goes far beyond games with rules. The extract below shows a little boy of nearly 4 faced with authority, so often the source of constraints and rules, engaging in a series of exchanges nearly all of which are either enunciations of rules, appeals for reasons for rules, or appeals against implied breaches of rules and concludes with a sequence in which the experience of the preceding interactions is translated into projected future behaviour and imbedded in a complex way within an elaborate social overture.

Example 4   Michael (3;11) and Susy (2;5), later Steven (2;6)
Mic and Sus are using dough in the home corner. Mic is making cakes. Sus is watching him and is sucking her dummy, she always has this in her mouth whatever she is doing.
Mic leans across and takes the dummy. Sus cries immediately, the Playgroup Leader bustles towards the disturbance—

Mic justifies	1. Mic:	She's a little baby to
He appeals to two underlying		have, to have a dummy.
rule-like presuppositions:		She's a little cry baby.

(a) only babies have dummies
(b) it's babyish to cry.

P.L. directs and justifies   2.   P.L: Don't take Susy's dummy
with presupposed rule (c) you   Mic. She likes it.
should not deprive people of
things they like.   dummy

Mic wipes the dummy over the   3.   Mic: You don't want your dirty   episode
table to make it dirty, and   old dummy, it's dirty.
appeals to another presupposed
rule (d) dirty things should
not be put in the mouth.

P.L overrides Mic, and   4.   P.L: Give me the dummy
pacifies Sus.   Michael. There you are
                                      Susy.

Mic goes back to his pastry.   5.   Mic: I'll make a picture.
P.L. Watches Sus and Mic for
a minute.   sharing

Mic takes all the dough, but   episode
then hesitates and turns to
P.L., and gives a new interpretation of rule (c) what Sus had
she might want, what she wants,
she ought to have.

Appeal to authority.   6.   Mic: (to P.L.) She had all this
                                      before, didn't she? D'you
                                      think she wants a bit?

P.L. accepts and directs   7.   P.L: I think she would Mic, you
then gives new direction with   give Sus half. You look
another rule (d) boys should look   after her. Boys have to
after girls/little children.   look after little girls.

Mic asks justification.   8.   Mic: Why?

P.L. justifies with new rule   9.   P.L: Because they are bigger
(e) the big and the strong   and stronger.   sex
look after the little and weak.   role
Mic looks doubtful, P.L. attempts   episode
to re-establish relationship, and   10.   P.L: (to Sus) Mic's going to
leaves them. Sus looks sulkily   look after you Sus.
at Mic and does not answer his
question. He pushes the cake   11.   Mic: (to Sus) Wanna play?
tray towards her, she takes it
and throws it away.

Mic appeals against breach of   12.   Mic: (to P.L.) Know what? I
rule (f) gifts should not be   give, I give her that
rudely refused.   thing, an' she threw it.

P.L. does not hear Mic—he
was perturbed at Sus's reaction.

He gives her a piece of dough. Sus pushes it away. (Mic searches visually for P.L.)	13. Mic: (to Sus) There you are.
	14. Sus: No!
Ste enters and looks at Sus. Mic evokes rule (a) and (b) to exclude Sus. Ste looks blankly. Mic goes off. He collects a chair for Ste, and puts it beside his own. They sit and play together. There is no conversation.	15. Mic: (to Ste) She's got a baby's dummy.
	16. Mic: (to Ste) There you are Ste, everytime you know, I'll sit near you and I'll play with you.

social
rejection
and new
social
overture

This series of exchanges shows the remarkable persistence of an underlying frame of reference which is highly structured with behavioural norms. Each of the four episodes has a different interpersonal context, a different context of activity and a different topical focus. There are four successive changes of relationship as the Michael/Susy interaction gives way to the Michael/ Playgroup Leader interaction, with Susy as third person, and then to the Michael/Susy interaction with the Playgroup Leader brought in on appeal, followed by the Michael/Steven interaction. It is the roles played in these interactions which dominate the speech acts of the speakers and seem to invoke and animate the frame of rules. The manifest frame of reference, the dummy, the play cooking with dough, have a less dynamic significance, providing the contingent stimulus of props and scenery rather than substance to the interaction.

The roles being played in this interaction are social roles already heavily tinged with the differentia of age, sex and authority. It is the contention of this chapter, however, that however early these differentiating concepts take root, they are built in to a still more fundamental set which contain defining characteristics of human persons. No doubt there are physical dimensions of the concept of a person such as those studied by Lewis (1975) and dimensions of overt behaviour, such as walking, eating, sleeping and so on. It is, however, the psychological dimension that is explored here, the representations which the child has of perceptions, intentions, experience and memory in others. It is not claimed that this psychological knowledge is reflected upon as a whole, so that the child knows he has a concept of a person, any more than he knows he has the concept of a thing. The child's knowledge is the underlying substratum of his success in interacting with persons before he has knowledge of his knowledge of persons. As Piaget recently pointed out *pris de conscience* or knowledge of know-how comes a long time after the know-how is successfully established (Piaget, 1976). What is claimed is that there is a gradual building up of hypotheses and expectations and rules which act as a working psychology, that same naïve psychology which Heider discussed at length (Heider, 1958). This naïve psychology has constants which allow generalized prediction about human beings as a whole and variable features which allow prediction of the probable behaviour of individuals. These variable features later generalize into dimensions of variation in a more complex model of human character.

What is constant tends to be taken for granted or presupposed, and therefore is more difficult to make salient. This is no doubt why research in this area which is usually based on differentiating characteristics tends to be so unsatisfactory. If a child is asked to name a friend and then tell the investigator something about him, he is unlikely to mention that his friend is alive, stays the same person, can remember things, can see things or can talk, or even that he can walk, sleep and eat. The child is much more likely to name some differentiating characteristic, such as "he has a swing" or "he plays with me" (Secord and Peevers, 1974). It would be most unwise to conclude from this that the child's concepts of persons are adequately represented much less exhausted by such a description, for it is a basic characteristic of language, built into its formal structure, that speakers concentrate on new information taking the old information as part of the presupposed background.

CONSTANT FEATURES IN THE MODEL OF A PERSON

What then might the constants of the child's psychological model be? It would appear from the previous analysis of the main features of language as such, that at least the following psychological dimensions have begun to form as the child builds up communicative skill.

    (1) Persons have identity over time despite changes in location, behaviour and appearance.

    (2) Persons are self moving or animate, and influence over the course of their behaviour has to be negotiated by invoking interest or a shared frame of constraint.

    (3) Persons identify each other and can react to each other.

    (4) Persons can see, feel, hear, touch and smell, i.e. they have a perceptual field.

    (5) Persons intend their actions.

    (6) Persons conceptualize and construct their world in roughly similar ways.

    (7) Persons have moods and states such as anger and fear, and also wants, likes and dislikes.

(8)   Persons can send and receive messages based on gestures and words which are related to context in stable ways.

(9)   Persons have an action potential, i.e. things they can and can't do.

(10) Persons can retain previous experience and structure their present behaviour by it.

(11) Persons can replicate previous behaviours in new contexts.

(12) Persons share sets of rules about what is appropriate within particular frames of action.

Without the establishment of at least some elements in this framework, the social and communicative behaviour of young children could not be explained. Looked at in this way, much of the apparently routine, habitual and even ritualized nature of the baby-caretaker interactions noticed in recent studies may be seen as laying the foundation for the invariancies on which stable expectations and hypotheses can be built and to which future experiences can be assimilated. Accommodation to the different, the variable and the new can then develop from a foundation in established cognitive schemes. If such schemes are not securely built either through misfortune or mismanagement or some endogenous defect in the developing child, the whole system of social skills and affective understandings is put at risk for reasons which are as much cognitive as affective. This in turn may imperil the complex system of cultural transmission, distorting it and creating areas of inefficiency. If there is one thing which is a constant message in the new work on caretaker-child interaction, it is the centrality of the interpersonal relationship in the transmission of meaning.

ORIGINS OF THE CHILD'S MODEL OF THE SOCIAL WORLD

The growing literature on the social apprenticeship of young babies and on prelinguistic and protolinguistic communication is beginning to illuminate this interpersonal generation of meaning. Several striking examples appear in this volume. The most visible process is the way the mother can be seen to attribute meaning to the behaviour of her infant. She persistently reads meaning into her baby's behaviour, and then reads out an interpretation on which she bases her own response (Newson, 1974). Not only that, but she enters into vocal dialogue with her child interpreting his signals as statements, often putting them into her own words and taking vocally both parts in the communication exchange. The work of Catherine Snow (1975) records this process with great sensitivity showing that the mother's model of communication as a two way process is not only implicit in her monitoring of the baby's behaviour and her adjustment to what she considers to be its meaning but is also modelled as a verbal exchange, the mother responding to the behaviours verbally, and also translating the behaviours verbally. Alternating behaviour, i.e. the periods of monitoring followed by periods of acting, may be an inbuilt characteristic of elaborate nervous systems, but at the human level it has produced a turn-taking vocal dialogue so delicately structured that Lewis and Freedle (1973) conclude that "the communication network even of the twelve week old baby and its mother is a non-random, sequential and situationally determined system".

Even at this early stage, then, there is intentional emitting of signals, signalling in a vocal channel, perception of signals and feedback on their effects, together with interpretation of signals on the adult side and expectations concerning the effect of signals on the side of the child. Whether the child can interpret the adult's signals except in a global way or as signs for routine interactions is not certain, but the more predictable the maternal signalling in relation to context, the more capable it becomes of generating expectation and interpretation. The content of the interactions is closely interlinked with the child's biological states, and it is likely that the whole of the early network is soaked in affectivity, the main focus of interest being persons, their states and actions.

Young babies also take notice of non-animate objects in their environment, from an early stage, but it is the introduction of that object environment into the intersubjective network between mother and child to create a field of reference that constitutes the next essential step in communication. Synchronous visual tracking between the mother-infant dyad allows the mother to feel that there is a world as well as a relationship to be shared (Schaffer, 1974; Newson, 1974). At first it is the careful monitoring of the child's direction of gaze that feeds this into her interpretative system, but later the child can track into the mother's line of vision (Scaife and Bruner, 1974). As soon as objects are touchable and graspable, these can also enter the communication net in increasingly elaborate exchanges (Bruner, 1975). Furthermore the child is carried into a variety of different environments both inside and outside the home, and so a spatial field and the things and persons in it become possible objects of shared attention and of communication. Bates and her colleagues (1975) suggest that this field of reference is not firmly built into the interpersonal network until the end of the first year when they begin to notice that their subjects start to co-ordinate behaviour towards things with behaviour towards persons so that things could be used to get the attention of persons. Bruner (1976) also places the beginning of pointing behaviour, or early deixis, at the end of the first and the beginning of the second year. The two key features of communication, the exchange of meaningful action, and the contextualization of that action within a field of reference are established before the conventional "first word" appears. To use Halliday's magical phrase, the baby has already learned how to mean (Halliday, 1975).

CONCLUSION

The analysis presented here moves the story a little further on to children who have learned to operate the main functional systems of language, and have acquired a degree of skill in communication. It is argued that this skill itself is an index of the child's knowledge of other persons. This skill displays his ability to make hypotheses about the communicative competence of persons, hypotheses about their perceptions, their concepts, their intentions, inclinations, moods and states, their memories and systems of rules. The child's image of the world is mirrored twice, once directly and again as a representation of the representations of others. His image of himself is also mirrored twice, once with direct knowledge of his internal states, and again by his representation of his behaviour in the eyes of others. Each image modifies and extends the other. This is by far the most elaborate and by far the most compelling of our human intellectual systems. It is the one which has the most power to influence for good or ill our coping pattern in all the manifold activities of the social world. It forms the articulating skeleton of feelings and relationships, it outlines and defines our own humanity. Surely it is time that the cognitive psychologist came face to face with the young naïve psychologist, and turned his sophisticated techniques to building a more adequate model of the growth of man's concept of man?

References

Aarts, F. G. A. M. (1971). On the distribution of noun phrase types in English Clause Structure. *Lingua* **26**, 281-293.

Adelson, E. and Fraiberg, S. (1974). Gross motor development in infants blind from birth. *Child Development* **45**, 114-126.

Alaniz, M. (1973). A search for a developmental sequence in the acquisition of drawing abilities: a study of children's spontaneous drawings. Unpublished manuscript, University of California, Los Angeles.

Allport, D. A. (1975). The state of cognitive psychology: A critical notice of W. G. Chase (Ed.) *Visual Information Processing* (New York: Academic Press): *Quarterly Journal of Experimental Psychology* **27**, 141-152.

Amsterdam, B. (1972). Mirror self image reactions before age two. *Developmental Psychobiology* **5**, 297-305.

Apostel, L. (1971). Further remarks on the pragmatics of natural language. In Y. Bar-Hillell (Ed.) *Pragmatics of Natural Languages.* Dordnecht: Reidel.

Aronson, E. (1974), quoted in T. Bower: Competent New Borns. *New Scientist* **61** (889), 672-675.

Asch, S. E. (1952). *Social Psychology.* Engelwood Cliffs, New Jersey: Prentice-Hall.

Atkinson, M. (1974). Prerequisites for reference. Paper read at B.A.A.L. Seminar, University of Newcastle-upon-Tyne.

Austin, J. L. (1961). In J. O. Urmson and G. J. Warnock (eds) *Philosophical Papers.* Oxford: Oxford University Press.

Austin, J. L. (1961). In J. O. Urmson and G. J. Warnock (Eds) *Philosophical Papers.*

Baer, D. M., Peterson, R. F. and Sherman, J. A. (1967). The development of imitation by reinforcing behavioural similarity to a model. *Journal of Experimental Analysis of Behaviour* **10**, 405-416.

Bastian, J. (1965). Primate signalling systems and human languages. In J. DeVore (Ed.) *Primate Behaviour.* New York: Holt, Rinehart and Winston.

Bates, E. (1976a). *Language and Context: the Acquisition of Pragmatics.* New York and London: Academic Press.

Bates, E. (1976b). Pragmatics and sociolinguistics in child language. In D. Morehead and A. Morehead (Eds) *Directions in Normal and Deficient Child Language.* Baltimore: University Park Press.

Bates, E., Camaioni, L. and Volterra, V. (1975). The acquisition of performatives prior to speech. *Merrill-Palmer Quarterly* 1975, **21**, 205-226.

Bates, E., Benigni, L., Bretherton, I., Camaioni, L. and Volterra, V. (1977). From gesture to the first word: on cognitive and social prerequisites. In M. Lewis and L. Rosenblum (Eds) *Origins of Behaviour: Communication and Language.* New York: Wiley.

Bateson, G. (1973). *Steps to an Ecology of Mind.* Frogmore, St. Albans: Paladin.

Battison, R. (1974). Phonological deletion in American Sign Language. *Sign Language Studies* **5**, 1-17.

Becker, E. (1972). *The Birth and Death of Meaning.* (2nd edn). London: Penguin.

Bell, R. Q. (1968). A reinterpretation of the direction of effects in studies of socialization. *Psychological Reviews* **75**, 81-95.

Bell, S. M. and Ainsworth, M. D. S. (1972). Infant crying and maternal responsiveness. *Child Development* **43**, 1171-1190.

Bellugi, U. and Fischer, S. (1972). A comparison of sign languages and spoken language. *Cognition* **1**, 173-200.

Berger, P. L. and Luckman, T. (1967). *The Social Construction of Reality.* Harmondsworth: Penguin Books.

Berlin, I. (1969). A note on Vico's concept of knowledge. In G. Tagliacozzo (Ed.) and H. U. White (Co-ed.) *Giambattista Vico: an International Symposium.* Baltimore: John Hopkins.

Berlin, I. (1976). *Vico and Herder.* London: The Hogarth Press.

Bernal, J. F. and Richards, M. P. M. (1973). In A. S. Barnett (Ed.) *Ethology and Development.* Little Club Clinics in Developmental Medicine No. 47, Spastics Society and Heinemann.

Bernstein, B. (1971). *Class, Codes and Control,* Vol. I. London: Routledge and Kegan Paul.

Bernstein, B. (1972). *Class, Codes and Control,* Vol. II. London: Routledge and Kegan Paul.

Bernstein, N. A. (1967). *The Co-ordination and Regulation of Movement.* London: Pergamon.

Bever, T. G. (1970). The cognitive basis for linguistic structures. In J. R. Hayes (Ed.) *Cognition and Language Learning.* New York: Wiley.

Bierwisch, M. (1970). Semantics. In J. Lyons (Ed.) *New Horizons in Linguistics.* Harmondsworth: Penguin Books.

Bloom, L. (1970). *Language Development: Form and Function in Emerging Grammars.* Cambridge, Mass: The MIT Press.

Bloom, L. (1973). *One Word at a Time: the Use of Single Word Utterances before Syntax.* The Hague: Mouton.

Bloom, L., Lightbowm, P. and Hood, L. (1975). Structure and variation in child language. *Monographs of the Society for Research in Child Development,* 40 (2, serial No. 160).

Bloomfield, L. (1933). *Language.* New York: Henry Holt.

Bloomfield, L. (1961). A set of postulates for the study of language. In S. Saporta (Ed.) *Psycholinguistics: A Book of Readings.* New York: Holt, Rinehart and Winston.

Blount, B. (1971). Socialization and prelinguistic development among the Luo of Kenya. *Southwestern Journal of Anthropology* **27**, 41-50.

Blum, A. (1974). *Theorising.* London: Heinemann.

Blurton-Jones, N. (1972). Comparative aspects of mother-child contact. In N. Blurton-Jones (Ed.) *Ethological Studies of Child Behaviour.* Cambridge: Cambridge University Press.

Boas, F. and Deloria, E. (1941). Dakota Grammar. *Memoirs of the National Academy of Sciences*, Washington: Government Printing Office.

Bolles, R. C. (1975). *Theory of Motivation* (2nd edn). New York: Harper and Row.

Bower, T. G. R. (1966). The visual world of infants. *Scientific American* **215**, 80-92.

Bower, T. G. R. (1972). Object perception in infants. *Perception* **1**, 15-30.

Bower, T. G. R. (1974). *Development in Infancy*. San Francisco: Freeman and Co.

Bower, T. G. R. (1975). Competent newborns. In R. Lewin (Ed.) *Child Alive*. London: Temple Smith.

Bower, T. G. R. (1977). Concepts of development. *Actes de XXIeme Congres International de Psychologie, Paris, 18-25 Juillet, 1976*. Paris: Press Universitaires de France (in press).

Bower, T. G. R. and Paterson, J. G. (1972). Stages in the development of the object concept. *Cognition* **1**, 47-55.

Bower, T. G. R. and Wishart, J. G. (1972). The effects of motor skill on object permanence. *Cognition* **1**, 165-172.

Bower, T. G. R. and Wishart, J. G. (1977). Towards a unitary theory of development. Paper read at Conference on *Origins of the Infant's Social Responsiveness*. Nantucket, 1976. Hillsdale, New Jersey: To be published by Lawrence Erlbaum Associates.

Bowerman, M. (1973). Structural relationships in children's utterances: Syntactic or semantic? In T. E. Moore (ed.) *Cognitive Development and the Acquisition of Language*. New York and London: Academic Press.

Bowerman, M. (1975). Cross-linguistic similarities at two stages of syntactic development. In E. H. Lenneberg and E. Lenneberg (Eds) *Foundations of Language Development*, Vol. I. New York and London: Academic Press.

Bowerman, M. (1976). Word and Sentences: uniformity, individual variation, and shifts over time in patterns of acquisition. Paper presented to the Conference on Early Behavioural Assessment of Communicative and Cognitive Ability of the Developmentally Disabled. Orcas Island, Washington.

Bowerman, M. (in press). The acquisition of word meaning: an investigation of some current conflicts. In N. Waterson and C. Snow (Eds) *Proceedings of the Third International Child Language Symposium*. London: Wiley.

Bowerman, M. (in press). Semantic factors in the acquisition of rules for word use and sentence construction. In D. Morehead and A. Morehead (Eds) *Directions in Normal and Deficient Child Language*. Baltimore: University Park Press.

Bowlby, J. (1969). *Attachment and Loss: Vol. 1. Attachment*. London: Hogarth Press.

Braine, M. D. S. (1974). Length constraints, reduction rules and holophrastic processes in children's word combinations. *Journal of Verbal Learning and Verbal Behaviour* **13**, 448-456.

Braunwald, S. R. (in press). Mother-child communication: the function of maternal language input. In W. von Raffler-Engel (Ed.) *Child Language Today*.

Brazelton, T., Koslowski, B. and Main, M. (1974). The origins of reciprocity: the early mother-infant interaction. In M. Lewis and L. Rosenblum (Eds) *The Effect of the Infant on Its Caregiver*, pp. 49-77. London: Wiley.

Bricker, W. A. and Bricker, D. D. (1970). A programme of training for the severely handicapped child. *Exceptional Children* **37**, 101-112.

Broch, O. Russenorsk. (1927). *Archiv fur slavische Philologie* **21,** 209-262. (as cited in Slobin, 1975).

Bromley, D. B. (1975). Development of the child's understanding of behaviour and environment. Paper delivered at a Conference of the International Society for the Study of Behavioural Development: Guildford.

Brown, R. (1956). Language and categories. In J. S. Bruner, J. J. Goodnow and G. A. Austin (Eds) *A Study of Thinking.* New York: Science Editions Inc.

Brown, R. (1958a). How shall a thing be called? *Psychological Review* **65,** 14-21.

Brown, R. (1958b). *Words and Things.* New York: The Free Press.

Brown, R. (1968). The development of wh- questions. *Journal of Verbal Learning and Verbal Behaviour* **(7),** 279-290.

Brown, R. (1970). The first sentences of child and chimpanzee. *Psycholinguistics: Selected Papers*, pp. 208-231. New York: Macmillan Company.

Brown, R. (1973). *A First Language: The Early Stage.* Cambridge, Mass: Harvard University Press.

Brown, R. and Fraser, C. (1964). The acquisition of syntax. In U. Bellugi and R. Brown (Eds) *The Acquisition of Language.* London and Chicago: University of Chicago Press.

Bruner, J. S. (1966). On cognitive growth II. In J. S. Bruner, R. Olver and P. M. Greenfield (Eds) *Studies in Cognitive Growth.* New York: Wiley.

Bruner, J. S. (1968). *Processes of Cognitive Growth: Infancy.* Worcester, Mass: Clark University with Barri Publishers.

Bruner, J. S. (1969). Biological functions of infant-mother attachment behaviour: general discussion. In A. Ambrose (Ed.) *Stimulation in Early Infancy.* London and New York: Academic Press.

Bruner, J. S. (1971). The growth and structure of skill. In K. J. Connolly (Ed.) *Motor Skills in Infancy.* London and New York: Academic Press.

Bruner, J. S. (1972) The uses of immaturity. In G. U. Coelho and E. A. Rubinstein (Eds) *Social Change and Human Behaviour.* Bethesda: National Institute of Mental Health.

Bruner, J. S. (1973a). *Beyond the Information Given.* New York: W. W. Norton and Co.

Bruner, J. S. (1973b). Organization of early skilled action. *Child Development* **44,** 1-11.

Bruner, J. S. (1974). Organisation of early skilled action. In M. P. M. Richards (Ed.) *The Integration of a Child into a Social World.* Cambridge: Cambridge University Press.

Bruner, J. S. (1975). The ontogenesis of speech acts. *Journal of Child Language* **2,** 1-20.

Bruner, J. S. (1976). From communication to language—a psychological perspective. *Cognition* **3,** 255-287.

Bruner, J. S. (in preparation). Language and experience. In R. S. Peters (Ed.) *John Dewey Reconsidered.* London: Routledge and Kegan Paul.

Bruner, J. S. and Bruner, B. M. (1968). On voluntary action and its hierarchical structure. *International Journal of Psychology* **3,** 239-255.

Bruner, J. S. and Koslowski, B. (1972). Visually pre-adapted constituents of manipulatory action. *Perception* **1**, 3-14.

Bruner, J. S. and Sherwood, V. (1975). Early rule structure: the case of peekaboo. In J. S. Bruner, A. Jolly and K. Sylva (Eds) *Play: Its Role in Evolution and Development*. Harmondsworth: Penguin Books.

Buechel, E. (1970). *A Dictionary of the Teton Dakota Sioux Language: Dakota-English, English-Dakota, with Consideration to Yankton and Santee*. Pine Ridge, S.D.: Holy Rosary Mission.

Bullowa, M. (1967). The start of the language process. Paper presented at the Xth International Congress of Linguists, Bucharest.

Bullowa, M. (in press). *Before Speech: The Beginnings of Human Communication*. Cambridge: Cambridge University Press.

Burlingham, D. (1961). Some notes on the development of the blind. *Psychoanalytic Study of the Child*, Vol. XVI, 121-145. New York: International University Press.

Busfield, J. (1974). Family ideology and family pathology. In N. Armistead (Ed.) *Reconstructing Social Psychology*. Harmondsworth: Penguin Books.

Carmichael, L. (1926). The development of behavior in vertebrates experimentally removed from the influence of external stimulation. *Psychological Review* **33**, 51-58.

Carnap, R. (1942). *Introduction to Semantics*. Cambridge, Mass: Harvard University Press.

Carpenter, E. (1966). Image making in arctic art. In G. Kepes (Ed.) *Sign, Image and Symbol*. London: Studio Vista.

Carpenter, S. (1974). The mother's face and the newborn. *New Scientist* **61** (890).

Carson, M. and Abrahamson, A. (1976). Some members are more equal than others: The effects of semantic typicality on class-inclusion performance. *Child Development* **47**, 1186-1190.

Carter, A. (1974). The development of communication in the sensori-motor period: A case study. Doctoral dissertation, University of California, Berkeley.

Carter, A. (1975a). The transformation of sensori-motor morphemes into words: A case study of the development of "here" and "there". *Papers and Reports on Child Language Development* **11**, 31-48.

Carter, A. (1975b). The transformation of sensorimotor morphemes into words: A case study of the development of "more" and "mine". *Journal of Child Language* **2**, 233-250.

Carter, A. (in press a). The development of systematic vocalisations prior to words: A case study. In N. Waterson and C. Snow (Eds) *Proceedings of the Third International Child Language Symposium*. London: Wiley.

Carter, Anne L. (in press b). The disappearance schema. In E. Keenan (Ed.) *Studies in Developmental Pragmatics*. New York and London: Academic Press.

Carter, Anne L. (in press c). Prespeech meaning relations: An outline of one infant's sensorimotor morpheme development. In P. Fletcher and M. Garman (Eds) *Studies in Language Acquisition*. Cambridge: Cambridge University Press.

Carter, R. T. Jr (1974). *Teton Dakota Phonology*. University of Manitoba Anthropology Papers, Winnipeg, Manitoba.

Cattell, P. (1940). *Infant Intelligence Scale Record Form*. New York: The Psychological Corporation.

Cazden, C. B. (1965). Environmental assistance to the child's acquisition of grammar. Unpublished doctoral dissertation, Harvard University.

Chafe, W. L. (1970). *Meaning and the Structure of Language.* Chicago: University of Chicago Press.

Chein, I. (1972). *The Science of Behaviour and the Image of Man.* London: Tavistock.

Chomsky, N. (1965). *Aspects of the Theory of Syntax.* Cambridge, Mass: MIT Press.

Chomsky, N. (1968). *Language and Mind.* New York: Harcourt, Brace and World.

Cicourel, A. V. (1973). *Cognitive Sociology.* Harmondsworth: Penguin Books.

Cicourel, A. V. and Boese, R. (1972a). Sign language acquisition and the teaching of deaf children. In D. Hymes, C. Cazden and V. Johns (Eds) *The Functions of Language: an Anthropological and Psychological Approach.* New York: Teachers College Press.

Cicourel, A. V. and Boese, R. (1972b). The acquisition of manual sign language and generative semantics. *Semiotica* **3**, 225-256.

Clark, E. (1973a). What's in a word? On the child's acquisition of semantics in his first language. In T. E. Moore (Ed.) *Cognitive Development and the Acquisition of Language.* New York and London: Academic Press.

Clark, E. (1973b). How children describe time and order. In C. Ferguson and D. Slobin (Eds) *Studies in Child Language Development.* New York: Holt, Rinehart and Winston

Clark, E. (1973c). Non-linguistic strategies and the acquisition of word meanings. *Cognition* **2**, 161-182.

Clark, E. (1974). Some aspects of the conceptual basis for first language acquisition. In R. Schiefelbusch and L. Lloyd (Eds) *Language Perspectives: Acquisition, Retardation and Intervention.* Baltimore: University Park Press.

Clark, H. H. (1973). Space, Time, Semantics and the Child. In T. E. Moore (Ed.) *Cognitive Development and the Acquisition of Language.* New York and London: Academic Press.

Clark, H. H. and Lucy, B. (1975). Understanding what is meant from what is said: a study in conversationally conveyed requests. *Journal of Verbal Learning and Verbal Behaviour* **14**, 56-73.

Clark, R. A. (in preparation). The ontogeny of communication. Ph.D. Thesis, University of Hull, England.

Clerk, R. (1974). Performing without competence. *Journal of Child Language* **1**, 1-10.

Clerk, R. (in preparation). What's the use of imitation.

Clerk, R., Hutcheson, S. and Van Buren, P. (1974). Comprehension and production in language acquisition. *Journal of Linguistics* **10**, 39-54.

Collis, G. M. and Schaffer, H. R. (1975). Synchronisation of visual attention in mother-infant pairs. *Journal of Child Psychology* **16**, 315-320.

Condon, W. S. (1974). Speech makes babies move. *New Scientist* 6 June, 1974.

Condon, W. S. and Sander, L. S. (1974). Neonate movement is synchronised with adult speech. *Science* **183**, 99-101.

Corrigan, R. (1976). The relationship between object permanence and language development: how much and how strong? Paper presented to the *Child Language Research Forum*, Stanford University.

Cullen, J. M. (1972). Some principles of animal communication. In R. A. Hinde (Ed.) *Non-Verbal Communication.* Cambridge: Cambridge University Press.

Davenport, R. K. (1967). The Orang-utan in Sabah. *Folia Primatologica* **5,** 247-263.

Davis, K. (1947). Final note on a case of extreme social isolation. *American Journal of Sociology* **52,** 432-437.

Davison, A. (1974). Linguistic play and language acquisition. *Papers and Reports on Child Language Development* **8,** 179-187.

Decarie, T. G. (1965). *Intelligence and Affectivity in Early Childhood.* New York: International University Press.

Dewey, J. (1896). The reflex arc concept in psychology. *Psychological Review* **3,** 13-32.

Donaldson, M. and Balfour, G. (1968). Less is more: a study of language comprehension in children. *British Journal of Psychology* **59,** 461-472.

Dore, J. (1975a). Holophrases, speech acts and language universals. *Journal of Child Language* **2,** 21-40.

Dore, J. (1975b). *The Development of Speech Acts.* The Hague: Mouton.

Dore, J. (in press). Oh them sheriff: a pragmatic analysis of children's responses to questions. In C. Mitchell Kerman and S. Ervin-Tripp (Eds) *Child Discourse.* New York and London: Academic Press.

Dore, J., Franklin, M. B., Miller, R. T. and Ramer, A. L. H. (1976). Transitional phenomena in early language acquisition. *Journal of Child Language* **3,** 13-27.

Douglas, J. (1971). *Understanding Everyday Life.* London: Routledge and Kegan Paul.

Douglas, M. (1966). *Purity and Danger.* Harmondsworth: Penguin Books.

Drach, K., Kobashigawa, B., Pfuderer, C. and Slobin, D. I. (1969). The structure of the linguistic input to children. Working paper No. 14, Language-Behaviour Research Laboratory, Berkeley.

Duckworth, W. L. H. (1910). A Note on sections of the lips of primates. *Journal of Anatomy and Physiology* **44,** 348-353.

Edwards, D. (1973). Sensory-motor intelligence and semantic relations in early child grammar. *Cognition* **2** (4), 395-434.

Edwards, D. (1978). The sources of children's early meanings. In I. Markova (Ed.) *Language and the Social Context.* London: Wiley.

Eimas, P. D. (1976). Speech perception in infancy. Paper delivered at the XXIst International Congress of Psychology, Paris.

Eimas, P. D., Siqueland, E. R., Jusczyk, P. and Vigorito, J. (1971). Speech perception in infants. *Science* **171,** 803-806.

Eisenberg, R. B. (1969). Auditory behaviour in the human neonate. *International Audiology,* 34-45.

Emde, R. N. and Harrison, R. J. (1971). Endogenous and exogenous smiling systems in early infancy. *Journal of Child Psychiatry* **11,** 177-200.

Escalona, S. (1971). Basic modes of social interaction: their emergence and pattering during the first two years of life. *Merrill Palmer Quarterly* **18,** 205-232.

Fairbairn, W. R. D. (1949). Steps in the development of an object theory of personality. *British Journal of Medical Psychology* **22**, 26-31.

Fant, L. J. (1972). *Ameslan: An Introduction to American Sign Language.* Silver Springs, Md., National Association of the Deaf.

Fantz, R. L. (1971). The origin of form perception. *Scientific American* **204**, 66-72.

Feldman, H. (1975). The spontaneous creation of a lexicon by deaf children of hearing parents, or, there is more to language than meets the ear. Unpublished Ph.D. dissertation, University of Pennsylvania.

Ferguson, C. A. (1976). Learning to pronounce: the earliest stages of phonological development in the child. *Papers and Reports on Child Language Development* **11**, 1-27.

Ferrier, L. (1975). Dependency and appropriateness in early language development. Paper presented at Third International Child Language Symposium, London.

Fillmore, C. J. (1968). The case for case. In E. Bach and E. J. Harmes (Eds) *Universals in Linguistic Theory,* pp. 1-90. New York: Holt, Rinehart and Winston.

Fischer, K. W. (1974a). Cognitive development as problem-solving: the meaning of decalage in seriation tasks. Paper presented at the Fifth Annual Interdisciplinary Conference on Structural Learning, Philadelphia.

Fischer, S. (1974b). Sign Language and linguistic universals. In C. Rohrer and N. Ruwet (Eds) *Actes du Collogue Franco-Allemand de Grammaire Transformationelle.* Tubingen, West Germany: Max Niemeyer.

Flapan, D. (1968). *Childrens Understanding of Social Interaction.* New York: Teacher's College Press.

Flavell, J. H. (1974). The development of inferences about others. In T. Mischel (Ed.) *Understanding Other Persons.* Oxford: Blackwell.

Flavell, J. H., Botkin, O. T., Fry, C. L., Wright, J. W. and Jarvis, P. E. (1968). *The Development of Role-taking and Communication Skills in Children.* New York: Wiley.

Forman, G. E. (1971). Scattered thoughts on the origins of the concept of similarity with focus on motor patterns as constrained by the bilateral symmetry of the human anatomy. Unpublished manuscript, State University of New York at Buffalo.

Forman, G. E. (1972). The role of bilateral symmetry of the human anatomy in the early development of logic. Colloquium presented at York University (March 1972).

Forman, G. E., Laughlin, F. and Sweeney, M. (1973). The development of jigsaw puzzle solving in preschool children; an information processing approach. Demonstration and Research Centre for Early Education. *Papers and Reports* **5** (8).

Forman, G. E., Kuschner, D. and Dempsey, J. (1975). Transformations in the manipulations and productions with geometric objects: an early system of logic in young children. Centre for Early Childhood Education, University of Massachusetts, Amherst.

Fouts, R. S. (1973). Acquisition and testing of gestural signs in four young chimpanzees. *Science* **180**, 978-980.

Fraiberg, S. (1968). Parallel and divergent patterns in blind and sighted infants. *Psychoanalytic Study of the Child* **23**, 264-306. New York: International University Press.

Fraiberg, S. (1971). Intervention in infancy: A program for blind infants. *Journal of the American Academy of Child Psychology* **10,** 381-405.

Fraiberg, S. and Adelson, E. (1973). Self-representation in language and play: observations of blind children. *Psychoanalysis Quarterly* **42,** 539-562.

Friedman, L. A. (1976). The manifestation of subject, object, and topic in American Sign Language. In C. N. Li (Ed.) *Subject and Topic.* New York and London: Academic Press.

Frishberg, N. (1975). Arbitrariness and iconicity: historical change in American Sign Language. *Language* **51,** 676-719.

Fromkin, V. (1975). An update on the linguistic development of Genie. In D. P. Dato, (ed.) *Developmental Psycholinguistics: Theory and Applications.* Washington, D.C.: Georgetown University Press.

Furness, W. (1916). Observations on the mentality of chimpanzees and orang-utans. *Proceedings of the American Philosophical Society* **45,** 281-290.

Gardner, B. T. (1976). Language in apes from the perspective of comparative psychology. Paper given at the XXIst International Congress of Psychology, Paris.

Gardner, R. A. and Gardner, B. T. (1969). Teaching sign language to a chimpanzee. *Science* **165,** 664-672.

Gardner, R. A. and Gardner, B. T. (in press). Comparative psychology and language acquisition. In K. Salinger and F. Denmark (Eds) *Psychology: the State of the Art.* Annals of the New York Academy of Sciences.

Garfinkel, H. (1967). *Studies in Ethnomethodology.* Englewood Cliffs: Prentice Hall.

Garvey, C. (1976a). Contingent queries. Unpublished manuscript: Johns Hopkins University.

Garvey, C. (1976b). Some properties of social play. In J. S. Bruner, A. Jolly and K. Sylva (Eds) *Play. Its Role in Development and Evolution.* Harmondsworth: Penguin Books.

Gauld, A. and Shotter, J. (1977). *Human Action and its Psychological Investigation.* London: Routledge and Kegan Paul.

Geertz, C. (1966). The impact of the concept of culture on the concept of Man. *Bulletin of the Atomic Scientists* **12,** 2-8.

Gelb, I. J. (1952). *A Study of Writing: The Foundations of Grammatology.* Chicago: University of Chicago Press.

Geschwind, N. (1970). The origin of language and the brain. *Science* **170,** 940-944.

Gesell, A. and Amatruda, C. S. (1947). *Developmental Diagnosis.* New York: Paul B. Huber.

Giddens, A. (1976). *New Rules of Sociological Method.* London: Hutchinson.

Ginsburg, B. E. (1976). Evolution of communication patterns in animals. In M. E. Hahn and E. C. Simmel (Eds) *Communicative Behavior and Evolution.* New York and London: Academic Press.

Gleitman, L. R. and Gleitman, H. (1970). *Phrase and Paraphrase.* New York: W. W. Norton.

Gleitman, L. R. and Rozin, P. (1977). The structure and acquisition of reading I: Relations between orthographies and the structure of language. In A. S. Reber and D. Scarborough (Eds) *Toward A Psychology of Reading.* Hillsdale, New Jersey: Lawrence Erlbaum Associates.

Goffman, E. (1971). *Relations in Public.* London: Allen Lane, Penguin Press.

Goldin-Meadow, S. (1975). The representation of semantic relations in a manual language created by deaf children of hearing parents: A language you can't dismiss out of hand. Unpublished Ph.D. dissertation, University of Pennsylvania.

Goldin-Meadow, S. (1977). Structure in a manual language system developed without a language model: language without a helping hand. In H. Whitaker and H. A. Whitaker (Eds) *Studies in Neurolinguistics,* Vol. 4. New York and London: Academic Press.

Goldin-Meadow, S. and Feldman, H. (1975). The creation of a communication system: A study of deaf children of hearing parents. *Sign Language Studies* **8**, 225-234.

Goldin-Meadow, S. and Feldman, H. (1977). The development of language-like communication without a language model. *Science* **197**, 401-403.

Goodall, J. (1963). Feeding behaviour of wild chimpanzees. *Symposium of Zoological Society of London* **10**, 39-48.

Goodall, J. (1965). Chimpanzees of the Gombe Stream Reserve. In I. De Vore (Ed.) *Primate Behavior: Field Studies of Monkeys and Apes.* New York: Holt, Rinehart and Winston.

Goodall, J. (1968). A preliminary report on expressive movements and communication in the Gombe Stream chimpanzees. In P. Jay (Ed.) *Primates: Studies in Adaptation and Variability.* New York: Holt, Rinehart and Winston.

Goodnow, J. and Levine, R. (1973). "The grammar of action": sequence and syntax in children's copying. *Cognitive Psychology* **4**, 82-98.

Goodson, B. D. and Greenfield, P. M. (1975). The search for structural principles in children's manipulative play: a parallel with linguistic development. *Child Development* **46**, 734-746.

Greenberg, J. H. (1966). Some universals of grammar with particular reference to the order of meaningful elements. In J. H. Greenberg (Ed.) *Universals of Language.* Cambridge, Mass: MIT Press.

Greenfield, P. M. (1973). Who is "Dada"? Some aspects of the semantic and phonological development of a child's first words. *Language and Speech* **16**, 34-43.

Greenfield, P. M. and Schweider, L. (in press). Building a tree structure: the development of hierarchical complexity and interrupted strategies in children's construction activity. *Developmental Psychology.*

Greenfield, P. M. and Smith, J. (1976). *Communication and the Beginnings of Language: The Development of Semantic Structure in One Word Speech.* New York and London: Academic Press.

Greenfield, P. M. and Westerman, M. (in press). Some psychological relations between action and language structure. *Journal of Psycholinguistic Research.*

Greenfield, P. M., Nelson, K. and Saltzman, E. (1972). The development of rule bound strategies for manipulating serrated cups: a parallel between action and grammar. *Cognitive Psychology* **3**, 291-310.

Grice, H. F. (1968). Utterers meaning, sentence meaning and word meaning. *Foundations of Language* **4**, 225-242.

Griffin, D. R. (1976). *The Question of Animal Awareness.* New York: Rockerfeller University Press.

Griffiths, P. D. (1974). *That there* deixis I: *that*. Mimeo. Department of Language, University of York.

Griffiths, R. (1954). *The Abilities of Babies*. London: London University Press.

Gruber, J. S. (1973). Correlations between the syntactic constructions of the child and of the adult. In C. A. Ferguson and D. I. Slobin (Eds) *Studies of Child Language Development*. New York: Holt, Rinehart and Winston.

Guanella, F. M. (1934). Block building activities of young children. *Archives of Psychology* **174.**

Guess, D., Sailor, W., Rutherford, G. and Baer, D. M. (1968). An experimental analysis of linguistic development: the productive use of the plural morpheme. *Journal of Applied Behaviour Analysis* **1,** 297-306.

Guillaume, P. (1927). Les debuts de la phrase dans la language de l'enfant. *Journal de Psychologie* **24,** 1-25.

Habermas, J. (1970). Introductory remarks to a theory of communicative competence. In H. P. Dreitzel (Ed.) *Recent Sociology No. 2*. London: Macmillan.

Habermas, J. (1972). *Knowledge and Human Interests*. London: Heinemann.

Halliday, M. A. K. (1973). Early language learning: a socio-linguistic approach. Paper presented at IXth International Congress of Anthropological and Ethnological Science, Chicago.

Halliday, M. A. K. (1975). *Learning how to mean: Explorations in the Development of Language*. London: Arnold.

Halliday, M. A. K. (1976). Learning how to mean. In E. and E. Lenneberg (Eds) *Foundations of Language Development*. London and New York: Academic Press.

Hamilton, A. (1970). Nature and nurture: child rearing in North-Central Arnhem Land. M.A. Thesis, University of Sydney. Australian Institute of Aboriginal Studies, Canberra.

Hamlyn, D. W. (1974). Person-perception and our understanding of others. In T. Mischel (Ed.) *Understanding Other Persons*. Oxford: Blackwell.

Harlow, H. (1949). The formation of learning sets. *Psychological Review* **56,** 51-65.

Harré, R. (1970). Powers. *British Journal of Philosophical Science* **21,** 81-101.

Harré, R. (1974a). Some remarks on "rule" as a scientific concept. In T. Mischel (Ed.) *Understanding Other Persons*. Oxford: Blackwell.

Harré, R. (1974b). The conditions for a social psychology of childhood. In M. P. M. Richards (Ed.) *The Integration of a Child into a Social World*. Cambridge: Cambridge University Press.

Harré, R. and Secord, P. F. (1972). *The Exploration of Social Behaviour*. Oxzford: Blackwell.

Harris, P. (1971). Understanding one another before we speak. Unpublished paper, Harvard University.

Harris, Z. S. (1951). *Methods in Structural Linguistics*. Chicago: University of Chicago Press.

Harrison, B. (1961). A study of Orang-utan behaviour in the semi-wild state. *International Zoo Yearbook* **3,** 57-68. London: Zoological Society of London.

Hayes, C. (1952). *The Ape in Our House*. London: Gollancz.

Hayes, C. (1970). A chimp learns to talk. In R. Kuhlen and G. Thompson (Eds) *Psychological Studies of Human Development.* New York: Appleton-Century-Crofts.

Heider, F. (1958). *The Psychology of Interpersonal Relations.* New York: Wiley.

Herodotus. (1942). *The Persian Wars. c. 460 B.C..* G. Rawlinson (tr.). New York: Random House.

Hess, R. D. and Shipman, V. C. (1965a). Early experience and the socialisation of cognitive modes in children. *Child Development* **36,** 869-886.

Hess, R. D. and Shipman, V. C. (1965b). Early blocks to children's learning. *Children* **12,** 189-194.

Hewes, G. W. (1973). Primate communication and the gestural origin of language. *Current Anthropology* **14,** 5-32.

Hewett, F. M. (1965). Teaching speech to an autistic child through operant conditioning. *American Journal of Orthopsychiatry* **35,** 927-936.

Hinde, R. A. (1974). *Biological Bases of Human Social Behaviour.* New York: McGraw Hill Book Co.

Hinde, R. A. and Stevenson-Hinde, J. (1976). Towards understanding relationships: dynamic stability. In P. P. G. Bateson and R. A. Hinde (Eds) *Growing Points in Ethology,* pp. 471-479. Cambridge: Cambridge University Press.

Hockett, C. F. (1966). The problem of universals in language. In J. H. Greenberg (Ed.) *The Problem of Universals in Language.* Cambridge, Mass: MIT Press.

Hogan, L. (1898). *A Study of a Child.* New York: Harper.

Holzman, M. (1972). The use of interrogative forms in the verbal interaction of three mothers and their children. *Journal of Psycholinguistic Research* **1,** 311-335.

Huber, E. (1931). *The Evolution of Facial Musculature and Facial Expression.* Baltimore: John Hopkins University Press.

Hull, C. L. (1943). *Principles of Behaviour.* New York: Appleton-Century-Crofts.

Huttenlocher, J. (1975). The origin of language comprehension. In R. L. Solso (Ed.) *Theories in Cognitive Psychology.* Hillsdale, New Jersey: Lawrence Erlbaum Associates.

Huttenlocher, J. and Strauss, S. (1968). Comprehension and a statement's relation to the situation it describes. *Journal of Verbal Learning and Verbal Behaviour* **7,** 300-304.

Huttenlocher, J., Eisenberg, K. and Strauss, S. (1968). Comprehension: relation between perceived actor and logical subject. *Journal of Verbal Learning and Verbal Behaviour* **7,** 527-530.

Hymes, D. (1971). Competence and performance in linguistic theory. In R. Huxley and E. Ingram (Ed.) *Language Acquisition: Models and Methods.* London and New York: Academic Press.

Hymes, D. (1964). Introduction: Toward ethnographies of communication. *American Anthropologist* **66,** 12-25.

Ingram, D. (1971). Transitivity in child language. *Language* **47,** 888-910.

Ingram, D. (1974). Stages in the development of one-word utterances. Paper presented to the Child Language Research Forum Stanford University.

Ingram, D. (1975). Piaget's data: a chronological record of Jacqueline, Lucienne and Laurent. Mimeo, University of British Columbia.

Ingram, D., Ingram, J. and Neufeld, W. (in preparation). A longitudinal study of the language development during the sensorimotor period.

Isaacs, W., Thomas, J. M. and Goldiamond, I. (1960). Application of operant conditioning to reinstate verbal behaviour in psychotics. *Journal of Speech and Hearing Disorders* **25**, 8-12.

Itani, J. (1963). Vocal communication of the wild Japanese monkey. *Primates* **4**, 11-66.

Jaffé, J., Stern, D. N. and Parry, J. C. (1973). "Conversational" coupling of gaze behavior in prelinguistic human development. *Journal of Psycholinguistic Research* **2**, 321-329.

James, W. (1890). *Principles of Psychology*. Vol. 2. London: Macmillan.

Kagan, J. (1971). *Change and Continuity in Infancy*. New York: Wiley.

Kalnins, I. and Bruner, J. S. (1973). The co-ordination of visual observation and instrumental behaviour in early infancy. *Perception* **2**, 307-314.

Kaplan, E. (1969). The role of intonation in the acquisition of language. Unpublished doctoral dissertation, Cornell University.

Kawai, M. (1963). On the newly acquired behaviors of the natural troop of Japanese monkeys on Koshima Island. *Primates* **4**, 113-115.

Kawai, M. (1965). Newly acquired pre-cultural behavior of the Japanese monkeys on Koshima Islet. *Primates* **6**, 1-30.

Kaye, K. (1976). Infants' effects upon the mothers' teaching strategies. In J. C. Glidewell (Ed.) *The Social Context of Learning and Development*. New York: Gardiner Press.

Kaye, K. and Brazelton, T. B . (1971). Mother-infant interaction in the organisation of sucking. Paper given to Society for Research in Child Development, Minneapolis.

Keenan, E. (1974). Conversational competence in children. *Journal of Child Language* **1**, 163-183.

Kellogg, R. (1969). *Analyzing Children's Art*. Palo Alto: National Press.

Klopfer, P. H. (1976). Evolution, behavior and language. In M. E. Hahn and E. C. Simmel (Eds) *Communicative Behaviour and Evolution*. New York and London: Academic Press.

Koch, S. (1959). Epilogue. In S. Koch (Ed.) *Psychology: A Study of a Science*. Vol. 3, pp. 729-788. New York: McGraw-Hill.

Koch, S. (1961). Psychological science versus the science humanism-antimony: intimations of a significant science of man. *American Psychologist* **16**, 629-639.

Kohlberg, L. (1969). Stage and sequence: the cognitive developmental approach to socialization. In D. Goslin (Ed.) *Handbook of Socialization Theory and Research*. Chicago: Rand McNally.

Konner, M. J. (1972). Aspects of the developmental ethology of a foraging people. In N. J. Burton-Jones (Ed.) *Ethological Studies of Child Behaviour*. Cambridge Cambridge University Press.

Kortlandt, A. (1960). Behaviour research on the evolution of apes and man. *Archives Neerlandaises de Zoologie* **XIII**, 585-586.

Kortlandt, A. (1962). Chimpanzees in the wild. *Scientific American* **206**, 128-138.

Kortlandt, A. (1965). Discussion contribution to A. L. Bryan's paper: "On the essential morphological basis for human culture". *Current Anthropology* **6**, 320-326.

Kortlandt, A. (1973). Discussion contribution to: G. W. Hewes: "Primate communication and the gestural origin of language". *Current Anthropology* **14**, 13-14.

Kuhn, T. S. (1962). *The Structure of Scientific Revolutions.* Chicago: University of Chicago Press.

Labov, W. (0000). The reading of the -ed suffix. In Levin, H. and J. Williams (Eds) *Basic Studies on Reading.* New York: Basic Books.

Labov, W. (1971). On the adequacy of natural languages: I. The development of tense. Unpublished paper.

Lackner, J. R. (1976). A developmental study of language behavior in retarded children. In D. M. Morehead and A. E. Morehead (Eds) *Normal and Deficient Child Language.* Baltimore: University Park Press.

Lakoff, G. (1971). On generative semantics. In D. D. Steinberg and L. A. Jakobovity (Eds) *Semantics: An Inter-disciplinary Reader in Philosophy, Linguistics and Psychology.* Cambridge: Cambridge University Press.

Lane, H., Boyes-Braem, P. and Bellugi, U. (1976). Preliminaries to a distinctive feature analysis of handshapes in American Sign language. *Cognitive Psychology* **8**, 263-289.

Langer, S. (1967). *Mind: An Essay on Human Feeling.* Vol. I. Baltimore and London: John Hopkins Press.

Lashley, K. S. (1951). The problem of serial order in behaviour. In L. A. Jeffres (Ed.) *Cerebral Mechanisms in Behaviour: the Hixon Symposium.* New York: Wiley.

Latif, I. (1934). The physiological basis of linguistic development and the ontogeny of meaning 1, II. *Psychological Review* **41**, 55-85, 153-176.

Lawick-Goodall, J. van (1971). *In the Shadow of Man.* Boston: Houghton Mifflin Co.

Lee, C. L., Brody, L., Matthews, W. S. and Palmquist, W. (1974). The development of interpersonal competence strategies of social exchange. Symposium presented at A.P.A. annual convention, New Orleans, Sept. 1974.

Lehiste, I. (1970). *Suprasegmentals.* Cambridge, Mass: MIT Press.

Lenneberg, E. H. (1967). *The Biological Foundations of Language.* New York: Wiley.

Levelt, W. J. M. (1975). What became of LAD? *Peter de Ridder Press Publications in Cognition 1.* Lisse, Netherlands: Peter de Ridder Press.

Lewis, M. and Brooks, J. (1975). Infants' social perception: a constructivist view. In L. B. Cohen and P. Salapatek (Eds) *Infant Perception from Sensation to Cognition,* Vol. II. New York and London: Academic Press.

Lewis, M. and Freedle, R. (1973). Mother-infant dyad: the cradle of meaning. In P. Pliner, L. Krames and T. Alloway (Eds) *Communication and Affect: Language and Thought.* New York and London: Academic Press.

Lewis, M. and Rosenblum, L. (Eds) (1974). *The Effect of the Infant on its Caregiver.* New York: Wiley.

Lewis, M. M. (1936). *Infant Speech: A Study of the Beginnings of Language.* New York: Harcourt, Brace Jovanovich.

Lézinne, I. (1973). The transition from sensorimotor to earliest symbolic function in early development. *Research Publications of the Association for the Research in Nervous and Mental Disease* **51**, 221-231.

Liberman, A. M. (1970). The grammars of speech and language. *Cognitive Psychology* **I**, 301-323.

Lieberman, P. (1975). *On the Origin of Language.* New York: Macmillan.

Lieven, E. (1975). Conversations between mothers and young children: Individual differences and their possible implication for the study of language learning. Paper presented at Third International Child Language Symposium, London.

Lieven, E. (1976). Turn-taking and pragmatics: two issues in early child language. Paper presented at Nato Conference "Psychology of Language". Stirling University.

Lieven, E. and McShane, J. (1977). Language is a developing skill. In D. Chivers and J. Herbert (Eds) *Recent Advances in Primatology.* Vol. 1. New York and London: Academic Press.

Lightholler, G. S. (1928). The facial musculature of three Orang-utans and two Cercopitheciae. *Journal of Anatomy* **63**, 19-81.

Lindner, G. (1898). *Aus dem Naturgarten der Kindersprache.* Liepzig. Grieben.

Lock, A. J. (1976). Acts instead of sentences. In W. von Raffler-Engel and Y. Lebrun (Eds) *Baby Talk and Infant Speech.* Lisse, Holland: Swets and Zeitlinger B.V.

Lock, A. J. (in press). *The Guided Reinvention of Language.* London and New York: Academic Press.

Lovaas, O. I. (1966). A programme for the establishment of speech in psychotic children. In E. Wing (Ed.) *Early Childhood Autism.* London: Pergamon Press.

Luria, A. R. (1975). Scientific perspectives and philosophical dead-ends in modern linguistics. *Cognition* **3**, 377-385.

Lyons, J. (1968). *An Introduction to Theoretical Linguistics.* Cambridge: Cambridge University Press.

Lyons, J. (1973). Deixis as the source of reference. *Work in Progress* **6**, 92-115. Department of Linguistics, Edinburgh University.

Mahler, M. (1963). Thoughts about development and individuation. *The Psychoanalytic Study of the Child* **18**, 307-323.

Maratos, O. (1973). The origin and development of imitation in the first six months of life. Unpublished Ph.D. Thesis, University of Geneva.

Maratos, O. (1977). Trends in the development of imitation in early infancy. In H. Nathan (Ed.) Proceedings of the O.E.C.D. Conference on *Dips in Learning.* St. Paul de Vence, March 1975. Paris (in press).

Marler, P. (1965). Communication in monkeys and apes. In I. DeVore (Ed.) *Primate Behaviour: Field Studies of Monkeys and Apes.* New York: Holt, Rinehart and Winston.

Marler, P. (1969). Vocalisation of wild chimpanzees: an introduction. *Proceedings of the Second International Congress of Primatology.* Atlanta. Vol. 1, 94-100.

Marler, P. and Tamura, M. (1964). Culturally transmitted patterns of vocal behavior in sparrows. *Science* **146**, 1483-1486.

Masangky, Z. S., McClusky, C. A., McIntyre, C. W., Sims-Knight, J., Vaughen, B. E. and Flavell, J. H. (1974). The early development of inferences about the visual percepts of others. *Child Development* **45**, 357-366.

Mead, G. H. (1934).*Mind, Self and Society.* Chicago: University of Chicago Press.

Menn, L. (1976). Pattern, control and contrast in beginning speech: a case study in the development of word form and function. Unpublished Doctoral dissertation, University of Illinois.

Menzel, E. W. (1973). Leadership and communication in young chimpanzees. In E. W. Menzel (Ed.) *Precultural Primate Behaviour.* Basel: S. Karger.

Merleau-Ponty, M. (1964). The child's relations with others. In *The Primary of Perception.* pp. 96-158. Evanston: North Western University Press.

Merleau-Ponty, M. (1970). *Themes from the Lectures at the College de France* (trans. John O'Neill). Evanston: North Western University Press.

Miller, D. L. (1973). *George Herbert Mead: Self, Language and the World.* Austin: University of Texas Press.

Miller, G. A., Galanter, E. and Pribram, K. H. (1960). *Plans and the Structure of Behaviour.* New York: Holt, Rinehart and Winston.

Miller, P. H., Kessel, F. S. and Flavell, J. H. (1970). Thinking about people thinking about . . . : a study of social cognitive development. *Child Development* **41**, 613-624.

Moerk, E. (1975). Piaget's research as applied to the explanation of language development. *Merrill-Palmer Quarterly* **21**, 151-169.

Morehead, D. M. and Ingram, D. (1976). The development of base syntax in normal and linguistically deviant children. In D. M. Morehead and A. E. Morehead (Eds) *Normal and Deficient Child Language.* Baltimore: University Park Press.

Morehead, D. M. and Morehead, A. E. (1974). From signal to sign: a Piagetian view of thought and language during the first two years. In R. Schiefelbusch and L. Lloyd (Eds) *Language Perspectives: Acquisition, Retardation, and Intervention.* Baltimore: University Park Press.

Morris, C. W. (1938). Foundations of the theory of signs. In *International Encyclopedia of Unified Science,* Vol. 12. Chicago: Chicago University Press.

Morris, C. W. (1946). *Signs, Language and Behaviour.* New Jersey: Prentice-Hall.

Murphy, C. M. and Messer, D. J. (1977). Mothers, infants and pointing: a study of a gesture. In H. R. Schaffer (Ed.) *Studies in Mother-Infant Interaction.* London and New York: Academic Press.

McCarthy, D. (1954). Language development in children. In L. Carmichael (Ed.) *Manual of Child Psychology.* New York: Wiley.

McCawley, J. D. (1968). The role of semantics in a grammar. In E. Bach and R. T. Harms (Eds) *Universals in Linguistic Theory.* New York: Holt, Rinehart and Winston.

McNeill, D. (1966a). Developmental psycholinguistics. In F. Smith and G. A. Miller (Eds) *The Genesis of Language.* Cambridge, Mass: MIT Press.

McNeill, D. (1966b). The creation of language by children. In J. Lyons and R. J. Wales (Eds) *Psycholinguistic Papers.* Edinburgh: Edinburgh University Press.

McNeill, D. (1974). Sentence structure in chimpanzee communication. In K. J. Connolly and J. S. Bruner (Eds) *The Growth of Competence.* London and New York: Academic Press.

McTear, M. (1976). Repetition in child language: imitation or creation? Paper presented at Nato Conference "Psychology of Language". Stirling University.

Macfarlane, A. (1974). If a smile is so important. *New Scientist* 25 April 1974.

Macfarlane, A. (1977). *The Psychology of Childbirth.* London: Fontana/Open Books.

MacKinnon, J. (1974). The behaviour and ecology of wild Orang-utans, *Pongo pymaeus. Animal Behaviour* **22,** 3-74.

Macmurray, J. (1957). *The Self as Agent.* London: Faber and Faber.

Macmurray, J. (1961). *Persons in Relation.* London: Faber and Faber.

MacNamara, J. (1972). Cognitive basis of language learning in infants. *Psychological Review* **79,** 1-13.

MacReynolds, L. (1969). Application of timeout from positive reinforcement for increasing the efficiency of speech training. *Journal of Applied Behaviour Analysis* **2,** 199-205.

Neisser, U. (1976). *Cognition and Reality.* San Francisco: Freeman.

Nelson, K. (1973). Structure and strategy in learning to talk. *Monographs of the Society for Research in Child Development* **149,** 38 (1-2).

Nelson, K. (1974). Concept, word and sentence: Interrelations in acquisition and development. *Psychological Review* **81,** 267-285.

Nemai, J. and Kellerman, G. (1929). Das Stimmorgan des Orang-utan. *Z. Anat. Entw. Gesch* **88,** 697-709.

Newell, A., Shaw, J. C. and Simon, H. A. (1958). Elements of a theory of human problem solving. *Psychological Review* **65,** 151-166.

Newport, E., Gleitman, G. and Gleitman, L. R. (1977). Mother, I'd rather do it myself: Some effects and non-effects of maternal speech style. In C. E. Snow and C. A. Ferguson (Eds) *Talking to Children: Language Input and Acquisition.* Cambridge: Cambridge University Press.

Newport, E. L. and Ashbrook, E. (1977). Development of semantic-syntactic relations in the acquisition of American Sign Language. (Manuscript) University of California at San Diego.

Newport, L. and Bellugi, U. (1977). Linguistic expression of category levels in a visual-gestural language. To appear in Rosch, E. (Ed.). Hillsdale, New Jersey: Lawrence Erlbaum Associates.

Newson, J. (1974). Towards a theory of infant understanding. *Bulletin of the British Psychological Society* **27,** 251-257.

Newson, J. (1977). An intersubjective approach to the systematic description of mother-child interaction. In H. R. Schaffer (Ed.) *Studies in Mother-Child Interaction.* London and New York: Academic Press.

Newson, J. and Newson, E. (1975). Intersubjectivity and the transmission of culture: on the social origins of symbolic functioning. *Bulletin of the British Psychological Society* **28,** 437-446.

Newson, J. and Newson, E. (1976). On the social origins of symbolic functioning. In V. P. Varma and P. Williams (Eds) *Piaget, Psychology and Education.* London: Hodder and Stoughton.

Newson, J. and Pawlby, S. (1972). Imitation and preverbal behaviour. Department of Psychology, Nottingham University.

Newson, J. and Paulby, S. (1975). On Imitation. Paper presented to an Inter-university Colloquium at Nottingham University.

Newson, J. and Shotter, J. (1974). How babies communicate. *New Society* **29,** No. 618, 345-347. 8 August 1974.

Ninio, A. and Bruner, J. S. (1977). Achievement and antecedents of labelling. *Journal of Child Language* (in press).

Ninio, A. and Lieblich, A. (1976). "The grammar of action": "phrase structure" in children's copying. *Child Development* **47,** 846-849.

Nokony, A. (1977). Meaning development in one child acquiring Dakota-Sioux as a first language. Unpublished M.A. Thesis. Vancouver, B.C: University of British Columbia.

Olson, D. (1970a). Language and thought: aspects of a cognitive theory of semantics. *Psychological Review* **77,** 257-273.

Olson, D. R. (1970b). *Cognitive Development: the Child's Acquisition of Diagonality.* New York and London: Academic Press.

Palmer, R. E. (1969). *Hermeneutics.* Evanston: North Western University Press.

Papousek, H. (1967). Experimental studies of appetitional behaviour in human newborns and infants. In H. W. Stevenson (Ed.) *Early Behaviour: Comparative and Developmental Approaches.* New York: Wiley.

Pawlby, S. (1977). A study of the nature and structure of imitative sequences observed in interaction between mothers and their infants. In H. R. Schaffer (Ed.) *Studies in Mother-Infant Interaction.* London and New York: Academic Press.

Peirce, C. S. (1932). *Collected Papers.* C. Hartshorne and P. Weiss (Eds) Cambridge, Mass: Harvard University Press.

Philips, J. (1973). The syntax and vocabulary of mother's speech to young children: age and sex comparisons. *Child Development* **44,** 182-185.

Piaget, J. (1926). *The Language and Thought of the Child* (Trans. M. Gabin). New York: Meridian.

Piaget, J. (1932). *The Moral Judgement of the Child.* London: Routledge and Kegan Paul.

Piaget, J. (1951). Pensee egocentrique et pense sociocentrique. *Cah. int. Sociol.* **10,** 34-49.

Piaget, J. (1952). *The Origins of Intelligence in Children.* New York: Norton.

Piaget, J. (1954). *The Child's Construction of Reality.* New York: Basic Books.

Piaget, J. (1955). *The Language and Thought of the Child.* Cleveland, Ohio: The World Publishing Company.

Piaget, J. (1962). *Play, Dreams and Imitation in Childhood.* London: Routledge and Kegan Paul.

Piaget, J. (1969). *The Mechanisms of Perception.* London: Routledge and Kegan Paul.

Piaget, J. (1970a). Piaget's Theory. In P. H. Mussen (Ed.) *Carmichael's Manual of Child Psychology.* New York: Wiley.

Piaget, J. (1970b). *Structuralism*. New York: Harper and Row.

Piaget, J. (1974). *La Prise de Conscience*. Paris: Presses Universitaires de France.

Piaget, J. and Inhelder, B. (1969). *The Psychology of the Child*. London: Routledge and Kegan Paul.

Ploog, D. and Melnechuk, T. (1969). Are apes capable of language? *Neurosciences Research Programme Bulletin* **9**, 599-700.

Plooij, F. X. (in press). How wild chimpanzee babies trigger the onset of mother-infant play and what the mother makes of it. In M. Bullowa (Ed.) *Before Speech: the Beginnings of Human Communication*. Cambridge: Cambridge University Press.

Popper, K. R. (1963). *Conjectures and Refutations*. London: Routledge and Kegan Paul.

Popper, K. R. (1972). *Objective Knowledge: An Evolutionary Approach*. Oxford: Clarendon Press.

Prechtl, H. F. R. (1953). Die Kletterbewegungen beim Saugling. *Mschr. Kinderheilk* **101** (12), 519-521.

Prechtl, H. F. R. and Beintema, D. (1964). *The Neurological Examination of the Full-term Newborn Infant*. London: The Spastics Society Medical Education and Information Unit in association with William Heinemann Medical Books Ltd.

Premack, D. (1971). On the assessment of language competence in the chimpanzee. In A. M. Schrier and F. Stollnitz (Eds) *Behaviour of Nonhuman Primates*, Vol. 4. New York and London: Academic Press.

Preyer, W. (1895). *The Mind of the Child*. New York: Appleton.

Pribram, K. H. (1971). *The Languages of the Brain*. New Jersey: Prentice Hall.

Quirk, R., Greenbaum, S., Leech, G. and Svartvik, J. (1972). *A Grammar of Contemporary English*. London: Longman.

Rambaugh, D. and Savage, S. (1977). Paper presented to the American Association for the Advancement of Science.

Reynolds, P. (1968). Evolution of primate vocal-auditory communication systems. *American Anthropologist* **70**, 300-308.

Reynolds, V. (1976). *The Biology of Human Action*. Reading: Freeman.

Richards, K., Spears, D. and Richards, M. P. M. (Eds) (1972). *Race, Culture and Intelligence*. London: Penguin.

Richards, M. P. M. (1971). Social interaction in the first weeks of human life. *Psychiat. Neurol. Neurochir.* **74**, 35-42.

Richards, M. P. M. (1974a). Development of psychological communication. In K. J. Connolly and J. S. Bruner (Eds) *The Growth of Competence*. London and New York: Academic Press.

Richards, M. P. M. (1974b). First steps in becoming social. In M. P. M. Richards (Ed.) *The Integration of a Child into a Social World*. Cambridge: Cambridge University Press.

Riggs, S. R. (1893). Dakota grammar, texts and ethnography. *Contributions to North American Ethnology*, **IX**. Washington: Government Printing Office.

Rigler, D. and Rigler, M. (1975). Persistent effects of early experience. Paper presented at Meeting of Society for Research in Child Development, Denver, 1975.

Risley, P. (1966). The establishment of verbal behaviour in deviant children. Paper presented at the Meeting of the American Association on Mental Deficiency, Chicago, Illinois.

Robinson, B. W. (1967). Vocalisation evoked from the forebrain in *Macaca mulatta*. *Physiology and Behaviour* **2,** 345-354.

Romanes, G. J. (1888). *Mental Evolution in Man: Origin of Human Faculty.* London: Routledge and Kegan Paul.

Romanes, G. J. (1897). *Essays.* C. Lloyd Morgan (Ed.). London: Longmans, Green and Co.

Rosch, E. H. (1973). On the internal structure of perceptual and semantic categories. In T. E. Moore (Ed.) *Cognitive Development and the Acquisition of Language,* pp. 111-144. New York and London: Academic Press.

Rosenstein, J. (1964). Concept development and language instruction. *Exceptional Children* **30,** 337-343.

Rozin, P. and Gleitman, L. R. (1977). The structure and acquisition of reading II: The reading process and the acquisition of the alphabetic principle. In A. S. Reber and D. Scarborough (Eds) *Toward a Psychology of Reading.* Hillsdale, New Jersey: Lawrence Erlbaum Associates.

Rozin, P., Poritsky, S. and Sotsky, R. (1971). American children with reading problems can easily learn to read English represented by Chinese characters. *Science* **171,** 1264-1267.

Rumbaugh, D. M., Gill, T. V. and Glaserfield, E. von. (1973). Reading and sentence completion by a chimpanzee. *Science* **182,** 731-733.

Rutter, M. (1972). *Maternal Deprivation Reassessed.* Harmondsworth: Penguin.

Ryan, J. (1973). Interpretation and imitation in early language development. In R. A. Hinde and J. Stevenson-Hinde (Eds) *Constraints on Learning.* London and New York: Academic Press.

Ryan, J. (1974). Early language development: towards a communicational analysis. In M. P. M. Richards (Ed.) *The Integration of a Child into a Social World.* Cambridge: Cambridge University Press.

Ryle, G. (1949). *The Concept of Mind.* London: Hutchinson.

Sacks, H., Schegloff, E. and Jefferson, G. (1974). A symplest systematics for the conversation. *Language* **50,** 696-735.

Sankoff, G. and Laberge, S. (1973). On the acquisition of native speakers by a language. *Kivung* **6,** 32-47.

Sapir, E. 61968). The psychological reality of phonemes. In D. Mandelbaum (Ed.) *Selected Writings of Edward Sapir.* Berkeley, California: University of California Press.

Saussure, F. de (1960). *Course in General Linguistics.* London: Owen.

Scaife, M. and Bruner, J. S. (1975). The capacity for joint visual attention in the infant. *Nature* **253,** 265-266.

Schaerlaekens, A. (1973). *The Two-word Sentence in Child Language Development.* The Hague: Mouton.

Schaffer, H. R. (1971). *The Growth of Sociability.* Harmondsworth: Penguin Books.

Schaffer, H. R. (1974). Behavioural synchrony in infancy. *New Scientist* **62** (892), 124-126.

Schaffer, H. R. (1974). Early social behaviour and the study of reciprocity. *Bulletin of the British Psychological Society* **27**, 209-216.

Schaffer, H. R. (1977a). *Studies in Mother-Infant Interaction.* London and New York: Academic Press.

Schaffer, H. R. (1977b). Early interactive development. In H. R. Schaffer (Ed.) *Studies in Mother-Infant Interaction.* London and New York: Academic Press.

Schaffer, H. R., Collis, G. and Parsons, G. (1975). Vocal interchange and visual regard in verbal and preverbal children. Paper presented at Loch Lomond Symposium Strathclyde (September 1975).

Schantz, C. U. (1975). The development of social cognition. In E. M. Hetherington (Ed.) *Review of Child Development Research.* Vol. 5. Chicago: University of Chicago Press.

Schlesinger, H. S. and Meadow, K. P. (1972). *Deafness and Mental Health: a Developmental Approach.* Berkeley: University of California Press.

Schlesinger, I. M. (1973). Relational concepts underlying language. Paper prepared for NICHD conference on Language Intervention with the Mentally Retarded, Wisconson Dells (June 1973).

Schneirla, T. C. (1972). The relationship between observation and experimentation in the field study of behaviour. In L. R. Aronson, E. Tobach, J. S. Rosenblatt and D. S. Lehrman (Eds) *Selected Writings of T. C. Schneirla.* San Francisco: Freeman.

Schutz, A. (1953). Common-sense and scientific interpretation of human action. *Philosophy and Phenomenological Research* **14**, 1-38.

Schutz, A. (1967). *Collected papers I: The Problem of Social Reality.* The Hague: Martinus Nijhoff.

Schutz, A. (1972). *The Phenomenology of the Social World.* London: Heinemann.

Schutz, A. and Luckmann, T. (1974). *The Structures of the Life-World.* London: Heinemann.

Scupin, E. and Scupin, G. (1907). *Bubis erste Kindheit.* Leipzig: Grieben.

Scupin, E. and Scupin, G. (1910). *Bubi im vierten bis sechsten Lebensjahr.* Leipzig: Grieben.

Searle, J. (1969). *Speech Acts: An Essay in the Philosophy of Language.* Cambridge: Cambridge University Press.

Secord, P. F. and Peevers, B. H. (1974). The development and attribution of person concepts. In T. Mischel (Ed.) *Understanding Other Persons.* Oxford: Blackwell.

Segal, H. (1975). *Introduction to the Work of Melanie Klein.* London: Hogarth Press and Institute of Psychoanalysis.

Seligman, M. E. P. (1970). On the generality of the laws of learning. *Psychology Review* **77**, 406-418.

Seuren, P. A. M. (1976). Language and communication in primates. Paper given at the 6th congress of the International Primatological Society, Cambridge, England.

Shafton, A. (1976). *Conditions of Awareness.* Portland, Oregon: Riverstone Press.

Sheldon, A. (1973). The role of parallel function in the acquisition of relative clauses in English. *University of Minnesota Working Papers in Linguistics and Philosophy* **1** (1).

Shields, M. M. (1974). The development of the modal auxiliary system. *British Educational Review* **26** (3), 180-200.

Shields, M. M. (1976). Yes and No, a study of negation and affirmation in discourse of children between three and five. *Proceedings of the 4th International Congress of Applied Linguistics.* Stuttgart: Hochschule Vestag.

Shotter, J. (1973). Acquired powers: the transformation of natural into personal Powers. *Journal for the Theory of Social Behaviour* **3**, 141-156.

Shotter, J. (1974). The development of personal powers. In M. P. M. Richards (Ed.) *The Integration of a Child into a Social World.* Cambridge: Cambridge University Press.

Shotter, J. (1975). *Images of Man in Psychological Research.* London: Methuen.

Shotter, J. (in press). Towards a social psychology of everyday life: a stand-point 'in' action. In M. Brennar, P. Marsh and M. Williams (Eds) *The Social Contexts of Methods.* London: Croom Helm.

Shotter, J. and Gregory, S. (1976). On first gaining the idea of oneself as a person. In R. Harré (Ed.) *Life Sentences.* Chichester: Wiley.

Shinn, M. (1900). *The Biography of a Baby.* Boston: Houghton Mifflin.

Sinclair, H. (1971). Sensorimotor action patterns as a condition for the acquisition of syntax. In E. Ingram and R. Huxley (Eds) *Language Acquisition: Models and Methods,* pp. 121-130. New York and London: Academic Press.

Sinclair, H. (1973). Language acquisition and cognitive development. In T. E. Moore (Ed.) *Cognitive Development and the Acquisition of Language.* New York and London: Academic Press.

Slobin, D. I. (1973). Cognitive prerequisites for the development of grammar. In C. A. Ferguson and D. I. Slobin (Eds) *Studies in Child Language Development.* New York: Holt, Rinehart and Winston.

Slobin, D. I. (1975). The more it changes . . . on understanding language by watching it move through time. In *Papers and Reports on Child Language Development* **10.** Department of Linguistics, Stanford University.

Slobin, D. I. and Welsh, C. A. (1973). Elicited imitation as a research tool in developmental psycholinguistics. In C. Ferguson and D. I. Slobin (Eds) *Studies of Child Language Development.* New York: Holt, Rinehart and Winston.

Smedslund, J. (1969). Meanings, implications and universals: towards a psychology of man. *Scandinavian Journal of Psychology* **10,** 1-15.

Smith, D. M. (1973). Creolization and language ontogeny: A preliminary paradigm for comparing language socialization and language acculturation. In C. J. W. Bailey and R. W. Shuy (Eds) *New Ways of Analyzing Variation in English.* Washington, D.C.: Georgetown University Press.

Smith, W. J. (1965). Message, meaning and context in ethology. *American Naturalist* **99,** 405-409.

Smith, W. J. (1969). Messages of vertebrate communication. *Science* **165,** 145-150.

Snow, C. (1972). Mothers' speech to children learning language. *Child Development* **43,** 549-565.

Snow, C. (1975). The development of conversation between mothers and babies. In G. Gazder and S. Levingson (eds) *Pragmatics Microfiche (1.6, A2).* Department of Linguistics, Cambridge University.

Snow, C. (1976). The conversational context of language acquisition. Paper delivered at the Psychology of Language Conference, Stirling, June 1976.

Snow, C. (1977). Mother's speech research: from input to social interaction. In C. Snow and C. A. Ferguson (Eds) *Talking to Children: Language Input and Acquisition.* Cambridge: Cambridge University Press.

Snow, C. and Ferguson, C. A. (1977). *Talking to Children: Language Input and Acquisition.* Cambridge: Cambridge University Press.

Snyder, L. (1975). Pragmatics in language deficient children: prelinguistic and early verbal performatives and presuppositions. Unpublished Doctoral dissertation, University of Colorado.

Spitz, R. A. (1965). *The First Year of Life.* New York: International University Press.

Spitz, R. A. and Wolff, K. M. (1946). The smiling response. A contribution to the ontogenesis of social relations. *Genetic Psychology Monographs* **34,** 57-125.

Stark, D. and Schneider, R. (1960). Larynx. In H. Hofer, A. H. Schultz and D. Starck (Eds) *Primatologia: Handbook of Primatology,* Vol. III, Part 2. Basel: Karger.

Stern, D. N. (1974). Mother and infant at play: the dyadic interaction involving facial, vocal and gaze behaviours. In M. Lewis and L. Rosenblum (Eds) *The Effect of the Infant on Its Caregiver.* London: Wiley.

Stokoe, Jr. V. C. (1960). Sign language structure: an outline of the visual communications systems. In *Studies in Linguistics, Occasional Papers* **8.**

Stout, G. F. (1938). *A Manual of Psychology.* London: University Tutorial Press.

Strauss, A. (Ed.) (1956). *The Social Psychology of George Herbert Mead.* Chicago: University of Chicago Press.

Strauss, A. (Ed.) (1964). *George Herbert Mead: On Social Psychology.* Chicago and London: University of Chicago Press.

Strawson, P. F. (1950). On referring. *Mind* **59** (237), 320-344.

Strawson, P. F. (1964). Intention and convention in speech acts. *Philosophical Review* **73,** 439-460.

Sugarman, S. (1974). A sequence for communicative development in the pre-language child. Mimeo, University of California, Berkeley.

Sugarman-Bell, S. (1978). Some organisational aspects of preverbal communication. In I. Markova (Ed.) *The Social Context of Language.* London: Wiley.

Swingle, P. G. (Ed.) (1973). *Social Psychology in Everyday Life.* London: Penguin.

Taylor, C. (1971). Interpretation and the sciences of man. *Review of Metaphysics* **25,** 3-57.

Taylor, R. (1966). *Action and Purpose.* Englewood Cliffs: Prentice Hall.

Tervoot, B. T. (1961). Esoteric symbolism in the communication behaviour of young deaf children. *American Annals of the Deaf* **106,** 436-480.

Thomson, J. and Chapman, R. S. (1975). Who is "daddy" (revisited): the status of two-year olds' over-extension in production and comprehension. In *Papers and Reports on Child Language Development* **10,** 59-68.

Trân Duc Thao (1973). *Recherches sur l'orgine du language et de la conscience.* Paris: Editions Sociales.

Trevarthen, C. B. (1972). In E. C. Carterette and M. P. Friedman (Eds) *The Handbook of Perception.* New York and London: Academic Press.

Trevarthen, C. B. (1974a). Infant response to objects and persons. Paper presented at the Annual Conference of the British Psychological Society.

Trevarthen, C. B. (1974b). Conversations with a two-month old. *New Scientist* **62** (896), 230-235.

Trevarthen, C. (1974c). The psychobiology of speech development. In E. H. Lenneberg (Ed.) *Language and Brain: Developmental Aspects. Neurosciences Research Program Bulletin* **12**, 570-585.

Trevarthen, C. (1975). Early attempts at speech. In R. Lewin (Ed.) *Child Alive.* London: Temple Smith.

Trevarthen, C. (1977a). Descriptive analyses of infant communicative behaviour. In H. R. Schaffer (Ed.) *Studies in Mother-Infant Interaction.* London and New York: Academic Press.

Trevarthen, C. (1977b). Basic patterns of psychogenetic change in infancy. In H. Nathan (Ed.) Proceedings of the O.E.C.D. Conference on *Dips in Learning,* St Paul de Vence, March 1975. O.E.C.D. Paris (in press).

Trevarthen, C. (1977c). Communication and cooperation in early infancy: a description of primary intersubjectivity. In M. Bullowa (Ed.) *Before Speech: The Beginnings of Human Cooperation.* Cambridge: Cambridge University Press.

Trevarthen, C. and Hubley, P. (1977). Developments from prereaching to reaching in the first six months after birth (in preparation).

Trevarthen, C., Hubley, P. and Sheeran, L. (1975). Psychological actions in early infancy. *La Recherche* **6**, 447-458.

Tulkin, S. R. and Kagan, J. (1972). Mother-child interaction in the first year of life. *Child Development* **43**, 31-41.

Urwin, C. (1976). Speech development in blind children: some ways into language. Paper presented at *Internationales Symposium des Blinden-und-Sehschwachen-Verbandes der DDR.*

Uzgiris, I. and Hunt, J. McV. (1975). *Assessment in Infancy.* Urbana-Champaign: University of Illinois Press.

Vereeken, P. (1961). *Spatial Development: Constructive Praxia from Birth to the Age of Seven.* Cyroningen: Walters.

Vygotsky, L. S. (1962). *Thought and Language.* Cambridge, Mass: MIT Press.

Vygotsky, L. S. (1966). Development of the higher mental functions. In *Psychological Research in the USSR.* Moscow: Progress Publishers.

Wada, J. and Rasmussen, T. (1960). Intracarotiel injection of sodium amytal for the lateralisation of cerebral speech dominance. Experimental and clinical observations. *Journal of Neurosurgery* **17**, 266-282.

Waddington, C. H. (1975). *The Evolution of an Evolutionist.* Edinburgh: Edinburgh University Press.

Wall, C. (1974). *Predication, a Study of its Development.* The Hague: Mouton.

Waterson, N. and Snow, C. (in press). *Development of Communication: Social and Pragmatic Factors in Language Acquisition.* London: Wiley.

Watson, J. S. (1966). The development and generation of "contingency awareness" in early infancy: Some hypotheses. *Merrill-Palmer Quarterly* **12**, 123-135.

Watson, J. S. (1977). The perception of contingency as a determinant of social responsiveness. Paper read at Conference on *Origins of the Infant's Social Responsiveness*, Nantucket, 1976. To be published by Lawrence Erlbaum Associates: Hillsdale, New Jersey.

Watzlawick, P., Beavin, J. H. and Jackson, D. D. (1967). *Pragmatics of Human Communication*. New York: Norton.

Weiss, P. (1939). *Principles of Development*. New York: Holt, Rinehart and Winston.

Wells, G. (1973). *Coding Manual for the Description of Child Speech*. Prepared for the Bristol Study of Language Development in Preschool Children: Bristol.

Werner, H. (1940). *The Comparative Psychology of Mental Development*. New York: Harper and Row.

Werner, H. and Kaplan, B. (1963). *Symbol Formation: An Organismic-Developmental Approach to Language and the Expression of Thought*. New York: Wiley.

Williamson, S. (in preparation). Acquisition and input in Tamil. Doctoral dissertation, University of Pennsylvania, Philadelphia, Pa.

Winnicott, D. W. (1965). *The Maturational Process and the Facilitating Environment, Studies in the Theory of Emotional Development*. London: Hogarth Press and Institute of Psychoanalysis.

White, R. W. (1959). Motivation reconsidered: competence motivation. *Psychological Review* **66,** 297-333.

Wills, D. (1970). Vulnerable periods in the early development of blind children. *Psychoanalytic Study of the Child* **25,** 461-480. New York: International University Press.

Winch, P. (1958). *The Idea of a Social Science and its Relations to Philosophy*. London: Routledge and Kegan Paul.

Wittgenstein, L. (1953). *Philosophical Investigations*. Oxford: Blackwell.

Wolff, P. (1963). Observations on the early development of smiling. In B. M. Foss (Ed.) *Determinants of Infant Behaviour*, Vol. 2. London: Methuen.

Wolff, P. (1969). The natural history of crying and other vocalisations in early infancy. In B. M. Foss (Ed.) *Determinants of Infant Behaviour*, Vol. 4. London: Methuen.

Wood, D. and Ross, G. (1972). Guided skill acquisition. Unpublished paper: Harvard University.

Wood, H. (1970). Problems in the development and home care of preschool blind children. Unpublished Ph.D. thesis, University of Nottingham.

Wundt, W. (1900). *Voelker psychologie: I Die Sprache*. Leipzig: W. Engelmann.

Young, J. Z. (1970). *Introduction to the Study of Man*. London: Oxford University Press.

Young, R. M. (1973). In J. Miller (Ed.) *The Limits of Human Nature*. London: Penguin.

Zalazo, P. R. (1977). The year-old infant: A point of major cognitive change. In H. Nathan (Ed.) Proceedings of the O.E.C.D. Conference on *Dips in Learning*, St Paul de Vence, March 1975. O.E.C.D: Paris (in press).

Index

ORIGINAL
VINCENT
MOTORCYCLE

Other titles available in the *Original* series are:

ORIGINAL
VINCENT
MOTORCYCLE
by J P Bickerstaff

Photography by James Mann
Edited by Cyril Ayton

FRONT COVER

The Rapide was perhaps the most popular model, and none was more successful than the Series C. With its sleeker covers, hydraulic damping and Girdraulic forks, it was current during the peak manufacturing years of 1949-52.

HALF-TITLE PAGE

The famous legend cast into the crankcase. The dual names of HRD and Vincent are inextricably entwined in this story, but after 1949 the machines became known simply as Vincents rather than Vincent-HRDs.

TITLE PAGE

When the Black Shadow appeared in 1948, its 150mph speedometer was the stuff of dreams. This big dial, shown in early form with markings at 10mph increments, is often seen on lesser Vincents, but correctly belongs only on a Black Shadow.

BACK COVER

The Black Shadow is the true icon in Vincent lore. On the bike's launch in 1948 the factory claimed a top speed of 128mph, making the Shadow as fast as anything a speed-hungry enthusiast could buy.

Published 1997 by Bay View Books Ltd
The Red House, 25-26 Bridgeland Street
Bideford, Devon EX39 2PZ, UK

Series edited by Mark Hughes
Type and design by Chris Fayers & Sarah Ward

ISBN 1 870979 83 4
Printed in Hong Kong
by Paramount Printing Group

CONTENTS

INTRODUCTION

HRD and Vincent are names of legend in motorcycling, names which fired the imagination and dreams of riders when the bikes were in production, and which still have that effect even now, long after their heyday.

Howard Davies spent his time in a World War I POW camp dreaming of making motorcycles, and of winning in the Isle of Man TT races, where he had already achieved a second place for the Sunbeam team in 1913. Less than ten years later, in 1925, he rode his own factory-built HRD to claim the Senior TT trophy. While Howard was achieving his ambition, Philip Vincent was a schoolboy and, like Davies, dreaming about making his own motorcycle. Just three years later, he had taken over the ailing HRD name and started on the long haul towards producing 'The World's Fastest Standard Motorcycle' – the vee-twins for which the names of HRD and Vincent, in conjunction, are most famous.

In the era after World War II, the Vincent-HRD was an expensive machine representing the peak of ambition for many a young demobbed serviceman, who would happily spend his service gratuity on a Vincent (if he could get one). Other motorcyclists, such as my own father, simply admired the bikes from afar. Forty and more years after the last Vincent left the Stevenage factory, these machines remain among the most coveted of motorcycles.

Of course, dreams can also turn into nightmares. Howard Davies had to liquidate his firm in spite of his successes, and although he paid off his debts he was not able to salvage his own trademark. Phil Vincent faced the same problem twice, having to call in the Receiver in 1949, resulting in a restructuring of his company, but eventually selling off the firm to Harper Engines in 1958, some time after motorcycle production ceased.

As for owners, well, they too can find their dreams a little sullied. A big-twin Vincent at its best can be a joy, but many restorers discover that a Vincent in pieces adds up to more pieces and more work than they have bargained for – or, if the bike is a runner, that their purchase is definitely not in its prime. In these situations they do not always have the perseverance (or money) to discover and undo the damage wreaked in 40-50 years. It is not an easy matter to arrive at a sweet-running Vincent from an accumulation of old and worn-out parts, but doing so can be extraordinarily rewarding.

The first Vincent twins were made before World War II and began the Vincent legend, although a mere 80 of these Series A Rapides were produced. For the post-war era, the Rapide was completely re-designed, emerging as the sleeker, more reliable and equally fast Series B Rapide – even on its compulsory diet of infamous low-octane Pool petrol. The Series B proved fast enough, straight out of the crate, to break national records in many countries, and even, with a little tuning, to break the world speed record (Bob Burns achieved no less than 167mph with a sidecar and

The first Vincent-HRD twins were made in 1936, but only in small numbers, so are rarely seen. The 998cc vee-twins produced 45bhp, and achieved a top speed of 110mph, and were the first models to be given the name Rapide. These Series A Rapides were the inspiration for the post-war big-twins.

Mercury crest was used throughout the life of the HRD and Vincent companies. Its origins lie with the Isle of Man TT trophy, and it was adopted by Howard Davies as his trademark. This rare version is the original form used by his company, HRD Motors Ltd, on the Wolverhampton-built motorcycles.

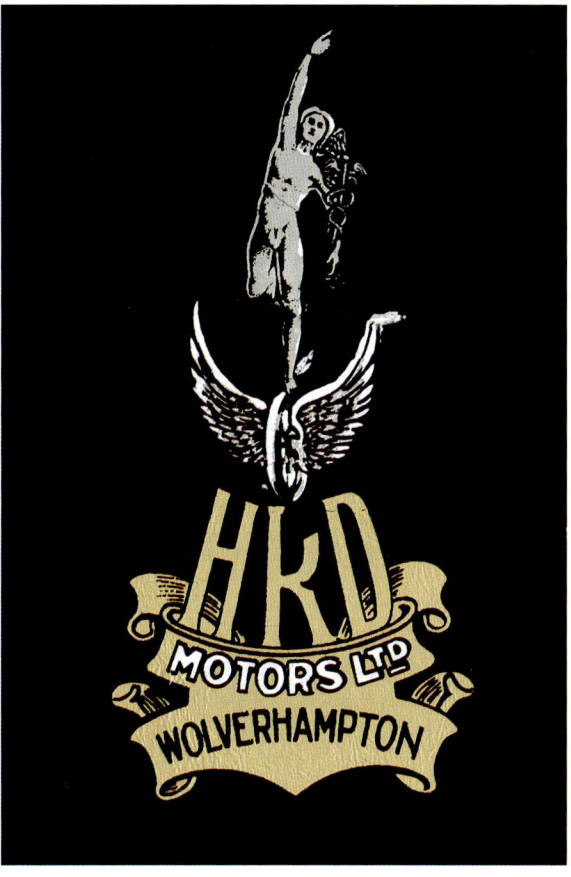

The HRD trademark originated in the initials of Howard Raymond Davies, a distinguished TT rider who started HRD Motors Ltd in Wolverhampton in 1924. Young Philip Vincent, who bought the moribund company in 1928 and moved it to Stevenage, added his name in tiny letters above the HRD trademark (right), which was then used for a further 30 years. Vincent's own name finally took pride of place (below) after his 1949 promotional tour of the USA, where the motorcycle market was becoming increasingly important. He discovered that the letters HRD caused confusion in the land of the Harley-Davidson, so thereafter his motorcycles were sold under this motif.

Russell Wright attained 182mph solo in 1955).

These machines were expensive, at £450, when other British (parallel) twins were on sale at only a shade over £300. For 20 years after production ceased in 1955, a good Black Shadow, the sports version of the Rapide, was as fast as anything a motorcyclist could buy, but of course it became increasingly old-fashioned. When prices for the ageing bikes fell, they could be bought, thrashed, modified or even cannibalised, for the sought-after engines, by any lad with a few pennies to rub together. The engines were used for racing, put into Norton's legendary Featherbed frame to make Norvin hybrids, or, around 1970, were sometimes installed in a purpose-built Egli-Vincent spine-type frame – a combination briefly marketed by Roger Slater as the Shadow 70. Prices continued to fall until the 500cc single-cylinder Vincents could not be given away; but the twins never quite reached that state, and their engines survived under many a workshop bench awaiting a time when they would be sought-after, rebuilt and treasured again.

In the modern classic bike world the Vincent has been revived and is again one of the most illustrious names among motorcycle marques. They present a challenge to restorers, are prized by collectors, displayed at shows, and ridden by a new generation of owners for pleasure. Mostly, such riding is confined to attendance at rallies and shows, but the machines can do much more, and there are Vincent riders who still use their machines long and hard. At least 100 Vincent-HRD models from 1926 to 1955 were on view at an international rally in New Zealand in 1995, 40 years after the bikes went out of production, and 40 years after the world records mentioned above were broken on the Tram Road near Christchurch, where the enthusiasts assembled to pay homage.

Riders like these take good care of their machines, but are more concerned with practicality than originality, so that 12-volt electrics, stiffened-up brakes and softened suspensions are all, on occasion, adopted.

Even *concours* enthusiasts utilise the replacement stainless steel fittings available, and have usually either built up their motorcycles from a pile of bits or restored a tired victim of many different (sometimes indifferent) owners.

Either way, rebuilds to truly original specification are almost as rare as untouched-since-manufacture original Vincents. Newcomers and specialists alike have to work hard to disentangle what a factory-fresh bike would have looked like compared with the shiny Vincents which currently dominate the classic bike world and *concours* competitions. The purpose of this book is to try to outline the history and development of the post-war Vincents, to pick out, describe and illustrate the way they were in their prime, and to help the present-day restorer to decide on the level of originality to be aimed for, and how to get there.

It is neither necessary nor desirable to rebuild to any given standard – especially that of absolute 'originality'. Anyone who has listened to tales of Vincent factory workers wielding their files and hammers would cringe at replicating all that went on at the works. The factory did not introduce modifications just for fun; it did so to make the machines work better, or sometimes just to make them work at all. Restoring a 1946 machine to strictly 1946 specification, therefore, would be a somewhat retrograde step; even the factory encouraged owners to bring their machines up-to-date during the years of production.

Factory paintwork and plating were generally of good quality, but, even so, runs in the paint were not unusual. Chromium plating was very little used except for special show models, but price and availability prevented as much use of stainless steel as Phil Vincent would have liked. A bike from a 1950 showroom floor would be unlikely to win a modern *concours*, where flawless paintwork and over-polished crankcases win prizes. To win the average *concours*

Specially made 5in 150mph speedometer proclaimed to the world that the Black Shadow was the only motorcycle which could outrun the Smiths standard 120mph instrument. Many of these prized Shadow clocks were fitted by private owners to glamorise their humbler 110mph Rapide models.

d'élégance, most models are prepared using the stainless fittings which are now usually supplied as spares and then highly polished.

Truly original machines, still fitted with rubber-covered wiring, fabric-covered cables, Miller electrics and so on, are rare indeed. Restoration to exactly original specification would truly be a challenge, especially when trying to replicate original tyre treads and markings. Of course, for riding regularly in today's conditions modern rubber is a necessity and uprated electrics (accepting modern 12-volt bulbs

ACKNOWLEDGEMENTS

Grateful thanks must be given to the owners who made their motorcycles available for the various photographic shoots without which this book could not have been prepared.

Stuart Towner (Model J); Richard Scudder (A Rapides); Dave Quartermain (B Rapide); Dave Stovin (C Rapide); Jeff Glasserow (Red Rapide); Bernie Stovin (D Rapide); Michael Whitehead (D Rapide); Arvid N. Myhre (Export Rapide); Bob Culver (B Shadow); Ian Lang (D Shadow); Ted Davis (B Meteor and Black Prince); Ray Smith (Touring Comet); Peter Elvidge (Comet and sidecar); Glynn Baxter (Grey Flash); Ted Croft (Black Knight); Bill Ewington (Black Prince); Bob Dunn (Workshop and Picador)

Thanks are also due to Dave Hills for reviewing and correcting the initial manuscript for technical accuracy, and to editor Cyril Ayton for his part in bringing this book together. The bulk of the photography was carried out by James Mann in the UK and the US, supplemented by further work from Rowan Isaac. Lest James or Rowan are thought to be responsible for any less-than-perfect colour photographs appearing in the following pages, I should add that a few illustrations have come from my own archive and show very rare machines and obscure items which had necessarily to be snapped with whatever Box Brownie happened to be to hand at the time.

Vincent engines have continued to attract Special builders through the years. Ken McIntosh of New Zealand has fitted a vee-twin into his spine frame, patterned on those marketed by Fritz Egli from the late 1960s, to create a competitive classic racer.

Interest in Vincent motorcycles was confirmed in 1995 when 300 participants took more than 100 Vincent-HRDs from around the world to the New Zealand International Rally. The majority, ranging from the my own 1926 side-valve to a just-completed Egli-style Vincent Special, were then put to work transporting rallyists around the islands for an average of over 2000 miles.

and a large rear light) make much more sense than a 1940s lighting system.

Whatever one's choice, there is no need to be apologetic. Post-war, some 13,000 machines were made, so the world can spare an odd Rapide, Comet or Shadow to be restored, raced, customised or simply maintained and ridden, to whatever specification and standard one may choose. In fact, so good is today's spares back-up, and the many engineering facilities now available for reclaiming old and damaged machinery, that the number of complete Vincents on the road and in collections is rising all the time.

My own involvement with Vincents goes back a long way. My father was of that motorcycling generation which saw the Vincent as the most glamorous and fastest motorcycle on the market – and totally out of range of most pockets. By 1962, Vincents had been out of production for seven years and secondhand prices were at an all-time low. When my father had a small tax windfall he grasped the opportunity to buy a well-worn Rapide which then became our family transport, hauling a large Rankin sidecar.

I remember going to a motorbike meeting at which I tried standing on the Vincent's kick-starter while Dad watched the bikes. Eventually the engine slipped over compression – and burbled into life! I did not know how to stop it and had to fetch Dad, who was quite annoyed. Not so much with me, but with the bike, because it would not usually start for him quite so easily!

In my college days I acquired a pre-war 500 Comet single which gobbled up a few years of effort before it actually ran, and then I eventually inherited my father's Rapide, registered PUB 335, when he gave up riding. By this time, however, it was in that proverbial tea chest, awaiting the mythical rebuild. The rebuild had to be completed on a student's shoe-string budget, but since then it has been my magic carpet, providing me with over 200,000 miles of both basic transportation and more exotic holidaying around Europe. It has brought me into contact with many of my closest friends, and shaped my life in the process.

Along the way I have collected and learned a lot of Vincent lore from books and magazines, from knowl-

The author's Touring Rapide, PUB 335, rebuilt from a tea chest of parts, reaches the first 100,000 miles. Chromium-plated handlebars should be raised, and black-enamelled (left); but originality comes second to usability (below, loaded up and on tour) in Bickerstaff's view.

edgeable enthusiasts, even from one-time factory personnel. And, of course, I have learned some of it the hard way. That original Comet taught me a lot about four-stroke motorcycles, and although PUB has been remarkably good to me, it has not gone 200,000 miles without some maintenance and repair – and a couple of rebuilds along the way. Into *Original Vincent*, therefore, I have put as much relevant knowledge as I can.

No-one, however, can produce a book like this straight out of their head, and I thank again those who have helped me with new facts for the text, and all the owners who have spared time and made their machinery available for photography. It has been fascinating for me, too, to track down representative bikes, especially those still fitted with now-obsolete parts. I salute the perseverance of those who have shunned the easiest rebuild routes in order to find those rare original parts and, especially, I salute those who have refused to rebuild at all and instead maintain a bike in its original paint and plating for as long as possible. I apologise to anyone whose name I should have included in the list of acknowledgements, but forgot!

Notwithstanding the help which I have been given, responsibility for accuracy, or otherwise, in this book is entirely mine. The Vincent-HRD was not a mass-produced item, manufactured to exact specification. Development was a continuous process and individual customer, or dealer, requirements would often be accommodated. In the years since production ceased, drawings and records have been dispersed, and memories have faded. It is, therefore, not possible to describe every original feature, and option,

for the standard models, much less for individual machines (although owners of machines up to engine number 99,999 can obtain a copy of the original order/build/dispatch record for their particular bike from the Vincent HRD Owners Club). *Original Vincent* is as accurate and detailed as I can make it, and any errors, I repeat, are entirely my responsibility.

Jacqueline Bickerstaff
April 1997

THE SERIES A MACHINES

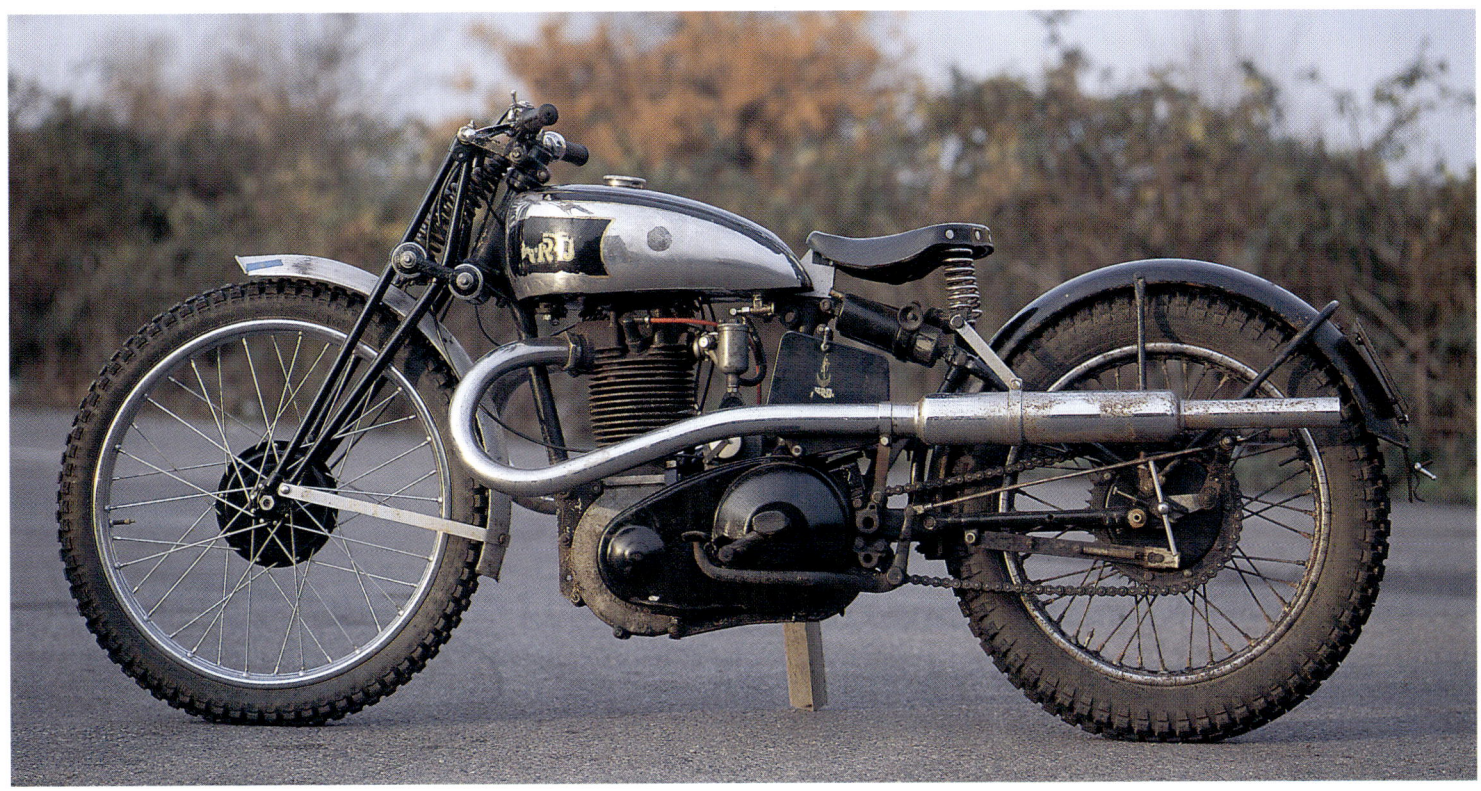

The 1933 Model J pre-dates Vincent's duo-braked models with their twin drums in each wheel. Other features to become familiar on the Series A machines have already become apparent, with open diamond tubular frame and triangulated rear suspension with friction-damped spring boxes sited under the saddle.

This line-up of rigid-frame HRD machines, assembled at the Vincent Owners Club's 1995 annual rally, represents approximately half the surviving examples of the Wolverhampton machines built by Howard Davies' original company, HRD Motors Ltd, from 1924 to 1928.

'A Great Adventure' was the heading used in September 1925 for a *Motor Cycling* article containing Howard Davies' account of the background to setting up his own motorcycle manufacturing company. Howard Raymond Davies had started his successful riding career before World War I, in the veteran era when almost any small cycle shop could assemble its own motorcycles using proprietary engines and cycle-type frames built up with standard catalogue lugs. Riding Diamond, Sunbeam and AJS motorcycles, he amassed a large selection of trophies, but less successful rides on Clyno and OEC finally moved him to take the brave step of making his own machines.

By this time, in the 1920s, somewhat larger finance, manufacturing and selling resources were required to turn out a successful motorcycle, but it was still possible to buy top-class components and fittings, including the all-important power unit. Davies had the stature for the endeavour: he had won the 1921

Senior TT on his Junior AJS (the only man ever to win the Senior on a 350) and he had good contacts throughout the industry. The small staff which he assembled was able to turn out a newcomer to the market whose stylish lines and saddle tank were much copied and helped to set the shape of motorcycles throughout the 1930s. Davies himself provided the ultimate testimonial and advertisement for his new HRD motorcycles by riding one to a Senior TT victory first time out in 1925!

For a while it looked as though the fairy-tale might continue, with the strength of sales necessitating a move in Wolverhampton to larger premises later in 1925, and then with another TT win for HRD in the 1927 Junior, when the rider was Freddie Dixon, of JAPs, adding to countless other competition successes. However, 1926 was the year of the General Strike, and the Depression years were looming; buyers for expensive luxury or sporting motorcycles such as the HRD began to dry up.

The under-capitalised firm was unable to weather the storm. After producing over 800 machines in its short three-year existence, HRD Motors Ltd went into voluntary receivership. Although all the creditors were eventually paid off, Davies was unable to regain control of his own trademark, which went with the rest of the business to Ernie Humphries, of the OK Supreme concern. Thereafter, Davies took very little part in the world of motorcycles, working instead for Swallow Sidecars and other manufacturers in the car business, and subsequently for himself, as a manufacturers' agent. Only in his retirement years was he to be occasionally reunited with one of his HRD motorcycles, for demonstration rides at Vintage Motor Cycle Club events.

THE VINCENT–HRD CO LTD

At the same time that HRD Motors was closing its doors, the young Philip Conrad Vincent (often to be known simply as PCV) was just embarking on his own Great Adventure, and one which would raise the combined names of Vincent and HRD to great heights. While still at Cambridge University, he patented and built the original triangulated rear suspension layout that was to feature on every Vincent-HRD and Vincent he would produce. After completing a Vincent Special prototype (with an adjustable steering-head angle which enabled him to experiment with frame geometry), he left Cambridge determined to set up as a motorcycle manufacturer.

Backing from his family, which had a cattle ranching business in Argentina, enabled him to acquire premises in Stevenage, Hertfordshire, where he was aided by the steadying hand of family friend Frank Walker, who was appointed as managing director. To launch a new machine, it was thought wise to acquire an established name. Thus, early in 1928 the trade-

mark, goodwill and a few remaining HRD component parts were purchased for £500 from Ernie Humphries, who had decided that it was not a propitious time to re-launch the marque and had contented himself with building a few complete machines and selling some other assets.

The Stevenage company was promptly named Vincent-HRD, with 'Vincent' in very small letters over the top of the bold HRD logo, where it remained until 1950 when 'HRD' was eventually dropped. From published catalogues, it is apparent that the fledgling Vincent-HRD company copied the sleight-of-hand favoured by its predecessors in illustrating a 'four-model' range by the expedient of photographing one of three Show models from the reverse side. Such trickery and touching up of photographs were widespread in the industry, and catalogues are therefore very unreliable sources of photographic detail; road test reports illustrating real motorcycles should be preferred, and private photographs are better still. This is certainly true of the HRD and Vincent catalogues, some of whose year-on-year alterations, touching up and inaccuracies can be divined by careful comparisons.

The original Vincent Special was an ugly duckling indeed. Even the cleaned-up production models with all-welded frames had tubes running conspicuously from steering head to rear-fork pivot, as well as rear springing to worry the conservative buying public. As a result, initial sales of these new Vincent-HRDs were slow, but perhaps that was not such a bad thing, coinciding with the Depression, for the small firm at least had only small outgoings and a very small number of buyers to find for the expensive machines.

One such sale, in 1929, certainly did not bring a financial reward, but nevertheless changed the fortunes and whole future of the company. It was of a side-valve 600 JAP-engined machine built to a specification laid down by John Gill of Bradford. Inspired by travelogues he had read, this young man was bent on adventures of his own. He aimed to ride the HRD and sidecar around the world – and carry a passenger too! It was a pioneering trip, because even petrol was not regularly available everywhere and Shell, the sponsors, had to arrange depots for him in remote places. After various difficulties, and a number of calls on Vincent-HRD for more (financial) support, he successfully returned to England from his travels. Although this was all good publicity for the company, what really changed the firm's fortunes was not so much Gill's trip but, rather, a change of passenger halfway through.

In Melbourne, Australia, Walter Stephens had abandoned the unsprung and uncomfortable rear pillion pad and was replaced by Philip Edward Irving (widely known as PEI), who grasped the opportunity as a way – a very character-building way – to get to England and the wider horizons that the UK had to offer. PEI was a talented young engineer destined to exert a

The earliest Vincent-HRDs used an odd-looking all-welded and triangulated frame, with tubes running either side of the engine. This 1929 500cc Touring model is possibly the earliest survivor among Philip Vincent's motorcycles and is almost identical to the 600cc side-valve used by John Gill on a round-the-world trip.

In the early years JAP proprietary engines were used by both HRD Motors and successors The Vincent-HRD Company. Large petrol tank cutaways were needed to accommodate the tall overhead valve JAPs, as can be seen on this 1933 Model J. PCV did not like chromium plating, and so the panels are of stainless steel.

tremendous influence on the evolution of the Vincent, as well as contributing to Velocette and AJS motorcycles and, much later, building a world championship racing car engine. Working with PCV intermittently over the next two decades, PEI allied his pragmatic and experienced engineering skills with the other Phil's determination and inventiveness to produce the most successful Vincent-HRD designs.

PROPRIETARY-ENGINED MODELS

The early triangulated frame design had proved a bar to sales and so Phil Irving's first task, undertaken in 1931, was to complete a more conventional looking frame design in time for the autumn London Olympia Show. The new model, with open diamond front frame and revised rear frame triangle, utilised conventional brazed lug construction, and even some inherited HRD lugs, to economise on costs. With its spring boxes tucked away under the saddle and a more normal looking petrol tank, the machine had the appearance of a conventional rigid model, which led to a welcome increase in sales.

A series of innovations followed, with, first, the introduction of a patented semi-sprung rear seat in 1933 to improve the lot of the pillion passenger (whose previous pad on the unsprung rear mudguard had been even more punishing than most contemporary arrangements), and then with duo-brakes – drums on both sides of each wheel – to provide excellent fade-free braking. Although this was the time of the Great Depression, innovation throughout the industry continued unabated as factories fought

simultaneously to improve and cheapen their products in order to maintain sales. For its power units, Vincent-HRD still relied on proprietary engine suppliers, mostly JAP in the early years, later increasingly switching to Rudge Python units; a few models were also built with Blackburne and Villiers engines.

In 1934 Teddy Prestwich of JAP persuaded Vincent-HRD to adopt JAP's new racing engine for a factory team entry in the Isle of Man Senior TT. Race machines had by this time deviated a long way from being lightly tuned, same-as-you-could-buy touring models; Vincent was perhaps hoping not so much for a win as to gain some respect for his motorcycles and to counter the suspicion with which rear suspension systems were still regarded. The result, however, was disastrous, with failures in all the engines in practice and during the race, in which all three riders entered by the firm eventually retired. This undermined Vincent-HRD's faith in JAP as engine suppliers at just the time that PCV's then main engine supplier, Rudge-Whitworth, was axing delivery of the Python engine range. The solution was clear: Vincent-HRD would have to design its own engine!

SERIES A SINGLES

Between the June TT races and the November Olympia show the new engine was drawn up, patterns, casings and machining were completed, and the new Series A models assembled ready for public scrutiny – a landmark step which turned the motorcycle assemblers into true motorcycle manufacturers.

For their own engine, PCV and PEI settled on a 500cc overhead valve design, using a high camshaft position (also referred to, confusingly, as semi-overhead camshaft by the motorcycle press of the day) which was at the time coming into fashion, but was later only retained by Velocette and Vincent (both firms of course much influenced by Phil Irving). As ever, PCV and PEI were not satisfied with simply following a well-trodden path, but came up with their own distinctive design incorporating many unique features. The high camshaft was driven by a large bronze idler wheel from the crankshaft pinion and operated widely splayed pushrods parallel to the valves, each enclosed in a separate tube. PCV and PEI further shortened the pushrods, and indeed the whole

Vincent-HRD introduced its own 500cc ohv engine in 1934 (above left). A vertical single-cylinder design, it incorporated features which would remain as trademarks through all subsequent designs, such as the 84mm × 90mm bore and stroke and the high-camshaft valve-operating mechanism. Cast iron cylinder and head with external oil pump and pipes were used only on the Series A engines. The first models to use Vincent's own engine were the Meteor and Comet, although these names were not adopted until 1935. This 1938 Comet (above) has duo-brakes – twin 7in drums front and rear – as standard equipment, and pillion seat and footrests, which were optional extras.

The Series A single was also produced as a stripped racing machine, when it was known as the TT Replica. Improved ribbed brakes, light alloy mudguards and handsome stainless steel oil and petrol tanks were features. This is the only known example fitted with the factory's big-fin light alloy cylinder head.

engine, by arranging forked rockers to bear on collars halfway along the valve stems between upper and lower guides. The rationale here was not entirely that of lightening the valve gear, but also to reduce side thrust and permit bulky hairpin springs to be accommodated externally, away from temper-sapping heat. In spite of the exposed valve springs and collars, the engine could fairly be described by the standards of the time as having 'fully enclosed valve gear'.

The Series A engine was a single-cylinder pushrod unit of 499cc featuring the 84mm by 90mm bore and stroke which would be retained on all subsequent Vincent engines. Cast iron was used for the cylinder and head on roadster engines, but for the TT Replica engines (also fitted to the Comet Special models) a bronze head was cast from the same patterns, and a composite cylinder consisting of a cast iron liner fitted in an aluminium alloy muff was adopted. The crankshaft followed conventional lines, with large internal flywheels carrying a roller-bearing big end and running on ball and roller main bearings.

Crankcase design was slightly less conventional. A normal, vertical, split was used but on the drive side a steel insert was fitted to carry the main bearings. The ball-race had to be a slip fit on that side, to accommodate a rather complex arrangement of shims between the spring-loaded ball-race and bearing housing, while the crankshaft was located from the timing side. On the timing side, too, assembly arrangements were unusual, with no removable timing cover as such but, rather, a series of small access holes provided at the half-time pinion (closed by the oil pump), the idler spindle (also closed by the oil pump) and an assembly slot in the top face (machined level

with the crankcase mouth). The twin-lobe camshaft ran in plain bushes fitted into the split recesses at this point, and then a separate light alloy casting, carrying the cam followers and pushrod tube recesses, finally closed off the timing case.

In this way, the camshaft was accommodated above the level of the crankcase mouth. From the camshaft, short pushrods, with adjustable cups or ball ends (according to the year), operated the straight, forked rockers and valves. The valves ran in bronze lower guides and cast iron upper guides, but to provide the flange on which the forked rockers could bear required a complex valve assembly including stepped valve stem diameters, a threaded top collar and a locking plate to prevent the valve unscrewing. A built-up gear-type oil pump was fitted externally, driven by the large idler gear spindle at just less than one-third engine speed.

Early engines featured a bulge at the front of the timing case, where the oil scraper and pick-up was sited. This did not prove satisfactory, and was rapidly altered to provide a scraper, sludge trap and oil pick-up at the lowest point, just to the rear, where it remained throughout production. No engine-shaft shock absorber was fitted as the Burman clutch incorporated rubber buffers; a novel self-extracting arrangement was applied to the engine sprocket to facilitate breaking the taper fit during dismantling, and a fine 0.375in pitch duplex primary chain was selected.

There was little difficulty in building new models around these new engines, because the mounting points of the previous Python engines had been duplicated in the new design, and the existing frames and forks, wheels, and semi-sprung seating could therefore be easily adapted. The frame was of conventional brazed-lug construction, with the front section an open single-loop diamond in which the engine plates and crankcase formed an integral part. Behind the gearbox, a casting carried large taper-roller pivot bearings for the triangulated rear suspension which differentiated Vincent-HRD machines from the usual rigid-frame motorcycles of the period. The rear triangle was built up of brazed tube and lugs, and, with the spring units discreetly fitted under the saddle, the appearance was not much different from that of a conventional machine – something which PCV had learned was necessary if his machines were to sell to more conservative motorcyclists. At the front suspension was provided by friction-damped Brampton girder forks.

Braking was provided by twin 7in single leading shoe drums fitted to each wheel, referred to as duo-brakes in Vincent-HRD literature and advertising. These were bolted to composite alloy and iron hubs. Separate spoke flanges were used instead of following the common practice of using the drum flange, in order to avoid the drums being pulled out of round by varying spoke tension. By the time the Series A models were first shown in 1934, the rear brakes were operated by a cross shaft and twin rods; at the front, a single cable from the handlebar lever actuated a fork-mounted balance beam controlling twin cables which conveyed equal pressure to the two brakes through movement of the beam.

These new models quickly displaced the older pro-

EDK 187 (above) is probably a fairly typical example of a Series A Rapide. Contrasting colours indicate that it is fitted with light alloy cylinder muffs and cast iron heads, while the brakes feature the plain drums and black, steel brake plates used on the Comet and Meteor models. The standard pattern of duo-brakes (left), used on singles and twins 1934-39, consisted of plain 7in drums on each side of the wheel. Holes drilled in the flange were for attachment of the drive sprocket when the drum was fitted to a rear wheel. Steel brake plates carried the ⅞in wide brake shoes and featured two brake anchor pins, so that the plate could be used either side of the wheel.

Some Rapides, such as DUR 99, were fitted with lighter and improved TT Replica brakes. MCR1 regulator on top of the toolbox indicates automatic voltage control (AVC) of the dynamo output, a new feature introduced by Lucas in the late 1930s. Items listed as extras on the single-cylinder models, such as the pillion seat and footrests, and the prop stand, became standard fittings on the Rapide.

prietary-engined machines from the range. Not only did the Series A engine prove popular with the public, but it also performed well in the 1935 Senior TT, powering the bikes that finished seventh and ninth, thereby vindicating the factory's decision to design and make its own engine.

The single-cylinder models were marketed in four states of tune, and at the prices given for 1937. The Meteor was the mildest, with a 1 1/16in carburettor and a black-enamelled petrol tank, and also the cheapest, at £89 10s. The Comet at £96 came in slightly more tuned form with a 1 1/8in carburettor, and was comprehensively equipped with a handsome maroon and stainless steel panelled petrol tank. A TT Replica model was also listed at £118, featuring a tuned engine with bronze head fitted into stripped and lightened cycle parts, and with special components such as ribbed, composite iron/alloy brake drums. The same racing engine could also be ordered, fitted into road-going cycle parts, as the hybrid Comet Special, for the clubman or speed merchant.

SERIES A RAPIDE

'From little acorns do great oak trees grow' – and so it was with the vee-twin Rapide. In this case the little acorn was a pair of tracings lying on Phil Irving's drawing board – presumably a dyeline print and its transparent master. Idly juggling these, one on top of the other, Irving suddenly realised that he was looking at a vee-twin, and, furthermore, one that could be made using existing components, which would fulfil

the requirement for high performance without recourse to a fussy and highly tuned engine such as that fitted in the TT Replica and Comet Special models.

Of course, many factories had turned out singles and vee-twins alongside each other in the past, using the same machining techniques but different castings, cams, and so on. The attraction of the arrangement on PEI's drawing board lay in the centres of the Comet camshaft, with its large idler placed fortuitously 23 1/2° rearward. Simply by adopting a 47° cylinder angle, very close to the conventional 50° of most vee-twins, Irving could arrange a second camshaft to occupy a mirror-image position around the large idler (approximately where the magneto pinion was located on single-cylinder models), and produce the Rapide engine using the same cylinders, heads and valve gear. He could even machine the new crankcases on the jigs used for the production singles.

It was this production efficiency which made it possible for the small factory to contemplate the model at all, and which dictated twin carburettors and the unusual forward-facing rear exhaust, where other vee-twin manufacturers had almost exclusively chosen to have a rear cylinder head with a conventional rearward-facing exhaust and a single carburettor. Practicalities and the evolutionary process were at work shaping the distinctive big-twins to come. A fast 1000cc model, and especially one with this unusual look and layout, gave Vincent-HRD a new identity among motorcycle manufacturers, rivalling that of Brough Superior with its big twins.

The new model was named the Rapide. The works set up the first photographs using a frame originally built to house a JAP vee-twin for record-breaker Eric Fernihough. However, this frame did not provide enough room even to fit the rearmost valve springs properly, and so it was not the first model to run. The Rapide was announced to the public and shown at the 1936 motorcycle show. Apart from its twin-cylinder 998cc high-camshaft engine, the Series A Rapide's general specification closely followed that of its single-cylinder stablemates.

The frame and suspension were altered only in detail, with a slight increase in wheelbase, from 55in to approximately 58in, and a heavier front down tube to the diamond frame. Vincent triangulated fork rear suspension and friction-damped Brampton forks were retained. A new petrol tank, usually finished in black with stainless steel panels, had twin filler caps because it had to carry oil as well as petrol, since the space previously occupied by an oil tank was now full of engine! Vincent duo-brakes – twin 7in drums on each wheel – were, naturally, retained. But while some machines were fitted with standard roadster drums and steel back plates, others were fitted with the TT Replica pattern of ribbed composite drum and light alloy back plate, to give improved braking and weight-saving.

The massive engine retained the single's 84mm by 90mm bore and stroke dimensions, and was fitted with two high camshafts operating the same short pushrods, straight, forked rockers and valves running in split valve guides, with external hairpin springs – again as on the single-cylinder engines. And like the singles, it featured an external bolt-on gear-type oil pump, somewhat prone to leak oil back into the sump when the bike was standing. And, of course, there were even more external pipes on the twin than on the single. The Rapide thus soon gained its alternative name of 'Plumber's Nightmare', an insult which was taken to heart – with the result that the oiling system was not replicated post-war!

Bottom-end and crankcase construction followed similar lines to the single-cylinder engines, being split along the centre of the front cylinder so that the extra engine width was all accommodated on the right-hand side. Similar flywheels, with different balancing holes, were built up around a longer crankpin which permitted the use of existing connecting rods, side-by-side, each with a separate roller-bearing big end. The resulting 1½in offset of the cylinders was regarded as an aid to cooling, and also eased the clearances around the rear cylinder's forward-facing exhaust port and the front cylinder's rearward-facing inlet port. Nevertheless, exhaust pipe plumbing was a tight fit, and the front carburettor had to be arranged with its mixing chamber horizontal (instead of vertical) in order to fit it in. Weight and bulk were further problems requiring attention on the big-twin.

Some light alloy components were available from

The lighter brakes with stiffer, ribbed drums used on TT Replica models and some examples of the Rapide. Clearly seen is the composite construction of the drums, consisting of finned, cast iron rings providing the braking surfaces, bolted to light alloy back plates. Light alloy was also used for the brake plates, which had a modified anchorage to suit the TT-pattern Brampton front fork.

Another standard fitting on the Series A Rapide model only, emphasising its luxury specification, was the Smiths eight-day clock mounted opposite the 120mph speedometer. Unsprung location on the front fork cannot have been beneficial to the mechanism. Also visible in this photograph is the unusual pattern of Amal ignition and twin choke levers, secured by integral hinged clamps and a screw.

the TT Replica singles and so most of the twin-cylinder engines were built with the composite cylinders, consisting of iron liners pressed into light alloy muffs. The factory was in the process of developing light alloy cylinder heads, although these had only been used on the works racers and were never listed, even for the TT Replica models. The intention was to use them on the Rapide; the show model had them fitted, but only one production machine ever appears to have been sold so equipped, the remainder having the

DXR 853, owned by Richard Scudder, is a very rare model fitted with light alloy cylinder heads, the only twin or production machine known to have been supplied in this form, although some works TT Replicas were built with light alloy heads, and were eventually sold off. Brakes on this model are of yet a third type, indicating how difficult it is to define a standard specification.

heavier cast iron heads. Compression ratio, timing and 1¹⁄₁₆in carburettor size were all taken from the mildest (Meteor) state of tune in order not to over-stress cycle parts or brakes.

Transmission by Burman was retained for the twin, but gearbox internals were of a special heavy-duty pattern, and a different clutch was fitted which required a revised aluminium alloy primary chaincase cover with a deeper clutch chamber. The second camshaft occupied the position originally used on the single-cylinder engine for a magneto drive, and so the front camshaft spindle was extended to drive a 12-tooth sprocket (with self-extracting nut) and ½in by ⁵⁄₃₂in chain in a short chaincase to the magneto. This was a Lucas Magdyno, fitted with a cam ring modified for the Rapide to accommodate the unusual 47° cylinder angle. Limitations of space left little alternative to mounting the Magdyno low (and upside-down) at the front, on a platform formed by the engine plates.

The Series A Rapide was an expensive model, at £142, so only a few were made; the official number is 78, but since at least two engine numbers appear to have been duplicated at the factory, the exact number is in doubt. Also lost in the mists of time is information on racing Rapides, for the works reputedly only prepared one racing model, as ridden by 'Ginger' Wood at Donington, but magazine reports show that P. M. Aitcheson also campaigned a race-prepared

model. Not that most owners needed a tuned version, for the standard Series A Rapide boasted a top speed of 110mph, sufficient to achieve a Brooklands Gold Star for lapping the Weybridge circuit at over 100mph, which is exactly what private owner Jim Kentish did by recording 106mph with his Rapide, while Ted Frend proved the model's top speed by lapping at 110mph.

What is a matter of fact is that the Burman gearbox inherited from the singles could not cope. Stronger gears inside the box had been specified but already Burman bearings were bastard sizes mixing Imperial and metric dimensions to get big enough items into the castings, so there was no room for improvement there; and, furthermore, the clutch was simply overwhelmed. In the factory handbook, the rider was warned not to open the throttle until the clutch was fully home and biting; in racing conditions the unit slipped, burned and broke. This was why the post-war models were given an in-house design of gearbox and the unique self-servo clutch.

Weight-saving, as achieved in the alloy cylinder heads, was much needed but as three different patterns of light alloy head are known to exist perhaps it was too early in their development, and the engineers were still learning how to fit valve seats satisfactorily into the soft material. All this development, and the production run of the Series A Rapide, was cut short by the outbreak of war in 1939.

WARTIME

Neither in price nor performance were Vincent-HRDs suitable for use in war. A good overhead-valve 500 from another manufacturer could be bought for £50 (far less than £142 for a Rapide or £90 for a Comet in 1937), and dispatch riders were not expected to travel at 100mph (although I am sure they would have loved to have been given the chance). In any case, the factory could never have turned out a realistic quantity of machines for the War Department. So the Stevenage shop floor undertook more basic general machining contracts, such as the manufacture of fuses and land-mine casings, as well as components for the aeroplane industry.

However, this was not enough to fully occupy the fertile mind of PCV or the time of his senior engineers and development staff. He had recently patented a novel twin-crankshaft two-stroke design incorporating twin power cylinders, a separate double-acting charging cylinder, six pistons (two in each cylinder) and 'uniflow' gas transfer techniques. The 'Men from the Ministry' were no match for PCV's salesmanship and, ever confident of the soundness of his ideas, he landed a number of development contracts for engines based upon the patents. A 500cc version developed to power airborne lifeboats for dropping to shipwreck survivors was the most suc-

cessful, but, even so, only a small initial batch was ever produced (shortly after the end of hostilities), of which some still survive. Plans were also being laid for the resumption of motorcycle production even before the war finished, mostly in such spare time as PCV and PEI could find 'out of hours'.

Unlike most motorcycle factories which would resume production with variants of their pre-war models, Vincent-HRD made a prior announcement that it would be dropping the well-proven singles and moving to peacetime production with a completely redesigned version of the 998cc Rapide, already described as 'The World's Fastest Standard Motorcycle'. Press announcements said that design work was well advanced before the war ended, and appeared to confirm this with a photograph of the complete motorcycle published late in 1945. In fact, the first machine was not completed until well into 1946 (a fact which makes clear, again, that advertising literature should not be trusted); and subsequently it was discovered that this one-that-never-was had been created by skilful artistic preparation from a full-size engineering drawing. Nevertheless, it depicted probably the prettiest Vincent-HRD ever, marrying the clean post-war power unit with skinny girder forks and a stainless steel panelled tank similar to that of the pre-war models. No wonder that returning servicemen could hardly wait to spend their gratuities on it.

The power unit of Richard Scudder's Rapide reveals how close the rear inlet valve spring is to the rear down tube, the factory having lengthened the frame as little as possible in order to keep wheelbase reasonably short. The Burman BAPH gearbox is similar to that used on the Series A single-cylinder models but features different-specification internals. Engine number V1002 – presumably this is the motorcycle show model which was known to have been prepared with light alloy cylinder heads, which can be clearly seen. Space for the front carburettor, placed between the cylinders, is severely restricted. Oil pipes, petrol pipes and exhaust pipes reveal why the model became called 'The Plumber's Nightmare'.

All-alloy unit-construction engine and gearbox was ahead of its time in 1946, but helped to keep the machine's weight down. Aluminium was also a plentiful material, whereas steel was in short supply. The unpolished crankcases of this engine, number 99 produced in mid-1947, were cast — according to a Phil Irving quotation — from a mixture of 'all sorts of the available aluminium scrap' but this engine has nevertheless proved good for 50 years of work and still carries its owner and his family on their holidays each year.

POST-WAR CONDITIONS

Conditions were difficult for manufacturers after the war. Government edict required that most of their production be exported, for foreign currency, even though there was no lack of demand at home where buyers often had to settle instead for secondhand or refurbished ex-WD machines. Steel, especially, was in short supply, rationed by the Ministry of Supply and not always available even when allocated to manufacturers. Companies soon learned to take anything they could get, bartering among themselves to finish up with what they actually needed, and Vincent-HRD was no exception.

Aluminium, however, was not rationed, and with the ending of warplane production the aluminium manufacturers suddenly needed new markets. This did not necessarily mean that the available alloys were of mythical aircraft quality, and indeed Phil Irving later described the DTD424 alloy widely used in his design work as being 'a metallic fruit salad made by melting all sorts of the available aluminium alloy scrap into a medium-strength general-purpose material'. The extensive use of light alloys in the post-war Rapide, foreshadowed by the example of the A Rapide, undoubtedly assisted in keeping weight down but was also an astute move from the point of view of sourcing raw materials – typical of PEI's pragmatism. It also accorded well with PCV's dislike of chromium plating as a means of brightening up a motorcycle. He proudly advertised that his new model featured among its virtues four brakes, a spring frame and stainless steel.

Although the Rapide was aimed at 'sportsmen and enthusiasts', as it had to be, carrying a price 50% higher than that of most other heavyweights, and although it boasted a 110mph top speed, borne out in numerous road tests, it still had to be able to run on the 72-octane Pool petrol which was decidedly inferior to the fuel available pre-war. Most Rapides, therefore, left the factory with compression plates lowering the nominal 6.8:1 compression ratio to an actual 6.45:1.

The machinery on which the earliest post-war models were made was mostly old and well worn. Many battles had to be fought with the firm's bankers before new automatic machines were installed to increase production. But by then the sellers' market had been missed and it was too late to prevent the company going into receivership, in 1949. Vincent owners everywhere have Mr E.C. Baillie to thank for the very existence of their machines, for it was he, appointed as Receiver, who decided that the firm could be saved and brought back to life; the majority of bikes were in fact made during the subsequent period, 1949 through to 1952.

Even though the factory did expand, and acquired newer machinery, it was always small by industry standards. Vincent-HRD could never aspire to the facilities, development resources or mass-production techniques of larger marques such as BSA, Triumph and AMC. Instead, they had to rely on the ingenuity of a small band of enthusiastic design and development engineers, and the skills of their machinists and fitters. It is against such a background that Vincent-HRD motorcycles should be judged, and appreciated.

RAPIDE (SERIES B, C & D)

The first Series B Rapide was presented to the press on 27 April 1946 – a remarkably early debut for an extensively new design developed in only a few years. It was to be the base model of the post-war range, for Vincent-HRD made the decision to drop the successful singles and aim instead at the exclusive, high-performance end of the market with the only British big vee-twin offered to the public after the war.

'Offered to the public' is a term which perhaps requires qualification, to reflect the difficult trading conditions of the late 1940s. Many of the pre-war marques were listed as returning to the market, in the 1946-47 press, only to fall by the wayside after producing just a few machines, a feat possibly achieved by using up old parts stock. But the UK buyer found it very difficult to obtain a machine even from the manufacturers who did successfully resume production, because they were under instruction from the government of the day, as previously mentioned, to

export a large proportion of their output. The first Rapides were exported in rotation to various overseas agents. The despatch book reads like a world gazetteer, so varied were the first destinations – USA, France, Denmark, Australia, New Zealand, Turkey, Czechoslovakia.

The earliest production machine off the line (number five) was dispatched on 18 September 1946 to Cimic of Buenos Aires, reflecting the Vincent family's Argentine home and ranching interests. Exports to Argentina grew rapidly, with sales both to the public and to official bodies becoming a major part of the Vincent-HRD export market until political changes in the country led to a complete halt on trade. Many of those early Rapides in Argentina were kept running, in the complete absence of an official source of spare parts, on a mixture of excellently crafted local parts and some very crude and agricultural repair methods.

Nevertheless, a number of these machines have

For its return to civilian production after World War II, Vincent-HRD offered the brand-new 998cc vee-twin Series B Rapide. Although developed from the Series A

twin, it was extensively re-designed in materials and constructional details, and achieved a notably 'clean' appearance. Dave Quarter-main's example is

representative of the very first production machines: Brampton girder front forks were fitted, as on the pre-war models, and the plain, all-black brakes confirm that this model

preceded the date of introduction of spun-aluminium water excluder rings; other early characteristics are the prominent cast-in oilways in the HRD-embossed

timing cover and the bare kick-starter foot piece which, it is believed, is as supplied new. The bar-end mirror is not a period item but indicates that this Rapide is used regularly.

survived the intervening years and are now being re-exported and restored again to their former glory. The Cimic Rapide engine F10AB/1/5 has been rescued in a completely wrecked state by Alex Noftsger of Georgia, USA, and rebuilt, to be known in future as 'Cinco'. Engine F10AB/1/3, currently in a rebuild belonging to Al Mark of Los Angeles, was supplied originally to V.L. Martin of California and was the first number in the order book, but was only completed 12 days later. No doubt both customers were told that they had 'the first' Rapide! The bare crankcases of number four exist in Australia, so it is clear that the very first production engines have survived for over 50 years. Unfortunately the works prototype, number 1EX, was used for other development experiments, having its gearbox sawn off, and no longer exists, while little is known today about the allocation of number two.

The Series B Rapide was a dramatically new motorcycle featuring extensive use of light alloys, unit construction of engine and gearbox, a unique frame-less method of construction, and a host of other novel features. To the engineer, however, it could be seen to embody tried and tested Vincent-HRD ideas. The high-camshaft engine retained the distinctive short pushrods, splayed to run parallel to the valves and operating forked rockers, although the exposed hairpin springs were gone and a simpler coil spring system had been devised. The new frameless con-struction incorporated the well-proven patented rear suspension, seat-support linkage and duo-brakes. Indeed, some parts, from a piston to a complete front wheel, were identical or interchangeable with those of pre-war models.

Overall, the new B Rapide was a smaller, better balanced and much cleaner design than its A Rapide ancestor. Gone were all the external oil pipes, with only a conventional pair remaining, taking oil to and from the dry sump. PCV was not to have his master-piece referred to as 'The Plumber's Nightmare' again.

Dave Stovin restored this 1951 Series C Rapide to a high level of originality by searching out new old stock (NOS) parts in preference to more readily obtainable pattern replacement parts. Finish is probably better than new, although the factory did produce such highly polished models for shows and the showrooms of major dealers. Front crashbar and rear carrier have been fitted to facilitate the bike's use for touring; crashbar is a Britax-style chromium-plated single bar, while combined carrier and pannier racks are Craven items specially developed with integral pivots to provide partial springing of the load. Both were period accessories often fitted by owners to new Vincents.

Final version of the Rapide was the Series D, with softer suspension and tall, fully sprung seat, which was re-introduced in 1955 to satisfy public demand.

An integral oil pump and prominent but neat cast-in oilways (above left) ensured that the Series B Rapide would not inherit the old Series A nickname of 'The Plumber's Nightmare'. Only the minimum of feed and return oil lines to the combined frame member/oil tank remained. Later timing covers, whether embossed HRD or, after 1949, Vincent, like this one (above), were smoothed out to provide an even cleaner look (and more easily polished covers). Similar changes were applied to the gearchange cover. Machines made late in 1949 were sometimes delivered with the manufacturer's name polished off the timing cover and some inspection caps (originally cast with the HRD motif). Here is an example (left), with plain timing cover and clutch cap.

ENGINE & TRANSMISSION

ENGINE The all-alloy vee-twin engine retained the proven 84mm by 90mm pre-war bore and stroke dimensions, but with the cylinder angle opened out to a more standard figure of 50° in order to accommodate '50°' magnetos. The earliest illustrations of the Rapide to appear in the weekly motorcycle magazines show a platform-fitting BTH magneto, but no machines were ever built that way and a change had to be made to accommodate the Lucas flange-fitting magneto instead, as Lucas was presumably the only electrical company still willing to grind 50° cam rings and provide magnetos adapted for a vee-twin.

Massive sand-cast crankcases, in DTD424 aluminium alloy, housed both engine and gearbox components, the unit construction providing both a much cleaner outline and a strong assembly to support the frameless layout. As a conservative measure, the early B series engines (prior to 1310) utilised hollow studs to retain the cylinder heads and secure the gasketless 'double-ground' cylinder head joint. Separate concentric inner studs screwed into the crankcases were used to retain the steel head brackets and carry frame stresses. Later engines used simpler and cheaper one-piece waisted studs, which proved equally satisfactory.

Iron-linered alloy cylinders were deeply spigoted into the crankcases and aluminium was also used for the cylinder heads, which required higher-specification RR53C (or Y-alloy) material, heat-treated for strength. The heads featured shrunk-in valve seats, with austenitic cast iron used for the inlets and wrought aluminium-bronze for the exhausts, both of these materials having the high expansion rates necessary to remain tight in their housings when hot. The exhaust valve guides, machined from aluminium-bronze, were of larger outside diameter than the otherwise similar inlet guides: the explanation is that PEI was allowing for the possibility of using sodium-cooled valves, as proven in aero engine use. In practice, the DTD49B exhaust valves proved eminently satisfactory, and sodium cooling was never used. Silicon-chrome-steel inlet valves were specified, and both inlet and exhaust seatings were cut with 30°

Each of four valve caps above the pushrod tubes individually exposes one of the rocker adjusters (tappets). Conventional detachable rocker box was avoided by sliding each rocker, assembled with bearing, into a cylindrical tunnel behind its valve cap and locating it longitudinally with an extension of the rocker feed bolt retaining the oil banjo directly above each cap.

angles, not the 45° used by most of the industry.

Although both cylinders featured rearward-facing carburettors and forward-facing exhausts, the front and rear head castings were different from each other on B and C models. The precise reason for this has never been discovered, but the most likely explanation appears to lie in the position of the separate float chamber carburettors: on the Amal Monobloc-equipped Series D models both heads were the same (two 'front' heads), but with such an arrangement the older 276 and 279 carburettor types with separate float chambers would have fouled the dynamo clamp and drive-pinion housing. Early cylinder heads had no webs between the fins but these were soon introduced to reduce 'ringing', and the finish of the castings was also much improved. The head design avoided having a separate rocker box by the ingenious use of slide-in Duralumin rocker bearings in tunnels machined into the heads, but oil drainage proved to be marginal and grooves in the rocker bearings soon had to be added (from engine 193) to alleviate the problem. Nevertheless, an oiled-up front sparking plug remained a not uncommon Vincent-HRD malaise when a Rapide was ridden slowly in traffic for too long.

The Rapide crankshaft followed the factory's previous practice in being a built-up assembly with side-by-side connecting rods. Mainshafts, in EN24, were pressed into the part-finished flywheels (made from 40-ton steel forgings), after which the flywheels were finish-ground off the shafts. A long EN36 case-hardened crankpin was pressed in, carrying two identical EN16 connecting rods, and also retained by nuts. This allowed a very high degree of alignment to be achieved, which was necessary for free running in the four widely spaced main bearings. The flywheels were extensively drilled before assembly to achieve a balance factor of 45%. The standard big-ends featured three rows of crowded 3mm by 5mm rollers, usually 45 per row; a variety of different caged big-end designs has subsequently become available from the various Vincent specialists.

The oiling system was not a carry-over from the pre-war models. Instead of the old gear pump, an integral Pilgrim combined rotary-reciprocating pump was adopted, and built into a tunnel machined into the crankcases. Worm-driven from the crankshaft, this pump drew oil through a felt filter housed in a chamber at the front of the crankcases, with all oilways being internal drillings except for the feed and return lines to the separate oil tank/upper frame member. Oilways up through the cylinder head joints were avoided by leading the return line across the cylinder heads through banjos attached to hollow rocker feed bolts above each tappet cover, with valve gear oil supply draining down the pushrod tunnels after doing its work. Hollow cam spindles provided lubrication to the cam bushes, and also to the cylinder walls via drillings in the timing cover. A further drilling, which contained the pressure relief valve, fed a bronze quill in the hollow timing-side mainshaft, to distribute oil to the crankpin and, thence, the big-ends. A sludge trap was formed by an undercut in the crankpin machining, but this was barely adequate and could fill with swarf and carbon in spite of the efficient felt filter – although with the coming of detergent oils this has ceased to be a problem. Original oil recommendation was SAE 40 in summer or SAE 30 in winter, but additional recommendations covered very cold and very hot conditions (SAE 20 for Arctic temperatures and SAE 50 for the tropics). Good quality modern 20-50 multigrades are probably satisfactory, provided that changes are still made at recommended intervals.

A number of small modifications were made to the lubrication system during Series B production, with a change from bronze to steel for the oil pump worm (from engine 375), revisions to the crankpin drilling (from engine 380), and fine metering wires being introduced in the inlet rocker feed bolts to reduce oil flow and keep the holes clear (from engine 1128). Oil-restrictor discs were introduced behind the rubber seals in the timing cover on late engines (from engine 9238), only to be made obsolete by a revision in the cover drillings (from engine 10,000); but they can usefully be fitted to earlier engines to redistribute the oil.

Other beneficial changes were made inside the timing chest. Many Bs had large idlers manufactured in bronze, but these were later changed to an RR77 wrought-aluminium component which was intended to quieten the engine by maintaining closer gear clearances, since its thermal expansion more closely matched that of the crankcases. In practice, this made little difference to noise levels; reliability, however, is much improved by using steel idlers patterned after those developed for use in the racing Lightning engines. Bronze idlers were sized, and selected for minimal timing gear backlash, but with the introduction of the alloy idlers adjustment was made by selection of sized crankshaft pinions (although for a time both bronze idler and crankshaft pinions were sized and selected for fit). Cam wheels and half-time pinion were machined from EN24W nickel-chrome-molybdenum steel, and lever-type cam followers from EN36 case-hardening steel. Various small idler designs were used, which on B and C models also formed part of the timed breather valve for exhausting crankcase compression through a hollow spindle and out of a banjo at the front of the engine. Bronze, cast iron and aluminium alloy were all used as sleeve materials in a steel pinion. But the only really unsatisfactory variant was a one-piece cast iron design, in which the gear wheel would sometimes shed its teeth – very few of these were made. Eventually, the timed breather on the Series D Rapide was discarded entirely and a simple atmospheric breather substituted, using a modified front valve cap and increased clearances around the upper valve guide, to ease the passage of

This engine (above), which had spent years in a barn, was opened up for this photograph, probably for the first time since assembly. Large idler drives the two high camshafts, and the spindles on which the gears run are supported by the outrigger plate, which avoids loads being transferred to the cover and thus aids oil-tightness. These Rapide bare cases (below) are of the earlier pattern, with the 3½in dynamo cradle cast in. Early-pattern cylinder studs use separate inners and tubular outers (machined only at the ends). Integral rotary oil pump gear is visible through the main bearing outer race.

Bronze large idler, of which two different patterns are shown (left), proved a little fragile and was replaced by high-expansion items forged in RR77 hiduminium wrought alloy (centre). These are capable of long service but are not very tolerant of running badly meshed. Most reliable is the steel idler (right), originally produced for the Black Lightning but now readily available as a replacement part.

Most Series B crankcases (above left) were embossed with the HRD motif. Engine number 16 indicates that this Rapide (owned by Dave Quartermain) dates from 1946; it was one of only four supplied to the home market that year. The first sand-cast crankcase *casings (above right) did not carry the words 'Made in England', an omission used by US customs to restrict imports. For a time the legend had to be stamped in manually, as seen here, until the various patterns could be modified (customs demanded that many parts,* *not just the crankcases, should be marked). After 1949 crankcases continued to be sand-cast, but the patterns were altered to produce the legend VINCENT (below left), putting Philip Vincent's own name in pride of place and finally breaking the link back* *to Howard Davies. Late Series C and all Series D crankcases (below right) were stronger and lighter die-castings. These are recognisable by a number of detailed differences from the sand-cast cases, such as the flashing visible just under the engine number stamping.*

air. Series D models also incorporated a new one-piece large idler spindle to replace the older composite pattern in which the steel shaft would sometimes loosen in its light alloy flange.

More visible changes occurred in the main castings, with at least three variants of main crankcases being used. B and C cases were sand-cast while late C and D cases were a lighter die-casting. Early B cases had a cast-in cradle for the 3½in diameter dynamo but this was soon changed (at engine 746) to the later pattern of bolt-on cradle for the 3in unit. Until late in 1949 the cases bore the legend 'HRD' below the front cylinder, but thereafter this was changed to read

'Vincent'; the decision to drop the old name and call the machines Vincent in future was taken in order to prevent confusion with Harley-Davidson in the increasingly important American market. Detailed differences exist on the die-cast 1954 cases, including support for the gearbox cam-plate spindle, flashing where the dies joined, and the background on which the engine number was stamped. The various covers changed even more conspicuously, leading to the quite distinctively different looks of early and late machines. The sand-cast timing and gearchange covers of early B models featured proud oilways and a clutch actuating arm bulge, while the die-cast items

had much cleaner, smoother contours. The fluted cast gearbox filler cap used on early models was replaced by a turned and knurled item on later models. The round clutch cover had to be quickly changed for one with a flat at the bottom, to prevent grounding during exuberant cornering. Valve and inspection caps, as well as the timing cover, also had the 'HRD' legend replaced by 'Vincent' late in 1949. The valve caps appear to have been redesigned slightly at the same time, as Vincent-embossed caps provide slightly greater clearances.

For a while in 1949/50 machines were supplied with plain valve caps and covers but, contrary to previously published explanations, it seems unlikely that many were built this way, for there is little pattern to be discerned in the order of their engine and frame numbers. Rather, the explanation may derive from the unfortunate timing of the decision to change the name to Vincent-HRD. It took place at a time when sales were falling disastrously, and machines had to be stockpiled all around Stevenage. Thus when a sale was made the works tried to collect and ship the HRD-embossed motorcycles first, because the new name was rapidly making them obsolete, and certainly few have a history of being in stock very long. By contrast, many late 1949 Vincent-embossed machines remained in stock for up to six months between completion and delivery. By early 1950 it was no longer possible to deliver an HRD without it being obvious to the customer that this was an 'old' machine, but the stockpile was not yet cleared of them. Solution: when pulling out an HRD from stock, buff off the name from the timing cover and various inspection caps, and pop on a fresh tank with the new transfers (no doubt returning the original to the paintshop). It would look to the customer as if his bike was fresh off the production line!

Crankcases were normally left as cast, although mated up in matched sets complete with covers, and then fettled to provide neat joins. The various covers and caps were polished on Rapides, and in the case of the Vincent-embossed variety the name on the timing cover was picked out with a black background inside the surrounding rectangle. Covers were retained with cheese-headed Whitworth screws, and the normal finish for these was cadmium plating, although many restorations have been converted to stainless steel hexagon-cap head screws (commonly referred to as Allen screws). BSF and Whitworth were the normal threads used inside the engine.

Although special threads, such as on mainshafts, adopted the cycle thread pitches of 20tpi and 26tpi, restorers should note that they were usually cut using 55° Whitworth threadform tools and not 60° CEI (Cycle Engineering Institution, also referred to as BS Cycle).

FUEL SYSTEM & CARBURETTORS The early line drawings published in 1945 indicate that minor changes were made before production began. Those illustrations showed flange-fitting carburettors, but in practice the Rapide was fitted with 1 1⁄16in clip-fitting Amal Type 276 carburettors with separate float chambers. A pair of light alloy adapters converted the carburettors' clip fitting to the two-stud flat face machined on the cylinder heads.

Standard (short) straight-arm float bowls were used on the earliest machines, but these were soon changed for longer than normal arms to provide improved access and a less crowded installation. When the first Series Bs were made, only the right-handed mixing-chamber version was in production, which meant that the front carburettor throttle-stop adjuster was very awkwardly sited between carburettor and cylinder

Rear carburettor installation leaves little room for cables and fuel lines (above left). Twin outlet banjo allows left- and right-side carburettors and petrol taps to be interconnected. Standard Amal short-arm float chambers were used only on early production machines, with longer float chambers adopted as soon as they were available to allow more clearance, particularly around the throttle-stop adjuster. In 1946 only a right-handed version of Amal's 276 carburettor was available (above), which meant that the throttle-stop adjuster ended up out of sight behind the carburettor and between the two cylinders. As soon as Amal introduced a left-handed body, it was adopted to solve the problem.

Most B and C Rapides were fitted with the left-handed 276 carburettor body (above) on the front cylinder, and also the longer-arm float bowl which provides greater clearance around the throttle-stop adjuster. Series D Rapides used a pair of identical 1⅛in Amal Monobloc carburettors (above right) with integral float chambers. Both were mounted on the left side of the machine, but once again Amal initially made only the right-handed version, making the adjusters inaccessible. Fuel lines were also revised on the Ds, using twin-outlet banjos.

fins, but this was rectified as soon as a left-handed version became available. Both versions were preferable to the A Rapide arrangement which had necessitated the front mixing chamber being horizontally mounted under the tank, and this may have contributed to the different front and rear head designs, with the front head adopting an inlet port well to the left (this also promotes desirable swirl in the gas flow). The separate float chamber 276 carburettor, however, would have been difficult to accommodate on the same side at the rear, because of the proximity of the new dynamo drive boss; this may have determined the design of the different rear cylinder head casting, with its inlet port on the right. When the Series D was designed with the new flange-fitting Monobloc carburettors (Amal number 376/31), using appropriately revised adapters, their more compact integral float-chamber design made it possible to use two front heads and place both, identical, carburettors on the left-hand side.

On Bs and Cs the front carburettor (276CJ/1DO and later 276DQ/1DV) featured a bottom-feed float chamber, while the rear carburettor (276CH/2DS) used the top-feed type. Two Ewarts plunger-type taps were fitted to the petrol tank, earlier taps having plungers screwed for replacement and adjustment of the separate corks, with later versions being permanently riveted together. B and C taps and carburettors were fully interconnected by cadmium-plated copper or brass banjo and T-sections linked with flexible canvas-reinforced black rubber tubing, so that one tap could be used as a reserve, except when riding very fast, when many owners preferred to open both taps to be sure of sufficient petrol flow. By the standards of the period, the Vincent was quite thirsty. Series D machines used black plastic fuel lines (but this did not improve their thirst…).

GEARBOX Although nobody at Vincent-HRD had much experience of gearbox or clutch design, the troubles previously experienced with the transmission in the Series A 1000cc models determined PCV and PEI to design their own transmission. Taking gearbox design in-house brought a host of benefits, enabling the much stronger and cleaner unit-construction technique to be used for the power unit. This then provided more than adequate support for a cross-over gearbox, with the final drive chain on what was traditionally the 'wrong' (right-hand) side, and that in turn allowed both clutch and final drive sprockets to be close to their respective bearings.

Inside the primary chaincase, which could be well sealed as there was no sliding gearbox adjustment to accommodate with the fixed-centres 'unit' layout, the sprockets could be located with precision. This permitted use of a fine-pitch triplex chain from the 35-tooth EN32 case-hardened engine sprocket to the 56-tooth nickel-chrome cast iron clutch sprocket. Adjustment was devised using a spring-blade tensioner with an external adjuster screw to tension the blade, and a chain inspection cap to check it through. Inside the gearbox, large pinions, machined from EN36 nickel-chrome case-hardened steel, were carried on substantial shafts running in ball-bearing journals.

Thus far the design was very successful, and required few changes. Only a few machines were made with the original 24-tooth second gear pinion, which was replaced by a stronger 23-tooth item cut on the same blank (from engine 309), and the single-blade tensioner was eventually changed (for the Series D engines) to a twin-blade design requiring a few modified mating parts. Some gears made of alternative steels during the 1951 Korean crisis, when nickel was in short supply, proved to be inadequate and had to be replaced by the factory; otherwise the gears wore satisfactorily well.

In other respects, however, the gearbox and transmission were not initially so successful, and early models required skilled factory fitters to select, fit and assemble a satisfactory gearbox. Original drawing modification notes indicate that a lot had to be learned about clearances, tolerances and cam plate contours before a gearbox could be reliably assembled from a random set of stores parts. Indeed, Phil Vincent's own riding career was ended by a crash when an early gearbox tightened up – a very serious occurrence since even lifting the clutch does not release the locked wheel which results. With the standard gearbox and rear sprockets (21-tooth and 46-tooth respectively) a top gear ratio of 3.5:1 resulted, with intermediate ratios of 4.16, 5.5 and 9:1.

Inside the gearchange cover the selector mechanism required, and still requires, proper adjustments carried out in the correct order, and preferably parts in good condition, to allow it to work properly. The resulting gearchange is fairly slow; if hurried, it is somewhat prone to 'over-change', a tendency which can be reduced by various factory and non-standard modifications; but jumping out of gear usually indicates wear or maladjustment. Early gearboxes, however, were subject to a string of minor but very significant modifications which should certainly be incorporated in any rebuild – notwithstanding any desire for originality.

The first two variations of selector cam plate are best replaced by the later G32/2 type, with modified slots (from engine 1590). The very earliest are definitely museum pieces because the first batch had to be hand-sorted to find 20 sufficiently accurate items, which were 'signed' by the chief inspector, Mr Sharland. Even when machining problems were rectified, the design of the early plates was such that hand-grinding the indents deeper and general polishing by fitters were necessary, to get an acceptable change. Gearchange adjustment was, and remains, very fiddly but is accurately described in various manuals and gives satisfactory results if the instructions are followed. The heavy components have a tendency to keep moving and 'over-change' if rapid gearchanges are made, as indicated earlier. This situation can be improved by lightening parts such as the cam plate, but this was never standard on Rapide models. A modified pawl carrier centraliser (a bent bit of sheet metal, G61/1) was introduced on late models (from engine 9669) but its use is advised only at rebuild times because adoption of this item on an old engine whose components have become sloppy can result in a previously satisfactory box 'under-changing'.

The gearbox compartment is separate from the engine and primary chaincase, and requires two pints of engine oil. However, users of multigrade oil would be wise to choose a separate type of gearbox oil, since it runs much cooler and a multigrade may stay at its

Fairly conventional four-speed gear cluster (above) was used, but gears were made larger than in most motorcycle gearboxes in view of the factory's unhappy experience with Burman gearboxes in the Series A Rapide. The other variation from traditional British practice was the crossover design, with the clutch driving the gearset via the splined shaft on the right, and output to the sprocket via the splined sleeve gear on the left. Gearbox filler cap (left), sited towards the back of the rear cylinder, also hides a dipstick for checking gearbox oil level. Early fluted pattern of cap, made from an aluminium alloy casting, was replaced by this later pattern of cap, turned from light alloy bar, knurled and then stamped (or in this case mis-stamped) with its legend. Initially the Rapide gear lever (left) was pivoted from the footrest hanger, to follow the footrest through any riding position adjustment, using this complex, adjustable ball-jointed linkage to the gearchange shaft. Gradually, wear would introduce backlash into the system, so first the owners, and later the factory, discarded it for a pedal bolted directly to the gearchange shaft.

Removing the clutch cover (right) reveals the outer, pilot clutch which is capable of driving the machine at modest speeds but whose main job is to operate the twin leading shoe servo clutch behind the pilot. Initial movement of the pilot clutch twists the spider of the unique Vincent servo clutch (far right) and throws out the shoes. Under power, these form a twin leading shoe arrangement and multiply the grip of the light-action pilot clutch. This engine, which has been standing for many years, has leaked oil through the seals and thoroughly wetted its shoes.

Major parts of the clutch. Right is the drum which bolts to the clutch sprocket (with a boss passing through an oil seal into the dry clutch housing). Into this goes, first, the servo shoe clutch assembly of shoes, shoe carrier, links and spider (below), followed by the single-plate clutch which provides a light drive and operates the inner clutch via the spider.

minimum viscosity. Oil retention in the gearbox is generally good, with garter-type oil seals on both sides; the result is that wear of pinions and bearings is low, although the Oilite bushes sometimes loosen in the sleeve gear. Provision was made for checking the oil level with a dipstick, located under the gearbox filler cap, but the level indication proved to be undesirably high and the recommendation was changed to a lower position on the dipstick flat, rather than altering the flat itself. Some care is needed to prevent oil creepage along the clutch shaft, and it is also worth-

while inserting a cork in the normally unused cross-shaft tunnel from the primary chaincase – provided to allow fitting of a left-hand kick-starter, particularly useful for foreign sidecar combination riders. Very few machines were actually so supplied, but in modern times left-hand kick-starter levers have become available again.

SERVO CLUTCH The Vincent self-servo clutch must be one of the most misunderstood (and complicated) parts of the machine. The factory faced a serious problem when the pre-production clutch insisted on slipping at full throttle, although the development prototype tried out on a Series A Rapide had worked well in its intended wet-chaincase environment. The clutch was relocated into a separate dry compartment, but this added an unwelcome inch in width and three more oil seals to the design. Even the two Phils, whose later written accounts of the problem agreed thus far, never came up with a good explanation of what had gone wrong, or a better solution, with the result that Vincent twins – and Vincent owners – have had to live with the extra complication ever since.

The clutch, in principle, consists of a 6in twin leading shoe brake operated by initial movement of links connected to a light and simple single-plate conventional clutch, also nominally of 6in diameter, and using Ferodo inserts. All, in theory, were well-proven engineering devices offering a substantial mass and surface area for dissipation of heat during periods when the clutch might be slipped, but the assembly

Triplex chain takes drive from an engine-shaft shock absorber (ESA) to the clutch sprocket. Chain tension in the unit-construction engine/gearbox unit is maintained by the adjustable spring blade tensioner below the bottom run. On the clutch sprocket the middle row of teeth is relieved to allow the dynamo drive sprocket to engage. Even so, it is clear that only one or two teeth on the dynamo sprocket carry the load – an undesirable feature.

Cam-type engine-shaft shock absorber used an array of 36 small springs in concentric pairs, instead of one large one, because of spring steel shortages experienced immediately after World War II. Originally it was intended that the clutch should be bolted to the sprocket in the oil bath chaincase. However, clutch slip problems forced a late change to extend the chaincase cover between the sprocket and clutch, using a large oil seal running on the sprocket centre boss.

was also complicated, unconventional and expensive to produce.

Nevertheless, pre-war experience of slipping and burned-out clutches had made it imperative that a more substantial yet light-to-operate design be found – and the Vincent clutch succeeded in fulfilling those requirements. If it slips, oil has probably got in (it does not take much to promote slippage); if it grabs, the shoe pivot holes are probably worn; and if erratic action or drag occurs, it is possible that the centralising springs have broken up. It is even just possible to assemble the clutch with the 1¼in wide shoes backwards, their arrows pointing the wrong way, so that it becomes an ineffective twin trailing shoe device. Not surprisingly, the clutch does not work very well like that, but none of this catalogue of faults, which may occur after 40 years of use and abuse, can really be held against the design. In fact, the linings will often outlast the shoes to which they are affixed, and the works had very little need to make any modifications after that first pre-production panic.

A very early change from three to six springs (at engine 70) was attributed by PCV to a need for more 'feel' by riders, but by others to insufficient strength to guarantee the shoes returning, with a slightly stiff clutch cable. The clutch shaft was unsealed on early machines, but oil creeping along the threads could get into the clutch; a nut with a ground face bearing on a sealing washer was introduced to solve that problem (from engine 594, with a Dowty-type seal being introduced at engine 656). On Series D models, the nut and the mating shaft were altered to accept an O-ring seal, the whole assembly being interchangeable

with its predecessor, but not the individual parts. Virtually the same result can be obtained by removing the rubber from a used Dowty seal and replacing it with a new, suitably sized O-ring at each reassembly. The clutch-shoe pivots were changed to use circlips instead of nuts (from engine 853), for production efficiency and reliability, and in 1952 a change was made to a more oil-resistant Duron lining material; this does not mean that it works when oil-soaked, only that the

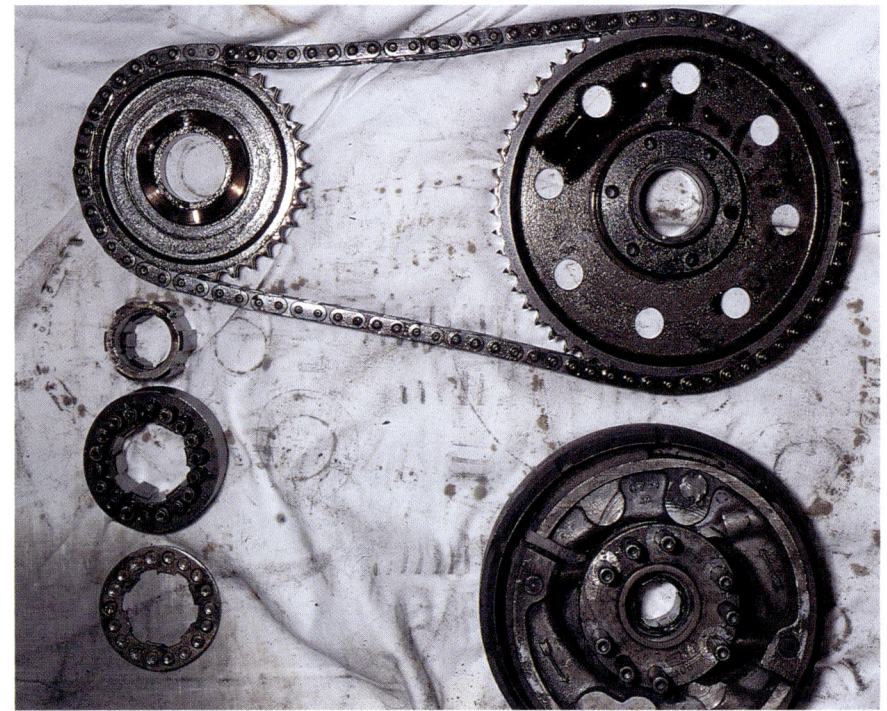

material can be successfully degreased, which was not always the case with the original woven material. A small number of machines were made with a lightened version of the ribbed cast iron clutch drum; these had apparently been specially cast for competition models but proved a little weak in the harsh conditions of racing and high revs, and so were used up on the more softly tuned Rapides.

A number of owners have modified clutch drums to use the one-piece Lightning-type friction disc instead of the normal plate with separate Ferodo inserts. There is little need to revert to standard since this modification is hard to undo, has proved to be very satisfactory, and the friction discs are still available. Apart from this, the only well-proven clutch requirements appear to be maintaining the original design in reasonably good condition, or to make a wholesale replacement with a complete multi-plate clutch conversion! Over the years, a number of these have been developed, based on Norton, Triumph, Suzuki and Ducati clutches. But the most popular clutch remains the original Vincent self-servo design.

Smoothing the drive from engine mainshaft to the clutch, the equally unconventional engine shock absorber (ESA) was never completely satisfactory. It was originally intended to use the cam-type shock absorber with a conventional single spring, although the factory had no previous experience of using an ESA because the pre-war models had used clutch rubbers for the shock-absorbing medium. However Vincent-HRD could not obtain the spring steel required for an intended post-war design, so PEI came up with his unconventional alternative, using a cam design with 18 small holes to accept a ring of small springs – quickly doubled to 36 by filling each hole with a concentric pair of little springs. No doubt he was influenced by his experience at Velocette where a ring of similar springs had been used in the clutch, but perhaps their job with lower power Velocettes had not been so arduous. Breakage of the little ESA springs was always somewhat excessive, and owners soon determined that the spring retaining plate should be replaced backwards, so that the spring recesses provided would not be operative. This enabled the springs to squirm around freely instead of getting trapped; nevertheless, replacement parts continued to be supplied with the recesses expensively machined out. Even with this modified assembly method, spring life, especially that of the tightly wound inners, was lamentably short; it seemed that whenever a chaincase was disturbed replacement of some springs was likely.

For the Series D models, a larger and heavier assembly, accepting 44 instead of 36 springs, was designed, which was an improvement, and it could be fitted to earlier models, although individual parts could not be mixed. Thicker and stiffer pressure plates for the B and C versions are now available, but these will only help if the other parts are still in good con-
dition. The small springs have to telescope into their drilled recesses during compression, but they are only able to do this if no angular motion takes place during the intended axial motion. When all the splines were new, very little angular rock could take place, but with the accumulation of wear in the splines the springs are repetitively pulled out of line as they compress; they become trapped, and break. Although the spline wear is not enough to affect component strength, and many rebuilders therefore re-use the parts, in fact the wear is responsible for a significant shortening of spring life, which has exacerbated the poor reputation of this admittedly 'marginal' design.

CYCLE PARTS

FRAME & REAR SUSPENSION How to shorten, stiffen and lighten their big-twin motorcycle for the post-war era? PCV wrote in his reminiscences: 'What isn't present takes up no space, cannot bend, and weighs nothing – so eliminate the frame tubes!'

The Series B Rapide was therefore designed to use the unit-construction engine/gearbox as its main stressed member, with the rear fork pivoted directly behind the gearbox. This location for the fork spindle minimised its separation from the gearbox sprocket centre, which in turn lessened variations in chain tension throughout suspension movement. Because of concerns about the relative weakness of cast aluminium and the novelty of the arrangement, a small engine plate on the left and the alloy gear change back plate on the right were used to spread the loads from the fixed ½in diameter spindle over a larger area of the crankcase casting.

The Vincent-HRD rear suspension system was retained, foreshadowing the modern cantilever arrangement at a time when awful plunger systems represented most manufacturers' first steps away from the rigid frame. The triangulated rear frame member (RFM) continued to be manufactured as a brazed lug and tube construction, as it had been on the Series A and earlier machines. However, the RFM was extensively revised in detail and carried the ¾in bore taper-roller pivot bearings, a reversal of pre-war practice which had been to mount the bearings in a special casting of the main frame.

The early fork, recognisable by its straight seat-support lugs, had limited clearance for large-section tyres such as 4.00-19in, and so was lengthened by ½in, to 18in, in 1949 (at frame 3900). To maintain the correct seat-support geometry while being assembled on the old jigs, this revised RFM utilised the curved seat-support lugs by which the later item is easily recognised. Some of the early seat-support stays used stainless steel or alloy straight sections, but the latter did not prove strong enough, and cadmium-plated steel was substituted. As late as 1950, Series B machines were made on which the only rear suspension damping was provided by the small friction liners

in the seat stay lower alloy clamps. The drums in which these linings operated were prevented from turning by 2BA screws on the earliest Bs, but these were soon changed to ¼in BSF. Series C models, the first batch of which were made in 1948, featured a hydraulic rear damper of Vincent-HRD's own manufacture but required no change to the RFM. For the Series D, the RFM was altered again, with relocated spring box lugs to mate with the new single Armstrong spring/damper unit which gave a 30% increase in rear suspension travel, to 6in.

A combined oil tank and upper frame member (UFM) represented the residual main frame on B and C models. Originally this was to have been an all-welded assembly, and such prototypes can be seen in works photographs, but problems with distortion could not be overcome, and instead a sheet metal tank bolted to a forged or cast steering head by close-fitting high-tensile bolts or studs was adopted. This assembly, usually treated as inseparable, mated with a pair of cylinder head brackets, each bolted on top of its respective cylinder head by additional nuts on extended holding-down studs.

Three types of B and C steering head exist. The earliest forged type (with a curved bottom) and the later malleable casting both featured a forked end to straddle a plain front cylinder head bracket to which it was rigidly bolted by a single stud. Originally the

front cylinder head bracket was identical to the rear one, but from 1951 a revised steering head casting was produced with a simple bottom lug to fit inside a revised slotted cylinder head bracket used on the front cylinder head. This must only be used with longer sleeve nuts (1in long), in order that they should engage fully, with the short (⅞in long) nuts retained for the rear head lug only; in both cases the fit must be tight if frame integrity is to be maintained. At the rear of the oil tank the holes for the rear bracket were slotted, and fitted with matching precision-fit sleeves, to allow the alloy power unit to expand when hot. A special assembly routine is required at this point, with the sleeve nut being tightened fully, then released one flat (one-sixth of a turn) before fitting and tightening the locknut.

From frame number 3500, the spring box rear cross tube was slotted to enable the Series C hydraulic damper to be fitted, but many earlier UFMs were also modified to update them, which was a factory-recommended policy. For the Series D, the UFM was completely revised, and no longer carried the oil. A simple tube, with brazed lugs at each end, was bolted to a slightly modified version of the Series C malleable steering head casting, taking less under-tank space and, most importantly, accommodating the longer suspension strut needed to keep up with the rest of the industry, which had at last discovered

The unit-construction engine/gearbox replaces a conventional tubular front frame – hence no downtubes are visible. Steering head is bolted directly to the front cylinder head bracket, and via the oil tank backbone to the rear head bracket. Triangulated swinging arm is pivoted on a spindle at the rear of the gearbox, with suspension units under the saddle. Seat-stay geometry supporting the rear of the seat was calculated as a compromise between pillion passenger springing and seat height.

Under-seat spring boxes were black enamelled on early models but later the inner covers were cadmium-plated. Above the spring boxes the tool tray slides in runners under the seat.

Links supporting the seat incorporate drum-type friction dampers at their lower ends, adjusted by alloy knobs. On Series B machines these provide the only rear damping; when the knobs were screwed down tight for a heavy load or sidecar, the 2BA screws below the centre bolt could shear; later machines were fitted with larger ¼in BSF bolts. Here, straight lugs supporting the links indicate that this is the earlier 17½in rear fork, and not the later 18in fork that has curved lugs.

On Series D models the combined oil tank/upper frame member was replaced by a simpler and slimmer tubular stay triangulating the steering head forging back to the rear head bracket. Series D engines also use a simple atmospheric breather provided by a modified valve cap over the front inlet valve spring. The position and pattern of the horn on Series D models is visible.

hydraulically damped swinging-arm rear suspension. The UFM of the D models was not as robust as its predecessor; old UFMs must be inspected for corrosion or cracking at the rear, usually due to an accident or use with a sidecar.

Sidecars were still an important means of transport for many people in the 1950s, and large-capacity motorcycles usually featured integral sidecar-mounting points. On the Rapide, three such attachment points were built in to accept ⅝in diameter studs carrying eyebolts or ball-joints. The front upper stud fitted into a boss in the head lug, and the front lower into the tubular front-stand pivot assembly. At the rear, a suitable tube was welded into the UFM of B and C models to accept a long eyebolt, and similar provision was made in the rearmost lug of the D's design. At the lower rear, there was no integral provision; for that position a bolt-on triangular lug was produced, threaded to accept a standard ball-joint fitting. Although apparently bolting to the rather insubstantial pillion footrest plates, in fact the forward apex of the triangle was retained directly by the rear-frame pivot axle, and thus the mechanical loads were adequately supported. Alternative rear suspension springs listed for the purpose were of 264lb/in (0.324in wire diameter) instead of the standard 189lb/in (0.300in wire diameter).

STEERING & FRONT SUSPENSION For the Series B models little change was made to the pre-war steering and front fork set-up (see page 16). In part, this was to reduce the design workload at the Vincent-HRD works, and it also off-loaded the steel supply problem to Brampton, the girder fork manufacturers. The HRD Brampton 1946-pattern forks, however, were not interchangeable with the pre-war version, because the pivot centres were slightly altered, and the design was improved by the provision of replaceable bronze bushes at the pivot points. Fitted with a brake anchor lug on each side, these forks were special to Vincent-HRD, and the fork links were usually stamped 'HRD'.

Two versions of top link exist (identical to the pre-war items), of 3⅜in length between spindle centres for solo use or 3in length (to reduce fork trail) for sidecar use; the latter should not be used in a solo set-up. The fork links were one of only a few places where 26tpi CEI threads were utilised, left-handed on the left and right-handed on the right, so that side-play adjustment could be made simply by turning the spindles after releasing the various lock-nuts. The main spring should be 9¾in long and the 180lb/in version (0.360in wire diameter) is best, although many Rapides were originally supplied with 160lb/in springs, and occasionally 170lb/in.

The girder-type forks could only be a stop-gap because they rapidly became out of date and out of fashion as almost all other manufacturers adopted new telescopic fork designs. PCV and PEI, however, would not contemplate telescopics, not least because their lateral stiffness was inferior even to girders which, being triangulated only fore and aft, could bend sideways under heavy sidecar usage. To side-step this dilemma, they designed the Girdraulic fork which distinguishes the C series machines from the Brampton-equipped and friction-damped B models.

As intimated by the name, this fork married the general principles of the older link-type fork, with its well braced legs, to the benefits of longer, hydraulically damped travel usually offered by telescopics. In the absence of proprietary hydraulic dampers, these too were of Vincent design. A single damper was used in the front fork, and an identical item was added between the rear spring boxes to control the rear suspension, for further improvement of comfort and roadholding. The frame number prefix for Series C machines was altered to RC, by which they can be recognised even though many Bs (prefix R) were updated by their owners or the factory. The new fork continued to rely on the basic parallel-link principle but with one-piece links and separate blades forged in L40 alloy by the Bristol Aircraft Co Ltd to provide lateral as well as fore and aft strength. Provision for sidecar hauling was completed by the ingenious use of eccentrics for the lower-link pivots, which simultaneously reduce trail and increase spring pre-load when turned forward. This turning is actually not as easy to do as it may seem, but can be done single-handedly at the roadside if necessary, as I discovered when attempting to ride with a newly collected sidecar. Laziness had led me to set off still with solo-trail engaged. Sheer fear from the resulting low-speed steering wobble prompted me to screw the steering damper down – and then to stop and learn how to adjust the forks a mere couple of miles later! Thereafter, the outfit was a delight to ride.

Series C Rapide Girdraulics were fitted with two concentric 15in long springs in each telescopic spring box, and the Vincent-manufactured hydraulic damper, but slightly softer suspension was provided on the D Rapide with single 16½in long springs and a leak-free proprietary Armstrong damper. The damper was fractionally shorter than the Vincent item and so longer 1in eyebolts replaced the previous ⅝in eyebolts; the correct length of eyebolt *must* be used with each type of damper. Many machines have subsequently been fitted with Koni dampers, which should be used with the short eyebolts.

The standard handlebar on all models of HRDs and Vincents was always black enamelled. Known as 'HRD straights', the standard Series B and C bars are ⅞in diameter and 25in long, and have the ends bent back by 20°. The Series D specification added an extra 1½in to the length, and longer 27in sidecar bars were also available. On the left bar was located the pressed steel clutch lever, normally embossed 'Amal', and the solid exhaust-valve lifter, usually supplied by Bowden, together with the Bakelite Miller dipswitch or, later,

a chrome-plated item. On the right bar was the pressed steel Amal front brake lever, twin Amal choke lever assembly and chrome-plated horn button (of unidentified make). Ball-ended levers had not come into use but many bikes have subsequently been fitted with them. Note that the standard nipple-to-pivot centres figure is ⅞in; the alternative 1⅛in size provides a less spongy front brake action but is much less suited to use on the clutch side. Rubber handlebar grips of unknown make were normal for the period, plastic grips having yet to become popular.

For the Series B models, friction-damped girder-type front forks – proprietary items supplied by Brampton – were retained. These became very rare due to owners updating their motorcycles with the later forks, but are now much sought after.

Unique Vincent Girdraulic forks combined strong, forged light alloy legs and well-proven link action of girder-type forks with long, soft springs each side and hydraulic damping (using a single middle strut) as used in the telescopic forks widely adopted in the late 1940s.

In the middle of the bars, an alloy knob identical to that on the seat stays controlled the Vincent-manufactured friction steering damper, a conventional fitting for the period and one which should be used on the Vincent ('lightly biting' was the advice). The original Vincent single-plate design is less satisfactory than the twin-plate damper adopted in 1953 (from frame 11937); as the conversion is very easy, many earlier machines have been modified over the years to incorporate the later twin-plate arrangement, which is to be recommended.

BRAKES The twin-drum duo-brakes remained a feature of the post-war design, closely following Series A practice. A short cable replaced the pre-war direct mechanical contact, connecting the foot pedal to the rear brake cross-shaft just behind the RFM pivot bearings. From there, ordinary rod operation of the rear drums resulted in uncompensated action.

At the front, brake operation was compensated to distribute the braking evenly between the two drums, by a balance beam just under the steering head. To reiterate the principle of this system, when the inner cable operated one drum, the outer, anchored to the beam, operated the second by rocking the beam and pulling a short cable on the other end.

Early Series Bs were fitted with pressed steel drums, which were soon changed (from frame 3050) to nickel-chromium cast iron, for better friction and wear properties. Quite why the factory went through the earlier phase is not clear, since it had experienced the same problems with pressed drums on the Series A duo-brakes a dozen years before.

Close-fitting spun aluminium water excluders were riveted to the brake back plates of all except the earliest Series B machines, and these are invaluable for keeping the brakes dry and effective. From 1952, a water excluder was added also on the left-hand rear drum, except on Series D models which had only a single, sprocket-side rear brake, to which a small deflector was added. In compensation the Series D drum was made of ribbed cast iron to maintain braking efficiency.

WHEELS & TYRES Simpler and lighter die-cast light-alloy hubs were adopted post-war compared to the complex Series A bolted-up design, and these were no longer interchangeable, as the rear one was made wider to strengthen the resulting spoke pattern. Both wheels used identical ⅜in id Timken (or SKF) taper-roller bearings which have a very long life, but should be shimmed — on the hollow axle — with a very small clearance to allow for expansion of the alloy hubs. Early bearings were 0.848in wide (K09074/K09196) but later changed to 0.75in (K09067/K09195); the later type can be used in the earlier wheel with appropriate spacers, as indeed the factory did. The rare metric bearings, fitted temporarily in 1951 during the Korean crisis shortages, cannot be replaced with Imperial-size bearings, as both hub and hollow axle were specially machined to suit.

Pressed steel spoke flanges featured keyhole-shaped piercing, which permitted individual spokes to be replaced without dismantling the wheel, and a four-cross spoke pattern was always used by factory wheel-builders. The ⅜in by ⅜in Renold chain ran on the 'wrong' side of the machine — because of the cross-over gearbox — to a sprocket bolted to the brake drum flange. Some machines were supplied with an alternative sprocket size on the other side, enabling a quick change to be made from solo to sidecar gearing by

Vincent handlebars originally were black-enamelled, not chromium-plated like many modern replacements. Alloy knob in the middle operates the steering damper and should be set just biting. Exhaust valve lifter lever on the left bar must be carefully positioned if it is not to chip the tank's paintwork on full left lock.

Duo-brakes (far left), with plain drums very similar to pre-war pattern, were used on B and C Rapides, but simpler construction of hub, cast in light alloy, was devised. Polished spun-aluminium water excluders, seen here, were added early in Series B production to help keep rain out of the brakes. D Rapide had a single rear drum (left) of ribbed Shadow pattern, attached by 10 bolts; standard 40-hole four-cross spoke pattern is clearly visible.

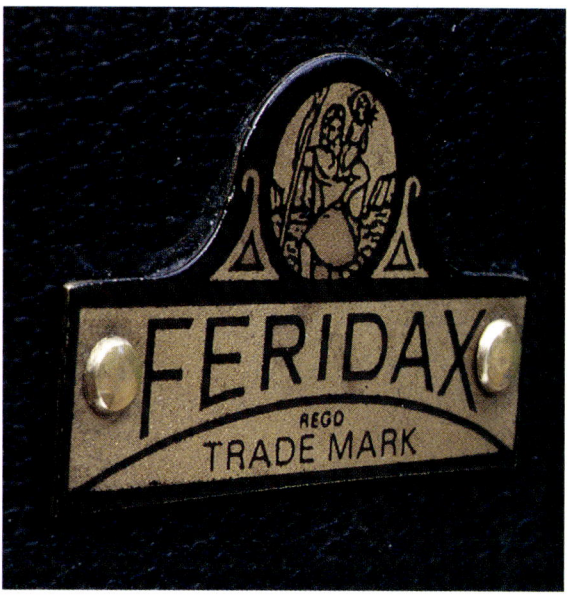

A dualseat, supplied by accessory manufacturer Feridax, whose trademark is printed on the rear of this example, was a novelty in 1946 but within a few years had almost completely replaced the mattress saddle throughout the motorcycle industry. Feridax sometimes marked their product with a riveted-on metal label, either a plain rectangular item or this more elaborate version (above right). Sometimes their name or trademark was printed on the cover instead, and sometimes no trademark appeared at all. Under the seat of B and C models is the slide-in tool tray (below) accommodating large, small and tube spanners, screwdrivers, pliers, greasegun and tyre levers. The two special spanners are 'K1' (in tray, for inspection caps) and 'K3' (foreground, for steering head and exhaust nuts). The tyre pump fitted separately in lugs under the petrol tank.

reversing the wheel and inserting extra chain links as necessary. Early Bs had a noticeably wider chainguard than the more usual 1¼in width version supplied thereafter, but whether this was simply due to a change of supplier or to secure a little more tyre clearance is not known.

Dunlop 3.00-20in front and 3.50-19in rear tyres were the standard size for B and C series, except for Argentina where Cimic requested equal-size 3.50-19in wheels front and rear, which became the standard for that country in 1948. Series D models adopted fatter 3.50-19in and 4.00-18in wheel sizes, for increased comfort, and no doubt because the 20in size was already becoming obsolescent by 1954. Avon tyres were always fitted to Series D models by the factory, which selected the ribbed Speedster for use on the front wheel and the studded Supreme on the rear – except for a number of machines sent to Elder Smith in Melbourne who requested the bikes to be dispatched without tyres, tubes or batteries. The modern H-rated Avon Speedmaster is a suitable replacement in looks and performance for the front tyre, and one of very few available in 20in size. The corresponding SM MkII is suitable for the rear, but cosmetically bears less resemblance to the original Supreme than some other tyres available in 19in and 18in sizes. Another popular replacement for the rear tyre, also from Avon, is the Roadrunner AM21 in 100/90 or 110/90 sections (the latter a tight fit which may not prove practical under Touring mudguards), and the equivalent AM20 front (in 90/90 H 19 size) can be used on Touring and Series D models, with their smaller front wheels.

The normal finish for the 40-hole Dunlop rims was chrome with black cellulose centres (an area difficult to polish and plate), and ³⁄₃₂in wide red lines delineating the boundary. The pattern is a throwback to the veteran era of motorcycling when rim brakes were used which could not be permitted to bear on

enamel. There were exceptions to this finish, with some US dealers requesting plain chrome, and in 1952, during the Korean war which resulted in a nickel and chrome shortage, when rims were finished in plain black, with red lines. Spokes of 10swg (front) and 9swg (rear) were normally used, plain or butted as available, and zinc-coated with cadmium-plated steel nipples. The more common plated brass nipples have proved to be perfectly satisfactory, but the plain spokes are too light, and butted ones are currently difficult or impossible to find, so heavier plain spokes in 9swg and 8swg have often been supplied as replacements. Stainless steel spokes and rims have also made an appearance on the replacement market but were never available during the life of the marque.

SEAT, MUDGUARDS & FUEL TANK A dual seat, shaped like a double saddle, was still a very novel idea in 1946. The seat was manufactured by accessory makers Feridax rather cheaply in plywood, with a strip-metal mounting frame underneath, Dunlopillo foam filling and a Rexine covering. At least two patterns of Rexine fabric were used, the earlier type having a coarser pattern, and variations also existed in the cut and stitching pattern.

The dual seat was supported at the front from a pivot formed by a stud and spacer running in a UFM cross-tube. At the rear, the two seat stays, provided with friction-damper linings and adjustable clamps at their lower ends, perpetuated the arrangement seen with the semi-sprung pillion seat patented in pre-war years. When Feridax attached their name to the seat, it was in the form of either a riveted plate (of which there are two patterns, the early rectangular version superseded by a later similar one, with the trademark added above) or printed lettering (which also appears to have existed in at least two patterns, with small or large letters); but some seats had no identification at all. The change to fully sprung seating on the Series

Series D seat is completely different from its predecessors. The same tapered-profile seat fitted to the enclosed Knight and Prince models, it is supported by a fully sprung rear sub-frame. Access to oil tank and Lucas regulator is by swinging the seat forward.

From their earliest days, Vincent and HRD machines utilised the Figure of Mercury emblem, representing the TT race trophy. These three styles (from the top) were used in turn on the petrol tank before 1950 (while the stylised HRD trademark was in use), between 1950-52 (using the Vincent scroll instead of the HRD legend), and after 1952 (when The Vincent HRD Co Ltd was reformed as Vincent Engineers (Stevenage) Ltd).

Variations of petrol tank exist. Usually these relate to the size of carburettor cutaway, which progressively increased as Shadow and then TT carburettors had to be accommodated. The top tank here, however, has a distinctly different profile to the standard item below it. Recovered from Argentina, it could be a local copy but detail and quality suggest it is an early hand-made tank produced before a press tool was completed.

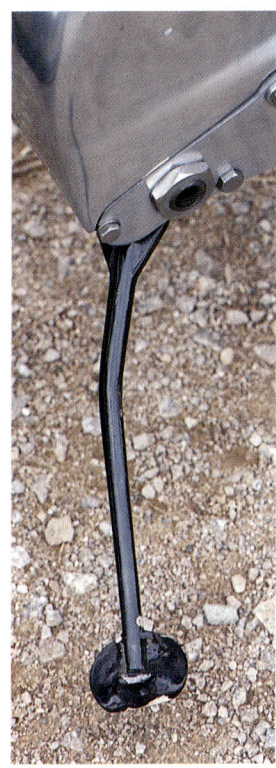

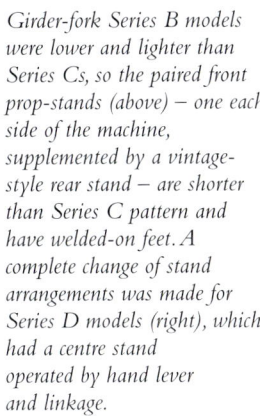

Girder-fork Series B models were lower and lighter than Series Cs, so the paired front prop-stands (above) — one each side of the machine, supplemented by a vintage-style rear stand — are shorter than Series C pattern and have welded-on feet. A complete change of stand arrangements was made for Series D models (right), which had a centre stand operated by hand lever and linkage.

D models necessitated a higher mounting, made more ugly by adapting the enclosed model's plain seat on to a simple 'after-thought' sub-frame.

On Series B and C Vincents, with no frame as such, and the RFM moving up and down, there was nowhere obvious to put the passenger's footrests. On the pre-war models this difficulty had simply been glossed over, with clamp-on footrests being supplied as optional extras, for bolting to the unsprung RFM. But a Series A passenger needed to be a hardy soul, perched on a little, square, semi-sprung pillion pad, and with his/her feet unsprung! For the Series B design the seating was much improved, and pillion footrest plates were bolted to the engine, on which fully sprung pillion footrests (and the silencer bracket) could be hung. Since Series D models had a rear sub-frame it was possible to move the pillion rests to loops formed as part of the sub-frame, making a little more room available for the centre stand mechanism.

Under the seat of B and C models a tool tray slid into runners formed from steel sheet. The normal tool kit included four large open-ended spanners (⅜in-⁷⁄₁₆in BSW, usually by Jenbro), four smaller spanners (0-3 BA, ⅛in BSW, and a magneto spanner), four tube spanners (0.92in, 1.10in, 1.30in and plug size), pliers, screwdrivers, grease gun and two special spanners. These latter are known as K1, which fits various inspection caps, and K3, which deals with exhaust-pipe nuts. For punctures, two tyre levers were provided in the tool box, with an inflator carried in lugs on the underside of the petrol tank. In the case of Series Ds, which carried a different, self-contained tool box on the rear sub-frame, the tyre pump too was carried inside the tool box.

For Rapides of all series, large-section polished alloy mudguards were specified, 5in front and 6in rear, retained by conventional tubular stays to the front forks, and rigidly mounted to the RFM with similar stays at the rear. This looked normal enough in 1946, but was *passé* when still in use on the D Rapide of 1955. As shown in the first publicity photographs, very early Series B models did not have the middle vertical stays on the rear mudguard, and support proved to be inadequate. Mudguards soon cracked and the factory had to send out modification kits for fitting by dealers; the original set-up, therefore, should not be replicated.

The substantial alloy hinge and old-fashioned drop-down rear stand enabled the rear wheel to be removed quickly, and without tools, since the wheel axle featured a tommy bar; but strength and technique are required to put the bike on to the stand. However, prop stands on both sides at the front avoided the need to use the rear stand at every stop. The shorter B prop stands (with welded-on feet) had to be replaced with longer stands to suit the higher static position of the Girdraulic-equipped C models, but, even so, the use of 'D' springs, wear of the pivots or use on steep cambers may result in excessive lean — so owners often carry a piece of wood to put under the stand foot. For the Series D, the old stands were replaced by a hand lever operated centre stand, with ordinary mudguard stays retaining the rear flap and a modified lower front mudguard stay providing a form of stand for front-wheel removal if necessary – such as for puncture repair. On the B and C front mudguard the lower stay is the shorter of the two, and its mounting lugs should be uppermost, while on the forward stay the lugs should point rearward.

Petrol tanks on early Series Bs had only a small cutaway to accommodate the front carburettor, but this was later enlarged to a standard size which would take in the larger Shadow carburettor, or even the TT instruments used on specially prepared machines, although at the cost of slightly diminished tank capacity, to 3⅓ gallons. A further modification required to the petrol tank was the fitting of two 'ears' at the lower rear to accept a stud and bracing tube to prevent resonance and cracking (from frame 2408), a modification which should be applied to pre-1948 tanks even at this late stage. The Series D tank used the same pressing and shape (for economy of tooling), but with a smaller frame cutaway and no hole for the oil tank filler, so that its capacity was increased to four gallons.

Gold leaf was used to line the tank, and drawings have been published showing the correct position for the two length-wise lines. But the D-shape border to HRD transfers appears to have been somewhat variable and is best judged from old photographs as well

On Series D machines the magneto was replaced by distributor and coil. The distributor fits in the position previously taken by the magneto, driven in the same way from the timing gears, but is protected by a cheaper, painted steel cover. Coil is crudely bolted alongside front cylinder. This machine has an additional weather shield.

In 1946 Vincent-HRD adopted the most powerful motorcycle dynamo available (right), the 50 watt 3½in diameter Miller instrument for which a cradle was cast into the crankcase, as seen here. Soon, however, they had to fall into line with other manufacturers and standardise on a 3in diameter dynamo, with consequent changes to the crankcase casting to accept a bolt-on cradle. In both cases the Miller voltage regulator cartridge was mounted directly to the top dynamo clamp. A six-volt black rubber battery, with external terminals (far right), was the standard fitting, as originally supplied by Exide. Lucas Altette horn was mounted on a spacer from one of the sidecar adapter holes. In-line connectors in the wiring are of original, finely threaded, Miller screw-together pattern, insulated with rubber sleeves.

as from faithful restorations. Three patterns of tank-top Mercury crest were used. HRD-embossed machines up to 1949 had the version with the HRD legend, then from 1950 it was changed to carry the Vincent scroll, while in 1953 it changed again to reflect the company restructuring as Vincent Engineers (Stevenage) Ltd instead of PCV's original Vincent-HRD Co Ltd. All patterns are available in a waterslide pattern which is much easier to apply than the old Gold-size type originally used.

ELECTRICAL EQUIPMENT & INSTRUMENTS

IGNITION & TIMING Lucas KD2 magnetos were used until engine 104, when the KVF type became standard. Both were equipped with automatic ignition timing adjustment provided by the magneto pinion drive automatic timing device (ATD), and post-war models therefore had no need for an ignition lever on the handlebar.

To assist the magneto in providing sparks at equal firing intervals (not ideal for a magneto), the twins utilised platinum points assemblies of slightly smaller diameter than the standard tungsten assemblies, and now harder to find. Early magnetos had equal-size 35mm bearings at both ends, but the more common later versions have a larger 40mm bearing at the drive end, no doubt adopted by Lucas for improved robustness. It is not unusual to find a magneto marked K2F

on a rebuilt machine, since there is little difficulty in converting this much more common parallel-twin magneto for vee-twin use by fitting the appropriate ring cam and slip ring. It is, however, desirable to move the safety gap screws which are on the opposite corners of the clockwise KVF from most (ie, anti-clockwise) K2Fs. The standard timing figure of 39° used for all series of Rapide equates to $^{31}/_{64}$in BTDC.

Series D Rapides were fitted with coil ignition, using a DKX2A distributor mounted where the magneto had previously been, under a sheet metal cover, and a coil on the left-hand side of the engine. KLG (the initials of Kenelm Lee Guinness, one of motoring's early pioneers) FE70 plugs were normally supplied on new Vincents; an equivalent in the more commonly available Champion range is N5 or N5C.

DYNAMO, WIRING, LIGHTS & HORN The 1946 Miller 3½in D9S 6-volt, 50-watt dynamo represented the best specification available on the British market when it was adopted for the Rapide. However, the motorcycle industry in general was not willing to redesign to this increased size, and eventually Miller had to revert to the 3in D6, while maintaining the nominal specification – no doubt making life for the smaller instrument very hard. Initially, the Vincent factory accommodated the smaller dynamo with an eccentric adapter until a revised design of crankcase with a bolt-on 3in cradle could be made available.

Separate dynamo drive, gear or chain, was avoided

The 1946, '47 and many '48 models featured an imposing 8in headlamp (below left) similar to that used on Series A models. The later 6½in headlamp (below right) for the home market came with two patterns of glass: one is a simple, coarsely fluted glass similar to that used with the 8in lamp; the other, shown here, features finer fluting (for better beam control) and the Miller diamond trademark.

by copying a layout used on Indians, in which the dynamo was mounted just above the clutch sprocket. By cutting back the middle row of teeth on the clutch sprocket, it was possible to mesh a dynamo sprocket (with odd-looking squared-off teeth) from above, 28 teeth providing a 25% increase over engine speed. The reduced contact area on the clutch sprocket was of no consequence because more than enough engaged teeth remained, but for the dynamo sprocket the reverse chain curvature put the load almost entirely on one tooth. With a correctly meshed sprocket, even this was of little consequence (the dynamo load being less than 1% of engine power), but it does become significant when trying to uprate the electrics with different generators.

The most satisfactory conversions replace the dynamo with a jack-shaft, to belt-drive a remote generator – exactly like the original Indian set-up. The

Achilles heel of the system, however, was the two-stage Miller regulator cartridge, which was neither as sophisticated as the corresponding Lucas automatic voltage control (AVC), with its integral current and temperature compensation, nor as easy to adjust. Indeed, a correct full adjustment procedure was never published in the general motorcycle press because it required factory jigs, and only a minor 'tweak' was ever described in handbooks. All too often, therefore, the AVC controlled too much or too little, and the hard-pressed Exide battery gradually boiled or went flat. Even on a restoration, it is advisable to convert the system to utilise either the Lucas AVC, or an electronic regulator which can often be hidden in an original Miller cartridge housing. This also enables the inside of the dynamo to be simplified by removal or bypassing of its internal cut-out, and most Vincent Miller dynamos have been so modified. Many have

Headlamp switch (above left) is a throwback to the days of third-brush dynamos and features a charge (CH) position which has no effect (ie, duplicates OFF) because battery charging is automatically controlled. Switch lever is awkward to reach on Series B models, with speedometer centrally placed on Brampton forks. Series D adopted a completely different headlamp (above): an 8in Lucas housed both lighting and ignition switches (left and centre respectively), ammeter with integral ignition warning light (right), and a revised 120mph Smiths speedometer.

Stop light (far left) as a standard fitting was another forward-looking feature in 1946, but illumination is poor in both 'stop' and 'tail' halves. Removing the internal separator helps a little, but basically the stop light cannot be brought up to modern standards. Earliest round pattern of stop light switch by Miller (left) incorporated its own mounting bracket; this 1946 machine does not have the forward mudguard stay to which the later switch was fitted.

The Rapide's 3in diameter Smiths chronometric 120mph speedometer (above) was moved to the top of the right-hand Girdraulic fork leg on Series C models. This position also improved accessibility to the headlamp switch, fitted in this case with the later streamlined lever. Export models could be fitted with a speedometer calibrated in kilometres; this 180kph version (right) was the equivalent of the 120mph instrument.

also been converted to 12-volt systems able to power modern quartz-halogen lamps by adoption of specialist regulators (such as the JG or KTec which persuade original 6-volt dynamos from Miller or Lucas to generate current safely at 12 volts.

Series D Rapides were fitted as standard with the 'long' 3in Lucas E3L 60-watt dynamo, using slightly modified drive components to adapt to the parallel instead of taper shaft, and with the RB107 regulator, but many of these too have been converted to 12 volts. A change of bulbs and, in the case of a D, of the ignition coil is required for 12-volt use, but normally the horn can be retained although it should be re-adjusted to prevent overheating through excessive current consumption.

The original horn on Series B and C models was the Lucas Altette, type HF1234, fitted on the left pillion footrest plate. A number of variations of this design exist, originally with the adjuster at the rear, a locknut being introduced in 1951, at which time some non-adjustable horns were also made; and later in the 1950s the adjuster was moved to the front of the horn, under the central dome nut. The exact pattern of the chrome surround dome nuts also varied. On Series D models, a smaller Lucas HF1441 horn was bolted behind the steering head lug where it cannot easily be seen.

Wiring on the magneto-equipped motorcycles was very simple, and few connectors were needed, but the original Miller connectors were delicate, and presumably expensive, devices. Fabricated from 8mm AF brass, the two halves were threaded ⁵⁄₃₂in by 40tpi and insulated with a ½in diameter rubber sleeve; two were used in the rear light and horn wires respectively. At the dynamo a single-pin plug (blue wire) provided for disconnection, and at the battery wires could be disconnected from the terminals – red wire to the positive terminal, and negative earth (B and C series). Black hard-rubber-cased Exide 13 amp-hour batteries were standard on B and C models (the Series D adopting a 'dry' Varley battery which absorbed its electrolyte in porous separators), at first with external terminals; later patterns featured terminals under the top cover. Original wiring was rubber covered, and, for protection and neatness, the two wires to the rear lamp were threaded down either side of the mudguard stay/lifting handle and under the hinge. The coil ignition D Rapide had a more complex wiring system (not correctly illustrated in many of the published diagrams), a positive earth electrical system, and Lucas bullet-type connectors.

Early Bs had the large and imposing Miller 8in diameter headlamp with fluted glass. This was changed in 1948 for a 6in lamp, smaller than the Lucas 7in lamp of the period but nevertheless sometimes referred to as 7in; to add to the confusion, this headlamp actually measured 6½in. Most of the smaller lamps had a coarsely fluted glass, but some late editions had a finer pattern with the Miller insignia moulded into the centre. For many export markets a slightly larger Miller 7in shell fitted with a narrower split rim was supplied, and would accept more readily available lighting units such as the Lucas F700 or American GE equivalent. Many US export models were delivered with a sealed-beam light unit; this should not be confused with the 1950s Lucas sealed-beam units which used separate fixed-focus flanged bulbs and were properly described as pre-focus units.

All Miller headlights contained the ammeter and the robust Bakelite Miller lighting switch with its inoperative 'CH' position, left over from the pre-war third-brush charging control systems. Early switches featured a small pointer and square lever design, which changed to a more symmetrical and streamlined pattern on later items. The early ammeters sometimes simply had the Miller 'Lighthouse' symbol, but more commonly they bore a legend giving rate-of-charge information about the controlled charging system.

With the Series D Rapides, the factory changed over to Lucas equipment, adopting that company's 8in headlamp (reverting to the early B lower headlamp stay size to support it) and matching Lucas switch and ammeter. The large headlamp was also able to accommodate the 120mph Smiths speedometer, which remained very similar to the B and C fitting, with a trip spindle extended out of the back of the shell through a grommet. A stepped rim (Lucas part 553453) accepted the 7in Lucas F700 pre-focus light unit. Headlamp shells were always painted to match the machine – usually black, of course.

At the rear, all B and C models featured the round Miller 30E rear lamp with chromium-plated 'STOP' bezel. This was an innovation at the time, but its twin-bulb divided construction resulted in an even smaller illuminated area of rear lamp than was provided by the single-bulb equivalent, which means that most original lamps have, at the least, been converted by removal of the divider, application of light-coloured paint and sometimes a change of bulb-holder to accept more modern combined stop/tail bulbs. For night riding, a larger lamp is desirable, such as the Lucas 564 used on the D Rapide. Three types of stop switch exist, although the early Miller circular switch used on the first few hundred Rapides is now almost impossible to find. Most common is the square Lucas part fitted by two 2BA screws, one to the rear mudguard stay and the other into a specially tapped frame bolt. The Series D, however, adopted a switch on the front fork bridge plate, operated by movement of the balance beam, so providing the front brake activation of the stop light which many owners had requested.

SPEEDOMETER & DRIVE The standard speedometer fitting was a 3in diameter 120mph Smiths S433/3/L but export models often had the equivalent metric 180kph head marked S433/7/L. A pressed, T-shape bracket retained the instrument on Brampton

Right-angle speedometer gearbox is driven by a gear pressed on to the wheel hub, protected but unlubricated, inside the right-hand front brake drum. Note the peg behind the wheel nut which prevents it from turning when the tommy-bar spindle is tightened or loosened. A spanner is not needed and should not, in normal circumstances, be used on Vincent wheel nuts.

forks by a pair of ⁵⁄₁₆in bolts – longer bolts will touch the spindle and lock up the forks! The bracket both raised and angled the speedometer for improved visibility and clearance around the headlamp, but period photographs suggest that a plainer, flat bracket may also have been used. On Series C models a simpler bracket made of two steel strips retained by a bolt on top of the blade, and the spindle-padbolt nut on the front, secured the speedometer head to the right-hand Girdraulic fork blade. On Series D Rapides the speedometer head was mounted into the headlamp, retained by a U-shaped bracket.

Series B and C fork mountings required a 25in cable, but the D headlamp mounting called for a longer 27½in cable. In all cases, a 1.5:1 right-angle gearbox (Smiths part 25971) affixed to the right-hand front brake plate took its drive from a pair of unlubricated gears inside – a very vintage arrangement improved slightly by being inside the brake drums, away from rain and grit. Modern replacement nylon pinions wear much better than the original steel ones in this situation, and they also fail more 'gracefully' in the event of a problem such as a seized speedometer drive gearbox (which usually occurs through lack of lubrication).

OPTIONAL SPECIFICATIONS

LUGGAGE EQUIPMENT Special pannier equipment *was* produced to fit all B and C models, but in fact little of it saw light of day and original or reproduction examples are extremely rare. The design utilised under-seat pivot blocks to take the weight, and links between the pannier frame and RFM to provide the rest of the stability and to maintain a sprung installation, even in the absence of a fixed rear frame section to which attachments could be made. The detachable cases were leather-covered (although Rexine-covered

Touring specification, originally developed for Argentina, was often ordered for American customers, as well as being popular in the UK. This Series C Touring Rapide is an export model, and has the 7in headlamp with sealed-beam light unit which uses a slightly narrower chromium rim than home market lamps.

examples also exist) and were tapered to provide a neat set-up, with the weight low and well forward. The resulting capacity was quite small, yet it was still often necessary to use heavily cranked alternative footrest pieces to provide enough room for the pillion passenger's feet. Few such sets of equipment were ever fitted and they quickly became obsolescent.

A larger-capacity pannier set was devised in 1953, and was described by Service Manager Paul Richardson in *Vincent Motorcycles*. The arrangement was reputedly so ugly that the factory's Ted Hampshire refused to fit the panniers when preparing show bikes, and few, if any, were sold. Most owners chose instead to buy proprietary equipment, most popular being Craven Silver Arrow panniers, mounted higher and further back on specially developed Craven articulated frames, which also provided an integral rear carrier facility.

TOURING SPECIFICATION A number of importers demanded special specifications, larger section tyres often being required. The first use of larger steel valanced mudguards is thought to have been at the request of Argentine authorities, after which a Touring specification alternative to the standard was listed for all roadgoing models prior to the introduction of Series D machines.

Touring specification included 3.50-19in WM2 front and 4.00-18in WM3 rear wheel sizes, shod with Avon Speedster and Supreme tyres, as with the standard sizes. Larger section and deeply valanced mudguards were fitted front and rear, requiring wider versions of the standard mudguard stays. A further variation of handlebar was evolved for the touring specification, still in black enamel, but wider, and with a conventional raised bend, to be known by the works as 'cowhorn' pattern. These bars required a longer throttle cable but otherwise interchanged with the standard bars.

Overall weight was increased by about 15lb with the Touring components fitted. In the 1948 catalogue the Rapide model fitted with the 7in split-rim headlamp and full Touring equipment was referred to as 'The export model'.

ACCESSORIES Few accessories were listed, but among these was a Feridax locking twistgrip which was available from 1954 but rarely taken up because the problem of motorcycle theft was still relatively uncommon in Britain. Feridax was very active in promoting a range of accessories; their simple Perspex-blade screens were advertised in the general motorcycle press, and in the Vincent Owners Club magazine (MPH), with the result that a number of touring and commuting machines were so equipped by their owners. Vokes air filters were also listed as an option by the works, again rarely taken up in the damp climate of Britain but of more relevance to dustier overseas markets.

SIDECARS Provision for sidecar fitting had figured highly in the design of the post-war Rapide, and indeed many were so fitted at home and abroad, from sleek sports 'chairs' to large double-adult family transport 'coachbuilt' models (a euphemism for simple plywood-constructed bodies). Vincent-HRD listed a sports sidecar in its 1949 catalogue, available in both left- and right-handed versions, for home and foreign customers in countries driving on the right (there were still many countries driving on the left in 1949). The sidecar, not of Vincent's manufacture, was the Blacknell Bullett Sports model normally listed at £83 12s 6d and supplied by sidecar makers Blacknell Sidecars Ltd (of Albert Avenue, New Nuthall, Notts).

COLOURS The great majority of Series B, C and D Vincents were finished in plain black, with gold lining and transfers – a contrast to the earliest models of 1928 which PCV had presented in green with nickel-plated frame or alternatively with a purple and cream tank. He had then learned from experience that motorcyclists could be very conservative people. However, some 'foreigners', especially Americans, were a little more flamboyant, and requested special finishes.

Enough Series C machines were supplied in a 'Chinese Red' finish for this to be regarded as a standard specification, but on request other paintwork finishes were produced, including blue and two-tone black and red. Precisely what colour was Chinese Red? Du Pont Centari Flame red (code NAV2346), a strong scarlet colour, is often recommended, but one original colour photograph I have seen suggests a slightly deeper red.

The enamelling shop normally dipped items to be painted, but this was confined to the standard black finish. When other colours were specified, they had to be applied by spraying because there was not enough demand to justify tanks of coloured paints. Some dealers also demanded extra chromium plating, such as on plain plated wheel rims, while Chilean importer José Amat persuaded PCV to supply machines with chromium-plated petrol tanks.

Some machines were also prepared to a 'show finish', although it seems unlikely that this in fact described one particular standard. Rather, it is likely to have meant extra attention to the matching of covers, extra polishing, and chromium plating of parts more usually finished in cadmium. 'Show finish' models were prepared not only for the annual Earls Court industry show, but also for dealers at home and abroad, no doubt with varying amounts of attention, according to the particular member of staff preparing the bike and the individual dealer's influence. There would thus have been quite a number of motorcycles produced with this extra attention to detail each year.

The Vincent was designed specifically with sidecars in mind. A four-point fitting was normally used, and a popular arrangement featured ball joints at both lower mountings, as seen on this Rapide. Long eyebolts for the top mountings could be used in lugs built into the UFM.

Home market machines required a holder for the licence (tax) disc. The standard item was this simple accessory from Miller, the electrical system makers.

'Chinese Red' was the only common variation from black finish ever specified and was almost exclusively supplied to the American market. Deep mudguards, fatter tyres and raised handlebars (known at the works as 'cowhorns') gave an appropriate look that was frequently specified for the US market, particularly after the tie-up with the Indian Sales Corporation of Springfield. The Black Shadow speedometer would not have been an original fitting on this Rapide.

BLACK SHADOW

Early in 1947 two special Rapides were prepared, listed as 'HRD racing combination' and 'HRD racing solo'. The first was built for Jack Surtees, father of World Champion John Surtees, and fitted with customer-supplied carburettors, handlebars and an oversize 4.00-18in Dunlop rear tyre.

Both machines had modified engines, with 1⅛in carburettor adapters, triple (instead of dual) valve springs, extensive polishing of connecting rods and cases, and so on, and both had stripped cycle parts, including cut-down mudguards, and the stands removed. The solo version (engine 71) additionally had lightened flywheels and was to remain a works bike raced very successfully by George Brown,

together with his existing works 500cc 'Speedway'-engined racer which, although also very successful, did not look like anything that the factory had on sale. Christened 'Gunga Din', the solo, F10AB/1A/71, was completed on 3 April 1947, but the precise completion date of Jack Surtees' bike was not recorded, although it was delivered just a few days later, on the 14th. Because of the extensive modifications, the engines of both machines were given the modified number 1A to distinguish them from the standard Rapide (type number 1). The 1A symbol later came to be known as White Shadow although originally meaning 'modified Rapide'.

Gunga Din went on to be the prototype develop-

JRO 102 is the original road test Black Shadow tested by Charles Markham in Motor Cycling in May 1948. Top speed was recorded as 122mph, but of the average speed over a 360-mile trip, Markham wrote, 'I dare not print'. It has survived for almost half a century, and has been returned to a very high level of originality in the hands of arch enthusiast Bob Culver.

For its road test report published in April 1948, The Motor Cycle *sent Editor Arthur Bourne and JRO 102 on a 2400-mile tour across the Alps to Italy. Problems reported were failure of the drive to the new 5in 150mph speedometer and difficulty in starting if the engine was flooded. The tester reported, 'It is a magnificent motorcycle'. Current owner Bob Culver thinks so too, and to prove it he repeated Bourne's trip 40 years later.*

ment bike for both the Black Shadow and the later racing Black Lightning. The Surtees engine, too, appears to have had an interesting life, starting off in frame R2069 but later being rebuilt, again as a very special engine, this time with close-ratio gears, and installed in frame 2690, which went to Chilean José Amat in April 1948. The engine, originally number 70, appears to have been renumbered F10AB/1A/700 at the time, an interesting example of the factory being first even in 'fiddling' numbers with the crafty extra zero – one wonders whether Amat knew it was a 'recycled' engine?

The prototype Black Shadow bore engine number F10AB/1B/558 in frame R2549, and was completed on 16 February 1948. According to reference books, Black Shadow frame numbers are suffixed with a B, but this appears not to have happened until a little later. Similarly, although the name Black Shadow was adopted for the new model, advertising remained confused for some time as to whether this was its full name. The new Girdraulic-equipped version was described in the 1948 catalogue as the 'Series C Rapide Black Shadow model', and other variations of naming were used in advertisements of the time.

The first Black Shadow was road tested by Charles Markham in *Motor Cycling* in May 1948 and was reported as having achieved 122mph, compared with the factory's claimed top speed of 125mph (other road tests obtained similar speeds, between 122mph and 128mph). This machine later caught fire, but although reported as 'burned out', the damage was not very serious. It was rebuilt by Ted Hampshire at the works for his own use, sold on later, and still survives.

ENGINE & TRANSMISSION

ENGINE Engine modifications for the Black Shadow were relatively minor, involving larger carburettors, higher compression ratio pistons, some additional polishing of internal components and, on earlier models only, an additional (third) inner valve spring inside the standard springs. However, the evidence accruing was that the additional spring poundage was unnecessary, and merely increased loading (and wear) of the cams and valve gear, so the fitting of triple valve springs was dropped.

The combination of better spring materials, and the isolated spring chamber which Vincent's twin valve guide arrangement provided, had beaten the

overheating problems which had dictated the use of exposed hairpin springs on the Series A Rapides (and various other high-performance machines). The cams were standard Rapide type, MkI at first, and then modified-contour MkIIIs – with quietening ramps – from 1952. Production cams were routinely checked and those showing 'longer' timings with larger overlap were set aside for Black Shadows, leaving the remainder to be fitted to Rapides. From the introduction of the Black Shadow, therefore, it could be argued that fewer exceptional Rapides were likely to have left the factory.

Big ends too were nominally the same as on the Rapide, but slightly differently executed. All the existing parts were used, the same built-up crankshaft – with long crankpin and side-by-side rods – enabling the cylinders to be offset for cooling of the rear cylinder and providing clearance for its forward-facing exhaust port. The factory, however, obviously did not expect such careful running-in from Black Shadow owners as from Rapide owners, and called up different clearances in the big ends of the two models. In order to produce assemblies to close limits, without making parts production excessively difficult and expensive, many components were manufactured and then graded according to size, upon inspection. Tables

Black Shadows are much more common in Series C than Series B form because the Girdraulic forks and C specification were introduced in the same year as the new model. However, shortages of new parts, and the C's raised price, resulted in Series B Shadows continuing alongside new Series Cs through 1949.

listed the gradings which could be used. In the case of Black Shadow big ends, fewer permutations were allowed, giving slightly finer control of clearances, although those clearances were actually larger than average on the Rapide assemblies. Rockers, connecting rods and other parts were polished before assembly into Black Shadows, although the evidence is that this extra finishing was carried out more often, on more parts and more enthusiastically on earlier models than on later ones.

The other major item which changed inside the engine was the piston. Rapides were fitted with a nominal 6.8:1 Specialloid piston with extensive radial ribbing supporting the piston crown (Vincent part number E7/6), although engines were usually fitted with compression plates that reduced the compression ratio to 6.45:1. For the Black Shadow model a higher compression 7.3:1 Specialloid piston was specified (part number E7/7), but on 72-octane petrol this made the engine prone to pinking unless careful throttle control was exercised, a problem which gradually disappeared as petrol quality improved. Special-

loid pistons carry the maker's name in relief on the sides under the gudgeon pins.

Later after-market replacement pistons from Hepolite, popular in the 1950s and '60s, generally replicated original Specialloid parameters, but have short cast-in slots either side of the gudgeon pin holes and no ribs internally. Early versions had narrow slits cut between the slots, but the reduced support and heat path led to distortion; later pistons were supplied without the slits and were perfectly satisfactory. When Specialloid and Hepolite versions became obsolete, Omega pistons were developed to fill the gap, and were normally available only in 7.3:1. Like the Hepolites, these were machined all over externally, but without slots, and provided internally with two ribs to support the piston crown. These too have ceased production, and have been replaced by Omega-manufactured die-cast pistons colloquially called 'Kempalloids', after Ron Kemp who helped develop and market them. Produced in more modern LM13 alloy, and with narrow compression rings, these pistons run with closer clearances than their predecessors and

All-black finish and the big 5in speedometer make the Black Shadow instantly recognisable. Series C specification was introduced late in 1948 and the change from HRD to Vincent trademark occurred late in 1949 – so, for the year between, Cs continued to be supplied badged as HRDs.

It was often said that a rear view was all that most road-users could expect to see of a Black Shadow in its heyday. The large speedometer placed centrally in front of the rider was claimed to be easier to read, and to distract the rider's view ahead for a shorter time. Imposing appearance for the new sports model was ensured by the black finish of the engine/gearbox unit (right). Superior cooling was claimed for the black finish, but the thickness and polish of the paintwork meant there was probably little difference. Die-cast timing cover in 1949 still bears the HRD legend but has hidden oilways and smoother contours than earlier sand-cast version.

have better oil-control rings for improved oil consumption. Omega manufactured 'Kempalloid' pistons are available only as 7.3:1.

All modern petrols exceed the octane rating of Pool on which Vincents originally had to run, or even the 80-octane Pool replacement, and so the Black Shadow's 7.3:1 ratio makes good sense for any Vincent engine – although a few Rapide owners like the flexibility of a lower ratio.

The last major, and rather dramatic, aspect of the Black Shadow engine was the overall black finish of its crankcase, covers, cylinders and heads. The process consisted of 'pyluminising', which was a chromate anti-corrosion and primer finish, over which stove enamelling was carried out using Pinchin & Johnson enamel at 200°F for two hours. In practice, it proved possible to utilise castings of poorer finish on the more expensive Black Shadow models because there was more opportunity to dress and fill underneath the

paintwork. Although it was argued that the black finish improved heat dissipation of the higher performance engine, the primary advantage of the finish was its visual impact, ensuring that the Black Shadow would remain memorable, even though not all the factory staff had supported the idea initially.

FUEL SYSTEM & CARBURETTOR Together with the increased compression ratio, the Black Shadow's performance improvement was primarily obtained by installing larger 1⅛in Amal 289 series clip-fitting carburettors. Cylinder heads remained the same, apart from blending and polishing of the ports for improved

Bare Black Shadow crankcases (above left) clarify details such as cylinders and heads being retained by long through-bolts. Large circular 'door' behind clutch allows gear cluster to be withdrawn without splitting case. Crankshaft (above) is a conventional built-up assembly with integral flywheels similar to most singles. Longer crankpin takes side-by-side con rods, and drilling is required to balance rod and piston assemblies. This knife-edge rig is used for checking balance. Different pistons (left) have been available over the years. From left, original Specialloid, after-market Hepolite, Omega and 'Kempalloid' (die-cast).

Rear carburettor installation (above), a 1⅛in Amal 289, looks indistinguishable from that of the humbler Rapide, as it uses identical float chambers, taps and fuel lines. The important cross stud, which braces ears at the rear corner of the petrol tank, is just visible. Except for some early models and Series Ds, most Black Shadow front carburettors (above right) were brass bodied, as on the single-cylinder Comet. It was not originally so obvious as in this view of a polished body, because Amal carburettors were supplied with a silver-painted finish.

gas flow, but to accept the 289 carburettors the alloy Rapide flange-to-clip adapters were replaced by new bronze adapters able to accommodate the larger bore size. Front carburettor numbers were 289M/1DO (early) or 229E/1DV (late), and the rear was 289N/2DS. Note that the first part of the number refers to the mixing chamber, including the particular jetting, while the second part refers to the float chamber. A rebuilt carburettor or one built from spares may now therefore carry the right numbers and have almost every part wrong, or carry the wrong numbers and be completely right.

As with early Rapides, the early Shadows were fitted with two right-handed carburettors, because there was not a suitable left-handed version in the Amal range at the time. This was soon corrected by Amal who supplied the appropriate pattern manufactured in brass, which remained as the finish throughout production. Presumably the small number of users

of this pattern and size of carburettor never justified preparation of the die required for the normal zinc-alloy casting, and so it remained sand-cast in brass throughout its life. The rear carburettor, like both Rapide instruments, was in the normal zinc-alloy die-casting, but both zinc and brass instruments were supplied by Amal in a painted silver-sheen finish that was very thin and soon wore through. Many are now polished in the base metal, but the original finish is easily seen on old carburettors in places where cleaning rags rarely reach, such as just above the mixing chamber nut or under the throttle-stop screw, albeit no doubt yellowed by age and petrol contamination.

Series D Black Shadows were fitted with the integral float-chamber Amal Monobloc carburettors in 1⅛in size (type 389/10). These flange-fitting carburettors required different adapters and fuel lines from their predecessors – the same items used on the enclosed Black Prince model (see page 108); fuel lines

Few Black Shadows used the early complex gearchange linkage. The works followed private owners in changing to a simple lever directly mounted to the gearchange shaft (left). Fine serrations for setting the angle, and alternative foot-piece holes for reach, ensured adequate adjustment to follow any alteration in footrest setting. Girdraulic forks (below) incorporate a friction steering damper similar to that fitted to the earlier Brampton forks. This single-plate design was improved in 1953 with a twin-plate modification. The eccentric is in the solo position, but a simple adjustment will convert the forks for sidecar use; in contrast, Bramptons required extensive work, a replacement spring and shorter fork links to effect the same change.

Black Shadow rear suspension was unaltered from that of the Rapide. Cadmium-plated rear spring box inners became standard when the Black Shadow was introduced, but modern restorers often chromium-plate the inners or adopt replacement items in polished stainless steel.

and taps were also common with those on the Black Knight model. Vokes air filters, of a rather crude triangular pattern, were only available on the open D models such as the Black Shadow because they would not fit under the cowlings of the enclosed variants.

GEARBOX & CLUTCH Altered layshaft first gear and double-gear pinions raised the bottom gear ratio from 9:1 to 7.2:1, giving overall ratios of 3.5:1, 4.2:1, 5.5:1 and 7.2:1, which the factory referred to as 'intermediate ratios'. After mid-1951 (from engine 7076), the Black Shadow reverted to the lower ratio, because it eased pulling away for solo riders, and was much more suitable for pulling sidecars, to which a surprising number of Black Shadows were hitched.

Although early teething troubles had been overcome with improvements to the cam-plate contours and notches, the gearbox was still a little prone to 'over-changing' when changes were rushed, as sporty riders were inclined to do. Drilling the cam-plate (G32/3AS) reduced its inertia and provided a worthwhile improvement, and so this modification was carried out on the Black Shadow. The heavy clutch also affected the gearchange, and for the Shadow the clutch shoe carrier (C3/1) was drilled, and occasionally the pawl carrier actuator too (G66/1AS).

Handlebar layout of the Vincent, from left: clutch and exhaust valve lifter, dipswitch, twin air levers (choke), front brake and throttle twistgrip. Twin-pull twistgrip is a popular modification, but the original layout used a normal single-pull twistgrip and junction box under the tank. Drilled steering damper knob is also a minor modification; it saves no weight, but does improve hand grip a little.

CYCLE PARTS

FRAME, STEERING & SUSPENSION No changes were made, or considered necessary, to the basic frame structure for the higher performance model, although attention was given to improving the braking. The works favoured a rather light 160lb spring on the Series B Rapide Brampton forks, but for the Black Shadow models they often fitted the heavier – and more suitable – 180lb spring.

BRAKES & WHEELS Although the Rapide's brakes were excellent by the standards of the day, braking was the one area where the works considered that improvement should be made, to suit the extra performance of the Black Shadow model. After all, the 7in duo-brakes had been originally developed for a range of mid-1930s 500cc singles. In particular, anti-fade properties would be more tested by the high speeds expected of the Black Shadow, and so more heat dissipation was required than even the existing duplicated drums provided. The same basic layout was retained (and thus most of the same parts in production), but with new ribbed cast iron drums all round to stiffen the action and increase both the mass of metal and the surface area available for keeping the drums cool.

Unlike the Rapide drums, which are interchangeable all round (except, in some cases, for being undrilled for the rear sprocket), Shadow drums were made differently for front and rear wheels. The front drums had a smaller flange, and the rear drums a full-size flange, to accept the chain sprocket, but no rib close behind it, in order to clear the sprocket-retaining bolt nuts. Additionally, rear drums were given ten instead of five hub-mounting bolts, requiring a differently drilled hub, although the exact reason for this precaution remains obscure. Possibly there was some concern about the shock-loading strength of the cast iron drum (or even of the high-tensile hub bolts), but in fact the alloy hubs, or occasionally the drum flanges, fail before the hub bolt attachment.

A new lining material, Ferodo MR41, was also introduced on the Black Shadows as a further piece of detailed attention, together with heavier Bowdenex outers for the front brake cables.

SEAT, MUDGUARDS & FUEL TANK Although model names were commonly used in advertisements, Series B and C machines did not carry any model indication in transfers, lining or badges; the Black Shadow's all-black power unit was statement enough to distinguish it from the humble Rapide. When the 1955 Series D Black Shadow was introduced, however, the figure of Mercury transfer on the top of the petrol tank was joined by a transfer proclaiming 'Black Shadow', to further distinguish it from the Rapide.

Re-siting the oil tank to the side on the fully sprung seat frame of the Series D models, and the smaller UFM cutaway, increased the petrol tank's capacity to four gallons and resulted in a cleaner tank top relieved of the earlier oil filler hole and cap.

No changes were required for the seat or mudguards of the Black Shadow.

ELECTRICAL EQUIPMENT & INSTRUMENTS

IGNITION & TIMING Nominally, the Black Shadow utilised the same electrical system as its sister Rapide model. At the launch of the new sports version it was

announced that special 'laboratory tested' Lucas magnetos would be used, and indeed early engine build sheets confirm that this was the case, with individual magneto numbers being recorded. From the first two special engines and the prototype, all Black Shadows received the KVF magneto even though Rapides were still being built with the KD2 type, but the KVF soon became standard throughout production.

Timing recommendation for the Shadow was marginally altered to 38° from the Rapide's 39° BTDC ($^{15}/_{32}$in and $^{31}/_{64}$in respectively), and was retained right through production to the Series Ds equipped with coil ignition.

DYNAMO, WIRING, LGHTS & HORN The prototype Black Shadow was fitted with a smaller 3in diameter Miller D6 dynamo in an eccentric adapter rather than the 3½in diameter D9S standard unit. The reason for the change is not recorded but may have reflected concern about the heavy inertia of the larger unit and the attraction of a reduction in both internal mechanical stresses and drive sprocket loads which the smaller unit could be expected to exhibit, compensating for the higher engine speeds and livelier acceleration which Shadow owners would have on tap. Whatever the reason, the 3in item was the standard Black Shadow fitment, and was later adopted throughout the range either because the D6 proved as good as the D9S or because Miller discontinued the D9S, or both.

Thereafter, through B, C and D Series, the Black Shadow shared exactly the same electrical specification as its Rapide equivalent, although, having been introduced two years later than the Rapide, when the

Duo-brakes were uprated for the faster Black Shadow, with ribbed drums for better heat dissipation. Note that drums are different front (above left) and rear (above): only the fronts have the same five-hole fixing as Rapide drums, and losing one rib at the rear, with ten-hole fixing, left room for the sprocket bolts. Spokes seen on this front wheel are to the original 40-hole, cross-four pattern, but rear wheel's stainless spokes laced in a cross-three pattern are incorrect.

B and C models have twin petrol and oil filler caps (above), the oil filler neck coming through a hole in the petrol tank. Original petrol tank cap was slightly domed, manufactured by Ceandess (name stamped on the brass-work inside); original oil tank caps were usually stamped with oil recommendations. Series D Black Shadow livery (below) was the same as that of the Rapide model. To differentiate the models, the Black Shadow was given an additional tank-top transfer to augment the Mercury crest; it was the only open Vincent to declare its model identity.

Tommy bar wheel spindle, mudguard hinge and spring clips on the torque arms aid rapid rear-wheel removal. No tools are necessary, as the chain can be lifted off, although cleaner hands may result from using pliers to release the chain's spring clip. Popular Avon SM tyre is the replace-ment nearest to the original Supreme, but its zig-zag tread pattern is entirely different to the older tyre's block tread. Substantial cast aluminium mudguard hinge (right) never wears out or rots, but in salty conditions it will seize on its stud.

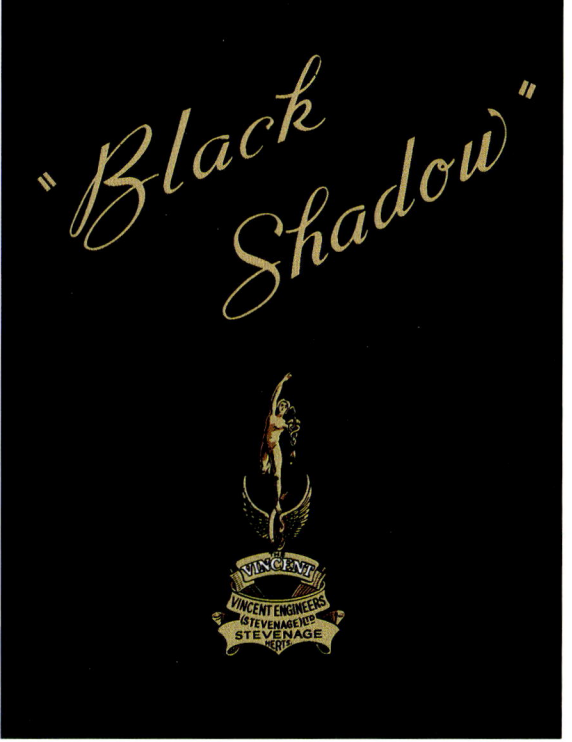

All Black Shadows used a 3in dynamo clamped in a bolt-on cradle (left). Series B and C models had the 50-watt Miller D6 seen here, Series Ds the similar 60-watt Lucas E3L unit. Black Shadow's upright speedometer (below far left) obscured the switch, but with the smaller 6½in headlamp there was room for a gloved hand. Two patterns of No. 75v ammeter exist; this type with the Miller trademark is generally the later one. Genuine Miller headlamp rims have diamond-shape Miller trademark pressed into the top. Perished insulation (left) shows this to be original rubber-covered wiring. Crude-looking bent strip wire termination is also factory original, for use with this type of outside-terminal battery. Knurled aluminium knob makes battery removal quick and easy. The square-pattern Lucas stop light switch (below left) had long replaced the round Miller item when the Black Shadow was introduced. It is attached to the forward mudguard stay by 2BA screws, the lower one screwing into a special frame bolt with a 2BA thread tapped into its head.

Two versions of the 5in 'Shadow clock', as the 150mph speedometer is known colloquially. Early type (above), now extremely rare, was housed in a deep pressed steel case and marked at 10mph intervals. Later type (above right), sleeker and more common, is housed in an aluminium casting (of which two slightly different patterns exist, to match two types of right-angle gearbox at the rear), and is marked at every 20mph – the 100mph reading beloved of 'ton-up boys' was of little consequence to the Black Shadow rider…

8in diameter Miller headlamp was obsolescent, only a small number of Shadows were equipped with that size of lamp, most receiving the 6½in lamps (or 7in export size).

SPEEDOMETER & DRIVE The crowning glory of the Black Shadow was its huge 5in diameter 150mph speedometer, a proud boast to the world of its prowess when 80mph speedometers were adequate for most 1940s motorcycles, and when the 120mph version as used on the Rapide would suffice for sports models of all makes for another 10 years or more. But Vincents wanted something better for the Shadow, the sales line being that a larger dial more directly in front of the rider was needed in order not to distract him at the high speeds he might reach.

Such large dials were in use in cars, so PEI was able to come up with a prototype fitting which, as he described in his autobiography, used a housing made from an aluminium saucepan – a typical example of Irving pragmatism! The early speedometer was indeed housed in a deep pressed steel case and had rather dense markings, but was soon replaced by the much neater type with a cast aluminium case and bold white-on-black markings at 20mph increments from 10mph to 150mph. The magic 'ton' did not even warrant a marking on the Shadow clock…

As an alternative to the Imperial 150mph speedometer (Smiths S515/L), export models could be fitted with the metric 240kph equivalent (S515/K/L). The large speedometer was centrally placed on an aluminium bracket bent up almost vertically to make the dial easy to read, similar arrangements being used on B and C models but differing in the width between mounting holes, respectively to suit Brampton and Girdraulic fork bolt centres. The position and angle required longer cables (25½in for the Series B and 27½in for the Series C), and a right-angle gearbox behind the speedometer head. The early pattern, taken from the Smiths car component list, had an exposed shaft, and gained a reputation for causing broken cables when the machine was wheeled backwards. It was replaced by a revised pattern, a miniature version of the brake plate mounted gearbox; however, earlier pattern speedometers will not accept the later gearbox without modification.

The Series D Black Shadow did not feature the 5in speedometer, having instead a 150mph version of the ordinary 3in instrument (S576/L), reflecting the fact that the internal mechanism of the two types was actually substantially the same. Fitted into the 8in headlamp with a U-clamp, just as on the Rapide model, it required the 27½in cable. A metric option

Vokes air filters (above) were listed as an optional extra; this example has come from a 1951 original and unrestored US export Black Shadow. Twin rear drums (left) enabled Vincent owners to fit alternative sprocket sizes, for a quick change of gearing (between solo and sidecar use, for example). This wheel is of mixed parentage; it could be a Rapide wheel uprated with ribbed Black Shadow drums, or a Black Shadow item rebuilt with a replacement five-hole Rapide hub. Many dealers affixed their own transfers (below) to the machines they sold, as an additional form of advertising. Conway Motors, whose dealer plate is riveted to the front mudguard of this Shadow, was one of Vincent-HRD's earliest and best known dealers, and remains so to this day.

(S576K/L) continued to be available, although few Series Ds were sold overseas. The Series D had grown portly, and probably slower than its predecessors on which more production care was lavished. The competition by 1955 boasted suspension of the quality of a Vincent's and performance at least approaching the Shadow's. With the loss of the glorious dinner plate sized speedometer, the D Shadow was only a shadow of its former self...

usually the basis for specially prepared racing or record-breaking models. Between these dates, however, a 'specially prepared' model would have been based on, and referred to as, a Black Shadow – as was F10AB/1B/900, sent to V.L. Martin in California with big carburettors and experimental MkII cams. This was the bike on which Rollie Free commenced his Vincent-mounted record-breaking, having previously used Indian machines.

OPTIONAL SPECIFICATIONS

Options for the Black Shadow models were as for the Rapide. Although the heavier Touring specification might seem anomalous on the sports version of the Vincent, it was available, and was chosen by some customers. Equally, the Black Shadow was often hitched to a sidecar, in an era when a sidecar outfit was likely to represent family transport, so the sidecar 'triangle' fitting, and larger sprocket (or indeed twin sprockets on the reversible rear wheel), would be specified. Colours and special requests would always be considered, from individuals or dealers, but it was mostly Rapides that were made in special colour schemes.

Tuned Vincent-HRDs were sometimes sold for record-breaking. Before mid-1948 these would have been called specially prepared Rapides. After the launch of the limited production racing Black Lightning model in February 1949, the Lightning was

METEOR (SERIES B)

Prototyped and shown in 1948, the Meteor did not actually enter production until late in 1949, shortly before the change to the Vincent trademark. Nevertheless, because of its short production run, most Meteors were badged as HRDs, like this example belonging to ex-factory development engineer Ted Davis.

Although there are many similarities, of course, between the post-war Meteor and Comet, I feel that these 500s, in any case inevitably overshadowed by the big-twins, deserve individual treatment in *Original Vincent*, even at the cost of some duplication in description and specification.

The Series B Meteor is a little-known, and possibly under-rated, model primarily because it was made in quite small numbers; only about 180 machines were manufactured in total. It was in the second half of 1948 that Vincent began to think about re-introducing a 500cc model. The 1946 Rapide had been joined by the Black Shadow earlier in 1948. Both were expensive, the Rapide priced at over £300 and the Black Shadow at over £400 (including purchase tax of about £75 for the former and £90 for the latter). By comparison, BSA and Triumph 650cc models cost around £200, and exotica such as the BSA Gold Star, Norton International and Triumph Grand Prix were generally between £240 and £340.

The Vincent-HRD factory had been very busy during the year, with the design of the Girdraulic fork for the Series C specification and other projects, but they were spurred on to complete the 500cc design

quickly by the reintroduction of the motorcycle show at Earls Court in 1948, where they naturally wanted to make a good impression. It would have been relatively easy to create a new version of the pre-war Comet because there was a 500cc engine available as a result of the Speedway engine project undertaken earlier in the year. The Speedway engine design consisted of a light alloy Series B cylinder and head on a modified Series A bottom end (a little more complicated than it sounds, on account of differences in the number of holding-down studs and varying cam positions), and on test it had appeared to be quite successful mechanically. Later the project foundered on marketing issues. However, the Speedway engine required a conventional frame, as used in the one-off works Cadwell racer ridden very successfully by George Brown, and Vincent did not wish to return to brazing up tubes and lugs. Such practices would not have fitted in with the firm's production facilities (or advertising), nor would they have saved money by using a large proportion of common parts with the twins. Hence a plan was evolved to design a model having a frameless construction like this twin's, with wheels, mudguards, tank and accessories, and a new

engine, all offering commonality with the twins.

As had been the case with the Series A range, a softer and cheaper Meteor was to be marketed together with a slightly more expensive and responsive Comet. But differentiating the two was something of a problem. Before the war, costs had been cut from the Meteor by omitting the pillion equipment (now integral with Vincent's post-war seat design), the speedometer (a post-war legal requirement) and the stainless steel tank panels (by 1948 Vincent tanks were all enamelled as standard); the only 'extra' that could now be omitted was the prop-stand. Something else had to be done to differentiate the Meteor and Comet models, and to justify a price difference without killing the market for the higher priced (and more profitable) model.

The decision was made that the Meteor would only be manufactured in Series B form, with the proprietary Brampton girder fork, while the Comet would adopt Series C specification, with hydraulic damping and the more expensive Girdraulic fork. Girder forks had still been commonplace on new

motorcycles in 1946 when the Rapide entered production, but most manufacturers had subsequently introduced their own telescopic designs – by 1948 girders were obsolescent. When the Meteor went into production nearly a year later its girder forks were clearly out of date, a fact which must have contributed to the model's short production run.

The first Meteor was finished very late in 1948, although exactly when is uncertain; it must have been available for the motorcycle show, but was shown as completed in the factory records *after* the date of the show. It was not uncommon for entries to be made after the event, in the case of prototypes and specials, presumably because the engineers got to work first and the books were only filled in when completed work needed to be accounted for to the money men. PEI has recorded that orders were very slow. This appears to be confirmed by the lack of attention which was given to the 500cc models, though PEI said that they slipped very easily into production. In fact, production did not start until August 1949, when there was a sales slump – a situation not helped by the

Meteor was the lower-cost version of the two 500cc single-cylinder models. It was only available in Series B form, with girder forks. A block of wood highlights the fact that the Meteor does not feature front prop-stands.

Engine unit of the 500cc singles bears a strong family resemblance to the 1000cc twins, which was an aid in both marketing and production. The distinctive diamond-shape timing cover, for example, is the twin's casting, but with rear cylinder oilways left undrilled.

Although Meteors were all Series Bs, and had only a short production run, some were made after the change of trademark. Engine number prefix F5AB/2 indicates that this Vincent-badged engine is a Meteor and not a Comet.

The Meteor engine became F5AB/2 because it was preceded by the rare Speedway motor F5AB/1. The Speedway project fell through and only a small pre-production batch was ever made, and sold off into various one-off projects. This example has been rebuilt in a speedway frame and indicates what the engine originally looked like in its intended application.

accountants insisting on a price increase which effectively killed sales. Rapides were being put into stock in buildings all around Stevenage. Although Black Shadows were not being stockpiled, this was primarily because they were being made in much smaller numbers, more or less to order only. No doubt it seemed a good time to get on with making the 500s, to see if they would sell better at lower prices than the big twins.

The first of the production Meteors was F5AB/2/2613, in frame R/1/4513, delivered to Trivellato of Brazil in a batch of machines including another three Meteors. For a while Meteor models were made in similar numbers to Comet 500s, but

Vincents considered that the lower power of the 500cc models could be adequately catered for with a proprietary gearbox (above), at a much lower cost than the factory's own limited-volume product. The latest BAP version was selected from pre-war supplier Burman. Inside the primary chaincase a proprietary five-spring Burman clutch was used. Access to the pressure-plate adjuster and spring screws was via a cover plate (above right) like that used on Series As. This plate appears to exist in three HRD variants: with and without the scroll bar over heavy lettering (usually found pre-war) and with finer lettering (usually post-war). It is not clear when each was introduced, or why.

eventually they were dropped, while the Comet continued. Perhaps the price margin was not enough, because a Meteor was still an expensive 500 at £247 13s – only £25 cheaper than the Comet. Perhaps the girder forks were just too old-fashioned to be acceptable any longer; perhaps Brampton lost interest in making the girders once the Series B models gave way to the Series C, and the quantities required by possibly their last major customer fell. And yet the Brampton girders were probably the biggest asset of the Meteor; lighter and giving a lower riding position than Girdraulics, they partially overcame the excess weight burden inevitable in adopting the cycle parts of a 1000cc twin on 500cc models.

The factory did list a Series C Meteor, illustrated in a 1950 catalogue (although the photograph shows clear marks of being retouched). I have also heard claims of ownership of a C Meteor, but I have never seen one. Only a complete trawl through factory records would reveal how many, if any, of such a model might have been produced; it would undoubtedly be a very small number. The factory would have

had little incentive to make a model with almost the same production costs as the similar Comet, but a lower selling price. It may, however, have had to fulfil orders after the supply of Brampton forks ceased, and C Meteors could have been one way to do so.

ENGINE & TRANSMISSION

ENGINE The new engine followed the design of the twin very closely, adopting the same cylinder, head and valve gear design – even the camshaft was the rear camshaft of the twin. At the bottom end, the same shafts and timing gears were adopted, with flywheels cut from the same blanks, but with smaller balance-weight areas to allow for the reduced weight of the shorter crankpin and single connecting rod and piston. The cylinder retained the same 25° forward slope as the front cylinder of a twin, to provide the same head-bracket mounting position and support the steering head and UFM.

A few minor modifications were required, such as

a shorter oil filter because the narrow crankcases provided a shorter filter housing. Rather more important changes included extra pinions in the timing case to drive the dynamo, relocated in the vacant space behind the cylinder. The same lubrication system was used as on the twins; indeed the timing cover was machined from the same casting, with the unused oilways simply left undrilled.

FUEL SYSTEM & CARBURETTOR For the soft-tuned Meteor model an Amal 1¹⁄₁₆in 176DQ/1DV carburettor was adopted, identical to the later Rapide front carburettor and fitted to the same front cylinder adapter. Amal had by this time produced the left-handed version of the 276 series, so the Meteor did not have to suffer an inaccessible throttle-stop screw on its carburettor, as had the early Rapides. Connection of the twin Ewart petrol taps to the single float chamber was achieved either by utilising a banjo with twin pipes (Vincent part A77), as shown in catalogue photographs, or an adapter (Vincent part A75) which trapped the first banjo and provided a further extension on which to fit the second banjo and usual retaining nut, double-decker fashion. Naturally, a simple single throttle cable replaced the triple cables and junction box system required on the twin-cylinder models.

GEARBOX & CLUTCH With rather less horsepower to cope with, the single-cylinder models were able to use a proprietary gearbox, as the Series As had done previously. Doing so meant lower weight and lower cost; reputedly, Burman could supply a complete gearbox at the same price that Vincent-HRD paid for a set of gearbox forgings for its own limited-production design. The unit adopted was Burman's BAP, a design widely used by other manufacturers at the time; but this does not mean that a Burman gearbox from another make of motorcycle will fit. Each manufacturer could specify a different version; variations in casing (to accommodate different pivot arrangements) and mainshaft (to match different chainlines) were the most important factors.

A conventional multi-plate clutch was also sourced from Burman, but without the shock absorbing rubber inserts previously used on Series A models, since this time the multi-spring Vincent-HRD shock absorber was being used on the engine mainshaft. Burman had improved its clutch somewhat since the Series A. Whereas the pre-war version used a four-spring steel pressure plate, the post-war version featured a five-spring cast light alloy pressure plate. Five friction plates (with fabric inserts) and six plain plates were used; these latter exist in ¹⁄₁₆in and ¹⁄₃₂in thicknesses, and the thin plates can be useful when new friction plates appear too thick.

A single-row ½in by ⁵⁄₁₆in chain sufficed for primary transmission; no tensioner was required since the separate gearbox could be moved fore and aft in

conventional fashion. Although the engine and gearbox were not of unit-construction design, the alloy primary chaincase was utilised as a stressed member, to retain frame integrity, aided by engine plates on the drive side.

CYCLE PARTS

FRAME & REAR SUSPENSION The Meteor, like the Comet, displayed some compromises in frame construction. The Rapide had been based on a frame-less design, using the massive unit-construction engine/gearbox as a stressed component. The singles, however, had a separate gearbox, and no rear cylinder

Meteor used the same 1946-pattern Brampton forks as other Series B machines and full duo-brakes front and rear. Fork spindles carry left- and right-hand threads, and the square ends allow them to be turned for adjustment of side play (until thrust washers only just spin). The lower mudguard stay doubles as an emergency front stand.

Friction damping of the Brampton forks is adjusted by this Bakelite knob (above). Tightening it tensions the spring blade under the fork link and applies pressure to friction discs under the chromed trim. Similar friction plates for the steering damper are just visible under the steering head. Two patterns of exhaust valve lifter lever were used (above right). This earlier brass type is straighter than the more common curved Bowden-supplied item; and note that it uses 3/16in Whitworth attachment screws rather than the 1BA screws found on all other levers and on the twistgrip.

to complete triangulation of two cylinders and the oil tank/UFM.

This was overcome by incorporating a bolt-in aluminium casting in place of the missing rear cylinder. The semi-tight fitting in the slotted top anchorage was not necessary, using this bolt-up construction, in the way that it had been with the hot and rigid twin engine. Engine plates bolting the engine and gearbox together would not have provided the lateral rigidity called for in the frameless construction, so a stress-bearing primary chaincase was incorporated providing support for one side of the rear fork spindle, with a conventional engine plate on the timing side. As on the twins, the designers erred on the side of caution, incorporating a steel reinforcement around the spindle anchorage to guard against risk of fatigue of the aluminium alloy chain-case casting. On the right-hand side, it was then adequate to use a conventional engine plate. The result was a design that looked just like a twin, but with the rear cylinder replaced by the alloy beam. In short, it had the desired family look.

In theory, the Meteor simply inherited the rest of its frame from the Rapide. In practice there were a few small changes required, reflected in the move from R to R/1 as the frame numbering prefix, the number appearing both on the steering head and the

left-hand rear fork lug. The same oil tank and front steering head lug were utilised, with most Meteors having the forked pattern of head lug current when they were made.

At the rear, however, some variation was caused by the change of final drive from the right-hand side to the left of the machine. A new chainguard was required, and its mounting had to be accommodated on the lifting handle – achieved simply by turning that item round. However, this compounded a brake cable problem resulting from the Meteor having adopted the longer pre-war type of footrest hanger which had no pedal and cable lugs; the repositioned chainguard occupied the position where the brake cable on the twins operated the brake cross-shaft. The prototype and earliest production singles, therefore, used a long brake pedal pivoted off the pillion footrest plates and operating the cross-shaft through a rod and linkage. This was not ideal: soon a change to the left-hand footrest hanger was made, to incorporate a cable anchorage and pivot able to accept the same pedal as used on the twin. The cable had to be longer, and operated the cross-shaft on the other (right-hand) side of the machine. This in turn meant that the Meteor's rear fork had to be slightly different from a Rapide's, with the cable anchorage on the right instead of the left. When the longer 18in RFM was adopted in 1949, a revised form of bolt-on cable anchorage was designed; its matching socket was fitted to both sides of the RFM so that this form of rear frame (with the curved seat stays) could be standardised on all 500cc and 1000cc roadster models.

Rear springs, of course, were a little lighter for the singles, using 0.276in gauge springs (121lb/in each) instead of the 0.300in (189lb/in each) springs fitted to the Rapide.

STEERING & FRONT SUSPENSION No changes were required for the front of the machine, where the same Brampton forks were used as on the B Rapide. A 160lb spring was normal for the Meteor, where it was probably more suitable than it was on the Rapides to which it was also often fitted. The 500cc model was, of course, lighter than the 1000cc; the dimensions of the primary cases and engine plates also resulted in a slightly shorter wheelbase, so the Meteor has an altogether different feel to the B Rapide, and is lighter in its steering.

WHEELS & TYRES Identical wheels and tyres were fitted to singles and twins, except that on the Meteor wheels there were no balance weights, no doubt partly because it was felt they were less important on the lower-performance model, and partly to knock off extra pennies from production costs. Naturally, the rear wheel was fitted the opposite way round (the duo-braked wheel being reversible anyway), but the same ⅜in by ⅜in Renold chain size was used. Eventually a 48-tooth sprocket became standard wear for the singles, but it appears that this did not take place immediately and early 500s, perhaps including many of the Meteors, had the same 46-tooth sprocket as the twins.

SEAT, MUDGUARDS & FUEL TANK The Meteor's seating, mudguards and petrol tank were identical to those on other models at the time. Meteors, however, were manufactured with crankcases embossed with both HRD and Vincent, so the petrol tanks too wore HRD and Vincent transfers during the short life of the model.

Although the mudguards were the same as on other models, the rear lifting handle had the chain-guard-mounting lug fitted on the opposite side from that of the twins (at least on the prototype, although the factory eventually realised that the twin's lifting handle could be used fitted the opposite way round), and the Meteor had a special lower front mudguard stay. This was a tubular type, retained by a single finger nut, and bent up to be usable as a front stand, if necessary – such as when the front wheel had to be removed for a puncture repair. This was provided because the Meteor model did not have the other models' rather complex twin prop-stand arrangement, which converts to a front stand when necessary. Omission of the front engine plates and stands also

The same QD rear wheel and hinged mudguard were specified on the Meteor as on the other models. Quick release of brake rods was ensured by use of this slotted motion block with spherical end. After slackening the wing nut a turn or two, the lever could be pushed forward by hand and the motion block pulled out. The brake rod would then drop clear.

meant that the Meteor was not fitted with the alloy magneto cowl which these items normally supported on the twins.

ELECTRICAL EQUIPMENT & INSTRUMENTS

IGNITION & TIMING A single-cylinder version of the Lucas magneto fitted to the twins was adopted for the Meteor. The model CM2 was fitted with normal tungsten (instead of platinum) points since the device did not have to produce two sparks per revolution at the odd angles of a vee-twin. Timing was set at 38° BTDC (¹⁵⁄₃₂in), as for the Black Shadow models – presumably reflecting the 6.8:1 compression ratio (compared with 6.45:1 Rapide and 7.3:1 Black Shadow figures). On the Meteor model alone, the magneto had to face the elements – mainly spray from the front wheels – naked and unprotected at the lower front of the engine.

DYNAMO, WIRING, LAMPS & HORN The smaller 3in diameter, 6-volt, 50-watt Miller D6 dynamo was adopted from the start, and the crankcases were cast to accept it behind the cylinder, driven from the timing chest by gears. With more room to spare on the singles, the battery and horn were repositioned, the former being turned sideways and the horn mounted alongside, using the rear sidecar hole in the oil tank/frame member and filling what would other-

Only on the Series B Meteor was the magneto (and oil filter cap) fully exposed to the elements (below), as a result of omitting front prop-stands, engine plates and magneto cowl assembly, in the interest of cost-saving. The Meteor used the same Smiths 120mph speedometer (below right) and central mounting bracket as the Series B Rapide, although its performance might just have been accommodated by the 80mph version. The bakelite knob above the steering head adjusts the Brampton steering damper.

wise have been a rather empty space. With adaptations to suit these new positions, the wiring system was otherwise the same as on the twin-cylinder models.

The prototype Meteor was fitted and photographed with the large 8in Miller headlamp, but it is not clear how many further Meteors used this size, as production did not start until eight months later, by which time the smaller lamp was the standard fitting throughout the range. The prototype Meteor was built without a stop lamp switch – no doubt a little more cost-saving – but it is not certain whether production Meteors were sold in this form; a different, though cheaper, lamp would have had to be stocked, and the factory C Meteor illustration (already mentioned as being an unreliable retouched photograph) did show the switch fitted.

SPEEDOMETER & DRIVE The speedometer was the same 120mph (S433/3/L) or 180kph (S433/7/L) component as used on the Rapide. Although the Meteor could barely outrun the lower 80mph versions of the almost universal Smiths Chronometric speedometer, it looked better in the showroom with the 120mph dial, and Vincent-HRD's stores did not have to stock a different type. Right-angle drive from a gear on the front hub and mounting to the Brampton fork followed Rapide practice.

OPTIONAL SPECIFICATIONS

No options were offered for the Meteor model, which had only a short production run.

COMET (SERIES C)

The Series C Comet 500 was conceived and advertised at the same time as the B Meteor, late in 1948. Although in some ways the two models were respectively half a Rapide and half a Shadow, in other respects the factory had to keep a critical eye on costs: the 500cc motorcycle market was much more hotly contested than that for 1000cc models, and buyers expected to pay much less for a 500 than for a 1000. Thus the Comet did not inherit the Shadow's ribbed brakes, and certainly not the big 5in speedometer, which remained exclusive to the Black Shadow.

In the late 1940s, as in later years when collectors began to value old motorcycles, there were people who were intimidated by the price and complexity of the bigger models. For them the single-cylinder Comet represented a much more realistic opportunity of owning a Vincent (only a few of the early Comet models were badged as HRDs). It remained an expensive motorcycle (£273 including £58 purchase tax in 1949), so it was important for the factory to maintain a de luxe specification.

The cut-down Meteor perhaps fell below the necessary standard and soon faded away. Accordingly, the Comet was equipped with the new Girdraulic forks and front prop-stands, and presented an up-to-date appearance with its dual seat, a fitting which was only just beginning to come into use on motorcycles generally. Although the Comet at 390lb was slightly heavy in comparison with rigid-frame machinery, it compared quite well with contemporary 500s which had plunger or swinging arm rear suspension – indicating, incidentally, just how effective the frameless construction had been in keeping down the weight of the powerful Rapide. The Comet's performance, with a top speed of 85-90mph, was sprightly when the model was introduced to the market in 1949 and remained competitive through to 1954, even though no development took place in the intervening years.

Two prototype Comets were prepared, the first earmarked for Jack Surtees and the second being the works development model. It seems likely that the works model was still in development when entered into the books in January 1949, probably to keep the

From its introduction, in 1948, the Comet was presented in Series C form with the new Girdraulic forks and hydraulic damping. No Series B version was produced, since the more modest Meteor filled that niche.

Comet shares wheels with the Rapide, having duo-brakes with plain drums and not the ribbed Shadow drums. Rear wheel sprocket (a large sidecar size here) is on the left side of the single, to suit the conventional gearbox, instead of on the right as on the twin with its cross-over gearbox.

accountants happy. The 'Surtees' bike was not listed as completed until March, nor delivered until September, but it was prepared and used as a show model between these dates. As with the Meteor, it seems that initial orders were not encouraging enough to spur the factory into production, promised for March 1949. Production in fact only began later in 1949 when the factory was trying to counter the slump in sales caused by the accountants setting prices of the twins too high. Once in production, though, the Comet proved popular on the home market. It was also exported overseas but was not so well known abroad as the more famous Rapide and Black Shadow models, with which records were being broken around the world.

ENGINE & TRANSMISSION

ENGINE The same basic engine unit was utilised in Meteor and Comet models, although the more common Comet engine number was differentiated

by type symbol F5AB/2A, the addition of the final A indicating a slightly modified specification (the larger carburettor, for example). The type symbols 2 and 2A respectively for Meteor and Comet resulted from this being the second post-war 500 design, F5AB/1 having already been used for the preceding Speedway motor (see pages 67, 70).

Crankcases for the 500s accepted the same cylinder, head, valve gear and camshaft as the Rapide, and the original moulds were embossed 'HRD' before the change to 'Vincent' very soon after production commenced. The crankshaft was made in the same way as for the twins, using the same shafts and flywheel blanks, but was, naturally, machined and balanced differently, as well as having the shorter crankpin for the single big end. The narrower cases, with only the single cylinder opening, were sand-cast, thick and heavy, and, with the narrower crankshaft, made up a very strong bottom end. Indeed, so sturdy was the Comet engine that it powered the fastest Vincent sprinter ever, outperforming even George Brown's famous Nero and its supercharged successor,

Touring specification was not exclusive to the Rapide; Ray Smith's Touring Comet is an excellent example of the specification as applied to the 500cc model. Fatter tyres (3.50-19in front, 4.00-18in rear) match black steel Touring mudguards, which are wider than standard Birmabright light alloy mudguards and require different stays; ribbed front and studded rear tyres are more reminiscent of the original Avon Speedster and Supreme fitments than most modern tyre combinations. Both the loop-type crashbar and the Craven carrier could have been added in the early 1950s, but Fibreglass top box is of a later era.

Only this solitary Series D Comet is known to have been sold by the factory. In common with the other open D models, it features a revised upper frame member, separate oil tank under the fully sprung seat, fatter tyres and Lucas electrics with coil ignition.

Super Nero. The Comet-based and supercharged Mighty Mouse of Bryan Chapman achieved a record-breaking 8.81secs standing quarter-mile time and was the fastest 500 in Europe in 1977, some 25 years after its engine was originally made.

Inside the standard Comet timing chest, things were perhaps not so robust; the alloy idler, used in all but the earliest engines, can be replaced with a steel idler just as usefully as with the twin-cylinder models, and the alloy small idler introduced for the singles also proved less than ideal and is best replaced by a modern idler in an alternative material. The steady plate was

made in steel because smaller centres and less heat were expected to give less differential expansion, and together with the spindles proved quite adequate and trouble-free.

The lubrication system, almost identical to that of the twins, proved more satisfactory on the singles, no doubt partly because of the developments which were already in place by 1948/49 (such as grooved rocker bearings), and also because the same-size rotary-reciprocating Pilgrim pump had only one big end and cylinder to supply, leading to a greater flow and safety margin.

The compression ratio adopted for the singles was 6.8:1, using the same E7/6 pistons as in the Rapide, but without compression plates. No doubt the 7.3:1 E7/7 pistons of the Black Shadow were avoided because, at the time, fuel was still of low octane and even a Black Shadow throttle had to be opened gently to avoid pinking, whereas the Comet had less power and therefore was expected to be ridden harder. Very little change was required in Comet engines over the period of production, and what there was arose mostly as a result of twin-cylinder model modifications (eg, changes in piston clearances).

A very few Series D Comet engines were prepared by the works, which had three enclosed Victor versions on display at the 1954 motorcycle show. One such Victor was eventually sold privately and a second one was stripped by the works to produce the sole Series D Comet before also being sold. Three more engines appear to have been fitted into C cycle parts and sold, of which some survive.

FUEL SYSTEM & CARBURETTOR A 1⅛in Amal 229F/1DV carburettor was adopted for the Comet, identical to the Black Shadow's 229E/1DV except for the main jet which on the Comet was 200 instead of 180. The bronze front cylinder manifold of the Black

Sloping 500cc Comet engine bears a strong family likeness to the twins. Comet had a relatively long production run; nearly all were produced after 1949 and, therefore, badged as Vincents. The same Burman BAP gearbox and clutch was adopted for the Comet as for the Meteor.

Comet crankcases are much smaller than those of the twin, since they do not include a gearbox. Cylinder studs are of later one-piece pattern; the waisting not only saves a little weight but also improves distribution of mechanical stresses.

The Comet has a larger 1⅛in carburettor and a higher 6.8:1 compression ratio than the similar Meteor engine, to endow it with a little more power. Comet also gained a new polished aluminium cowl to protect its magneto. The round clutch inspection cover was changed yet again at the end of 1949, to read 'Vincent' instead of 'HRD'.

The factory built three enclosed Victor 500s, one of which is believed to have been sold, with another having remained 'unclothed' to become the sole D Comet; at least three D Comet engines in C cycle parts were sold. All would have been fitted with this 1⅛in Amal Monobloc 289M/1DO carburettor.

Lower-poundage 'Comet' springs were introduced for the 500cc models; rear suspension otherwise was the same as on the big twins. A Comet rear mudguard is pressed to clear the single's left-side chainguard instead of the twin's right-side chainguard, and the deeply valanced Touring mudguard is not easily converted to or from a twin's standard mudguard.

Shadow was also a required fitting on the Comet; and, as on the Shadow's front cylinder, the carburettor remained a brass item throughout the model's life. A few Series D specification engines using the 1⅛in Amal Monobloc were prepared for prototypes of Victor and Comet models and were sold to the public in a mixture of D and C/D machines.

A 1948 works photograph shows the Comet model using fuel pipes very similar to those of the twins, with a T-piece on the left-hand tap providing for interconnection to the right-hand tap from one branch and to the carburettor from the other. This arrangement appears again in later catalogues. However, the 1948 photograph is very suspect (a *twin's* magneto cowl is shown, for example), and examination of the later catalogues shows that the same photograph has been retouched and re-used, and is not a reliable guide to contemporary specification. Two fuel pipe arrangements were used: the long adapter (Vincent part A75) to accept two unions each with a flexible pipe to one petrol tap, and the twin outlet union (Vincent part A77) to accept a flexible pipe from each tap.

GEARBOX & CLUTCH A single-row replacement for the triplex Rapide engine sprocket accommodated ½in by ⅜in chain drive to the conventional five-spring multi-plate clutch, as used on a number of

The same mudguard stay is used on the Comet as on the twins, but turned round to place the chainguard anchorage lug on the left side instead of the right. This means that the lifting handle is just behind the hinge, instead of just in front. This Lucas rear lamp, not original but of a similar period, is much more suitable for night work than the Miller.

being embossed HRD (covers exist with, and without, the additional bar over the lettering), while most Comets were produced after the name change and, therefore, with 'VINCENT' proudly cast into this cover plate.

CYCLE PARTS

FRAME & REAR SUSPENSION Because of its inclined cylinder, the Comet was able to utilise the same upper and rear frames featured in the other models in the range, fitted with hydraulic damping, and completed with the single-cylinder frame tie running vertically above the gearbox. This frame tie completed the triangulation which would otherwise have been lacking (because there was no rear cylinder). The frame tie, unlike that missing cylinder, was not subject to heat, and therefore the top bolt was fully tightened instead of being relieved to provide a sliding joint. Reflecting the Series C specification and single-cylinder adaptations, the frame number prefix allocated was RC/1/.

The two prototypes were made early enough to feature a 1948-style short rear frame and painted

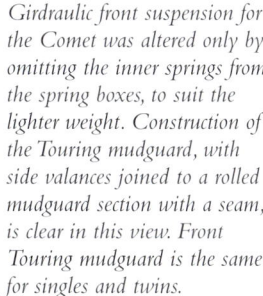

Girdraulic front suspension for the Comet was altered only by omitting the inner springs from the spring boxes, to suit the lighter weight. Construction of the Touring mudguard, with side valances joined to a rolled mudguard section with a seam, is clear in this view. Front Touring mudguard is the same for singles and twins.

other makes of motorcycle of the period. The Burman BAP gearbox provided both major weight and cost savings by comparison with the Rapide gearbox and proved quite adequate for the 28bhp Comet. Although the gearbox, too, was common to other marques, and hence made in large numbers by Burman, each manufacturer had its own variant; the top-pivot Vincent fitting, with its own length of mainshaft, was not interchangeable, complete, with other variants, but shared all wearing parts.

The primary chaincase was fully enclosed and load-bearing, with a polished cover. The clutch inspection cover was dimensionally the same as the pre-war magneto inspection cover, a few early models

The 500cc single's dynamo is clamped in a cradle behind the cylinder and driven from the timing gears. This dynamo is the 60-watt Lucas E3L, fitted as original equipment on Series Ds, and is seen on the unique Series D Comet.

The same S433/3/1 Smiths speedometer was used on the Comet as on Rapide and Meteor models. Simple steel attachment brackets are used to mount it to the Girdraulic forks, and night-time illumination is provided by a bulb in the screw-on bulb-holder underneath. The small knurled knob resets the trip mileometer.

spring boxes, which therefore appear in many factory illustrations; but production machines were all made after the longer rear frame and plated spring boxes had been adopted in 1949. The same peculiar long brake pedal was used on the prototype Comets as on the Meteor, operating through a short rod linkage, but it was extremely rare on the production models; the standard arrangement of cable operation from a footrest hanger-mounted pedal, as fitted to the twins, quickly came into use.

Lighter rear springs of 0.276in wire (121lb/in), instead of the 0.300in wire (189lb/in) Rapide variety, were adopted for the lighter bikes; later these were discontinued and the heavier springs installed.

STEERING & FRONT SUSPENSION The Comet model was made in Series C form from the start, and therefore had the Girdraulic front forks. To suit the model's lighter weight, these forks were fitted only with outer springs of 15in length, and omitted the inner springs used on the heavier twins. HRD straight handlebars (in black enamel), control levers and electrical switches remained as on the Rapide, except that a single-lever Amal choke control was fitted in place of the twin-lever version.

WHEELS & TYRES Rapide wheels were adopted on the Comet model, with plain brake drums instead of Shadow drums, to control production costs. The Comet was a lighter machine and had less need of the extra benefits of the heavier and more expensive ribbed rums, and the factory's choice was certainly

A 500cc Comet is quite adequate to pull a sidecar, in this case a slightly younger Watsonian Palma. However, Vincent owners, used to 1000cc behemoths, consider 500cc rather insufficient for the task.

validated when *Motor Cycling* magazine achieved a record stopping distance of 21ft from 30mph in its 1950 Comet road test. Early Comets did not have a balance beam stop and would often have one brake just caressing the drum (as did all the Brampton-equipped B models); then the balance beam stop was added to the left-hand side of the bridge plate, and a return spring to the right brake cam lever, properly to locate all four brake shoes when in the 'off' position. The same Avon 3.00-20in Speedster and 3.50-19in Supreme tyres were used as on other models, except for the Touring variants (and the two or three Ds), which had 1in smaller rims and tyres.

SEAT, MUDGUARDS & FUEL TANK No changes to the seat, mudguards or tank were made for the Comet, which used the same components as other models. Although original works pictures showed a rear lifting handle specially adapted for the singles (with a chainguard mounting on the left), the factory

soon realised, as mentioned earlier, that the twins' lifting handle could be reversed for use on the singles, and so Comets were made that way, with the handle being set a little further back. Certainly for a short person this proves to be an advantage when trying to lift the bike on to the stand. All 500cc models were made after the petrol tank tie-bolt modification was introduced.

ELECTRICAL EQUIPMENT & INSTRUMENTS

IGNITION & TIMING As with all the other Series C models, Comet ignition was by magneto, the first models using a Lucas CM2, shortly replaced by the K1F – a single-cylinder version of the KVF adopted for the twins in 1948/49. Tungsten points were standard in the single-cylinder magnetos, which did not require the platinum points of the KVF to boost a weak spark. Comet timing was set at 39° BTDC – equivalent to $^{15}/_{32}$in piston movement.

DYNAMO, WIRING, LIGHTS & HORN Like the Meteor, the Comet adopted the 3in Miller dynamo from the start, using the same cartridge two-stage regulator as all the other B and C models. Wiring, too, was virtually identical to that on both Meteor and twins. And the same Lucas Altette horn was used, hanging from the rear of the upper frame member.

Prototype machines were originally built with the large 8in headlamp, but even the factory illustrations always showed the smaller lamps that were fitted to production models. The rare D Comet engine (F5AB/3A/ prefix) used the Lucas E3L 60-watt dynamo adopted for the Series D range, and similar wiring to the D twins. Details of the fittings on the C/D hybrids are not known.

SPEEDOMETER & DRIVE The normal Rapide speedometer in 120mph Imperial (S433/3/L) or 180kph metric (S433/7/L) form was used on the Comet. All Comets were fitted with Girdraulic forks and the speedometer was mounted on the right-hand fork leg using the same twin steel strip brackets as on

the Rapide. Similarly, the front-wheel drive, right-angle gearbox and 25½in cable were unaltered from components on other existing models.

OPTIONAL SPECIFICATIONS

LUGGAGE EQUIPMENT The Comet featured the same seat and rear frame arrangement as other B and C models, and therefore accepted the same luggage-carrying frames, whether the rare Vincent-HRD manufactured frames or proprietary variants such as Craven.

TOURING SPECIFICATION Touring specification could be requested on any Vincent, but was usually featured only on Rapide and Comet models. Comets supplied in this form had the fatter 3.50-19in front and 4.00-18in rear wheels, valanced steel mudguards and 'cowhorn' handlebars. Probably not so many Touring Comets as Touring Rapides were made, but a number of Comets still exist in this trim.

Four-point sidecar attachment was designed in (above left), with integral lugs provided everywhere except at the rear lower point, for which a triangular bolt-on adapter was listed. Eyebolts have been used at all four points in this attachment; the multiplicity of clamps and fittings is fairly normal for a sidecar installation. Upper anchorage of the Girdraulic spring box is on this eccentric (above); for sidecar use the eccentrics, either side, are turned forward, as here, which reduces fork trail and increases spring load in one operation.

BLACK LIGHTNING & GREY FLASH

Most Black Lightnings went abroad but this one was supplied via Humphreys of London, and may have been intended for sidecar racing as it is fitted with front engine plates and a cross-tube. This original photograph provides many details of modifications and original fittings (every Lightning was different). The large petrol tank is modified from a standard steel item, with an extra section welded on top (and the joins smoothed out by an artist's brush on the print).

Racing machines were frequently made to individual requirements, rarely to a simple catalogue specification. Original material can thus be especially valuable in establishing what might, or might not, have been done by the factory to its racing products. In this section some original black and white photographs of Black Lightning and Grey Flash machines are presented. It may, however, be appropriate to offer a warning about original material which the restorer might think could be relied upon implicitly. Far from it. 'The camera never lies' is the biggest lie of all.

Catalogues had to be available at shows, but most factories would be in a last-minute panic over the more important matter of the preparation of the show models. Howard Davies, indeed, had to bribe his way into Olympia with the first HRDs, after-hours on the night before opening day. So how did they manage the show 'literature' of catalogues and pre-show illus-trated publicity for the press? Updates to existing ranges could be accommodated by the drawing office artist, with minor changes being drawn in and major changes (such as a new front fork) calling for 'cut-and-stick' techniques. Vincent-HRD catalogues show all the hallmarks of both practices. If necessary, a new model could be drawn from scratch, which the factory did in 1931 (when introducing the diamond-frame models with Python engines) and again in 1945 (to promote the coming Rapide).

More reliable, therefore, are photographs taken by the press, for these were generally of real machines. But the press had their own artists, trained to 'massage' pictures to look good, by painting in highlights or removing unsuitable backgrounds. The photograph of the 1954 Lightning, for example, displays shinier exhausts and fatter spring boxes than would have been seen, at the time, on a Lightning. Even more dramat-ically, examination reveals that the machine was photographed complete, with its petrol tank on, and was then 'undressed' by painting out the tank and cutting-and-sticking on the spine UFM! Evidence? A control cable which turns into a plug lead at one end, and goes nowhere at the other. See if you can spot any clues. Most valuable of all photographs would be a private owner's picture of his pride and joy, followed by any album photograph; but bear in mind that as time passes owners, too, carry out modifcations to their machines.

BLACK LIGHTNING

The fully race-prepared Black Lightning model was introduced at the 1948 Earls Court motorcycle show. Two previous machines could be regarded as the prototypes. The works racer Gunga Din, originally built as a modified Rapide (engine 1A/71), was altered over time to try out ideas, raced by George Brown, and generally put to all kinds of duty. It was, in effect, a development model, first for the Black Shadow and thereafter for the Black Lightning. The second prototype, again a Series B, was John Edgar's machine supplied for Rollie Free's early record-breaking runs in the USA. This was supplied fully prepared for speed work (plus road-going equipment for fitting afterwards) to the specification which would become known as Black Lightning. However, the decision to market such a model had not been taken, and the name had yet to be coined, when 1B/900 was built. So it was recorded as a Black Shadow even though it was subsequently widely referred to, even by the factory, as a Black Lightning.

At the 1948 motorcycle show Vincent-HRD introduced the Series C hydraulically damped suspension, and so all the racing models (Grey Flash as well as Black Lightning) were built as Series Cs – with two possible exceptions. One Lightning, supplied to Elder Smith (Australia) in 1949, may have been a Series B; and a late Lightning appears to have been built to Series D engine specification but supplied in Series C cycle parts.

The first recorded Lightning was F10AB/1C/1320 sent to Cimic in Argentina in January 1949. This machine has survived and has recently been brought to Britain by John Kinley, who is restoring it. In fact, most of the 30 or so original Lightnings built have survived the intervening years, but note that a few Lightning engines were built for use in small racing cars, and complete 'Lightning' motorcycles have subsequently been constructed around these engines.

With a nominal top speed of 150mph, the Black Lightning could be considered to have underlined the legend 'The World's Fastest Standard Motorcycle'. This was further emphasised when New Zealanders Bob Burns and Russell Wright broke world records for sidecars (at 162mph) and solos (at 185mph) in 1955 on Wright's Black Lightning.

GREY FLASH

At the 1948 show the ordinary 500cc Meteor and Comet models were shown for the first time but were not to enter production for some months. A racing variant was not conceived until the following year, when the Grey Flash was announced for the 1949 show. Unlike the Lightning, which was listed as a pure racing model, the Grey Flash could be ordered as a stripped racer (£330), as a fully road-equipped model (£349), or as a dual-purpose mount with full road equipment but supplied also with racing extras, when it was priced at £362.

The first recorded Grey Flash, also known as the 'Eppynt racer' after the Welsh venue of its first race outing, was dispatched to Ross Motors of Hinckley and was subsequently very successfully campaigned by their rider, J.P.E. 'Johnny' Hodgkin. Another Grey Flash of significance was F5AB/2B/3520, supplied in August 1950 to John Surtees, who was himself an apprentice at the Vincent works. Vincent dealer Jack Surtees' name has already appeared in these pages in connection with specially prepared models for his sidecar racing exploits. Young John was not only going to follow in his father's footsteps, but was, of course, to surpass his achievements with World Championship wins on two wheels and four. A dual-purpose Grey Flash, fitted with the No.16 gearbox and supplied stripped but with silver-finished lighting equipment to match, provided some of his earliest racing miles. On this machine he began to make his mark in road racing before moving on to works Norton and MV Agusta machinery.

In 1950, too, four special Grey Flash models were prepared as works entries for that year's Senior TT. This occurred in the middle of the factory's deepest financial crisis, but the Receiver (E.C. Baillie) had determined to salvage the company and considered that such an entry would be a good way to demonstrate to the public that Vincent was still in business. The bikes had very special big ends and oversize valves, but gave trouble in practice and were quickly rebuilt to a slightly more conservative and well-proven specification. Best performance – and the only finish – was by Ken Bills in 12th place (race average 83.79mph, fastest lap 85.3mph). While it was not competitive with the works Nortons, the Grey Flash had made a creditable showing that was over 8mph faster than the best pre-war TT figure recorded by a Vincent.

After the races one of these team bikes was rebuilt, using parts from the others, and dispatched as a rare 'Black Flash' to Trivellato of Brazil. Just over 30 Flashes were built; ascertaining an exact number is difficult because two were recorded as being rebuilt as Comet models before sale, and at least one machine was noted as a 'Racing Comet' but had its engine built and numbered as a Flash by the engine builder. If the works were not always sure of a machine's designa-

Another period photograph provides more original specification details and indicates the pitfalls of relying on catalogues and press photographs. Alloy rims – 21in front, 20in rear – carrying Avon racing tyres are clearly seen. When this photograph was taken the machine had its petrol tank on, but for some reason a photograph showing the spine was required, so the petrol tank was painted out. An upper frame member cut from another picture was stuck on, and then the artist smoothed over the joins.

After breaking 150mph on John Edgar's Black Shadow/Lightning, Rollie Free bought his own Black Lightning, seen here restored and resplendent with 2in racing pipes. He had a streamlined shell made but it rendered the machine unstable and he was thrown off at speed. Undaunted, Free removed the shell and continued his runs, to raise the US record to 156mph (which he subsequently raised again, to over 160mph). Free's Lightning is currently owned by the US-based Team Obsolete. Marty Dickerson, in the background, is a contemporary record-breaker to Rollie Free, who was still breaking records on his Grey Flash in 1996.

Glynn Baxter's 1950 Grey Flash is used for classic racing and therefore has had to be modified in some respects. Wheels are smaller, with slightly wider alloy rims, to accept available new tyres. ACU regulations demand ball-ended handlebar levers, a silencer and an oil-catch bottle.

This original photograph of George Brown is marked '1950 TT'. This Grey Flash, however, does not look like one of the specially prepared TT models – in particular, it has a Burman, not an Albion, gearbox. This is probably the works development Flash listed as having been built with a pre-war Burman, and taken to the Isle of Man as a practice/spare bike. Frame tie has been replaced by tubing and the brake balance beam pivot is braced – a modification subsequently adopted by many Vincent owners.

tion, then it is even more difficult for the historian! As with the Lightning engines, some Flash engines were built for car use, rather than for installation in complete motorcycles. However, these 'car' units are generally distinguishable by their engine numbers: where Grey Flash bike engines carried numbers with an F5AB/2B/ prefix, those supplied separately (mostly to Kieft Cars) received an F5AB/2C/ prefix.

ENGINE & TRANSMISSION

ENGINE The same basic tuning principles were applied to single and twin engines; indeed, it was the availability of Lightning parts which made the consideration and development of a 'tuned Comet' practicable. Higher-lift MkII cams, polished high-tensile (85-ton Vibrac) connecting rods, triple valve springs, opened-out and polished ports, and raised compression ratios suitable for the fuel specified (petrol, alcohol, etc) were normally featured. Some machines were fitted with special 'big-port' heads and larger valves, but this was much rarer, and the plain big end is only known to have been fitted to John Surtees' Grey Flash, apart from its trial use in the works 500cc TT entries. Since the variability of engine tune makes it impossible to describe a standard-build specification, the reader is referred to *The Denis Minett Notebook*, which contains the published notes of the man who prepared and repaired many of the special and racing engines.

FUEL SYSTEM & CARBURETTORS The most common carburettors on both Black Lightning and Grey Flash models were Amal 32mm 10TT9 clip-fitting instruments, but other sizes could be specified, and were. Early Grey Flashes, for example, were built with 1³⁄₁₆in versions on double-flanged adapters, and later Amal manufactured a small batch of 1⁷⁄₁₆in carburettors especially for Manx Norton and Vincent racers. Jetting would vary according to the fuel selected, with extremely large jet sizes required for

alcohol fuels. Taper-cock petrol taps were normally fitted to the racing machines, instead of the cork-plunger type used on roadsters.

GEARBOX & CLUTCH The Black Lightning retained Vincent's own gearbox and unique self-servo clutch; however, extensive detailed modifications were carried out to improve the speed and reliability of gearchanging. Backlash was increased by grinding off alternate dogs to make engagement quicker and easier. The cam-plate was drilled to reduce inertia, speeding the change and reducing the tendency to flywheel on past the gear position.

In the clutch the shoe carrier was drilled for lightness, and the roadster's metal plate with friction inserts was replaced by a one-piece friction disc from Ferodo. The width of the ears on the replacement disc was increased, for extra strength, and the cast iron clutch drum slots were opened up to suit. Many owners altered their roadster's clutch to this pattern, and friction plates to suit can still usually be obtained.

Gear ratios were normally those of the earlier Black Shadows (with high bottom gear), although a special close-ratio set of gears (obtained with a specially cut 19-tooth G6/1) was also listed.

For the Grey Flash model the alterations to gearbox and clutch were much more dramatic. Burman had always been suppliers to Vincent-HRD, and initially a Burman gearbox was considered. At least one bike, works experimental machine F5AB/2BX/2921, was fitted with a pre-war Burman racing gearbox, but exactly where this fits in the development schedule is not clear as it was only recorded when being renumbered and altered. However, Burman could no longer supply these special 'boxes, nor the wide range of gear ratio options which a competitive machine would need. So the decision was taken to fit the Grey Flashes with the rival Albion product. This necessitated a number of changes, since the mounting points were not the same for both makes of gearbox.

An obvious result is the slightly odd angle at which

HRD cases and the wide, forked steering head lug indicate that this is a 1949 Black Lightning. It is believed to be the works development model 'Gunga Din'. Larger TT carburettors are the most obvious deviation from the standard engines, the dynamo is of course removed, and weight has been saved by omitting the front engine plates and stands.

This Grey Flash (right), destined for Moorkens in Belgium, was extensively polished and chromed, most likely for display. A blanking plate has been used to seal the dynamo drive hole and the machine has been assembled with cap-headed (Allen) screws rather than the usual cadmium-plated cheese-headed screws.

Racing engines had stronger, steel idlers and the ATD was omitted from the magneto drive in favour of a simple dog to drive a rev counter (below). Some tuners extensively drilled the timing gears and/or narrowed them. Rocker arrangements are clearly seen with some rockers fitted to the tunnels, other tunnels empty, and a rocker and bearing assembly on the bench in front of the right-hand engine. These are not factory-prepared engines but the work of later tuners; gearboxes have been removed, to be replaced probably by AMC units.

Racing models usually used lever type petrol taps instead of the cork plunger type fitted on road machines. Carburettors were usually 32mm 10TT9, but currently Glynn Baxter's Flash has an Amal RN. Frame tie (replacing the twin's rear cylinder) is clearly visible, a special pattern on the Grey Flash to mate with the Albion gearbox.

The Grey Flash adopted an Albion gearbox instead of the Burman fitted to the Comet and Meteor 500s, because Albion could offer a better choice of close ratios. The No. 16 gearbox, with aluminium casing, was original equipment on most road-equipped and dual-purpose Flashes.

Rear suspension of the racing models was Vincent's normal triangulated fork with some lightening carried out – the rear stand lugs have been cut off this Grey Flash, and various parts drilled. Rear sprocket teeth are thinned to accept the narrower and lighter ⅜in × ¼in racing chain.

the Albion 'box fits in the Vincent. A revised and re-machined frame tie was necessary, together with some different spacers. Two different versions of the Albion were specified, No.5 and No.16, although not uniquely – a No.20 is known to have been supplied too. The No.5 'box, used on the stripped racing Flashes, was made of Elektron (magnesium alloy) and was some 7lb lighter than the No.16. For the road-equipped and dual-purpose Flashes, the No.16 with kick-starter and a more robust aluminium alloy casing was specified. In both cases the matching Albion clutch with a rubber cush-drive was fitted, giving the Grey Flashes a particularly smooth transmission.

CYCLE PARTS

FRAME & REAR SUSPENSION Frame and suspension arrangements remained very much as on the road-going models, featuring, of course, Vincent's own triangulated fork rear suspension. This was fitted from the start with the new hydraulic damper, but also retained the friction dampers in the lower castings of the seat stays. However, some Grey Flashes were produced with fully sprung seats mounted on stays extended to the footrest plates, and with the rear frame seat stay lugs removed.

Modifications to the frames consisted primarily of drilling heavyweight areas, such as the steering head forging and the rear frame pivot-bearing casing. Drilled footrest plates, redesigned and relocated footrests and control pedals were all developed to give a more appropriate riding position for speed, and to reduce weight.

STEERING & FRONT SUSPENSION With the 1000cc and 500cc racing machines introduced in

Glynn Baxter's Grey Flash has been prepared with a fully sprung rear seat. Like some original owners, he has discarded one rear brake and all the cross-shaft mechanism, using instead direct cable actuation of the remaining brake. Simple chain adjuster bolts, instead of the road bike's finger adjuster, are correct for a racing machine.

1948 and 1949 respectively, it was appropriate for these bikes to be fitted with the new hydraulically damped Series C suspension and Girdraulic front forks from the start. A modification applied to many front forks was the milling away of metal on the inside face of the fork legs, where stresses were lowest, although it appears that no drawings for this work were made.

A rare exception to the rule that Vincent-HRD always supplied black-enamelled handlebars occurred with the Grey Flash. The works still did not specify chromium-plated bars, but provided silver-finished handlebars to match the Flash (no pun intended) paintwork.

BRAKES Four brakes, two on each wheel, were retained on the racing machines, with ribbed drums adopted for optimum braking. For lightness and stiffness, new brake plates, incorporating air scoops, were prepared and cast in lightweight Elektron. Because of the poor ageing and fatigue resistance of this magnesium alloy, old items should at least be crack-tested; many machines have been fitted with more recent replacements, copied from the originals but manufactured in aluminium alloy.

In the case of the Grey Flash, some owners chose to discard one rear brake, considering the bike overbraked and therefore carrying excess weight. The front brakes of some Black Lightnings prepared for

The light grey finish of the Flash clarifies the bolted-up construction of the steering head forging into the sheet steel box-section oil tank. The petrol tank is rubber-mounted on bushes in the tank ears, which are expanded by a predetermined amount when the stepped retaining bolt is screwed fully home.

Except for one or two possible Series B Lightnings, racing machines were all Series Cs with Girdraulic forks. These were often lightened by milling away material on the inner faces on the low-stressed centreline, as seen here (through the wheel spokes). Brake-plates on this Flash are modern aluminium copies of fragile Elektron originals.

record-breaking, not racing, were completely removed, with braking effort confined solely to the rear where one drum was needed to carry the drive sprocket. Record-breakers, of course, are much more concerned with going than with stopping.

WHEELS & TYRES Normally, the racing models were fitted with larger diameter wheels, 3.00-21in front and 3.50-20in rear (or 3.25-20in on some Grey

Flashes), which suited the racing pattern tyres available from Avon; but the standard sizes of 3.00-20in and 3.50-19in could also be specified.

Alloy wheel rims were usually fitted and two patterns are known to have existed: early rims have narrow flanges and those of 1951 show wider outer flanges. Hubs were usually polished, and some machines had chromium-plated spoke flanges, and even chromium-plated spokes. This extra plating may

have been applied only to those machines that were also prepared as show models; out of such small production numbers a significant proportion would have also been exhibited at trade shows or in dealer showrooms.

SEAT, MUDGUARDS & FUEL TANK The racer's seat was built up in the same way as the standard seat, using the same metalwork, but usually featured a simpler, plain-profile plywood base and a thinner foam rubber seat squab which allowed for more variation in riding position. Some seats were built with a rear hump to help keep the rider on board, but many were simply plain. The seats were usually mounted on the standard seat stays to the RFM, incorporating friction damping at their lower ends, but some Grey Flashes were prepared with fully sprung seats mounted on longer stays to the footrest plates, and with the RFM lugs removed. Road-going and dual-purpose Grey Flashes, of course, were fitted with standard seat, footrest and mudguards equipment.

Stripped models had their mudguards cut down front and rear.

Petrol tanks had larger cutaways underneath to accommodate the large TT carburettor(s), and were sometimes beaten to establish grooves and flutes in the top surface in order to clear forks or handlebars. Larger tanks were sometimes made, and at least some of these were prepared by cutting and welding on extra sections (cut from the standard pressings) to a standard tank.

Black Lightnings were normally supplied in all-black finish, with the engines black-enamelled and polished in the same way as the Black Shadow. The Grey Flash alone adopted a new colour scheme appearing to originate from the finish of the front forks on an early model which were anodised to a grey colour (most Grey Flash forks were *enamelled* grey). The new finish was further extended by using dull chromium plating on the petrol tank and many smaller steel parts, and a grey colour for painted sections (which were, presumably, sprayed since the

Original racing brake-plates were cast in Elektron, an extremely light magnesium-based alloy. Features special to these plates include screwed-on air scoops, integral cam-lever bosses with stiffening ribs and bolted-in (not riveted) shoe pivots. Water excluders were machined from the casting, except for the drive-side rear brake-plate, where the sprocket prevented it. The Grey Flash, like Black Lightning, was fitted with ribbed drum duo-brakes front and rear.

Reg Dearden's Black Lightning was originally supplied late in 1949, but returned to the factory to have a supercharger fitted in mid-1950 – a job which required a 4in lengthening of the wheelbase and many special parts. Note that the machine, built for record-breaking, has no front brakes and only a single rear brake. It is believed Dearden's intended rider was Les Graham; the project foundered when he was killed. The machine is seen here at a Canadian rally in 1977, still on original tyres, when current owner Mike Manning ran it briefly.

Lucas magnetos were the standard fitting on post-war Vincent-HRDs, even on the Black Lightning, with its special KVF TT instrument. An exception was the Grey Flash, which was usually fitted with the BTH TT magneto seen here.

production numbers involved would certainly have been too small to justify the use of dip tanks).

ELECTRICAL EQUIPMENT & INSTRUMENTS

IGNITION & TIMING Manual magnetos were adopted for racing machines, usually a Lucas KVF TT for the Black Lightning and a BTH TT for the Grey Flash; but Scintilla magnetos were occasionally used on twins and Lucas TT magnetos on singles. Omission of the ATD unit from the magneto drive made provision of a rev counter drive relatively easy, with a dog drive to a right-angle gearbox mounted on the magneto inspection cover of both singles and twins. An 8000rpm Smiths rev counter was normally fitted.

DYNAMO, WIRING & HORN Road-equipped and dual-purpose Grey Flashes were specified with the same full lighting equipment as that of the sister Comet models. Stripped Grey Flashes and Black Lightnings were not fitted with wiring, a horn or a dynamo, which was replaced by blanking plates (in steel and light alloy variants) to provide oil-tightness. Although the Black Lightning was not listed in road-equipped form, one or two were supplied fully equipped in this way, using Rapide-style components.

OPTIONAL SPECIFICATIONS

The Grey Flash was offered in three forms: stripped for racing, fully road-equipped as a sporting mount, and as a dual-purpose machine which the clubman could use on the road or convert for track use. However, customers could request special features. With a production output of only a little over 30 machines, it is difficult to talk of a standard specification and options.

In the case of the Black Lightning, this is even more true. There was much less opportunity to race in a 1000cc class than as a 500. The big twins were usually bought and prepared for record-breaking after discussions between the purchaser and Phil Vincent. As mentioned, fully road-equipped models could be supplied while, at the other extreme, a specially lengthened Black Lightning complete with supercharger was prepared for Reg Dearden (although ultimately it was never used in anger).

BLACK KNIGHT & BLACK PRINCE (SERIES D)

By 1954 the motorcycle world had moved on, compared with 1946 when the Series B Rapide was introduced. All the major manufacturers had brought in higher performance (parallel) twin-cylinder models as top of the range machines, with singles mostly retained as modest-cost transport, and side-valves almost gone from the scene. Cycle parts, too, had undergone a revolution, with rigid frames becoming a thing of the past, temporarily fashionable plunger rear springing rapidly giving way to the swinging arm type, and telescopic front forks being almost universal.

The Vincent factory – the company name was changed to Vincent Engineers (Stevenage) Ltd after restructuring in 1953 – had expanded its range with the Black Shadow and Comet models in 1948, and introduced the Series C suspension improvements in the same year. The following years, 1949 and 1950,

Fully enclosed Black Knight, with windscreen and handmuffs, provided even more protection from the elements than the previous Touring version of the Rapide. Revised suspension and engine specification made it a more refined package too – but the public did not rush to buy.

A line-up of Black Knights and Black Princes at the 1995 40/40 rally, held to commemorate the 40th anniversary of the Series D machines, when 40 or more fully enclosed models were assembled. The site for the event was the old Vincent factory in Stevenage; the half-timbered building is the original Vincent works used from 1928 onwards.

were spent substantially in increasing production, although the racing Black Lightning and Grey Flash models had also been developed; in fact, most Vincents were produced in the years 1949 to 1951.

Behind the scenes, however, the factory had been working on a Government contract to develop a 65bhp fuel-injected version of the vee-twin engine. The Picador, as it was called, was required to power ML Aviation's U120D target aircraft. Phil Vincent hoped that this would provide a significant throughput for the production line and enable motorcycle production to be continued, even though the post-war boom in two-wheelers was declining again. The contract was eventually cancelled, apparently because radio-controlled technology was not sufficiently advanced to control the aircraft. Only a small number of Picador engines were built. Some later appeared on the surplus market, to leave behind a legacy of high performance and non-standard parts.

To the motorcycle world it seemed that Vincents had been standing still. A major move forward was

required, and so Series D development was undertaken. The factory took the almost unprecedented step of asking customers' advice, via a questionnaire published in the journal of the already active and thriving Vincent-HRD Owners Club. The factory itself, like many before, began to think in 'middle-aged' terms of a refined touring machine. The result was the 1954 show-stopping range of fully enclosed models, with the Victor, Black Knight and Black Prince superseding the Comet, Rapide and Black Shadow respectively.

It was a brave move and won Vincent a lot of publicity in the motorcycle press – but not many sales. First, the factory had great difficulty in sourcing Fibreglass enclosures of adequate quality at this early period in the development of this new material. Second, and more serious, the necessary customers did not materialise. It was a popular belief that motorcyclists wanted cleaner, enclosed models, and many of the major factories explored the same path. But the motorcycling public in fact proved to be very conser-

vative. Only the innovative 250cc Ariel Leader achieved any real success. History shows that the Series D models were 40 years before their time, and only in the 1990s have manufacturers like Honda (with the Pan-European) and BMW (with the K1100RT) begun to find even a small market for extensively enclosed motorcycles. In 1955, therefore, Vincent had to beat a hasty retreat with the all-enclosed D range, and re-introduce 'open' versions under their old titles of Rapide, Black Shadow and

Comet – although the last named, like its enclosed version, never saw series production.

In the enclosed range, the Black Knight took over the mantle of the open Rapide model as a powerful, long-legged touring model. With superior weather protection and a more refined response on the road, due to improved ignition, carburation and transmission shock absorber, the Black Knight represented an advance over its open predecessor.

As the successor to the Black Shadow, previously

The 1955 season Series D range gave all models the same full-enclosure treatment; thus the Black Prince replaced the Black Shadow in the line-up. Comparison of this Black Prince with the similar view of the Black Knight shows how little visual difference there is between the models; contrast this with the distinct identity

the Black Shadow had been given, compared with the Rapide, by its black finish and imposing speedometer. Restricted supplies of the new Fibreglass components, and public demand, soon resulted in the return of the Black Shadow, in Series D form, alongside the Black Prince.

billed as 'The World's Fastest Standard Motorcycle', the enclosed Series D equivalent was the Black Prince, but this machine tried to be two different things at the same time – a sports model and a refined tourer. The buying public was proving to be unenthusiastic about fully enclosed motorcycles – and especially so in the case of the 'traditional' buyers of sports models. The Black Prince had little to distinguish it from its slower, and visually similar, Black Knight stablemate and simply never made the impres-

sion that the Black Shadow had done before it.

When the naked Black Shadow and Rapide had to be re-introduced and sold alongside the newer models, the intended roles of the different models became even less clear. Nevertheless, the Black Prince was a true Grand Tourer, representing a dramatic and courageous move forward in motorcycle design – but it was too early! Even sports fairings, copied from the race track, had yet to make their mark.

The Series D models had a number of improved

features compared with the preceding machines, and owners of earlier Vincents have often adopted some of these to give greater comfort with longer-travel, softer suspension. The looks of the enclosed models were, at the least, an acquired taste in a world of naked motorcycles. The open versions looked exactly what they were – hastily assembled lash-ups based on parts not designed for the purpose.

Only about 400 Series D Vincents were made in total, and just less than half that number were the enclosed Black Knight and Black Prince models. The 500cc bikes were not proceeded with, in either enclosed Victor or open Comet guise, although both were prototyped and shown, and the Victor was even included in the company's 1955 catalogue.

The exact performance of these late models is difficult to establish, as they were made in relatively small numbers for only a year, and the road test reports which appeared were mostly of the 'impression' variety rather than formal timed tests with detailed facts and figures. 'Rab' Cook, an experienced journalist, and knowledgeable about the marque, reported in *Motor Cycling* that he believed his new Black Prince would prove to be as fast as colleague Eric Ballantine's new D Black Shadow ridden at a crouch. However, history suggests that later Black Shadows struggled hard to match the performance of the earlier, carefully assembled jobs, and that the Ds were made in such small numbers that dodges – such as carefully selecting the longest timing camshafts from production tolerances – could not have been as generally employed as in earlier years. With improvements in fuel (meaning reduced pinking if the engine was handled unsympathetically) and low-speed running (by virtue of the improved shock absorber and ignition), the Black Prince was perhaps less highly strung than the early Black Shadows, and may have been regarded more as a slightly faster de luxe version of the Black Knight than as a true sports model.

At the end of 1955, it was announced that motorcycle production was to cease at Stevenage. Bruce Main-Smith road tested a pre-war A Rapide together with a last-of-line D Black Prince for *Motor Cycling*. The last production Vincent was a Black Prince, engine number F10AB/2B/11134, frame number RD13034B/F, completed on 16 December 1955.

ENGINE & TRANSMISSION

ENGINE Quite major changes were introduced in the engine/gearbox unit, although the Picador developments were not generally incorporated, apparently because of service problems (eg, the Picador crankshaft required heavy presses which were not generally available at motorcycle dealers and repairers). The most obvious changes were the use of two 'front' cylinder heads and the adoption of coil ignition in place of the magneto. Using only one cylinder head

casting no doubt helped production costs, especially as volumes were much reduced, and appears to have become possible with the adoption of the more compact Amal Monobloc carburettor.

New die-cast crankcases with thinner sections were utilised on the Ds, although they had in fact already appeared on late C models, and saved 9lb. It might seem odd that money was spent on expensive dies so late, and for such a small run of castings, but in fact the order had been raised before the financial troubles of 1950. When the Receiver was called in he discovered that work on the dies had already been started at the sub-contractors (John Dale) and so it was allowed to proceed to an eventual conclusion in 1953. Late cases are not only lighter than the earlier sand-cast cases but also stronger in some strategic places such as at the cam-plate spindle boss. Unfortunately, machining quality was not maintained so well, and crankcase mouths were often machined a little on the loose side, while pushrod tube seal recesses were not always square, and in the worst cases had to be re-machined to obtain good oil sealing.

Internally, the engine was almost unaltered, with a Series C flywheel assembly and MkIII cams with quietening ramps, as featured in the later Cs. However, some of the D engines appear to have been badly prepared. The works admitted that some machines could barely approach 100mph and would benefit from being re-timed one tooth earlier. For the enclosed D models the covers, but not the main crankcases, were black enamelled to blend in with the Fibreglass enclosures.

The lubrication system inside the engine was unchanged, but different external piping was necessary to reach the separate oil tank mounted in the rear skirt, replacing the old combined oil tank/frame member. The connecting oil pipes were routed close to the cowl pivot (or rear sub-frame pivot on open Rapides) to minimise disturbance and flexure when raising the seat for access or wheel removal.

One change made was to the breathing of the engine, which had never been totally satisfactory. Condensation and filling of the primary chaincase afflicted some machines and oil consumption had never been outstanding (especially since factory service manager Paul Richardson persuaded the works to increase piston clearances a fraction, to reduce the incidence of seizures on new machines). The timed breather system was blanked off, and instead a revised front inlet valve spring cap was fitted, with a ¼in BSP fitting to accept a banjo and the breather pipe. To allow air flow through this route, a modified upper valve guide seating was also necessary.

The triplex chain primary drive was retained, and also the rather unmechanical arrangement of the dynamo sprocket dipping into the middle-row top run above the clutch sprocket and driving through only one or two teeth. Some Series D cases had the dynamo hole machined out with the same tapered

Under their cowlings, the Black Knight and Black Prince models were powered by Series D developments of the 998cc Rapide and Black Shadow engines respectively. Black-painted covers on unpainted castings matched black Fibreglass cowlings, and using the same colour scheme on open Series D models minimised production variations.

recess as C cases, but some were left plain and machined with a parallel recess at this face; the explanation for the difference is not known and the case numbers of the 'plain' examples do not appear to run in sequence. An improved chain tensioner with twin blades, requiring slightly different end abutments, was used, as was a revised engine-shaft shock absorber (ESA). This latter retained the previous multi-spring design, but had a revised cam profile and was larger, to accommodate 24 instead of 18 concentric pairs of springs, giving each pair an easier life. Revised thrust washers and an ESA nut were all that was needed to fit the new components to the unaltered mainshaft, and thus the later ESA can be fitted to earlier series machines, undoubtedly giving longer spring life.

Compression ratios continued unchanged from the earlier models, with 6.45:1 for Black Knight and Rapide and 7.3:1 for Black Prince and Black Shadow versions. This was probably because the early Black Shadows (and even Comets with their 6.8:1 ratio) had

needed a careful hand to avoid pinking on the poor petrols of the late 1940s and early '50s, and so the factory preferred to retain the more tolerant engine characteristics that the newer fuels provided rather than try to gain extra horsepower at the expense of temperamental engine manners, particularly on the Prince and Shadow models. This policy, together with the improved shock absorber and the surer low-speed firing resulting from use of coil ignition, produced engines which responded better at low speeds and appeared to have more torque, even though valves, cams and compression ratio were all unaltered.

FUEL SYSTEM & CARBURETTORS New Amal Monobloc carburettors, with integral float chambers, were adopted for the Series Ds. Identical 1¹⁄₁₆in type 376/31 units were used front and rear on the Black Knight and Rapide models (body part number 376/003), with the Black Prince and Black Shadow being fitted with the larger 1¹⁄₈in type 389/10

Similarity of the 65bhp Picador target aircraft engine with the motorcycle engine is obvious when looking at these crankcases. A similar triplex primary drive was retained, but where the motorcycle engine had a gearbox and clutch, the Picador featured a simple bevel box (missing from this example), which became the front of the aircraft unit and drove the wooden propeller.

The original engine shock absorber (ESA) featured an 18-hole cam accepting 36 small springs in concentric pairs (far right). This was the standard fitting on all B and C engines, but for the Series D engine the ESA was redesigned and the cam enlarged to accept 44 springs in 22 holes (centre). The Picador ESA was different again, with 26 holes (left).

Carburettors adopted for the enclosed Black Prince (and open Series D Black Shadow) were 1⅛in Amal Monoblocs. Only right-handed Monoblocs were available at the time, so the adjusters are hidden on the inner sides. Original Amal silver-painted finish is well illustrated on the rear carburettor, where chipped and peeled areas provide a contrast with the darker zinc alloy base metal colour.

Monoblocs (body part number 389/002). New manifolds were required to suit the flange-fitting carburettors, with their 2in bolt centres (holes $^{11}/_{32}$in diameter), different items being required for the 1$^1/_{16}$in bore of the Black Knight and the larger 1$^1/_8$in bore of the Black Prince.

The Monobloc design was more compact than its predecessors, enabling Vincents to use the 'front' head on the rear cylinder where carburettor space was restricted by the dynamo drive boss. Different petrol pipes and unions were required for the new carburettors, and a simpler arrangement than that of the B and C models was used. One black plastic pipe connected each tap to one carburettor, and a third pipe linked the two carburettors via the twin pipe unions. All Monobloc carburettors were zinc-based die-castings and, unfortunately, were only initially available in right-handed form, so the throttle stop adjusters were on the 'wrong' side of the body for the Vincent. Once again tickover adjustment was an awkward task for the Vincent owner, as it had been with the original Series Bs.

Originally, Monobloc carburettors were fitted with copper and brass floats, and nylon float needles, but the later plastic floats and Viton-tipped needles are more satisfactory. Although Vokes air filters, of a rather crude triangular pattern, were available for the open models, these would not fit under the cowlings of the enclosed models, which could not, therefore, be supplied with filters.

GEARBOX Little change was considered necessary in the clutch or gearbox, which had proved robust enough. The early Series B gearchange problems had been adequately overcome, although the 'box still did not respond very well to fast changes, and the revised pawl carrier with bent-up ears to restrict pawl motion had only been introduced as late as 1953 (Vincent part G61/1).

Similarly, the clutch continued to receive only minor modifications, with Stellite used to reduce wear on the actuating lever in 1953, and a divided clutch pushrod, with a ball bearing separating the halves, introduced in 1954. In spite of the advent of Duron clutch linings (reputed to be oil-resistant) in 1953, a significant modification introduced with the Ds was revised oil sealing for the clutch mainshaft, to keep oil away from the linings. Instead of the old Dowty bonded seal an O-ring was used, but a revised gearbox mainshaft and clutch nut were also required to match. The complete assembly can be used on earlier models, but the parts are not individually interchangeable, and converting earlier models is rarely worth the expense and labour involved. All die-cast crankcases, used on a few late Cs as well as all Ds, had the stronger gearbox cam-plate spindle boss, for experience had shown that the previous sand-cast cases could be damaged in this area, usually by the spindle vibrating loose and/or brutal gear-changing.

The final drive, by $^5/_8$in x $^3/_8$in chain, was retained unaltered. The Black Knight, Black Prince, Rapide and Black Shadow models used common gear ratios that replicated standard B and C Rapide ratios.

SERVO CLUTCH No changes had been made to the servo clutch, although road testers found it to be sweeter than on earlier models. This impression no doubt resulted from the other improvements, such as better primary-drive shock absorber components, and the good low-speed running provided by coil ignition and the new Monobloc carburettors.

CYCLE PARTS

FRAME & REAR SUSPENSION Major changes were introduced with the Series D, under the cowlings as well as externally, in order to improve suspension and comfort. The starting point was a new upper frame member (UFM), which no longer acted as an oil tank and could, therefore, be made smaller than its predecessor. In fact, the same steering head lug was used, simply machined a little differently; but instead of the bolt-on, box-section oil tank, a simple 1$^1/_8$in tube was substituted, with appropriate lugs on each end. Its smaller size allowed a much smaller cutaway to be used in the petrol tank and, more importantly, it accommodated the much longer proprietary Armstrong combined spring/damper unit. This unit, which replaced the older Vincent-designed damper and twin spring boxes, gave increased rear suspension travel of approximately 6in. The new UFM, however, did not prove to be as strong as the old one, and some have been known to crack, probably because of the extra stresses of sidecar use or accident damage.

Although superficially similar to the earlier rear frame member (RFM), the Series D version was in fact much altered, and is not interchangeable with the earlier RFMs. The single spring/damper unit required closer lugs for attachment at the RFM, and spring clips instead of nuts were used on the attachment studs at both ends of the unit. The seat-stay lugs were omitted, since a fully sprung arrangement was adopted for all the Series D variants, supported directly from the pivot-bearing spindle instead of on seat stays from the rear fork.

Also omitted on the rear fork was machining of the cross-tube bosses previously used for the twin brake cross-shaft, and of the left-hand torque arm anchor, because only a single drum was utilised on the D. A few early Ds had chainguard bosses on both sides, in expectation that the single-cylinder Victor model would be made, with its conventional chain line. But this was soon dropped when the decision was made not to proceed with the 500s. No doubt cost entered into the decision to use only a single rear drum, but technically there was also the advantage that deleting one drum, and also the old rear stand, reduced unsprung weight. Since improved suspension was a

Two nuts at the lower front corner of the rear cowling release it to swing up, with a prop provided to hold it aloft when work is in progress on the rear wheel. Tubular support frame can be seen bonded inside the cowling. A single Armstrong rear damper controls the suspension on both Black Knight and Black Prince models.

major aim, and the heavier Touring-size tyres and rims were being adopted, this method of achieving a good unsprung-to-sprung weight ratio was of some importance.

The obsolete style of rear stand was also retired because all the D models featured a new centre stand operated by a hand lever, along the lines of the device fitted to pre-war Rudge-Whitworth machines. The stand lever pivoted on a modified footrest hanger and operated the tubular stand via links and pins, the whole being of simple construction and fabricated without lugs or castings. Although not directly transferable to B and C machines, because of interference with their second rear brake, the design has been copied in slightly modified form by private owners and fitted to a number of earlier machines.

STEERING & FRONT SUSPENSION Girdraulic forks were retained for the Series Ds, but with softer springing provided by longer, 16½in single springs instead of the 15in springs of the Series Cs, and oil nipples to improve lubrication of the bushes. Proprietary hydraulic dampers had become readily available, and so the old Vincent design was replaced with an Armstrong sealed-for-life component. Both the stroke and the fully extended length of the Armstrong were marginally shorter than the original Vincent damper. To compensate for the Armstrong's shorter overall length, longer 1in eyebolts were used in place of the Series C's ⅜in bolts; these should *only* be used with the shorter damper units. The D's front suspension, therefore, was softer but slightly shorter in travel than that of the preceding Cs.

The steering damper, too, received attention, with the twin-disc form being adopted – a recommended modification for earlier machines. The straight HRD form of handlebar was retained and was still black-enamelled, but it was lengthened by 1½in to 26½in. Handlebar levers and fittings remained as before, except for a change of dipswitch with the adoption of Lucas electrical equipment throughout, and mounting the twin choke levers upside-down on the enclosed models.

The new cowlings made the front of the Black Knight and Black Prince models look very different from their predecessors; but underneath relatively little had changed, as could be seen on the open Rapide and Black Shadow. Unsprung weight was, however, reduced by having only the Fibreglass front mudguard fitted to the unsprung part of the forks. The remainder of the front cowling also carried the head-lamp which had previously been supported on stays from the fork legs and had bobbed up and down as part of unsprung weight. The front end, therefore, gained some improvement in springing/damping to match the revised rear assembly.

BRAKES, WHEELS & TYRES To provide addit-ional comfort, and no doubt because the 3.00-20in size previously used for the front wheel had become obsolete, the Series D machines adopted Touring specification wheels of 3.50-19in front and 4.00-18in rear. Tyres remained of Avon manufacture, with a ribbed type at the front and a block-tread pattern at the rear.

All Series D models dispensed with duo-braking on the rear wheel, adopting instead the lighter arrangement of a single drum, but utilising the ribbed Shadow type for its improved stiffness and heat dissi-pation. This drum carried the sprocket, and was fitted with a new short water-excluder. On the other side, a simple bearing cover replaced the usual brake-plate assembly, to keep dirt out, and shorter hub bolts were required to retain the spoke flanges. To clear the rear cowl, the rear brake operating lever was cranked and fitted pointing downwards instead of upwards, as on

previous models, and operated by a longer brake cable with its anchor screwed into the torque arm fitting (the same item once used on the early, short Series B RFM). Some cost-cutting was evident in the adop-tion of a plain wheel spindle, with hexagon head, instead of the previous stainless steel tommy bar, and simple ¼in BSF chain adjuster bolts in place of the complex finger adjusters employed on Bs and Cs.

The Black Knight used twin Rapide-type plain 7in drums on the front wheel. It was thought that only the higher-performance Black Prince enclosed model warranted twin ribbed 7in Shadow drums, although all Ds utilised the same WM2 section rims and 3.50-19in Avon Speedmaster front tyres. The wheels of the enclosed models were fitted with a plain

Inside the curve of the windscreen is a dashboard containing the instruments and a smaller version of the transfers found on front and rear cowlings. Screen and dashboard turn with the steering and the Girdraulic forks bob up and down underneath. Series D petrol tank has only a single cap.

The Black Knight (above) continued to use the Rapide's twin plain front brake drums. Old speedometer drive gear inside the right-hand drum was retained, but with a different right-angle gearbox and cable run on the enclosed models. As the higher-performance model, derived from the Black Shadow, the Black Prince has two ribbed Shadow drums (above right) in its 3.50-19in front wheel. A large Black Prince transfer adorns the cowling.

hexagon-headed axle in place of the stainless steel tommy-bar axle of the earlier models, providing a small reduction in unsprung weight; the plain axle was also cheaper to produce. It remains important, however, to undo the axle from the bolt end, and not to try to turn the nut, which is positively located by the machined fork end.

SEAT, MUDGUARDS & FUEL TANK A completely new seat was required to blend in with the rear enclosure. The result was a simple, tapered shape made from a steel pressing. The seat pivoted at its nose, from a bracket attached to the tank bolts, to reveal the oil tank filler, the voltage regulator and a little storage space for tools. It rested upon the rear cowling and

integral sub-frame, and was retained by a ball catch at the rear. Early D seats utilised spring steel inserts but later models relied entirely on a foam seat squab. The same seat was used for the open D Rapide and D Black Shadow models, on a hastily designed fully sprung seat frame whose only virtue seems to be that it accommodated a capacious toolbox opposite the oil tank. Scries Ds were supplied with a set of tools similar to that found on earlier models, but in the case of the Ds the toolbox was long and thin enough to accept the tyre pump, and so the pump lugs under the petrol tank were omitted.

A short rear mudguard was fitted to the rear frame to complement the rear cowl, which kept rider and passenger clean. However, it does allow a lot of road

Rear wheel (opposite) on both Black Knight and Black Prince is fitted with a single ribbed brake drum. The cam-operating lever points downward and is directly operated by the brake. Cowling largely protects the brake from rain, but a small, part-circular water excluder on the bottom of the brake plate provides protection from wheel spray. A baffle on the short mudguard also keeps spray from the rear of the engine, and the electrics.

Under the seat (right), which hinges forward on release of a catch, is the oil tank filler cap, the Lucas regulator (AVC) and space for the tool roll and small spare parts. On the cowling behind the tapered seat is one of the two large transfers (below), the other being on the nose of the front wheel cowling. For the Black Knight, the symbol used above the Vincent scroll is a Knight's axe.

filth to accumulate inside the cowl and on various parts, so many owners have fitted a more extended mudguard, using a pair of stays, as on the B and C models. At the front of the machine the old Birmabright light alloy mudguard was replaced by the black Fibreglass cowl, which formed a deeply valanced and efficient mudguard. Brackets retained this Fibreglass moulding to the fork bridge plate at the top, and at the bottom it was bolted to a loop-type stay. As on the Meteor, which also had no prop-stands, this loop-stay served double duty, acting as a front stand for wheel removal and puncture repairs.

The fuel tank was manufactured from the same basic pressing as the B and C tanks, because press tools were too expensive to replace unnecessarily. It was fitted to the machine at the same mounting points, except that no distance piece and tie bar were fitted at the rear, tank stiffness having been adequately increased by the reduced UFM cutaway. However, the underside panel was completely revised, with a much smaller tunnel for the UFM, and no opening for an oil filler, as the oil tank had been re-located. This resulted in a considerable increase in petrol capacity, from 3⅓ gallons to 4 gallons. No lining was applied to the tank on enclosed models (the lining being placed instead on the enclosures), and there were no 'Vincent' transfers on the side of the tank.

COWLINGS The cowlings provided the visual impact of the Series D Vincent range, giving the bikes the

Front view demonstrates the weather protection afforded to the Prince or Knight rider. This Black Prince is not fitted with the detachable hand-muffs which the original catalogue described as optional extras; it is very rare to find an enclosed model which does not have them. Three-quarter view (opposite) of LRO 927 shows that the side panels, with their built-in legshields, also make effective air scoops to provide cooling air for the big-twin engine inside.

aspect of a fully clad war-horse, which no doubt helped to suggest the titles Victor, Black Knight and Black Prince.

At the front, both the mudguard and the screen cowlings were fork-mounted, turning the headlight with the steering. Above the mudguard, which has already been described, a complex cowling supported the steeply curved windscreen, enclosing the instrument cluster in a dashboard above the headlamp mounting. The moulding also provided a built-in, forward-facing number plate, and attachment points for hand-muffs to shroud the rider's hands. These were described in the catalogue as optional extras but appear to have been supplied as original equipment in most, if not all, cases.

The side panels fulfilled a multiplicity of functions: they were not there simply to hide the working parts. At the front they formed legshields, the protruding beaks being an important part of this function, and they also served as an air scoop and tunnel to provide

cooling for the engine. Hidden under the front, and providing the forward mounting points, was a substantial loop-type crashbar to protect both the rider and those rather fragile panels.

The rear cowling was bonded directly to the rear sub-frame, which was composed of three interconnected loops also providing pick-up points for pillion footrest, oil tank and luggage equipment mounting. The complete cowling could be pivoted upwards (after first raising the seat, and loosening the lower sleeve nuts) for access to the rear wheel and other mechanicals, a prop-stay being provided to hold it up.

The year 1954 was very early in the development of Fibreglass for use in mainstream production. Few motorcycle manufacturers followed Vincent's lead until some years later, leaving development of the material to the proprietors of add-on fairings and panniers. Vincent experienced difficulty in sourcing mouldings of adequate finish and quality.

According to Phil Vincent, the production mould-

Distinctive 'beaks' on top of the legshields (above left) are important in protecting the rider from the elements. Air flows were investigated by sticking on tufts of wool to make them visible, and these beaks were added to stop a flow of air and water over the top of the legshields. Front cowl (above) incorporates a number plate panel sized to suit the six-figure British number plate of the time. Detachable hand-muffs are retained by three bolts, as is the deeply curved windscreen. Modern replacements for the screen have been made in clear and smoked acrylic; this dark screen serves to make the machine even more imposing.

Coil ignition was adopted for the Series D models, with the single coil crudely mounted above the primary chaincase, and a new distributor and sheet metal cover replaced the previous magneto and cast aluminium cover. On enclosed models this is all hidden behind a side panel, partly supported by lugs on the crashbar that is an integral part of the machine's specification.

ings were finished in Pinchin & Johnson synthetic enamel, baked at 150°F, although George Aylott of the paintshop says that stoving caused bubbling under the Fibreglass, and the mouldings were spray finished. Lining consisted of a simple stripe each side in ³⁄₁₆in wide gold leaf, starting on the front mudguard, continuing briefly along the side panel beaks, and then along the side panel, before sweeping across and down the rear cowl.

The same cowlings were used on Black Prince and Black Knight models, except for the first prototypes in which contours differed in a few details from the final design; for example, an altered lower line to the rear cowlings, and the shape of the legshield beaks, designed to catch spray. Details of the lining were also identical on the two models; but there was some difference in the transfers. On the Black Knight large transfers depicting a Knight's axe behind the Vincent scroll and the wording 'Black Knight' adorned the top of both front mudguard and rear cowl, while a smaller

version of the same transfer was affixed to the dashboard. The Black Prince featured a Prince's helm above the Vincent scroll and the legend 'Black Prince', with large transfers on front mudguard and rear cowling, and a smaller version on the dashboard.

ELECTRICAL EQUIPMENT & INSTRUMENTS

IGNITION & TIMING The owner survey carried out by the factory before deciding on the Series D enhancements had revealed requests for easier starting, so it was decided to switch from magneto to coil ignition. Although widely used on cars for decades, coil ignition was distrusted by riders familiar with the under-powered and neglected electrical coil ignition systems found on a minority of motorcycles. However, through the 1950s coil ignition finally replaced the magneto as a result of lower production costs and somewhat improved generators, although Vincents never gained the benefit of later and more reliable alternators, and featured a dynamo to the end.

A Lucas DKX2A distributor system was adopted (Lucas part number 40455A) which could be fitted directly where the magneto had previously been, driven by the same Tufnol gear as earlier models, but without the ATD mechanism. Parts for this distributor, which incorporated a bob-weight ATD mechanism internally, are now hard to find but the condenser and points remain readily available (Lucas numbers 400308 and 400415 respectively). Points gap was 10–12 thou. The large 6-volt GQ coil was mounted on a plate on the left-hand side of the crankcase by long nuts, an arrangement hidden by the panels of the enclosed models, but gaining no cosmetic Brownie points on the open versions. The HT leads were tied to the oil pipe on the left, and fed behind the head bracket to reach the plug in the front end from the rear. Timing for both Black Prince and Black Knight models was listed by the factory service manager as 38–40° (½in–½in BTDC) 'according to the particular engine and conditions of use'. There was no change to the plug recommendation, which remained as KLG FE70 ¾in reach type, with a 25 thou points gap.

DYNAMO, WIRING, LIGHTS & HORN A completely new electrical system was adopted for the Series D range, identical on Black Knight and Black Prince models, and varying only slightly in layout for the open Rapide and Black Shadow variants. Although 50 watts had been the best available in 1946, this was no longer true in 1954; and, in any case, Miller was fading from the motorcycle electrical equipment market.

The solution was to adopt Lucas equipment throughout. The E3L 'long' dynamo fitted into the same 3in cradle as the previous Miller instrument, but, oddly, the taper-shaft model (as used on BSA and AJS/Matchless) was not adopted; instead, Vincent chose the parallel-shaft type favoured for Magdyno units. Possibly this was because the taper-shaft model would not slide quite as close to the primary chaincase as the Miller, and slightly different drive parts would have been required, which would inevitably have got mixed up with the earlier type, to the detriment of the primary drive. The parallel-shaft dynamo had to have a completely different sprocket carrier, simply made but clearly not interchangeable by mistake with the Miller drive components. An RB107 automatic voltage control (AVC), containing both regulator and cut-out, was used, fitted into the rear cowling under the seat; MCR2 and RB108 types are equally suitable.

The Lucas white-face ammeter, fitted into the dashboard panel, featured an internal ignition warning light, and, of course, the panel also housed an ignition switch, something not previously fitted to

Rounded Lucas 529 rear lamp was selected for the enclosed models, to match the curve of the rear cowling, on which a large model transfer was affixed.

Vincent-HRDs. New wiring looms were also required; these differed between open and enclosed models, although the exact reasoning for some of the differences is not clear. An HF1441 horn was fitted behind the steering head lug. A front brake operated stop light switch picked up power feed from the horn terminal, conveniently sited in this forward position, but the wiring diagrams issued by the factory were in error regarding the switch wiring, showing an arrangement that would not work.

Unlike the open models, which retained a separate 8in headlamp, the enclosed models had a Lucas F700 pre-focus unit fitted into the cowling, which was fully sprung but still turned with the front wheel – something on which PCV was adamant. The Lucas F700 was often referred to as a 'sealed-beam' unit because

Dashboard comparison. Black Knight instrumentation (top) consists of lighting and ignition switches, white-faced ammeter (incorporating red ignition warning light) and Smiths S467/3/L 120mph speedometer. Black Prince layout (above) is identical, except for Smiths S652/L 150mph speedometer. Whereas all other Vincent speedometer needles rotate from 1 o'clock to 11 o'clock, the Black Prince's needle moves from 7 o'clock to 5 o'clock. Model transfers, just visible, also differed.

of its crimped-in glass and non-adjustable bulb, but it should more correctly be referred to as a 'pre-focus' unit since a sealed-beam unit constitutes an integral, non-replaceable bulb, as indeed had been fitted to US export models for some years. A modest 30/24-watt British pre-focus bulb was normal for the period and was then very common, but it is now somewhat rarer, especially in 6-volt form. At the rear, the tiny Miller stop/tail lamp was finally abandoned for a larger Lucas lamp with plastic lens using the conventional 6-volt 6/18-watt stop/tail bulb (now obsolescent, but an interchangeable 6-volt 5/21-watt type remains readily available). On the enclosed models the lamp was a type 529 whose curved profile matched the rear cowl profile better than the more popular 564 used on the open Ds. The lighting switch was fitted into

the dashboard panel, retained by a spring clip, and exists in a variety of slightly different forms.

SPEEDOMETER & DRIVE The vintage-style front wheel gear drive for the speedometer was retained, mounted on the right-hand brake back plate, but with minor changes to suit the revised cowlings. A different right-angle gearbox was utilised, with a slightly longer reach and mirror image casting, driving through a longer 37in speedometer cable to reach the revised speedometer location.

The speedometer was positioned in the middle of the dashboard on both Black Knight and Black Prince models, but different patterns were required for the two. The Black Knight was fitted with a 120mph speedometer, but again of slightly different pattern from that used on preceding Rapide and Comet models; the Smiths number was S467/3/L, or S467/7/L for the 180kph export version. A special speedometer head was employed for the Black Prince, which required a 150mph fitting to match its Black Shadow type of performance. It was a normal 3in instrument fitted with '150mph' internals; the Smiths number for it is S652/L. A metric 250kph version was listed as S652/K/L; however, as so few Ds were exported, this one is very rare.

OPTIONAL SPECIFICATIONS

Only about 100 each of the Black Prince and Black Knight enclosed models were produced, so there was little opportunity for optional specifications to be developed. Original factory records for the Ds no longer exist, and therefore there is no certain way of checking back as to whether special customer-specification versions were made. One optional item which was offered was a deflector for the windscreen on the enclosed models. Sourced from Feridax, this item could be clipped to the top edge of the screen to raise its effective height for tall riders.

LUGGAGE EQUIPMENT Luggage equipment was envisaged for the enclosed D models, which had been designed as luxury touring machines. The rear enclosure frames carry built-in mounting points, but no touring equipment ever materialised.

TOURING SPECIFICATION The fully enclosed specification of the Black Knight and Black Prince models featured all the extra weather protection and comfort previously provided with Touring specification equipment, which therefore became obsolete on the introduction of the Black Knight and Black Prince.

COLOURS No variations of colour scheme are known; all Black Knight and Black Prince models were finished in the standard black, with gold lines.

BUYING A VINCENT

Restoring a Vincent can be a long and expensive business, but there is no shortage of available advice and help. There are numerous books in print detailing the history and technicalities of the machines, and additional titles which are out of print but can be unearthed through advertisements or at autojumbles. A thriving Vincent-HRD Owners Club exists and there are several firms specialising in the manufacture and supply of parts or the restoration of engines or complete motorcycles; these are widely advertised in the classic motorcycle press and the club magazine *MPH*. Buying the machine in the first place represents a different challenge, not least because it may consist of a single transaction – and with the high price of Vincents, it also represents an opportunity for a single, expensive mistake. The prospective owner has some decisions to make before even commencing to look seriously for a bike, in particular what, where, and how to buy. What to buy encompasses both the model and its condition. This may be dictated by financial considerations, or by the buyer's own needs. One person may be looking for a machine to ride and rally immediately, while another may be more concerned to exercise engineering and restoration skills in the challenge to get another 'heap of scrap' running and roadworthy again.

On paper there are plenty of pre-World War II models to choose from, but pre-Series A machines are so rarely for sale that advice and pricing information are of little use. The Series A models command somewhat similar prices to the post-war versions, except that the A Rapide is much rarer, and therefore more expensive, than its later counterpart. Useful advice can only be offered on the choice of post-war models. The choice between single- and twin-cylinder models will certainly affect price, and of course price may indeed be an influencing factor, but it would be unwise to allow that factor alone to dictate a choice. The singles never had and never will have the aura of the big-twins; so if 'legend' is the driving force then a twin it must be. On the other hand, the singles boasted excellent performance and quality in their time. Their more lightly loaded mechanics generally prove more reliable, in spite of the bikes perhaps having to be ridden harder, and their performance and gearing will prove much more suitable for slow Vintage rallies. If, therefore, ownership of a Vincent-HRD alone is the requirement, then a Comet (or Meteor) may make an excellent choice and will be much less daunting to maintain than one of the twins. Let me recap a little. Three single-cylinder models were made. The Grey Flash was usually supplied for racing, although a road-equipped 'dual-purpose' specification model was also listed; both are rare, as well as expensive. The Series C Comet is by far the most common and easily obtained single, and indeed the most easily obtained Vincent of all. The girder-fork Meteor model was a cheaper, lower-specification model in its day but is now hard to find and can probably command a slight price premium over the Comet.

There is a much greater range of twin-cylinder models to choose from, or aim for, depending on one's point of view. The legendary 150mph Black Lightning was catalogued only as a racing model (although one or two road-equipped Lightnings were supplied); it was made in very small numbers, and anyone with the determination to find and afford one probably needs no general-purpose help. Series A Rapides, too, only rarely become available, so a determined monitoring of every relevant publication and auction, and any private contacts, generally offer the only avenues. Road-going models include the enclosed Black Prince and Black Knight models, and Rapides and Shadows in all post-war series. Although Prince and Knight were made in similar limited numbers, the former (nominally an enclosed Shadow) is regarded as more desirable; but both are expensive and difficult to find. Rapides and Shadows, however, are easily found in the motorcycle press, at specialist dealers, and at auction, as well as by private contact through clubs. A Shadow is probably the most generally sought-after Vincent of all. Series C models of the twins are the most common, and generally make the most satisfying buy. Series Ds offer improved comfort but are regarded as ugly by many. The Bs are both lighter and lower than later variants, but the suspension friction damping is more primitive, as are the Brampton girder forks – in the rare event that they are still in place.

What to buy, however, does not merely relate to the particular model but also to its condition. Here there is no one answer, because of the differing needs of different people. Those without mechanical aptitude, or time, must necessarily buy a ready-restored, or at least running, machine. New restorations are generally the shiniest; but in all other respects let the buyer beware! Even when a rebuild is backed up by receipts, the purchaser cannot be sure that all the parts were in fact fitted, or that they were *correctly* fitted – or that a large hammer wasn't employed in their fitting. There are now a number of stolen machines in circulation. Engine and frame numbers should be carefully examined for any sign of tampering; and where possible, it is also wise have some check run on them. In all cases, evidence of the seller's identity should be checked, and a receipt obtained for the transaction. A running machine with some mileage logged offers some insurance against the worst errors, as does purchase through a professional dealer, who may charge a higher price but also has legal responsibilities which offer some protection to the buyer.

The alternatives to a complete and running Vincent include a complete or near-complete but not running machine, or simply a box of bits (a 'basket case'). Someone's unfinished rebuild can give a new owner a head start, but you should always ask yourself why the former owner gave up – and whether you

Can you tell if this is a complete machine? Courtesy of Manfred Kinne, Germany, this is a picture of a Series A Meteor, dismantled but plated and painted ready for reassembly. Apart from ordinary sizes of nuts and bolts, I suggest that this is indeed a complete machine.

have any more stamina (or money) than he did. An old and neglected model, or a worn-out runner, may not appear to be a promising start, but provided that the price is reasonable it *can* represent the best of all worlds. If it is all in one piece, that almost guarantees completeness, and although you will undoubtedly need to spend money on it, at least the initial price you pay should reflect that. A box of parts is likely to prove the most expensive and difficult route to acquiring a Vincent that will be finally fit for the road, but at least the expense can be spread over a long period. For many this may be the only viable option. Boxes of parts are notorious for being incomplete, but fortunately almost any part can now be obtained new, which means that non-availability of critical components is no longer a bar to completion of a project. However, a careful study is vital because some major items, such as crankcase, heads and flywheels, are so expensive that their absence may make a rebuild impractical. *Condition* is a different matter; naturally, good condition of all parts is desirable but almost anything can be repaired and restored, provided that the initial purchase price is low enough to make the

task of repair or restoration worthwhile.

How and where to buy has already been touched upon, with some mention of purchase through advertisements or auctions. But there are other considerations. UK buyers will almost certainly look to home sources, as perhaps will those living in the old colonial countries to which many machines were exported, although if currency exchange rates are favourable they may also choose to check UK outlets and accept the inevitable shipping costs. In Argentina, with a poorer exchange rate, there should still be the remnants of 1947 exports to be found! Although a few Vincents were imported into Japan, these were mostly Comets, which were all that even well-off Japanese could afford in 1950, and the very few twins originally seen in that country were usually imported by servicemen stationed there. Nowadays, however, exchange-rate values are reversed. Japanese buyers find it easier to look to the UK for a purchase and, as with a number of other foreign buyers, they have found that even the potentially poor buy obtained by 'buying blind' through dealers or agents amounts to better value than either scheduling a personal visit or

Very few original and unrestored Vincents still exist for reference. This 1951 Black Shadow was stored in a Texas barn for many years, as indicated by faded fabric-covered cables and original Avon Speedster front tyre. Plain black steel mudguards were never catalogued: were these fitted by factory, dealer or owner?

near-futile attempts to respond to advertisements before home buyers have snapped the machines up.

ENGINE & TRANSMISSION

If the machine is complete and running, listen to the engine. Do not worry immediately if it is noisy (a Vincent has been described as sounding 'like two gas stoves being dragged over cobbles') but, rather, try to identify the noises. A general clatter, especially from the timing chest, is normal, but whines are not, and no individual tap should normally stand out from the rest, although front exhaust tappet noise can sometimes be discerned. Whines usually come from the dynamo drive or an overly tight meshing of cam wheels and large idler. Neither is desirable; both indicate poor assembly and both should be corrected. Oil consumption – at least when the engine is running on original parts – has never been especially good, but a Vincent should not leak oil. The standard twin's clutch feels very fierce to the uninitiated but should not drag or slip (the Comet clutch, of course, being of conventional multi-plate type, has conventional operating characteristics).

When the machine is in boxes its mechanical condition is more easily examined (and usually found to be poor), but the main objective is to ensure completeness. Major items need to be present: a pair of crankcases (check the mating numbers), preferably

with covers and bearing housings in good condition and certainly with no bits sawn off; a pair of flywheels (the new owner noting that Comet flywheels differ from those of twins and that conversion is impractical); a full set of gears and shafts (or Burman 'box, in the case of singles – and note that the mainshaft is not the same as that used in Burmans fitted to other makes); cams and gearwheels; and a complete set of clutch parts (remember that there are a lot of parts in a Vincent twin's clutch…). Although items such as studs, nuts and case screws may seem unimportant, there are so many that a 'basket case' deficient in such trivia will present a significant problem to the rebuilder.

What price the remains of this Norvin, on view at an auction? Engine has clearly been partly dismantled; so is it nearly complete, or an empty shell? What is it worth? At an auction, time to decide is limited, and remember that you have to pay a buyer's premium of perhaps 10 per cent on top of your actual bid. Avoid getting carried away!

Vincents for sale come in all imaginable forms. This Series D engine has been chopped (gearbox cut off) and rebuilt with a modified mainshaft to mate with a vintage Morgan three-wheeler chassis. It sold quickly to a Dutch buyer.

CYCLE PARTS

On a running machine front-fork condition can be cursorily checked by pushing against the front brakes, or pushing with the front wheel set against a wall (steering damper slackened off), before sampling the machine on the road. Play in head bearings, spindles and eccentrics will quickly become apparent. Very slight play at the spindles and eccentrics may be tolerated – it leads to a characteristic 'click' as the steering is turned – but major wear should be corrected using readily available parts. The forks should move up and down easily even with pressure on the handlebars. Completely seized forks are not unknown (or safe). Vincent brakes were good in their day, even if they are not up to modern disc-brake standards; the front-brake lever should not come back to the bar, and certainly it should not be possible to push the bike along with the brake applied. Poor brakes and any assurance that 'they were always like that' should be taken as a reflection on the vendor's competence, and not on that of the brakes in original condition. In the worst cases a test ride should be taken with caution. But most poor Vincent brakes can be materially improved by simple adjustments, although new parts may be required for full improvement.

Once upon a time cycle parts were of little value, and when machines were broken up they were thrown away. This is no longer the case. Major cycle parts are difficult to find and expensive secondhand.

A 'basket case' should therefore contain at least a complete UFM and steering head (preferably still firmly in one piece), an RFM (preferably with no cracks at the right rear fork lug, although these are repairable), a pair of wheel hubs, and a complete set of front-fork parts. Girdraulic forks are complex, and expensive to replace, so a pair of blades, a head-stem and clip, and a pair of fork links are minimum requirements; but the condition of spindles is not of any consequence since these are readily replaced (similar provisions apply to the rarer Brampton girders). Bare wheel hubs are simple alloy spools, fitted with taper-roller bearings, but complete hubs include brake drums, plates, shoes, shims, spindles, and so on, and since the majority of models featured four brakes (ie, four drums, four brake-plates, and eight brake shoes) replacement of all these is not to be taken lightly.

Whether the prospective purchase is complete and running or is a basket case, the best way to ensure a sound purchase is to take the advice of an acknowledged expert in this marque which has so many differences and foibles compared to more common British bikes of the same period. Where this is not possible, the next best thing is not to set expectations too high. On a running machine expect to find things wrong, or at least not to your taste, and in need of bedding down. With a basket case, expect to have worn or missing parts, and to spend at least as much money again on the task of re-assembly. Eventually the motorcycle will be worth it.

DATA SECTION

SERIES A (1934-39) SPECIFICATIONS

	METEOR	COMET	COMET SPECIAL	TT REPLICA	RAPIDE
ENGINE PREFIX	M	C	TTC	TTR	V
BORE & STROKE (MM)	84 × 90	84 × 90	84 × 90	84 × 90	84 × 90 twin
CAPACITY (CC)	499	499	499	499	998
COMPRESSION RATIO	6.8:1	7.3:1	8:1	8:1	6.8:1
BHP/RPM	25 @ 5300	26 @ 5600	28 @ 5600	34 @ 5800	45 @ 5500
MAGNETO/GENERATOR	BTH Mag-generator	Miller Dynomag	Miller Dynomag	BTH TT magneto	Lucas MNVI 47°
IGNITION TIMING	42° (¹⁷⁄₃₂in)	42° (¹⁷⁄₃₂in)	40° (½in)	42° (¹⁷⁄₃₂in)	42° (¹⁷⁄₃₂in)
SPARKING PLUG	KLG F70	KLG F70	KLG F100	KLG F220	KLG F70
VALVE TIMING (DEGREES)					
INLET OPENS BTDC	40	44	48	48	40
INLET CLOSES ABDC	52	56	60	60	52
EXHAUST OPENS BBDC	65	68	71	71	65
EXHAUST CLOSES ATDC	33	38	42	42	33
CARBURETTOR & SETTINGS	Amal 76/022	Amal 89/011	Amal 10TT	Amal 10TT	6/30 front 76/022 rear
BORE	1¹⁄₁₆in	1⅛in	1⁵⁄₃₂in	1⁵⁄₃₂in	1¹⁄₁₆in
MAIN JET	170	180	330-350	360	180 front/170 rear
NEEDLE JET	Std	Std	Std	Std	Std
NEEDLE POSITION	3	3	0.109	0.109	3
SLIDE	6/4	29/4	6	7	6/4
GEAR RATIOS	SOLO SIDECAR	SOLO SIDECAR			
TOP	4.6 5.5	4.6 5.5	4.3	4.3	3.58
THIRD	5.8 6.9	5.8 6.9	5.0	5.0	4.51
SECOND	7.4 9.3	7.4 9.3	6.2	6.2	6.49
BOTTOM	12.4 14.7	12.4 14.7	7.8	7.8	9.55
PRIMARY CHAIN	0.375 duplex	0.375 duplex	0.375 duplex	0.375 duplex	0.375 duplex
PITCHES	94	94	94	94	94
DRIVE CHAIN	⅝ × ⅜in	⅝ × ⅜in	⅝ × ⅜in	⅝ × ⅜in	⅝ × ⅜in
PITCHES	108	108	108	108	108
WHEELS FRONT	3.00 × 20in (26 × 3)	3.00 × 20in (26 × 3)	3.00 × 20in (26 × 3)	3.00 × 20in (26 × 3)	3.00 × 20in (26 × 3)
REAR	3.25 × 19in (26 × 3.25)	3.25 × 19in (26 × 3.25)	3.25 × 19in (26 × 3.25)	3.25 × 19in (26 × 3.25)	3.25 × 19in (26 × 3.5)
BRAKES FRONT	twin 7in plain drums	twin 7in plain drums	twin 7in plain drums	twin 7in ribbed drums	twin 7in ribbed drums
REAR	twin 7in plain drums	twin 7in plain drums	twin 7in plain drums	twin 7in ribbed drums	twin 7in plain drums
PETROL TANK CAPACITY	3¼ gall	3¼ gall	3¼ gall	5 gall	3½ gall + ½ gall oil
WHEELBASE	55in	55in	55in	55in	58in
DRY WEIGHT	385lb	385lb	385lb	335lb	430lb
TARGET SPEED	75-80mph	85-90mph	87-92mph	102-110mph	105-115mph

NUMBERING SYSTEMS

ENGINE NUMBERS

Vincent owners regard the engine as the most important part of the motorcycle, and therefore the engine number as determining the model and year, when non-original parts have been fitted or a machine has been built up from a mixture of parts or models. After World War II, the Vincent-HRD factory adopted a code and numbering system which carried a great deal of information in the engine number. The number appears on the left-hand side of the crankcase just below the (front) cylinder barrel.

A typical engine number is in the form F10AB/1/8180 (1000cc Rapide). The code is interpreted as follows:

Engine type symbol F = 4-stroke, T = 2-stroke
Capacity (in 100cc) 10 = 1000cc, 5 = 500cc, 0.5 = 50cc (eg, Firefly cyclemotor)
Material symbol A = aluminium alloy (a few special engine types used M for magnesium alloy)
Purpose symbol B = bicycle (other options include M for marine or U for utility)
Design number (divider) Between the obliques, a new number for a fresh design or an added letter for modification to a design, as follows. **1000cc** /1/ = Rapide, /1A/ = White Shadow, /1B/ = Black Shadow, /1C/ = Lightning, /2/ = D Rapide or Black Knight, /2B/ = D Black Shadow or Black Prince (some /3/ crankcases were sold by Harper

The engine number is located just below the (front) cylinder, on the primary chaincase side. When buying, the number should be examined carefully – if in doubt, check with the Vincent Owners Club. However, do not automatically assume that irregular stamping is a fake; this engine is a genuine Grey Flash (/2B/) in spite of the odd-size stampings.

Engines, and some /4/ crankcases by Holders, successors to Vincent Engineers, and /5/ HRD-embossed cases have also been manufactured by Bob Culver/Derek Sayer). **500cc** /2/ = Meteor, /2A/ = Comet, /2B/ = Grey Flash, /3A/ = D Comet or Victor (numbers appear to start at 2 because 1 is for the rare Speedway motor)
Engine number Commencing at 3 and ending at 11134 (excluding /3/, /4/ and /5/ replacement cases/engines)

A prospective buyer is well advised to look at the number carefully, because it is all too easy to 'upgrade' a model by stamping in an extra character, and there are even stolen Vincents in circulation. However, do not automatically assume that an irregular stamping is a fake. The first part of the number was stamped on routinely before machined castings were put into stores, whereas the final designation and serial number were only stamped when the engine was built – and frequently with different stamps. If in doubt, check with the Vincent Owners Club.

FRAME NUMBERS

Frame numbers, too, indicate the original model information in code, all commencing R as a result of being derived from the initial Rapide design. It should be noted that both upper frame member (UFM) and rear frame member (RFM) were stamped with matching numbers, although some present-day machines have been built up with non-matching parts. The UFM is usually stamped on the left-front of the steering head, and the RFM on the left-hand rear lug. Most machines were delivered from the factory with a frame number 1900 larger than the engine number, although this is not an absolute rule, and many earlier models had a difference of, for example, 1990. The numbers decode as follows:

Prefix series R = Series B, RC = Series C, RD = Series D
Design number (divider, 500cc only) /1/ = Meteor or Comet, /1A/ = Grey Flash
Frame number Usually 1900 larger than the engine number
Suffix B = Black Shadow, F = Black Knight, B/F = Black Prince

The frame number is found on the left-hand side of the steering head, alongside the figure of Mercury transfer.

Because Vincents were built up from separate upper and rear frame members (UFM and RFM), both parts are stamped with the frame number. A check on the rear number, situated on the left rear fork end, will show whether it matches the commonly used number on the steering head. If not, the machine may have been built up from parts.

PRODUCTION MODIFICATIONS

Modification	Engine	Frame	Year
Six clutch springs instead of three	70		1947
KVF magneto introduced	104		
Grooved rocker bearings (front inlet only until engine 2340)	193		
23-tooth second gear replaces 24-tooth	309		
Modified gearchange selector pawl spring	350		
Steel oil pump worm	375		
Crankpin drilling revised (two holes instead of six)	380		
Lucas stoplight switch replaced Miller		2340	1948
Petrol tank lugs and tie-bolt added		2408	
Clutch nut with ground face and Dowty seal	594/656		
Crankcase modified to accept a bolt-on dynamo cradle	746		
Circlips replace nuts to retain clutch shoes	853		
Cast iron brake drums introduced		3050	
Metering wires ('joggle wires') fitted to inlet rocker feedbolts	1128		
Solid cylinder holding-down studs replace concentric type	1310		
Lock washers added to retain idler and breather spindle nuts	1314		
Modified breather valve	1400		
Slotted cross-tube introduced on UFM		3500	1949
Rear spring boxes plated instead of enamelled		3616	
Revised gearbox cam plate, G32/2	1590		
Adjustable rear chain oiler introduced		3800	
Longer (18in) RFM introduced		3900	
First Vincent embossed crankcases	3090		
Stainless steel pushrods	3132		
One-piece idler (single-cylinder models)	3477		
Alloy idler gear (Comets from engine 3815)	4548		
HRD type Mercury crest replaced by Vincent type			late 1949
Triple valve springs dropped from Black Shadow	5336		1950
Steering head lug modified and head bracket slotted (FT3/2)		8614	1951
High first gear dropped for Black Shadow model	7076		
MkIII cams with quietening ramps	8343		1952
Drain plug introduced on Burman gearbox		10497	
Modified ratchet shaft and bevel in gearbox (G39/1, G40/1)	8509		
Forged gearchange actuating arm (G66/2)	8697		
Pushrod bush (G111) omitted from clutch shaft	8821		
Duron clutch linings introduced			1952
Oil restrictor discs fitted behind timing case seals	9238		
Modified gearchange pawl carrier	9669		1953
Stellited clutch lever (G91/1)	9701		
Twin disc steering damper replaced single disc type	11937		
Timing cover drillings revised, restrictor discs omitted	10000		
Divided clutch pushrods (G96/1) and ball bearing	10021		
Vincent-HRD Mercury crest replaced by Vincent Engineers type			1953
Series D range replaces Series C			Motorcycle show 1954

PART NUMBERS

The part numbering code used by the factory has been retained by most Vincent-HRD specialists, and is therefore still very useful. The system had the useful property of using prefixes which indicated roughly where on the machine the part belonged, acting as a cross-check with the description, and also indicating where a common part has been 'borrowed' from elsewhere in the design. Simple nuts and bolts received a simple number only (a remnant of an abortive numbering scheme which threatened to give the four identical brake shoes four different numbers!). The suffix system has been usefully extended by modern parts suppliers to indicate variations from the original design.

Prefix C = clutch, E = engine, ET = engine (twin), F = frame, FF = front fork, FT = footrest, G = gearbox, H = hubs, K = tool kit, O = oil pump, PD = primary drive, PR = proprietary parts (eg, Lucas, Burman)
Number
Suffix number When a part was redesigned or modified, it was given a /1 suffix, and this number increased with any subsequent modification. Usually the later part is an improved modification, but occasionally it is an adaptation for use elsewhere on the machine (eg, A22/1 is the long version of the oil banjo bolt A22, for use at the oil filter position)
Suffix letters F = front, R = rear, AS (sometimes S) = assembly, (S) = service exchange, PM = part machined (ie, not ready for use)
Modern suffix An expansion of the original numbering for modern replacement parts: SS = stainless steel version, mod = design modified from original

DATING

Year	Engine	Frame
1946	19	2019
1947	400	2300
1948	1400	3300
1949	4980	6880
1950	5730	7630
1951	8250	10150
1952	9570	11470
1953	10000	11900
1954	10300	12200
1955	11134	13034

* Numbers given are the last made for the year.

SPECIFICATIONS OF 1946-55 MODELS

	B RAPIDE	C RAPIDE	D RAPIDE	B SHADOW	C SHADOW	D SHADOW
BORE & STROKE	84 × 90 twin	84 × 90 twin	84 × 90 twin	84 × 90 twin	84 × 90 twin	84 × 90 twin
CR	6.45:1	6.45:1	6.45:1	7.3:1	7.3:1	7.3:1
BHP/RPM	45 @ 5300	45 @ 5300	45 @ 5300	55 @ 5700	55 @ 5700	55 @ 5700
MAGNETO	KVF GM1	KVF GM1	(see Black Knight)	KVF GM1	KVF GM1	(see Black Prince)
CONTACT GAP	0.012in (0.3mm)	0.012in (0.3mm)	(see Black Knight)	0.012in (0.3mm)	0.012in (0.3mm)	(see Black Prince)
IGNITION TIMING	39° (31/64in)	39° (31/64in)	(see Black Knight)	38° (15/32in)	38° (15/32in)	(see Black Prince)
SPARKING PLUG	KLG FE70	KLG FE70	KLG FE70	KLG FE70	KLG FE70	KLG FE70
QUOTED EQUIVALENT	Champion N5	Champion N5	Champion N5	Champion N5	Champion N5	Champion N5
GENERATOR	Miller D6, 50w	Miller D6, 50w	Lucas E3L, 60w	Miller D6, 50w	Miller D6, 50w	Lucas E3L, 60w
BATTERY	Exide 13a-h	Exide 13a-h	Varley 14a-h	Exide 13a-h	Exide 13a-h	Varley 14a-h
LAMPS : FRONT	6v 24/24w, bayonet	6v 24/24w, bayonet	6v 30/24w, prefocus	6v 24/24w, bayonet	6v 24/24w, bayonet	6v 30/24w, prefocus
REAR	6v 6/18w, offset pin	6v 6/18w, offset pin	6v 6/18w	6v 6/18w, offset pin	6v 6/18w, offset pin	6v 6/18w
VALVE TIMING						
INLET OPENS	40-42° BTDC	40-42° BTDC	(see Black Knight model)	40-42° BTDC	40-42° BTDC	(see Black Prince model)
INLET CLOSES	60-64° ABDC	60-64° ABDC		60-64° ABDC	60-64° ABDC	
EXHAUST OPENS	70-72° BBDC	70-72° BBDC		70-72° BBDC	70-72° BBDC	
EXHAUST CLOSES	28-33° ATDC	28-33° ATDC		28-33° ATDC	28-33° ATDC	
CARBURETTOR	276CJ/1DO front	276DQ/1DV front	376 Monoblocs	280M/1DO front	229E/1DV front	380 Monoblocs
& SETTINGS	276CH/2DS rear	276CH/2DS rear		289N/2DS rear	289N/2DS rear	
BORE	1 1/16in	1 1/16in	1 1/16in	1 1/8in	1 1/8in	1 1/8in
MAIN JET	170	170	220	180	180	250 (or 270)
NEEDLE JET	Standard	Standard	376/072	Standard	Standard	376/072
NEEDLE	n/a	n/a	376/063	n/a	n/a	389/063
NEEDLE POSITION	3	3	2	3	3	2
SLIDE	6/4	6/4	4	29/4	29/4	4
GEARBOX	Vincent	Vincent	Vincent	Vincent	Vincent	Vincent
GEAR RATIOS: TOP	3.5	3.5	3.5	3.5	3.5	3.5
THIRD	4.16	4.16	4.16	4.16	4.16	4.16
SECOND	5.64	5.64	5.64	5.64	5.64	5.64
BOTTOM	9.1	9.1	9.1	7.25	9.1 (engine 7076)	9.1
CLUTCH	Vincent servo	Vincent servo	Vincent servo	Vincent servo	Vincent servo	Vincent servo
PRIMARY CHAIN	0.375in triplex	0.375in triplex	0.375in triplex	0.375in triplex	0.375in triplex	0.375in triplex
PITCHES	94	94	94	94	94	94
DRIVE CHAIN	5/8 × 3/8in	5/8 × 3/8in	5/8 × 3/8in	5/8 × 3/8in	5/8 × 3/8in	5/8 × 3/8in
PITCHES	106	106	106	106	106	106
WHEELS: FRONT	3.00 × 20in	3.00 × 20in	3.50 × 19in	3.00 × 20in	3.00 × 20in	3.50 × 19in
REAR	3.50 × 19in	3.50 × 19in	4.00 × 18in	3.50 × 19in	3.50 × 19in	4.00 × 18in
BRAKES: FRONT	twin 7in plain drums	twin 7in plain drums	twin 7in plain drums	twin 7in ribbed drums	twin 7in ribbed drums	twin 7in ribbed drums
REAR	twin 7in plain drums	twin 7in plain drums	twin 7in ribbed drums	twin 7in ribbed drums	twin 7in ribbed drums	twin 7in ribbed drums
OIL CAPACITY &	6 pints	6 pints	5 pints	6 pints	6 pints	5 pints
TARGET CONSUMPTION	200mpp	200mpp	200mpp	200mpp	200mpp	200mpp
PETROL TANK	3 1/2 gall	3 1/2 gall	4 gall	3 1/2 gall	3 1/2 gall	4 gall
TARGET MPG (KM/L)	55-65	55-65	n/a	55-65	55-65	n/a
WHEELBASE	56 1/2in	56 1/2in	56 1/2in	56 1/2in	56 1/2in	56 1/2in
DRY WEIGHT (CLAIM)	455lb	455lb	455lb	458lb	458lb	458lb
TARGET SPEED	110mph	110mph	110mph	125mph	125mph	125mph

COMMON SCREW THREADS

In addition to building motorcycles, the Vincent factory did a great deal of general engineering work, and possibly for this reason they did not adopt the traditional cycle threads (also known as CEI and BSCy) which were widely used by British motorcycle manufacturers at the time. Instead, they utilised the normal engineering threads in use at the time before widespread adoption of the Unified (American) threads or Metrication. Nevertheless, a wide range of thread types is to be found on the Vincent, reflecting the haphazard way in which thread standardisation historically occurred, and these can be confusing to owners.

Most fasteners, even the common, bought-out items, had a turned finish, not the stamped and rolled threads of modern parts. Before World War II, those specially made fasteners which could not be bought out were sometimes 'Parkerised' (a chemical blacking process) to provide some corrosion protection. Post-war, however, cadmium plating was extensively used, even on the special parts, except where stainless steel components could be fitted. Chromium plating was very little used, except where standard on bought-out items, although show models were often prepared with chromium instead of cadmium.

Cadmium plating is now regarded as environmentally unfriendly, but zinc plating is a satisfactory substitute. Stainless steel fasteners are widely supplied as spare parts, and cap-head screws (commonly called Allen screws) are very popular, but neither were used originally. Note that the combination of aluminium and stainless steel is much more active electrochemically than the original aluminium and steel/cadmium combination. Especially in wet and salty environments, corrosion must be expected unless care is taken to use barrier grease or paint on assembly.

BRITISH STANDARD FINE (BSF)

This series of screw threads, intended for general use, has a Whitworth form (55° thread angle, rounded root and crest). It is widely used on the various nuts and bolts holding a Vincent together, and on special-purpose parts. Enthusiasts will find taps and dies in at least 1/4in, 5/16in, 3/8in and possibly 1/2in sizes very useful.

7/32in × 28 tpi 1000cc clutch drum screws

1/4in × 26 tpi A large number of small fasteners and studs, control lever pivot screws, brake rods, carburettor parts, rear chain adjusters, 500cc clutch screws, damper knobs, D distributor cam hollow bolt

5/16in × 22 tpi Numerous fasteners and studs, gear lever foot-piece, footrest and kick-starter pivots, tank bolts, Girdraulic spring box bolts, oil pump screw, gearchange cover screws, rear stand tommy bar

3/8in × 20 tpi Larger fasteners and studs, rocker feedbolts, magneto and dynamo drive nuts, UFM spigot nuts, seat stay eyebolts, propstand pivot bolts, Girdraulic padbolts

7/16in × 18 tpi Girdraulic spindles, rear spring box eyebolts, kick-starter foot-piece plug

1/2in × 16 tpi Footrest hanger/RFM pivot stud, cylinder head bracket nuts, Burman gearbox studs, wheel spindles and nuts

SPECIFICATIONS OF 1946-55 MODELS

	METEOR	COMET	GREY FLASH	BLACK LIGHTNING	BLACK KNIGHT	BLACK PRINCE
BORE & STROKE	84 × 90	84 × 90	84 × 90	84 × 90 twin	84 × 90 twin	84 × 90 twin
CR	6.45:1	6.8:1	8:1	to order	6.45:1	7.3:1
BHP/RPM	26 @ 5300	28 @ 5800	35 @ 6200	70 @ 5600	45 @ 5300	55 @ 5700
MAGNETO	K1F GM2	K1F GM2	TT (by BTH)	KVF TT	GQ coil & KDX2A distributor	
CONTACT GAP	0.012in	0.012in	0.010in	0.010in	0.010-0.012in	0.010-0.012in
IGNITION TIMING	38° (15/32in)	38° (15/32in)	42° (17/32in)	38° (15/32in)	38-40° (15/32-1/2in)	38-40° (15/32-1/2in)
SPARKING PLUG	KLG FE70	KLG FE70	KLG FE220	KLG FE220	KLG FE70	KLG FE70
QUOTED EQUIVALENT	Champion N5	Champion N5	Champion N3	Champion N3	Champion N5	Champion N5
GENERATOR	Miller D6, 50w	Miller D6, 50w	D6, if fitted	not fitted	Lucas E3L, 60w	Lucas E3L, 60w
BATTERY	Exide 13a-h	Exide 13a-h	-	not fitted	Varley 14a-h	Varley 14a-h
LAMPS : FRONT	6v 24/24w, bayonet	6v 24/24w, bayonet	As for Comet	not fitted	6v 30/24w, prefocus	6v 30/24w, prefocus
REAR	6v 6/18w, offset pin	6v 6/18w, offset pin	if fitted		6v 6/18 w, offset pin	6v 6/18 w, offset pin
VALVE TIMING						
INLET OPENS	40-42° BTDC	40-42° BTDC	55° BTDC	55° BTDC	0.110in inlet lift @ TDC, opening	
INLET CLOSES	60-64° ABDC	60-64° ABDC	68° ABDC	68° ABDC	0.190in inlet lift @ BDC, closing	
EXHAUST OPENS	70-72° BBDC	70-72° BBDC	73° BBDC	73° BBDC	0.220in exhaust lift @ BDC, opening	
EXHAUST CLOSES	28-33° ATDC	28-33° ATDC	50° ATDC	50° ATDC	0.065in exhaust lift @ TDC, closing	
CARBURETTOR	276DQ/1DV	229F/1DV front	10TT9	10TT9	376 Monoblocs	389 Monoblocs
& SETTINGS				front & rear		
BORE	1 1/16in	1 1/8in	32mm	32mm	1 1/16in	1 1/8in
MAIN JET	170	200	1700 (alcohol)	360 (petrol)	220	250 (or 270)
NEEDLE JET	Standard	Standard	0.120 (alcohol)	0.109 (petrol)	376/072	376/072
NEEDLE	n/a	n/a	n/a	n/a	376/063	389/063
NEEDLE POSITION	3	3	4	4	2	2
SLIDE	6/4	29/3	7	7	4	4
GEARBOX	Burman	Burman (Trials)	Albion	Vincent	Vincent	Vincent
GEAR RATIOS: TOP	4.64	4.64 (4.64)	4.87	3.27	3.5	3.5
THIRD	5.94	5.94 (6.82)	5.75	3.89	4.16	4.16
SECOND	8.17	8.17 (9.20)	6.82	5.26	5.64	5.64
BOTTOM	12.4	12.4 (14.6)	10.36	6.77	9.1	9.1
CLUTCH	Burman multiplate	Burman multiplate	Albion multiplate	Vincent servo	Vincent servo	Vincent servo
PRIMARY CHAIN	1/2 × 5/16in	1/2 × 5/16in	1/2 × 5/16in	0.375in triplex	0.375in triplex	0.375in triplex
PITCHES	64	64	64	94	94	94
DRIVE CHAIN	5/8 × 3/8in	5/8 × 3/8in	5/8 × 1/4in	5/8 × 1/4in	5/8 × 3/8in	5/8 × 3/8in
PITCHES	108	108	108	106	106	106
WHEELS: FRONT	3.00 × 20in	3.00 × 20in	3.00 × 21in	3.00 × 21in	3.50 × 19in	3.50 × 19in
REAR	3.50 × 19in	3.50 × 19in	3.50 × 20in	3.50 × 20in	4.00 × 18in	4.00 × 18in
BRAKES: FRONT	twin 7in plain drums	twin 7in plain drums	twin 7in ribbed drums	twin 7in ribbed drums	twin 7in plain drums	twin 7in ribbed drums
REAR	twin 7in plain drums	twin 7in plain drums	twin 7in ribbed drums	twin 7in ribbed drums	single 7in ribbed drum	single 7in ribbed drum
OIL CAPACITY &	6 pints	6 pints	6 pints	6 pints	5 pints	5 pints
TARGET CONSUMPTION	250mpp	250mpp	n/a	n/a	200mpp	200mpp
PETROL TANK	3 1/2 gall	3 1/2 gall	3 3/8 gall	3 3/8 gall	4 gall	4 gall
TARGET MPG (KM/L)	80 (28)	75-80 (26-28)	35 (12.5)	n/a	n/a	n/a
WHEELBASE	55 3/4in	55 3/4in	55 3/4in	56 1/2in	56 1/2in	56 1/2in
DRY WEIGHT (CLAIM)	386lb	390lb	330lb	380lb	460lb	460lb
TARGET SPEED	80mph	90mph	110mph	150mph	110mph	125mph

BRITISH STANDARD WHITWORTH (BSW)

This series of screw threads is of coarse pitch, especially suitable for use in weaker materials such as light alloy. The Whitworth thread form (55° thread angle, rounded root and crest) is used, and is a memorial to Joseph Whitworth who led the way in precision measurement and standardisation without which provision of off-the-shelf spare parts would not be possible (**On a Uniform System of Screw Threads**, Joseph Whitworth, 1841). Useful tap and die sizes are 3/16in, 1/4in and 5/16in Whit.

5/32in × 32 tpi Petrol tap plunger stud (adjustable type)

3/16in × 24 tpi Clutch cover screws, magneto inspection cover screws, Miller regulator attachment studs, big end oil feed quill blanking screw

1/4in × 20 tpi Timing cover screws, primary chaincase screws, gearbox cover plate screws, steady plate studs, 500cc inner chaincase countersunk screws

5/16in × 18 tpi Carburettor adapter and magneto studs (inner ends only, outer ends 5/16in BSF), timing cover blanking screws, exhaust lifter spindles, Burman gearbox cover studs, 1000cc gearchange back plate countersunk screws

3/8in × 16 tpi Crankcase blanking screw, 500cc inner chaincase bolt

7/16in × 14 tpi Brampton fork spring nut

BRITISH STANDARD PIPE (BSP)

BSP threads sizes are mysterious to the uninitiated, because their nominal sizes refer to the bore size of a pipe for which the thread is suitable. The actual threads are thus much larger than the designation suggests, but retain the Whitworth thread form. Pipe threads were routinely used on carburettor and petrol fittings, and for drain plugs. Note that Vincents chose to use the 1/8in size for certain mechanical items where a very fine thread was required, no doubt because they already possessed the tooling, rather than a 3/8in CEI thread, which a 1/4in pipe thread is easily confused with; note that a CEI thread must not be used lest damage be caused.

1/8in (0.383 × 28 tpi) Rocker adjusters ('tappets'), 1000cc clutch adjuster, cylinder jet holder, Vincent damper filler plug, oil pressure release valve cap

1/4in (0.518 × 19 tpi) Oil and petrol unions, oil banjo bolts, engine and gearbox drain plugs, gearbox pawl spring plug, exhaust lifter ferrule, chain oiler pipe adapter

3/8in (0.656 × 29 tpi) Oil tank stop valve body, gearbox cam plate spindle

1/2in (0.825 × 14 tpi) Gearbox filler neck (crankcase end)

BRITISH ASSOCIATION (BA)

This series of threads was favoured by the electrical and instrumentation industries, and its odd dimensions may reflect an early connection with continental practices. Whatever the reason, the pitches reflect a mathematical series, starting at 1mm, and the thread form is 47 1/2°, with rounded root and crest. The 0BA size, which occurs on speedometer and rev counter cases, is easily mistaken for 1/4in BSF but is significantly different. The use of BSF (or BSW) is not satisfactory, but it will be found that a 6mm ISO (metric) fastener is an almost perfect fit.

6BA (0.110 × 47.9 tpi/0.53mm) Magneto contact breaker spring screw, headlamp shell brass blade screw

5BA (0.126 × 43.1 tpi/0.59mm) Amal 276 and 289 top ring spring retaining screws

4BA (0.142 × 38.5 tpi/0.66mm) Petrol tap plunger retaining screw, Vincent damper cover screws, 5in speedometer gearbox retainer plate screws, D distributor screws

3BA (0.161 × 34.8 tpi/0.73mm) Magneto contact, contact breaker through-bolt, safety gap screws

2BA (0.185 × 31.3 tpi/0.81mm) 1000cc clutch screws, exhaust lifter spindle nuts, brake switch screws, brake lamp spring anchor, brake torque arm spring screws, magneto end screws, D distributor pinion screws and points screws, Monobloc float cover screws

1BA (0.209 × 28.2 tpi/0.90mm) Control lever clip screws, Altette bezel studs, twist-grip friction screw, carburettor throttle stop and air screws, chain oiler adjuster, Monobloc pilot jet

0BA (0.236 × 25.4 tpi/1.0mm) 3in speedometer head attachment, Altette horn mounting studs

Cycle Threads (CEI, BSCy)

The cycle industry developed a range of fine-pitch thread standards for general purposes and specialist applications (eg, steering columns, spokes). These were especially suitable for the light-gauge wire and tube construction methods used in the industry and were inherited by the motorcycle industry, where the additional asset of resistance to loosening under vibration was no doubt appreciated.

Originating with the Cycle Engineers Institute, many of these thread standards were adopted into the British Standards as BSCy. Threads from less than 1/4in to over 1in all utilised the same 26 tpi thread pitch, but an alternative of 20 tpi was also provided for use in the larger sizes. Thread form for cycle threads is 60°, with rounded root and crest.

Prior to World War II, Vincent-HRD used cycle threads fairly extensively on Series A and earlier models. In the post-war era, however, the factory largely avoided them, except when re-using old designs or when compatibility demanded. However, suppliers of bought-in components were still using these threads, so a number of cycle thread applications are to be found on a Vincent, especially on the Series Bs.

1/4in × 26 tpi Not used (almost indistinguishable from 1/4in BSF).

5/16in × 26 tpi Girdraulic handlebar cap studs (bottom only, top 5/16in BSF), 1000cc choke lever, Series B gearchange linkage, front brake adjusters, Burman gearbox adjuster bolts, various Brampton fork fittings

3/8in × 26 tpi Primary chain adjuster, brake cams, torque arm retaining screws, big end quill, Brampton head clip bolt and various damper parts, Burman sector spindle and kick-starter

7/16in × 26 tpi Gearchange ratchet retaining nut, Brampton fork damper screw, Brampton fork top spindles (left-hand thread on left side)

1/2in × 26 tpi Bottom speedometer drive cable nut, Brampton fork bottom spindles (left-hand thread on left side)

3/4in × 26 tpi 1000cc clutch nut

11/8in × 26 tpi Steering column and head nut (Brampton and Girdraulic)

Spoke threads are a specialist set of thread sizes developed in the cycle industry for use with material dimensioned to the Standard Wire Gauge (swg) – which is not related to the American Wire Gauge (awg). Note that spoke threads are rolled, usually on to cold-drawn wire, so that the finished thread outside diameter is larger than the raw material from which it is made, resulting in a lighter and stronger component than thread cutting. It is not practical, or wise, to attempt to copy and thread spokes on a lathe.

8 swg (0.176in × 32 tpi)	8 swg (0.160in dia) spokes, valve-lifter adjuster).
9 swg (0.157in × 40 tpi)	9 swg (0.144in dia) spokes.
10 swg (0.141in × 40 tpi)	10 swg (0.128in dia) spokes.

20 tpi Threads

Large-diameter parts were routinely threaded at 20 tpi. These parts were normally lathe turned, and Whitworth thread form was used, no doubt to make use of the readily available thread chasers, and to avoid mix-ups.

7/16in × 20 tpi Front exhaust cam follower spindle (1000cc)

9/16in × 26 tpi Cylinder head studs and nuts, D rear- and centre-stand bolts, 500cc left-hand footrest locknut and tie-bracket bolt

3/4in × 20 tpi Hollow axles, engine mainshafts, battery carrier cross-tube, E80 thin nuts, ESA nut, inlet valve guide lock-ring, sidecar bracket, rear fork end lugs (if machined)

1in × 20 tpi Pushrod tube gland nuts

1 1/4in × 20 tpi Oil pump plug, Vincent damper gland, 1000cc clutch plate plug (C26), 1000cc gearbox sprocket nut, gearbox filler (1000cc and 500cc)

1 7/8in × 20 tpi Valve caps, 1000cc gearbox and chaincase inspection caps, exhaust pipe nuts

2 1/8in × 20 tpi Oil-filter cap

2 9/16in × 20 tpi Gearbox bearing lock-ring

ISO Metric

The only metric thread an owner normally meets on a Vincent or HRD is the spark plug thread (14mm × 1.25mm pitch).

Unified National Coarse & Fine (UNC & UNF)

During World War II the Unified series of threads gained widespread use in Europe, particularly in the motor industry. The motorcycle industry was slower to adopt them, with the BSA/Triumph/Ariel group starting to change over in the late 1950s. The Unified threadform is 60° with nominally flat roots and crests. UNC threads are virtually interchangeable with BSW in most (but not all) common sizes, but the same does not apply to UNF-BSF. It is very undesirable to allow UNF fasteners to get mixed up with British threaded components, because they can be very difficult to distinguish without thread gauges. For example, the 5/16in size is 18 tpi in BSW, 22 tpi in BSF, 26 tpi in BSCy and 24 tpi in UNF – a nightmare if mixed up in the same box!

Glossary

ATD	Automatic timing device
AVC	Automatic voltage control
BA	British Association (thread)
BSCy	British Standard cycle (thread)
BSF	British Standard fine (thread)
BSP	British Standard pipe (thread)
BSW	British Standard whitworth (thread)
Butted	local thickening of wire or tubular components to reinforce a point of high stress
CEI	Cycle Engineers Institute (thread)
ESA	Engine shock absorber
Elektron	Proprietary magnesium-based light alloy material for castings
HRD	Initials of Howard Raymond Davies, founder of the original HRD Motors Ltd
ISO	International Standards Organisation
MPH	Journal of the Vincent HRD Owners Club
PCV	Popular shorthand for Philip Conrad Vincent, manufacturer of the Vincent motorcycle
PEI	Popular shorthand for Philip Edward Irving (also known by his pen name 'Slide Rule')
RFM	Rear frame member, the triangulated swinging arm of the Vincent
swg	Standard wire gauge
tpi	Threads per inch
UFM	Upper frame member, the residual main frame of the Vincent
UNC	Unified National coarse (thread)
UNF	Unified National fine (thread)

Vincent Specialists

The VOC Spares Co Ltd
The Wharf, Burford Lane, Lymm, Cheshire WA13 0SL, UK; tel 01925 753367, fax 01925 758455

Conway Motors
Unit D, Fox Pitt Farm, Shingle Barn Lane, West Farleigh, Maidstone, Kent ME15 0PN, UK; tel 01622 820635

Maughan & Sons
42 Townend, Wilsford, Grantham, Lincs NG32 3NY, UK; tel 01400 230212

Bob Dunn
Coggra Fold Farm, Bradley Fold Road, Bradley Fold, Bolton, Lancs, UK; tel 01204 391322

Ron Kemp
Ty-Vin, Llanddewi, Llandrindod Wells, Powys LD1 6SE, UK; tel 01597 851542

Grays Motorcycle Centre
63 Southend Road, Grays, Essex RM1 5NL, UK; tel 01375 370066

Mathews Motorcycles
15 Knox Gardens, Clacton-on-Sea, Essex, UK; tel 01255 427663

Classic Restorations Holland
Zesstedenweg 217A, 1613 Je Grootebroek, Holland; tel 02285 16697

Sid Biberman
510 Thole Street, Norfolk, Virginia 23505, USA; tel 804 588 3001

Magri Motorcycles
1220 Pennsylvania, San Francisco, California, USA; tel 415 285 6735